COLLECTIONS OF THE
CONNECTICUT HISTORICAL SOCIETY
VOLUME XII

Lists and Returns
of
Connecticut Men
in the
Revolution

1775-1783

Connecticut Historical Society

HERITAGE BOOKS
2008

HERITAGE BOOKS

AN IMPRINT OF HERITAGE BOOKS, INC.

Books, CDs, and more—Worldwide

For our listing of thousands of titles see our website
at
www.HeritageBooks.com

A Facsimile Reprint
Published 2008 by
HERITAGE BOOKS, INC.
Publishing Division
100 Railroad Ave. #104
Westminster, Maryland 21157

Originally published by the
Connecticut Historical Society
Hartford
1909

International Standard Book Numbers
Paperbound: 978-0-7884-0312-5
Clothbound: 978-0-7884-7514-6

OFFICERS OF THE SOCIETY.

Elected May 26, 1908.

PRESIDENT, SAMUEL HART.

<table>
<tr><td rowspan="8">VICE-
PRESIDENTS,</td><td>JAMES J. GOODWIN, HARTFORD.</td></tr>
<tr><td>SIMEON E. BALDWIN, NEW HAVEN.</td></tr>
<tr><td>JONATHAN TRUMBULL, NORWICH.</td></tr>
<tr><td>MORRIS W. SEYMOUR, BRIDGEPORT.</td></tr>
<tr><td>CARL STOECKEL, NORFOLK.</td></tr>
<tr><td>FRANK FARNSWORTH STARR, MIDDLETOWN.</td></tr>
<tr><td>ELLEN D. LARNED, THOMPSON.</td></tr>
<tr><td>E. STEVENS HENRY, ROCKVILLE.</td></tr>
</table>

RECORDING SECRETARY,   ALBERT C. BATES.
CORRESPONDING SECRETARY, W. DeLOSS LOVE.
TREASURER,   JOHN E. MORRIS.
LIBRARIAN,   ALBERT C. BATES.
AUDITOR,   EDGAR F. WATERMAN.

MEMBERSHIP COMMITTEE,
- SAMUEL HART, *ex officio*.
- JULIUS GAY.
- HORACE E. MATHER.
- JANE T. SMITH.
- ALBERT C. BATES.
- GEORGE S. GODARD.
- HENRY A. CASTLE.
- EDWIN P. TAYLOR.

LIBRARY COMMITTEE,
- SAMUEL HART, *ex officio*.
- FRANCIS H. PARKER.
- THOMAS S. WEAVER.
- J. COOLIDGE HILLS.

PUBLICATION COMMITTEE,
- SAMUEL HART, *ex officio*.
- ALBERT C. BATES.
- LEVERETT BELKNAP.
- FORREST MORGAN.

COMMITTEE ON MONTHLY PAPERS,
- P. HENRY WOODWARD.
- FRANCIS PARSONS.
- ARTHUR L. SHIPMAN.

LISTS AND RETURNS

OF

CONNECTICUT MEN

IN THE

REVOLUTION.

1775-1783.

HARTFORD
CONNECTICUT HISTORICAL SOCIETY
1909

CONTENTS.

INTRODUCTION.

This Society published in 1901, as the eighth of its series of Collections, a volume of "Rolls and Lists of Connecticut Men in the Revolution, 1775-1783." As explained in its introduction, the material in that volume supplemented what had already been published in 1889 in the officially issued "Record of Service of Connecticut Men in the War of the Revolution, 1775-1783."

The material herewith issued as the twelfth volume of Collections, with the title Lists and Returns of Connecticut Men in the Revolution, 1775-1783, is intended to supplement what has already been published in the two volumes mentioned above.

The major part of this volume, as its title might indicate, is composed of officially written lists and returns of soldiers who were serving in the Continental regiments of the "Connecticut Line." There are also some rolls of companies in service which had not previously been printed, particularly in 1782 and 1783. Comparatively few new names of soldiers or additional records of service are printed in this volume. Its chief value will be found to consist in the addition in the case of a great majority of the soldiers, of the name of the town from which the soldier came. This will supply much sought for information, and in many cases will doubtless serve to identify the soldier.

Many of the statements made in the introduction to the volume of Rolls and Lists apply equally well to this volume. A part of the copy was made by Mr. Thomas, and all of the cards for the index were written by Miss Gay. All comparison of index cards and reading of proof of both text and index has been done by the editor. Much the same method has been used in indexing as in the former volume. All surnames have been indexed exactly as they appear in the text; but in the case of Christian names, where both a correct and an incorrect spelling of the same name appeared, both are indexed under the correct spelling.

The sources from which the material in this volume has been printed are, with the addition of volume 39 of the Revolutionary War series in the State Library, practically the same as those used in the previous volume of " Rolls and Lists " and enumerated in the introduction to that volume.

A word of explanation seems advisable regarding the rolls of Col. Samuel B. Webb's regiment for 1782 and 1783, which are found in volume 39 of the Revolutionary War series, and are here printed on pages 303-344. These rolls were formerly in the Comptroller's office and have but recently been transferred to the State Library, where they have been arranged and bound. They are not original rolls of the period which they represent, but are comparatively modern copies, perhaps made about 1843. The source from which they were copied is not now known. The majority of them are written in a free running hand which leaves not a few of the letters in the names poorly formed and doubtful, while many of the names are closely written, owing to the copyist's anxiety to crowd them into the limited space on a certain uniform size of paper. Apparently the copyist was sometimes careless in his writing and set down letters which could not by any possibility be construed as forming a name. Monthly muster rolls of the staff and of the different companies in this regiment for some or all of the months of February, March, May, June, July, September, October 1782, December 1782-January 1783, and February 1783, are preserved in these copies. In this volume only the earliest roll in each year of each of these companies has been printed. The later monthly rolls have been compared with this, and differences, except occasional unimportant variations of spelling, are noted on the printed page. Thus it appears that the name of the same person is found on one roll as Chester Upham and on another as Christopher Upham (page 307), or on one roll as Amos Gustin and on another as Amos Griffin (page 310). Whether or not these differences appeared on the original rolls is a matter for conjecture. In numerous instances a name after having appeared on several successive monthly rolls is dropped from succeeding rolls without any mention being made of the man's discharge, desertion, or transfer to another company (such as John Gimson, page 311). Such disappearances are noted on the printed page, as well as the occasional appearance of names on later which are not found on earlier rolls (such as David Clark, page 312). By printing the earliest roll and thus noting the differences found on later rolls the wearisome repetition which would have occurred in printing practically the same roll a half dozen times has been avoided.

Much of this volume is made up of official lists which had themselves been copied and compiled from other lists, made up probably by the town's authorities in the absence of the persons named in the lists. In making such a compilation the opportunity for error is great, and not a few of the names as they appear in the lists and are here printed are evident errors. In some instances the true name is very evident, although badly misspelled; but in others not even by the trial of a phonic pronunciation can the real name be guessed.

In printing these documents it has been impossible to avoid some duplication of names and services, but it has been thought better to allow occasional duplication than to run any risk of omission.

ALBERT C. BATES,

Chairman of the Publication Committee,
and Editor of this Volume.

THE SOCIETY'S LIBRARY, DECEMBER 16, 1908.

CONTINENTAL REGIMENTS, 1775.

RETURNS OF MEN IN SERVICE.

[*See Record of Connecticut Men in the Revolution, pages 34-94.*]

[Each of these Returns, sent in to the State authorities from the different towns, is signed by the Selectmen of the town from which it is sent and gives the names of persons resident in that town who had been employed in the Continental service in 1775, and who under a law passed in December of that year were exempted from the payment of certain taxes to the State. Some of the Returns give the number only and not the names of those who had been in service.]

[*State Library, Revolution 6, 1-131.*]

BOLTON

Richard Skinner
Zenas Skinner
Ebenezer Wright
Benjⁿ Griswold
Joseph Carver
Simeon Griswold
William Richardson

Ruben Searls
Edward Paine
Jeremiah Chapman
Zadock How
Roswel Paine
Jedediah Lenord
Asa Lenord

BRANFORD

Benjamin Bartholomew
Mason Hobart
Levi Baldwin
Caleb Frisbie
Ralph Hoadly
Gideon Bartholomew
Titus Frisbie
Zaccheus Maltbie
John Palmer Jun'
Barnebas Palmer
Timothy Barker
Benjamin Butler
Aaron Baldwin
Ephraim Rogers

Artemas Johnson
Jacob Rogers
Walter Butler
Stephen Wade
John Negus
Alling Smith
Ephraim Chidsey
Roswell Chidsey
Andrew Burr
Samuel Whedon
John Mallery
Reuben Johnson
Samuel Hoadly, Jun'
William Baldwin

Andrew Morris
Philemon Rogers
James Barker Junr
Hooker Frisbie
Simeon Linsly
Joseph Whedon
John Whitne Junr
Joseph Jones
Robert Stewart
William McQueen
Oliver Lanfere Junr
John White
Asher Sheldon, Junr
John Guy
Joseph Russell
Joseph Willford
Josiah Fowler Junr
Benjamin Henshaw
Jonathan Byintun

Benjamin Norton
Solomon Talmage
John Bunnel
Abraham Bunnel
Wooster Harrison
Asahel Harrison
Levi Rose
Abraham Cook
Mark Mazuzen
Joel Howd
Levi Rogers Junr
Rufus Rogers
Ebenezer Foot
John Lodewick Abberhart
Ebenezer Byintun
Jairus Harrison
Matthew Butler
Jacob Page
Luther Page

DERBY

Adam Vorse
Benjamin Tomlinson
Charles Whittelse
David Tomlinson
William Tucker
David Canfield
Ebenezer Hitchkook
Enos Jones Prindle
Eben^r Turill Witemore
Amos Fooks
Jonathan Brown
Georshom Bearsley
Gideon Tomlinson
Abijah Beard
Hezekiah Woodin
Jonathan Lyman
Elezer Durand
Jabez Pritchard

John Smith
Isaac Durand
Samuel Hull
Samuel Durand
Edward Basset
Joseph Lum
Isaac Tomlinson
Oliver Chatfield
Ritchard Haters
Abraham Basset
William Tomlinson
William Clark
William Woshbon
William Woodin
Reuben Canfield
Caleb Chatfield
Gideon Cande
Bowers Woshbon

DURHAM

John Jones
Joseph Smith
Phin^s Parmele
Jacob Clark
Sexton Squier
Asa Brown
Aaron Camp
Gideon Chittenden
Zebulon Lewis Clark
Amos Fowler
Amos Davis
Dan^{ll} Bishop
John Meeker
David Ward

Eben^r Squier
Eph^m Clark
Joseph Snow
John Stocking
Benjn Sutlief
Benjn Tainter
Jon^n Wells
Charles Parmele
Hez^h Parmele
Phin^s Picket
Sam^{ll} Savage
Sam^{ll} Seaward
Abr^m Shelley
Abiathar Fowler

CONTINENTAL REGIMENTS, 1775. 3

Eben^r Hall
Nathan Hall
Husted Hinman
Benjn Hogins

Wm Johnson
Jon^n Loveland
Sam^{ll} Lucas
Jared Whedon

EAST HADDAM

Warreu Ackley
Gideon Brainard
Jonah Brainard
Henery Cone
Elisha Adams Fowler
Timothy Hosmer
Hezekiah Mack
Joseph Rolo
Elias Lay
Aron Lyon
William Harvey
John Harvey
John Attwood
Timothy Fuller
Zechariah Gates
Jonah Gates
Luther Barney
Simeon Spencer
John Peek
Gabriel Ely
Samuel Smith
Isaac Taylor
Nathaniel Beebe
Matthew Smith 3^d
Bethuel Fuller
Phenihas Cone
Roberson Williams
Ethan Pratt
David Fox Jr

Israel Cone
Jonah Cone Jr
Duren Whittlesey
Nathan Harvey
Ezra Harvey
Silas Ackley
Elihu Huntley
Joshua Fox
Noah Huntly
Nathan Beebe
Daniel Gates 3^d
Noadiah Emmons
Jonathan Kneeland
Joseph Knolton
Daniel Shepperson
Jesse Willey
David Spencer
Samuel Chapman
Levi Crosby
William Beckwith
Samuel Post
Amaziah Spencer
Robert Harvey
Elihu Minor
Oliver Cone
Barzileel Ackley
Timothy Fuller 2nd
Ezra Beckwith
Zachariah Rolow

FAIRFIELD

Joseph Squire
Wm Jenings
Andrew Thorp
Ebe^r Knap
John Parret Jn^r
James McKay
John Persons
David Burr 3^d
Judson Sturges
Thomas Elwood
Hill Stirges
Wm Carter
Levey Mallery
David Anibell
Lyman (?) Jenings
David Stirges Ju^r
Nath^{ll} Taylor
Nehemiah Phypeney (?)

John Knap
John Perrey
Jonath^n Spears
Nath^{ll} Spears
Nehemiah Fowler
John Williams Jn^r
Isaac Jervis
Nathan Thorp
John Fuller
Sam^{ll} Squire 2^d
Hez : Goold
Peter Morehouse
Aaron Hubbell
Ezekel Canfield
Ichabod Canfield
Wm Remong
Steph^n Guyar
Gideon Holibord

Andrew Bennitt
Dan^ll Bennitt
Hez: Bennitt
John Sherwood
Joseph Batterson
Wm Batterson
John Batterson
George Batterson Jn^r
Russel Disbrow
Simon Disbrow
Gabrel Allen
Abrahm Wincop
Joshua Baker
Andrew Baker
Edmon Ogden
Nath^ll Johnson
John Johnson
Joseph Elwood
Nath^ll Godfrey Jn^r
Ezra Wood
Sam^ll King
Joshua Couch
George Moser
James Coal
Thomas Couch
Moses Stirges
Peter Winton
James Redfield
Gershom Banks
Joseph Bradley
John Blakman
Joseph Thorp
Jehial Sherwood
Thomas Goodsel
Joseph Frost
Thad^s Stapels
John Staples
Dan^ll Roberson
Amos Williams
John Mills
James Goodsel
Chancey Downs
Dan^ll Ketchem
Josiah Jenings
Cresterfey Godfrey
Edman Ogden
Eliphalet Gray
Frances Hutinock
Hezekiah Bears
Joel Gilbord
John Squire
Joseph Dickson

Joseph Whitlock
Joseph Green Jn^r
Enoch Towner
Silas Hanes
Joal Jenings
Sam^ll Bradley
Gershom Hubbell
John Gilbord
Justice Bradley
David Bradley
Elisha Bradley
Beter Stocker
Stephen Straten
Dan^ll Squire
Nehemiah Thorp
Fayweather Brothwell
Wolcutt Bennitt
Wheeler Cable
Thomas Duffey
Soloman Green
Liman Gray
Wm Hubbell
Jos: Hubbell Jn^r
Benj^m Hall
Zach Sherwood
Wm Hawley
Nathan P^t Jackson
Eliphalet Jenings
Richard Lacey
Isaac Odell
Eben^r Meaker
David Morehouse
Ezra Morehouse
Isaac Stephen
Eurial Morehouse
Isaac Hubbell
John Beardslee
Justice Jenings
Jeremiah Johnson
Nehemiah Cable
Onesimas Bradley
Asa Bradley
Fenias Squire
Shubal Goraham
Stephen Holibod
Dan^ll Blackman
Dan^ll Silliman
James Jambers
Reuben Chapman
Moses Dimon
Seth Webb
Elijah Cable

GUILFORD

James Bishop
Son of Wait Monger
Indented Indian servant of
    Simeon Chittenden
Son of Gideon Hoppen

Nath^ll Allis Ju^r
Thos Bevin
Jedidiah Cruttenden
Salmon Cruttenden
Gilbert Cruttenden

Zachariah Doud
Ruben Doud
Tim° Field
Chris^tr Foster
Sam^ll Hoit
Pember Josselin
Jon^a Murray
Wait Munger
Jn° Parsons
Noah Scrantom
Ab^m Scrantom
Tim° Wilcox Ju^r
Charles Norton
Eber Hall
Joseph Rowlason
Jared Scrantom
Saml Acaly
John Hill
Moses Hill
Josiah Fowler Junr
William Fowler
Dan^ll Chittenden Junr
Neriah Bishop
Simeon Chittenden Junr
John Ball
Benjamin Norton
Josiah Fowler
Luke Field
Amos Tole
Nathan Meigs
Son of Josiah Fowler
Timothy Field
Joel Dudly
Jn° Scovell Jr
Dan^ll Scovell
Willm Willasey

George Ferrol
Jared Chittenden
Danl Murray
Joseph Parmele Jr
Ezra Griswold
Reuben Shelley Ju^r
Jonathan Handy
Philemon Hall
Zebulon Benton
Thalmeno Bishop
Isaac Chalker
Roswell Woodward
David Hull
John Johnson Ju^r
David Morse
Two sons of Willm Parmele
Son of Peter Vaill
Son of Jairus Handy
Johnson Bishop
Zebulon Cruttenden
Thomas Dudley
Thomas Griswold
Jn° Harris
Mark Hotchkiss
Moses Doud
Jn° Doud
Barnabas McKeine
Levi Lee
Son of Westall Scovill
Dan^ll Stone J^r
Isaac Stow
Son of Seth Stone
David Dudley 3^d
Eben^r Bragg
Timothy Scranton

HADDAM

John Smith
John Arnold and Son
Robert Clark
James Young
Abner Tibbald
Richard Wakely
James Cone
Jacob Baily Junr
Abraham Tyler
William Smith
Elisha Spencer
Reuben Smith
Daniel Ray
Gideon Baily Ju^r
Jonathan Bordman
Samuel Brooks
William Baily
Asaph Young
John Baily Ju^r
Joseph Clark

Ephraim Sawyer
Cornelius Higgins J^r
Bezaliel Shailer
Arnold Hazelton
Eleazer Bate
John Russel
Timothy Baily
Gideon Baily
Aaron Thomas
William Porter
Giles Cone
Gideon Goff
Josiah Arnold
Elias Cone
Timothy Towner
Joseph Smith
Aaron Brainerd
Charles Hazelton Ju^r
Augustus Lewis
Amos Baily

Abraham Brooks Ju^r
David Brainerd
Joseph Dickerson
Jonathan Clark
Joseph Lungrel Rowley
Joel Hubbard
Jacob Baily & Son
Reuben Bates

Samuel Cone
Samuel Marsh
Sylvenus Clark
Seth Arnold
Thomas Brainerd
Reuben Brainerd
Jabez Baily

[It is not actually stated that these men from Haddam were in service in 1775, but it is to be presumed that they were from the fact of their taxes being abated and the list being placed with lists of persons from other towns who did serve.]

HARTLAND

Euriah Church
Charles Phelps
Elisha Giddings
Joshua Giddings
Asa Andrews
Abel Moses
Phinehas Parkins
Jason Parkins
Samuel Phelps
Daniel Bill
Daniel Benjamon
Daniel Bushnel
Titus Alling
Nathaniel Alling

Jonathan Wilder
Timothy Tiffaney
Thomas Sill
Ezekel Beach
Ashbell Beech
Obed Crosby
Ephraim fox
James Hungerford
Josiah Meeker
Preeda Stephens
Childs Taylor
Timothy Couch
William Williams

HARWINTON

Abnur Willson
Jese Poter or Jesse Potter
Oliver Phelps
Hezekiah Phelps
Daniel Cook
Ashbel Poter or Portter
Solomon Buller or Butler
Hezekiah Leach
Abraham Catlin
Sam^{ll} Weson or Weston
James Olcut Jr
    or James Olcut
Benja^m Barbur
Sam^{ll} Lambart
Jabez Frisbey
Elijah Loomiss
Enos Scoot or Enes Scot
Alyn Haydon
Eli Catlin

Isaiah Butler J^r
Christopher Jouson
Timothy Barbur
Simian Barbur
    or Simon Barbor
Zimry Skinnor
White Griswould
Sam^{ll} Phelps J^r
George Loomiss
Joseph C Hawley or **Holley**
George Jones
Sam^{ll} Wesson Jr
    or Sam^{ll} Weston Jur
Sam^{ll} Jonson
Jonathan Cook
Asa Griswould
Lavinas Holt
Amus Gilbert

MIDDLETOWN

Ebenezer Blake
Paul Bunn
Wm Butler
Othniel Clark

Barachiah Fairbanks
Joseph Farnsworth
Richd Hamlin
Samuel Johnson

Charles Knowles
*Col° Return J. Meigs
Wm Mitchell
Tim° Starr Junr
Elijah Tuells
*Samuel Tuells
Joseph Willis Junr
Charles Whiting
Ely Butler
James Dewey
James Johnson
Simeon Savage
Stephen Sage
Elnathan Thrasher
Aaron White Junr
Peet. Galpen
Selah Hubbard
Ithuriel Hulburd
Timothy Hubbard
Elijah Loveland
Abijah Peck Junr
Jesse Peck
Elisha Peck
Roger Riley
Elisha Savage
Danl Willcocks
Daniel Cornwell
Elisha Cornwell
Frederick Winthrop
Christo^r Whitebread
Josiah Atkins
Nehem^h Barns
Freelove Blake
Edward Crowell
Solomon Crowell

Edmund Fairchild
Wid° Babbits Son
Benj^a Babbit
Ebenezer Field
David Hull
James Johnson 2^d
Elihu Lyman
John Roberts Junr
Amos Wetmore
Henry Bonfoy
Ashbell Cornell
Butler Gilbert
Joseph Harris
Joseph Lung
Comfort Marks
Danl Sizer
Abraham Sage
Ichabod Swaddle
Sol° Hubbard
Dean Hubbard
Jn° Hubbard
Caleb Johnson Jr.
Lemuel Lee
George Seaton
Joseph Driggs Junr
Jesse Gilbert
Hez^a Goff Junr
Hez^a Hubbard Junr
Wm Lucas
Nathl Miller
Saml Markham
Edward Powers
Charles Plum
Simeon Roberts
Joseph Starrs Son

NEW FAIRFIELD

Samuel Nichols
Phineas Bardsly
Bille Trowbrdge
Talmage Hall
John Lacy
Jonas Brath (?)
Daniel Trowbridge
Stephen Gregory
Joseph Barss
Elish Hibbard
John Hendrick
John Mourhouse
John Mitchel
Neil Clerk
Abel Cosher (?)
John Hulbard
Ezra Hubbel

Elijah Crane
Joseph Osburn
Timothy Taylor
Abel Sherwood
David Wakman
Moses Knap
Amon Bebee
Joseph Dubury (?)
William Phelps
Amos Hubbel
John Osborn
Barzilla Brown
Benjamin Bennet Ju^r
Joel Botchford
Abraham Nichols
William Towner
Benjamin Giddings

---

*His tax was abated for the service of two persons.

Calib Pitt
Stephen Jurden
Seth Lacy

John Perkhust
John Hambleton

NEW HAVEN

Elias Townsend
Evlyne Pierpont
Caleb Ball
Nathaniel Bishop
Mases Potter
Saml Squire
James Richards
Willm Alling
Robert Simpson
John Jocelin
Joseph Moulthrop
Saml Perkins
Saml Peck
Joseph Collings
Henry Sanford
Jacob Barns (?)
Hugh (?) Clark
Eldad Hotchkiss

Walter Wilmot
John Andrews
Martin Clark
Thomas Gardiner
John Miles
Eliakim Sperry
Sam^{ll} Smith
Benjn Smith
Eliphalet Barns
Yale Todd
Eben^r Allin
Fredrick Harding
Son of Freeman Huse, now
    (1777) prisoner in Great
    Britain
Son of Asa Smith died in the
    Continental Service.

NEWTOWN

Jo^s Smith
Jabez Botsford
Henry Fairman
Clement Botsford
Nathl Little
George Peck
Wm Allen
Abel Baldwin
John Botsford
Jo^s Booth
Isael Burritt
Wm Barnett
Levi Bostwic
Isaac Bloodgood
Amos Benedict

Mat^t Clark
Francis Drake
Jesse Fairchild
Enoch Hubbel
James Fairchild Junr
Stephen Hawley Junr
George Murry
Peter Prindle
Abijah Prindle
Aaron McGregory
James Bennitt
Jonathan Hurd
Andrew Northrop
Philo Beardsle

NORWALK

Addams Joshua
Betts Thomas J^r
Betts James
Bassey Peleg
Bassey Silas
Bouton Eleazor
Benedict John J^r
Benjamin James
Brown Nathan
Benedict Thomas J^r
Betts Thomas
Brown Daniel
Betts Rheuben
Baker James

Brown Jonathan
Clenton Joseph
Cole Alvin
Chard Joseph
Chard Samuel
Chase Jared
Deforest David
Elles J. Bard
Fox Jonathan
Grummon Nehemiah
Gilbert Gershom
Gilbert Thadeus
Griffith William
Gates Samuel

Gregory Elias
Gregory Ezra
Hendrick Nathan
Hyat Abraham
Hyat Alvin
Hoyt Thomas
Hanford Theop* 3d
Hanford Theop* Jr
Hanford Stephen
Hoyt Nathan Jr
Hoyt Joseph Jr
Hoyt Justice
Hubble Thadeus
Hendreck David
Hulburt Stephen
Hanford Eleazor
Jones Thomas
Johnson John
Keeler Samuel 3d
Kellogg Jonat
Keeler Isaac
Keeler Lockwood
Lockwood David
Lockwood James
Morehouse Michael
Mead Mathew
Mallery Giles
Mead Elias
Marvin Ozias
Morehouse Thomas
Meeker Stephen
Nash Ebenr Jur

Olmsted Silas Jr
Raymond Wm
Richards John
Raymond Jonat
Reed Nathan
Reed Abraham
Reed Hezekiah
Rockwell Joseph
Raymond Benjn
Scribner Elias
Smith Daniel
Seymour William
Sherrod Mathew
Selleck Jacob
St John Nehemiah
St John Nehemiah Jr
Starling Thadeus
Scribner Zacheus
Sloan Allexander
Scofield Peter
Scribner Abraham
Selleck James
Tuttle Levi
Taylor Levi
Taylor Elijah
Tuttle Peter
Wright J. Allyn
Whitlock Oliver
Whitlock Nathan
Wyat Henry
Gregory Isaac

PRESTON

Col John Tyler
Col Samll Mott
Capt Edward Mott
Capt Nathan Peters
Capt Jeremiah Halsey
Lieut Nathaniel Gove
William Whitney
Jedediah Whitney
Silas Brewster
Nathll Larabe
Josiah Witter
Phineas Freeman
Samll McDaniels
Elijah Park
Giles Tracy
Benjn Freeman
Cyrus Ames
Levi Tracy
Matthias Ames
Jonas Satterlee
Dick Fitch
Thomas Meech
Amasa Standish
Jesper Black

Solomon Story
Peter Ellis
Eli Hill
Thos Averill
Gager Freeman
Prentis Avery
Manasseh Prentice
Walter Fanning
Danl Smith
Joseph Stanton
Joshua Meech
Charles Miles
Jason Rude
Moses Park
Ezekiel Tracy
Willim Butler
Joseph Swan
Danll Freeman
Nathan Freeman
Elisha York
Danl Yerrington
Sanford Hrreck
Isaac Herreck
Preserved Brumbly

Bethuel Brumbly
Dan¹ Bellus
Thoˢ Bellus
Mathew Coy
Ephraim Coy
Mathew Ray
Abel Bennit
Elijah Stanten
Jacob Averill
John Benjamin
Rozel Benjamin
Thoˢ Aldridge
Peleg Sweet
Thaddeus Downer
Uriah Beman
Simeon Rouse
Asa Kinne
Jacob Kinne
John Poolman
Sam¹ Wheler
Peleg Billings
Joseph Billings
Jacob Burton
Robart Halley
Joseph Northrop
John Peterson

Elijah Phillops
Henry Walton
Nathan Walton
Allen Geer
Jonathan Averill
Sam¹ Huntington
Steven Gates
John Wheler
Moses Smith
Leuis Huit
Peres Tracy
Joshua Woodward
Asa Burnam
Elijah Johnson
David Green
Asa Story
Jonas Boardman
Roger Coit
Farewell Coit
Elish Belcher
Nathan Belcher
Lem¹ Geer
John Gates
David Green
Rouse Bly

SIMSBURY

Elisha Cornish Juʳ
Timothy Humphry
Wiliam Andrus
Azriah Willcox
Solomon Buel
Elijah Barber
Eli Tuller
Levi Piney
Aron Piney
Asahel Strickland
John Willson
Ebenezer Brown
Oliver Case
Stephen Terry
Benjamin Slarter
John Roundey
Richard Andrus
Daniel Merrill
Daniel Barber
Jacob Tuller
Roderick Adams
Jonathan Montecu
Oliver Adams
Samuel Barnard
Joseph Grimes Jʳ
Joel Humphry
John Alderman
Elijah Nobel
James Eno
Roger Willcox

Abel Adams
Stephen Langatha
Amoziah Barber
Shubal Moses
John Fletcher
Elisha Harington
Moses Liley
Jesse Russel
Thomas Phereton
Stephen Harington
Jonathan Humph Jʳ
Joseph Tuller
Eseck Allen
Luthar Lawrence
Theophilus Humpʳ
Elijah Tuller
Timothy Woodbridg
Martin Case
Jacob Davis Jʳ
Permenio Adams
Benjamin Bodwel
Thomas Phelps Jʳ
Theophilus Woodbrig
Jared Ingram
John Pettibone
William Andruss
Daniel Johnson
Benjamin Holcom
Levi Dibol
Noadiah Holcomb

Levi Frisby
Ebenezer Lamson
Eli Holcomb
Jacob Hays
Seth Hays
Seth Holcomb
Azriah Holaday
Amos Holaday
Timothy Cossit
Micah Case
Daniel Buttolph
Samuel Dewolf
Zebinah Burr
Luke Hays
Nath[ll] Griffen
Elijah Evens
Asahel Hays
Oliver Hays
Elishama Holcomb
Israel Mesenger
David Mesenger
Thomas Totton
Wiliam Hays 3rd
John Valance
John Drake Ju[r]
Richard Gay Ju[r]
Reuben Clark
John Hill 2[d]
Thomas Winchel J[r]
Edmun Murfey
Rufus Mason
Judah Phelps
Phinehas Wolworth
Joseph Burrill
Joseph Hinkston
Reuben Wollworth
Jehial Winchel
Simeon Winter
Abner Warner
Ebenezer Mereman
Arunah Moore
Theophilus Hide

Israel Warner
Daniel Warner
Benjamin Adams
Jonathon Morgan
William Case
Abraham Case J[r]
Benjamin Dyar
George Humphry
Oliver Humphry
David Hill
Solomon Humphry J[r]
Gideon Mills
John Pooler
Pliney Case
James Andrus
Seth Willcox
Joseph Willcox
Daniel Barber
Eliphilit Curtis
Samuel Millar
Othaniel Gillet
Nathaniel Johnson
Solomon Curtis
Job Barber
Ephraim Mills
William Tailor
John Matson
Aron Mesenger
Ruben Mesenger
David Clerk
James Ward
Thomas Wright
Henry Edwards
Jacob Pettibone
Daniel Barber
Nathaniel Piney
Hezekiah Andrus
Michael Willson
Jonathon Couch
Elijah Holcomb
Moses Holcomb

SOMERS

Abraham Coy
Peter Piney
John Russel
William Elmer
Roburt Pease 2[d]
Matthew Bewel
Daniel Kibbe
David Ritchardson
Amisa Buck
James Kibbe 2[d]
Jesse Ritchardson
Jacob Brown
Bildad Kibbe

Joseph Root
Abner Pease
Moses Pelton
Reuben Sikes
Elijah Sexton
William Parsons
Joseph Sexton
Eliacom Wardwell
Ritchard Pease
Edward Laurance
Samuel Right
Daniel Burchard
David Pease

John Orcutt
Amasa Allin
Jacob Orcutt
John Fairman

Levi Hamblin
Stephen Jones
Alexand Brown

TOLLAND

Comfort Carpenter
Hemon Bocor
Elijah Chapmon
Luke Washbon
Joel Stimson
Elias Newton
Samuel Steel
James Steel
John Abbot
Elijah Bradley
Jonathan Burros
Josiah Benton
Jonathan Benton
Samuel Benton
Azariah Benton
Asa Baldwin
John Carlton
Darius Carlton
Richard Carlton
Ebenezer Cook
Edward Dimock
Isaac Fallows
Christopher Francis
Simeon Griswold

Ebenezer Grant
John Huntington
Abner Hatch
Dan Hatch
Andrew Minor
Andrew Minor Junr
Rufus Price
Joshua Parks
Fyrus Preston
Ammi Poalk
Perez Steel
Elisha Stibbins
Isaiah Sparks
Simon Stimson
Nehemiah Sabins
Stephen Failor
Jabez West
Eliab Lad
Willobe Lowil
Ira West
Elijah Johnson
Samuel Price
Elijah Price

VOLUNTOWN

Serg^t Perez Briggs
" John Wylie
" Moses Wylie
" David Dorrance
Corp. Daniel Hopkins
" Jonathan Millet
" Joseph Bowdish
" William Kasson
" Joseph Gordon
Comfort Titus
William Hopkins
Amos Babcock
John Braughton
Joseph Randall
Simean Stevens
Benoni Kinne
Elijah Hodge
James Swift
Charles Swift
William Clerk J^r
James Wylie J^r
William Smith
Ichabod Shaw
William Stewart

Benjamin Rhoades
Elijah Fayr
Joseph Kennedy
Robert Campbell
Noble Campbell
Allen Stephenson
Nathan Dennison
James Kiegwin
Thomas Kiegwin
Amos Kiegwin
Nathan Coy
Robert Jameson J^r
George Gordon J^r
Job Bennet
Joseph Sweet
William Gray
William Bennet
John Bennet
Sampson Williams
Negro Ceaser
Mark Croswell
John Lowden
David Campbell
Anthony Eames J^r

Mark Eames Ju^r
Isaac Eames
Jonathan Chilson
Benjamin Burden

Gideon Tower
Alexander Williams
Elisha Eagleston
Andrew Jillson

WALLINGFORD

A list of the Mens Names that Was out With me in the Year 1775.

Ephraham Chamberlin
Joseph Shailor
Daniel Hall
John Mansfield
Moses Hall 2^d
Aaron Hull
Samuel Orsburn
Titus Hall
Aaron Persons
Samuel Collins
Ephraim Merriams
John Anthony
Thadeous Averet
Amos Austin
Benjamin Austin
Jared Benham
John Butlar
Titus Brockitt
Ira Bartholomew
Abel Barns
Samuel Benham
Elisha Cowls
Joel Cowls
Elisha Curtis
James Corbit
Benj^m Chittenden
Israel Daton
Thomas Dudley
Amos Davis
James Frances
Giles Griswell
John Griswould
Rufas Hall
Sam^{ll} Hough
Caleb Hull
Saml Hall
Enos Hall
Charles Hall
Asa Hall
Simeon Hopson
Raphel Hulbart
Jonah Hill
Phenihas Hough
Israel Hall
Moses Hall 3^d

Sam^{ll} Johnson
Aaron Ives
Thomas Janes
Levi Ives
Dan Johnson
Saml Johnson 2^d
Epaphras Nott
Phenihas Lyman
John Meriam
Joel Mattoon
Saml Mattoon
Ichabod Merriman
Barnibas Moss
Enos Mix
Saml Miles
Benj^m Preston
Edmond Parker
Benj^m Parker
John Perce
Elisha Perker
Phenihas Peck
Gidion Roys
Joseph Roys
Jonathan Slead
Miles Sperry
John Slead
Daniel Smith
Seth Smith
Abel Thorp
Elihu Thompson
Charles Tuttle
Jesse Vorse
Joseph Ward
Joseph Wolcott
Moses Warner
Ebenezar Warner
Nash Yale
Joseph Yale
Jonathan Yale
Elihu Lewis
Daniel M Mullin
Thadeous Carter
Timothy Hart
Gedeon Bristol
Isaac Shepard

A true list of the Mens Names that Went out of Wallingford With me in 1775 which Belong^d to this town

Certified pr Isaac Cook Junr   Wallingford Sep^t 2^d 1777

14 REVOLUTION LISTS AND RETURNS.

Wallingford December 1ˢᵗ 1777

These May Cartifie that the Following Persons Ware in the Service with Me att Boston in the Year 1775

Timothy Moltrop
Linus Hopson
Pren (?) Hopson
Samˡˡ Hopson Jur
Ambrose Avered
Cornelus Koberling (?)
Giles Cook
Arch Allin
John Frances
John Booth
Amos Frances
Samuel Culver Juʳ
Thomas Mix Juʳ
Street Yale

Amasa Yale
Daniel Sled (?)
Titus Hart
Archabel McNale
Abram Hall
Joel Hall
Isaac Doolittle
Enos Page
Ruben Bristol
Ichabod [?]
Samˡˡ Bunnil
Wᵐ Munrow
Rubin Tyler
Josiah Mix

Certified pr Me Street Hall

WINDSOR

Job Allyn
Jonathan Loomis
Increase Mather
Roger Rowel
Jacob Judd
George Wolcott
John Roberts
Elnathan Filley
Elijah Marshall
Phenihas Drake 3ᵈ
Isaac Pinney Junʳ
William Phelps 3ᵈ
Lanslott Phelps
Elijah Griswold
Martin Holcomb Junʳ
Solomon Clark Junʳ
James Wilson
Israel Warner
Edward Barnard Jnʳ
Zacheus Phelps
John May
Luke Thrall
Oliver Winchell
Theophilus Hide
Ashbel Stiles
Thomas Haydon
Martin Denslow
Samuel Wing
Ezekiel Thrall
Oliver Clark
Samˡˡ Gibbs
David Gibbs
Eleazer Gaylord

William Davice
Alpheus Munsell
Lemuel Welch
William Parsons
Elias Brown
Cornelius Russell
Daniel Eley
Samuel Munrow
Aaron Lyon
Nathˡ Stanley
Shubel Barber
Jesse Thrall
Roger Mills
Ruben Loomis
Thomas Allyn Junʳ
William Manley
Moses Cook
David Filley
Jonathan Bidwell
Moses Drake
Simeon Grayham
"Two Heads"
Stephen Fosbury
John Fosbury
Joseph Fitch
Jonah Gillet Junʳ
Jonathan Gillet
Ezekiel Case
John Rowell Junʳ
Isaac Skinner
Thcmas Gillet
Abiel Wilson
Aaron Webster

ALARM SERVICE, 1775.

CAPT. BORDMAN'S COMPANY

Wee yᵉ Subcribers Beloning to Capᵗ Bordmans Company Beeing Cald out att two alarams to Defend yᵉ See Ports to Wit on yᵉ 7 Day of August 1775 yᵉ 2 on yᵉ first Day of Sepᵗʳ in yᵉ year 1776 Wee Do hereby acknowledge that Wee and Each of Vs have Recd our Wages as it Was allowed Pr yᵉ Pay table May yᵉ 6 1777

Roger Billing
Nathan Stanton
Abel Stanton
William Hartshorn
Thomas Rix
Thomas Bellows
John Cogswell
Nathan Cogswell
Benajah Cook
John Cook Juʳ
Remengton Seers
Israel Herrick
Ezra Benjamin
Gideon Ray
John Ray
Elisha Guile
Amos Hutchinson
Nathan Burton
Isaac Burton
Pearly Brown
Abial Benjamin Juʳ
Elijah Lester
James Hatch
James Rix
Theophilus Rix
David Bordman

Christᵒ Smith
Alexʳ Stewart
Daniel Rix
Eleazar Prentice
Peleg Sweet
Hezekiah Boardman
Samˡˡ Bliss
Christo. Babcock
Ebenezer Herrick
Jedediah Ensworth
Henry Burton
Joseph Wilbur
Thomas Wilbur
Banjmin Asten
Jese Banjmin
Elias Brown
Barton Cooke
David Benjamin
Preserved Brumbly
Isaac W. Stanton
John Cleaveland
Spencer Kinne
Ezra Kinne
Amos Hutchson
Joseph Starkweather

[The above names are all autographs.]

Captain Joseph Bordman and his Company was from Northern Preston now the town of Griswold [Added in a modern handwriting.]

ROLLS AND RETURNS, 1776.

CAPT. WELLES' COMPANY

[*See Record of Connecticut Men in the Revolution, page 396.*]

Apprisement of the Soldiers guns under Com^d of Capt Saml Welles

Capt Saml Welles
Abraham Tallcott
George Tallcott
Richd Smith
Jesse Churchel
Josiah Lumis
Josiah Stevens
Serj^t Benjn Stevens
Benjn Howard
Frances Nichalson
Barnabas Fuller
Thomas Brooks
Ashbil Webster
Steven Couch
Peter Stevens
David Hubbard
John Morley
Jon^th Loveland
David Nigh fifer
Edward Potter
Elijah Covel
Jon^th Covel

Joseph Bidwell
Jon^th Gains
Leu^t Thos Hollister
Serj^t Aaron Hubbard
Elijah Hubbard
Josiah Brooks
Saml Daniels
Joseph Churchel
Eliz^r Hubbard
Ebez^r Benton
Saml Hills Junr
Wm Densmore
Timothy Stevens
Aaron Hollister
Josiah Hollister
Timothy Wood
John How
Elemuel Tubbs
Hez^h Wickham
Nathan Nichalson
Thos Morley
Elez^r Goodale

Glastonbury 18th 1776

[*State Library, Revolution 6, 173.*]

2

CAPT. PEASE'S COMPANY

[See Record of Connecticut Men in the Revolution, page 439]

A Muster roll of Capt Abial Peess Company

Capt Abial Peese
Lieu John Pomry
Lieu Israel Converse
Ens. Abner Wood
Serj Issacher Jones
Serj Samuel Hail
Serj Samuel Edson
Serj John Warner
Corp Stephen Jones
Corp Benajah Kent
Corp Sam^{ll} Warner
Drum Erastus Peese
Fifer Sylvanus Peese
Uriah Austin
Reuben Bradly
Samuel Blogget
Josiah Bradly
David Brace
John Comes
Oliver Chapin
Serel Chafe
Reuben Cooly
Daniel Chapens
John Carpenter
Uriah Clough
Jonathan Cross
Philander Denslow
John Dimmick
Simeon Dimmuck
Samuel Davis
Lemuel Davis
Nathan Edson
Josiah Edson
Joseph Edson
Benjamin Edson
Samuel Eaton
John Ferinan (?)
Natⁿ Fuller
Elijah Fay
John Goudy
Samuel Goudy
William Goudy
Josiah Gibbs
William Green

Joshua Hudson
John Hamlin
Levi Hamlin
Moses Horton
Nat^l Hide
Israel How
Abner Hathway
Eleizer Jones
Ephraim Jonson
Abel Kent
Philip Langdon
Juston Lombord
James McCluer
Joel Noble
Timothy Noble
Shadrach Norton
Joseph Pearman
Nathaniel Pomroy
Russel Prat
Abner Pease
Peter Peese
San^{ll} Peese
Joel Peese
Augustus Peese
Jonathan Parks
Sanford Richardson
Jesse Richardson
Abijah Remington
Elijah Robins
Ezra Saxton
James Spenser
Joseph Saxton
Isaac Shepherd
Jonathan Shead
Eliphalet Spenser
Ebenezer Thresher
Amos Torry
James Ward
John Ward
Simeon Webster
Nathan Webster
Ebenezer Walker¹
Samuel Warms (? Warner)
Levi Woolworth

[Indorsed]   A Muster Roll of Capt Abial Peas's Company at New London in the year 1776

[*State Library.*]

CAPT. BARNS' COMPANY.

A Pay Role for a Number of Capt Barns Company in the State of Connecticut who marched to New York from Waterbury in August Last and Home again. [Other documents show the date to be 1776.]

Names	When arivd	When returd home
Lieu⁴ Lazarus Ives	Aug⁴ 18	Sep⁴ 14
Serg⁴ Aaron Fenn	''	''
Corp Benjamin Barns	''	''
Cephas Ford	''	19
Paul Griggs	''	''
Elnathan Ives	''	''

[*State Library, Revolution 10, 181.*]

CANTERBURY RETURN

[*See Record of Connecticut Men in the Revolution, page 412.*]

Arms & Accoutraments bo⁴ hired, or impress⁴ by the Select Men of Canterbury & delivered to Soldiers of that Town for Camp⁴ 1776

to whom d⁴	of whose Company
Tracy Cleveland	Capt Bacons
Warren Williams	''
Dan¹ Kendal	''
Solem⁴ Cleveland	''
John Curtis	''
Asa Burges	''
Rich⁴ Parsons	''
David Addams	''
Abner Addams	''
Nehem⁴ Parrish	''
Jacob Staples	''
Elkanah Smith	''
Silas Gates	''
Philip Withy	''
Nath¹ Carver	''
Pender Jennison	''
David Smith	''
Elijah Spencer	''
Rufus Downing	''
John Gro (?)	''
Nath⁴ Williams	''
Tm⁰ Hall	
W⁴ Shaw	Capt Elderkin
Eph⁴ Goram	''
Curtis Cleveland	Capt Cutlers
Dan¹ Cushman	Capt Sharps
Tho⁴ Cotten	''
Eben⁴ Kingsly	''
Rufus Baker	''
Ja⁴ Bennet	''
Oliv⁴ Perkins	

[*State Library, Revolution 6,166.*]

CONNECTICUT LINE, 1777-1781.

[*See Record of Connecticut Men in the Revolution*, pages 125-298.]

SUPPLIES, 1777-1779.

An Alphlabitical Account of the Names of those who have Reciv⁴ Supplies from Towns, there Value at the Stated Price of 1776, & the Value of the Money Lodg⁴ by the Soldjer, together with the Name of yᵉ Town to which they belong.

[In December 1776 the Assembly passed an act fixing and stating the price of sundry articles of provision and other commodities. The following August another act was passed permitting soldiers to deposit a certain proportion of their wages with the selectmen or a committee of the town in which they resided who were authorized to expend the sum so deposited in the purchase "at the stated price" of provisions and supplies for the support of the family of the soldier making such deposit.]

	Names	Town
	Allen Daniel Capᵗ	Ashford
6	David	Derbey
2	Ebenʳ	Fairfield
6	Thomas	"
2	Moses	"
	Jonathan	Newhaven
4	Samuel	Suffield
5	Amos	Sharon
1	Ashur	Mansfield
4	Adams David Junʳ	Canterbury
4	David Doctʳ	"
D	Samuel	"
	John	Farmington
A	Jonathan	Greenich
4	William Lieuᵗ	Hartford
7	Asael	Norfolk
1	Andrus Thomas	East Haddam
	William	East Windsor
3	Theodore	Farmington
3	Obediah	"
9	James	Groten
9	Ezra	Newhartford
3	Asa	Weatherfield
1	Ackly Thomas	East Haddam
0	Andeson William	East Windsor
1	Thomas	Lime

	Names	Town
	Abbe Thomas Cap[t]	Enfield
8	Eleazer	Hartford
1	Jeduthan	"
1	John	Mansfield
8	Albert Thomas G. Serj[t]	Farmington
	Avory Thomas Lieu[t]	Groten
1	Simeon Ens[a]	"
1	Annew Andrew	"
1	Arnold Jehiel	Haddam
8	Augustus Cesar	Hartford
5	Angur George	Middletown
A	Aken James Serj[t]	Newhaven
A	Alley William	"
7	Aspenwall Aaron	Norfolk
7	Caleb	"
1	Auldredg W[m]	Preston
2	Austen Richard	Suffield
	Antoney John	Wallingford
4	Brandon Charles	Ashford
	Barker Sam[ll] Cap[t]	Branford
7	Barber Nath[ll]	Torrington
6	Bunnel Abraham	Branford
6	Bagdon Cezar	"
	Bacon Abner Cap[t]	Canterbury
6	William	Midletown
4	Nehemiah	Pomphret
5	Henery	Voluntown
8	Bowers Benajah Corp[l]	Chatham
8	Ephraim	"
8	Benj[a]	"
9	Butler Peter	
6	Walter	Greenich
8	John	Labenon
8	Steaphen	Saybrook
	Biggelow Eli	Colchester
4	Bill Jonathan	"
	Beriah Cap[t]	Norwich
	Blancherd Robbin	Colchester
8	Jacobe	Stamford
8	Brigham Paul	Coventry
7	Bishop David	Danbury
7	Thalmenus	Guilford
A	Nathan[ll]	Newhaven
	Nathan[ll] Leiu[t]	Norwich
	Baldwine Silas	Derbey
7	Calib Leiu[t]	Killingsworth
	Henery	Saybrook
8	Booth Henry	Enfield
5	Burr Daniel	Fairfield
8	Buckley Seth	"
9	Edward Cap[t]	Weathersfield
5	Bradley Eliphalet	Fairfield
2	Nathan	"
5	Philip B. Col[o]	Ridgfield
6	Daniel	Wallingford
A	Oliver	Newhaven
2	Beers Hezekiah	Fairfield
	Brown Jonathan Cap[t]	Farmington

	Names	Town
0	Brown Wᵐ	Midletown
7	Charles Corpˡ	Newfairfield
8	Henery	Newhaven
8	Jacobe	Summers
	Charles	Stonington
1	Joshua	"
	Oliver	"
5	Ebenʳ	Tolland
9	Edward	Weathersfield
0	Josiah Leiuᵗ	E Windsor
5	Judah Dᵒ	"
8	Barns Daniel Capᵗ	Farmington
9	Thomas	Midletown
	James Lieuᵗ	Newfairfield
A	Solomon Serjᵗ	Newhaven
6	Moses	Wallingford
	David	"
8	Daniel	Waterbury
D	Brunson Roger	Farmington
5	Asa	"
8	Bates John	"
6	Eleazer	Haddam
6	Amos	"
6	Danˡˡ	"
8	David	Stanford
6	Bonfoy Benunuel	Haddam
	Brainord Encrease	"
6	Boardman Jonathan	"
0	Moses	Middletown
6	A. Samˡˡ	"
3	Barnard John Capᵗ	Hartford
9	Brewer Daniel Serjᵗ	"
3	Bevens Ebenʳ	"
	Buckland Steaphen Capᵗ	"
D	Bull Eppiphras Capᵗ	"
9	Bushnal Daniel	Hartland
4	Baxter Aaron	Hebron
3	Francis	E Windsor
7	Barnum Liuᵗ	Kent
7	Steaphen Serᵗ	"
7	Amos Corpˡ	"
	Burnum Asa	Litchfield
	Joseph	Lyme
	Asa	Preston
7	Barlow John	Kent·
1	Betts James	Labenon
8	Badcock John	"
1	Ball Humphry	"
1	Blackman Jonathan	"
	Elijah Capᵗ	Middletown
4	Beckwith Phineas	Lyme
1	Ickeabud	Newlondon
4	Bogue Ickabd	Lime
	Blake Ebenʳ	Middletown
6	Bull John Lᵗ	Guilford
7	Billens Steaphen Lᵗ	Groten
1	James	Stonington

	Names	Town
6	Benton Edward Serj^t	Guilford
	Bailey Gideon L^t	Haddam
6	Jacobe	"
	Robert	"
1	Brightman Henrey	Groten
8	Bristol Jonathan	Milford
5	John	Windsor
6	Benjamin	Wallingford
6	Bens Thomas	Milford
4	Bend John	Norwich
7 '	Bottom John	Litchfield,
8	Bouten David	Stamford
2	Bissel John	E Windsor
	Beeman Jonathan	
	Friend	Washington
[ ]	Baker Bartholemew	Redding
6	Edward	Newhaven
[ ]	Beebe Boanerges	Newlondon
6	Joel	Milford
1	Ammon	Norwich
2	James Capt	Stratford
1	Bolles James	Newlondon
	Brind Edward	Haddam
6	Belden John	Milford
	Burk John	"
0	Basset Joshua	Mansfield
2	William	Waterbury
2	Barrows Jacobe	Mansfield
1	Bugbe John	"
1	Bennet Joshua	"
1	Benjⁿ	Norwich
	Berdsley Phineas Capt	Newfairfield
2	Brocket Hezekiah	Newhaven
6	Blakslee Zealous	"
6	Britton Samuel	"
7	Bostwick Eben^r	Newmilford
	Buns Isaiah Sr(?) Washington	"
7	Buns Isaiah Jr(?) Newmilford	Washington
	Bewel David	Newmilford
2	Buck Josiah	"
7	Botsford Joel	Newtown
4	Briant John	Norwich
0	Brewster Hezekiah	"
5	Bigsbe Elias	Reading
1	Brumly W^m	Stonington
A	Benjamins John	Stratford
	Burrus Josiah	"
6	Blodget Artimas	Salisbury
9	Blinn Abraham	Weathersfield
9	Justus	"
	Burnap Benjⁿ	Windham
7	Bingham John	"
	Abishai	"
2	Bartholomew John	Woodstock
2	Bruce Eli	"
	Brown Nathan	Norwalk
8	Bouton John	Norwalk

	Names	Town
8	Bedient Mordica	Norwalk
8	Beers Jesse	"
8	Comstock Sam[ll] Cap[t]	Norwalk
8	Cheney Eben[r] Corp[l]	Ashford
7	Richard	Kent
7	Culver Aaron	Canaan
8	Timothy	Farmington
4	David	Hebron
	Daniel	N. London
7	Chambers Will[m]	Canaan
4	Cleaveland John Serg[t]	Canterbury
	Timothy Leiu[t]	"
2	Moses Leiut	"
7	Josiah	Sharon
2	John	Stanford
1	Jonas	Colchester
4	Cady Abijah	Canterbury
	Darius	Stonington
1	Carter Reuben	Canterbury
8	Aaron	Chatham
4	Edward	Colchester
	James	Lebanon
4	Coburn Samuel	Canterbury
D	Cushman Daniel	"
	Cole Marcus Leiut	Chatham
	John Leiut	Farmington
9	Samuel	Hartford
7	John	Waterbury
	Clapp Nathan	Coventry
5	Chapman Collens	Danbury
4	Joseph Leiu[t]	Norwich
6	Dan[ ] Serj[t]	Saybrook
	John	"
6	Cook Thomas	Durham
4	Case	Norwich
8	Joel	Waterbury
1	Clark Samuel	E Haddam
8	Lyman	Farmingtown
1	Samuel	Haddam
0	Aaron	"
8	Abraham Serj[t]	Hartford
8	John	Labenon
5	Othniel Leiu[t]	Midletown
9	Joel	Newhaven
A	David Serj[t]	"
6	Marten	"
4	Jacobe	Norwich
4	James	Weathersfield
8	Richard	Waterbury
	Asael Ens[n]	Woodstock
9	William	Newlondon
	Churchel Elijah	E Windsor
2	Chandler Joseph	Enfield
5	Coggin David	Fairfield
9	Cable W[m]	"
	Curtice Amos	Farmington
8	Daniel	Hartford

	Names	Town
7	Curtice George	Kent
8	Steaphen	Waterbury
8	Camp Isaac	Farmingtown
8	Samuel	Waterbury
8	Sam^{ll} Junr	"
	Phineas	Woodbury
3	Canada David	Glastenbury
3	Crary Richard	"
	Conlee John	"
7	Convers Thomas Capt	Goshun
	Chase Walter	Haddam
8	Case Richard	Hartford
0	Church Samuel	Haddam
	Eben^r	Woodbury
6	Cone Elisha	Haddam
5	Ozias	Middletown
	Joseph	"
5	Daniel	"
3	Combs William Serj^t	Hart^d & Weathf^d
9	Corney Maleciah	Hartford
9	Cadwell Matthew S^t	".
1	Simeon	Stoningtown
	Coleman Noah Doct.	Labenon
1	Colefox Wm Ens^a	Newlondon
	Chappel Joshua	"
1	W^m 3^d Corp^l	"
	Comfort	"
9	Ameziah	Labenon
	Curtice	Salisbury
1	Corwin Selah	Lime
	Jonathan	Norwich
	Selah	Norwich
9	Crittenden Gideon	Middletown
5	Cahales Cornelius alias Frost Sam^{ll}	Milford
4	Conant Sam^{ll}	Mansfield
3	Calib	"
A	Coshall Thomas	Newhaven
7	Canfield Elijah	Newmilford
1	Comestock Gid^a	Norwich
	John	Saybrook
8	Car James alias Miller	Norwich
4	Cleff Lem^{ll} Capt	Plainfield
5	Cooley Nathan	Redding
5	Ruben	Somers
3	Comestock Sam^{ll}	Seybrook
5	Cummes W^m	Ridgfield
	Cottrel Nathan	Stonington
5	Cynamon Thom^s	"
	Collins Wm Lock	Stratford
6	Clanghorn Eleaz^r Leu^t	Salisbury
9	Crane Curtice	Weathersfield
5	Coy Sam^{ll}	Windsor
8	Calkens Israel	Waterbury
7	Chamberlin Eph^m	Wallingford
1	Chadwick John	Lime

	Names	Town
8	Cole Alben	Norwalk
2	Davinson W^m	Ashford
	Robert	Greenwich
6	Isaac	Milford
6	John	Washington
4	Dawner Ezra	Bolten
2	Caleb	E Windsor
2	Duggins James	Canterbury
	Downing Steaph^a	.'
	Christopher	Norwich
8	Doubleday Joseph	Coventry
A	Dixon George	Danbury
	Durfe Thomas	Fairfield
	Disborough Justus	"
8	(?) Joshua	"
2	Dimon Moses	"
2	John	Woodbury
8	Dutton Oliver Serj^t	Farmington
	Titus Serj^t	Waterbury
3	Dunham Cornelus	Farmington
	Dealing Sam^ll	Glastenbury
A	Davis Isaac	Greenwich
9	Daniel	Groten
8	Jonathan	Waterbury
	Steaphen	"
7	Daton Richard	Groten
	Israel	Newhaven
6	Davis James	"
9	Eben^r	Weathersfield
6	Dowd Moses	Guilford
7	Demming Wail	Goshun
	David Leiu^t	Hartford
1	Darrow Christoph^r	Hartford
4	Delibar James	"
9	Day Westbrook	"
	Die Dan^ll	Kent
	Dodg Daniel	Lyme
	Nathan	Colchester
1	DeWolf Steaphen	Lime
1	Edward	"
	Dewey James	Midletown
1	Dextor John Corp^l	Mansfield
6	Doyle Hugh	Newhaven
	Dickermon Joseph	"
7	Dunwill William	N Milford
7	Dailey James	"
	Drinkwater W^m	"
4	Durke John Col^o	Norwich
	Benj^a Leiu^t	Windham
	Jeremiah	"
	Dudley Zebulon L^t	Saybrook
1	Davel John	Stonington
1	Dennison Amos	Voluntown
5	Denslow Marten	Windsor
2	Dimmok Joseph	Willington
8	Dunbar Amos } alias Joel Brunson }	Waterbury
	Miles	"

	Names	Town
0	Danzy W^m	Newlondon
1	Daniels Ezekiel	"
	Douglass Solomon	"
1	Richard Lieu^t	"
5	Deforest Saml Ens^n	Norwalk
	Eams Everet	Danbury
3	Earl W^m	Enfield
2	Evans Abiathar	Hartford
	Sam^{ll} Junr	"
8	Henery	"
	Edgcomb Ezra	Newhartford
	Evan Isaac	Preston
8	Elmer Calib	Harrington
5	Daniel	Sharon
2	W^m	Somers
3	Ells Edward Capt	Midletown
1	Ellis John Chaplan	Norwich
6	Eagleston David	Newhaven
5	Eaton Solomon	Tolland
8	Easton Eliphalet	Woodbury
4	Edwards Nath^{ll}	Waterbury
	Elderken Vine Capt	Windham
2	Fountaine Enos	Stamford
6	Foot Eben^r	Branford
6	Ezra	Derbey
7	Eben^r	Harrington
A	Isaac Serj^t	Newhaven
8	Elijah	Newtown
8	Freeman Elisha	Canaan
	Jack	Colchester
6	Frank	Derbey
	Sampson	Glastenbury
3	Sifax alias Mosely	"
0	Edward	Groten
7	Guy	"
0	Micael	"
	Freeman Providence	Newlondon
3	Fitch Rufus	Canterbury
6	Joseph Trumbull	Salisbury
6	Fits Gerald Henery	"
	Fox John	Colchester
8	Elisha	Farmington
9	Asa	Glastenbury
	Jacobe Leiu^t	Norwich
1	Joshua	E Haddam
6	Farmer Th^o Ens^n	Derbey
2	Fuller John	Fairfield
5	Fegoe Peter	"
4	Fargoe W^m	Newlondon
	Fowler Nehemiah	Fairfield
	Caleb Corp^l	Guilford
	French Samuel	Fairfield
A	Fletcher Joseph	Greenwich
0	Fanning Elisha	Groten
4	Charles Leiu^t	Norwich
8	Frisbey Benjn	Torrington
7	Franklin Samuel	Killingsworth

	Names	Town
9	Flowers Elijah	Newhartford
4	Foster Zephaniah	Lebanon
3	John	Midletown
7	Benj[n]	Sharon
5	Fisher Cristoper	Midletown
7	Isaac	Sharon
6	Frances James	Midletown
6	John	Wallingford
2	Franklen Jehial	Woodbury
5	Frost Sam[ll]	
	alias Cornelu Cabales	Milford
1	Fenton Jonathan	Mansfield
2	Solomon Leiu[t]	"
	John	Willington
6	Ford Daniel	Newhaven
1	Fellows Joseph Ens[n]	Stongton
1	Nath[ll]	"
5	Forgarson Dan[ll]	Salisbury
8	Fattendon John	Waterbury
8	Fulford John Serj.	"
	Farnum Ruben	Windham
	Filets Francis	Woodbury
9	Fay Gershome	Winchester
9	Tim[o]	"
9	W[m]	"
9	Filley Remembrance	"
5	Fenn Dan[ll]	Washington
1	David	Colchester
1	Farnsworth Nath[ll]	"
6	Garret John	Branford
	John	Newhartf[d]
1	Goff Sam[ll]	
	alias Rich[d] Faiman ?	Chatham
3	Geer Elihue	Enfield
hired	Giddens Richard	Chatham
1	Gladding W[m]	Haddam
1	Gray James	Newlondon
7	Elijah	Groten
1	Goodfaith David	Newlondon
4	Gardiner David	Newlondon
1	Sherman	Norwich
	De Tubs	"
9	Gilbert Joseph	Newhartford
9	Theodore	"
7	Obediah	Stratford
7	Green Sam[ll]	Canaan
8	Josiah	Fairfield
	William Cap[t]	Hartford
	Robart	Voluntown
8	John Corp[l]	Woodstock
	Gates Nath[ll] Leiu[t]	Canterbury
3	Graham Joseph	Chatham
6	{ Grimes Silus }	Saybrook
	{ Cyrus }	"
3	Gutrich Levey	Chatham
7	David	Sharon
	Ephraim	Weathersf[d]
3	Graves Peter	Colchester

	Names	Town
	Graves Simeon	Waterbury
5	W^m	Midletown
	Grant Azeriah	E Windsor
6	James	Saybrook
3	Griswold Joseph	Infield
8	White	Harwington
D	Glover John	Fairfield
2	Goodsill Eppiphras	"
7	Grover Phineas L^t	Glastenbury
3	Amasa	Killingly
2	Jacobe	Stratford
5	Goold John	Goshun
8	Gridley Seth	Harwington
1	Gross Samuel	Lebanon
6	Gilston Jacobe	Midletown
5	Gillson Eleazer	Sharon
A	Gibson Sam^ll	Newhaven
4	Goodale Jacobe	Pomphret
D	Guyant Luke	Preston
8	Granger Samuel	Suffield
	Phineas	"
0	Gibs Josiah	Summer
3	Sam^ll Leiu^t	Windsor
1	Griffen James	Stoningtown
9	Giffin Simon Serj^t	Weathersfield
	Gorum Sam^ll	Stratford
0	Gaylord Benj^a	Waterbury
		& Torington
1	Hardy Nathaniel	Ashford
	Hall William	"
3	Israel	Enfield
5	Stephen	Fairfield
7	Stephen Capt	Guilford
7	Philemon L^t	"
7	David	Danbury
	Samuel Corp.	Killingworth
7	Talmadge Ens^a	N. Fairfield
6	Rufus	Wallingford
	Nathaniel	Waterbury
	William	N. London
0	Howe Zadock L^t	Bolten
9	Joshua	N. Haven
	Hubbard Elihue	Chatham
8	John Ens^a	Branford
3	Hezek. L^t	Middletown
0	Roswell	"
6	Harrison Jairus Sg^t	Branford
	William Corp^l	Lebanon
	Hoadley Saml	Branford
8	Higby Elihu	Canaan
7	Holembok John L^t	Branford
	Hale Aaron L^t	Chatham
1	Higgins Heman	"
3	Jesse	"
	Cornelius	Haddam
6	Humphry E. Capt	Derbe
6	Elijah Capt	Woodbury

Names	Town
Hotchkiss Levi Lᵗ	Derbe
8 Zadock Capᵗ	Farmington
7 Ira	Guilford
6 Hawkins Zadock	Derbe
6 Hinman Hustead Cor.	Durham
1 Holmes Eliphat Capᵗ	E. Haddam
A Nathaniel	Greenwich
8 David Doctʳ	Woodstock
Harvey Ithamar Capᵗ	E Haddam
1 Ezra	"
5 William	Saybrook
Hagar Simeon Serjᵗ	Enfield
A Hubbel, William Lᵗ	Fairfield
A Isaac Lᵗ	"
7 Hutonet Francis	Fairfield
7 Hilton Atkinson	"
6 Hosmer Timᵒ Doctʳ	Farmington
3 Hart Jonathan Adjᵗ	"
7 Benjamin	Wallingford
8 Hayden David	"
Thomas Lᵗ	Windsor
4 Hill Daniel	Glassenbury
7 Ebenʳ Capᵗ	Kent
4 Hill Phillip	Lebanon
4 John 2ᵈ	Symsbury
3 Holden John	Glassenbury
A Hays Abraham	Greenwᶜʰ
Titus	Hartland
A Harriot Israel	Greenwich
1 Harrinton Isaac	Groten
3 Elisha	Symsb
Hannabal Joseph	Groton
Joseph	Stonington
0 Holley Joseph	Groton & Preston
8 Hally Abraham	Stanford
Hawley C. Joseph	N. Milford
7 Handy Samuel Serjᵗ	Guilford
8 Heath Peleg Lᵗ	Hartford
8 Hadlock Reuben	"
9 Hooker William	"
6 John	Milford
8 Hodge Asael Capᵗ	Harwinton
6 David	Milford
7 Holdridge Hezekiah Col.	Hebron
Hyde Rufus	Lime
4 James Ensⁿ	Norwich
1 Horron John	Lyme
1 Hayns, Jonathan	"
1 Hudson Eleazer	"
John	Stonington
5 Henshaw Willᵐ Lᵗ	Middlet.
6 Hull David	"
6 Giles Serjᵗ	Salisbury
7 Samuel	N. Haven
8 Oliver	Saybrook
James	Waterbury
Stephen	Woodbury

	Names	Town
3	Harris John	Middletown
1	John	Mansfield
3	Champlin	Colchester
6	Hine Titus	Milford
1	Huse Bodwell	N. Haven
6	Howel Nicolas	"
	Harden Frederick	"
	Hunt Richard	"
7	Hamlin Joel	Norfolk
5	Hopkins Henry	Redding
4	Harmon John Capt	Suffield
7	Herrick Libeus	Stonington
4	Hazard Jeffry	"
	Hiscox Thomas	"
	Hawks Hannah p Son	"
2	Hallop Joseph	Stratford
2	Hinkley Ichabod Capt	Tolland
2	Heacock Samuel Serj^t	Stanford
	William Junr	Waterbury
8	Elisha	"
	David	Woodbury
	Hastings John	Wallinford
8	Hait Joseph Col	Stanford
	Houghton James	Union
2	Hoyt Philemon Serj^t	Willington
6	Samuel	Wallingford
0	Peter	N. London
	Hendry Daniel	"
	Hatch Hemon Corp	Willington
	Hitchcock Lemuel L^t	"
8	Thomas	"
	Hambden William	Woodstock
9	Howard George	Farmington
1	Halloway William	N. London
	Jones Joseph	Branford
1	Daniel	Lebanon
3	Thomas	Pomph.
9	Aaron	Saybr.
3	Eleazer	Somers
6	Jasper	Stratford
5	Isaiah	"
	Thomas	Wallingf^d
	Henry	N. London
hired	Jennings Elnathan	Chatham
4	Johnson James	
6	Willm	Durham
2	Nathaniel	Fairfield
[ ]	John	Farmington
8	William	Greenwich
6	Isaac	Guilford
5	Jonathan Col.	Middlet.
3	David	"
6	Abrah^m Corp.	N. Haven
1	Benjamin	Plainfield
8	Nathaniel	Stanford
	Robert	Sharon
2	Elihu	Tolland
6	John	Wallingf^d

	Names	Town
	Judd Daniel Serj^t	Colchester
3	William Capt	Farmington
8	Stephen	Waterbury
2	Bruster	"
	Jackson P. Nathan L^t	Fairfield
1	Thomas	Preston
8	Jesup Nathaniel	Greenw.
9	Jarrels Thos Serj^t	Hartford
1	Jolly William	N. fairfield
5	Jackknife Robert	Stonington
1	Ingram Mary p Son	"
8	Judgson Joseph	Woodbury
	Jordan John	Washington
6	Jocelin John	N. Haven
	Jacobs M.	Norwich
7	Knap Timothy	Goshen
5	James	N. Fairfield
2	Usel	Stamford
5	James	"
3	Keeney Benjn	Hartford
6	Kimbal Abrah.	Middletown
	Kinning Thomas	N. Fairf^d
4	King George	N. Haven
9	Orry	Stratf^d
8	Kimberly L^t	N. Town
	Kirtland Capt	Saybrook
	Karril John	Symsb
5	Kelsey Noah	Sharon
9	Kilby Christopher	Weathersf^d
3	Lyon Henry	Ashford
2	Samuel	Fairfield
3	Abiel	Pomphret
0	Asa Q. M.	Woodstock
1	Thomas	N. London
	Lane William	"
	Lee Levi	"
	Elisha Capt	Lime
1	Ezra L^t	"
8	Abner	Woodbury
8	Lester Andrew	Cant.
7	Luke Phineas	Cornwell
5	Ludeman John	Danbury
4	Lord John	"
6	Jabez	N. Haven
6	William	Saybrook
9	Jeremiah Serj^t	"
	Loomis Moses	E. Windsor
9	Israel	Hartford
2	Lockwood Stephen	Fairfield
A	Moses	Greenwich
	Saml Capt	"
2	Timothy	Stamford
5	Eliph. Serj^t	"
4	Moses Serj^t	Weathersfield
9	Lamb Joseph	Glassenb.
9	Loveland Thomas	"
8	Elisha	"
	Levi	"

3

	Names	Town
7	Layre Jacob	Goshen
	Lukus Samuel	Hartford
7	Leet Allen	Killingw.
7	Lambskins Benjᵃ	Kent
1	Lay Richard	Lyme
6	Asa Leiut.	Saybrook
8	Lung Joseph	Middletown
7	Lacey F. Fairchild	N. Fairfield
5	Josiah Capᵗ	Newtown
6	Levingsworth Eli Majʳ	N. Haven
	Lines John	"
1	Leeds Thomas	Stonington
1	Lewis Valentine	"
	Ebenezar	Wallingfor
	Samuel Serjᵗ	Waterbury
8	Lunsbury Peter	Stamford
	Larrebee Willet	Salisbury
2	Luce Jonathan	Tolland
3	Lilly Ebenezer	Union
5	Lamberten Obed	Windsor
5	Lawrence Amos	"
	Littlefield Ebenʳ	Windham
A	Leverick Gabriel	Fairfield
2	Lockwood Gersham	Norwalk
	Miner Silvester	N. London
	James	"
1	Elihu	E. Haddam
	Andrew	Tolland
1	Munro John	N. London
1	Manwaring George	"
0	Mallerson Benjᵃ	"
	Mac Fall William	N. London
9	Merrils Cypron	N. Hartford
9	Aaron	"
8	Asher	Hebron
	Cyprian	Farming.
	Marcy Thomas	Ashford
	Miller Daniel	Chatham
8	Daniel	"
5	John	Glassenb.
8	Charles Lᵗ	Hartford
1	Nathan	Lyme
8	Nathaniel	Weathersfᵈ
4	Markham Joseph	Chatham
	McCorn William	"
1	Matthews James	Danbury
8	William	Midletown
7	Robert	Newhaven
1	Mitchel Samuel	E Haddam
2	John Serjᵗ	Fairfield
	George	Norwich
1	Murfe Thomas	E Haddam
1	Mott Samuel	E Haddam
9	Adam	Winchester
6	Mobs Piercey	E Haddam
5	Morehouse David	Fairfield
7	Meeker Steaphen	"
2	Daniel	"

	Names	Town
	Meeker Steaphen	Reading
2	Mills Joseph	Fairfield
D	Samuel Leiu^t	Simsbury
2	Murry Abraham	Derbey
	Noah Serj^t	Kent
6	Moses Jonas	Derbey
2	Mix John	Farmington
A	Tim^o Leiu^t	Newhaven
4	Thomas Junr	Wallingford
3	Momosuck Daniel	Farmington
	McDowel Alexand^r En.	Glastenbury
9	McLane Matthew	Groten
	Mc Donald John	"
4	Mc Danield James	Preston
7	Miles Isaac Serj^t	Goshun
A	John Leiu^t	Newhaven
7	Charles Leiu^t	Preston
	Mattocks Sam^{ll}	Hartford
3	Mahar James	"
3	Mize William	"
	MacOrlander Leiu^t	Hebron
6	Mc Lane Jacobe	Salisbury
4	Mc Gregor John Capt	Plainfield
1	Mc Censey James	
	alias George	Stonington
2	Mc Anotter John	Stamford
	Mauenborough Jedadiah	Hebron
3	Marble Thomas	"
5	Marshal Elisha	Harrington
	More John Junr	Kent
3	Wm Junr	Union
5	Mason John	Litchfield
	Munger Daniel	"
6	Billey	Salisbury
6	Mather Elias Leiu^t	Lyme
	Maccoy Allexander	"
6	Meigs Return Col^o	Midletown
	Marks Comfort	"
6	Mansfield Jos^h Capt	Newhaven
6	Dan	"
6	John Leiu^t	Wallingford
	Munson Wm Capt	Newhaven
6	Levy Lieu^t	Wallingford
6	Moultrup Joseph	Newhaven
6	Steaphen	Newhaven
6	Mallery Amos Corp^l	"
A	Melone Daniel	"
6	Marten Lewis	"
4	George	Windham
	Moss John	Newhaven
6	Daniel	"
1	Manning W^m	Norwich
2	Phineas	Stafford
	Wm Capt	Woodstock
4	Marsh Peter	Plainfield
5	Abner	Killingley
1	Meach Joshua	Preston

	Names	Town
2	Millington Sam[ll]	Stafford
9	Migat Zebulon	Weathersfield
4	Munn Isaiah	Colchester
5	Mead Jasper L[t]	Norwalk
	Nash Eben[r]	Norwalk
6	Norten Benj[n] Ens[n]	Branford
A	Jedadiah	Chatham
7	Rufus Corp[l]	Guilford
7	Elon	"
5	Joseph	Goshun
0	Newton Isaac	E Windsor
2	Elias	Tolland
8	Ezekiel	Washington
	Nickerson Urana	Greenwich
6	Niger Phillip	Guilford
6	Newel Robert	Saybrook
7	Nichols Sam[ll]	Newfairfield
	Negro Briston	Saybrook
	Cuff	Colchester
4	Nelson Daniel	Suffield
6	Nugent John	Stonington
8	Nichols Sam[ll]	Norwalk
6	Otis Joseph	Branford
A	Oryon alias Rian Jerem	Danbury
6	Okeain Jeremiah	Derbey
5	Osburn Stratten	Fairfield
	Oswold Col[o]	Farmington
8	Olmstead James Ens[n]	Hartford
	Oharra Tim[o]	Newhaven
7	Orvis Eleazer	Norfolk
	Olin W[m]	Norwich
6	Owen Eliphalet	Salsbury
	Owen Alvin	
	alias David Thrall	Windsor
2	Orcut Calib Serj[t]	Willington
8	Olds Aaron	Woodbury
6	Oliver	Washington
6	Post Abner	Saybrook
2	Pool Daniel	Ashford
6	Potter Steaphen Cap[t]	Branford
3	Lemuel Corp[l]	Farmington
	Israel Leiu[t]	Newhaven
6	Moses	"
4	Pelton George	Chatham
0	Eben[r]	Groten
	David	"
2	Benj[n]	Guilford
3	Parks Daniel	Chatham
	Price Levy	Cornwell
	Rufus Leiu[t]	Tollan
	Picket Thomas	Danbury
6	Prichard James	Derbey
8	George Jun[r]	Waterbury
A	Prindle J Enos	Derbey
8	Abijah	Newtown
2	Porter Hezekiah	E Windsor
9	Amos	Haddam

	Names	Town
3	Porter Eleazer	Hebron
3	Nathan	Mansfield
5	Daniel	Windsor
2	Pierce Daniel	E Windsor
2	Parsons David Capt	Enfield
2	Jonathan	"
A	Theodocious	Greewich
	Perkens Daniel Junr	Enfield
5	Patching Elijah Corp^l	Fairfield
1	Purcivael Paul Q M	Farmingtown
6	Powers James	"
0	Thomas	Midletown
8	Nathan	Woodstock
	Pees Peter Serj^t	Glastenbury
1	Pomp Samuel	Groten
1	Jacobe alias David	"
	Peck Zebelon	Goshun
2	Silas	Lime
	Silas Junr	"
0	Ariel	Midletown
	Darius Leiut	Norwich
A	Charles Serj^t Aro	Wallingsford
3	Pomeroy Ralf Leiu^t	Hartford
	Benjn Doct^r	Hebron
7	Phelps Charles	Hartland
	Pieffer Lazarus	Hebron
	Perry Silvanus	Killingsly
7	Elisha	Ridgfield
	Eben^r Serj^t	Windham
4	Palmer Elijah	Lebanon
5	Benjn	Litchfield
1	W Jonathan Leu^t	Stonington
5	Plant Timothy	Litchfield
	Prentice Jonas Capt	Newhaven
	Parmele Jeremiah Capt	Newhaven
A	Parker Edmond	"
9	Samuel	Stratford
5	John	"
6	Elisha	Wallingsford
3	Benjn	"
	Eliab	Waterbury
6	Isaac	"
7	Peet Lemuel	Newmilford
	Polly Alpheus	Lebanon
7	Plumb Ameriah	Norfolk
1	Peter	Norwich
4	Perigo W^m	"
0	Pollard W^m	"
8	Isaac	Woodbury
1	Pratt Ethan	Saybrook
0	Russel	Somers
2	Pearman Joseph	Suffield
4	Peters Peter	Stoningtown
6	Phillups Thomas	Stratford
5	Parkinson Dene	Stamford
5	Pellet Enos	Sharon
2	Preston Tiras	Tolland
8	Amasa	Waterbury

	Names	Town
	Patterson Andrew	Tollan
5	Pinney Aaron	Windsor
5	Prior Abner Cap[t]	"
7	Page Tim[o]	Wallingsford
	Parde Jonathan	Waterbury
	Pendleton Daniel	"
3	Parrish Eliphas	Windham
1	Quindley Thomas	Newlondon
4	Quash Catoe	Colchester
4	Quy Libeus alias Negro	Norwich
4	Robertson James	Newlondon
9	Ephraim	Coventry
	John	Midletown
	Jared Leiu[t]	Newhaven
	Samuel Q M	"
6	Thomas	"
4	Elias Leiu[t]	Windham
	Simeon Jun[r]	"
1	Sam[ll]	"
1	Richards Steaphen	Newlondon
1	W[m] Cap[t]	"
4	Rogers Peter	"
1	Asael	E Haddam
A	James	Greenwich
1	Lemuel	Lime
1	Joseph	"
9	Roberts Elisha	Newhartford
3	Nathan	Colchester
7	Benj[n]	Newfairfield
	Abial	Waterbury
8	Joel	"
8	Ranne Jabesh	Chatham
3	Steaphen	"
4	Rowley Jesse	Colchester
	Roswell Jeremiah	Danbury
	Rigs Laban	Derbey
6	James	"
2	Raymond W[m]	Fairfield
2	David	"
	Sam[ll]	Reading
	Rows Amos	Farmington
1	Rouse Simeon alias Oliver	Preston
7	Jabez Serj[t]	Windham
8	Rundle John	Greenich
3	Randol Elijah	Windham
A	Ritch Edward	Greenich
9	Risley Steaphen	Hartford
7	Reed Benj[n]	Hartland
1	Enoch Cap[t]	Lime
1	Nathan	Mansfield
	Ruben	Norwich
4	Oliver	Pomphret
A	Rumbelo Thomas	Killingworth
6	Rosseter Sam[ll]	Litchfield
	Roach John	Lime
5	Remmington Steaphen	Ridgfield
4	Rising James	Suffield

	Names	Town
8	Russel Giles Col°	Stonington
8	Wm Junr	Stratford
9	Ashur	Weathersfield
5	Rust Jonathan	Sharon
5	Robbers Joseph	Voluntown
9	Riley John Leiu^t	Weathersfield
	Root Nathan Leiu^t	Willington
8	Rice Nehemiah Capt	Waterbury
	David	Willington
7	Ripley Charles Serj^t	Windham
2	Rood Simeon	Woodbury
A	Ryon Jeremiah alias Green (?) Junr	Redding & Danbury
	Steaphens Aaron	Newhartford
	Peter Junr	Canterbury
	Roswell	Farmington
3	Tim°	Glastenbury
	Aaron Capt	Killingsworth
2	Peter	"
6	W^m	Newhaven
6	Elijah	Saybrook
	Seymour Elias discharged	Newhartford
	Shipman John	Saybrook
	Samuel Leu^t	"
2	James Serj^t	"
	Stannard Jasper	"
5	Samuel	Litchfield
3	Smith Peter	Ashford
3	Abijah	"
6	Jordan	Branford
4	Ezra Leu^t	Chatham
D	Asaph	Farmington
3	David	"
0	John Leiu^t	Haddam
	George Ens^n	Hartford
5	Henery	Litchfield
4	Enoch	Lime
6	Wm Leiu^t	Milford
3	John Junr	Mansfield
6	Ambrus	Newhaven
5	Henery	Pomphret
	Job Leiu^t	Ridgfield
1	Daniel	Stoningtown
8	Isaac	Stamford
5	Isaac Junr	"
7	Daniel	Wallingford
7	John	Waterbury
8	Levy	"
	Samuel	"
8	David Major	
	James	Windham
2	Daniel Corp^l	Woodstock
2	Spaldin Ephraim	Ashford
	Shaw William	Canterbury
4	Jonathan	"
	Benj^a	"
4	Richard	Stoningtown
5	Schallem Abraham Serj^t	Chatham
0	Stocken Marshal	"

	Names	Town
1	Stark Tim°	Colchester
1	Samuel	"
	Steaphen	"
	Steaphen	Hebron
	Simons Isaac	Infield
9	Eli	Colebrook
3	Simmons Samuel	Cornwall
	James	Stonington
7	Swift Heman Col'	Cornwall
	Robert	Groten
6	Strong Eliakim Serj'	Durham
7	John Serj'	Guilford
1	Barnabas	Lebanon
5	David Leiu'	Sharon
6	Phineas	Salisbury
6	Seward Samuel	Durham
	Daniel	Milford
	W^m	"
6	Nathan	Waterbury
6	Squire Saxton D M	Durham
6	Abiathur	"
	S. Samuel	Farmingtown
6	Daniel	Newhaven
A	Stent. Samuel	"
	Spencer David Leiu'	E Haddam
	Obediah	Hartford
1	Ichabud Leiu'	Lime
	Salley James	E Haddam
2	Sturges Moses Leiu'	Fairfield
3	Steel Josiah	Farmingtown
	Smithers William	Glastenbury
7	Simbo Prince	"
0	Staunten Amos Cap'	Groten
4	Suntsemun Aaron	"
	Speers John	"
	Starts alias States	"
6	Sharper Tuis	"
	Sharp Joseph	Milford
4	Benjamin	Pomphret
0	Sterry Silas	Groten & Preston
1	Solomon Amos	Groten
	Shortman William	"
4	Sholes Nathan	"
5	Sealey John	Goshun
3	Segwick Samuel	Hartford
3	Scot Elijah	Harwington
2	Shelley alias Kelly John	Litchfield
1	Lemuel	Stoningtown
8	Eben' Serj'	Stratford
5	Stone Josiah alias Joseph	Litchfield
	David	Wallingford
1	Sill David Col°	Lime
1	Selden Ezra Cap'	"
4	Saunders John	"
7	Wm Serj'	Newfairfield
6	Sawyer Asa	Lime
0	Sullard Jacobe	"

	Names	Town
4	Sumner John Col°	Midletown
0	Savage Abijah Cap¹	"
6	Starr David Leiu¹	"
1	Josiah Col°	Newmilford
6	Sizer Jonathan	Midletown
6	Steward John	Milford
8	Sanford Sam¹¹ Cap¹	"
6	Thomas	Newhaven
7	James	Newlondon
	Ezekiel	Waterbury
1	Shumway John Cap¹	Mansfield
	Sherman Wᵐ Cap¹	Newhaven
6	John Leiu¹	"
	Sperry Chauncey	"
6	Sugden Abraham	"
6	Stockwell Abel	"
A	Simpson Robert	"
6	Shepard John	"
7	Stilwell Steaphen	Newmilford
7	Sturdevant Nathan	Norfolk
	Sydleman John	Norwich
	Spicer Samuel	"
1	Stilman Robert	"
	Starkweather Asa	"
4	Stoddard Joshua	Plainfield
3	Enoch	Weathersfield
8	Nathan Cap¹	Woodbury
8	Ely	"
4	Shadden John	Pomphret
	Stoel Elisha	"
	Seers Obediah	Preston
5	Sherwood Nehemiah	Reading
2	Speers Elijah	Suffield
4	Sowas Richard	Stoningtown
	Searl Constant	"
	Suncheman Nath¹¹	"
A	Sunderland John	Stratford
	Scofield Selah	Stanford
5	Sᵗ John James	"
2	Sabens Nehemiah	Tolland
3	Summit Prince	Voluntown
	Sprague James Leiu¹	Union
6	Shaler Joseph Leiu¹	Wallingford
8	Southmaid	Waterbury
	Scovel Steaphen	"
9	Steaphen	Winchester
D	Shelden Elisha Col•	Sharon
5	Scribner Asa	Norwalk
	Thomas Abselom	Newlondon
5	Steaphen	Chatham
3	Patrick	Hartford
A	John	Newhaven
6	Samuel	"
	James	"
6	Ephraim	
5	Taylor John	Newhartford
5	Baruck	Fairfield

	Names	Town
3	Taylor Ephraim	Hebron
3	Thomas	Union
8	Simeon	Woodbury
6	Towner Jacobe	Branford
2	Tickens Tiras	Canterbury
4	Tarble W^m	Colchester
7	Tanner Tryal Leiu^t	Cornwall
8	Thomson Nathaniel Serj^t	Coventry
A	Isaiah Leiu^t	Farmington
6	David Serj^t	Guilford
D	Appiphras	Saybrook
	Tomlinson David Ens^n	Derbey
9	Treat John	Glastenbury
3	Tryon Ezra	"
A	Townd John	Greenich
6	Teal Sam^{ll}	Guilford
5	Tuttle Levey	Litchfield
8	Ezekiel	Waterbury
	Tim^o	Waterbury
8	Jabez	"
	Tim^o Ens^n	"
	Hezekiah	"
	Peter	Norwalk
7	Trowbridge John Serj^t	Newfairfield
6	John Leiu^t	Newhaven
5	Eben^r	Newmilford
A	Troop John Leiu^t	Newhaven
4	Benjn Maj^r	Norwich
6	Tolls Elnathan	Newhaven
3	Tounsend Solomon	"
A	Todd Yale	"
7	Tubs Nathan	Norfalk
	Tracey Hezekiah Leiu^t	Norwich
1	Wm Ens^n	"
4	Moses	"
1	Tyler Nathan	Preston
6	Tooley Andrew	Saybrook
6	Tupper Wm Corp^l	Salisbury
5	Thrall David alias Alven Owen	Windsor
8	Thayr Asa	Waterbury
8	Terril Joel	"
	Trowbridg Sam^{ll}	Norwalk
8	Taylor Elijah	"
3	Verry Jonathan	Chatham
8	Vaun Daniel	Lebanon
6	Verguson John	Newhaven
8	Upson Ezekiel	Waterbury
4	Wright Elisha	Newlondon
3	John	Chatham
8	Simeon	Hebron
	Isaiah	"
5	James	Litchfield
	Ezekiel	Norwich
	Weekes Joseph	Newlondon
1	Wiley Edward	"
1	Willey Jonathan	E Haddam
4	Wales Eben^r Leiu^t	Ashford

	Names	Town
3	Waters W^m	Ashford
A	W^m	Greenwich
3	Warren John	Bolten
8	Abraham	Farmingtown
6	White John Ens^n	Branford
6	Joseph	Derbey
6	Samuel	Newhaven
6	Oliver	Saybrook
3	Wood Jacobe	Chatham
3	Lemuel	Enfield
6	Elisha	Newhaven
2	Thomas	Somers
3	Whitney Daniel S M	Colchester
	Henery P M	Derbey
4	Williams John	Colchester
1	Thomas	E Hadam
A	Richard	Fairfield
0	Henery Leiu^t	Groten
0	Uriah Serj^t	Groten
9	Dan^{ll} Serjt	Weathersfield
8	Obed	Waterbury
	Wix Uriah	Cornwall
4	Wack Frederick	Colchester
6	Warner Eben^r Serj^t	Derbey
3	Robert Capt	Midletown
6	Worster Henery	Derbey
	Thomas Capt	Newhaven
2	Washburn Benjn	Derbey
8	Samuel	Stratford
6	Watrus Richard	Derbey
6	Wakeley Jonathan	"
1	Watken Ephraim	Easthadam
1	Wheeler Joshua	"
6	Thomas	Guilford
5	David	Stonington
0	Wallace Ab^{rm}	Eastwindsor
0	Wadsworth J B Doct^r	"
5	Roger Leu^f	Hartford
2	Ware Dan^{ll} Serj^t	Enfield
2	Webb Hezekiah	Fairfield
	Jonathan	Norwich
A	Gideon	Wallingford
4	Nath^{ll} Capt	Windham
D.	Wainwright Sam^{ll}	Farmington
7	Thomas	Sharon
	Willcox James	Farmington
	James	Harwington
3	Welten Benjn	Farmington
	Steaphen Junr	Waterbury
	Webster Joshua Serj^t	Glastenbury
A	Wessels Herculus	Greenwich
A	Wilson David	"
1	George	Lime
6	John	Newhaven
A	Warrin Henery Leiu^t	Greenwich
A	Whiting Sam^{ll} Leiu^t	"
3	Whitmore Lemuel S^t	"

	Names	Town
7	Wyard Thomas	Goshun
3	Wyllys Sam[ll] Col[o]	Hartford
4	Eben[r]	Midletown
6	Joseph	"
5	Wattles Roswell Serj[t]	Hartford
	Way Hammon	"
3	Walters Thomas	"
	Walter W[m]	Newhaven
D	Silas	Norwich
1	Woodworth Jedadiah	Lebanon
4	Benj[n]	"
	Ward William	"
1	Waid John	Lime
	Marten	"
7	Wilder Aaron	Newfair[d]
D	Wilds Jonathan	Newhaven
7	Wilkeson Iccabud	Newmilford
9	Jesse	Winchester
	Whitley W[m]	Newmilford
7	Watson Tetus Cap[t]	Norfolk
1	Waterman Eben[r] Jun[r]	Norwich
	Wedge Joshua	"
9	Warden Isaac	Saybrook
1	Walter	Stoningtown
7	Waterhouse Steaphen	Saybrook
2	Widger John	"
3	Woodbridg Theoph[l]	Simsbury
5	Woodward Oliver	"
	Woodward Oliver	Windsor
8	Walker Nathan[ll]	Stafford
A	Robert Cap[t]	Stratford
8	Elisha	Woodbury
	Nathan alias Zacheriah	"
2	Wallbridg Ames Maj[r]	Stafford
1	West John	Stoningtown
	Joseph	Windham
2	Wardwell Jacobe	Stamford
8	W[m]	"
2	Weed Benj[n]	"
5	Thadeus Leiu[t]	"
	Western Benj[n] Ens[n]	Weathersfield
9	Wells Joshua	"
5	Wedg Josoph	Windsor
5	Wing Samuel	"
	Waldow Albigence	Windham
8	Welch Luke	Woodbury
	Micael	Washington
	Moses Wairing	Norwalk
	Wilcox Elias	"
8	Williams John	"
1	Yerrington Jesse	Groten
7	Yale Waitotite	Sharon
	Nash	Wallingford
	Yates W[m]	Salisbury
	Zander Gad	Newhaven

The Characters annexed to the Names of the Men in carrying the Supplies into the Acc[ts] to denote what Reg[t] they belong to viz:

1st Regt	.	.	.	1	Col[o] Webb's	. .	9
2 Do	.	.	.	2	Col[o] Shirburn's	. .	0
3[d] Do	.	.	.	3	L[t] Dragoons	. .	D
4th Do	.	.	.	4	Artillery .	. .	A
5th Do	.	.	.	5			
6th Do	.	.	.	6			
7th Do	.	.	.	7			
8th Do	.	.	.	8			

[Indorsed] Alphabet of Family Supplies in 1777, 8 & 9.

Alphabetical List of Persons in the Connecticut Line who rec[d] Family Supp[s] before 1780

[*State Library, Revolution 30, 1.*]

RETURNS OF MEN IN SERVICE, 1777-1779.

[The Archives relating to the Revolution volume 30, numbers 51–147, consist of returns from the various towns, giving particularly the names of soldiers serving in the Continental Line from these towns whose families had received supplies from the town during the years 1777, 1778, 1779. Many of the returns give, in addition to those whose families had received supplies, the names of other soldiers serving from the respective towns during those years. The names of those whose families had received supplies are carefully checked with a cross, and such names comprise the "Alphabetical List" which forms the first document in the same volume of the Archives, and is printed in this volume beginning on page 21. The names of such soldiers as are not thus checked are here given under their respective towns.]

ASHFORD

Names of Officers and Soldiers Single

Daniel Eldrige Lei[t]
Benj[a] Dimmuck Se[r]
Samuel Allen
Lemuel Allen
David Peck
Dyer Brown
Ephraim Aery In the Light Dragoons
Jason Crofford
Joseph Ingly
Jonathan Crane
Comfort Tyler
Jedediah Smith
Abijah Brooks J[r] Dead
Eleaser Russell
John Lane
Eleaser Smith
Asa Davison Dead
Elias Dimmuck
Elias Robinson
Jonathan Bullock
Paul Davison
Joseph Snell

John Watkins
Stephen Eaton
Robert Patterson
James Hale
Josiah Bicknall
William Southworth
Joseph Southworth
James Eaton
Eleasor Owen
Robart Hale
Caleb Hendee Ju[r] In his Excellency Gen[ll] Washingtons Gard
Joseph Hunter
Joshua Knowlton
James Grant
Chester Rogers
Amos Dowsett
Lawrence Dowsett
Tytus Prescoot Negro Dead
Tone Smith Negro
Aaron Keyes Negro

CANAAN

Col. Swifts Reg[t]
Simon Tubbs
Isac Smith
Samson Hunt
John Curtis
Richard Bishop
Joseph Cowles

Col. Chandlers or Rusels Reg[t]
Serj. Joshua Whitney
Thomas Stevens
William Mix
Serj. Elias Lee
Stephen Stevens
Warren Grizwold Deceased
Abner Miller
Bille Laurance
David Preston

COLCHESTER

Gideon Chapman
Asahel Newton Junr
Ezekiel Daniels
John Smith
Gideon Fox
Amos Fox
John Hall
Cuff Wells
Dolphin Kellogg
Esau Kellogg
Joshua Frank
Hendrick Townsend
Asher Carter
James Dodge
Nehemiah Daniels
Joshua Isham
Jeremiah Stanton

Jesse Brown
Ephraim Deathic(?) Ju
John Roberts
Robert Douglas
Frederic Bowman
Nathan Scovel Junr
Joseph Thompson
William Jones
Samuel Loomis Ju^r
Thomas Pilgrim
James Morgan Junr
William Gardner
Charles Brown
Ebenezer Billings
Israel Johnson
Joseph Whood (?)
Elijah Taylor

CORNWALL

Abraham Grimes
Peres Bonney
Joshua Hartshorn
Silas Dibble
} Those were Detached the 26th July 1778 to serve till the 15th of Jany 1780

DANBURY

[The following men received bounty.]

Ezra Ketcham
David Hall
Thad^s Starr
John Barnum
Noah Barnum
Willm McLean
Noah Taylor
Natha^{ll} Robinson
Roben Negro
Variah Negro

James Guthery
Jesse Peck
Joshua Taylor
Willm Griffeth
Jonathⁿ Dickeman
Benjaⁿ Sillick
Willm Porter
Ebenezer Barnum
John Curtis
Collins Chapman

DERBY

Reuben Blake
David Chapman
David Hull

Daniel Nichols
Charles Perkins

The Above five Men are now serving in the Continental Army have not Received any bounty from the Town

[The following men received bounty.]

Joseph Smith
Eleazer Durand
Gawham (? Garsham) Bardsley
John Dow

Willlam Whitney
John Allen
Thomas Cook
Joseph Fairchild

Philo Lewis (?)
William Smith
James Luch
George Waterous
Levi Chatfield
Benjamin Black
Abner Riggs
Walter Wooster
Philow Wooding
Amos Fox

Thomas Phillips
Bether Nicols
John Hatchet
Edward Warren
Andrew Waterous
Moses Reggs
Daniel Brown
Jeremiah Woodin
Joseph Tomlinson
Ebenezer Durand

EAST WINDSOR

Soldiers in the Continental army now in service E: Windsor

North Society Souldᵉˢ

Francis Baxter
Alexʳ Tomson
Erastus Booth
Elnathⁿ Fitch
John Hadlock
John Pierce

John Bissel
Israel Orsborn
Aaron Fargo
Moses Elsworth
Zepheniah Baits
Abel McIntire

Elenton Soulders

Lᵗ Josiah Brown
Doctʳ B Wadsworth
Serjᵗ Warham Foster
Russel Prat
Willᵐ Anderson
Zedekiah Peek
Samˡˡ Taylor
Danˡˡ Pierce
Elihu Bissel
Stephen Bartlet
Wᵐ Brown
Jude Brown
Levi Charter
John Indian

Abram Wallis
Chancy Foster
John Taylor Junʳ
Wᵐ Wallis
Hez Elsworth
Abner Slade
David Clark
Ezra Leonard
Benoni Hills
John Newel ffilr (?)
Zebulon Burroos
Joseph Kingsberry
Eliphalet Lord
Benjⁿ Hubbard Indⁿ

East Windsor 1st Parish Soldiers

Lᵗ Erast. Wolcutt Prisʳ
Abiel Allin
Tomo Chapin
John Gaylord
Wᵐ Jones
Leonard Munro
Mark Filly
Samˡˡ Hadlock
Thomˢ Raymond
Jonath Fowler

Christopher Horton
Elijah Churchil
Israel Strong
Stepⁿ Dorman
Hez Porter
Leonard Rogers
Abel Negro
Gurdon Munsil
Porter Negro

[The families of Bissel, Beaman, Andrss, Grant and Wadsworth appear to have received supplies, although the names are not checked in the list.]

ENFIELD

Serj' Jabez Parsons
Benj" Butler
Tho' Root Jun'
Othniel Allen
Eben' Pease 3ᵈ
Simeon Pease
Benjᵐ Henington
John Ward
Tho' Hale Jun'
Hiram Hall
Amasa Allen
David Bullen Ju'
David Phelps Jun'
Eben' Aames

Isaac Markham
Tho' Justus Davis
John Graham
William Thomson
Nathan [iel ?] Ros [e ?]
John Delaney
Benjᵐ Baxter
Joel Mᶜ griggry
Benj" Bugbee
James Erl
Levi Terry
Isaac French
Jared Simons
James Russel

FARMINGTON

Ezekial Curtis Eight Months Man
Solⁿ Welton Eight Months Man

Hezekiah Stanley
William Davice
Serj' Luke Wadsworth
Thomas Green
Ebenezer Lee
Samuel Adams
Hartwell Barns
Samuel Coe
Zeb" Woodruff
Josiah Lensley
Steph" Brunson
Thomas Collet
John Corner
Timothy Wells
Elisha Wells
James Tayler
Wise Barns
Hosea Gridley
Asa Brunson Ju'
William Lee
Elijah Porter
Paul Welman
Serj' Joel Smith
Phinehas Judd
Cornelius Dunham Ju'
Mark Mildrum
Jason Hitchcock
Sam' Hitchcock
Elisha Heart
Tim° Heart
Steph" Hotchkiss
Roger Lewis
David Jaaroms
Levi Frisby
David Enos
Benoni Brunson

Tim° Bibbins
Isaac Byington
James Foster
James Mitchel
Joseph Patterson
Semion Persons
Asher Heacox
David Heyden Jun'
James Cole
Ebn' Hills
Wᵐ Smiley
James Tryon
Israel Winchel
John Smith
James Couch
Amos Barns
Mark Newell
Bliss Heart
Prince Negro
Joshua Smith
Steph" Chapman
Isaac Hall Negro
Solⁿ Tuttle
Solⁿ Buck
Sam' Ingham
Corp' Ichabod Hawley
Normon Newell
Jese Mathews
Hubbard Mathews
Pharoah Gomer
Dan' Allyn Negro
Moses Merriman
Eben' Darren
Wᵐ Woodruff
Levi Hatchcock
Reubin Cole

4

Elisha Linkton
Aaron Moree
Eliakim White
Gad Negro
Dick Negro
John Andrus
Josiah Cole
Kitt Moore
Joel Welton
Elix^r Dorchester
Elijah Royce
Elisha Webster
Robert Cook
George St George
Abel Scipeo
Ira Winchel
Luther Adkins
Lemuel Potter
Nathan Gellett
Roswell Webster
Saml Comstick
Wm Mathews
Ichabod Bailey
Reuben Heart
Reuben Peck

Tom Negro
Charles Woodruff
Elisha Bailey
Liverpole Wadsworth Negro
Elijah Heart
Nathan Savage
John Wintworth Strong
Jacob Teal
Jonthⁿ Lankton Negro
Jonthⁿ Brigham
Joseph Teal
Barabas Clark
Jeremiah Gillett
Prince Denison
Peter Keehole
Wm Robbards
Salmon (?) Root
Levi Hamlin
Isaac Fisk
Riverius Newell
Constant Robbards
Thomas Twist
Mingo
Paul Williams
Simion Adams

GOSHEN

Stephen Mix
Simeon Hall Deceased

York Negro Deceased
John Willoughby Deserted

GROTON

Serg^t Eben^r Morgan
Serg^t Daniel Nikerson
Serg^t Joseph Bently
Joseph Cornish
Jesse Starr
John Pemberton
Moses Stoddard
Saml Backer
Cuff Negrow
Abel Wassonks
Isaac Rogers
Joseph Meson
Joseph Queekets
George Buckmaster
Elisha Avery
George Avery J^r
Wheler Shouls
Amos Latham
John Burnham
Wm Paul
Asa Baley
John Pomp
Cato Robison
Abraham Pharoah

Serg^t Robert Allyn
Serg^t Thos Malison
Bildad Edward
Andrew Wiger
Robert Williams
Thos Williams
Andrew Backer
Daniel Wiger
Wm Davis
Jonathan Ruff
John Dabol 3^d
Andrew Forseth
Diariah Elderkin
John Williams
Solomon Williams
Nathⁿ Williams
Nathⁿ Smith
Ezekiel Billing
Simⁿ Comstock
Gilbert Edgcom
Roswil Parish
Natha^l Noys
Chris^r Chester
Joseph Willey

Wᵐ Devenport
Nathˡ Solomon
Jack Negro
Israel Brown
Robert Stanton
Rufus Holdredge
Jacob Williams
Joseph Williams
David Fanning
Nathan Fanning
Thoˢ Gallup
Prentice Gallup
Elisha Stoddard
Lemuel Chester
Ralph Williams
Jonathan Mongo
Asa Lamb
Joseph Colver
Thoˢ Fanning

Nathan Stoddard
Nathanel Bellows
Gershom Brown
Fraderic Park
Aaron Sholes
James Park
Constant Avery
Benjⁿ Petice
James Pelton
Danel Stoddard
Danel Holway
Cyrus Killam
Fraderick Stoddard
Ebenʳ Pollerd
James Pattison
Miner Allyn
Fraderick Fanning
John Brown

GUILFORD

George Ranney
Amos Hall
Abraham Woodard
Nathan Megs
Ebinezer Hoadley
Thomas Hall
Benjamin Waterous
James Wand
Ebinezer Cook
Jared Chittenden
Bela Scovel
Chandler Renton
Benjamin Kirkham
William Kirkham
Ambrous Norton
William Stone
Gad Negro
Jonathan Nonesuch
Nathˡˡ Smith
Thomas Sanford
Jonothan Parker
William Bayley
Jehial Doud
Jonathan Arnall

Solomon Doud
Cuff Negro
David Adhins
Moses Hill
William Chittenden
William Rowleson
Timothy Stephens
Samuel Akerly
Samuel Teal
Zebulon Benton
Xyper Tyley
Torrey Scrantom
Benjamin Crampton
Timothy Scrantom
Joel Bishop
Elnathan Seward
Calvin Crampton
Josiah Adkins
Joseph Terrey
William Beadle
Jonothan Wilcox
Isaac Hotchkiss
Nathˡˡ Smith
Pompy Negro

HADDAM

A List of Soldiers Belonging the Town of Haddam in the Continental
Army that had no families to be Supplyed

Serᵗ John Baily
Serᵗ Jeremy Baily
Cesor Chapman
Shumer Wilcox Dead
William Porter dead
William Baily

Timothy Smith Deserted
James Smith deserted
Timothy Brainerd deserted
David Thomas deserted
James Brooks
Joseph Porter

Wells Smith
Abner Porter Discharged
Aaron Porter dead
Ashbil Bradly
John Nickols
Cudjo Negro
Ebenezer Wilcox dead
London Sawyer
Nathⁿ Cook
Jesse Cone
Stephen Burr
Hezʰ Clark

Henry Smith
Lemuel Pratt
Christopher Baily
Timothy Baily
Gurdon Baily
Noadiah Cone
Serᵗ Lowdon Baily
Daniel Crane
Oliver Cone Deserted
Jerathmeul Bonfoy Deserted
Seth Spencer
Wᵐ Clark

HARTFORD

Battalion Men that have received nothing but Bounty

Peter Philips
Stephen Fox
Elijah Porter
Moses Porter
Jonathan Arnold
John Vibart
Eliphalet Hills
David Wood
Samuel Easton
Levy Risley
Seth Kellogg
John Whiting Jʳ
William Whiting
Jonathan Shepard
Isaac Merrill
Benjᵃ Flowers
John Turner
James Chadwick
Joseph Day
John Adams
John Watson Jʳ
David McLean
James Parks
Grove Kellogg

Thomas Spencer
Hezekiah Goodwin
Asa Seymour
Thomas Wells
Timothy Andruss
Abdiel Flowers
Wᵐ Whistler
Zadock Sealey
Robert Culbert
Richᵈ Jackson
Daniel Miller
Benjᵃ Jobb
Wᵐ Henry
Wᵐ Tryon
Benjᵃ Webster
Robert Stiles Junʳ
Davis Johnson
Simeon Hosmer
Asa Bunce
William Hinsdale
James Barnard
Horrace Kellogg
Theodore Chamberlain

KILLINGWORTH

Lieuᵗ Joseph Willcox
Serjᵗ George Griswold
Serjᵗ Caleb Turner
Serjᵗ William Linn
Serjᵗ Nathaniel Crane
Corpˡ Philip Redfield
Drumʳ Barnabus Wellman
Drumʳ James Parmele
Fifer Benjamin Wright
Benjamin Tooly
Asa Buel
Reuben Chittenden
James Chittenden
Zenas Griswold

Jesse Jones
John Kelcey
Samˡˡ Nettleton
Elias Redfield
Daniel Willcox
John Crane
Paul Wellman
John Wellman
Oliver Kelcey
Hubbel Steevens
Benjamin Pelton
William Gaylor
William White
Abel Hull

John Chittenden
John Lewes
Edward Griffin
John Chatfield
William Wellman
Oliver Teal
Constant Parmele
Reuben Wright

Joseph Hull
Daniel Dwolf
Giles Willcox
Joshua Kelcey
George Hull
Joseph Teal
Richard Jackson
Joel Crane

The following is an account of those that are Dead & Discharged

Serj^t Orel Turner Died April ye 8 1777
Hollum Nettelton Died May ye 10 1777
John Hall Died August ye 23 1777
Eber Chittenden Died January ye 26 1778
Job William Died March 1778
Silvanus Merry Died March ye 24 1778
Stephen Blachly Died April ye 8 1778
Jensourah Evarts Died January ye 9 1778
Zepheniah Clark Died Septem^r 1777
William Nettelton Died January ye 7 1778
William Tooly Ded
John Tooly Dead
Daniel Carter Dead
Tites Teal Dead
Abraham Steevens Discharg^d
Samuel Steevens Discharg^d
Eliakim Steevens Discharg^d
Simon Steevens Deserted

LITCHFIELD

Ephraim Bates L D.   Jno Shether Capt. L D.

Alphabetical List of Soldiers who have already or probably may here-
after receive the said annual Pay of 20/ p^r Month Viz.

[That amount was voted by the town April 15, 1777, to each soldier
who should inlist to make up the towns quota of 92. The families of those
checked (x) received supplies.]

Giles Alcock
Cash Africa
John Bottom
Enos Barns 2
Enos Barns 3^d
Ambrose Barns
James Columbus
Abial Canfield
Simon Crosby
John Cowl
Eldad Camp
Dyar Cleaveland
Abel Culver
Isaac Clough
Putnam Catlin
Reuben Craw
Joseph Collyer
Rufus Fancher
John Farnam

Aaron Fox
Sylvanus Graves
Isaac Grant
George Hamilton
Amos Herick
Tucker Hart
Abel Hitchcock
Medad Hotchkiss
John Johnson
Samuel Kilborn
Abraham Kilborn
David Kilborn
Peter Kelcy
x John Kelly
Jared Knapp
John Larow
x John Mason
Ashbel Mason
Eli Mix

Nicholas Manjent
x Daniel Munger
x Benjamin Palmer
· Paul Price
x Timothy Plant
Isaac Parker
x Samuel Rossetter
John Royal
Thomas Roberts
Simeon Ross
x Josiah Stone
Jonathan Smith
John Smith
x Henry Smith
David Seelye
John Seelye
Seeley
John Simpson
x Samuel Stannard
Enoch Sperry
David Strickland
John Sweet
x Levi Tuttle

Benjamin Taylor
Samuel Todd
John Vaughn
Samuel Vaughan
Samuel Waugh
Thaddeus Waugh
Samuel Woodcock
James Wright
Philemon Wilcocks
Ebed Meleck
Jaek Negro
George Dixon
Reuben Smith
Thomas Owen
Isaac Trowbridge
Benjamin Bissell
William Sales
Anthony McDaniel
John Breck
Asa Laraby
Willet Laraby
Peter Hawley
Adam Stevenson

MANSFIELD

[All of the following named persons received a grant of additional pay from the town. There are no check marks against those of whom it is noted that their families received supplies, to indicate that the names have been carried into the other list.]

John Dextor
Charles Wood
Joshua Bennet
Aaron Royce
Elijah Royce
Luther Chaimberlane
Benjⁿ Lylley
Nathan Reed
John Turnor
John Bugbe
Steaphen Dunham
Josiah Conant Junʳ
Jonathan Fenton
John Smith
John Eldredg
Asael Dunham
Lummim Case
Darius Dextor deceased
James Dextor
Roger Freeman
Luther Eaton
John Baker
John Hartshorn Junʳ
Jacobe Barrows
Iccabud Hovey
Benajah Geer
John Abbe
Nathˡˡ Cary Junʳ

John Marten
Ashur Allen
Phineas Allen
Diarca Allen
Samuel Conant deceased
Calib Conant
Elijah Baldwine
Wᵐ Dodg
Willord Church
Jonathan Nichols Junʳ
Ezra Phelps
Benjⁿ Bugbe
Amariah Crane
Wᵐ Storrs
Jeremiah Gillit
Bigsbe Rogers
Nathan Porter
John Balch Junʳ
Ebenʳ Snow Junʳ
Jonathan Snow
Joshua Basset
Jeshua Davis
James Strong
Daniel B. Perkens
Daniel Bosworth
Josiah Burt
John Harris

Supplies for the Families of the Soldjers belonging to the Town of Mansfield

Joshua Basset
Sam¹¹ Conant
John Harris
Calib Conant
Nathan Porter
John Smith Junʳ
Jonathan Fenton
Jacobe Barrows

Capᵗ John Shumway
Ashur Allen
Lieuᵗ Solomon Fenton
Nathan Reed
John Bugbe
Joshua Bennet
John Abbe
John Dextor

NEW MILFORD

The following is the Names of those men who are intitled to the Bounty granted by New Milford agreeable to the Inclosed Vote Viz.

[The bounty voted was £12 for the first year and £6 each year for the second and third year's service.]

Oliver Bostwick
William Whitely
Charles McDonald
Liffe Sanford
William Drinkwater
Ralph Smith
Ebenezar Drinkwater
Ichabod Wilkinson
Ebenezar Bostwick
Mathew Wildman
William Dunwell
Joseph Clarke
Elijah Canfield
Abijah Moger
Garshom Nichols
Isaiah Bunce
Shubal Phillips
Eli Nichols
Lemuel Peet
Ebenezar Keeler
Chileab Palmer
David Cole

Samuel Phillips
Jeruel Phillips
Abraham Barns
Mingo Treat   27

David Merwin
William Foot
Goodman Noble
Theophilus Comstock
Eleazar Hendrick
John Knap
Daniel Rogers
Liverius Hawley   8

David Beach
David Bostwick
Stephen Wheeler
Ebenezar Trowbridge   4

James Bennit
Joseph C. Hawley

NB. The first mentioned 27 men Inlisted in Capᵗ Elizur Warners Company in Col° Swifts Regiment, and the nex 8 Inlisted in Capᵗ Halls Compʸ in the same Regᵗ. And the next four Inlisted under Capᵗ Eli Catlin in Col° Bradleys Regᵗ — but what Compʸ the other two belong to is not Ascertained.

NEW HARTFORD

A Return of Supplies Made the Officers and Soldiers In the Continental army belonging To the Town of New Hartford

Elijah Flower Serjᵗ
Joseph Gilbert   "
Theodore Gilbert Private
Ezra Andruss

Aaron Steevens
Elias Seymour
Elisha Robbarts
Cyperon Merrill

Aaron Merrill   Ezra Edgcomb
John Taylor   John Garrit

[None of the above names have check marks showing that they have
been carried into another list.]

POMFRET

Major Thomas Grosvenor   Lem^{ll} Fling
Capt Stephen Brown dead   Willm Earls
Ens^a Silas Holt   John Whealer
Elias Jones   Billings Sabin
Ebenezer Gilbert   Sam^{ll} Cleaveland
Benjamin Bufinton   James Jones
Sam^{ll} Glass   Willm Lashbrooks
Rowland Cotton   Lewis A Negro Man
John Bryant   Willm Ervin
Abiel Varnum   Thos Hill
Willm Cleaveland   Ezra Goodell
Jonathan Hill   John Wampee
Joseph Griffin J^r   Elijah Cheney Deserted
Obadiah Brown   Silas Covel
Abner Chapman   Ezekil Loomis
Dick A Negro Man   Sam^{ll} Millington
Jacob Hovey   Jahazaniah How
Beezer Owen   Jos Holms
Jesse Earls   John Barker
James Paine Fitch   Joseph Ross
Amasa Copeland   Sam^{ll} Bugbee
Joseph Gunner   Abner French
Simeon Camp   Elias Robertson
John Lilly   Zenas Harthaway
Sam^{ll} Cady   Cyrus Cartwright
General Putnams Negro Man   Ebenezer Grow
Jonas Newport   James Grant
Oliver Goodell   Nathaniel Stowell
Willm Wanslow   Cesar A Negro Man
Willm Cart   Jonathan Crain
John Cheney Deserted   Caleb Conant
Andrew Morrison   Jonathan Bullock

PLAINFIELD

Reuben Bryant   Nathaniel Sabins
Amos Bennet   Jacob Heard
Jonathan Whipple

RIDGEFIELD

Capt St John Thomas Keeler
Lieut Keeler   John Condrick
Levi Keeler   Ezekiel Whitney
Jeremiah Keeler   Lewis Jacklin
Elijah Weed   Solomon Ren
Barack Nickerson   Abraham Resegue
Eliphaz Nickerson   Daniel Benedict
Elisha Lincoln   Nehemiah Olmsted

Jeremiah Osburn
Gilburt Brush
Thomas Hutcherson
Thomas Warson
Sylvarnus Sealey
Hezekiah Hawley

John Hitchcock
Micajah Weeks
James Stanton
Benjamin Bennit
Stephen Meeker

SALISBURY

L' Noah Lee

L' James Coon

SHARON

Stephen Wells
Amos Allin
Jonas Knap
William Stewart
James Loughlin
Timothy Brockway
Nathaniel Tyler
James Knap
Jonathan Tobias
Ezekel Whitney
Zelophehead Williamson
  (? Withamson)
William Low
Derias Gray
David Row
Samuel Gray
Josiah Strong

Abner Colkin
Cornelius Hamlin
Jabez Lewis
Joseph Strong
Daniel Elmer Jun
Henery Stephens
Nathaniel Richard
James Tobias
Derias Calkin
Jude Bill
Adonijah Pangborn
Amasa Warner
Phinehas Benjaman
Ephelit Smith
Azerial Acley
Henery Mackintire
Joseph Tucker

STAFFORD

Maj' Ames Walbridge
L' Silas Blogget
Josiah Edson
Nathan Edson
Joseph Wheston
Joseph Edson
Joseph Green
Porter Walbridge
Joshua Wheler
Tim° Wheler
Zadock Wheler
Hezekiah Wheler
Tim° Luce
Isaac Pinny
Nehemiah Washbon
Benj" Washbon
Solomon Tupper
Robert Thomson
Joshua Walbridge
Steph" Whileaker (?)
Obediah Walker
Phillup Kibbe
Benj. Buller

Asa Buller
Elijah Russele
Nathan Kent
Ben Jon Orcutt
Sam¹ Worner
Steph" Moulton
Thoms Worner
Alva West
Joseph Cross
Chester Morse
Reuben Putman
Jacob Green Ju'
Sim" Webster
Nathan Washbon
Isaac Cushmon
Israel Butler
Benj Rennals
William Brown
Tim° Herington
Zach Green
Nath¹¹ Cushmon Ju'
David Green
Nathan¹ Foster

STRATFORD

Josiah French
Benjamin Brayzer
London Good Luck p^d to
   Jn° Willcockson
Joseph Usurp Negro to
   David Willcockson
John Gilbert
John McKensey
Abel Cuff
Richard Handy
Gideon Seley
Miles Dixon
Lemuel Seley
George Leman
William Beden
Elisha Pulford
Daniel Hawley's Negro
John Willcockson Junr
John Bennitt
Jeremiah Blackman
Stiles Curtiss's Negro Amos
John Edwards's " Ceaser
Toney — Negro
Heber Smith
Pompy Moss
Nathaniel Beach
David Sillick
Abijah Perrey
John Blackman
David Jackson
John Turney's Negro
David Duclos
Abijah Beardslee
Andrew Porter
John Benjamin Mitchel
Samuel Blackman
Samuel Whitney
Jehiel French
Robert Welch
John Bassitt
Elihu Blackman
Nathan Thompson
Daniel Jones
Samuel Pulford
John Waklee
Jeremiah Ryan
Daniel Sherwood
Stephen Hall
Robert Simmons
John Titus
Caleb Chatfield
Timothy Blackman
Daniel Barlow
Amos Saunders
Alexander Fairchield
Lewis Anjevine

John Beers Junr
Charles Burritt
Timothy Chapman
Abraham Hawley
Nathaniel Booth
Gersham Turney (? Tumey)
John Crawford
John Downes
James Downes
William Daskam
David Eves
Nathan Hawley Junr
David Hurd
Benjamin Beach
Peter Lewis a free Negro
Isaac Brown
Joseph
Gideon Seeley
John Munrow
Robert Freeman, Negro
Benjamin Hilton
Benjamin Waklee
James Hide
John Beardslee Junr
Jesse Dickinson
John Peet
Jesse Smith
Eli Nichols
Samuel Waklee
David Barlow Junr
Samuel Henman
Ephriam Seeley
Richard Hawley
James Wayland Junr
Daniel Munrow Junr
Samuel Maning
Silus Glassgow
Jesse Primas
Thomas Ivers for his Negro
   Jack
Joel Beers
Joseph Loaring
Prosper Wetmore
Joseph Waklee
Timothy Gauney
Richard Damenery
Nathan Turell
Benjamin Benjamin
David Wells
Bryan Montecue
David Willcoxson, for Josiah
Joseph Cleark
John Chops p^d Ezra Hawley
Ned Sherwood p^d Levi Jack-
   son
John Beach p^d for his Negro

Grant Johnson
Isaac Dickerson
Joseph Hubbert
Ephraim Mollato

Silus Nickols paid him for
his Servant
Samuel Richmond

TOLLAND

Serg^t Ebanez^r Stebins
Ammi Paulk
Martin Davis
Willm Huntington
Willm Johnson
Isaac Squire
Abel Crandel
John Proc^t Burrus

William Sole
Shubal Dimock
Edy Hatch
Simon Stimson
George Hubbard
Joseph Sparks
Amos Harris
David Pierse

TORRINGTON

Sam^{ll} Keley Ju^r
Cleark Roberts
Ambros Fyler
Ebenezer Scovil
Ebenezer Leach
Isaac Day
John Towee
John Camp
Coonrod Weaver
Seth Stannard
Daniel Farmen
Bennajah Abrow

Timothy Fay
Samuell Jones
Remembrance Filley
Amos Jarols
John Whrite
Ithurel Flowers
Aaron Merells
Daniel Beneduk
A Negro Man
Gemalial Omsted
George Nottingham
Rivaous Newell

UNION

Sergn^t Nehemiah Cage (? Case)
John Laflin
George Dillaba
James Walker
Samuel Peirce
John Wright
Joseph Snell

James Laflin
Nehemiah Pecker
Benjamin Bullen
John Smith
Luthar Loomis
Joshua Ephraim
Eleazer Pagan (?)

WALLINGFORD

Almond Munson
Amasa Tharp
Amos Tharp
Saml S. B. Hotchkiss
Orange Munson
Lent Munson
Charles London
Jno Hulbert
Elihu Cook
Johnson Cook
Warren Cook
Enos Mix
Andrew Andrews
Jesse Vose

Saml Wright
Jno Sled
Selah Stedman
Joseph Clark
George Cook
Saml Blakslee
Benaiah Hall
Ja^s Brown
Israel Dodge
Hull Shepherd
Toney Negro
Roswel Beach
Joel Cook
Willm Cook

Sam¹ Perkins
Jesse Peck
James Tibbel
Daniel Cady
Willᵐ Parker
Reuben Moss
Amos Mix
Sam¹ Spencer
Isaiah Moss
Lieut. Giles Curtis
Thos Dudly
Timothy Parker
Jnᵒ Parker
Hiel Peck
Joseph Wolcott Jr
Charles Heydon
Asa Beach
James Miles
Israel Johnson
Sam¹ Parsons
Wait Yale
Amos Parker
Anthony Goodsill
Abram Parker
Charles Merriman
Eliakim Johnson
Lieut. Lem¹ Hitchcock
Ebenezʳ Lewis
Thoˢ Hitchcock
Timʸ Parker, Serg.
David Stone
Jnᵒ Anthony, discharged
Enoch Merriman
Benj. Ford
Benj. Raxford
Elisha Hall
Seth Smith
Joab Sanderson
Ephᵐ Meriam
Edmᵈ Merriam
Jotham Hall
Jonathª Ford
Levi Robinson
John Pierce
Jotham Rice
James Coburn
Joseph Coburn
Asaph Merriam
Sam¹ Collins
Moses Hall 3ᵈ
Lem¹ Willcox
Barnabas Mitchel
Elisha Bishop

Samson Smith Negro
Boston Negro
Chatham Freedom Negro
Lemmon Cumber Negro
Andrus Moor
Ruel Affrica Negro
William Buntin
Benj. Johnson
Dan¹ Johnson Hall
Aaron Hall
Timothy Hart
Abel Tharp
Timothy Page
Titus Hart
Luke Kerns
Sam¹ Spellman
Thaddeus Todd
Sam¹ Jones
Luther Johnson
Medad Potter
Benoni Moss
Elisha Parker Jr.
Willᵐ Prout
Peter Sibbels
Benj. Hendric
Thoˢ Davis
Ebenezer Brockitt
Adam Molatto
Dick Freedom Negro
Asa Bellamy
Abel Clark
Amos Andrews
Joel Willmott
Elmer Russel
Charles Kimberly
Levi Hitchcock
Levi Bunnel
Job Tyrrel
Prince Negro
Ambrose Hine
Titus Atwater
Job Negro
Chauncey Lewis
Peter Negro
Sharp Negro
Nath¹ Tyler
Levi Tyler
Eldad Porter
Willᵐ Grant
Abel Lewis
Divan Clark
Jnᵒ Perkins

WINCHESTER

William Leach
Steaven Hurlburt
Jese Wilkenson

Adam Moot
Timothy Fay
Wiliam Fay

Seth Stanard
Remembrance Filley
David Hudson
Pebody Stanard
Steaven Scovils

Gershom Fay
Levi Welkenson
Jonathan Preston
Prince Neagro

WOODBURY

Sam¹ Lamfear
Jethro Tona
Galloway Peter
James Parks
Moses Hawkins
Wᵐ Stanclift
James Negro
Samuel Cofrin
Elisha Hubbert
Aaron Curtiss
Frederick Barnce
John Slauter
Henry Wakely
Shem Doel
Gideon Bristol Junʳ
David Hecock
John Bulford
John Hubbart
Moses Strickland
Lewis Hurd
Daniel Potter
Sheldon Potter
Timothy Hinman
Joseph Stiles
Cummy Simons
James Sharp
Simeon Barns
Abel Wakely
John Thompson
William Bondy
Aseph Hurlbut
James Abenathy
George Fields
Ephraim Seley
John Clarke
Pomp London
John Turrel
Benjⁿ Avery
Jonathan Twist
James Brown
Ira Way
Matthew Read
Tint Gillis
Elisha Perry
Zuar Bradley
John Herrick
Jnᵒ Davenport
Robert Smith
Michael Robin
Anthony Stoddard
Gideon Hurd Junʳ

Abiel Linsley
Jehiel Bradley
Benjⁿ Wheeler
George Hows
Julian Easton
Titus Negrow
Joseph White
Aner Adee
Joseph Walker Junʳ
Solomon Reynolds Junʳ
Benjⁿ Hinman 3ᵈ
Aquila Sturgiss
Peter Johnson
Hezekiah Keeler
Enoch Thomas
Phineas Palmer
Daniel Stephens
David Reynolds
Justus Reynolds
David Dixon
Amos Clerk
Samuel Jackson
Jared Dixon
Stephen Ranney
James Hucker
Daniel Tucker
Alexander Mills
Joseph Blakesley
Hinman Wooster
Sam¹ Lee
Charles Sheldon
David Robinson
Wᵐ Beamont
Moses Church
Jonathan Munger
Robin Negrow
George Bannister
[   ] Hurlbut (?)
Barnabas Blenney
Peter Kellis
Elijah Pixlie
Jnᵒ Laflin
John Nails
Samuel Wilson
Freeman Judd
Benjⁿ Buel
Eliphalet Downs
Tom Gage
Isaac Bloom
Thomas Mitchel

TOWN BOUNTIES ETC., 1777-1779.

[The Archives relating to the Revolution 30, numbers 8-50, consist of returns from the various towns, giving particularly the names of soldiers serving in the Connecticut Line, who received "Town Bounties etc. before 1780," from the towns for which they served. The returns are dated about April 1,1779, and include from the beginning of the year 1777.]

BOLTON

Leut Zadock How
Ezra Downer
John Worner
Sam^{ll} Lilington
Enoch Carter
Sam^{ll} Loomis
Solomon Chappel
Isaac Jones
Ezra Chapen
Zepheniah Thayer
Hiel Chapen
Roger Loomis

Levit Millard
Joseph Spencer Dec^t
Ebe^r Dart
Nath Taylor
Elijah Howard
Josiah Bordman
Joshua Flint
Andrew Loomis
Jerijah Thayer
Donnety
Moredock McLane Dec^t
Asa Lanord Deserted

CANAAN

Col^o Rusels Regiment
Serjent Joshua Whitney now Ensⁿ
Serj^t   Elias Lee
Serj^t   Aaron Brownel
Bille Lawrance Drum Maj^r
David Preston
Samuel Peirce
William Mix
Elisha Freman
John Watson
Andrew Lester
Thomas Stevens
Abner Miller
Stephen Stevens

Of Col^o Meiggs Reg^t
Ozias Baker
Himan Coole

Of Capt Bucklands Matrosses
Neil McNeil

Col^o Swifts Reg^t
Leu^t   John Holombeck
Serj^t   William Fellows

Isaac Smith
William Chambers
Samuel Green
Simon Tubbs
Isaac Higby
Seth Curtis
Peter Serdam
Samuel Hunt
Serj^t Rusel Hunt
Nathaniel Douglass
Aaron Culver
Benjamin Scovel
Richard Bishop
Timothy Woodford
John Curtis
Eben^r Church
John pervett

David Preston
Joseph Cowles
John Curtis
Richard Bishop
Samson R Hunt
Nathaniel Douglass
Timothy Woodford

Aaron Culver
Aaron Brownel
Elish Freman
Andrew Lester
Thomas Stevens

William Mix
Elias Lee
Stephen Stevens
Abner Miller
Bille Lawrance

CANTERBURY

Andrew Hebbard
Ser¹ Joen Cleveland
Sam¹¹ Coburn
Thomas Harris
Jacob Cleveland
    Isaac Basset
Daniel Edwards
James Litchfield
Daniel Durfee
Sam¹¹ Glass
Reuben Lilliee
John Lillie
Abiel Farnam
Jerule (? Jerub) Mott
Sam¹ Thomson
Dan¹ Fitch
Sam¹ Stoddard
Israel Dodge
David Adams
Abijah Cady
Tius Tykins Indian
Frederick Curtiss
John Jeffards
Cap¹ Abner Bacon
Leiut. Tim° Cleveland
Doct. David Adams
Serj¹ Eben² Felch
Thomas Austin hired Jon¹Bill
James Johnson
John Ames Samson indians man*
John Ames
James Dixon
Jeriel Dodge
William Shaw
Elijah Munroe
Nathaniel Edwards
Jedidiah Brown
Nathan Lester
Elias Shaw
Aaron Faulkner

James Duggin
Josiah Burnham
Benj³ Shaw
Rufus Fitch
Roger Green
James Morse
Francis Perkins
Robert Herrick
Reuben Carter
Peter Stevens
Ser¹ Nathaniel Gates
Nathan Stevens
Walcott Justin
Leiu¹ Moses Cleveland

Light horse men { Sam¹ Adams / Dan¹ Cushman / Tho⁸ Cushman / Elisha Litchfield

The following are Men died in the Service hired for three years & during the war viz

James Wharf
Silas Gates
Amos Brewster
Josiah Munroe
Joseph Bond
Jona¹ Shaw
James Clark
John Shaw
Nehemiah Munroe
John Cleveland Jr
Stephen Farnam
Prince Lillie
Lee Woodward
Jeremiah Reed
Clark Herrington
Ezekiel Herrington
Jedidiah Adams
Bartlet Bingham

CHATHAM

L¹   Ezra Smith
L¹   Marcus Cole
L¹   Aaron Hale
Serg¹ Benj³ Bowers
Serg¹ Ab^m Schallenx

Serg¹ Levi Goodrich
Serg¹ Nath¹¹ Montgomery
Serg¹ Elnath³ Geanings
Serg¹ Abner Cole
Serg¹ Richd Giddins

---

*John Ames partly erased and Samson indians man added in another handwriting

Serg^t James Johnson J^r dead
Corp^{ll} Benaj^h Bowers
Corp^{ll} John Paine
Corp^{ll} Ebur Stocking
Corp^{ll} Nath^{ll} Cook
Corp^{ll} Jos^h Markham
Corp^{ll} Othniel Brainard
Corp^{ll} Wm Stocking
Lemuel Goodrich
Bethuel Goodrich
Jonathan Verry
Jonathⁿ Stocking
Peter Butler
Wm Cook
Reuben Schallenx
Elihu Mott Dec^d
W^m McCorne
Seth Knowles
Wm Grey
Giles Knowles
Jos^h Andrews
Jos^h Graham
Ephraim Bowers
Jno Graham
Josiah Davies
Stephen Ranney
Jacob Wood
Jacob Wood J^r
David West J^r
Joshua Morgan Dec^d
Marshal Stocking
Stephen Thomas
Elijah Whiting
Dan^{ll} Robarts
Joel Doolittle
Jabez Ranney
Ephraim Brigs
George Brown Dead
Thomas Brown
Daniel Pelton
John Gill
Thos Fitz Simons
Charles Martin

James Shields
John Wright
Heman Higgins dead
Jesse Higgins dead
Jesse Higgins Jr dead
Benjⁿ Benjamin dead
Nathⁿ Powers
Thos Rich
Joseph Rich
Peter Sharman
George Pelton
William Exton
Followdan Damewood
Joel Green
John Goodrich
Sam^{ll} Rich
Nath^{ll} Rich
Dan^{ll} Parks
Sam^{ll} Goff J^r
John Parks
Ezra Smith Junr dead
Abel Abel
Tim^o Chipman
Sylv^r Smith
Thomas Sorow
John Strong
Dan^{ll} Millar
Elihu Hubbard
Lem^{ll} Rich
Joseph Chace
Aaron Carter
Benjⁿ Troubridge
Ichabod Lucas
Zebadiah Briggs
Sam^{ll} Freeman
Thomas Hodge
Robert Stiles
Sam^{ll} Goff
Beriah Stiles
Joshua Goff
Martin Stiles
Hewet Aloord
Rhoderice White

COLEBROOK

Eli Simonds
Joseph Simons

Samu^{ll} Philleps
Abial Canfield

COVENTRY

Capt Paul Brigham
Serj^t Eleazer Loomis
Serj^t Nathaniel Thompson
Corp^l James Barnabee
Robert Lane
John Savory
Conant Sawyer

Ephraim Robertson
Joseph Doubleday
Asael House
Samuel Burden
Joseph Badcock
Joseph Doubleday Junr
Noah Chappell

Benjamin Grover
Nathaniel Rose Desarted
John Brown
Aaron Stimson of Toland
Elias Newton of Toland
Elisha Stebbins of Toland
Nathan Walker of Staford
Richard Davenport
Jonathan Delano of Toland
Philip Lewis of New London
Nathaniel Harris
Jules Burns
Isaac Kellogg
Daniel Edwards

Richard Carlton of Toland
Serj't Amos Avery
Justus Brewster
John Bill
Roger Welch
William Bourns
John Parker
Nathan Parker
Job Leson
Jesse Leson
Evens of Hartford
Cristian name] un-
known
Jerijah Shair of Bolton

DURHAM

L't Charles Burrit
Ser' Eliakim Strong
Ser' Benjamin Sutliff
Co'r Hust : Henmin
Co'r Sam'll Lucas
Du'r Saxton Squire
Du'r Phinehas Squire
Du'r Reuben Brown
Du'r David Brown
Du'r John Bishop
Fif'r Sam'll Brown
Fif'r Nathaniel Brown
Eliakim Hull
Timothy Dunn
Warrop Murry
William Lucas
Simeon Mallery
Phinehas Miggs
Seth Strong

Sam'll Seaward
Enos Crane
John Meaker
Nathan Keelsoy
William Carr Ju'r
Bryan Rosseter
Skiler (?) Goddard
Gideon Chrittendon
Thomas Cook
Abiather Squir
Amos Davis
William Johnson
John Handcox
Sharp Negro
Cato Negro
Des't (?) Robart Kneel
Des't (?) Gashom Brown
De'd (?) Cyrus Newton
De'd (?) Joseph Hickcox

ENFIELD

Cap't David Parsons
Cap't Tho's Abbe
Serj't Jabez Parsons
Serjt Dan'll Ware
Serjt Simeon Hager
Joseph Chandler
Henry Booth
Joseph Griswold
Jonathan Parsons
Isaac Simons
Irael Hall
Benj'n Butler
Tho's Root Jun'r
Othniel Allen
Ebenezer Peese 3'd
Simeon Pease
Benj'n Herrington
John Ward

Tho's Hale Jun'r
Hiram Hall
Amasa Allen
David Bullen Jun'r
David Phelps Jun'r
Ebinezer Ames
Isaac Markham
Tho's Justus Davis
John Graham
William Thomson
Nathaniel Rose
John Delaney
Benj'n Baxter
Joel M'cgriggay
Benj'n Bugbee
Lemuel Wood
Jams Erl
John Phips

Dan¹¹ Perkins Jun'
Ichabad Meacham Jun'
   Matrosses
Jonathan Terry Jun' Listed
   and Since Dead
Levi Terry
Isaac French
William Erl
Jared Simons

Eben' Perkins

   Hired by two Men
James Russel
Richard Fairman
Stephen Butler
Asa Hall
William Prier
Tho' Athington

FAIRFIELD

*Maj' Albert Chapman
*Cap' Josiah Lacey
*Leu' Isaac Hubbel
*Leu' William Hubbel
*Leu' N. Peet Jackson
*Leu' James Chapman
Leu' Daniel Bradley
*Jos^h Disborow Serg'
*Moses Sturgis   "
*Stephen Hall   "
*Richard Williams "
*Atkisson Hillton "
*Tho' Allen
*Ebn' Allen
*Stephen Lockwood
*Nath¹¹ Johnson
*Moses Allen
*William Raymong
*David Raymong
*Joseph Mills
*Justice Disborow
Benjamin Allen
Eliphalet Allen
William Johnson
John Johnson
Gershom Jeacocks
Isaac Elwood
Nathan Elwood
Joshuah Jeacocks
Henry Disborough
Abraham Sturgis
Nath¹¹ Sturgis
Ezra Wood
Joseph Batterson
James Batterson Jun'
Jonathan Poor
Simon Disberow
Stephen Batterson
John Couch
Abraham Couch
Gideon Hulbert
Nathan Taylor
Francis Hebbern
*Daniel Bennit

*John Mitchel Corp¹
Joseph Mosier
*Eppaphras Goodsel
*Eliphalet Bradley
Nathan Bradley
Aaron Sturgis
Hez^h Webb
Peter Stocker
Aaron Whaley
Ezekiel Thorp
Aaron Thorp
John Beaher (?)
Nathan Winton
Isbon Hubbell
John McMullin
*Jonathan Spears
John Gilbert
Daniel Barlow
William Jackson
Francis Hibbert
Tho' Stephens
*Francis Hutonot
Hez^h Whaley
Wakeman Hull
Augustus Sturgis
*John Fuller
*Daniel Burr
*Nehemiah Fowler
William Gold
Edward Field
Nathan Squire
John Lerone
Philip Frenchman
Lewis Grisson
Josiah Armstrong
Peter Fegro
*David Morehouse
*Elijah Patchin Corp¹
*Tho' Durfee Corp¹
Isaac Odell Serg'
*David Coggins
Burr Gilbert
Ebn' Meaker
Joseph Read Indian

*These are designated as Married Men

Simon Cheapeak Ind
Zackriah Sherwood
Paschall Southwell
Isaac Hubbel
Isaac Smith
*Barrack Taylor
Wolcot Patchin
Simeas (?) Shervin
Benjⁿ Stigley (? Higley)
John Hallett
Jo^s Prindel
James Hesket
*Seth Bulkley
David Jackson
Stephen Evens
John Hubbard
Stephen Clerk
John Downia
John Coggins
Benjⁿ Bennit
Peter Negro

Amos Marshell
David Barlow
Jonathan Edwards
Michael Bowing
Eliphalet Gray
Josiah Green
David Wallace
Isbon Jennings
Hezekiah Meeker
John Cook
Patrick Linch
Richard Clark

Teams Men
Nathan Bulkley Junr
Joseph Lyon Junr
Saml Staples Junr
Seth Webb
John Jennings Junr
Ephraim Beers
Alexander Weeks

GROTON

Capt Amos Stanton
Lt Henry Williams
Lt Stephen Billing
Lt Simeon Avery
Searg^t Limuel Whitman
Searg^t Uriah Williams
Searg^t Eben^r Morgan
Searg^t Daniel Nikerson
Elijah Gray
Robert Swift
Jesse Yerington
Saml Pomp
Robert Davis
Andrew Annew
John Mc Donel
John Spears
Jonas Sunseman
Tuis Sharper
Henery Britman
James Andrus
Daniel Davis
Ebenezer Pelton
Amos Solomon
Silas Stery
Joseph Holley
James Simon
Nathan Sholes
David Pelton
Joseph Bentley
Jesse Starr
John Pemberton
Richard Daton

Moses Stodard
Abel Wassonk
Isaac Roger
Joseph Meason
Joseph Quacheets
Elisha Avery
George Avery J^r
Wheler Shoules
Amos Latham
John Burnam
Wm Paul
Asa Beley
Cato Roberson
Robert Allyn
Thos Malison
Bildad Eadwards
Andrew Wigar
Robert Williams
Thos Williams
Andrew Baker
Daniel Wiger
Wm Davis
Jonathan Ruff
John Dabol
Andrew Foreseth
Diarka Elderkin
John Williams
Solomon Williams
Nathan Williams
Nathan Smith
Ezekiel Billing
Simeon Comstok

---

*These are designated as Married Men

Gilbert Edgcom
Roswell Parish
Joseph States
Natha¹ Noyse
Chris' Chester
Joseph Willey
Jack Negro
Elisha Fanning
Robert Stanton
Rufus Holdredge
Jacob William
Joseph Williams
David Fanning
Nathan Fanning
Prentice Gallup
Elisha Stodard
Lemuel Chester
Ralph Williams
David Chapman
Asa Lamb

Tho' Fanning
Nathan¹ Bellows
John Brown
Gershum Brown
Fradrick Park
Aron Shoules
James Park
Constant Avery
Benjⁿ Pettice
Daniel Stodard
James Pelton
Daniel Holway
Cyrus Kiltam
Fradrick Stodard
Eben' Pollard
James Patterson
Miner Allyn
Fradrick Fanning
Cato Negro

GOSHEN

Capt Thomas Converse
Liut William Starr
Zebul Peck
John Gould
Timothy Knap
James Brown
Jacob Lair
Serg' Jonathan Demming
Serg' Isaac Miles
David Hurlbut
Jonathan Wheaton
Joel Galord
Wait Demming
Obil Beach
Nathaniel Sizer
Abel Basset
Robert Morris
Javis Boney
Matthew Buckley

Simeon Hall
David Langly
John White
Joseph Norton
Caleb Miles
Justice Squire
Elisha Mix
Ebenezer Lewis
David Holms
Asa Brooks
Stephen Mix
Linas Moss
John Willoughby
John Sealy
George Tankard
Jack Negro
George Gardner
Thomas Wyard
How

HADDAM

Leiut Gideon Baily
L' John Smith
L' Cornelius Higgins
Serj' Loudon Baily
" Jeromy Baily
" Jesse Cone
" Jehiel Arnold
" Hezekiah Clark
" John Baily
Corp¹ Jacob Baily
" James Smith
Ashbel Bradley
Timothy Baily

Gurdon Baily
Robert Baily
Aaron Clark
Joseph Porter
Stephen Burr
Lemuel Pratt
Wells Smith
William Gladen
Elisha Cone
Oliver Cone
Samuel Church
Jerathmel Bonfoy
Benanuel Bonfoy

Noadiah Cone
David Thomas
Seth Spencer
John Nichols
Nathniel Cook
Timothy Smith
Daniel Crane
Henry Smith
William Clark
William Baily
Cudjo Negro

London Sawyer
Cesar Chapman
Amos Bates
Daniel Bates
Eleazer Bates
Christopher Baily
James Brooks
Jonathan Bordman
Amos Porter
Walter Chase
Timothy Brainerd

HARTFORD

Samuel Wyllys Col[a]
Christopher Darrow Maj[r]
Stephen Buckland Cap[t] Art[y]
William Green Cap[t]
Samuel Mattocks Cap[t]
John Barnard Cap[t]
Ralph Pomeroy Pay Master
William Adams "
Roger Wadsworth Lieu[t]
David Deming Lieu[t] Artl[y]
Charles Miller Lieu[t]
Peleg Heath "
George Smith Ensign
James Olmsted "
Daniel Brewer Serg[t]
William Combs "
Mathew Cadwell "
Thomas Jarrell "
Roswell Wattles "
William Mize
Daniel Curtis
Reuben Hadlock
Patrick Thomas
Obediah Spencer
Thomas Waters
James Mahar
Ebenezer Beevins
Samuel Sedgwick
Caesar Augustus
Abraham Clark
Israel Loomis
Stephen Risley
Abiather Evans
James Delibar
Samuel Evans Jun[r]
Samuel Lucas
Richard Case
Benjamin Keeny
Eleazer Abby
Malachi Corney
Hammon Way
John Adams
John Watson Jun[r]
David McLean

James Parks
Grove Kellogg
Thomas Spencer
Hezekiah Goodwin
Asa Seymour
Thomas Wells
Timothy Andruss
Abdiel Flowers
William Whistler
Zadock Sealy
Robert Culbert
Richard Jackson
Daniel Miller
Benjamin Job
William Henry
William Tryon
Benjamin Webster
William Hinsdale
Davice Johnson
Simeon Hosmer
Asa Bunce
James Barnard
Theodore Chamberlain
John Foster
John Bath
Samuel Hancy
Horrace Kellogg
John Turner
William Hooker
Joseph Day
James Chadwick
Peter Phillips
Seth Kellogg
John Whiting Jun[r]
William Whiting
Jonathan Shepard
Isaac Merrills
Benjamin Flowers
Samuel Easton
Jonathan Arnold
Eliphalet Hills
John Vibert
Stephen Fox
Moses Porter

Elijah Porter
Samuel Roberts Junr

David Wood
Levi Risley

Asa Burnhams family not belonging to the Town but being there were supplied.

HARTLAND

Enlisted out of the State
Major Theodore Woodbrige
Bartholomew Barrett
Cyrus Dubbs
Moses Wooster
Benjamin Darling
John Call
John Wheeler
John Harrison
Samuel Hall

Ruben Hail
Ser^t Benjamin Giddinge
Cor^l Obed Crosby

fifer   Joseph Gilbert
Benjamin Reed
Charles Phelps
Benonia Evans
David Rood
Edward Cowdry
Harris Fox
Daniel Bushnell
Titus Hays
Ebenezer Hall   Deceased
Jonathan Butler   Deceased
Richard Clemons Deceased
Samuel Wier   Deceased

HARWINTON

Caleb Elmore
Seth Gridley
Samuel Hinsdel
Elisha Hinsdel
James Wilcox
Joseph Halsted
Timothy Stedmon

Elijah Scott
Ethel Scott
Roswel Catlin
Thos Green
Ozem Cook
Joseph C. Hawley
Lieu^t Asahel Hodge

KILLINGLY

Jabez Kingsbury
Thomas Barns
Mathew Moffit
John Meason
John Meason J^r
Ward Walton
Daniel McDaniel
Cato Hunt
Serj^t Pennel Child
Charles Lebret
Joseph Robins
Joseph Sheffield
Abner Marsh
John Keith
Tom Black
Willm Jones
Archelaus Town
Jason Harris
Lemuel Barns
Amasa Grover
Comfort Redway
Benj^m Bobinson

Silas Rickard
Crummil Luther
Squir Knight
Oliver Jinks
Cornelus Havens
James Runalds
Jacob Runald
Willm Arven
Benj^m Cady ye 3^d
John Pike
Simeon Lenord
Jack Green a negro man
David Runalds
Willm Blanchard
Zibee Roberts
Jabez Leach
Jacob Bixby
Nath^{ll} Turner
Parker Adams
Sam^{ll} Hall
Philip Keach
Perley Herren

Jeremiah Wilkey
Willm Adams
Isaac Barrows
Josiah Barrows
John Russel
Solomon Johnson
Gidion Martain
Silas Rickard

Sam^ll Runalds
Squier Whitmon
Jacob Warren
Nicholas Shippy
Daniel Sweet
Joseph Starkweather
Lieut Silverus Perrey

KILLINGWORTH

Capt Aaron Steevens
Lieu^t Caleb Baldwin
Lieu^t Joseph Willcox
Serj^t George Griswold
Serj^t Caleb Turner
Serj^t William Linn
Serj^t Nathaniel Crane
Corp^l Sam^ll Hull
Corp^l Philip Redfield
Drum^r Barnabas Wellman
Drum^r James Parmele
Fifer Benjamin Wright
Joel Crane
Elifelet Clorck
Peter Steevens
Benjamin Tooley
Asa Buel
Reuben Chittenden
James Chittenden
Zenas Griswold
Jesse Joans
John Kelcey
Sam^ll Nettelton
Elias Redfield
Daniel Willcox
Sam^ll Franklin
John Crane

Paul Wellman
John Wellman
Oliver Kelsey
Eliakim Steevens
Hubble Steevens
Benjamin Pelton
Thomas Rumbelow
Allen Leet
William Gaylor
William White
Abel Hull
John Chittenden
John Lewes
Edward Griffin
John Chatfield
William Wellman
Oliver Teal
Constant Parmele
Reuben Wright
Joseph Hull
Daniel Dwolf
Giles Willcox
Joshua Kelcey
George Hull
Joseph Teal
Richard Jackson
Simon Steevens

MANSFIELD

Capt John Shumway
Ens^n Solomon Fenton
Jonathan Snow
James Step
Calib Conant
John Marten Junr
Bigsbey Rodgers
Diarca Allen
Amarah (?) Crane
Jeremiah Gellit Junr
Joshua Basset
Benjamin Bugbe
John Bugbe
Joshua Bennet
Asher Allen
John Dextor
Aaron Royce

Elijah Royce
Charles Wood
Steaphen Dunham
Nathan Reed
Benjn Lilley
Nathan^ll Hardey
John Smith Junr
Jonathan Fenton
Josiah Conant Junr
John Hartshorn
Phineas Allen
Asael Dunham
James Dextor
Luther Eaton
John Eldredg
Elijah Baldwine
Jonathan Nichols

William Dodg
Willard Church
Nath[ll] Cary Jun[r]
John Abbe
John Balch Jur
Nathan Porter
Benajah Geer
John Baker
Ichabud Hovey
Rodger Freeman
Lumey Case
Jacobe Barrows

Daniel Bosworth
Sam[ll] Herrington
Eben[r] Snow
Josiah Burt
Daniel B. Perkens
Isaac Park   Groton
Ralph Williams D[o]
Clement Minor   Tollan
Newport Molattow D[o]
John Saunders   Mansfield
Joshua Bassett Jun[r] D[o]

MILFORD

Samuel Bryan Marshall
Serj[t] Peter Hepburn
Isaac Davidson
Abel Hitchcock
Jared Hitchcock
Isaac Northrop
John Heath
Amos Mallery
Joel Bebee
William Goldsmith
Elisha Thares
John Naugason
Titus Hine
David Hodge
Benjamin Pritchard
Justus Woods
David Mallery
Samuel Stow
James Goldsmith
Amos Clark
John Peters
Congo Zado
Elijah Bryan
Samuel Green
Thomas Binns
Samson Church
Job Woodruff
John Hooker
Peter Negro
Jube Negro
Daniel Soward
John Peck Jun[r]
Phinehas Johnson
Tim[o] Johnson
Anguis M[c]Fee
Toney Prudden
Jeffery James

Sharper Rogers
Elnathan Tolls
Timothy Beard
John Gellitt
James Pene
Samuel Eells Jun[r]
Joseph Plumb Mertin
William Rusell
Elackander Burk
Samuel Dickerson
Joseph Sharp
Hezekiah Brackitt
John Morris
Pomp Cyrus
Anthony Fransway
William Ovitt
Elisha Lewis
Stephen Marchant
Jonathan Bristoll
Joseph Goldsmith
Benjamin Burn
Jeffery Rogers
John Stewart
William Soward
Gabril Leverick
John Jackson
George Clark
Elijah Clark
Joel Sperry
John Belden
Peter Bristoll
Samuel Frost
James Cebra
John M[c]Renneck
Cap[t] Charles Pond
Cap[t] Samuel Sanford
Lieu[t] William Smith

NEW MILFORD

Col[o] Josiah Starr
Lemuel Peet
Wiliam Dunwell

Ebenezer Bostwick
James Daily
Abijah Moger

Isaiah Bunce
Wil^m Drinkwater
Abram Barns
Ichabod Wilkenson

Elijah Canfield
Stephen Stilwell
Joseph C Hawley

NORFOLK

Titus Watson Capt
John Trobrig Cor^l
Moses Turner "
Elijah Knap "
Aaron Aspinwell
Asael Addams
Calob Aspinwell
Joel Hamblin
Nathan Tubbs
Levi Norton
Reuben Stevins
Sam^ll Orvis
Amiriah Plumb
Calob Sturdifunt

John Walter
Elnathan Seward
Abr^m Knap
Reufus Trall
Jeames Benidict
Hiland Hall
Bates Turner
Silas Cowles
Edward Fuller
Charles Walter
Wm Turner
Jonas Hubbard
Lem^ll Sperry

NORWICH

Jedidiah Huntington
    Brigadier General
John Durkee Colonel
Ebenezer Huntington Major
Benjamin Throop Major
Ebenezer Perkins Captain
Beriah Bill "
Rufus Abell
James Lord   Lieutenant
Nathaniel Bishop "
Darius Peck "
John Durkee Junr "
Andrew Griswold "
Silas Goodale "
Jacob Fox "
Hezekiah Tracy "
Charles Fanning "
Joseph Chapman "
James Hyde 3rd   Ensign
Reuben Pride "
Diah Hartshorn "
William Tracy "
John Ellis   Chaplain
Philip Turner   Surgeon
Nathaniel Gardner Surgeon's
    Mate
John Fanning   Surgeon's
    Mate
Jedidiah Waterman Junr
David Pelton
Eleazer Pond
John Bond
Uriah Polley
Prince a free Negro

Alexander McCoy
Aaron Bailey
Barzil Bowdril
John Vandewson
William Bacon
Allen Pratt
John Whiting
Andrew Simons
Jedidiah Richards
Abner Pitcher
Elias Moores
Solomon Goodrich
James Greer
Dyar Manning
Roger Manning
David Gardner
Elijah Pike
Phill a Negro
Charles Avery 3^d
Peter Granger
Israel Webster
Miles Avery
Morris Jones
Titus Teal
Luke Brown
John Howell
Joseph Waterman
Oliver Arnold Junr
William Branch
Ebenezer Snow Junr
David Hunn
Cato Grover
Jedidiah Hyde Junr
Phinehas Durkee

Oliver Rogers
Joseph Lathrop
Ephraim Whitaker
Case Cook
Stephen Lee
Christopher Palmer
John Patten
Asa Eams
William Manning Ju^r
John Frederick Ancraman
Francis Green
John Briant
James Carr alias Miller
Edward Moore
Cuffee Wells
Aaron Baxter
Thomas Powers
John Simpson
Oliver Teal
Absalom Thomas
Bristo Augustus
Daniel Thomas
Sherman Gardner
Peter Plumb
Elijah Vergison
Isaiah Wright
Jabez Kingsberry
John Mirach Whitney
Thomas Gardner
Abimeleck Uncas
Rufus Hartshorn Junr
William Hallowell
William Pollard
Joshua Williams
Elkanah Meech
Gideon Comstock
Reuben Read
Jason Corning
John Gaylord
Thomas Mix Junr
Samuel Roath Junr
John Jacob Sidleman
Frederick Avery
Thomas Patten
Asher Spicer
Robert Stillman
William Holdridge Junr
Roger Fitch
Timothy Raymond
Samuel Clark
Benjamin Bennet
Benjamin Mott
Francis Donity
Jabez Post
Stephen Calkin
John Reynolds
John Hyde Durkee
Joseph Mesum

Kedar a free Negro
Micha a free Negro
Moses Tracy
Nathaniel Hill
Samuel Spicer
Toby Pendall a free Negro
Lebbeus a free Negro
Hezekiah Brewster
Adon Ames
Elijah Thomas
William Densey
Ned a Negro Man
Solomon Lothrop
John Wompee an Indian
Ephraim Wheeler
Charles Adams
Andrew Harrington
Asa Rothbourn
Joseph Branch
Benjamin Craft
John Bishop Junr
Selah Corwin
Jonathan Corwin
Ephraim Durfey
Daniel Bennett
Amos Brewster
George King
Newport a free Negro
John Wight
Ceaser Stewart a free Negro
Daniel Hawley
Jeremiah Capron
Ebenezer Perrigo
Elijah Knight
James Kingsley
William Perrigo Junr
Israel Dodge
James Morse
Abner French Junr
Daniel Fitch
Francis George
Thomas Malcom
John Allen
Ebenezer Waterman Junr
Samuel Ladd Junr
Everet Eams
John Pond
William Moore
Richard Lyman
John Martin
Samuel Goold
Richard Penhallow
Amos Green
John a Negro
John Thompson
Ebo. Raimond a Negro
Solomon Huntley
Backus Fox a free Negro

Edward Simons
Ebenezer Broughton
Araunah Hackley
Abner Hurlbut
Abner Waters
Ebenezer Armstrong
Oliver Story
John Packard
Benoni Congdol
Luther Waterman
John Brown
Jacob Clark
Hunt Simons an Indian
Samuel Huntington
Abraham Brown
Lathrop Davis
Hiram Huntington
William Harriss
Levi Deains
Thomas Meach
Joseph Fox
William Hinson Jun'
Darius Woodworth
Andrew Harriss
Joshua Reynolds
Noah Peas
Peregrine Gardner
Rozwel Crocker
Eleazer Groto a Mulato
Robert Bartlet
Jeremiah Osgood
Russel Chapel
Ammon Beebee
Alpheus Polley
Simon Choichoi an Indian

John Swaddle
Asa Fitch
Jesse Forsyth
Joseph Robbins
Jabez Choat
Samuel Geer
William Davis
Thomas Trapp 3rd
Cooper Polegreen
Edward Ewen Jun'
Benjamin Brooks
Jonathan Snow
William Fargo
Frederick Fanning
John Gleason
Samuel Bolles
Joseph Freeman
Jonathan Colefox
William Taylor
Joseph Randall
Eli Widger
Nathan Shoals
William Harrison
Jacob Rand
Cornelius Griffin
Peter Rogers
Simeon Reynolds
Levi Wentworth
Samuel Lathrop
Roger Avery
Isaac Cocheits
Christopher Downing
George Mitchel
Daniel Tracy
Joseph Truman

PLAINFIELD

Maj' Wills Cleft
Cap' John McGriegier
Cap' Lieu' Lem[ll] Cleft
Serg' Asa Jones
   " W[m] Waterman
Joshua Stoddard
Reuben Briant
Amos Bennet
Phinehas Hulet
Sip Watson Negro
Jonathan Whipple
Benjamin Johnson
Ned Negro

Stephen Bennet
John Satterlee
Sam[ll] Stafford
Nath[ll] Sabins
Jacob Hurd
Lott Chase
Sam[ll] Deates Negro
Frederick Waldo
Peter Marsh
Abel Franklin
Cudgo Negro
Josiah Rogers
W[m] Meach

POMFRET

Jacob Goodell
Nehemiah Bacon
John Shadden
Abiel Lyon

Benj[n] Sharp
Oliver Reed
Thomas Jones
Elisha Stowell

Henry Smith
Jaazaniah How
Joseph Holmes
John Barker
Joseph Ross
Samuel Bugbee
Abner French
Elias Robison
Zenas Hathway
Cyrus Cortwhrite
Ebenezer Grow
James Grant
Nath¹¹ Stowell
Cezar Negro Man
Jonathan Craine
Caleb Conant
Jonathan Bullock
John Duggins
Elias Jones
Eben' Gilbert
John Cambell
Benjⁿ Buffington
Sam¹¹ Glass
Rawland Cotton
John Briant
Abial Farnam
William Cleavland
Jonathan Hill
Joseph Griffin
Obadiah Brown
Abner Chapman
Ebenezer Cheney
Dick a Negro Man
Jacob Hovey
Eleazer Owens

Nehemiah Buckin
Jesse Earles
James Pain Fitch (Dead)
Amasa Coussland
Joseph Gunner
Simeon Camp
John Lilley
Samuel Cady
Gen¹¹ Putnams Negro Man
Jonas Newport
Alvin Goodell
William Winslow
William Cart
John Cheney
Andrew Morrisson
Lemuel Fling
William Earl
Thomas Jones
John Wheeler
Billinds Sabin
Samuel Cleavland
James Jones
William Lashbrooks
Lewis a Negro Man
Henry Smith
Oliver Reed (Dead)
Elisha Stowell (Dsmissᵈ)
William Arvin
Thomas Hill
Ezra Goodell
John Wampee
Elijah Cheney
Silas Covel
Ezekiel Lomiss
Samuel Millinton

PRESTON

Lᵗ Charles Miel
Silas Storry
William Aldrish
Thomas Jackson
James McDanields
Simeon Rouse
Nathan Tyler
Luke (? Duke) Guyant
Obediah Seers
Serjᵗ Asa Burnham
Joseph Holly
Joshua Meech
Isaac Evens
Andrew McLorey
William Prince Neg°
Ezra Ames
Lemuel Herrick
Daniel Thomas
John Johnson
John Dugan

Christopher Avery
Abraham Patinger
Elisha Baldwin
Epʰᵐ Coye
Jospʰ Billing
Nathan Ayres
Jesse Benjamins
Seth Frink
Elisha Frink
Joab Burton
Serjᵗ Isaac Coit
Serjᵗ Daniel Coit
John Boardmun
Wᵐ Little
Jonᵗʰ Brown
John Austen
Luther Gates
Merit Rockwell
Thomas Frink
Theophilas Frink

Josp[h] Gideons
Joshua Bunday
Henry Burnside
Stephen Downer
John Potter
Serj[t] Ephrain Morgan
Asa Bowdish
Josp[h] Prentice
Zebulon Ames
Carpender Ellis
Reuben Park
Azariah Lorthup
Ephram Withy
Joseph Woodard
David Parke
Sam[l] Vallet
James M[c]Clain

John Stringer
Robert Bruce
Stephen Danield
John Paul
Elias Meason
Nathaniel Whitechurch
James Frink Jun[r]
Josiah Wood
Gideon Lynde
John Chambers
Nathaniel Holt
Thomas Hallet
Nathan Elies
John Ayer
Joseph Rowse
Constant Avery
Thomas Bundy

RIDGEFIELD

Col[o] Bradley
Lieu[t] Kafin
Cap[t] S[t] John
Lieu[t] Smith
Stephen Rementon
Levi Keeler
Jeremiah Keeler
Elipha Perry
Elijah Weed
Barack Nickerson
Eliphaz Nickerson
Elisha Lincoln
Thomas Keeler
Williams Cummus
John Condreck
Ezekiel Whitney

Lewis Jacklin
Solomin Ren (?)
Abraham Russego
Darius Benedict
Nehemiah Olmsted
Jeremiah Osborn
Gilbert Brush
Thomas Hutchenson
Thomas Wason
Sylvanus Sealy
Benjamin Bennett
Hezekiah Hawley
John Hitchcock
Mousiah (?) Weeks
James Stanton
Stephen Meaker

SALISBURY

Lieu[t] Elezer Claghorn
Serg[t] Giles Hull
Corp[l] John M[c]Lean
Corp[l] Daniel Eyarts
Corp[l] William Tupper
fifer Jacob M[c]Lean
Champeon Ackley
Artemus Bloget
Hildrick Barrot
James Bradley
Ozias Baker
Curtice Chappel
Jacob Coon
Thomas Chipman
Isaac Cool
Daniel Cammell
Nathanael Emmeson
Henery Fits Jerell
Daniel Forgerson

Joseph Trumble Fitch
Bezellel Farnum
Samuel Fisk
Benjamin Graves
Amasa Grinall
George Griswould
Samuel Griswould
Henery Hull
Daniel Hull
Moses Hull
Jonathan Hull
John Havens
John Hawley
Willard Larrebee
Thomas Lewis
Billy Munger
William Mattherson
Simeon Meigs
Eliphelet Owen

Phinias Strong
Benjamin Schophel
Peter Serdam
Gamalel Terry
Asa Owen
Martain Tubbs
Abraham Welden

Isaac Wellden
William White
Solomon Whitney
John Wield
William Yates
Job Towsley
Dan¹ (?) Bostwick

SAYBROOK

John Hart	Cap'
Asa Lay	Lieu'
Benoni Shipman	"
Henry Hill	"
Jeremiah Lord	Sarj'
James Shipman	"
Sam¹ Clark Jun'	"
Elias Pratt	"
Wm Lord	"
Wm Chapman	"
Wm Doty	"
Dann Chapman	"
Morris Jones	"
Stephen Ingham	"
James Foster	Corp¹
Benjn Mack	do
Sam¹ Williard	do
Sam¹ Beamont Jun'	do
Wm Bartholomew	do
Hezekiah Buckingham Jr (?)	do
Robert Newell	Private

Jediah Gladding
Jesse Chalker
Joseph Hand
Prince Doan
Jediah Chapman Jun'
Jediah Denison
Isaac Warding
Andrew Tooly
Wm Stephens
Zepheniah Bowers
Isaac Caby
James Springard
Limbo Negro
Pabady (?) Pratt
Adam Crammer
Jesper Pratt
John Widger Jun'
Asa Pratt Jun'

Ethan Pratt Jun'
Sam¹ Doty Jun'
Gideon Buckingham Ju'
John Nichols
Philip Daras
John Widger
Stephen Waterhouse
Sam¹ Hansan
Stephen Ludlow
Oliver White
Stephen Butler
Cyrus Grimes
Robert Newell Jun'
Wm Cooper
Aaron Jones
Jonathan Butler
Zebedee Brown
Gift Negro
Amos Lord

Soldiers Hir'd by Two Men
Oliver Hull
James Post
George Spencer
Constant Chapman
Thomas Quiba
Ebenezer Stevens
Cornilus Wright
James Grant
Wm Harvy
Elijah Stevens
Simeon Luis
Andrew Lewis
Benjn Sherman
Taber Smith
Ethan Pratt
Sam¹ Comstock J^r
Martin Dibble
Pearce White

SHARON

Lieu' David Strong
Nathaniel Whipel
Daniel Elmer
Josiah Cleaveland
Jonathan Russ
Robert Jonson
Ebenezer Gilson

Amos Allin
Wait Yale
Thomas Wanerite
Enos Pettet
David Goodrich
Isaac Fisher
Stephen Wells

Jones Knap
William Stewart
James Laughlin
Timothy Brockway
James Knap
Noah Kelsey
Jonathan Tobias
Ezekel Whitney
Zelphehead Williamson
William Low
Derias Gray
Derias Colkin
James Tobias
Jabez Lewis
Samuel Gray
Cornelius Hamlin
Josiah Strong
Abner Calkin
Jude Bill
Nathaniel Richards

Joseph Strong
Daniel Elmer Jun
Henery Stephens
Amasa Warner
Phin: Benjamens
Eliphelit Smith
Ariel Acley
Henery Mackintire
Joseph Tucker
Adonijah Pangborn
Lemuel Sherod
Ben Foster
John Goodrich
Eliphalit Everit
Daniel Avery
Isaac Pierce
Isaac Persons
Jonathan Tobias
Nathaniel Tyler
Negor by Name

SOMERS

The Regiment and Company of
Maj^r Walbridges Comp^n Col Shermans
Regiment.
    Serj^t Wm Elmer
    Thomas Wood
    Jacob Ward Junr
    Joel Pease
    William Maning
    Nathan Jones
    Dan^{ll} Bewel
    Wm Quirk
    Amos Lane an Indian su-
      posed to be Deserted.

Capt Blackmans Company
Col Sherlburns Reg^t
    Russel Pratt
    James Spencer
    John Hitchcock
    Levi Hamblin
    John Hamblin
    Josiah Gibbs

Isaac Shepard
Philip Langdon
Alex^r Baxter
John Ferman
Dan^{ll} Rice

Capt Wrights Comp^n
Col. Bradleys Reg^t
    John Orcott
    Ruben Coley
    Peter Pease

Capt Abeys Comp^n
Col. Willys Reg^t
    Jacob Brown
    John Cleveland
    Ichiel Gibbs
    James Taylor listed with
      Leut Chapman Toland,
      Supposed to be Deserted
    Eleazer Jones Deceast

SIMSBURY

Voluntarily Inlisted for three
  years or during the war
    Lieu^t Theophilus Wood-
               bridge
    Lieu^t James Andrus
    Stephen Langathe
    John Humphry
    Ezekiel Messenger
    John Hill 2^d
    Roland Linsey

Josiah Linsey
Israel Humphry
Hezekiah Phelps Ju^r
Samuel Church
Elisha Harrington
John Thorril
Benjamin Hays
Asa Hays
James Slaughter
Jacob Davis

James Kirtland now
           Discharged
William Talor
David Clark now Ded
Joseph Weed now Ded
Consider Holcomb Ju^r
Hired for three years or during
  the war
    Elisha Case
    David Egelstone
    Oliver woodword
    Thomas Phelps
    Benjamin Bodwill
    Josiah Higley
    John Farron
    Francies Olmsted
    Ebenezer Drake
    Uriah Pees now Ded
    Thomas Burn
    Zackery Prince now Ded
        Rec^d his freedom

Luke Guiant
Philister Pinney
David Eno Ju^r
Wm Clark
John Davis
George Hills
James Nocak
London Wallace (?)
Ashbel Olmsted
Samuel Spray
Jaben Bennet
William Clark
Samuel Spencer
James Gallet
Samuel Wampey
Calob Curtis
Elijah Clark
Gilbert Whitney
Benjamin Brewer now Ded
Jacob Holloday
A Negro name not known

STAFFORD

Maj^r Amos Walbridge
Serj^t Sam^{ll} Worner
  "   Josiah Edson
  "   Isaac Pinny
  "   Jos^h Green
Corp^l Jos^h Whiston
  "   Jos^h Walbridge
Nathan Washbon Drum^r
Fife Porter Wolbridge
Steph^n Moulton Bond musick
Asa Thompson
Phin. Manning
Nathan Edson
Robert Thompson
Benjn Washbon
Ebenez^r Snell
Joshua Wheler
Zadock Wheler
Hezekiah Wheler

Joseph Cross
Benj Reynalds
Steph^n Whiteaker
Tim^o Herrington
Sam^{ll} Millington 3^d
Nanh^{ll} Cushmon
Asa Butler
Israel Butler
Simeon Webster 3^d
Reuben Putman
Isaac Cushmon
Benjn Orcutt
David Green Ju^r
Benjn Butler
Philip Kibbe
Nath^{ll} Walker
Timothy Wheler Dest.
Nath^{ll} Foster Dest.

TOLLAND

Capt Ich^d Hinckley
Lt Rufus Price
Lt Elijah Chapman
Doc^r Jeremiah West
Serj^t Eben^r Stebens
Nehemiah Saben
Jonathan Delàno
Jonathan Luce
Elihu Johnson
Tirus Preston
Andrew Peterson
Elias Newton
Martin Davice
Wm Huntington

Wm Johnson
Solomon Eaton
Ebenezer Brown
Isaac Squire
Abel Crandal
J. Procter Burrows
Wm Sowl
Shoball Dimmick
Edy Hatch
Simon Stimson
Clement Miner
Rausel Miner
Jacob Haskal
John Crandal

George Hubbard
Elijah Benton
Joseph Sparks
Richard Carlton

Amos Harris
Ame Paulk
David Paine

UNION

In the Year 1777 Inlisted without any Hire
    Leiu^t James Sprague
    Serg^t Nehemiah Coye (?)
    John Laflen Junr
    George Dillabur
    Samuel Peirce
Hired for three years & have families
    Thomas Taylor
    James Houghton
    Ebenezer Lillie
    William Moor Junr

Hired for three years & have no families
    James Walker
    Benjamin Bullin
    John Smith
    Luthar Loomis
    Joshua Ephraim
    Eleazer Payon (?)
Hired to Inlist in ye year 1778 for three years
    James Laflen
    John Wright
    Joseph Snell
    Abraham Laflin
    Nehemiah Packer

VOLUNTOWN

3rd Comp^y allarm List
                Reg^t Listed into
  Peter Morras   Col Huntington
  Robert Green   "
  Henry Bacon   "
  Henry Carpentor   "
  Moses Culver   "
6 Comp^y alarm List
  Lem^{ll} Shelle   "
3 Comp^y Militia
  Robt Campbell   Col Durkee
  Nathan Coy   Col Prentice
  Zoath Tucker   "
  Peleg Shaw   "
  Joseph Robens   "
  Joseph Shely   Col Sherbum
  Richd Soles   "
  Joseph Peters   Col Wyllys
  Mark Crosswell   Col Prentice
  Prince Summut   Col Wyllys
  Ceser Negro   "

6 Comp^y Militia
  John Gray   Col Huntington
  Alex^r Williams   "
  Jaduthan Heard   "
  Wm Adams   Col Durkee
  Squir Wright   Col Huntington
  Wm Gray   "
  David Cady   "
  Wm Knight   "
7 Comp^y Militia
  Amos Denisen   "
  Phenis Ellis   "
  Wm Pierce   "
  David Coy   "
  Wm Beazel   "
  Emanuel Redrik   Col Durkee
  Christ^o Brown   Col Sherburn
  Heney Hall   Col Huntington

WALLINGFORD

Capt Eph^m Chamberlain
Lt Levi Munson
" Joseph Shailor
" John Mansfield
" Lem^l Hitchcock
Charles Peck Serj. Artill.
Jehiel Peck Serj. Art^y
Jesse Peck
Titus Hart
Aaron Hall

Abel Tharp
Thos Mix
Enos Mix
John Francis
Andrew Andrews Serj^t
Edmond Fields
Jesse Vose
Saml Wright
John Sled
Selah Stedman

Joseph Clark
Johnson Cook
Warren Cook
George Cook
Timothy Hart Serj'
Benjⁿ Hart
Saml Blakslee
Benajah Hall
James Brown
Perigree Dodge
      alias Israel Dodge
Hull Shepherd
Lt Giles Curtis
Joel Cook
Willm Cook
Toney Negro
Thos Janes
Roswel Beach
Elisha Parker
Jotham Rice
Moses Barns
Thos Dudly
John Parker
Timothy Parker
Joseph Wolcott Junr
Charles Heydon
James Prout
Asa Beach
James Miles
Danl Smith
Benjⁿ Johnson
Irael Johnson
Wait Yale
Amos Parker
Anthony Goodsill
Abram Parker
Elisha Parker
Eliakim Johnson
Charles Merriman
Danl Cady
Danl Bradly
Danl Johnson Hall
Willm Parker
Reuben Moss
Thaddeus Todd
David Hall
Elisha Hall
Asaph Merriam
Edm^d Merriam
Nash Yale
Lem^l Willcox
Joseph Coburn
Ja^s Coburn
Rufus Hall
Jonathan Ford
Levi Robinson
Benj. Ford
Jatham Hall
Benj. Rexford Ju^r
Moses Hall

John Anthony
Seth Smith
Barnabas Mitchel
Elisha Bishop
Lemon Cumber Negro
Boston Negro
Chatham Freeman Negro
Samson Negro
Gideon Webb
Abel Clark
Joel Willmot
Elmor Russel
Reuben Moss
John Johnson
Prince Hotchkiss Negro
Ambrose Hine
Job Hull negro
Chauncy Lewis
Nathan^l Tyler
Eldad Porter
Saml Jones
Medad Potter
Benoni Moss
Asa Bellamy
Aaron Clark
Amos Andrews
Ichabod Hitchcock
Levi Hitchcock
Benj. Bristol
Amos Mix
Saml Spencer
Isaiah Moss
Almond Munson
Amasa Tharp
Amos Tharp
Saml S. B. Hotchkiss
Orange Munson
Lent Munson
Charles London
John Hurlbert
Elihu Cook
Willm Prout
Abij: Ives
Dick Freedom Negro
Eben: Lewis
Saml Perkins
John Hasting
John Pierce Serjt.
Enoch Merriman Serjt.
Saml Collins
Eph^m Merriam
Willm Grant
Sharp Yale Negro
Abel Lewis
Dimond or Divan Clark
Peter Sibbels
David Barns
Danl Hummerston
Benj. Parker

WATERBURY

[The families of each of these
soldiers received supplies in
1778 or 1779.]

Asa Thair
Sam[ll] Camp
Isreal Calkins
Richard Clark
Jonah Mallery
Stephen Welton Jun[r]
W[m] Hickcox Jun[r]
John Cole
Eliab Parker
John Smith
Serg[t] Ezekiel Tuttle
Joel Cook
Serg[t] Sam[ll] Lewis
Sam[ll] Camp Jun[r]
Cop[l] Nemiah Royce
Stephen Curtis
Amos Dunbar
Obed Williams
William Southmayd
Ezekiel Sanford
Simeon Graves
Ens[n] Timothy Tuttle
Jonathan Parde

Dan[ll] Barns
Serj[t] Ezekiel Upson
George Prichard Jun[r]
Abial Robbards
Lue Smith
Joel Robbards
Jabez Tuttle
Stephen Judd
John Tattendon
Stephen Scovill
Sergt John Fulford
Sergt Titus Dutton
Sam[ll] Smith
Leiut Nath[ll] Edwards
W[m] Bassit
Jonathan Davis
Bruster Judd
Timothy Andrews
Elisha Hickcox
Nath[ll] Hall
Major David Smith
Isaac Parker
Stephen Davis
Stephen Curtis 3[d]
Hezekiah Tuttle
Dan[ll] Pendleton

WINCHESTER

George Hudson
Pabdy Stanard
Jonathan Preston
Prince Neagro
John Fay
Seth Stanard
William Leach
Steave Hurlburt

Levi Wilkenson
Steaven Scovils
Adam Mott
Remembrance Filley
Jesse Wilkenso
Garshom Fay
William Fay
Timothy Fay

WILLINGTON

Serj[t] Caleb Orcutt
Serj[t] David Hinckley
Serj[t] Richard Lord
Corp[l] Haman Hatch
Solomon Fenton
John Scriptor
Nath[n] Carpenter
Allen Carpenter
Corp[l] Adonijah Fenton
James Johnson
John Hinckley Drumer
Asa Stoel

John Scott
Fradrick Pearl
Jabez Flint
Joseph Cushman
William Blanchard
Gideon Noble fifer
David Johnson
Cop[l] Eliphelit Cushman
William Stiles
Joseph Dimick
David Rice

WINDHAM

Belonging to the 2[d] Society
Lieut Benj[n] Durke
John Burnam

Nathan Burnam
Benjamin Burnap
James Burnap

Calvin Burnap
John Frame
John Fuller
Abner French
Thomas Farnam
Abial Farnam
James Hale
Nathan Hovey
Philemon Holt
Nath¹ Martin
Meecham Jeremʰ
Meecham Jonaᵗʰ
Martin George
Parry Ebenʳ
Eliphaz Parrish
Jsaiah Rogers Dead
Ruben Farnam
Jonathⁿ Flint
Jacob Hovey or Roger Smith
Elijah Randall
James Smith or Sharper
                    Negro
Elias Bingham
Belonging to the first Society
Ebenezer Gray Lᵗ Colº
Nath¹¹ Webb Capᵗ
Amos Woodward
Levi Hibbard
John Bingham Sergᵗ
Timº Hibbard
Asa Hibbard Sergᵗ
David Young Drumer
Eleazʳ Robinson
Dyar Hibbard
Uriah Hibbard
Seth Larribe
Caleb Fitch
Elijah Backus
Ezek¹ Dunham
Garshom Dunham
Joseph Read
Mason Abbe
Jonah Palmer
Walter Chaise
Ephᵐ Terry
Ebeⁿ Hibbard
Elijʰ Linkon
Adriel Simons
Salomⁿ Tracy Sergᵗ
Elijʰ Spafford Sergᵗ
Benjⁿ Ripley
Joseph Johnson
Benaijⁿ Geers
John Holly

Joseph West Fief Majʳ
Comfort Foster
Abisha Bingham
Sam¹¹ Robinson
Sam¹¹ Murdock
Sam¹¹ Spencer Artificer
Josiah Read
Jnº Huntington
Jnº Spencer Sergᵗ Light
                    Horse
Abner Backus
Jabez Rouse Sergᵗ
Charles Ripley Sergᵗ
Andʷ Warner Corpˡ
Jnº Holliss
Richᵈ Howard
Wᵐ Placey ⎫
Jnº Leathercoat ⎪
Joseph Robbins ⎬ Indians
Joseph Meason ⎪
Silas Frink ⎭
Sam¹¹ Brown
Joseph Holcom of Windsor
Belonging to the third and fourth
    Societys
Albigenor Waldo Surgion
Sam¹¹ Cogswell 1ˢᵗ Lieut
Elias Robinson Ensign
Josiah Burnham Sergᵗ
Alfred Hurlbutt Sergᵗ
Thoˢ Hurlburtt Corpˡ
Nathan Morgan Fiefer
Fradrick Whiting Sergᵗ
Levi Deans
Edwᵈ Coburn
Peter Scovill
Joseph Ginning Juʳ
Zopher Robinson
Nath¹¹ Bennit
Thoˢ F. Gerrald
Asa Walden
Francis Pirkins
Benjⁿ Cary Juʳ
Jabez Pottage an Indian
Abel Robinson
Hezʰ Cary
James L. Flint
Turner Lille
Abner French
Elipaz Kingsley
            Lieut of yᵉ artificers
Levi Cary
Oliver Cary

WINDSOR

Dan¹¹ Bissell Junʳ
Obed Lamberton Jʳ
David Thrall

Joel Denslow Dead
David Gibbs
David Barber Jʳ

Joseph Saymour
Shubel Berber Dead
Ezekiel Clark Jr
Joseph Barnard
Simeon Moore Jr
Cor¹¹ Russell
Thomas Parsons
Ezra Beckwith
Oliver Woodward
Isaac Thrall
Tim° Hoskins
Palashel Wakefield
Amos Lawrance
Eb^zr Woolworth
Elias Brown
Stephen Loomis Jr
Martin Denslow
Sam¹¹ Wing Dead
David Daniels
Aaron Pinney Dead
Dan¹¹ Porter
Barzil Henry
Isaac Phelps Dead
Joseph Wing Dead
Allyn Pryor
Robert Westland Jr
Zeb. Hoskins
George Loomis
Phin Griswold
Neil McLean Jr
Tim° Phelps
Sherman Rowland
Mathew Holcomb Dead

Edward Negro Dead
Capt Abner Prior
Lt Seth Phelps
Lt Sam¹¹ Gibbs
Ezekil Case Jr
Sam¹¹ Marshall
Joseph Egelston
Levi Charter
Elihu Mills
Elias Crow
Nath¹¹ Egelston Jr
Isaac Egelston
Sam¹¹ Brown Jr
Abel Gillet Jr
Abel Cook Dead
Ephriah Loatwall
Isaac Chandler
Joseph Westland
Timothy Egelston
Will Munrow
Alvin Hurlbut
Sam¹¹ Coy Dead
Shubel Cook
Richard Cook
Wm Cook
John Brister
John Winchel
John Daset
Norman Fyler
Elihu Mather
Nath Mather
Jonth Bidwell Jr

WOODSTOCK

Serjt Jn° Bartholomew
Corp¹ Dan¹ Smith
 do   Theor Luther
Lemuel Allen
Wm Jepson
Wm Press
John Briant
David Lawrence
Denis Spencer
Asa Winton
Elihu Hebbard
Timothy Hebbard
Fifer Aaron Hebbard
Fifer Jn° Brock
Thoᵉ Spencer
Joᵉ Pagan
Nathan Powers
Dan¹ Evans
Jn° Vinton

Abrm White
Nath¹ Robins
Cato Negro
Jason Crawferd
Fredrick Green
Simeon Camp
Peter Saunders
Eli Bruce
Robert Chandler
Dan¹ Bowen
Paul Haradan
Q. M. Asa Lyon
Aas Hibbard
Richard Guile
Amasa Frissel

now Dead { Amos Bunnal
Corp¹ Jn° Greene
James Guile
Phelix Negro

COLCHESTER

[The heading of another part of this document seems to show that it covers service in the Continental Army " up to the first day of Jan'y 1780.]
   These following are the Names of Soldiers Belonging to the Town of Colchester Who are some of them hired by two men and part of them We Suppose are entitled to 5/ p month from the Towns but have not as Yet Recev^d any

John Burns	Amasa Brown
John Frederick	Lewis Ackley
Elisha Pomp	William Isham
Abijah Pratt	Joshua Goff
Jon^a Isham	Aaron Holmes
Nicholas Ackley	Aaron Chamberlin
Naomi Beebe	Ebenezer Isham
Dennis Gardner	Ephraim Judd
Labbeus Loomis	William Burnham
Robert Ransom	Arkelaus Free
Abner Chapman	Elisha Brown
William Baker	Isaac Brown
Peregreen Dodge	Samuel Kneeland
Roswel Chappel	Joel Fox
Edward Rathbun	
Jacob Rathburn	[Comptrollers Office]

WALLINGFORD

[The following names of Continental soldiers from Wallingford are found in another list among others already printed in this volume.]
   [These received £5 bounty each.]

Daniel Thade	Moses Marus
John Stead	Jesse Thorp (?)
Timothy Thorp	Saml Holt
Elijah Parker	

[These did not receive bounty]
   Benj Kendrich Decd   John Hastens

Edmon Field of this town has drawn a bounty from Waterbury.

[George M. Curtis, Meriden.]

PRISONERS.

The following is a list of the officers belonging to the State of Connecticut that were liveing and in Captivity on Longisland the 2nd of May 1777

Colo. Hobbey Greenwich
Colo. Heart Farmington
Maj. Wells Colchester
Capt. Bennedick Danbury
Capt. Bissel East Hartford
Capt. Percefeild Chatham
Capt. Trobridge N. Haven
Capt. Keeler Norwalk
Capt. Parit Milford
Capt. Couch Walingford
Capt. Smith Colchester
Capt. Beebe Litchfield
Capt. Wells Glasenbury
Lieut. Clark Danbury
Lieut. Trobridge Danbury
Lieut. Gove Preston
Lieut. Fanning Norwich
Lieut. Fitch Norwich
Lieut. Blacklidge Stratford
Lieut. Brainard East Haddam

Lieut. Eells Norwalk
Lieut. Grant Litchfield
Lieut. Gillit Hartford
Lieut. Brewster Preston
Lieut. Tanner Cornwall
Lieut. Orcut Willington
Lieut. Cleaveland Norwich
Lieut. Edwards Waterbury
Lieut. Cooke Torrington
Ens. Forsdich New London
Ens. Hall Derby
Ens. Bradford Plainfield
Ens. Taylor N. Fairfield
Ens. Burnham Danbury
Ens. Lyman Middletown
Ens. Bradford Haddam
Ens. Knowlton Ashford
Storrs Quartermaster Mansfield
Smith Wagonmaster

[*State Library, Revolution 11, 139*]

RETURN FROM 4TH BRIGADE OF MILITIA.

A Return of the Soldiers that have inlisted and been draughted or detached from the 4th Brigade of Militia in the State of Connecticut commanded by Brigadier General Siliman to serve in the Continental Army commanded by his Excellency General Washington. May 1, 1778.

Soldiers Names	Towns they belong to	Company	Regiment	Time they inlisted for	Detached to serve till
Stephen Meaker	Redding				
Elias Bigsby	"				
Nathan Coley	"				
Ephraim Bectley	"				
John Rumsey	"				
Eph^m Wheeler	"				
Eben^r Patchen	"	"	"		
Dan^ll Monroe	"	"	"		
Abijah Burret	"	"	"		
Bartholomew Baker	"	"	"		
Jeremiah Byne	"	"	"		
Sam^ll Raymond	"	"	"	for 3 years	1 Jany next
Peter Drew	"	Capt G. Morehouse	"	"	"
Nathl Morgan	"	"	"		"
Nathan Lyon	"	"	"		"
Moses Knap	"	"	"		"
Lazarus Beach	"	"	"		"
James Sanford	"	"	"		"
Dan^ll Hill	"	"	"		"
David Hill	"	"	"		"
Israel Rowland	"	"	"		"
James Adams	"	"	"		"
Enos Lee	"	"	"		"
James Green	"	"	"	dureing ye Warr	"
Nathan Rumsey	"	"	"	"	

Soldiers Names	Towns they belong to	Company	Regiment	Time they inlisted for dureing ye Warr	Detached to serve till
Nehemiah Sherwood	Redding	Capt G. Morehouse			
Ebenr Williams	"	"			
Henry Hopkins	"	"		"	
Gershom Fairchild	"	"		"	
Jabez Williams	"	"		"	
Ned Negroe				"	
Jack Negroe				"	
Nathll Booth				"	
Joseph Hubbard	Stratford	Capt Brinsmaid and Nichols	Colo Whiteing	"	
John Crawfoot	"	"	"	"	
John Downs	"	"	"	"	
James Downs	"	"	"	"	
Abell Peet	"	"	"	"	
Reuben Beach	"	"	"	"	
John Jones	"	"	"	"	
Gideon Seely	"	"	"	"	
Daniel Jones	"	"	"	"	
Daniel Averies	"	"	"	"	
William Dascomb	"	"	"	"	
Nathan Hawley	"	"	"	"	
Nathll Beach	"	"	"	"	
Ephraim Seely	"	"	"	"	
John Gilbert	"	"	"	"	
Ebenr Shelly	"	"	"	"	
Joel Mosier	"	"	"	"	
Gideon Hawley	"	"	"	"	
Joseph Wakeley	"	"	"	"	
Danl Sherwood	"	"	"	"	
Nero Negro	"	"	"	"	
Caesar Negro	"	"	"	"	
Tony Negro	"	"	"	"	
Peter Lewis	"	"	"	"	
Samll Hinman	"	"	"	"	

Name		Residence	Captain	Colonel	Term	Date
Jacob Grover	"	"	"	"	"	"
John Riggs	"	"	"	"	"	"
Abrah^m Hawley	"	"	"	"	"	"
Sam^ll Manning	"	"	"	"	For 3 years	"
John Sunderland	"	"	Capt J. Benjamen	"	During Warr	"
John Downing	"	"	"	"	"	"
Robert Freeman	"	"	"	"	"	"
Pinkerman Clark	"	"	"	"	"	"
Jack Freeman	"	"	"	"	"	"
Ebenezer Shelly	"	"	"	"	"	"
Sam^ll Osborn	"	"	"	"	"	"
Alex^r Fairchild	"	"	"	"	"	"
Sam^ll Richmad	"	"	"	"	"	"
Amos Saunders	"	"	"	"	"	"
Prosper Wetmore	"	Derby	not known	Col° Thompson	"	1 Jany next
Caleb Chatfield	"	Stratford	Capt P. Curtiss	Col° Whiteing	"	"
John Munroe	"	"	"	"	"	"
Sam^ll Lewis Junr	"	"	"	"	For 3 years	"
Israel Hawley	"	"	"	"	"	"
Jesse Dickerman	"	"	"	"	"	"
Isaac Dickerman	"	"	"	"	"	"
Sam^ll Parker	"	"	Capt S. Beardsly	"	Dureing y° Warr	"
Eph^m Quosh, Molatt	"	"	"	"	"	"
Lively Negro	"	"	"	"	"	"
Pomp Negro	"	"	"	"	"	"
Josman Negro	"	"	"	"	"	"
Joseph Negro	"	"	"	"	"	"
David Hard	"	"	"	"	"	"
Eben^r Smith	"	"	Capt J. Birdsly	"	"	"
Timothy Chatman	"	"	"	"	"	"
James Hide	"	"	"	"	"	"
Benjn Wakeley	"	"	"	"	"	"
Shubael Freeman	"	"	"	"	"	"
John Williamson	"	"	"	"	"	"
Gideon Leavensworth	"	"	"	"	"	"

Soldiers Names	Towns they belong to	Company	Regiment Col° Whiteing	Time they inlisted for	detached to serve till
Wallaston Hawley	Stratford	Capt J. Birdsly		During ye Warr	
William [Jedon	"	"		"	
Benjn Shelton	"				
John Nobles	"				1 Jan^r next
Abraham Noble	"	Capt Burroughs			
John Chaps	Fairfield				
Barack Taylor		"		"	
Burr Gilbert		"		"	
Ebenezer Meaker		"		"	
Thomas Durfee		"		"	
Seth Buckley				"	
Robert Simmons	Stratford	Capt S. Judson	"	"	
John Bennett	"	"	"	"	
John Beers	"	"	"	"	
Daniel Munroe	"	"	"	"	
David Minot	"	"	"	"	
Silas Glasgow Negro	"	"	"	"	
James Beers	"	"	"	"	1 Jany next
Isaac Hubbell	"	"	"	"	"
John Hopkins	Suratoga in N. York State	hired into Capt Booth's Comp^y	"	"	
John Basset	Stratford	Capt J. Booth	"	For 3 years Dureing ye Warr	
Benjamin Dean	"	"	"		
Jesse Primus	"	"	"		
Amos Temp	"	"	"		
Samuel Pulford	"	"	"	"	
Lewis Anjevine	"	"	"	"	
Ephraim Seely	"	"	"	"	
Briant Montegue	"	"	"		
Eli Lewis	"		"		
John Benjamen Junr	"	Capt Eb. Coe	"	"	1 Jany next
Jesse Smith	"	"	"	"	
David Barlow	"	"	"	"	
Isaac Brown	"	"	"	"	

Name	Residence	Enlisted by	Colonel	Term	Remarks
Orry King	"	"	"	"	
Josiah Barrow	"	"	"	"	
Joel Beers	"	"	"	"	
John Beardsley	"	"	"	"	
Samuel Whitney	"	"	"	"	
John Peet	"	"	"	"	
Jasper Jones	"	"	"	"	
Justus Seely	"	"	"	"	
Nath'll Beebee	"	"	"	"	
Daniel Mosier	"	"	"	"	
David Selleck	Stanford	not known	Col Mead	For 3 years	
Stephen Hall	Stratford	Ensign Nichols	Col'o Whiteing	Dureing y'e Warr	
Eli Nichols	"	"	"	"	
Henry Bayley	"	"	"	"	
Abell Mallet	"	"	"	"	
Sam'l Parker	"	"	"	"	
Truman French	"	"	"	"	
Abrah'm Fabrique	"	"	"	"	
Benj'n Bennitt 3d	"	"	"	For 3 Years	
Tim'o Blackman	"	"	"	"	1st Jan'y next
Daniel Barlow	"	"	"	"	"
David Watkins	"	"	"	"	"
Abijah Beardsley	"	"	"	"	
Sam'll Curtiss	"	"	"	"	
Asa Winton	"	"	"	"	
Jn'o Benjamen Mitchel	"	Cap't Leavensw'th	"	During y'e Warr	
Abijah Perry	"	"	"	"	
George Leaming	"	"	"	"	
Toney Freeman	"	"	"	"	
Peter Lewis	"	"	"	"	
Joseph Lawin	"	"	"	"	
George Hall	"	Cap't Tomlinson	"	"	1st Jan'y next
David Blackman	"	"	"	"	"
Jeremiah Blackman	"	"	"	"	"
Sam'll Blackman	"	"	"	"	

Soldiers Names	Towns they belong to	Company	Regiment	Time they inlisted for	Detached to serve till
	Stratford	Capt Tomlinson	Colo Whiteing	During ye Warr	
Miles Dickson	Stratford	Capt Tomlinson	Colo Whiteing	During ye Warr	
Richard Hawley	"	"	"	"	
Samll Riggs Mills	"	"	"	"	
Elisha Pulford	"	"	"	"	
Lemuel Seeley	"	"	"	"	
Nathan Thompson	"	"	"	"	
Samll Washborn	"	"	"	"	
Isaiah Wilcockson	"	"	"	"	
Robert Welch	"	"	"	"	
James Wayland	"	"	"	"	
James Hide	"	"	"	"	
Nehemiah Gearham	"	"	"	"	
Charles Burrit	"	Capt Sterling	"	"	
Samll Lewis Brooks	"	"	"	"	
Josiah French	"	"	"	"	
Richard Handy	"	"	"	"	
John McKenzie	"	"	"	"	
Samll Wakely Junr	"	"	"	"	
David Wells Junr	"	"	"	"	
Timothy Gauncey	not known	"	"	"	
Isaac Hubbell	Fairfield	"	"	"	
Zachariah Sherwood	"	"	"	"	
David Jackson	"	"	"	"	
David Morehouse	"	"	"	"	
Isaac Odell	"	"	"	"	
Elijah Patchen	"	"	"	"	
Burr Gilbert	"	"	"	"	
Transient Persons hired by Jeremiah Rines	Sratford	not known	not known	"	
Ephm Porter	"	"	"	"	
James Hamhidon	"	"	"	"	
Thomas Jacklin	"	"	"	"	
John Williams	"	"	"	"	
Richard Danbury	"	"	"	"	

Name				
John White	"	"	Fairfield	"
Ephraim Rose	"	"	"	"
William Braizier	"	"	"	"
John Titus	"	"	"	"
David Day	"	"	"	"
John Davenport	"	"	"	"
John Jones	"	"	"	"
William Lock	"	"	"	"
John Wright	"	"	"	"
Jonathᵃ Goodwell	"	"	"	"
Ashel Tirrel	"	"	"	"
Andrew Po rter	"	"	Fairfield	"
Daniel Burr	"	"	Cap' Barham	"
Richard Williams	"	"	"	"
Andrew Porter	"	"	"	"
Lewis Garrison	"	"	"	"
Joseph Armstrong	"	"	"	"
Phillip Frenchman	"	"	"	"
Peter Rowfiner	"	"	"	"
Seth Bulkley	"	"	"	"
Joseph Lorian	"	"	"	"
Wakeman Hull	"	"	Cap' Thorp	"
Augustus Sturgis	"	"	"	"
Stratton Osborn	"	"	"	"
John Fuller	"	"	"	"
Gilbert Dudley	"	"	"	"
Richard Williams	"	"	"	"
Nathan Squire	"	"	"	"
Peter Stalker	"	"	"	"
Daniel Bennitt	"	Col⁰ Mead	not known	Norwalk
Abrahᵐ Raymond	"	Col⁰ Whiteing	Cap' G. Burr	Fairfield
John Mitchel	"	"	"	"
Epaphras Goodsell	"	"	"	"
Moses Sturgis	"	"	"	"
Daniel Meaker	"	"	"	"

Soldiers Names	Towns they belong to Fairfield	Company Capt G. Barr Capt: Nash and Wakeman	Regiment Col^o Whiteing	Time they inlisted for During ye Warr For 3 years	Detached to serve till
Ezra Williams	Fairfield	Capt G. Barr Capt: Nash and Wakeman	Col^o Whiteing	During ye Warr For 3 years	
Jonathan Poor	"	"	"	"	
James Cole	"	"	"	"	
Stephen Lockwood	"	"	"	"	
Eben^r Allen Junr	"	"	"	"	
Alexand^r Wicks	"	"	"	"	
Joseph Batterson	"	"	"	"	
James Batterson Junr	"	"	"	"	
Stephen Batterson	"	"	"	"	
Wm Raymond	"	"	"	"	
Joseph Mills	"	"	"	"	
Nath^a Sturgis	"	"	"	"	
Isaac Elwood	"	"	"	"	
Abr^m Sturgis	"	"	"	"	
Joshua Jecocks	"	"	"	"	
Ezra Wood	"	"	"	"	
Joshua Disbrow	"	"	"	"	
Isaac Disbrow	"	"	"	"	
Henry Disbrow	"	"	"	"	
Simon Disbrow	"	"	"	"	
Gideon Hurlburt	"	"	"	"	
John Couch	"	"	"	"	
John Johnson	"	"	"	"	
William Johnson	"	"	"	"	
Justin Disbrow	"	"	"	"	
Abrah^m Couch	"	"	"	"	
John Crossman	"	"	"	"	
Ephraim Beers	"	"	"	"	
Gershom Jecox	"	"	"	"	
Moses Dimon	"	Capt Wheeler	"	Dureing ye Warr	
William Cable	"	Capt Silliman	"	"	
Tony Lyon a Molatt	"	"	"	"	
Nehemiah Turner	"	"	"	"	
Danl Wingfield	"	"	"	"	

Name	Residence	Captain	Discharge
John Fuller	"	"	"
William Gold	"	"	"
Peter Stalker	"	"	"
Samuel Chapman	"	"	"
Richard Williams	"	"	"
John Baker	"	"	"
John Lyon	"	"	"
Stephen Lyon	"	"	"
Asa Turney	"	"	"
Josiah Armstrong	"	"	"
Enos Jones Prindle	"	"	"
Dan'l Meaker	"	"	"
Paschal Churchet	"	"	"
Thomas Allen	Stratford	Cap' N. Seely	1 Jan'y next
Samuel French	"	"	"
Amos Freeman	"	"	"
Nathan Tirrell	"	"	"
John Jones	"	"	"
Enos Wheeler	"	"	"
Eben' Beech	Fairfield	"	"
Eleazer Hall	"	Cap' Bennitt	"
John Gilbert	"	"	"
Dan'l Jackson	Stratford	"	"
Isband Hubbell	"	"	"
Ebenezer Gilbert	"	"	"
Jedediah Hall	"	"	"
John Blackman	Fairfield	Cap' Lyon	1st Jan'y next
Nath'l Treadwell	"	"	"
William Jackson	"	"	"
Sam'l Lyon	"	"	1st Jan'y next
Daniel Vance	"	"	"
Thomas Treadwell	"	"	"
Hezekiah Fanton	"	"	"
Josiah Cable	"	"	"
John Stalker	"	"	"

Soldiers Names	Towns they belong to	Company	Regiment	Time they inlisted for
		Capt Lyon / Capt Hill	Col^o Whiteing	Dureing the Warr or 3 years / Detached to serve till 1st Jan^ry next
Gold Dimon	Fairfield			
Eliphalet Bradley	"			
Nathan Bradley	"	Capt Hill	Col^o Whiteing	Dureing the Warr or 3 years
Daniel Raymond	"	"	"	"
Sam^ll Turney Junr	"	"	"	"
Nathan Winton	"	"	"	Detached to serve till 1st Jan^ry next
Aaron Wayley	"	"	"	"
Hezekiah Webb	"	"	"	"
Joseph Mosier	"	"	"	"
Ezekiel Thorp	"	"	"	"
Aaron Thorp	"	"	"	"
Francis Swords	"	"	"	"
Peter Stalker	"	"	"	"
Hezekiah Wayley	"	"	"	"
Nath^ll Johnson	"	"	"	"
Michael Bowen	"	Capt Godfrey	"	"
Josiah Green	"	"	"	"
John Teen	"	"	"	"
Elip^t Gray	"	"	"	"
Bradley Dean	"	"	"	"
Thiah Beers	"	"	"	"
Dan^ll Canfield	"	"	"	"
Sam^ll Green	"	"	"	"
Benjamen Allen	"	Capt Dean	"	"
Atkinson Hilton	"	"	"	"
Francis Hutternock	"	"	"	"
Joseph Ogden	"	"	"	"
Stephen Hurlburt	"	"	"	"
Stephen Dickeman	"	"	"	"
Joel Gilbert	"	"	"	"
Stephen Lockwood	Ridgefield	not known	Col^o Beardsley	"
Ezekiel Hawley hired				

Name	State / Town	Captain	Colonel	Term	Date
Jonathan Edwards	{ Massachussets } Bay State Woodbury	not known Cap⁺ A. Mallary	not known Col° Moseley	During y⁰ Warr	
Stephen Hull	"	"	"	"	
Eliphalet Easton	"	"	"	"	
Samˡˡ Wilson	"	"	"	"	
Elisha Walker	"	"	"	"	
Phinehas Camp	"	"	"	"	
Tite Negro					
Isaac Pollard					
Freman Judd	Waterbury Woodbury	not known Cap⁺ Mallary	not known Col° Mosely		1ˢᵗ Janʳʸ next
Jabez Bacon	"	"	"		"
Ebenʳ Talman	"	"	"		
Daniel Bedson (?)	"	"	"		
Eli Stoddard	"	Cap⁺ T. Judson	"	"	
Zachariah Walker	"	"	"	"	
Chapman Judson	"	.	"	"	1 Janʳʸ next
Abiel Linsley Junʳ	"	"	"		"
John Slaughter	"	"	"		"
Abell Mix	"	"	"		
Adam Crammer	"	"	"		
Phinehas Demming	"	"	"		
Delucena Bacchus	"	"	"	"	
Simeon Tylor	"	Cap⁺ N. Hine	"	"	
John Davenport	"	"	"	"	
John Herrick	"	"	"	"	
Zuor Bradley	"	"	"	"	
Jonathan Twist	"	"	"	"	
Aner Adye	"	"	"	"	
Julian Easton	"	"	"	"	
Benjᵃ Avery	"	"	"	"	
Benjᵃ Wheeler Junʳ	"	"	"	"	
John Tirrell	"	"	"	"	
James Brown	"	"	"	"	
Gideon Hurd Junʳ	"	"	"	"	
Anthony Stoddard	"	"	"	"	

Soldiers Names	Towns they belong to	Company	Regiment	Time they inlisted for During ye Warr	Detached to serve till
Jehiel Bradley	Woodbury	Capt N. Hine	Col^o Mosely		
Truman Crissey	"	"	"		
Iri Way	"	"	"	"	
Michael Molatto	"	"	"	"	
Tim^o Gibbs	Newtown	not known	Col^o Beardsley		1st Jan^ry next
Matthew Read	"	"	"	"	"
John Burns	Woodbury	Capt N Hine	Col^o Mosely	"	"
Zachariah Prentice	"	"	"		"
Tim^o Tomlinson	"	"	"		
Elijah Sherman	"	"	"		
Nicholas Masters	"	"	"		
Chapman Judson Junr	"	"	"		
Reuben Hotchkiss	"	"	"		
Zachariah Beers	"	"	"		
Norman Easton	"	Capt E. Smith	"		
John Drummonds	"	"	"	"	
Simeon Barns	"	"	"	"	
Zadock Hawkins	"	"	"	"	
Zadock Hawkins Junr	"	"	"		
Jonas Hinman	"	Capt D. Hinman	"		1st Jan^ry next
Joel Hinman	"	"	"		"
Enos Hinman	"	"	"		"
Israel Curtiss Junr	"	"	"	"	
Charles Strong	"	"	"	"	
Elisha Hobart	"	"	"	"	
John Hobart	"	"	"	"	
David Hicock	"	"	"	"	
Gideon Bristol Junr	"	"	"	"	
John Bulford	"	"	"		
Moses Strickling	"	"	"		
Davis Demmonds	"	"	"		
Thomas James	"	"	"		
Edmund Washband	"	"	"	"	1st Jan^ry next
Stephen Stillwell	New Milford	Capt B. Bostwick	"		

Name				Residence	Captain
Dan¹¹ Dye	"	"	"	"	"
John Fish	"	"	"	"	"
Sam¹¹ Phillips	"	"	"	"	"
A man whose Name is unknown	"	"	"	"	"
James Daily	"	"	"	"	"
Nath¹¹ Durkee	"	"	"	"	"
James Bennitt	"	"	"	"	"
Oliver Bostwick	"	"	"	"	"
Josiah Buck	"	"	"	"	"
Joseph Clark	"	"	"	"	"
Christopher Cockran	"	"	"	"	"
Wᵐ Drinkwater	"	"	"	"	"
Theophˢ Cornstalk	"	"	"	"	"
A Person hired by some of } the Compᵞ his Name forgot }	"	"	"	New Milford	Cap' B. Stone
Ebenʳ Drinkwater	"	"	"	"	"
James Weeks	"	"	"	"	"
Lemuel Peet	"	"	"	"	"
John Frothingham	"	"	"	"	"
Wᵐ Foot	"	"	"	"	"
Matthew Wildman	"	"	"	"	"
Wᵐ Danwell	"	"	"	"	"
David Cole	"	"	"	"	"
Truman Wooster	"	"	"	"	"
Azariah Canfield	"	"	"	"	"
Chileab Palmer	"	"	"	"	"
Elijah Canfield	"	"	"	"	"
Francis Eustace	"	"	"	"	"
James Wilson	"	"	"	"	"
Robert Nichols	"	"	"	"	"
Perry a transint Person	"	"	"	"	"
Prince Gratis	"	"	"	"	"
Robert Smith	"	"	"	"	"
Israel Phillips	"	"	"	"	"
Shubael Phillips	"	"	"	"	"

Soldiers Names	Towns they belong to	Company	Regiment	Time they inlisted for	Detached to serve till
James Abernethy	New Milford	Capt A. Hurburt	Colo Mosely		
Luke Welch	"	"	"		
Shem Negro	"	"	"		
Wm Bryant	"	"	"		
David Blakeley	"	"	"	During ye Warr	1 Jany next
Phinehas Baker	"	"	"	"	"
John Gold	Woodbury	"	"		"
David Mallary	"	"	"		"
Jonathan Blakeley	"	"	"		"
Gideon Hurlburt Jr.	"	"	"		"
Robert Hurlburt	"	"	"		"
Thomas Calihan	"	"	"		"
John Hunt Junr	"	"	"		"
James Hawley	"	"	"		"
Simeon Hunt	"	"	"		"
Matthew Royce	"	"	"		"
Joseph Tonance	"	Capt D. Leavensw'th	"	During ye Warr	
Francis Field	"	"	"	"	
George Field	"	"	"	"	
Abell Wakely	"	"	"	"	
John Thompson	"	"	"	"	
Wm Bunday	"	"	"	"	
Joseph Westcott	"	"	"	"	
David Rumsey	"	"	"	"	
John Booth	"	"	"	"	
Aseph Hurlbutt	"	Capt N. Chapman	"	"	1st Jany next
Thos Squire 3d	"	"	"	"	"
Thos Weller	"	"	"	"	"
Dan Stephens	"	"	"	"	
Stephen Ranny	"	"	"	"	
Hinman Wooster	"	"	"	"	
Joseph Judson	"	"	"	"	
Charles Sheldon	"	"	"	"	
Wm Bennedict	"	"	"	"	

Eben' Church	"	"	"	"
George Howe	"	"	"	"
Justus Reynolds	"	"	"	"
Amos Clark	"	"	"	"
Alex' Mills	"	"	"	"
Robin Negroe	"	"	Cap' E. Hawley	"
David Dixon	"	"	"	"
Sam'll Lee	"	"	"	"
James Hooker	"	"	"	"
Jared Dixon	"	"	"	"
Sam'll Jackson	"	"	"	"
Aaron Olds	"	"	"	"
David Reynolds	"	"	"	"
David Robinson	"	"	"	"
Joseph Blackley	"	"	"	"
Phinehas Palmer	"	"	"	"
Dan'll Tucker	"	"	"	"
Moses Churchill	"	"	"	"
Hezekiah Keeler	"	"	"	"
Friend Beeman	"	"	"	"
Enoch Thomas	"	"	"	"
Jonathan Munger	"	"	"	"
Stephen Barnum	"	"	Kent	Cap' Mills
Sam'll Bates	"	"	"	"
Primus Hubbell	"	"	"	"
Cuff Comstalk	"	"	"	"
Cult Freeman	"	"	"	"
Thomas Warrups	"	"	"	"
Peter Warwehew	"	"	"	"
Dan'll Sucknuck	"	"	"	"
John Ashly	"	"	"	"
John Smith	"	"	"	"
Elijah Chapman	"	"	"	"
Benj'n Bolt	"	"	"	"
W'm Bradshaw	"	"	"	"

Soldiers Names	Towns they belong to	Company	Regiment	Time they inlisted for	Detached to serve till
			Col° Mosely	During yᵉ Warr	
Elipt Simpson	Kent	Capt Mills Capt A. Fuller			
Samˡˡ Chamberlain	"		"	"	
Jesse Merwin	"		"	"	
Amos Barnum	"		"	"	
Joseph Dixon	"		"	"	
Samˡˡ Hubbell	"		"	"	
Zenus Barnum	"		"	"	
Dorias Sperry	"		"	"	
Prentice Fitch	"		"	"	
Samˡˡ Fairchild	"	"	"	"	
John Main	"		"	"	
Danˡˡ Dye	"		"	"	
Joseph Hurd	Woodbury	Capt S. Hurlburt	"	"	
Ezekiel Newton	"		"	"	
Robert Burton	"	"	"	"	
Noah Hurlburt	"		"	"	
Tom Indian	"		"	"	
Job Molatto	"		"	"	
Roger Blaisdell	"		"	"	
James Hawley	"	"	"	"	1ˢᵗ Janʸ next
John Woodruff	"		"		"
Peruda Isbell	"		"		"
John Weeks	"		"		"
Joel Titus	"		"		
John Sears	"		"		
William Ingraham	"	Capt J. Farrand	"	"	
Isaac Lyon	"		"	"	
Enos Prindle	"		"	"	
Asa Durkee	"	"	"	"	
Peter Negro	"		"	"	
Danˡˡ Fenn	"		"	"	
Gamaliel Parker	"		"	"	
Oliver Olds, not joined		"	"	"	
Eleazer Ingraham	"		"	"	1ˢᵗ Janʸ next

Name		Residence	Captain		During y⁰ Warr or 3 years
Darius Fisher	〃	〃	〃	〃	
John Jordan	〃	〃	〃		
Thadᵉ Hicock Junʳ	〃	〃	〃	〃	
Calvin Hurd	〃	〃			
William Reynold	〃	〃			
Abijah Moger		New Milford	Capᵗ P. Yates	〃	〃
David Beech Junʳ	〃	〃	〃	〃	〃
James Beers	〃	〃	〃	〃	〃
David Sherman	〃	State of Vermont		〃	〃
Edward Fuller	〃	〃		〃	〃
Benajah Leonard		〃			〃
Wᵐ Blanchard					〃
David Rowe					〃
Danˡˡ Yarington					〃
Edward Grates					〃
John Frothingham					〃
Mingo Treet		New Milford	Capᵗ N Hine	〃	〃
Goodman Noble	〃	〃	〃	〃	〃
Jehabad Wilkinson	〃	〃	〃	〃	〃
Ebenʳ Bostwick	〃	〃	〃	〃	〃
Gershom Nichols	〃	〃	〃	〃	〃
Stephen Wheeler	〃	〃	〃	〃	〃
David Merwin	〃	〃	〃	〃	〃
Ebenʳ Trowbridge	〃	〃	〃	〃	〃
Liffie Sanford		〃	〃	〃	〃
Wᵐ Whitely		〃	〃	〃	〃
Eli Nichols			〃	〃	〃
Ralph Smith			〃	〃	〃
Danˡˡ Rogers				〃	〃
John Knap				〃	〃
David Bostwick				〃	〃
Solomon Bostwick				〃	〃
George Rush				〃	〃
Alexʳ Dulford				〃	〃

Soldiers Names	Towns they belong to	Company	Regiment Col° Mosely	Time they inlisted for During yᵉ Warr or 3 years	Detached to serve till
Abisha Dudley	New Milford	Cap' N. Hine			
Othniel Sax					
Asa Sprague	Kent	Cap' J. Sackett	,,	,,	
John Warren	,,		,,	,,	
Patrick Downs	,,		,,	,,	
Fredrick Temple	,,		,,		
Thomas Fenn	,,		,,		
Peleg Holmes	,,		,,		
Sam'l Hawes	,,		,,		1ˢᵗ Janᵞ next
Joel Whitlock	,,		,,		,,
John Thomas	,,		,,		,,
John Finney	,,	Cap' J. Carter	,,		
Eben' Focher	,,		,,	,,	
Eben' Hill	,,		,,	,,	
Lemuel Beeman	,,		,,	,,	
Elisha Beeman	,,		,,	,,	
Nathan Wheeler	,,		,,	,,	
Matthias Beeman	,,		,,	,,	
George Curtiss	,,		,,	,,	
John Beeny	,,		,,	,,	
John Brown	,,		,,	,,	
John Graham	,,		,,	,,	
Isaiah Bunce	New Milford	Cap' E. Couch	,,	,,	
Edward Finkins	,,	,,	,,	,,	
A man hired by Jos. Bostwick & and Son, Name forgot }	,,	,,	,,	,,	
Noah Murray	Kent	,,	,,	,,	
Joel Murray	,,		,,	,,	
A man, Name unknown hired p Joel Murray & Benjⁿ Adams }	,,		,,	,,	
Abraham Barns	New Milford	Cap' W. Cogswell	,,	,,	1ˢᵗ Janᵞ next
Tho° Davenport	,,	,,	,,	,,	
Bernard Davenport	,,		,,	,,	
Eleazer Hendrick	,,		,,	,,	

Name			1 Jan'y next
Sam'll Smith	"	"	
Henry Williams	"	"	
Elisha Mix	"	"	
Jesse Gratis	Kent	"	
James Taylor	"	"	
David Dains	"	"	
Asa Starkweather	"	"	
Michael Welsh	"	"	
Sam'll Beeman	"	"	
Tho' Woodward	"	"	
Edward Goodyear	"	"	
Asiah Roberts	"	"	
Sam'll Richards	"	"	
John Barlow	Woodbury	Cap' B. Treat	
Galloway Negro	"	"	
Tony Negro	"	"	
Jem Negro	"	"	
Justus Peirce	"	"	
David Dunning	"	"	
Zadock Henries	"	"	
Macock Ward	"	"	
Joseph Squire	"	"	
Simeon Rood	"	"	
Lewis Hurd	"	Cap' J. Sanford's	1 Jan'y next
Dan'll Potter	"	"	"
Solomon Reynolds	"	"	"
Sheldon Potter	"	"	"
Aaron Curtiss	"	"	
Tim' Hinman	"	"	
Joseph Stiles	"	"	
Aquilla Sturgis	"	"	
James Negro	"	Cap' E. Hinman	
Cummy Negro	"	"	
Jehiel Franklin	"	"	
W'm Stanclift	"	"	

Soldiers Names	Towns they belong to	Company	Regiment	Time they inlisted for During yᵉ Warr or 3 years	Detached to serve till
James Parks	Woodbury	Capᵗ E. Hinman	Colᵒ Mosely	During yᵉ Warr or 3 years	
Simeon Rood Junʳ	"	"	"	"	
Moses Hawkins	"	"	"	"	
Samˡˡ Lamphere	"	"	"	"	
Ezra Weed	Norwalk	Capᵗ Scovil	Colᵒ Mead	"	
Nathaniel Nash	"	"	"	for 3 years dureing yᵉ Warr	
James June	"	"	"	"	
Nathˡˡ Pardy	"	"	"	"	
Simeon Bouten	"	"	"	"	
William Waterbury	"	"	"	"	
David Keeler	"	"	"	"	
Asahel Green	"	"	"	"	
Richard Everet	"	"	"	"	
Abijah Arnold	"	"	"	"	
Stephen Hait	"	"	"	"	
Timᵒ Hathorly Hanford	"	"	"	"	
Ebenezer Benedict	"	"	"	"	
Matthew Marvin	"	"	"	"	
Nathan Brown	Norwalk	Capᵗ Eli Reed	"	for 3 years dureing yᵉ Warr	
Abrahᵐ Reymond	"	"	"	"	
Moses Waring	Stanford	"	"	"	
John Williams	"	"	"	"	
Abrahᵐ Hawley	"	"	"	"	
Bill Smith	"	"	"	"	1 Janʳʸ next
Dan Provost	"	"	"	"	
Bethel Hickock	"	"	"	"	
Jonathan Scovil	"	"	"	"	
Silvanus Scovil	"	"	"	"	
Ezra Bates	"	"	"	"	
Denny Parkenton	"	"	"	"	
David Bouten	Stanford	Capᵗ Scovil	"	"	
Charles Stewart	"	"	"	"	
John Cleveland	"	"	"	"	
Joshua Stone	"	"	"	"	

Name	Residence	Captain	Term	
Stephen Davenport	Norwalk	Capt E. Lockwood	"	1ˢᵗ Janʳʸ next
Hezekiah Rogers	"	"	"	"
William Jackson	"	"	"	"
Dover St John	"	"	"	
Nehemiah Hait	"	"	1ˢᵗ Janʳʸ next	
Stephen Scribner	"	"	"	
Samˡˡ Ketchum	"	"	"	
Nathan Jervis	"	"	"	
Stephen Meaker	"	Capt O. Marvin	During yᵉ Warr	
Nathan Taylor	"	"	"	
Gershom Lockwood	"	"	"	
Ozias Hanford	"	"	"	
Jesse Beers	"	"	"	
Peter Tuttle	"	"	"	
Josiah Taylor	"	"	"	
Noah Taylor	"	"	"	
Hezekiah Hawley	"	"	for 3 years	
John Teen	"	"	"	
Aaron Sturgis	"	"	"	
Moses Scribner	"	"	"	
Uriah Mead	"	Capt Clap Raymond	During yᵉ Warr	
Abin Cole	"	"	"	
Bartholomew Parsons	"	"	"	
John Bouten	"	"	"	
Nathaniel Sterling	"	"	"	
Jonathan Sesar	"	"	"	
Theophilus Mead	"	"	"	
Uriah Keeler	"	"	"	
Josiah Green	"	"	"	
Seth Hubbell	"	"	"	
Nathan Jackson Junʳ	"	"	"	
Wᵐ Jenkins	"	"	"	
Mordecai Bedient	"	"	"	
Calvin Jenkins	"	"	"	
Moses Scott	"	"	"	

Soldiers Names	Towns they belong to	Company	Regiment	Time they inlisted for	Detached to serve till
	Norwalk	Capt Clap Raymond	Col^o Mead	During ye Warr	
Isaac Olmstead	"	"	"	"	
David Parsons	"	"	"	"	
Osborn Parsons	"	"	"	"	
John Rockwell Junr	"	"	"	"	
Aser Patchen Junr	"	"	"	"	
Sam^ll Trowbridge	"	"	"	"	
Isaiah Whitney	"	"	"	"	
Gregory Thomas	"	"	"	"	
Sam^ll Green	"	"	"	"	
Aaron Cumstalk	"	Capt N. Gilbert	"	"	
James Whelpley	"	"	"	"	
Henry Keeler	"	"	"	"	
Jeremiah Mead	"	"	"	"	
Sam^ll Mead	"	"	"	"	
Sam^ll Holmes	"	"	"	"	
Justin St John	"	"	"	"	
John Johnson	"	"	"	"	
Nath^ll Hendrick	"	"	"	"	
Jonathan Nichols	"	"	"	"	
Pelatiah Lyon	"	"	"	for 3 years	
David Whitlock	"	"	"	"	
Zaccheus Scribner	"	"	"	"	
Moses Jackson	"	"	"	"	
Nathan Jackson	"	"	"	"	
Gershom Gilbert	"	"	"	during ye Warr	
Thad^s Gilbert	"	"	"	"	
Jasper Mead	"	"	"	"	
Sam^ll Deforest	"	"	"	for 3 years	
Matt. Gregory	"	"	"	during ye Warr	
Sam^ll Gates	"	"	"	"	
Asa Scribner	"	"	"	"	
Elijah Taylor	"	"	"	"	
Aaron Keeler	"	"	"	"	
Moses Gilbert	"	"	"	"	

Name	Place	Captain		Term
John Williams	"	"	"	
Azor Patchen	"	"	"	
Sam^ll Nichols	"	"	"	
Isaiah Betts	"	"	"	
Sam^ll Hyatt	"	"	"	
David Westcott Junr	"	Capt J. Gregory	"	1st Jan^ry next
John Harrison	"	"	"	"
Thomas Woodbridge	"	"	"	"
Jesse St John	"	"	"	"
Aaron St John	"	"	"	"
Aaron Keeler	"	"	"	"
Abijah Olmstead	"	"	"	
Levi Clinton	"	"	"	
Henry Selleck	"	"	"	
Simon Wood	"	"	"	
Matthew Gregory Junr	"	Capt U. Raymond	"	3 years
Aaron Raymond	"	"	"	
Joseph Bouten Junr	"	"	"	
Danl Brown	"	"	"	
William Garner	"	"	"	
Stephen Frost	"	"	"	
Zebulon Jackson	"	"	"	
James White	"	"	"	
Thomas Rowland	"	"	"	
Stephen Wood	"	"	"	
Stephen Kellog	"	Capt El. Raymond	"	1st Jan^ry next
Daniel Hait	"	"	"	"
James Seymour	"	Capt J^s Richards	"	"
Eli Tuttle	"	"	"	"
Wm Reed Junr	"	"	"	
Jacob Selleck	Stanford		"	
John Bissell	"		"	
Enoch Kellog	"		"	
John Paylar	"	Capt Morehouse	"	1st Jan^ry next
Barnabas Marvin	Norwalk		"	

Soldiers Names	Towns they belong to	Company	Regiment	Time they inlisted for	Detached to serve till
John Fillean	Norwalk	Capt Morehouse	Colo Mead	During ye Warr	1st Janry next
Elias Wilcox	"	"	"	"	
Ned Negro	"	Capt J. Raymond	"	"	1st Janry next
Eliakim Wareing		"		"	
Casar Negro	Stanford			"	
Transient Persons for	Norwalk			"	
John Sear	"			"	
Ebenr Nash Junr	"			"	
Wm Spurr	"			"	
Isaac Smith	"			"	
Robert Hunter	"			"	
Peter Merritt	"	"	"	dureing ye Warr or 3 years	
Wm Gorddin	"		"	"	
Wm Canady	"		"	"	
James Hamilton	"		"	"	
Saml Dickenson	"		"	"	
Wm Hill	"		"	"	
Joseph Thompson	"		"	"	
Stephen Wood	"		"	"	
David Pope	Stanford	Capt S. Hait	"	"	
John Margaro	"	"	"	"	
Benjamin Stoves	"	"	"	"	
Benjamin Byington	"	"	"	"	
Thomas Woodertory	"	"	"	"	
Nathan White	"	"	"	"	
Andrew Edmonds	"	"	"	"	
Ebenr Armstrong	"	"	"	"	
Ephm Waistcoat	"	"	"	"	
Stedly Eumun	"	"	"	"	
Wm Scott	"	"	"	"	
Joseph Thompson	"	"	"	"	
Thomas Mitchel	"	"	"	"	
Thomas Wood	"	"	"	"	

Cap[t] J. Bell

Cap[t] J. Lockwood

John Dickson
Benjamin Weed
John M[c]Numlly
Sam[ll] Hait
8
Stephen Brown
Jonas Weed
Francis Bell
John Weed
Dan[ll] Shay
Isaac Smith
Negro Man
William Canady
John Bishop
Benjamen Allen
Stephen Wood
George Shaver
Charles Powers
John Thompson
Joseph Ingly
James Phloman (?)
Eben[r] Hait
Andrew Doghardy
William Heldrig
Thomas Lewis
John M[c]Donald
Deliverance Conkling
Newton Crawford
James H. Wright
Thomas Mitchel
Thomas Wood
Bruster Bidd
Seth Winchel
Sam[ll] Welchard
Michael Kingsbury
Sam[ll] Clark

Soldiers Names.	Towns they belong to	Company	Regiment	Time they inlisted for	Detached to serve till
	Stanford	Capt J. Lockwood	Col^o Mead	During ye Warr	
David Wallis	Stanford	Capt J. Lockwood	Col^o Mead	During ye Warr	
Joseph Cheshire	"	"	"	"	
John Mather	"	"	"	"	
Joseph Boyinton	"	"	"	"	
John Ashley	"	"	"	"	
Benjamen Tarbox	"	"	"	"	
Two transient Persons } Names unknown	"	"	"	"	
Samuel Hickox	"	Capt S. Knap	"	"	
Sam^{ll} Wheeton	"	"	"	"	
Enos Fountain	"	"	"	"	
David Webb	"	"	"	"	
Seely Scovil	"	"	"	"	
Jacob Wardwell	"	"	"	"	
Samuel Bush	"	"	"	"	
Ushal Knapp	"	"	"	"	
Stephen Davenport	"	"	"	"	
Charles Selleck	"	"	"	"	
Tim^o Lockwood	"	"	"	"	
Josiah Smith	"	"	"	"	
Silas Scovil	"	"	"	"	
Jacob Blanchard	"	"	"	"	
George Mills	"	"	"	"	
William Wardwell	"	"	"	"	
Peter Lounsbury	"	"	"	"	
Borden Knap	"	"	"	"	
Thomas Newman	"	"	"	"	
Nathl Johnson	"	"	"	"	
Isaiah Smith	"	"	"	"	
Peter Smith	"	"	"	"	
Clement Loyd	"	"	"	"	
Austin Smith	"	"	"	"	
Isaiah Jones	"	"	"	"	
John Smith	"	"	"	"	

Name	Town	Captain	Term
Justin Whitney	"	"	"
James Waterbury	"	"	"
David Maltby	"	"	"
Nathan Knapp	"	"	"
Moses Webb	"	"	"
James Knap	"	"	"
Isaac Brown	"	"	"
James St John	"	"	"
George Finchley	"	"	"
Eliph¹ Lockwood	"	"	"
Ezra Green	"	Cap¹ Ch⁰ Smith	3 Years
Sam¹¹ Wareing	"	"	"
Caleb Smith	"	"	"
Stephen June	"	"	"
Jonathan Edwards	"	"	"
John Smith	"	"	Dureing y⁰ Warr
Joel Halt	"	"	"
Samuel Finch	"	"	for 3 Years
Eben' Webb	"	"	"
Eben' Wareing	"	"	"
Joseph Cowdry	"	"	"
David Austin	Greenwich	Cap¹ David Wood's	for 3 Years
Benjamen Reynolds	"	Cap¹ Ch⁰ Smith	"
Isaac Palmer	"	"	"
William Jemison	"	"	Dureing y⁰ Warr
Joseph Fletcher	"	Cap¹ Ed. Brown	for 3 Years
William Waters	"	"	"
Mead Marshall	"	"	"
Edward Ritch	"	"	"
Sam¹¹ Close	"	"	"
William Town	"	"	"
Isaac Davis	"	Cap¹ B. Green	"
John De Pew	"	"	Dureing y⁰ Warr
Henry De Pew	"	"	"
Abraham De Pew	"	"	"

Soldiers Names	Towns they belong to	Company	Regiment	Time they inlisted for	Detached to serve till
Francis De Pew	Greenwich	Cap¹ G. Peck	Col° Mead	for 3 years	
Ezekiel Daton	"	"	"	"	
Joshua Taylor Jun'	"	"	"	"	
Tho' Wheaton	"	"	"	"	
George Edgett	"	"	"	"	
Nath'l Holmes	"	"	"	"	
David Wilson	"	"	"	for 3 Years	
John Reed Jun'	"	"	"	"	
Abrah'm Sherwood	"	Cap¹ J. Anderson	"	"	
Moses Lockwood	"	"	"	"	
Jonathan Whelpley	"	"	"	"	
Charles Knap	"	Cap¹ G. Peck	"	"	
Peter Betts	"	"	"	"	
David Lockwood	"	"	"	"	
Jonathan Adams Jr	"	"	"	"	
Jeremiah Finch	"	"	"	"	
Sam'l Finch	"	"	"	"	
Joseph Lockwood Jr	"	"	"	"	
Jared Lockwood	"	"	"	"	
Sam'l Knap	"	"	"	"	
John Reed	"	"	"	"	
Timothy Lockwood Jr	"	"	"	"	
John Burley	"	"	"	"	
Sam'l Mead	"	"	"	"	
Jacob Blancher	"	"	"	"	
Joseph Judson	"	"	"	"	
Ebenezer Whelpley	"	"	"	"	
Dan'l Johnson	"	"	"	"	
Eliphalet Tilding	"	"	"	"	
Alexander Mills	"	"	"	"	
Jeremiah Rundell	"	"	"	"	
Amos Lockwood	"	"	"	1ˢᵗ Jan'y next	
Moses Peck	"	"	"	"	
Israel Reynolds	"	"	"	"	

Name	Company	Term
William Marshall	Cap' Odle Clase	for 3 Years
Nath¹¹ Brown	"	"
Nehemiah Wilson	"	"
Garret Hait	"	"
Joseph Traverse	"	"
Stephen Hall	"	"
Benjamin Rose	"	during yᵉ Warr
Samuel Johnson	"	for 3 years
John Reed	"	"
Israel Harret	"	"
James Vessels	"	"
Hercules Vessels	"	"
John Rundal	"	"
Willⁿ Johnson	"	"
John Brown	"	"
William Seaman	"	"
Richard Williams	"	"
John Town	Cap' J. Hobby	dureing Warr
Abraham Hayse	"	"
Gilbert Wilson	"	"
William Crudock	"	for 3 years
Iran Nickerson	"	"
John Mackrady	"	"
John Smith	Cap' D. Wood	"
Josiah Wood	"	"
Nath¹¹ Jessup	"	"
Joshua Barker	"	"
Silas Howe	"	"
Frederick Pole	Cap' J. How	"
Abᵐ Ferris	"	"
Theodotius Parsons	"	"
Jesse Parsons	"	"
Silvenus Conkling	"	"
Elijah Mead	"	"
Jonathan Mead	"	"

Soldiers Names	Towns they belong to	Company	Regiment	Time they inlisted for	Detached to serve till
Jesse Whitney	Greenwich	Capt J. How	Colo Mead	for 3 years	
John Taylor	"	"	"	"	
John Belshaserhes					
Joseph Marshall	"	"	"	Dureing Warr	
Samuel Banks	"	"	"	"	
Transient Persons hired for					
David Slater					
Transient Persons hired for					
George Nottingham	Greenwich			dureing Warr	
Jesse Purdy	"			"	
James Rogers				"	
Neal McCowen	"			"	
Wm Brown	"			"	
Jno Wienkleman				"	
James Richardson				"	
Danll Selleck	Danbury	not returned	Colo Beardsly	"	
John Barnum	"	"	"	"	
Jack Negro				"	
Thomas Names	"	"	"	"	
Aeral Ackley transient P. for				"	
James Blakely	Ridgfield	"	"	"	
Joseph Jackson	Danbury	"	"	"	
William Porter	"	"	"	"	
Wm Griffin				"	
Wm McLean	"	"	"	"	
Samll Barnum				"	
Noah Barnum				"	
Frederick Dikeman				"	
Uriah Clark's Negro				"	
William Taylor's Do				"	
James Matthews transient P. for				"	
Robert Bowman				"	
Andw Simons				"	
Caleb Maxfield	"	"	"	"	

Name	Residence	Returned	By whom	Term
Ezra Ketchum	"	"	"	"
Stephen Barber	"	"	"	"
Aaron Knap	"	"	"	"
William Hokhins	"	"	"	"
John Curtiss	"	"	"	"
Nath¹¹ Robertson	"	"	"	"
Jonathan Dikeman	"	"	"	"
David Hall	"	"	"	"
Jonath Williams } Transient Person }	"	"	"	"
Miner Allen	N. London	Not returned	not returned	"
Daniel Elmer	Sharon	"	"	"
Josiah Whitney	Ridgefield	"	"	"
Isaac Collen	Danbury	"	Col° Beardsly	Dureing yᵉ Warr
Thaddeus Starr	"	"	"	"
Joseph Moss White	"	"	"	1ˢᵗ Janʳʸ next
Nehemiah Dibble	"	"	"	"
Isaac Reed	"	"	"	"
Dan¹¹ Dikeman	"	"	"	"
Dan¹¹ Dibble	"	"	"	"
Christopher Glover	"	"	"	"
Comfort Benedict	"	"	"	"
Wᵐ Stone	"	"	"	"
Levi Starr	"	"	"	"
Levi Peck	"	"	"	"
James Stevens	"	"	"	"
Peter Starr	"	"	"	"
Benjⁿ Cozier	"	"	"	"
Wᵐ Patch	"	"	"	"
Isaac Barnum	Newtown	"	"	"
Joseph Hepburn	"	"	"	"
Israel Burrit	"	"	"	"
George Murray				3 Years
Thomas Brooks				"
Samuel Brooks				During yᵉ Warr

Soldiers Names	Towns they belong to	Company	Regiment	Time they inlisted for	Detached to serve till
Charles McDonald	New Milford	Not returned	Colo Beardsly	3 Years	
Ebenr Keeler	"	"	"	"	
Liverus Hawley	"	"	"	"	
Joseph Hawley	"	"	"	"	
Othniel Sax	"	"	"	"	
David Bishop	Danbury	"	"	dureing ye Warr	
Danll Osborn	Ridgefield	"	"	{ Dureing ye Warr } { or 3 Years }	
Elisha Gilbert	"	"	"	"	
Ebenezer Jacklin	"	"	"	"	
Thomas Sagar	"	"	"	"	
James Patrick	"	"	"	"	
Abrm Russigue	"	"	"	"	
Stephen Remington	"	"	"	"	
Nehemiah Olmstead	"	"	"	"	
Jeremiah Olmstead	"	"	"	"	
Joseph Jackson 2d	"	"	"	"	
Jeremiah Dean	"	"	"	"	
Darius Benedict	"	"	"	"	
Levi Keeler	"	"	"	"	
Jeremiah Keeler	"	"	"	"	
Bartholomew Baker	"	"	"	"	
Silvenus Seely	"	"	"	"	
Benja Bennett	"	"	"	"	
Hezekiah Hawley	"	"	"	"	
Elisha Perry	"	"	"	"	
Thos Keeler	"	"	"	"	
Elijah Weed	"	"	"	"	
Barack Nickerson	"	"	"	"	
Gilbert Brush	"	"	"	"	
Danll Canfield	"	"	"	"	
Lewis Jacklin	"	"	"	"	
John Street	"	"	"	"	
Thos Whitney	"	"	"	"	

Name			Dureing Warr		1ˢᵗ Jan'ʸ next
Ezekiel Whitney	"	"	"	"	
Eliaphas Nickerson	"	"	"	"	
Joseph Smith	"	"	"	"	
Elisha Lincoln	"	"	"	"	
Solomon Ben	"	"	"	"	
Reuben Craw	"	"	"	"	
Haman Craw	"	"	"	"	
Dan¹¹ Riggs	"	"	"	"	
Stephen Stillman		"	"	"	
Transient Persons inlisted for					
Joseph Sears				Dureing Warr	
Peter Kellis				"	
John Roberts				"	
John Hitchcock				"	
Micajah Weeks				"	
Tho⁵ Warson				"	
Wᵐ Mitchel				"	
James Burns				"	
Wᵐ Newton				"	
John Hayes				"	
John Butler				"	
Benjⁿ Dawns				"	
Tho⁵ Wasson				"	
Joseph Shaw				"	
Henry Williams				"	
Wᵐ Fleet			not returned	"	
Charles White			"	"	
Solomon Brown			"	"	
Tho⁵ Hutchinson			"	Danbury	
Fortune White a Negro				"	
Benjⁿ Knap				"	
David Knap				"	
John Knap Junᵣ				"	
Caleb Starr				"	

Soldiers Names	Towns they belong to	Company	Regiment	Time they inlisted for { Dureing yᵉ Warr or 3 Years }	Detached to serve till
Talmage Hawley	New Fairfield	"	"	"	
Charles Brown	"	"	"	"	
Elijah Beardsley	"	"	"	"	
Jnᵒ Fairchild Lacy	"	"	"	"	
Jnᵒ Hambleton	"	"	"	"	
Reuben Stevens		"	"	"	
Eliphᵗ Simpson	State of N. York	"	"	"	
Jonah Jones	"	"	"	"	
Aaron Wilder	"	"	"	"	
Benjᵃ Roberts	"	"	"	"	
James Wyllys transient P. for	N. Fairfield	"	"	"	
Wᵐ Bostwick	"	"	"	"	
Samˡˡ Stratton	"	"	"	"	
Jnᵒ Roberson	"	"	"	"	
Eleazer Waller	New Fairfield	"	"	"	
Thoᵐ Kenning	"	"	"	"	
Wᵐ Saunders	"	"	"	"	
Matthew Fowler	"	"	"	"	
Samˡˡ Nichols	"	"	"	"	
Ithiel Barns	"	"	"	"	
Eleazer Waller	"	"	"	"	
Francis Ferguson	"	"	"	"	
John Brown	"	"	"	"	
John Ryan	"	"	"	"	
Joseph Hodges	"	"	"	"	
Ezra Prindle	"	"	"	"	
Ebenʳ Perkins	N. Hampshire	"	"	"	
A Negro hired by Jonᵗʰ Giddings	N. Fairfield	"	"	"	
Toby Boston	"	"	"	dureing yᵉ Warr	
William Jolly	"	"	"	"	
John Cooper		"	"	"	

Name	Place	Term
Joel Botsford	Newtown	Dureing Warr or 3 Years
Wm Barnet	"	"
John Williams transient Person for N.T.	Newtown	"
James Sanford	Danbury	"
Ebenr Barnum	Newtown	"
Abell Booth	Danbury	"
Silas Barlow	New Milford	1st Janry next
Ichabad B. Palmer		"
Abm Wheeler	Newtown	"
Joseph Hatch	"	Dureing ye Warr
Abrahm Baldwin	"	"
Saml Fairweather	"	"
Saul Murry	"	"
Nathan Hubbell	"	"
Isaac Baldwin	"	"
John Kimberly	"	"
Andw Blackman	"	"
Wm Crawford	Danbury	"
Robert Nailor	"	"
John Curtiss	"	"
James Guthra	"	"
Prince Cromwell	"	"
David Coy transient P for	"	"
Amos Seely	"	"
John Fitcher	"	"
Patrick Brian	"	"
John Ludeman	"	"
John Finnigham	"	"
Mingo Jiles	"	"
Isaac Collen	"	{ Dureing Warr or 3 Years
Robin Starr Negro	"	"
Thaddeus Starr	"	"
David Bishop	"	"

Soldiers Names	Towns they belong to	Company	Regiment	Time they inlisted for	Detached to serve till
Joshua Taylor	Danbury	"	"	{ Dureing Warr or 3 Years }	
Jesse Peck	"	"	"		
Jabez Williams	"	"	"		
Collins Chapman	"	"	"		
Isaac Goarham	Redding	"	Col⁰ Whiteing	"	
Robert Welch	Stratford	"	"	"	
James Davis	Sharon	"	not returned	"	
Sam¹¹ Dibble	Danbury	"	Col⁰ Beardsly		1ˢᵗ Jan'y next
Asahel Benedict	"	"	"		"
Eben' Judd	"	"	"		"
Eleazer Bennedict	"	"	"		"
Zelotes Roberson	"	"	"		"
Clauson Hawley	"	"	"		"
Reuben Judd	"	"	"		"
Benjⁿ Williams	"	"	"		"
Sam¹¹ Crowfoot	"	"	"		"
Robert Anderson Jun'	"	"	"		"
Comfort Barnum	"	"	"		"
Abell Baldwin	Newtown	"	"	{ Dureing y⁰ Warr or 3 Years }	
Abijah Prindle	"	"	"		
Zalmon Prindle	"	"	"	"	
Matthew Clark	"	"	"	"	
Sampson Negro	"	"	"		
Jack Negro	"	"	"	"	
Toby Negro	"	"	"	"	
Elijah Foot	"	"	"		
Nathan Little	"	"	"	"	

The foregoing is a true and exact Return of the Soldiers inlisted and draughted from the 4th Brigade of Militia in the State of Connecticut for Continental Service according to the several Regimental Returns that have been made to me. The Term of Service is in many Instances left uncertain and I could not ascertain it because the Regimental Returns were uncertain, specifying it to be 3 Years or dureing the Warr. I am informed and believe that the Men in Many Companies that are engaged in the Carting Service and in the Companies of Artificers make a Part of the Soldiers returned in this Return; which I suppose to be wrong and where I found a Man's Name entered in any of the Returns as being entered in either of those Branches of the Service I have neglected to enter his Name in this Return. After all there are many others that belong to those Departments that are included as I am well but not Officially informed; Nor do I think that this Matter can be placed in its proper Light so as to know certainly how Many of them do & how many do not belong to the Battalions raised by this State, unless the General Assembly shall think proper to adopt some particular Method of Examination to ascertain it.

I am indebted to the Authority & Select Men of Newtown for the Materials wherewith to make a Considerable Part of the Return that respects Newtown Soldiers. There are in that Town Three or Four Companies that have no Officers: they have heretofore chosen their Officers, but of Persons so unfriendly that I am informed it has not been thought proper to give them Commissions; And there is at present no Probability that any Officers would be chosen by those Companies, that it would be thought proper to give a Commission to; as there are so many unfriendly Voters in those Companies, that are under Age and not obliged to take the Oath of Fidelity to qualify them to vote that (as I am informed) they will carry a Vote as they please: hence it comes to pass that we can have little or no Help from those Companies. I hope some Method will be adopted to give them such Officers as the Publick can have Confidence in, and then we may expect them to yield their Proportion toward filling up the Army and not before.

I find several Instances in the foregoing Return where the same Man is returned as a Soldier inlisted in Three or Four Companies in the same Town: and and to which of them he belongs I am not able to determine and so am obliged to let the same Man stand three or Four Times returned, because I don't know to which Company he belongs. And even if I had the Power to put this Matter right these Returns have come in so late that I have had no Time for it.

Fairfield May 8th 1778

G. SELLECK SILLIMAN Brigr Genl

The whole Number of Soldiers belonging to the Several Towns in the Brigade Selected from all the Returns and placed to their respective Regiments in the Brigade, etc.

Regiments	Towns in Each Regim' and other Places out of the Brigade returned	Number of Soldiers inlisted and detached from each Town &c.	Number of Soldiers inlisted from each Regiment
Col° Whiteings	Redding . .	33	
Do	Stratford . .	169	
Do	Fairfield . .	126	
Do	Derby . . .	1	
	Suratoga .	1	
	Massachussets .	1	
Total		331 . .	331
Col° Moseley	Woodbury .	165	
Do	New Milford . .	75	
Do	Kent . .	58	
Do	Waterbury . .	1	
	State of Vermont .	8	
Total		307 . .	307
Col° Mead's	Norwalk . .	137	
Do	Stanford . .	123	
Do	Greenwich . .	96	
Total		356· . .	356
Col° Beardsley's	Danbury . .	82	
	Newtown . .	30	
	Ridgefield . .	57	
	New Fairfield .	31	
	N. Milford in this Reg'	7	
	N. London . .	1	
	Sharon . . .	2	
Total		210 . .	210
			1204

The Above is the exact Amount of the Soldiers contained in the Return wrote on the first Thirty-two Pages of this Return.
May 8th 1778

G. S. SILLIMAN Brigr Genl

N. B. Since the Several Regimental Returns came in Asa Sherwood of Fairfield is inlisted into the Army during the Warr.

RETURNS FROM MILITIA, 1778.

FIFTH REGIMENT.

A Return of the Names of those Men who are Inlisted into the Continental Service from the 5th Regiment of Militia in the 5th Brigade in the State of Connecticut, The Towns to which they Belong & Compy Distinguishing the Names of those now in Continental Service as allso the Names of those Inlisted or Detached pursuant to Orders of January Last.

Windham

	Inlisted or Detachd
Capt N. Wales Compy	
Charles Ripley	now in Service
Jabez Rous	"
Andrew Warner	"
John Hobs	"
Richard Howard	"
Wm Placey } Indians	"
John Leathercoat }	"
Joseph Robens	"
Joseph Masa	"
Silus Frink	"
Saml Brown	
Capt Tinkers Compy	
John Bingham	now in Service
Asa Hibbard	"
Amos Woodward	"
Levy Bingham	"
Timo Hibberd	"
David Young	..
Eleazr Robinson	"
Dier Hibberd	"
Seth Larrobe	"
Calib Fitch	"
Elijah Baccus	"
Ezekiel Dunham	"
Gershom Dunham	"
Joseph Reed	"
Mason Abbe	"
Walter Chase	"
Jonah Palmer	"
Ephraim Terry	"
Ebenr Hibberd	"
Elijah Linkon	"
Adriel Simons	"
Solomon Tracey	"
Elijah Spafford	"
Frances Shellis	"
Benjn Ripley	

	Inlisted or Detach^d
Joseph Johnson	now in service
Benajah Geer	"
John Hayley	"
Joseph West	"
Comfort Foster	"
Sam^{ll} Robenson	"
Sam^{ll} Murdock	"
John Huntington	"
Vriah Hibberd	"
Capt Maltier Binghams	
Steaphen Calif	in C^l Service
Samuel Stubbs	"
Alven Ames	"
Asa Ames	"
Benjⁿ Lamb	now in Service
Jonathan Meacham	"
Simeon Robenson	1^t Jany 1779
Reuben Welsh Detach^d	1^t Jany 1779
Capt Perkens Comp^y	
Elus Vpton	Inlisted 1^t January 1779
Capt Sam^{ll} Bingham	
Elius Robenson	now in Service
Josiah Burnham	"
Thomas Hurlbut	"
Samuel Brown	"
Abner French	"
Turnor Lilley	Inlisted 1^t Jany 1779
Aaron Overton	"
Simeon Bunde	"
Daniel Doughtey	"
Luke Flint	"
Hez Hibberd	Drafted 1^t Jany 1779
Capt Jonathan Rudd	
Nathan Morgen	now in Service
Levy Dean	"
Edward Coburn	"
Peter Scovel	"
Joseph Jennings Junr	"
Zopher Robenson	"
Nathaniel Bennet	"
Th^o Fitsjareld	"
Asa Walden	"
Frances Perkens	"
Benjⁿ Cary Junr	"
Abel Robenson	"
Jabez Potage	"
Ephraim Robenson	Inlisted to ye 1^t Jany 1779
Elius Upton	"
Simeon Robenson Junr	"
Capt Eben^r Mosely	
Philemon Holt	now in Service
Eliphaz Parrish	"
James Burnet	"
Elijah Benton	"
Nathan Hovey	"
Jacob Hovey	"
Abner French	"

	Inlisted or Detach^d
Ruben Farnam	now in Service
Eben^r Perry	"
James Smith	"
Abner Ashley	Detach^t 1^t Jany 1779
Capt Wm Howard	

Mansfield

Capt Nath^ll Hall	Inlisted or Detach^d
Eleazer Conant	In Continental Service
Jonathan Snow	"
Caleb Conant	"
John Martin Junr	"
Joshua Basset	"
Joshua Davis	"
Asher Allen	"
James Strong	
Jonathan Davis	Detach^t until ye 1^t January 1779
Wm Campbel	"
Henery Balch	"
Samuel Sergeant	"
Joel Starkweather Junr	
Capt Eleaz^r Huntington	
Phineas Allen	In Continental Service
Diarke Allen	"
Samuel Conant	"
Elijah Baldwine	"
John Harris	"
Wm Dodg	"
Ezra Phelps	"
Jonathan Nichols Junr	"
Amariah Crane	"
John Abbe	"
Jeremiah Gillet	"
Willard Church	"
Wm Fitch Storrs	"
Bixbie Rodgers	"
Benj^a Rugbe	"
Nathan Porter	
Gideon Arnold	Detach^d until 1st January 1779
Matthew Warnor	"
Aarad Simons	"
Isaac Hall	
Capt Isaac Barrows	
Sam^ll Herrinton	In Continental Service
Eben^r Snow Junr	"
Daniel B. Perkens	"
Josiah Burt	"
John Balch	"
Nath^ll Cary Junr	"
Josh^a Basset Junr	"
Groton Isaac Park	
Andrew Hall	
Peter Davinson	} Drafted for ye 1st January 1779
Sam^ll Nichols	

9

	Cap¹ Whitmore	Inlisted or Detach^d
	Josiah Conant Junr	In Con¹ Service
	Jonathan Fenton	"
	John Smith	"
	John Saunders	"
	John Harde	"
	Isaac Cheets	"
Tolland	Clement Minor	"
	Jacobe Bosworth	"
	John Wampe	"
	Seth Chaimberlen	Detach^d until Jany 1779
	Moses Webster	"
	James Kidder	"
	Cap¹ Am^o Williams	
	John Dextor	In Continental Service
	Joshua Bennet	"
	John Bugbe	"
	Aaron Royce	"
	Elijah Royce	"
	Benjn Lille	"
	Nathan Reed	"
	John Turnor	"
	Charles Wood	"
	Luther Chaimberlen	"
Groton	Ralph Williams	
	Cap¹ Sam^ll Thomson	
	Benajah Geer	In Contin¹ Service
	Jon^o Baker	'
	Ichabod Hovey	'
	Rodger Freeman	"
	Jon^o Eldredg	"
	Leumy Case	"
	Luther Eaton	"
	Jacobe Bosworth	"
	Darius Dextor	"
	James Dextor	"
	Jacobe Barrows	"
	Dan^ll Bosworth	"
	Asael Dunham	"
	Robert Fox	"
	John Hartshorn	"

Ashford

Cap¹ Benjn Clark	Inlisted or Detach^d
Nath^ll Harde	In Con¹ Service
Chester Rodgers	"
Amos Dowset	"
Lem^ll Dowset	"
Philemon Holt	"
Eben^r Brown	"
Lem^ll Allen	"
James Grant	"
John Watkens	"
Th^o Morey	"
Robert Paterson	"
Aaron Kyes	"
Cyrus Chafe	"
John Abbot Junr	Drafted 1st Jany 1779

	Inlisted or Detach^d
Capt Caleb Hinde	
Robert Hale	In Continental Service
James Hale	"
Josiah Bicknal	"
James Eaton	"
Eleaz^r Owen	"
Jas. Southworth	"
Steap^n Eaton	"
Wm Wators	"
Wm Hall	"
Caleb Hende	
Joseph Hunter	
Wm Southworth	
Joshua Fenton	
Capt Squier Hill	
Abijah Smith	In Cont^l Service
Samuel Mosely	"
Jonathan Crane	"
Benjn Dimmock	"
Dan^ll Poole	"
Jedadiah Smi^th	"
Abijah Brooks Junr	"
Robert Lewis	"
Negro Tone	"
Daniel Smith	Inlisted for ye 1st Jany 1779
Comfort Tyler	"
Joab Enoe	Detached for Jany 1779
Capt Sim^n Smith	
Asa Davison	In Con^tl Service
Elias Dimmock	"
Elias Robenson	"
Eph^m Spalden	"
Wm Davison	"
Jon^o Bullock	"
Charles Kimboe	for 2 years
Sam^ll Rob (?)	Detach^d to Jany 1779
Clark Robinson	Detach^d to Jany 1779
Elius Chapman	"
Capt Benjn Sumner	
Eben^r Cheney	In Continental Service
Peter Smith	"
Charles Brandon	"
Sam^ll Allen	"
Henery Lyon	"
Eleaz^r Russel	"
Eleaz^r Smith	"
John Lane	"
Titus Negro	"
Benjn Coals Junr	Drafted for 1st Jany 1779
Cyrus Powers	"
Capt John Sumner	
Samuel Allen	In Continental Service
Joseph Engle	"
Eph^m Avery	"
David Peck	"
Obediah Brown	"
Aaron Bosworth	Drafted to ye 1st Jany 1779
Sam^ll Bolls	"
Elius Anderwood	"
Jonathan Howard	"

Coventry

	Capt John Arnold	Inlisted or Detach^d
	Eben^r Perkens	In Continental Service
	Joseph Atkens	"
	Joseph Doubleday	"
	Richard Deavenport Junr	"
	Mark Negro	"
	Jonathan House	"
	Habackock Turnor	"
Tolland {	Jonathan Dileno	"
	Richard Carlton	"
Labenon {	Nath^{ll} Harris	"
	Isaac Kellog	"
	Capt Jer^a Ripley	
	Asael House	In Con^{tl} Service
	Sam^{ll} Burden	"
	Daniel Edwards	"
	Joseph Badcock	"
	Joseph Doubleday Junr	"
	Noah Chapple	"
	Benjⁿ Grover	"
	John Brown	"
	Nath^{ll} Rose	"
Stafford	Nath^{ll} Walker	"
Tolland	Aaron Stemson	In Con^l Service
	Elius Newton	"
	Elish. Stebbens	"
Coventry	Elias Janes	Drafted until ye 1^t Jany 1779
	Capt Wm Wilson	
	Nath^{ll} Thomson	In Cont^l Service
	Amos Avory Junr	"
	John Bill	"
	Solomon Dean Junr	"
	John Parker Junr	"
	Sam^{ll} Evens	"
	Wm Burns	"
	Sam^{ll} Allen	"
	Nathan Parker	"
	Julius Burns	"
	Rodger Welsh	"
	Benjⁿ Buell Junr	"
	And^w Kingsbury	"
	Noah Porter Junr	Detach^d until Jany 1779
	Noah Grant	"
	Hez. Richardson	"
	Oliver Ladd	"
	Jon^a Johnston	"
	Ezekiel Wentworth	"
	Elijah Wright Junr	"
	Capt Ama^{sa} Rust	
	Robert Lane	In Continen^l Service
	Abrah^m Brown	"
	Justus Brewster	"
	Sam^{ll} Allen	"
	Dan^{ll} Rockwell	"
	Elisha Adams	Detach^d until Jany 1779
	John Ladd	"
	Josiah Porter	"

	Inlisted or Detach^d
Noah Carpenter	Detach^d until Jany 1779
Elijah Carpenter	" "
Nath^{ll} Eells	" "
John Thomson	" "

To Brigad^r Gen^{ll} J. Douglas Esqr of the 5th Brigade of Militia in the State of Connecticut. The within is a Return of those in the 5th Regiment in Said Brigade who are now in the Continental Service, Except Remov^d by Death or Discharge. Also the Names of those Inlisted or Detach^d to Serve in the Continental Service until the first of January next, together with the names of the Towns to which they belong, made agreeable to the Returns from the Respective Companies in Said Regiment, Those men who are Retund as belonging to Towns out of this Regiment were Hired Prinsipally by the Town of Coventry with Money Rais^d by the Inhabitents of Said Coventry, They having the hiest Asurance that Said Towns had furnished there Quota of Men before the Men were hired, as apears by the Returns. In Compliance With the Orders from the Honble the Gen^{ll} Assembly of this State of Jany Last. From your Hon^{rs} most Obed^t

Humble

Servt Exp Storrs Col^o

Mansfield ye 10th March

Anno Domⁱ 1778

[*Connecticut Historical Society*]

ELEVENTH REGIMENT

A Return of that Part of ye 11th Rig^t in Woodstock in State of Connecticut

Capt Frissell Company
for the war

| Asael Clark } | Woodstock |
| Cato Negro } | Ashford |

for three years

Abijah Bugbee }	Woodstock
Ely Bruce }	
Richard Gile }	

Inlisted untill January

Comfort Tuytor Transient Parson
James Dodg Woodstock

John Morse hired }	Benjⁿ Ballen of union 3 years
John Goodale ju^r }	
Hewlett Martain }	Detached
John Hewlett }	
Esre Chamberlin }	
Daniel Perry hir'd }	John Right of union 2 y^s

Capt Bowen Company
for 3 years

David Holmes	Woodstock
Willm Manning	Woodstock
Briant Brown	Woodstock
Willm Gibson	Woodstock
Paul Hernden	Tran^t Person
Lemuel Allin	Ashford
John Green	Woodstock
Nath^{ll} Robbins	Tran^t Person

David Lawrence
Willm Martin   } Detached
Joshua Lauton
   Capt Paine Comp^y
   for 3 years
John Bartholomew
Willm Press
Dennis Spenser   } Woodstock
Robart Chandler
Daniel Brown
James Chafee Ju^r
Richard Bolls
Philip Brown   } Detach^t
Richard Shapley
Jonas Haughton
Bille Manning Inlisted Jan^y
   Capt Stephen Lyons Comp^y
   for 3 years
Theophilus Luther
John Vinton
John Brock
Amos Burnal
Daniel Evans
Abraham White   } of Woodstock
Elihu Hebbard
Aaron Hebbard
Asa Lyon
Asa Winter
   Capt Stones Comp^y
   for 3 years
Timothy Hebbard
Thos Spenser
Nathan Powers   } of Woodstock
David Negrow
Josiah Pagan
John Lyon Detach^t until the First of Jany
   Part of Capt Lyon C^y
Daniel Smith   } Draughted
Asa Hebbard   Woodstock
Abijah Williams
   Capt Morris Company
   for 3 years
James Gould
Jason Crawford
Simeon Camp   } Woodstock
Poter Sanders
Fradrick Green
John Felen
John Bowen
Joseph Haward
John Wilson
Joseph Bartholomew   } Detached
Jethnel Perrin
Asa Morris
Stephen Abbot
Micah Barlow

      Killingly March the 10th 1778
            Willm Danielson Co^{ll}

A Return of that Part of y⁰ 11ᵗʰ Regᵗ in Killingly in State of
Connecticut

Capᵗ Larneds Company
for y⁰ War
John Kath
for 3 years
Elisha Mayo
Abnar Marsh
Archabel Town } All of Killingly
Lemuel Barrows
Tom Negrow
Willᵐ Jones
    Detached
Jonathan Lee
Joseph Alton

Capᵗ Convers Company
for 3 years
Solomon Johnson
Gideon Martin
Isaac Barrows
Josiah Barrows
Samˡˡ Runnels
John Russel
Silas Richards } All of Killingly
    Drughted
David Harscall
Nathˡˡ Mils juʳ
Chostor Convers
Thoˢ Eliot
Willᵐ Whitemore
Simeon Stone

Capᵗ Chandler
Charles Lebret
Penuel Child } for 3 years
Joseph Robins
Isaac Atwood
Nathˡˡ Bundy
Jacob White } Detachd until y⁰ 1ˢᵗ of January
Jacob Daly
    All of Killingly

Capᵗ Dikes Company
for the War
Cato Negroo
    Detached
James Roads } All of Killingly
Thoˢ Wever
Enos Smith
Penual Cady

Capᵗ J. Cady Company
for y⁰ War
Benjamin Cady
Jesse Robart
Joseph Walker
for 3 years
Amasa Grover
John Pike
John Lawrance } All of Killingly
James Reynolds
Jacob Reynolds
Willᵐ Arvin
Comfort Redaway
Benjⁿ Robison
Crumel Luther

Capt D. Cady's Comp^y

Thos Barrows ⎫
Mathew Moffitt ⎪
John Jones ⎬ for 3 years
Ravid Runnels ⎪
Thos Taylor ju^r ⎭

John Anderson ⎫
Oliver Kingsbury ⎪
John Kee ⎬ Detached to Sarve
Nath^{ll} Kee ⎪ untill Janery
Elezar Fairman ⎭

John Bush Inlisted till Jen^y.

All of Killingly

Capt Warrins Comp^y

Daniel Sweet ⎫
Jacob Warrin ⎪
Joseph Starkwether ⎪
Elijah Russel ⎬ for 3 Years of Killingly
Richard Hopkins ⎪
Nicholas Shippee ⎪
Simeon Russel ⎭

Tibbee Robarts Transiant Person
Squier Knight Plainfield

Jonas Baker ⎫
Willm Walton ju^r ⎪
Thos Wood ⎬ Detached to Sarve
Nath^{ll} Lovegoy ⎪ untill Jenuary
Ephriam Warren ⎭

Capt Hawkins
for 3 years

Ward Walton a tran^t Person

Willm Durfy ⎫
Henry Carpenter ⎬ Detach^d
Willm Straight ⎭

Capt Eaton

Jabez Kingsbury ⎫
John Robards ⎬ for 3 years Killingly
John Meegan (?) ⎭

Elijah Goar Detached

Part of Capt Stones Comp^y

Josiah Child ⎫ for 3 years
Joseph Sheffield ⎬ Killingly

Benj^a Fairbanks Detached
John Gilbart Groton
Inlisted until January

Michel Crosby ⎫
John Bond ⎪
Joseph Carrel ⎬ Transiant Parsons
Caleb Eady ⎪ Not in any Com^y
Zenus Hathaway ⎪
Willm Blanchard ⎭

Capt Greens Company

——Turner a Transiant Parson

Willm Adams ⎫
Jeremiah Wilkie ⎪
Jacob Bixby ⎪ for 3 years
Parker Adams ⎪
Perley Herrin ⎬ all of Killingly
Cornelus Havens ⎪
Jason Harriss ⎪
Philip Keach ⎪
Sam^{ll} Hall ⎭

Jonathan Porter
Lemuel Knap
Ebenezar Plumer
Henry Stone
Jonathan Aldrige } Detached
Aaron Alger
Willm Stockwell
Nath^ll Carril
  Part of the Granadear Comp^y
Barnew Tortolott
Comfort Woodart } Detached
Jose Joslen
Salvenus Perrey
Simeon Leonard } for 3 years
Jabez Leach
Jack Negrow } all of Killingly
Jonathan Jenkes
David Runnels
Joseph Jinkes
Jacob Leavens } Detached
Abijah Fleng

        Killingly March ye 10th 1778
               Willm Danielson Co^ll

A Return that Part of ye 11th Reg^t which belongs to Pomfrett in State of Connecticut
  In Continental Sarvis for three years or During the War

Capt. J. Williams	
Joseph Ross	Pomfrett
Salos Covel	"
Thos Hill	"
Oliver Read	"
Ezra Goodale	N. London
John Wamper	Pomf^t
Elijah Cheney	"
Jaazaniah How	"
Joseph Holmes	"
Thos Jones	Stafford
Sam^ll Millington	Lebanon
Ezekiel Lomis	Windham
Abiel Farnam	Pomf^t
Henry Smith	"
Joseph Griffin	
Capt Welds Company	Pomf^t
Elias Jones	"
[ ] Sabin	"
James Jones	"
Rowland Collon	"
Joseph Griffin	"
John Cheney	"
Joseph Ross	"
Jonathan Hill	"
Joseph Hunter	"
John Morrisson	"
Matthew Jackson	"
William Clevland	"
Ebenezer Gilbert	"
Willm Earl	
Willm Lashbrooks	Pomf^t for the war
Benj^a Buffinton	Tran^t Parson
John Briant	Norwich

Jonathⁿ Bullock	Tran^t Parson
John Campbell	Pomf^t
Capt S. Williams Company	
Jacob Goodale for 3 years	Pomfrett
Dick Negro "	"
James Indian for the War	
Nehemiah Bacon for 3 years	Pomfrett
Detach^d until 1st January	
Charles Putnam } for 3 years	
Amasa Deaolph }	
Luis Negrow 3 years	
Capt Crafts Company	
Silas Holt of	Pomf^t
Elisha Stowel	"
Abiel Lyon	"
John Shadden	"
Eben^r Owen	"
Elias Robinson	Ashford
John Fuller	Windham
Sam^{ll} Bugbee	Tran^t Parson
Negro Name unknown	
Jacob Havey	Windham
Caleb Conant	Mansfield
Willm Tarnham	Windham
James Eaton	Ashford
Thos Grosvenor	Pomfrett
Stephen Brown	"
Ebenezer Force	"
Capt Ingalss Company	
Lemuel Fling	Pomfrett
Benjamin Sharpe	"
Cyrus [ ]	"
Ebenezer Groo	"
Nath^{ll} Stoel	"
John Lille	Cantabury
Ceaser Negro	Pomf^t
During the War	
Zenas Harthaway	Pomf^t
James Grant	"
for 3 years	

James Duggin }
Sam^{ll} Cady
Amasa Copland
Alvin Goodale
Jesse Earl   } of Pomf^t
Capt Adams
Septimer Gardner
John Wheler

Part of Granadear Comp^y	
Obediah Brown	Trantion Parson
Ebenezar Cheney	Ashford
Abnar Chapman	Colchester
Abnar French	Canterbury
for three years	

Killingly March ye 10th 1778
Willm Danielson Co^{ll}

A return of the Non Comisond officers and Soldiers that Belonged to the 5th Brigade in the State of Connecticutt who are Now Engaged in the Continental Armey March ye 20th 1777

[*Connecticut Historical Society.*]

TWELFTH REGIMENT

A Return of the Men Raised for the Continental Army By The Town of Lebanon as Pʳ Returns

Jonathan Bill	Lebanon	for 3 years	
John Clark Junʳ	"	"	
Ameziah Chappel			
Thomas Doyle	Transient Person	"	Hired in Lebanon
James Denison Fish	Lebanon	"	
Rowswold Minor	"	"	
Charles Quameny	"	"	
John Crandol	"	"	
Michael Barry	"	"	
Jediah Woodworth	"	"	
William Williams Junʳ	"	"	
Joseph Laws	"	"	
Daniel Vaughan Junʳ	"	"	
Lemuel Case	"	"	
Samuel Groos	"	"	
Jonah Case	"	"	
Rowland Swift Junʳ	"	"	
John Allen	"	"	
John Bray	"	"	
Cash Negro Man	"	"	
Abraham Merefield	"	"	
John Groos	"	"	
Charles Wright	"	"	
Jonathan Richardson	"	"	
Walter Harris		"	
Samuel Robbenson	Windham	"	Hired by Lebanon
Elijah Bill	Lebanon	"	
Benjamin Luis	N. London	"	
Zepheniah Foster	Lebanon	"	
Phillip Hills	"	"	
Alpheus Polly	"	"	
Benjamin Butler	"	"	
Thomas Watles	"	"	Not Joined
Jabez Metcalf	"	"	
Amherst Bartlet	"	"	
Jared Hinckley Junʳ	"	"	
James Mckartey	"	"	
Rawswold Richardson	"	"	
Moses Clarke Junʳ	"	"	
Joshua Carpenter	"	"	
Joshua Franck a Melato	"	"	
Joseph Clark	"	"	
Benjamin Woodworth	"	"	
Ed. Webster	"	"	
Lemuel Washborn	"	"	
Jonathan Edgerton	"	"	
Richard Lyman 2ᵈ	"	"	
Stephen Hall	"	"	
Richard Lyman 3ᵈ	"	"	
Dan Metcalf	"	"	
Ignatious Waterman	"	"	
Jabesh Palmer Junʳ	"	"	Hereby Enlisted
Thomas Mershal	"	"	

David Bruce	Lebanon	for 8 years	
Gideon Geer	"	"	
Fitch Lanphear	"	"	
Ezrael Caswell	"	"	
Zera Page	"	"	
John Felows	Tollon	"	
Ammi Doubledee	Lebanon	"	
Jonathan Moredock	"	"	
Ariel Moredock	"	"	
Ephraim Terry 3ᵈ	"	"	
James Newcomb Junʳ	"	"	
Olliver Bemont	"	"	
Isaiah Tiffeny 3ᵈ	"	"	
Asa Richardson	"	"	
John Vaughan Junʳ	"	"	
Jesse Torry	"	"	
Jonah Groos	"	"	
Horton Lee	"	"	
Barnebas Strong	"	"	
James Bettis Junʳ	"	"	
Ollever Hyde	"	"	
Abner Doubledee	"	"	
Lothrop Davis	"	"	
William Ward	"	"	
Nathˡˡ Holebrook Junʳ	"	"	
James Barnibee	"	"	
Flaviel Clark	"	"	
John Rithbie	Transient Person	"	Hired by Lebanon
John Barnes	"	"	Hired by Lebanon
Vmphrey Ball	Lebanon	"	
Nathˡˡ Harris	"	"	
Ezekiel Loomis	"	"	
Phinehas Sprague	"	"	
John Pineo	"	"	
Timothy Woodworth	"	"	
John Huntington	Windham	"	Hired by Lebanon
Seth Doubledee	Lebanon	"	
Elijah Palmer	"	"	
William Bentley	"	During the War	
Isaac Bartlet	"	for 8 years	
Daniel Jones	"	"	
Daniel Ingraham Junʳ	"	"	
Shubel Otis	"	"	
Thomas Earl	"	"	
Allen Prat	"	"	
John Butler	"	"	
Bruister Chappel	"	"	
Uriah Polly	"	"	
Simeon Puffer	"	"	
Rawswold Bourn	"	"	
Noah Robbords	"	"	
Hoseah Burge	"	"	
Amos West	"	"	
Elisha Luther	"	"	
Samuel Helmes	"	"	
John Babcock	"	"	
Samuel Mordock	"	"	
Joseph Martin	"	"	
Daniel Puffer	"	"	

Isaac Kellogg	Lebanon	for 3 years
Judah West	"	"
Ezekiel Lyman Junr	"	"
Dan Lyman	"	"
Israel Webster	"	"
Ezrah Dorner (? Downer)	"	"
John Humphrey	"	"

Detached Men in Lebanon to Serve in Continental Army until Janry Next are —

In Capt. Sam^{ll} Dunham's Compy —
Phinehas Post
Samuel Bruister

In Capt. Elias Bliss' Company	In Lebanon 119	Enlisted
Edward Hawkins	7	Detached
Jonah Swetland	126	

Joseph Buckingham
Nath^{ll} Fitch
In Capt. Andrew Waterman's Company
Walter Mackaul

A Return of the Men In Hebron In The 12th Regiment In the State of Connecticut that have joined and Detached To join the Continental Army

Thomas Marble	Hebron	for 3 years	
Aaron Baxter	"	"	
Cesar Negro man	"	"	
Lazrus Puffer	"	"	
James Gallet	"	"	
Stephen Stark	"	"	
Ephraim Taylor	"	"	New Enlisted
Brister Negro man	"	"	
Joel Fox	"	"	
Samuel Rude	"	"	
William Hills	"	"	
William Danielson	Transient Person	"	Hired by Hebron
John Winship	Hebron	"	
Ephraim Bemus	"	"	
Cesar Negro man	"	"	
Joseph Indian Man	"	"	
Dan Blackman	"	"	
Eleazer Newcomb	"	"	
Aaron Bingham	"	"	
Joseph Larnord	"	"	
William Peters	"	"	
Eleazer Porter	"	"	
Isaiah Wright	"	"	
Abner Mack	"	"	
Solomon Guttrege	"	"	
James Prat	"	"	
Henry Goslin	"	"	
Jared Phelps	"	"	
Elexander Porter	"	"	
Beriah Skinner	"	"	
Joel Mack	"	"	
Homer Phelps	"	"	
Peter Negro man	"	"	
John Phelps	"	"	
Elijah Hutchinson	"	During the War	
Joseph Belcher	"	"	

Hezekiah Marks	Hebron	During the War
Reuben Merrils	"	for 3 years
Ashur Merrils Jun[r]	"	"
Joshua Bill	"	"
Elius Wires	"	"
Samuel Mack	"	"
Gill Belcher	"	"
Ely Phelps	"	"
Robert Cox	"	During the War
Osten Brown	"	for 3 years
Eleazer Brown	"	"
John Colver	"	"
Israel Gillet Jun[r]	"	"
Benjamin Mackinborough	"	"
Israel Stark	"	"
Thomas Skinner	"	"
Jedadiah Mackinborough	"	"
Simeon Wright	"	"
Abijah Gardner	"	"
Daniel Watrous	"	"
Wiman Parker	"	"
Joseph Chapman	"	"	Newly Enlisted
Ashur Merils	"	"
David Colver	"	"
Garner Gilbert	"	"
Daniel Polly	"	"

The Men Detached In Hebron to Serve in Continental Army untill Janry Next as p[r] Returns is

    In Capt Stephen Barber's Company
        Samuel Right
        Neziah Gilbert
    In Capt Simeon Edgerton's Company
        Samuel Raymond
    In Capt Thomas Terril's Company
        Joseph Larnord
    In Capt Joshua Phelp's Company
        Stephen Stiles Jun[r]   62 Enlisted
    In Capt Skinner's Company   14 Detached
        Zadock Man   ———
        Joseph Wain Case   76
    In Capt David Tarbox Company In Hebron
        Benjamin Archer Jun[r]
    In Capt Samuel Gilbert's Company
        Asa Hutchinson
        Ebenezer Hutchinson
        Amos Hall
        John Merrill
    In Capt David Miller's Company
        Eleazer Root
        Jeremiah Boles

The Whole of The Detached Men In Hebron to Serve In The Continental Army is 14

A true Return of the men Enlisted and Detached to join the Continental Army in Lebanon and Hebron in the 12th Regiment in the State of Connecticut According to Returns.   Errors Excepted

                Jeremiah Mason Colo
                   March 10th A.D. 1778

[Connecticut Historical Society.]

EIGHTEENTH REGIMENT.

A Return of Men Detach'd from the 18th Regiment of Militia in ye State of Connect Commanded by Jona Humphry Esqr Col to Join the Continental Army until Jan'ry Next   May 1778

Names of Men Detached	Names of Men hired Inlisted or Excused by Phisican	Town the hired, Inlisted or Detached men belong to	Time Engaged for	Compa Inlisted into	
Timo Phelps	Excused by ye Doctr				
Daniel Barber	Sd to have Marchd to Join Simsbury				
Joel Eno	hird Sariah Fox	East Hartford	1 Janry 1778		
Elipha Mitchel	hird Josiah Higley	of Simsbury	Do		
Elisha Griswold	Excusd by Phisisian				
Abijah Roe		of Simsbury			Taken by Recruiting officer
Elnathan Strong	hird London Wallas Jur	of Simsbury	1 Janry	Capt Wm Judd	Absconded
Wm Rothbone					
Jonah Rice	hird Heza Phelps 3d	of Simsbury	1 Janry	Capt Wm Judd	
Asa Priest	hird Keny	of East Hartford	During War	Capt Abbot	
Alexd Marshel	hird Elezr Abby	of Do	Do	Do	
Jared Merril	hird Isaac Loveland	of Glassenbury	Do	Capt Barnard	
Reubin Case	hird	Do	Do		
Ichabod Gilbert	hird London Free Body	Do	1 Janry	Capt Judd	
Stephen Perring	hird Dan Dibol	Do	Do	Do	
John Wright	Inlisted	Do	Do	Do	
Wm Shepherd Jr	Excusd dy Phisician	Do			
Joel Holcomb		Do	Do	Do	
Matthw Griffin		Do			absconded
Benja Reed	hird Joseph Sharp	Do	1st Janry	Do	
Ebenezr Holcomb		Do	Do	Do	
Joab Gillet	hird Rufus Case	Do	Do	Do	
Aaron Dibol		Do	Do	Do	
Aaron Cook					
Amasa Case Jur	hird James Keny	of Hartford	3 years	Capt Bard	
Luke Moor	sick Present	Simsbury			
Edwd Thomson Jur		Do			absconded

Names of Men Detached	Names of Men hired Inlisted or Excused by Phisicion	Town the hired, Inlisted or Detached men belong to	Time Engaged for	Comp[y] Inlisted into	Absconded
Reubin Phelps		Do			absconded
Eppap[h] Alderman	hir[d] Garshum Fay	Winchester	1st Jan[ry]		
Ozias Moor	hired	Simsbury	1 Jan[ry]	Cap[t] Judd	
Reubin Tuller	Inlisted	Do	1 Jan[ry]	Do	
James Beach	Inlisted	Do	During y[e] War	Capt Walbridge	
Asa Case	hir[d] James Noacoke	Do	3 years		
John Barber Jr	hir[d] Felix Curtis	Do	1st Jan[ry]	Cap[t] W. Judd	absconded
Amos Willcocks Jur	hir[d] Gilbert Whiting	Do			
Edw[d] Prouty	Excused by Phisian	Simsbury			
Eph[m] Sanden		Simsbury			
Ozias Higley	hir[d] Zenos Hays	Do	1st Jan[ry]	Cap[t] W Judd	absconded
Nich[o] Gosard	hir[d] John Gosard	Do	1st Jan[ry]	Do	
John Griffen	Inlisted	Do	Do	Do	
Micah Hays	hir[d] Benj[a] Hays	Do	Do	Do	
Jacob Hays	hir[d] Jacob Hallad[y]	Do	3 years		
Nat[a] Gillet	hir[d] Joseph D[o]Wolf	Do	1st Jan[ry]	Cap[t] W. Judd	
Benaj[a] Holcomb	hir[d] W[m] Thorn	Do	1st Jan[ry]	Do	
Noadiah Kendol	hir[d] Eben[r] Gosard	Do	Do	Do	
Reuben Hurlburt	hir[d] Ro[t] Case (?)	Do	Do	Do	
Joshua Holcomb Jur		Do			Absconded
Silas Phelps		Do			Absconded
Elisha Eno	hir[d] Israel Humphrey	Do	1st Jan[ry]	Cap[t] W Judd	
Ichabod Strickland		Do			absconded
Abner Griffen		Do			absconded
Isaac Eno	hir[d] Malachi Corning	Hartland	During y[e] War	Cap[t] W Judd	
John Moses	Jon[a] Mountigue	Simsbury	1st of Jan[ry]		
Abel Loomis	hir[t] Reubin Cadwell	Hartland	During y[e] War		
Jon[a] Adams Jur		Simsbury			
Jesse Negus		Do			Absconded
Daniel Gains	hir[d] Amos Holcomb	Do	1st January	Cap[t] Judd	Absconded
Joshua Austin		Do			absconded
Ezra Holcomb Jr		Do			

Name	Remark	Place	Time	Captain
David Phelps		Simsbury		
Daniel Stiles		Do		
Isaac Penfield	Inlisted	Hartland	1 Jan'y	Cap' W Judd
Jabez Gideons		Do	Do	Do
Aaron Warner	hired Samuel Church	Do	Do	Do
Stephen Richardson	Excus'd by Phisisian	Barkhamsted	Do	Do
Jonas Weed	Do	Do		
10 Samuel Eno		Do		
Amos Case	hired	Simsbury	During War	Cap' Champlon
John Backon	hir'd Jon° Andrus	Do	1st January	Do
Noah Holcomb	hir'd Jacob Davis 3d	Hartland	Do	Cap' W Judd
Joel Buttolph	hir'd Gideon Perkins	Farmington	During y° War	Do
Thomas Coble	hired	Simsbury	1st January	
Consider Holcomb Jur	Inlisted	Do	Do	
Elijah Holcomb	Do			

The Within & Above is a True Return of the Men Detached & Inlisted out of the 18th Reg't of Malitia in the State of Connect' as Recruits to fill up the Continental Army According to the Best of Our Knowledge

[Connecticut Historical Society]

TWENTY FIRST REGIMENT

A Return of the Solders Now in the Continental Army ; those Detach⁴
to Serve till the First Day of January Next or Inlisted for Said Term from
and belonging to the Towns of Canterbury Plainfield and Voluntown and
belonging to the 21ᵗʰ Regiment of militia in the State of Connecticut.

Men's Names Belonging to Canterbury — their Quota 76

    Capᵗ Sherebiah Butts's Compʸ

Rufus Fitch
Roger Green
Jacob Mott
Samˡˡ Thomson
Samˡˡ Stoderd
Jeremiah Read
Clark Herington
Ezekiel Herington
Robert Herrick } Inlisted for 3 years or During the War
Jed⁴ Adams
David Adams
Ruben Carter
Bartlet Bingham
Isaac Evens
Jed⁴ Green
Daniel Fitch
Westly Perkins

Wescut Perkins } Listed Feb 7 1778 for 3 years
Nathan Steavens

    Capᵗ Benjⁿ Bacon's Company

Thoˢ Herris
John Shaw
Jacob Cleavland
Nehemiah Monrow
Elijah Monrow
Isaac Basset
John Cleavland Juʳ } Inlisted for 3 years or During the War
Jedediah Brown
Nathan Lester
Nathˡˡ Edwards
Elias Shaw
Aaron Falkner
John Tefford
Rdugen(?) an Irish Man

    Capᵗ Wᵐ Hebbards Company

Elijah Burnam
Fredrick Curtice
Daniel Durfey
Stephen Farnam
Samˡˡ Glass
Ruben Little } Inlisted for 3 years or During yᵉ War
Prince Little
John Little
Lee Woodard
Benjˢ Shaw

    Capᵗ John Johnson's Company

Thomas Astin
James Whorfe
Silas Gates
Ebenezʳ Felch } Inlisted for three years or During the War
Abijah Cady
James Johnson
James Morse

Tias Ticker listed Feb 7 1778 for 3 years
Abel Williams { Inlisted till y⁰ 1ˢᵗ
Amon Stanton { Jany next
    Capᵗ Joˢ Ransfords Company
Amos Bruster ⌠
Isiah Monrow
Joseph Bond
Andʷ Hebbard ⟨ Inlisted for 3 years or During yᵉ War
Jonᵗʰ Shaw
James Clark
John Eames ⌡
James Dixson Listed till first Janʳʸ next
John Green   Detachᵈ   Do
    Capᵗ Aaron Fullers Company
Jeriel Dody ⌠
Wᵐ Shaw
John Cleavland ⟨ for 3 years or During yᵉ War
Samˡ Cobom
Abiel Farnam ⌡

Men's Names Belonging to Plainfield — their Quota 46
    Lieuᵗ Joshua Bottom's Company
Asa Jones ⌠
John Saterly
Jacob Heard
Samˡˡ Staford
Boaz Tyler   ⟨ Inlisted for 3 years or During the War
Isaac Heard
Nathˡ Sabens
James Dick
Wᵐ Benson
Joshua Simmon ⌡
John French ⌠
Stephen Spaulding ⟨ Detachᵈ till 1ˢᵗ Janʸ next
Rozel Aply ⌡
    Capᵗ Joshua Dunlap's Company
William Waterman ⌠
Joshua Stoderd
William Knight
Ruben Bryant
Amos Bennet
Phinehas Hulet
David Wheler   ⟨ Inlisted for 3 years or During the War
Epheram Dunlap
Manual Jones
Slip Watson
Lot Chase
Jonᵗʰ Whipple
John Clark ⌡
John Manly Listed till 1ˢᵗ Janʸ
Elijah Cook Detachᵈ
    Capᵗ Branch[ ] Compʸ
William Meach ⌠
John Jack
Jonᵗʰ Chipmon
Amos Clain   ⟨ for 3 years or During yᵉ War
Ned a Negro
Daniel Donvon ⌡
Elias Woodard Detachᵈ

Cap⁺ Waterman's
Benjᵃ Johnson
Andrew Spaulding
Stephen Bennet
Abel Franklin
Cuggo a Negro
Josiah Rogers
Gideon Wells Detachᵈ
Henry Backon   } inlisted till
John Thoˢ Trantom   } 1ˢᵗ Janʸ
Roger Avery of Norwich Do
Edward Tylar of Pomfret Do
Jesse Williams Groton

Men's Names Belonging to Voluntown—their Quota 48

Cap⁺ Moses Campbells Compʸ
Robert Campbell
Nathan Coy
Zoath Tucker
Joseph Robbens
Peleg Shaw   } Inlisted for 3 years or During the War
Mark Croswell
Prince Summit
Joseph Peters
Seaser a Negro
William Crary Detachᵈ
Jonᵗʰ Gates   Detachᵈ
Wheler Gallup Detachᵈ but has pecured one Richard Sholes to
Inlist into the Continental Army for 3 years under one Henry Williams Lᵗ
Cap⁺ John Dixsons Compʸ
William Gray
Robert Heard
John Gray
Jeduthen Heard
Alexᵈʳ Williams   } Inlisted for 3 years or During ye War
Wᵐ Adams Juʳ
Squir Knight
James Patrick
David Day
Robert Thomson
Ichabod Peevy
Amos Gore   } Detachᵈ
James Dixon
Cap⁺ Samˡˡ Robbens Compʸ
William Pierce
David Coy
Amos Deneson   } Inlisted for 3 years or During yᵉ War
Phinehas Allas
Abraham Herrington
Christopher Colegrove
Bennony Kinne
Moses Robens Juʳ   } Detachᵈ
Emmanuel Redrick
Phenies Lewis
Nathˡˡ Petyes Inlisted till 1ˢᵗ Janʸ next
Isaac Newton Detached but has procured one Christopher Brown
to inlist into yᵉ Continental Army for 3 years with Hʸ Williams Lᵗ

Cap⁺ Robert Dixsons Comp⁷

Moses Culver
Peter Morras
Henry Carpenter } Inlisted for 3 years or During y⁰ War
Robert Green
Henry Bacon
Jacob Patrick Detach⁴

Cap⁺ Ezra Cary Comp⁷

James Kinne
Jon⁺ʰ Hillard } Detach⁴
Gideon Palmer

Gideon Ray Detach⁴ but has procured one Christopher Billing to inlist in Room as p⁺ Certificate

Benjamin Gallup Detach⁴ but has procured one Lemuel Shelly in his Room as p Certificate.

Voluntown March 10ᵗʰ A D 1778

The above is a true List of the Names of the Solders now in the Continantal Army and that are now Detach⁴ or Inlisted to Serve in the Continental Army agreeable to the Return from the Several Captains in the above S⁴ towns belonging to the 21ˢᵗ Reg⁺ of Militia in the State of Connecticut (Excpt. Cap⁺ Smith's Company from which I have Rec⁴ no Return nor from Cap⁺ Timothy Backus)

Certif⁴ P

James Gordon L⁺ Col.

[*Connecticut Historical Society.*]

RETURNS FROM MILITIA, 1779.

SECOND REGIMENT.

A Return of the Non Commissioned officers and Privates in Listed in the Connecticut Line of Infantry in the Continental Army for the 10th Company in the 2d Regiment of Milisha in this State

Names of those Inlisted for three years or during the war	Regiments into Which they are Inlisted	Inhabitants of what town or Transient persons	Town Accounted for
Justus Wood	Meggs	New haven	New haven
Martin Clark	"	"	"
David Dorman	"	"	"
Samuel St Squir	Lamb	"	"
Abel Hitchcox	Meggs	Milford	Milford
Jared Hitchcox	"	"	"
Isaac Northrop	"	"	"
George Clark Jr		"	"
Elijah Clark		"	"
Samuel Champen	Lamb	Transient	New haven
Walter Booth	B Webbs	New haven	"
John Alling	"	"	"
Isaac Ford	"	"	"
Ephraim Thomas	R Meggs	"	"
Samuel Woods	"	"	"
John Vergurson	"	"	"
John [ ]	"	Transient	"
James Gainer	"	New haven	"
Elijah Osborn	Chanler	"	"
Thaddeus Thompson	Lambs	"	"
Brister Mix	Meggs	Transient	"
Richard Gore	"	New haven	"
Jesse Benjamin	Durkees	Preston	
Joseph Bonds	"	Canterbury	
Dan Chapman	Meggs	Transient	
John Johnson	"	Wallingford	
David Lounbuary	B Webbs	New haven	New haven
Joshua Meech	Huntingtons	Preston	

A true Return Test
Samuel Osborn
officer of said Co.

Dated at New Haven
the 7th Day of May A. D. 1779   [*State Library, Hebard papers, 36.*]

A Return of the Non Commissioned Officers & Soilders, Inlisted in the Continental Army, in the Connecticut Line of Infantry; as Returned by the Captains of the Several Companies in the 2d Regt of Militia in this State; belonging to Towns in this State, not Included in said Regt
Branford May 24th 1779

Soldiers Names	Regt Inlisted in	Inhabitants what Town	Town Acct for
Saml Lumis	Col. Wyllys	Colchester	N. Haven
John Mason	Col. Durgy	Killingworth	"
Amos Bruster	"	Canterbury	"

Soldiers Names	Reg^t Inlisted in	Inhabitants what Town	Town Acc^t for
Nathan Gillet	Col. Douglass	Farmingtown	N. Haven
Benj^a Wright	Col. Swift	Killingworth	"
Sam^ll Dickerson	Col. Webb	Norwalk	Milford
John McCannack	"	Fairfield	"
Jarib Mott	Col. Durgy	Canterbury	N. Haven
Abijah Bardsley	Unknown	Stratford	Derby
Charls Bradly	Col. Bradly	Sharon	"

The Soldiers Above Named is the Whole (Some few Transiant Persons Excepted) that is Returned in the 2^d Reg^t not belonging to the Towns Included in Said Reg^t. Certifyed P Edward Russell Col.

Since the within Return was Compleeted I have Rec^d A Return from Capt Horseey of Seven Men in Service, & belonging to and Counting for Derby. Names as follow^t

James Prichard	Ebenez^r Warner
Ebenez^r Durand	Henry Wooster
Daniel Nichols	Thom^s Philips
Philo Lewis	P E Russell Col

[State Library, Hebard papers, 35.]

A Return of the Non-Commissioned Officers & Privates inlisted in the Connecticut Line of Infantry, in the Continental Army for the Militia Company in the 2^d Regiment of Militia in this State.

Names of those Inlisted for three years or During the War	Regiments into which they are inlisted
Jonathan Brown	Col^o Meggs ye 6th
Daniel Brown	"
Richard Watres	"
Andrew Watress	"
[ ] Leach	"
William Whitney	"
William Smith	"
Joseph Smith	"
Jeremiah O Cain	"
Abraham Murry	2^d Battalion
Gersham Beardsee	Col^o Meggs ye 6th Batt^n
William Woshbon	Col^o Bradley
John Halchet	Col^n Meggs ye 6th
George Watress	Col^n Meggs ye 6th
David Chapman	"

Derby May 8th 1779   Capt Joseph Holbrook return

[Each man was an inhabitant of, and was accounted for the town of Derby.]

[Connecticut Historical Society.]

SEVENTH REGIMENT.

A Return of the Non commisoned Officers and Privates inlisted in the Connecticut line of Infantry in the Continental Armey for the 8th Company in the 7th Regiment of Militia in this State

Names of those inlisted for three years or during the war	Regiments into which they are inlisted	Inhabitants of what town or transient persons
Jasper Pratt	Col Willys	Saybrook
Taber Smith	unknown	"
John Widger	Col Charls Webb	"
John Widger Jur	Col Swift	"
John Tucker	Col S. Webb	"
Asa Pratt Junr	Col Megs	"
Reuben Buckingham	unknown	"
Ethen Pratt Junr	Col Prentice	"
Samuel Doty Junr	"	"
Hezekiah Buckingham	"	"
Gideon Buckingham 2d	Col Megs	"
W[m] Turner	Col Prentice	"
John Nickels	Col Megs	"
Martin Dibble	Col S. Webb	"
Stephen Waterhouse	Col Swift	"
Oliver Graham	Col Worner	"
John King	Col Megs	Transient

[All are accounted for the town of Saybrook]
Dated at Saybrook the 10 Day of May A D 1779
Dan Platts Commanding officer
of Said Company

[*State Library, Hebard Papers, 39.*]

A Return of the Non Commissioned Officers and Privates Inlisted in the Connecticut Line of Infantry, in the Continental Army for the 17th Militia Company in the 2[d] Regiment of Militia in this State

Names of those Inlisted for three years or during the war	Regiment into which they are inlisted	Inhabitants of what town or Transient person
William Cook	Col Lambs	New Haven
Danieal Ford	Col Megs	"
Noah Jonson	"	"
Rich[d] Mansfield	"	"
Sam[ll] Robinson	Col Hastens	"
Moses Potter	Col Megs	"
Abraham Cooper		
Charles Mansfield	Col Megs	"
Joseph Jonson		
Samuel Fraser	Col Megs	"
John Hicks	"	
Francis Clarage		
John O Briant	Col Megs	Transient
Ezekel Taphan	"	"
Joseph Dickerman	"	New Haven
Will[m] Wate	"	"
Timothy Potter	"	"
Eli Denslow	Col Russel	"

[Each man was accounted for the town of New Haven.]
Dated at New Haven the 8th Day of May 1779
John Gilbert Commanding Officer of
said Company

[*State Library, Hebard Papers, 41.*]

A Return of the Non-Comisioned Ofisers and Privite Inlisted in the Conneticut Line of Infantry in Continental Army for the first Company alarm list Seventh Regement of militia in this State Saybrook may 10 1779

Names of those in-listed for three years or During the War	Reg^t into which they Inlisted
Zebada Brown	Sam^ll B Webbs
Peter Floro	Return meaggs
Gift Freeman	Return maiggs
Jeremiah Lord	Sam B Webbs
William Lord	Return meggs
James Foster	Sam^ll B Webbs
Isaac Wardin	Sam^ll B Webbs
Olover White	Return Meggs
Robart Newell	Return meggs
Sam^ll Hanson	Sam^ll B Webbs
Jedidiah Gladin	Return meggs
Prosper Booth	Charles Webbs
Stephen Ludlow	Charles Webbs
Joseph Hand	Sam^ll B Webbs

[Each person was accounted for the town of Saybrook, and excepting James Foster a Transent Person each was an inhabitant of that town.]
Certified Elisha Chapman Cap 1 alarm Comp 7 Reg^t
[*Connecticut Historical Society.*]

SIXTEENTH REGIMENT.

A Return of the Noncomision officers and Souldiers inlisted into the Connecticut Line of the Continental army belonging to the 16th Regiment of militia as Returned by the Commanding officers of the Companies on ye 10th Day of May 1779

Names of those inlisted what town & Company

Captn Comfort Hoyts Com-
pany Danbury
Benjn Seymor Sellick
John Barnum
Benjn Numes
[ ]ben Lord
Amos Negro
James Long
Joseph Jackson

Captn James Clarks Company
Danbury
Andrus Simmons
James Mathews
Jack Negro
John Ludiman
Wm Griffith
David Row
Josiah Whitney
John Davidson
Uriah Negro
Uriah Acley
George Doolittle
Wm Porter

Wm MacLean
Sam^ll Barnum
Noah Barnum
Fradrick Diteman
Wm Negro

Capt Daniel Hecock Danbury
Sargt Joshua Taylor
Jesse Peck
Collaris Chapman
Isaac Gorham
Benjn Waters
Minor Allen
Cato Login
Robart Welch
Edward Godard
Jonas Gates
[ ] Flint

Captn Eph^rm Barnums Dan-
bury
Isaac Collar
Thad^us Starr
John McGlaffin

Names of those inlisted what town & Company

Joseph Perker
Robin Starr
Tobe Boston
James Davis
Jeremiah Russel

Captn Richard Shute Danbury
Minor Allen
John Nails
Aaron Knap
Ezra Ketchum
David Hall
Nath[ll] Robinson
Caleb Maksfield
Dan[ll] Elmer
John Curtis
Jon[ll] Diteman
John Williams
David Cay
W[m] Hopkins

Captn Richard Barnum's Danbury
Robart Nalor
James Gutherie
Mingo Giles
Fortin (? Foster) White
Prince Cornell
John Finnington
Amos Seelye
Patrick Rian
Joseph Plum
Steph[n] Rial
John Flisher
John Larabee

Captn Joseph Smith Newtown
James Sanford
George Clapham
Joel Botsford
Nathan Lummis
David Bishop
Stephn Benjamin
Mathew Marvin
Tho[s] Barnum
W[m] Barnet
W[m] Ryne

Captn Richard Smith Newtown
David Byshup
Tho[s] Brooks
Sam[ll] Brook
George Murry
Israel Burret

Joseph Hauley
Lyberias Hauley
James Waklee
Charles McDonald
Othniel Salks
Ebenz[r] Keeler

Capt Abel Botsford Newtown
Mathew Clark
Joseph Hatch
Nathan Hubbell
Isaac Baldwin
Sam[ll] Fareweather
Isaul (?) Murry
Andrew Blackman
W[m] Crawford
Hezekiah Meaker
Jacob Persons
Brester Judson

Captn Elijah Botsford Newtown
John Kimberlee
Zalmon Prindle
Wait Lewis
Lemuel Hubbell
Josiah Turrill
Smith Turrill

Captn George Turrills Newtown
Benjm Grgory

Captn John Botsford Newtown
Elijah Foot
Nath[ll] Little
Abijah Prindle
Peter Fairchild
Tobe Bennitt
Jack Botsford
Levi Wolfe
John Umphrey

Capt Benj[m] Sumers Newtown
Abel Baldwin Junr

Captn Peter Penfield Newfairfield
Sergt Talmage Hull
Benj[m] Robards
Corpl Charles Brown
John F Lacey
Ruben Stevens
Elijah Beardsley
Jonah Jonas

Names of those inlisted what town & Company

Captn Steph^n Pardee New-
  fairfield
Sergt John Trowbridge
Thos Cannan
Wm Briant
Eliezer Wallen
John Hamilton
Aaron Wilder

Captn Dan Towner New fair-
  field
Wm Jolly
Steph^n Stilwell
David Corbin
Edward Dunham

[*State Library, Hebard Papers, 40.*]

TWENTY-FIRST REGIMENT.

A Return of the Non Commissioned Officers and [ ] Connecticut [ ] Infantry in the Continental Army for the 21st Regiment of Militia in this State

Names of those Inlisted for three years or During the war	Regiments into which they are Inlisted	Inhabitants of What Town or Transient person	Town accounted for	Company Accounted for
2d Compy Alarm list				
Ebenezor Felch				
Silas Gates	Col Durkee	Canterbury	Canterbury	Capt Johnson
James Whorf	"	"	"	"
Thomas Austin				
Abijah Cady				
Thas Tiken Indian	Col Webb	Trant person	"	"
Francy Clergio	2d Battallion			
Samson Indian	Col Durkee			
Nathan Stevens	Col Webb	Canterbury	"	Capt Butt
5th Compy Alarm				
Andrew Hibbard	Col Durkee	Canterbury	Canterbury	Capt Raynsford
Jonth Shaw	"	"	"	"
John Ames				
[ ]h Munraw				
Joseph [ ]ond				
James Clark	Col Meigs			
Peter Stevens Jr	Col Durkee	Transt person	"	"
Nathan Smith				
2nd Compy Militia				
Rufus Fitch	Col Wyllys	Canterbury	Canterbury	Capt Butt
Roger Green	Col Huntington	"	"	"
Jarub Mott	Col Durkee			
Saml Thompson				
Saml Stoddard	Col Wyllys			
Jereh Read	Col Durkee			
Clark Herrington				
Ezekiel Herrington	"	"	"	"
Robert Herrick	"	"	"	"

Jedediah Adams
David Adams
Reuben Carter
Bartlet Bingham
Isaac Evens
Jedediah Green
Daniel Fitch
Francis Perkins
Walcut Justin
Nathan Stevens
] Clef]nd
Nehem Munro (?)
John Jeffords Indian
Isaac Basset
John Cleveland
James Duggan
Jedediah Brown
Elias Shaw
Nath'l Edwards
Elijah Munrow
Aaron Faulkner
Nathan Lester
Sam' Adams Light Dragoon
8th Company Militia
Josiah Burnham
Benj' Shaw
Frederick Curtis Jr
Daniel Durfey
Reuben Lilley
Abial Farnam
John Lilley
Sam'l Glass
Stephen Farnam

Col Hunting
Col Durkee

Col Wyllys
Col Durkee

Col Meigs
Col Durkee
"
"

Col Webb
Col Durkee

Col C. Webb

Col Wyllys
Col Durkee
"
"

Col Wyllys

Col Webb

Cap' B. Bacon

Cap' Hibbard

Canterbury

Canterbury

Names of those Inlisted for three years or during the war	Regiments into which they are Inlisted	Inhabitants of what Town or Transient person	Town accounted for	Company accounted for
Lee Woodward	Col Durkee	Canterbury	Canterbury	Capt Hibbard
Prince Lilley				
7th Compy Alarm list				
John Cleveland	Col Durkee	Canterbury	Canterbury	Capt Fuller
Wm Shaw	Col Meigs	"	"	"
Saml Coburn	Col Durkee			"
James Paine Fitch	"	Pomfret	Pomfret	"
Jerial Dody			Canterbury	
Israel Dodge		Canterbury		
10th Compy of Militia				
Saml Cleveland	Col Wyllys	Pomfret	Pomfret	Capt I Tylar
Nathll Edwards	Col Durkee	Canterbury	Canterbury	"
James Litchfield	"		"	"
James Duggan	"			
John Jeffords Indian Can[	"	Transt person		
Jy 18th May 1779			Obadiah Johnson Col.	
[ ] Compy Alarm list				
Daniel Donwon	Col Huntington	Transient person	Plainfield	Capt Branch
Jonath Chapman	Col Sherburn	Groton	Plainfield	"
Frederick Waldo	Col Durkee	Transient person	"	"
Amos Clain	Col Sherburn	"	"	"
John Jack	Col Wyllys	Plainfield	"	"
Wm Meach	Col Huntington			"
Ned Negro	Col Sherburn	Trant person		"
John McLarlene	Col Durkee			"
4th Compy Do				
Benja Johnson	Col Durkee	Plainfield	Plainfield	Capt Waterman
Stephen Bennet	"	"	"	"
Josiah Negro	"			"
Cuggo Rogers		N. London	"	"
Jesse Williams	Col Sherburn	Groton	"	"
Andrew Spalding	Col Durkee	Plainfield		"
Abel Franklin	"	Transt person		"

Name	Col.	Residence / Status	Residence	Company
Sam^ll Dexter Negro	"	Plainfield	Plainfield	Capt Bottom
Peter Marsh	"	Trans^t person	"	"
1st Comp^y Militia				"
Asa Jones	Col Durkee	Plainfield	Plainfield	
[Satterlee	"	"	"	
[Sabins	"	"	"	
Jacob Heerd	"	"	"	
Sam^ll Stafford	"	"	"	
James Dick	Col Wyllys	"		
Boaz Tylar	"	"		
Isaac Heerd	"	"		
Wm Renson	Col Sherburn	Trans^t person		
Joshua Cinnamon	"	Trans^t person		
John Baker	"	Groton		
Nath^ll Holt	"	Preston		
Amos Chapman	Col Prentice	Groton		
Sipeo Negro	"	Trans^t person		
4th Comp^y Militia				Capt Dunlap
Wm Waterman	Col Durkee	Plainfield	Plainfield	"
Amos Bennet	"	"	"	"
Reuben Briant	"	"	"	"
Joshua Stoddard	Col Huntington	"	"	"
Wm Knight	"	Trans^t person	"	"
Sip Watson	"	Plainfield	Voluntown	"
Cuy Shepard	Major Porter	Voluntown	Plainfield	"
Mark Loswell	Col Durkee	Norwich	"	"
Heze^h Kingsley	"	Trans^t person	"	"
John Clark	"	Plainfield	"	"
Phinehas Mulet	"	"	"	"
Jon^th Whipp[ ]	"	Trans^t person	"	"
Lot Chase	"	"	"	"
Abel Franklin	"		"	"
Peter Marsh	"		"	"

Plainfield Return　　Canterbury 18th May 1779　　Obadiah Johnson Col.

Names of those inlisted for three years or during the war	Regiment into which they are Inlisted	Inhabitants of What Town or Transient person	Town accounted for	Company Accounted for
3rd Compy Alarm list				
Peter Morris	Col Huntington	Transt person	Voluntown	Capt R. Dixon
Robert Green	"	Coventry	"	"
Henry Bacon	"	Voluntown	"	"
Henry Carpenter	"	Transt person	"	"
Moses Culver				
6th Compy Do				
Lemuel Shelle	Col Huntington	Indian	Voluntown	Capt Wm Edmonds
3rd Compy Militia				
Robert Campbell	Col Durkee	Voluntown	Voluntown	Capt Campbel
Nathan Coy	Col Prentice	"	"	"
Zoath Tucker	"	"	"	"
Peleg Shaw	"	"	"	"
Joseph Robbins	Col Sherburn	Groton	"	"
Joseph Halley	Col Wyllys	Voluntown	"	"
Richard Shols	Col Prentice	"	"	"
Joseph Patters	Col Wyllys	"	"	"
Mark Croswell				
Prince Summits				
[ ]Negro				
6th Compy Militia				
John Gray	Col Huntington	Voluntown	Voluntown	
Alexr Williams	"	"	"	
Jeduthun Hurd	Col Durkee		"	
William Adams	Col Huntington		"	
Squire Knight			"	
William Gray			"	
David Day	In Regt of Artificers		"	
7th Compy Militia				
Amos Dennison	Col Huntington	Voluntown	Voluntown	Capt S. Robbins
Phineas Ellis	Col Wyllys	"	"	"
Wm Pierce	Col Meigs	"	"	"
David Coye				

Wᵐ Bearzal	Col Huntington	"	"	"
Emmun-Rederax	Col Durkee	"	"	"
Christᵒ Brown	Col Sherburn	:·	:·	··

Voluntown Returns   Canterbury 13ᵗʰ May 1779   Obadiah Johnson Col

Names of the men	regᵗ Inlisted into	Inhabᵗˢ of wᵗ town	Town accounted for	Company accounted for
8ᵗʰ Compʸ of Alarm list				
Jabez Kingsbury		Killingly	Killingly	Capᵗ J Eaton
John Meazon Indian			"	"
John Meazon Jr Do			"	"
9ᵗʰ Compʸ of Militia				
Thomas Barrus	Col Durkee	Killingly	Killingly	Capᵗ D Cady
Matthew Moffitt	"	"	"	"

The above Companys Belong to Killingly.

[*Connecticut Historical Society.*]

11

UNKNOWN REGIMENT.

Col. N. Beardslee's Return May 1779

Captn W^m G Hubbell New
    fairfield
Wm Sanders
Mathew Fowler
Sam^{ll} Nichols
Abraham Nichols
Ethel Barns
Joel Botsford
Edward Dunham
Francis Foster
John Brown
Charles Farguson
Wm Scott
Miles Wolman
David Corbin
Tobe Negro
Ned Negro
Jona an indian
Eliphalit Simson
Ezra Prindle
Wm Jole

Captn Jonah Foster Ridge-
    field
Joseph Sears
John Robarts
Joseph Smith
Gibbart Brush
Elisha Lincoln
Ruben Cran
Amon Cran
John Condruy
Lewis Jacklin
Dan^{ll} Rigs
Elisha Perry

Captn David Olmstid Ridge-
    field
Steph Remington
Neh^h Olmstid
Jeremiah Olmsted
Joseph Jackson
Jeremiah Dean
Derias Benedic
Levi Keeler
Bartholomew Baker
Jeremiah Keeler
Selvinis Seelye
Benj^a Bennit
Hezekiah Hawley
Jeremiah Osburn
John Hitchcock
Thos Wason
James Barnes
John Hays
Benjn Downs

Joseph Shaw
Wm Platt
Charles White
Solomon Brown
Thos Hutchinson
Lucus Brown
James Stanton

Captn Knoles Sears Ridgefield
Sarg^t John Street
Thos Whitney
Ezekiel Whitney
Micajah Weeks
Eliphas Nicoson
Solomon Ren
Dan^{ll} Canfield
Wm Mitchel
Wm Newton
John Butler
Baruch Nicoson
Elijah Weed
[   ] Keeler
[   ] Dodge

Captn Isaac Hine Ridgefield
Nehemiah Sherwood
Mical Frank
Dan^{ll} Osburn
Sarg^t Elisha Gibbard
Ebenz^r Jacklin
Thos Seagor
Abraham Russigu
Wm Cummins
John Hitchcock
Micajah Weeks
Thos Wason
Wm Mitchel
James Barns
Wm Newton
John Hays
John Butler
Peter Kelue
Henry Williams

inlisted Since the 19th of April 1779
Town of Newtown
    Captn Elijah Botsfords Com-
      pany
    Wait Lewis
    Lemuel Hubbell
    Josiah Turrill
    Smith Tuttle

    Captn Jabez Botsfords Com-
      pany Newtown
    Levi Wolf

The Town of Newtown Dificent 25 men
Certified Pr Nehemiah Beardsly Col

[State Library, Hebard Papers, 37.]

SUPPLIES, 1780.

An Alphabetical List of the Names of the Officers and Soldiers in the Connec^t Line who have rec^d Family Supplies from the several Towns for 1780.

	Names	Towns to which they belong
4	Adams Wm Lieut.	Hartford
x	Abbe Jeduthan	"
3	Eleazer	"
3	Augustus Zezar	
x	Andrus Thomas	E. Haddam
x	Ackly Thomas	"
	Arnold Jehiel	Haddam
5	Angar George	Mdletown
3	Andrus Asa Serj.	Weathersfield
	Austin Richard	Suffield
4	Allen Samuel	"
5	Anderson William	E. Windsor
O	Andrus Thomas	Simsbury
O	Andrus W^m	"
A	Alley W^m	New Haven
H	Alling Jonathan	"
A	Akin James Serj.	"
3	Alvord G. Th^o Serj.	Farmington
3	Adrus Theodore	"
6	Atkins Josiah Jun	Waterbury
x	Thomas Anderson Lieut.	Lyme
*	Akely Samuel	Guilford deserted
2	Allen Moses	Fairfield
2	Allen Eben^r	"
x	Aldrich W^m	Preston
x	Avery Simeon Lieut.	Groton
x	Anew Andrew	"
9	Andrus James	"
9	Andrus Ezra	New Hartford
x	Allen Asher	Mansfield
x	Abbe John	"
4	Adams David Surg.	Canterbury
4	David	"
D	Sam^{ll}	"
7	Andrus Tim^o	Watertown
6	Blodget Artimas C^{ter}	Salsbury
2	Barrows Jacobe Corp.	Mansfield
x	Bugbe John	"
x	Basset Joshua	"
7	Brown Charles	Newfairfield
7	Bunce Isaiah	Washington
2	Basset W^m	Watertown
2	Buck Josiah	Newmilford
7	Bostwick Eben^r	"
7	Bewil David	"
*	Bissel Benjn	Litchfield Deserted
8	Brigham Paul Capt	Coventry
x	Ball Umphry	Lebanon
D	Bull Eppiphras Maj.	Hartford
	Buckland Steaphen Capt.	"

	Names	Towns to which they belong
3	Barnard John Capt.	Hartford
9	Brewer Daniel	"
3	Beevins Eben^r	"
3	Brown Jacobe	Summers
3	Brown Eben^r	Tolland
3	Booth Henery	Enfield
6	Blanchard Robbins	Colchester
6	Bates Amos	Haddam
6	Bonfoey Benanual	"
6	Boardman Jonathan	"
6	Bates Daniel	"
6	Bates Eleazer	"
6	Bailey Robart	"
6	Bacon W^m	Mdletown
9	Brown W^m	"
6	Boardman Sam^{ll} A	"
9	Barns Thomas	"
9	Boardman Moses	"
5	Brisler John	Windsor
x	Brown Elias	"
9	Brown Edward	Weathersfield
9	Blin Justus	"
9	Abraham	"
9	Bulkley Edward Capt.	"
3	Bowers Ephraim	Chatham
9	Butler Peter	"
3	Bowers Benjamin Serj.	"
3	Bowers Benaiah	"
8	Brown Josiah Lieut.	E. Windsor
3	Baxter Francis	"
8	Barns Daniel Capt.	Southington
7	Baldwine Calib Capt.	Killingsworth
	Brunson Rodger	Farmington
6	Baker Edward Serj.	New Haven
A	Barns Solomon Serj.	"
A	Burroughs Samuel	"
A	Bishop Nath^{ll}	"
3	Brown Henery Serj.	"
6	Blakesly Zealus	"
6	Bracket Hez.	"
6	Blakesley Jared	"
4	Beckwith Phineas Serj.	Lyme
6	Bunnell Abr^m	Branford
6	Bagdon Cezar	"
6	Belding John	Milford
3	Bristol Jonathan	"
6	Bebe Joe	"
H	Burk John	"
6	Bradley Daniel	Wallingford
Inv^d	Barns Moses	"
6	Bristol Benjamin	Cheshire
6	Barns David	"
6	Ball John Lieut.	Guilford
6	Benton Edward S^t	"
7	Bishop Almeno	"
5	Baker Bartholomew	Reading
3	Belding Moses	"

	Names	Towns to which they belong
7	Barnum Sam^{ll} Lieut.	Kent
7	Barnum Steaphen S^t	"
7	Amos Corp.	"
7	Barlow John	"
2	Bradley Nathan	Fairfield
	Eliphalet	" not in ye Ab.
8	Bulkley Seth	"
8	Bates David	Stamford
5	Barns Ambrose	Norwalk
7	Bedient Mordica	"
8	Bouton John	"
A	Benjamin John Lieut.	Stratford
Sm	Bebe James Capt	"
5	Bradley B Philip Col.	Ridgfield
x	Bebe Ammon	Norwich
x	Bennet Benjⁿ	"
9	Brewster Hez.	"
4	Briant John	"
	Blakesly Jeremiah	Danbury
7	Bishop David	"
7	Bingham John Serj.	Windham
W	Bingham Abishai S^t	"
	Burnap Benjⁿ	"
4	Bacon Nehem^a	Pomphret
7	Bill Judah	Sharon
7	Billings Steaphen Capt.	Groton
x	Brightman Henery	"
4	Benjamins Jesse	Preston
5	Chapman Collens	Danbury
7	Cleaveland Josiah	Sharon
4	Chapman Joseph Lieut.	Norwich
4	Cook Case	"
4	Clark Jacobe	"
	Comstock Gideon	
5	Cummins W^m	Ridgfield
	Collins L. W^m	Stratford
8	Comstock Sam^{ll} Capt.	Norwalk
*	Cole Alben	"
	Comestock Samuel	Saybrook
9	Crane Curtis	Weathersfield
3	Cones Wm Serj.	"
5	Chapman Albert Maj.	Fairfield
7	Chapman James Lieut.	"
5	Coggins David	"
7	Curtis George	Kent
	Cheney Richard	" Died Oct 1779
5	Cooly Nathan	Readding
7	Chaimberlane Ephraim Capt.	Wallingford
x	Clark Samuel	E. Haddam
6	Claghorn Eleazer Capt.	Salisbury
W	Chipman John Capt.	"
W	Coon James Lieut.	"
7	Church Eben^r	Woodbury
7	Convers Th^o Capt.	Goshen
8	Clark Ab^m	Hartford
8	Case Richard	"
9	Comey Mallehi alias Allen	"

	Names	Towns to which they belong
9	Cadwell Matth^w	Hartford
9	Cowls Sam^{ll}	"
8	Curtis Daniel	"
8	Clark John	Lebanon
5	Cooley Ruben	Somers
3	Cheney Eben^r	Ashford
W	Clap Nathan	Coventry
4	Cleft Lem^{ll} Capt	Plainfield
7	Canfield Elijah	New Milford
8	Camp Samuel	Wattertown
3	Crary Richard	Glastenbury
2	Chandler Joseph	Infield { Enter^d to Medad Pom- roy his Substitute
D	Churchill Elijah	"
4	Edward Carter	Colchester
6	Cone Elisha	Haddam
8	Sam^{ll} Church	"
8	Clark Aaron	"
5	Clark Othniel Lieut.	Middletown
	Cone Joseph	" Discharged 79
5	Ozias	"
5	Daniel	"
9	Crittendon Gid^n	"
	Carril John	Smsbury
3	Culver Tim^o	Southington
3	Carter Aaron	Chatham
O	Cary George	"
4	Cleaveland John Ens.	Canterbury
x	Carter Ruben	"
D	Cushman Dan^{ll}	"
x	Chatfield John	Killingworth
8	Camp Samuel	Waterbury
	Clark Lyman	Farmington
A	Curtis Dan^{ll} Junr	"
8	Camp Isaac	"
D	Churchill Elijah	E. Windsor
6	Cook Thomas alias Miles	Durham
6	Clark Martin	New Haven
A	Coshall Th^o	"
O	Clarriage Francis	"
	Clark Joel	"
x	Carwin Selah	Lyme
5	Cornelius Cohale al^s Sam^{ll} Foot	Milford
8	Cæsar Bristol	Newtown
6	Davidson Isaac	Milford
O	Daniels Sam^{ll}	"
3	Dunham Cornelius	Farmington
6	Dunn Tim^o	Durham
2	Duggin James	Canterbury
X	De Woolf Steaphen	Lyme
2	Davison W^m	Ashford
7	Dunwell W^m	New Milford
7	Dailey James (Sapper)	"
O	Dutton Titus Lieut.	Watertown
8	Davis Jonathan	"
8	Dunbar Miles	"
5	Denslow Marten S^t	Windsor

	Names	Towns to which they belong
7	Demmon Wait	Goshen
x	Darrow Christoph' Maj.	Hartford
2	Demmon John	Woodbury
6	Doud Moses	Guilford
x	Dextor John Serj.	Mansfield
	Downing John	Fairfield
6	Disborow Justin	"
	Joshua Ser'	"
8	Durfe Thomas	
9	Davis Eben'	Weathersfield
S	Donatis Francis	Preston
6	Doyle Hugh	New Haven
O	Dayton Israel	"
6	Davis James	"
	Dickerman Joseph Discharged	"
4	Durke John Col.	Norwich
	Durke Jeremiah	Windham
D	Dorman Gershom	Sharon
	Dickinson George	Danbury
5	De Forest Sam'l Lieut	Norwalk
7	Dalton Richard Corp.	Groton
	Davison Robert	"
9	Davis Daniel	"
5	Eaton Solomon	Tolland
5	Elmore Dan'l	Sharon
*	Evis Daniel	Stratford Desert.
6	Eagleston David	New Haven
x	Ellis John Chapln	Norwich
8	Easton Eliphalet	Woodbury
8	Elmon Calib	Harwington
2	Evans Abiather	Hartford
3	Henery	"
	Edwards Nath'l Lieut.	Watertown
6	Ely Elisha Capt.	Lyme
3	Eells Ed'd Capt.	Middletown
6	Foot Ezra	Darby
6	Farmer Th° Lieut.	"
5	Foot Sam'l alias Cohale Cornels	Milford
6	Eben'	Branford
*	Francis James	Middletown
5	Fisher Crestop'	"
3	Foster John	"
7	Franklin Sam'l	Killingsworth
6	Fowler Calib Corp.	Guilford
2	Fenton Solomon Lieut.	Mansfield
x	Jonathan	"
	Fitch Nehem*	Lebanon
4	Fuller John	Chatham
6	Ford Daniel	New Haven
	Marten	"
A	Fryar Charles	"
A	Foot Isaac	"
9	Flowers Elijah S'	New Hartford
8	Fox Elisha	Farmington
*	Fuller John	Fairfield Deserted
x	Farnsworth Nathan	Colchester
8	Fulford John	Watertown

	Names	Towns to which they belong
	Flag Jonathan	Hartford
7	Foster Benjª	Sharon
7	Fisher Isaac	"
6	Fitch Joseph Trumb¹¹	Salisbury
7	Freeman Sampson	Glastenbury
9	Fox Asa	"
6	Fields Edmund	Wallingford
6	Francis John	"
O	Fox Ebenʳ	" Chesʳ
9	Fay Gershom alias Moses	Winchester
9	Wᵐ	"
9	Tim•	"
9	Filley Remembrance	"
9	Fanning Elisha	Groton
8	Freeman Edward	"
8	Micael	"
8	Fields Francis	Woodbury
2	Franklin Jehiel	"
*	Forgo Peter	Fairfield
4	Fanning Charles Lieut.	Norwich
7	Grover Phineas Capt.	Glastenbury
8	Gibbs Josiah	Sommers
8	Gridly Seth	Harwington
7	Goodrich David	Sharon
5	Gelson Eleazer	"
D	Glover John	Fairfield
3	Graves Peter	Colchester
3	Griswold Joseph	Enfield
8	Grainger Samˡˡ	Suffield
2	Phineas	"
9	Gilbert Joseph Serj.	New Hartford
9	Theodore	"
	Gillet Adna	"
	Gibson Samˡˡ	New Haven
4	Grant James	Saybrook
6	Graham Cyrus	"
7	Gilbert Obediah	Stratford
	Gould John	Goshun
3	Gibbs Samˡˡ Lieut.	Windsor
D	Giants Luke	Preston
x	Goff Samˡˡ	Chatham
8	Graham Joseph	"
8	Goodrich Levi Serj.	"
[?]	Gladding Wᵐ	Haddam
9	Giffin Simon Sᵗ	Weathersfield
	Gillit Zacheriah Sᵗ	Southington
x	Gardiner Sherman Sᵗ	Norwich
[?]	David	"
5	Graves Wᵐ (Sapper)	Medletown
6	Gilson Jacobe	"
6	Garrit John	Branford
6	Gooldsmith Wᵐ	Milford
O	Green Joseph	"
6	Hinman Houghton	Durham
3	Harris alias Harrison Champlin	Colchester
	Hull Giles	Salisbury
8	Hecox E	Watertown

	Names	Towns to which they belong
7	Hill Eben' Capt	Kent
	Hager Simeon	Enfield
3	Hall Israel	"
A	Hubbel Isaac Capt.Lt.	Fairfield
A	William Lieut.	"
5	Hall Steaphen S'	"
7	Hutenot Francis	"
7	Hilton Atkenson	
3	Higgins W^m	Lyme
7	Hall David	Danbury
*	Howard Richard	Windham deserted
8	Hodg Asael Capt.	Harwington
7	Hamblin Joel	Norfolk
2	Hinckley Iccabud Capt.	Tolland
4	Hills Daniel	Glastenbury
3	Holden John	"
8	Heath Peleg L. Lieut.	Hartford
8	Hadlock Ruben	"
O	Hopson Linus	Wallingford
O	Hall Titus	"
7	Hart Benj^a	"
6	Hall Rufus	"
x	Holmes Eliph' Capt	E. Haddam
x	Harvey Ezra Corp.	"
5	Harvey W^m	Saybrook
8	Hull Oliver	"
A	Harris Henery	Stratford
2	Harrop or Harlop Joseph	"
2	Hawley Nathan	"
8	Hubbel Seth	Norwalk
8	How Zadock	Bolton
x	Harde Nath^ll	Ashford
3	Hall Robert	"
x	Hide R. W^m	Lyme
4	Hide James Ens.	Norwich
	Higgins Cornetuis Lieut.	Haddam
9	Hollis Joseph	Preston
7	Holdridg Hez. Col.	Hebron
3	Hubbard Hez. Lieut.	Middletown
3	Harris John	"
5	Henshaw Wm Lieut.	"
8	Hubbard Roswell	"
8	Hull David	"
6	Howell Nicholas	New Haven
9	Hull Sam^ll	"
O	Harden Fredrick	"
	Huse Boardwell	"
9	Howe Joshua	Farmington
6	Hosmore Tim° Doct.	"
8	Heyden David	"
	Howard George	"
3	Hart Jonathan Lieut.	"
	Hotchkiss Zadock	
7	Hall Stephen Capt.	Guilford
7	Philemon Lieut.	"
7	Handey Sam^ll S'	"
7	Hotchkiss Ira	

	Names	Towns to which they belong
4	Hill John	Simsbury
*	Harrinton Elisha	"
5	Hall Sam[ll] Corp	Killingworth
8	Hobart John Lieut.	Branford
6	Hoodley Sam[ll]	"
6	Harrison Jarus	"
6	Hooker John	Milford
6	Hodg David	"
6	Hine Titus	"
2	Hiccock Sam[ll] Lieut.	Stamford
2	Hait Joseph Col.	"
8	Holley Abraham	"
6	Humphry Elijah Capt.	Darbey
x	Hanes Jonathan	Stamford
5	Jones Isaiah	"
	Johnson Robert	Sharon
6	Abraham Corp.	New Haven
6	Joslin John	"
8	Judson Joseph	Woodbury
H	Jones Joseph	Branford
x	Jackson Th[o]	Preston
2	Johnson Elihue	Tolland
6	Johson Isaac	Guilford
x	Jones Daniel	Lebanon
5	Johnson Jonathan Col.	Midletown
H	Jones Th[o]	Wallingford
O	Charles	"
6	Johnson John	Cheshire
9	Jeralls Th[o]	Hartford
6	Jones Jasber	Stratford
*	Judd Brewster	Watertown
9	Jones Aaron	Saybrook
6	Johnson W[m]	Durham
8	Judd Steaphen	Waterbury
3	Judd W[m] Capt.	Farmingtown
*	King Orrey Deserted	Stratford
7	Knap Tim[o]	Goshen
O	King Hez	Wallingford
3	Keney Benj[n]	Hartford
6	Kimball T. Abraham	Midletown
9	Kilbey Christopher	Weathersfield
5	Kelsey Noah	Sharon
2	Kelley John	Litchfield
	King George	New Haven
8	Kimberly E Lieut.	Newtown
x	Lee Ezra Lieut.	Lyme
x	Lay Richard	"
9	Loomis Israel	Hartford
	Lyon Ezra	Ashford
7	Lambkins Benj[n]	Kent
5	Lawrance Amos S[t]	Windsor
5	Lamberton Obed	"
3	Lung Joseph	Midletown
2	Luce Jonathan	Tolland
9	Loveland Thomas	Glastenbury
3	Elisha	"
7	Leet Allen	Killingworth

	Names	Towns to which they belong
4	Lockwood Moses	Weathersfield
8	Lee Abner	Woodbury
6	Leavenworth Eli Maj.	New Haven
6	Lord Jabez	"
	Lines John	"
7	Lake Phineas	Cornwall
5	Lacy Josiah Capt.	Fairfield
A	Leverick Gabriel St	"
3	Lilley John	Canterbury
3	Ebenr	Union
9	Lord Jeremiah St	Saybrook
6	Lay Asa	"
H	Lee Noah Capt	Salisbury
5	Ludiman John	Danbury
2	Lewis Peter	Stratford
3	Marble Tho	Hebron
3	Mack Abner	"
D	Minor Elisha	Woodbury
7	Miels Charles Capt.	Preston
4	McDaniels Jams	"
O	Matthews John St	New Fairfield
D	Mills Samll Lt	Simsbury
2	Mecker Stephen	Redding
5	Mason John	Litchfield
Inv.	Munger Daniel	"
3	Moore Wm	Union
8	Mallery Jonah	Watebury
x	Macks Jeremiah	Danbury
x	Minor Elihue	E. Haddam
D	Morrison Wm	Weathersfield
3	Miller Nathll	"
9	Maggot Zebulon	"
4	Mix Thomas Jur	Wallingford
6	Munson Levi	"
6	Mansfield John	"
O	Matthews Eliada	Chester
4	Martin George	Windham
2	Mix John Lieut.	Farmington
3	Monossuk Daniel	"
	McDaniel John	Groton
*	Miller Daniel	Chatham Deserted
4	Markham Joseph	"
5	Meed Jeremiah	Norwalk
5	Jasper Lt	"
9	Merrils Cyprian	New Haven
9	Aaron	"
6	Mather Elias Ens.	Lyme
3	Miller Charles Lt	Hartford
	Meeker Daniel	"
3	Mize Wm	"
3	Mahar James	"
6	Meigs J Return Col.	Midletown
3	Mosely Sifax	Glastenbury
5	Morehouse David	Fairfield
2	McNutters John	Stanford
2	Manning Wm	Norwich
4	Mc Gregor John	Plainfield

	Names	Towns to which they belong
4	Marsh Peter Corp.	Plainfield
2	Murrey Abraham	Darbey
A	Mix Steaphen	Goshen
4	Munson Wm Capt.	New Haven
A	Miles John Capt	"
6	Mansfield Joseph Capt.	"
A	Mix Tim° L^t	"
7	Matthews Robert (Sapper)	"
6	Mallery Amos S^t	"
6	Malthrop Joseph	"
6	Mansfield Dan.	"
6	Malthrop Steaphen	"
x	Murphy Thomas	E. Haddam
x	Mitchel Sam^11	"
6	Northrup Isaac	Milford
9	Norton Sam^11	Hartford
5	Joseph	Goshun
A	Newel James	Farmington
A	Norton Jedadiah	Chatham
6	Benjn Ens.	Branford
7	Norton Rufus	Guilford
7	Elon	"
6	Niger Phillip	"
8	Nichols Samuel	Norwalk
5	Nickerson Barret	Ridgfield
	Nash Eben^r	Norwalk
8	Nutton Ezekiel	Washington
6	Newel Robart	Saybrook
5	Owen Alvin	Windsor
6	Oulds Oliver	Washington
6	Owen Eliphalet	Salisbury
Sm.	Osburn Nath^11	Stratford
2	Orcutt Calib S^t	Willington
6	Oatis Joseph	Branford
5	Olmstead Isaac	Norwalk
8	Olmstead James L^t	Hartford
A	Parker Edmund	New Haven
4	Perrigo W^m	Norwich
6	Potter Moses	New Haven
D	Amos	"
4	Powers Thomas	"
A	Prindle Y. Enos	Darbey
5	Petit Enos	Sharon
9	Porter Amos	Haddam
3	Parker Benjn	Wallingford
6	Elisha	"
A	Peck Charles	Cheshire
	Peckit Th°	Danbury Susquehannah Comp
2	Peirce Dan^11	E Windsor
x	Patterson James	Norwich
	Patchin Elijah	Fairfield
8	Prichard George	Waterbury
8	Powers Thomas	Midletown
8	Peek Ariel	"
3	Pomeroy Ralph	Hartford
x	Parseval Paul Q^m	Farmington } in list of
3	Potter Lem^11	" } Errors

	Names	Towns to which they belong
6	Powers James	Farmington
=	Pratt Isaac	" Six months man
	Palmer Benjⁿ	Litchfield
8	Parks Daniel	Chatham
6	Potter Steaphen Capt.	Branford
	Powers James	Southington
8	Pratt Russel	Somers
3	Porter Nathan	Mansfield
x	Pompey Samˡˡ	Groten
	Polly Alpheus	Lebanon
7	Perry Elisha	Ridgfield
x	Plumb Peter	No[ ]h
2	Parenan Joseph	Suffield
2	Preston Tirus	Tolland
6	Pratt Ethan	Saybrook
	Pool Daniel	Ashford
9	Parker Samˡˡ	Stratford
6	Phillips Thomas	"
O	Painter Gamaliel Capt.	Salisbury
O	Pendleton Danˡˡ Capt.	Watertown
6	Parker Isaac	"
8	Preston A	"
	Porter Daniel	Windsor
x	Prior Abner Maj.	"
7	Peet Lemˡˡ	New Milford
A	Purdey Jesse	"
2	Parsons Jonathan	Enfield
2	David Capt.	"
3	Perry Silvanus Lᵗ	Killingly
8	Prindle Abijah	Newtown
4	Quashe Cato	Colchester
4	Qui Lebbeus	Norwich
4	Rowley Jesse	Colchester
O	Reynolds John	Hartford
9	Risley Steaphen	"
6	Rosetor Samˡˡ	Litchfield
9	Roberts Elisha	New Hartford
Sm	Ramong Samˡˡ	Reading Sapper & Miner
A	Rian Jerry	"
7	Roberts Benjⁿ	New Fairfield
8	Ranney Steaphen	Chatham
8	Jabez	"
x	Reed Nathan	Mansfield
9	Roberson Ephᵐ	Coventry
	Rose Samˡˡ	"
	Remmington Steaphⁿ	Ridgfield
A	Rombelow Thomas	Killingworth
7	Rust Eppiphras	Cornwall
4	Riseing James	Suffield
8	Russell Wᵐ	Stratford
8	Rice Nehemiah Capt.	Watertown
x	Reed Enoch Capt.	Lyme
9	Roberts David	Midletown
4	Reynolds John	Norwich
9	Russel Ashur	Weathersfield
9	Ryley John Lieut.	"
6	Rozel Jeremiah	Danbury

	Names	Towns to which they belong
O	Rexford Benjn	Wallingford
6	Benjn Junr	"
5	Rust Jonathan	Sharon
7	Rouse Jabez S^t	Windham
4	Robinson Elias Ens.	"
	Simson Ju^r	"
3	Randol Elijah	"
H	Robinson Sam^{ll} Lieut.	New Haven
2	Rayming David	Fairfield
8	Robards Joel	Waterbury
7	Sanford James	Newtown see Danbury
6	Sherman John Lieut.	New Haven
6	Sanford Th^o S^t	"
6	Smith Ambrus	"
6	Sugden Abraham	"
6	Stockwell Abel	"
A	Sherman Edmund S^t	"
6	Shephard John	"
2	Steaphens W^m	"
5	Strong David L^t	Sharon
8	Smith John L^t	Haddam
3	Smith John	"
4	Joshua	"
7	Daniel	Wallingford
7	Sanford James	Danbury see Newtown
*	Stodard Enoch	Wethersfield deserted
6	Seward Nathan	Waterbury
8	Smith Lue	"
A	Simons Robert	Fairfield
5	Smith Isaac	Stamford
6	Starr David Capt.	Midletown
O	Sizer Wm Capt.	"
O	Savage Steaphen	"
6	Sizer Jonathan	" see David Hungerford
4	Sumner John Col.	"
8	Savage Abijah Capt.	"
x	Sill David L C	Lyme
x	Selden Ezra Capt.	"
x	Spencer Ichabud	"
4	Saunders John	"
*	Sullard Jacobe	"
6	Sawyer Asa	"
	Smith Enoch	"
8	Sanford Sam^{ll} Capt.	Milford
6	Smith W^m L^t	"
6	Steward John	"
8	Smith David Maj.	Watertown
*	John	" 7th Deserted
2	Spear Elijah	Suffield
8	Shilley Eben^r Serg.	Stratford
A	Sunderland John	"
7	Swift Heman Col.	Cornwall
7	Steaphens Aaron Capt	Killingworth
2	Steaphens Peter	"
	Smith Jobe L^t	Ridgfield
x	Shumway John Capt.	Mansfield
x	Smith John	"

	Names	Towns to which they belong
4	Smith Ezra L^t	Chatham
[ ]	Stockin Marshall	"
5	Schullena Abr^m S^t	"
x	Starr Josiah C Col.	New Milford
	Stilwell Steaphen	"
D	Sheldon Elisha Col.	Salisbury
6	Strong Phineas	"
O	Swetland Aa[ ] S^t	
*	Smith Abijah	Ashford deserted
6	Steaphens Elijah	Saybrook
2	Sabins Nehemiah Corp.	Tolland
9	Scovil Steaphen	Winchester
4	Shaw Benjamin	Canterbury
6	Steaphens Peter alias Asa	"
6	Squire Abiathur alias Ashar	Durham
6	Squire Saxton	"
6	Seaward Samuel	"
6	Strong Eliakim	"
3	Steaphens Tim^o	Glastenbury
7	Simbo Prince	"
7	Strong John L^t	Guilford
	Stannord Elijah	"
6	Swift Robert	Groten
6	Sharper Tuis	"
S	Sterry Silas	"
3	Shortman W^m	"
S	Stanton Amos Capt.	"
A	Squire Sam^{ll} Serj.	Southington
6	Smith Jordan	Branford
5	Scribner Asa	Norwalk
8	Stodard Eli	Woodbury
5	Stannord Sam^{ll}	" & Litchfield
5	Smith Henery	Litchfield
x	Sears Obediah	Preston
	Stark Sam^{ll}	Colchester
	Tim^o	"
O	Spencer John L^t	Hartford
9	Stone Th^o	"
3	Smith David	Farmington
D	Asaph	"
3	Steel Josiah	"
9	Steaphens Aaron	New Haven
5	Sherwood Nehem^a	Reading
7	Saunders W^m	New Fairfield
6	Shalor Joseph L^t	Wallingford
6	Sowers W^m	Milford
5	St John John Capt.	Norwalk
9	Simons Eli	Colebrook
A	Thomson Isaiah L^t	Farmington
5	Taylor John	New Hartford
7	Trowbridg John S^t	New Fairfield
6	Towner Jacobe	Branford
8	Taylor Elijah Ens.	Norwalk
[ ]	Tarble Wm Invalid	Colchester
6	Taylor Simeon	Woodbury
6	Thomson David S^t	Guilford
6	Teal Samuel	"

	Names	Towns to which they belong
[ ]	Tryon Isaac	Glastenbury
[ ]	Tiken Tias	Canterbury
[ ]	Thomson Epaphr[ ]	Saybrook
[ ]	Tooly Andrew	"
6	Tupper W^m S^t	Salisbury
5	Trowbridg Eben^r	New Milford
5	Thomas Steaphen	Chatham
7	Tubbs Nathan	Norfolk
3	Taylor Ephraim	Hebron
8	Thompson Nath^ll	Coventry
D	Tucker Jarvis	Milford
3	Taylor Thomas	Union
4	Throop Benjn Maj.	Norwich
4	Tracey Moses	"
x	Wm Ens.	"
*	Taylor Barrick	Fairfield
8	Thayer Asa	Waterbury
8	Tattendon John	"
A	Throop John L^t	New Haven
6	Trowbridg John L^t	"
A	Todd Yale	"
6	Thomas Ephraim	"
A	Thomas John	"
6	Tolles Elnathan	"
6	Thomas Samuel	"
6	Verguson John	"
8	Upson Ezekiel	Waterbury
8	Vaughn Daniel	Lebanon
3	Verry Jonathan	Chatham
3	Wright John	"
4	Woodsworth Benjn	Lebanon
x	Jedadiah	"
x	Willcox Philemon	Waterbury
6	Willson John	New Haven
6	Wood Elisha	"
D	Wilds Jonathan	"
6	White Sam^ll	"
O	Walter W^m	"
4	Webb Nath^ll Capt	Windham
7	Wainwright Th^o	Sharon
6	White Joseph	Darbey
O	Wilcox Jarius Capt.	Wallingford
A	Webb Gideon	Cheshire
S	Wallis Abr^m	E Windsor
S	Wadsworth B. Joseph Doc^r	"
9	Williams Daniel S^t	Wethersfield
9	Wells Joshua	"
x	Williams Thomas	E. Haddam
x	Willey Jonathan	"
x	Wadkins Ephraim	"
2	Wheeler Joshua	"
A	Williams Rich^d	Fairfield
x	Waterman Eben^r	Norwich
6	W[ ]	Midletown
3	Wa[ ]nor Robert Capt.	"
5	Weed Th[ ] Capt	Stamford
2	Wardwell Jacobe	"

	Names	Towns to which they belong
A	Willson David	Stamford
8	Waterbury W^m	"
x	Wade John	Lyme
x	Willson George	"
x	Wade Martin	"
8	Williams Obediah	Watertown
8	Washburn Sam^{ll}	Stratford
7	Wier Thomas	Goshen
5	Woodward Oliver	Simsbury
8	Woodbridg Theoph^s L^t	"
D	Wood Thomas	Sommers
	Worden Isaac	Stonington
2	Ware Daniel	Enfield
8	Welton Benjn	Farmington
8	Willcox James	"
D	Wainwright Sam^{ll}	"
8	Warren Ab^m	"
=	Welton Solomon	" Six months man
D	Ward John	New Hartford
7	Wilder Aaron	New Fairfield
6	White John L^t	Branford
8	Williams John	Norwalk
A	Wilcox Elias	"
A	White Eliakim	Southington
6	Wadsworth Theodore Do^r	"
8	Williams Henery L^t	Groton
8	Whitman Lem^l S^t	"
8	Williams Uriah S^t	"
6	Wheeler Thomas	Guilford
8	Warren John S^t	Glastenbury
9	Wilkenson Jesse	Winchester
9	Wording Isaac	Saybrook
6	White Oliver	"
7	Waterhouse Steap^n	"
4	Wales Eben^r L^t	Ashford
8	Waters W^m	"
7	Whitley W^m	New Milford
8	Wyllys Sam^{ll} Col.	Hartford
9	Wood Jonathan	"
8	Waters Th^o	"
4	Wack W Fredrich	Colchester
8	Whitney Dan^{ll}	"
8	Welch Luke	Woodbury
*	Wright James	Litchfield
X	Willcox Philemon	"
6	Yates William	Salisbury
	Yarrington Jesse	Groton
6	Yale Nash	Wallingford
7	Yale Wait	Sharon

Appendix

7	Aspenwall Calib	Norfolk
7	Aspenwall Aaron	"
7	Adams Asael	"

x denotes 1st Reg^t
2   "   2^d "

12

3 denotes 3ᵈ Regᵗ
4   "   4ᵗʰ "
5   "   5ᵗʰ "
6   "   6ᵗʰ "
7   "   7   "
8   "   8   "
9   "   Colᵒ Webs Regᵗ
D.   "   2ᵈ Lᵗ Dragoons
A.   "   Artilery
O.   "   Artificers
W.   "   Colᵒ Warners
H.   "   Colᵒ Hazens
L.   "   Coloᵒ Livingstons
S   "   Sherburns
*   "   Deserted
=   "   Short Recruit or 6ᵐᵒ m[   ]
Sm.   "   Sapper & Miner

FIRST REGIMENT — COL. STARR.

FIRST COMPANY — COL. STARR.

Pay Roll of the Short levies Col. Starr's Comp^y 1st C^t Reg^t

Names	Comm^t of service	Expiration of service	Towns
Isaac Lyman Serg^t	Aug. 1	Sep. 15	Lebanon
Oliver Kent	July 1	Oct. 25	Suffield
Asa Mason	"	"	Ashford
Zach^h Chapman	"	Nov. 20	Est Hadam
Willm Middleton	22	Dec. 3	Groton
Zebulon Fervin	1	"	Suffield
Jonah Rising	"	"	"
Peleg Watson	"	"	Windsor
John Lay	"	"	Lyme
Lawrence Dowsit	June 26	5	Ashford
Nath^{ll} Fenton	July 1	"	Mansfield
Azariah Hillard	15	"	Stonington
Joshua Reynolds	20	4	Norwich
Moses Fitts	1	5	Ashford
Ethen Rogers	15	"	Branford
Wm Royce	"	4	Ashford
David Carpenter	"	9	"
Ethen Barker	"	"	Suffield
Silas Dewey	"	"	"
James Lathrop	Aug. 1	"	Lebanon
John Holmes	July 1	"	Stafford
And^w Colegrove	5	"	Voluntown
Samuel Pitts	1	18	Ashford
Archib^d Greenfield	15	"	Lyme
Amos Dowsit	1	"	Ashford
Phil^n Andrews	"	"	Est Hadam
George Coit	"	"	Preston
Willm Campbill	"	25	Suffield

Decr 29th 1780   J. Tiffany, Ens^n

[*State Library, Revolution 17, 48.*]

SECOND COMPANY — LIEUT.-COL. SILL

Pay-roll for the new Levies in Lieu^t Col^o Sill's Comp^y 1st Connec^t Reg, 1780

Names	Comm^t of Service	Expiration of Service	Towns to which they Belong
Ebenezer Conant	July 15	Dec. 4	Hartford
Eleazer Barrows	June 26	31	Mansfield
Ethan Barrows	July 1	18	"
Robert Brown	15	4	Stonnington
Jonathan Bassit	June 26	18	Mansfield
Amos Conant	"	4	"
David Lawson	Aug. 3	18	Union

Names	Comm^t of Service		Expiration of Service	Towns to which they Belong
Nathan Conant	July		Dec. 8	Mansfield
Walter Carey	June	26	4	"
Nathan Cottrill	July	1	3	Stonington
Cato Cuffe		15	9	"
John Elsworth	"		13	Torrington
John Gifford		1	4	Norwich
Guy Lester	"		9	Lyme
Timothy Miner	"		"	"
Charles Miner	"		4	"
Edward Otis	"		31	"
Daniel Preston	"		13	Mansfield
Tuish Sharper		15	8	Groton
Morris Woodbourn	"		9	Stonnington
John Wilson		9	14	Hartford
John Wilson Junr	"		9	"
Stephen Thompson		6	4	Union

Joseph Clark Ensign

[*State Library, Revolution 17, 44.*]

FIFTH COMPANY.

Pay Roll of the Short Levies 5th Company 1st Connecticut Reg^t Decr 1780

Names	Commencement of Service		Expiration of Service	Towns they belong to
Asa Williams	July	15	Dec. 5	Hartford
George Woodbridge	"		"	"
Saml Deliber	"		"	"
George Abby	"		"	"
Joseph Kent		1	"	Stafford
Solomon Tupper		20	"	"
Timothy Dimmick	"		"	"
Daniel D. Wolf		1	"	Enfield
John Hellermegy	"		"	"
Joseph Stewart	"		"	East Haddam
Thomas Larroby	"		"	N London
Elihu Huntley		15	"	Lyme
Theophilus Rathbon	"		"	"
Joseph Emerson	"		"	"
Charles Wood		20	18	Stafford
Jabez Cary	"		9	Mansfield
Jacob Hills		1	"	Enfield
Gurdon Rogers	"		"	East Haddam
Elisha Lyman		15	11	Lebanon
Elisha Peck	"		13	Lyme
Asa Wilson		1	9	Enfield
Thos Keney		15	21	Hartford

Thos Anderson Leut

[*State Library, Revolution 17, 19.*]

CAPT. DOUGLASS' COMPANY.

Pay Roll of the New Levy' in Cap' Douglass Company 1ˢᵗ Connecticut Reg' 26ᵗʰ Dec' 1780

Names	Commen' of Service		Expiration of Service		Towns
Jonaᵗʰ Metcalf	July	1	Oct.	26	Lebanon
Guy Chapel		15	Dec.	9	N London
Jedʰ Cady		1	"	"	Mansfield
Abner Cady		"		4	
Stephen Eaton		"		"	
Stephen Ellis		"		"	Norwich
Ephraim Frost		"		"	Mansfield
Nathˡˡ Fitch		"		"	
Wᵐ Fagins		"		"	Groton
Joseph Herrick		"		"	
Cuff Hurlburt		13		"	Groton
Caleb Johnson		"		9	N London
Asael Kingley		1		"	
Elnathan Keys		"	Nov.	15	
Josiah Lockwood		5	Dec.	4	
Zadock Lee		1		"	Lebanon
Nathˡˡ Little		"		"	
Samˡˡ Mobbs		"		13	East Haddam
Timʸ McIntosh		"		"	Lyme
Abner Peck		15		4	Huntington
Henry Smith		5		9	Hadam
Asael Southwell		"		"	
Zackeus Spencer		1		4	Labanon
Jnᵒ West		"		18	
Badwell Watkins		"		4	
Shoram Stanton		15	Oct.	26	Groton

Ezra Lee Lieuᵗ

[*State Library, Revolution 17, 30.*]

CAPT. SELDEN'S COMPANY.

Pay Roll of the New Levies Captain Seldens Company 1ˢᵗ Connectieutt Regiment Dec' 1780

Names	Commen' of Service 1780		Expiration of Service		Towns they belong to
Oliver Brown	July	1	Nov.	21	Stonington Deserted Nov 21
Nathan Bebee	June	27	Oct.	27	East Haddam Deserted Oct. 24
James Chandler		"	Dec.	4	Ashford
Benedict Church		"		6	Voluntown
Elijah Cone		18		13	East Haddam
Edward Coney		15		3	Norwich
Samuel Garret		1		15	Stonington
Paul Harris	Aug.	1		9	Canterbury
Robert Jackson	July	1		21	Voluntown
Zephaniah Mitchel 2ᵈ		15		6	Colchester
Philip Meachum		1		9	Suffield
Stephen Mosher		"		"	Lyme
Elisha Royce		27		"	Ashford
Elisha Rogers		"		4	"

Names	Comment of Service 1780	Expiration of Service	Towns they belong to
Joseph Scott	July 1	Dec. 4	Willington
Benjamin Smith	15	15	Voluntown
Ezra Sibley	1	9	Willington
Simeon Snow	June 27	4	Ashford
Asahel Woodworth	July 1	3	Norwich
Stephen Butler	Sep. 22	15	Ashford
Zephaniah Mitchel	July 15	Aug. 17	Colchester

E Selden Capt

[State Library, Revolution 17, 25.]

CAPT. DORRANCE'S COMPANY.

Pay Roll of the New Levies Captain Dorances Comp^y 1st Connec^t Reg^t Decr 1780

Names	Commencement of Service	Expiration of Service	Towns they belong to
Joseph Kinney	July 1	Dec. 4	Preston
Ameziah Corwin	"	"	Lyme
Saml Daniels	"	"	"
Levi Hitchcock	"	"	Darby
Saml Utley	"	9	Woodstock
Elisha Wilcox	"	"	"
Pell Collins	"	"	Stonington
Abraham Wade	"	"	Lyme
Jabez Frink	"	"	Stonington
Stephen Jackson	"	"	Woodstock
George Jackson	"	"	"
Saml Davis	"	"	Stafford
Darius Woodworth	"	10	Norwich
Roswell Lamphier	"	"	"
Luther Skinner	"	"	Woodstock
Eliab Edson	"	11	
Jonah Cushman	"	13	Woodstock
Joseph Ransom	"	"	Lyme
Ichabod Allen	"	15	Stonington
John Gould	"	"	
Simon Newcomb	"	16	Lebanon
Richard Crosby	"	4	Mansfield

High Lands 22^d Decr 1780

David Dorrance Capt

[State Library, Revolution, 17, 13.]

CAPT. RICHARD'S COMPANY.

Pay Roll for the New Levies in Capt Wm Richards' Comp^y 1st Conn^t Reg^t 1780

Names	Comment of Service	Expiration Service	Towns they belong to
Thomas Attwood	July 1	Nov. 4	Mansfield
Nath^ll Ames	13	Dec. 12	Preston
Jno Abbee	7	Nov. 14	Windham
Ephraim Brown	15	Nov. 4	Stoning Town } gave certificate 17 Feby 1835

Names	Commen* of Service	Expiration Service	Towns they belong to
David Bennet	July 1	Oct. 26	Stoning Town
Jabez Breed	"	Dec. 11	"
Jnᵒ Center	"	9	Norwich
Wᵐ Daniels	"	4	East Haddam
Benjⁿ Diggins	15	9	Stoning Town
Richᵈ Dye	"	4	"
Joel Davis	"	9	Mansfield
Wᵐ Eaton	1	3	"
Wᵐ Glading	2	"	Haddam
Cesar Griswold	1	"	Lyme
James Mitchel	"	9	East Haddam
Abraim Niles	Sep. 1	4	Stoning Town
Jnᵒ Scott	"	13	Killingly
Joseph Cook Stubs	July 15	9	Stoningtown
Arnold Worden	1	"	"
Roger Woodworth	"	3	Lebanon
Stephen Wilcox	"	4	Stoning Town

Ezra Lee Lieuᵗ

[State Library, Revolution 17, 10.]

CAPT. SHUMWAY'S COMPANY.

Pay Roll of the New Levies Captain Shumways Company 1ˢᵗ Connecticut Regiment, Decʳ 1780.

Names	Commencᵗ of Service 1780	Expiration of Service 1780	Towns they belong to
Caleb Handee Sergᵗ	June 27	Dec. 14	Ashford
William Southward Corpˡ	"	4	"
Peter Ayers	July 13	"	Norwich
David Brooks	11	"	Wollingsford
Thomas Barrett	16	13	Woodstock
Joshua Baker	Aug. 27	11	Ashford
John Bugbee	1	13	Mansfield
Samuel Chaffee	July 5	4	Woodstock
Comfort Carpentor	1	9	Mansfield
Plina Camberlin	5	16	Woodstock
Oliver Chapman	"	4	"
Timothy Clark	1	9	Lebanon
Benjⁿ Daboll	15	16	Groton
Jeduthan Dimmick	1	9	Mansfield
Varny Fellows	"	11	"
Solomon Dimmick	Oct. 1	13	"
Phillip Dimmick	Aug. 21	4	
Benjⁿ Green	July 15	9	Preston
Gardner	11	16	
Jeremiah Hedges	1	11	Mansfield
Joseph Lamb	13	"	Willington
Benjⁿ Pirce	1	9	Mansfield
William Press	5	4	Woodstock
Thomas Rock	15	16	Groton
Joseph Scarborough	Aug. 21	9	Ashford
Samuel Smith	July 15	4	Norwich
Abel Sanders	"	"	Woodstock
Benjⁿ Tucker	5	9	"
Jesse Waldo	1	4	Mansfield

Simⁿ Avery Lieuᵗ

[State Library, Revolution 17, 45]

CAPT. REED'S COMPANY.

Pay Roll for the New Levies in Capt E Reeds Comp^y 1st Connecticut Reg^t 1780

Names	Comm^t of Service	Expiration of Service	Towns to which they belong
Timothy Aldrich	July 1	Dec. 4	Preston
John Baker	"	9	Mansfield
Maturen Hopkin	15	4	Woodstock
Robert Hammond	"	16 Mansfield	gave a certificate Novr 11, 1816
Nathaniel Hewit	5	4	Stonington
Robert Hewit	20	9	"
Edmond Halley	10	4	"
Jonas Kenny	"	"	Preston
Thomas Leeds	18	"	Stonington
Thomas Morrow	10	"	Norwich
Christopher Miner	June 29	"	Lyme
John Mielkin	July 18	18	Preston
Elijah Porter	15	"	Mansfield
Amos Royce	1	4	"
Gideon Rogers	8	9	Lyme
James Reives	9	18	"
Augustus Stores	10	9	Mansfield
Gilbert Shaw	"	4	Ashford
Obadiah Sears	"	9	Preston
Amos Thomson	"	4	Mansfield
Jared Tozer	"	"	Simsbury
Charles Hunt	Aug. 15	"	Lebanon
Manchester Halley	"	"	Preston
Phillip Prince	Sep. 1	18	Stonington

Enoch Reed Capt

[*State Library, Revolution 17, 50.*]

SECOND REGIMENT — COL. BUTLER.

FIRST COMPANY — COL. BUTLER.

Pay Roll of The Levies in the 1ˢᵗ Company 2 Connecticut Regiment Commanded By Zebulon Butler Colᵒ

Mens Names	Commencement of Time		To what time Paid		Towns To which they Belong
Nathanˡ More	Aug.	1	Dec.	8	Windsor
Zeanas Burnan	"			18	Hartford
Asbel Warren	"			9	Windsor
Isaac Bellows	"			18	Hartford
Charles Kinball	July	1		8	Ashford
Fradrick Tubbs	"			18	Newtown
Daniel Judd	"			12	Farmington
Jonathan Merrils	"			9	"
Joseph Munro	"			18	Danbury
Adoniram Benton	"			"	Goshen
Eli Bliss	"			12	Suffield
Joshua Symons	"			8	Tolland
Absalom Mooney		25	Oct.	1	Ridgfield
Joseph Pease		1	Dec.	8	Enfield
Thoˢ Hollister	"			9	Farmington
Samˡ Read	"			"	Tolland
Joseph Allyn	"			"	Danbury
Salvanus Booth	"			"	Farmington
Amos Clark	"			"	"
Samˡ Craft		18		8	Norwich
Willᵐ Stevens		16		18	New Haven
James Scariot		25		"	Hebron (?)
John Mooney		1		"	Ridgfield
Jack Gregory		25		9	Stratford
Manoah Crowel	Aug.	1		"	Tolland
Joel Perkins	July	1		18	
John Welman		25		8	Farmington
Hezekiah Porter	Oct.	1		9	Windsor

J. Hinckley Capᵗ Comdᵗ

[Indorsed] Pay Roll of the Short Levies in Colᵒ Butlers Company 2 Connect Regᵗ 1780

[*State Library, Revolution 17, 3.*]

SECOND COMPANY—LIEUT.-COL. HAIT.

Pay Roll of The Short Levies in Lt Col^o Haits Company 2^d Connecti^t Reg^t Commanded By Zebulon Butler Col^o

Mens Names	Commencement of Service 1780	To what time Paid	Towns To Which They Belong
Abiel Wolcutt Fifer	July 15	Dec. 9	Windsor
Jonathan Amedown	1	"	Willington
Saml Brocker	"	13	Simsbury
Abijah Phelps	"	8	"
Richard Andrews	"	13	"
Lemuil Wiard	"	8	Farmingtown
Archabel Cook	"	9	"
Lott Humphrys	"	"	Simsbury
Thos Wadsworth	"	13	Windsor
James Duggen	"	Nov. 15	Hartford
Mathew Peck	"	Dec. 8	Farmington
Jonathan Barber	"	"	Simsbury
Eliph^t House	Aug. 1	"	Farmington
Clement Minor	15	"	Tolland
Daniel Mack	July 1	"	Farmington
Wm Anderson	15	"	Willington
John Wate	"	"	Norwich
Joshua Button	"	8	"
Wm Mill Ross	"	"	Willington
Josiah Button	"	"	Farmington
Peter DeWolf	"	"	Symsbury
Joseph Tuller	"	9	"
Noah Miller	"	"	Farmington
John Booth	"	13	"
Nathan^l Andrews	"	"	"
John Turrel	"	"	"
Joseph Videto	"	"	N Milford
Oliver Lomis	20	"	Windsor
David Burnam	Aug. 15	"	Farmington
Eli Skinner	Sep. 1	"	
Justis Weed	"	9	Stamford
Solomon Lusk	"	13	
Simeon Rennels	"	8	Woodbury

J. Hinckley Capt Comd^t

[State Library, Revolution 17, 29.]

THIRD COMPANY—MAJ. WALBRIDGE.

Pay Roll of The Levies in Major Walbridges Company 2 Connec^t Reg^t Commanded By Zebulon Butler Col^o

Mens Names	Commencement of Time 1780	To What Time Paid	Towns To which They Belong
Daniel Brewer	July 1	Dec. 6	Hartford
Abel Bester	"	"	Stafford
Edward Burges	12	"	Enfield
David Booth	1	"	
Phin^s Brownson	"	"	Farmington
Austin Bishopp	"	13	Danbury
Reuben Bradly	"	6	Stafford
Zadock Benton	"	9	"
Saml Dunham	"	"	

Mens Names	Commencement of Time 1780		To What Time Paid	Towns To which They Belong
Daniel Eaten	July	1	Dec. 6	Windsor
Levi Eno	"		9	Simsbury
James Fisk	"		6	
Abel Goodrich	"		9	Danbury
Phil[n] Holt	"		22	Willington
Reuben Hill	"		6	Simsbury
Appleton Holster	Sep.	1	"	
Theodore King	July	1	"	Windsor
Noah Munro	"		13	Danbury
Sam[l] Parks		20	"	Tolland
Isaac Pratt		1	"	Farmington
James Powers	Sep.	1	6	
Daniel Roberts	July	1	"	Hartford
Isaac Rice	"		"	Meridan
Timothy Rositer	"		9	Harwington
Nathan[l] Tamage	"		"	Southington
Adrian Wadkins		18	6	Stafford
W[m] Fuller		1	13	
Eastus Hatch	"		6	New Haven
John Ford	"		"	Somers
Elias Baskam	"		"	Windsor

J. Hinckley Cap[t] Comd[t]

[State Library, Revolution 17, 26.]

CAPT. BETTS' COMPANY.

Pay Roll of The Short Levies in Cap[t] Betts Company 2 Connecticut Regiment Commanded By Zebulon Butler Col[o]

Mens Names	Commencement Of Time		To What Time Paid	Towns They Belong To
Jesse Dickison Fifer	June	26	Dec. 9	Stratford
Oliver Boge	July	5	"	Farmington
Levi Woodford	"		"	"
Calvin Judd	"		"	
Amos Andrews	"		"	"
Ephraim Monson	"		13	"
David Lee	"		9	"
Joseph Dutton	"		"	Windsor
Eleazer Payne	"		"	
Isaac Gillit	Sep.	7	13	"
Tho[s] Hadlock	July	5	9	Willington
David Fuller	"		"	"
John Hill	"		13	Coventry
Jonathan Benton	"		6	N Milford
Jn[o] Drinkwater	"		9	"
Job Terrel	"		6	Harwington
Aling Catling	"		9	N London
Reuben Grant	"		6	"
Jonathan Quivey	"		13	Farmington
Robert Coe	"		9	"
James Roberds	"		"	Harwington (?)
Joseph Cook	"		"	Tolland
Willial Barnard	"		"	"
Stephen Rossiter	"		"	"
James Gleason	Aug.	1	13	

J. Hinckley Cap[t] Comd[t]

[Indorsed] Pay Roll of the Short Levies in Cap[t] Betts Company 2 Connec[t] Reg[t] 1780.

[State Library, Revolution 17, 4.]

CAPT. ALDIN'S COMPANY.

Pay Roll of The Short Levies in Capᵗ Aldins Company 2ᵈ Connᵗ Regᵗ Commanded By Zebulon Butler Colᵒ

Mens Names	Commencement of Time	To what time Paid	Towns To which they Belong
Sam¹ Robards	July 1	Dec. 13	Winchester
John Balcom	"	"	New Hartford
Timʸ Alderman	"	9	Simsbury
Eber Higley	"	"	"
Ozias Hawley	"	"	"
Enos Holcum	"	"	"
Moses Wright	"	"	Danbury
Oliver Grant	"	"	Windsor
Amasa Rockwell	"	18	" .
Oliver Grant 2ⁿᵈ	"	"	Danbury
Josiah Hall	20	8	Somers
David Lotroop	1	13	Windsor
Solomon Savage	13	"	Middletown
Asa Ripnear	"	"	"
Jonathan Rice	22	9	Tolland
James Niles	20	"	Willington
Joseph Hale	22	"	Farmington
Freeman James	"	4	Willington
Theopˢ Hunt	"	"	New Milford
Ebenezer Smith	"	18	Fairfield
Ephᵐ Bidwell	26	"	Windsor
Amos James	Aug. 1	4	Willington
Anthony Kibby (?)	July 20	Oct. 18	Somers
Joseph Elmore	26	Dec. 13	Windsor
David Linn	Aug. 1	"	Killingworth
Israel Tuller	"	9	Simsbury
Timothy Anderson	"	16	Windsor
Lemuel Walter	Sep. 1	9	Winchester
Mathew Reynolds	July 12	Sep. 6	Woodbury

J. Hinckley Capᵗ Comdᵗ

[Indorsed] Pay Roll of the Short Levies in Capᵗ Aldins Company 2 Connᵗ Regᵗ 1780

[*State Library, Revolution 17, 8.*]

CAPT. TEN EYCK'S COMPANY.

Pay Roll of The Short Levies in Capᵗ Ten Eycks Light Infantry Company 2 Connᵗ Regᵗ Commanded By Zebulon Butler Colᵒ

Mens Names	Commencement of Time 1780	To what time Paid	Towns To which they Belong
Ede Hatch Dᵐ	July 1	Dec. 9	Toland
Eber Olford	"	4	Simsbury
Sam¹ Chase	"	" "	Toland
Zacheus Gillit	"	"	Farmington
Hezkʰ Huntington	"	9	Toland
Sam¹ Hitchcock	"	"	Farmington
Ambras Hitchcock	"	"	"
Ezek¹ Holcumb	"	"	Simsbury
Enoch Haze	"	"	"
Erastus Hills	"	"	Windsor
Elijah Hill	"	"	Simsbury

Mens Names	Commencement of Time 1780		To what time Paid	Towns To which they Belong
Geo. Blackburn	July	1	Dec. 9	Hartford
Josh Newbury	"		"	Windsor
Ebenr Snell	"		"	Stafford
Wm Rockwell	"		"	Windsor
Martin Dickins	"		"	"
Joel Slayter	"		"	Simsbury
Chancy Atkins	"		"	Farmington
Simeon Barns	"		"	"
Joel Holcomb	"		31	Simsbury
Danl Pardy	"		13	Farmington
Ezekl Beeman	"		"	Kent
Asa Brownson	"		"	Farmington
George Buck	"		"	Hartford
Daniel Andrus	"		"	Danbury
Jedh Blanchard	"		"	Simsbury

J. Hinckley Capt Comdt

[State Library, Revolution 17, 18.]

CAPT. PARSONS' COMPANY.

Pay Roll of The Short Levies in Capt Parsons Company 2 Connecticut Regiment Commanded By Zebulon Butler Colo

Mens Names	Commencement of Time		To what time paid	Towns they Belong to
Jonathan Allyn	July	1	Dec. 4	Hartford
Theophilus Allyn	"		9	
Ellihu Allyn	"		13	Danbury
Richard Abby	"		9	Enfield
Phinias Blodget		23	13	Windsor
Saml Billings		1	3	Somers
Peter Bugbee		20	"	Enfield
Jonathan Bement		26	13	Windsor
Ambras Cowdy		1	9	Hartland
Oliver Coe	"		17	Winchester
Peletiah Daniels	"		9	Hartland
David Dunham		20	"	Canaan
Nathan Fox		1	3	Simsbury
Levi French	"		9	Enfield
Uriah Gates	"		13	Hartford
Hills Gowdy	Aug.	1	9	Enfield
Saml Gowdy	July	10	"	"
Thamar Granger		1	"	Simsbury
Saml Halkins		29	"	Enfield
Saml Mott		1	31	Barkhanstead
Saml McGregory	"		Nov. 13	Enfield
Mathew Mansfield	Sep.	1	Dec. 18	Fairfield
Abner Pearce	July	1	13	Enfield
Aaron Pearce		10	9	"
Edward Pearce	"		"	"
Saml Spencer		23	6	Somers
Gideon St John	"		17	Canaan

J. Hinckley Capt Comdt

[Indorsed] Pay Roll of the Short Levies in Capt Parsons Company 2 Connectt Regt 1780

[State Library, Revolution 17, 27.]

CAPT. WOLCUTT'S COMPANY.

Pay Roll of Capt Wolcutts Company 2 Connecticut Reg^t Commanded By Zebulon Buller Col^o

Mens Names	Commencement of Time		To what time Paid		Towns to which They Belongs
Ezra Austin	July	17	Dec.	9	Wallingford
Justice Bissel		19		"	Windsor
Daniel Braymon	June	27		6	"
Seth Canada		24		"	Farmington
Enoch Crowel	July	12		13	Enfield
Lemuil Church		"		"	Killingly
Rufus Crain		19		9	Windsor
Benjn Elsworth	June	29		13	Danbury
John Gaylor		24		"	Farmington
Jered Smith		"		"	Wallingsford
David Grant	July	21		9	Windsor
Walter Holms	June	29		"	Stafford
Lemuel Higby	July	17		13	Wallingsford
Abner Johnson	June	29		9	Toland
Asaph Merrium	July	17		13	Wallingford
Erastus Merriam		"		6	"
Wyllin McKey		"		13	"
Elisha Peck	June	24		"	Southington
Seth Penfield		"		6	Farmington
Timothy Porter	July	12		9	Windsor
George Potwain	June	29	Nov.	7	"
Noah Pearce	July	19	Dec.	9	"
George Shipman		12		6	Lyme
Peter Wolcutt	June	29		13	Windsor
Simeon Rice	July	17		"	Willington
[Indorsed] 1780			J. Hinckley Capt Comd^t		

[*State Library, Revolution 17, 34.*]

CAPT. HINCKLEY'S COMPANY.

Pay Roll of The Short Levies in Capt Hinckleys Company 2 Connecticut Reg^t for the whole Term of there Service 1780

Mens Names	Commencement of Time		To what time Paid		Towns they Belong to
Sam^{ll} Steal Serj^t	July	1	Dec.	13	Toland } Promoted to a Serjt Sep. 1 80
William Eldridge		15		"	"
Samuel Pierce		1		"	Danbury
William Johnson		"		3	Tolland
Bruster Harris		"		"	"
Saml Ellis		"		"	Farmington
Allen Webster		18		"	Hartford
Ezra Nicholas		1		"	Danbury
Eleazer Hatch	Aug.	1		"	Toland
John Thompson	July	1		13	"
Ezra Raudin		"		"	"
Aaron Dilyno	Aug.	1		"	"
Ebenezer Pinney	July	20		"	East Windsor
Sandrus Perry		1		9	Danbury
Reubin Judd		"		"	"

Mens Names	Commencement of Time	To what time Paid	Towns they Belong to
Levi Barnam	July 1	Dec. 9	Danbury
John Steel	"	"	"
Job Hodgers	"	"	"
Daniel Gregory	"	13	"
Amos Lovland	"	9	Hartford
Sanford Williams	15	13	Norwich
Elisha Smith	"	"	"
Lott Burdges	1	"	Toland
Andrew Steel	15	9	East Windsor
Isaac Herrick	"	13	Fairfield
James Roberds	1	"	Farmington
Salvenas Gage	Aug. 1	9	Toland
Luther Delyno	July 1	Sep. 23	"

J. Hinckley Cap' Comd'

[*State Library, Revolution 17, 37.*]

THIRD REGIMENT—COL. WYLLYS.

FIRST COMPANY COL. WYLLYS.

Pay Roll of the Short Levy men who have Served in the Col⁰ˢ Company 3ᵈ Connᵗ Regᵗ for the Campaign 1780   December 22ᵈ 1780 Copied

Names	Commencement of Pay	to what time paid	Towns they Belong to
Lansford White	July 1	Dec. 9	Bolton
John Ward	"	5	"
Gideon Whitaker	"	3	Killingly
Daniel Hudson	"	12	Woodstock
David Ames	"	4	Killingley
Joseph Foster	"	12	Pomfret
Weaver Brown	2	"	"
Ithamar Oney	1	"	Killingly
Ebenʳ Atwood	"	"	"
Thomas Heath	Aug. 25	Nov. 14	Litchfield

Reuben Pride Lieuᵗ

[*State Library, Revolution 17, 68.*]

SECOND COMPANY — LIEUT. COL. GROSVENOR.

Pay roll of the short levies who have served in Lᵗ Col. Grosvenor's Co 3ᵈ Connecticut Regᵗ in the Campaign of 1780

Names	Comᵗ of Service 1780	Expirat of Service 1780	From what Town
Aseph Burley	July 10	Dec. 14	Hartford
Hezkʰ Barret	1	9	"
Ceaser Boeny	Aug. 10	4	Weathersfield
David Enos	July 1	"	Simsbury
Timothy Fisher	Aug. 15	10	Hartford
Nathˡ Merrills	July 1	18	"
John Randol	"	"	Pomfret
Ely Seymour	Aug. 15	4	Hartford
Elisha Seymour	"	11	"
Ardon Seymour	July 1	9	"
Wᵐ Sedgwick	Aug. 15	11	"
Charles Webster	July 1	18	"
Daniel Wadsworth	10	11	"
Timothy Heart	1	4	Farmington

Israel Johnson Serjᵗ
Ex Sam Richards P Master

[*State Library, Revolution 17, 68.*]

THIRD COMPONY MAJ. CLIFT.

Pay Roll of the Short Levy Men who have Served in Major Clifts Comp[y] the 3[d] Connec[t] Reg[t] in the Campain of 1780 Dec[r] 22[d]   Copied

Names	Commencement of Pay		To What Time Paid		Town they belong to
Abnor Brown	July	1	Dec.	5	New London
Elihew Benton		"		4	Winsor
Sam[l] Cleaveland		"	Nov.	9	Pomfret
Fredrick Cleaveland		"	Dec.	4	"
Gardner Cleaveland		"		"	"
Wardwill Green		"		"	"
Benj[n] Green		"		"	"
Rufus Gibbs		"		11	Winsor
Soloman Gilbert		"		13	Pomfret
Peleg Havens		"		4	Winsor
Andrew Morrison		"		13	Pomfret
Noah Pinney		"		4	Winsor
Preserved Redway		"		"	Killingly
Peltiah Tuttel		"		11	New London
Daniel Thomson		"	Oct.	25	"
Asa Cutter	Aug.	8	Dec.	9	Killingly
Cromwill Luther	July	1		10	"

Sylv[a] Perry Lieu[t]

[State Library, Revolution 17, 61.]

FOURTH COMPANY — CAPT. WARNER.

Pay Roll of the Short Levies that Have Served in the 4th Comp[y] 3[d] Conn[t] Reg[t] Part of the Year 1780   Copied

Names	Commenc[t] of Pay		to What Time Paid		Town Belonging to
Aseal Cheney	Sep.	11	Dec.	12	Chatham
Aseal Peck	June	3		"	Norwich
Joseph Kingsbury		30		"	"
Jasper Bentley		"		31	"
Benj[a] Greenslit		"		12	"
Aseal Bentley		"		4	"
Barnard Convise		"		"	"
Benj[a] Babbet	Sep.	14		20	Middletown
Manoah Hubbard		5		4	"
Thadias Bowe (? Boise)		"		"	"
Daniel Burton	July	7		14	Chatham

R. Warner Cap[t]

[State Library, Revolution 17, 64.]

FIFTH COMPANY — CAPT. EELLS.

Pay Roll of the Short Levies in the 5 Comp[y] 3[d] Connec[t] Reg[t] for the Campain the year 1780 Dec 1780 Cap[t] Eells's C[o]   Copied

Names	Commence of Pay		to what time paid		Towns
Aloan Begilow	July	15	Dec.	9	Hartford
Elias Clark		1		"	Winsor
Solomon Dunham		"		14	Farmington
Lem[l] Fox		15		9	Glasonb[y]
Eben[r] Gates		1		14	Colchest[r]
David Hollister		15		9	Glasenb[y]

18

Names	Commence of Pay	to what time paid		Towns
John Plank	July 15	Dec.	14	
Sam¹ Welch	1		10	
David Canady	"		14	Glasenbʸ
Abner Maten	"		"	
Josiah Brooks	15	Oct.	25	"
Asher Sexton	"	Dec.	10	
Joseph Levenie (?)*	"	Sep.	1	
Ebenʳ Ames	Sep. 1	Dec.	9	

Wᵐ Tryon Sarjᵗ
Ex Sam¹ Richards Lieuᵗ

[*State Library, Revolution 17, 65.*]

*This name crossed out in original document.

SIXTH COMPANY.

Pay Roll of the Short Levies who have served in the 6ᵗʰ Company 3ᵈ Connecᵗ Regᵗ for the Campaign 1780 December 26ᵗʰ 1780 Capᵗ Barnard's Co

Names	Commencᵗ of pay	to what time paid		Town they Belong
Timothy Sedgwick	July 1	Dec.	11	Hartford
Horatio Wales	"		31	"
James Ensign	"		4	"
Wᵐ Hinsdale	"		9	"
Rosel Fox	"		14	Glastenbury
Jacob Augustus	"	Nov.	11	Hartford
Asa Bunce	"	Dec.	9	"
Sam¹ Martin	"	Jan. 1 '81		
Ezra Ramsdil	"			

Ashbil Riley Serjᵗ
Exᵈ Sam¹ Richards P Master

[*State Library, Revolution 17, 66.*]

SEVENTH COMPANY.

Pay Roll of the Leveys in the 7 Compʸ 3ᵈ Connecᵗ Regᵗ in the Service of the United States, Commanded by Colᵒ Sam¹ Wyllys, December 24ᵗʰ 1780   Copied

Names	Comᵉᵗ of Pay	To what Time Payd		Town
John Blackmar	July 1	Dec.	14	Killingly
Abiel Chaffe	"		11	"
Charles Chaffe	"		11	"
Jonathan Congdon	"		11	N. London
Reuben Hamlin	"		10	Farmington
Reuben Harrison	Aug. 1		1	Wethersfield
Sam¹ Short	July 15		5	Killingly
Ezekiel Scott	1		14	Farmington
Lyman Clark	Aug. 20		"	"
Josiah Clark	"		17	"
Sam¹ Starbord	July 1	Nov.	8	Newtown

Thoˢ G. Alvord Serjᵗ
Exᵈ Sam¹ Richards Lieuᵗ

[*State Library, Revolution 17, 69.*]

CAPT. STILWILL'S COMPANY.

Pay Rool of the Short Levies who have serv'd in Capt Stilwills Comp^y Col^o Wyllys's Reg^t for the Campaign 1780 Copied

Names	Comm^t of Pay		To what Time Paid		Towns they Belong to
Lemuel Barrows	July	1	Dec.	12	Killingly
George Robertson	"			8	"
Ebenz^r Tolbert		15		"	"
William Turner		"		"	Gloucenbury
Hezek^h Wadworth		"		12	Hartford
Saml Dealing		"		"	Gloucenbury
Nathan Day		"	Oct.	25	Killingly
Saml Learnard	Aug.	1	Dec^t	9	"
Joseph Levine		"		12	"
John Friswell		15		"	Woodstock
William Chafee		1	Oct.	25	Bolton
Thos Fox		"		26	Gloucenb^y
John Brock, Fifer	July	1	Dec.	12	Woodstock

Camp Highlands Decr 22^d 1780 Elias Stilwill Capt

[*State Library, Revolution 17, 67.*]

Wm Clealand served in Capt Haits Co. 8^d reg. July 6 to Dec. 2, 1780

[*State Library, Revolution 17, 70.*]

FOURTH REGIMENT — COL. DURKEE.

FIRST COMPANY — COL. DURKEE.

Pay Roll of the Short Levy Men in Colᵒ Durkees Compʸ in the 4ᵗʰ Connecticut Regimemt Who have served the Campᵍⁿ '80

Mens Names	Commᵗ of Pay		To what Time Paid		Town they Belong to
Philip Martin	July	7	Dec.	10	Waterbury
Roman Freman		14		15	Windham
David Sampson	"			7	"
Peter Tacomwase		12	Sep.	6	Mohegan De-serted Sep. 6
Joshue Cooper	"		Dec.	10	"
Jacob Cooper	"		"	"	"
Joseph Squib		14		1	"
Cudgo Purkins		13		"	Windham
Jonson Sampson		14		7	"
Amon Fortin		11	Oct.	21	Lebanon
Prince Moredock		13	Dec.	15	Norwich
Pomp Negro		7		7	"
Mark Clark	Aug.	4		10	Seabrook
John Lines	July	12	Oct.	26	Windham
Jubiter Negro		7	Sep.	11	Norwich
Brister Negro		11	Dec.	10	"
Ceasar Negro		7	"	"	"
John George	Aug.	4		1	Mohegan

John Reynolds Serjᵗ

[*State Library, Revolution 17, 39.*]

SECOND COMPANY — LIEUT.-COL. SUMNER.

Pay Roll of the short Levys who have served in Lᵗ Colᵒ Sumners Company 4ᵗʰ Connecticut Regiment for the Campaign 1780

Names	Commᵗ of Pay		what time Paid		Towns to Which belong
Luke Flint	July	5	Oct.	25	Windham
William Hyde		16	Nov.	12	Norich
Elias Upton		1	Dec.	3	Windham
Othnell Luce		10		"	"
John Green		6		"	Norwich
David Canady	Aug.	15		4	Windham
Ezenas Hall	July	16		9	Ashford
Roger Burchard		8		"	Norwich
Ebenʳ Gennings		12		10	Windham
Zackeus Flint		10		"	Pomfret
Levy Dean	Oct.	1		"	Scotland
Jared Burgh	July	16		"	Chesseir
Wᵐ Yarington	Aug.	8		"	Scotland

Names	Comm⁺ of Pay		what time Paid	Towns to Which belong
Elizer Cutler	July	9	Dec. 10	Norwich
Jabez Downs		5	"	"
Echabod Blackman		10	"	Lebinon
Ezekiel Cleary		7	"	"
Asher Merrils	Aug.	15	12	Hebron
Richard Bostick	Sep.	7	"	"
Samˡ Mix	July	4	"	Waterbury
Joshua Ripley	Aug.	15	"	Windham

Joˢ Chapman Captᵗ Lᵗ

[*State Library, Revolution 17, 60.*]

THIRD COMPANY—MAJ. THROOP.

Pay Roll of the short Levys in Major Throops Compʸ 4ᵗʰ Connecticut Regiment who have served for the Campaign 1780

Names	Comm⁺ of Pay		To what time Paid	Towns they belong to
Elijah Chudle	July	1	Oct. 30	Narwich
Danil Buttan		"	31	Windham
Isaac Winter		"	Dec. 3	Pamfritt
Christopher Hall		28	6	Killingly
James Bishop		1	"	Durham
Erastus Warthington		"	10	Colchester
Amos Green		"	"	Killingly
Ebenʳ Sparks		20	"	"
Fraderick Goodell		1	"	Parmfrett
Seth Pope		"	12	Lebanan
Ebenʳ Groo		"	"	Pamfritt
Ebenʳ Brooks		"	13	Chissher
Jeremiah Lockwood	Sep.	15	14	Danbury
Thomas Patten	July	11	"	Narwich (?)
George Harris		1	"	Sey Brook
Aaran Chamberlin	Sep.	15	"	Colchester
David Belding	July	1	"	East Hadam
Sims Edgerton		"	6	Narwich
Nell Whittaker		"	Oct. 22	Killingly
Joseph Ensworth		"	Dec. 12	Woodstock
Aaran Putnam		"	2	Fairfield
Justice Whitlock	Sep.	1	14	
Thomas Perry		"	"	
Curtes Stodard		"	"	
Adanijah Root		"	"	

Lebbeus Loomis Lieuᵗ

[*State Library, Revolution 17, 36.*]

CAPT. PHELPS COMPANY.

Pay Roll of the short Levy Men who have serv'd in the Late Capᵗ Phelps's Company in the 4ᵗʰ Connecticut Regᵗ for the Campaig 1780

Names	Comm⁺ of Pay		What time Paid	Towns
Wᵐ Clark	July	1	Dec. 4	N London
Ezra Loomis	Sep.	1	10	
Solomon Loomis	July	1	"	

Names	Commt of Pay	What time Paid	Towns
Joseph Boyd'	Aug. 21	Dec. 16	
Tho' Simamons	"	10	
Sam' Dart	July 1	3	Bolton
Daniel Dorchester	"	10	"
Sam' Talcut	"	"	"
Sam' Tracy	6	"	Plainfield
Jesse Gilbert	1	4	Windham
Jno Thomas	Aug. 1	14	
Moses Hutchinson	"	Nov. 23	
Jno Keggin	July 10	Dec. 11	Plainfield
Job Philips	"	10	"
Guy Beckwith	1	9	
Eleazer Lewis	10	14	Volunta
Elnathan Stevens	20	11	
Tho' Addis	"	5	
Wm Bishop	"	Oct. 26	
Amos Davis	"	Dec. 14	
David Franklin	"	10	
Amos Gustin	"	"	
Hugh Canady	"	9	
Aaron Buell	"	14	Stratford
Ishum Simons	Aug. 5	10	
Nath' Rogers	July 1	3	Bolton
Luther Gates Drumr	Aug. 1	9	
Benjn Wells Fifer	July 20	14	Bolton
Joseph Loomis	1	Oct. 26	

Highlands 20th Decr 1780   S Holt Lieut

[State Library, Revolution 17, 15.

CAPT. McGRIEGIER'S COMPANY.

Pay Roll of the short levies of Capt McGriegiers Compy 4th Regt

Names	Commet of Service	To what time paid	Towns
John Allin	July 8	Dec. 4	Pomfret
Danll Spencer	"	11	"
John White	"	10	"
Asa Beech	10	"	
Griegory Smith	"	"	
Alexr Miller	12	4	Voluntown
Abel Franklin	13	"	"
Wm McRow	"	"	
Ruben Bryant	14	"	Plainfield
John Lovejoy	15	"	
Jeduthan Hurd	"	"	Plainfield
Charles White	22	10	Durham
Tho' Cooke	"	"	
Juvenal Winter	8	11	Pomfret
Ephraim Witter	Aug. 1	"	
Danll Davisson	"	"	
Joshua Kendall	4	"	Woodstock
Alven Answorth	"	4	"
Asa Lamb	6	10	Groton
Walter Griswold	"	Nov. 6	
Sluman Allin	July 8	Dec. 4	Pomfret
John Robinson	"	Nov. 5	"
Enoch Post	"	3	Norwich

[Arranged with rolls for 1780.]

[State Library, Revolution, 17, 17.]

CAPT. CLIFT'S COMPANY.

Pay Roll of the Short Levies of Capt Clifts Company 4th Conn^t Reg^t

Names	Comme^t of Service 1780		Expiration of Service		Towns
Simeon Robinson	July	14	Dec.	10	Windham
Daniel Ginnings		"		"	"
Thos Rindge		"		16	"
John Walden		12		9	"
Elijah Lilley		"		10	"
Seabury Manning		"		"	"
Garsham Hale		"		"	"
Garsham Hall 2^d		"		"	"
Joseph Waldon		5		9	"
Epaphras Curtis		"		10	"
Asa Benjamins		"		9	Norwich
Stephen Avery		"		"	"
Peter Roath		"		16	"
Amos Wentworth		"		10	"
Benjn Durfee		"		"	Stonington
Hezekiah Clift		"		5	Preston
Rufus Johnson		"		10	Windham
Robert Snow		"		"	Ashford
Enos Robins		"		15	Windham
Caleb Faulkner		14		10	"
Benjn Cary	Aug.	1		"	"
Joseph Rogers		"	Nov.	19	Litchfield
Isaac Rerde (?)		"	Dec.	10	Killingly
Jabez Bottom		15		"	Windham
James Fuller		"		"	Plainfield
Samuel Kimball		"	Oct.	26	Killingly
Stephen Ginnings		"		"	Windham
Elijah Farnom		"		"	"
Thad^s Burdseye (?)	July	16	Dec.	10	Stratford

Camp Decr 28th 1780   William Glenney Ensign

[*State Library, Revolution 17, 23.*]

CAPT. BUELL'S COMPANY.

Pay Roll for the Short Levy Men in Capt Buells Company Light Infintry in the 4th Connecticut Reg^t who have Searved for the Company 1780

Mens Names	Commencement of Pay		to what time paid		Towns they belong to
Danel Allen	July	9	Dec.	14	Waterbury
Anthony Burningham		1		"	Killingly
Isreal Bolch		8		"	Mansfield
Thedeous Burdsey		9		10	Stradford
Eliphelet Coburn		8		4	Norwich
Elijah Cook		"		10	Windham
Belliel Camp		9		14	Waterbury
Bibe Cotton		1		"	Pomfret
Ward Cotton		7		4	"
Semeon Carew		8	[ ]		Norwich
Samuel Hunn		"		10	"
Aseael Hotchkiss		9		14	Waterbury
Samuel Kimball		1		10	"

Mens Names	Commencement of Pay	to what time paid	Towns they belong to
Chester Lillee	July 8	Dec. 2	Windham
Jeremiah Meacham	"	14	"
John Marshel	1	"	Bolten
Jerod Pritcket	9	"	Waterbury
Nethanel Rogers	1	9	Bolten
Pirum Ripley	"	10	Norwich
Joseph Wright	8	12	Lebenon
David Saffard	1	10	Bolten
Samuel Taler	"	14	Pomfrit
James Ball	2	"	Bolten

Andrew Hibbard Serj⁴

[*State Library, Revolution* 17, 28.]

CAPT. FITCH'S COMPANY.

Pay Roll for the Short Levy men in Cap⁴ Fitch⁴ Company in the 4ᵗʰ Connec⁴ Reg⁴ who have served for the Campaign 1780

Mens Names	Commencement of Pay	to what time Paid	Town they belong to
Abel Baker	July 1	Dec. 8	Norwich
Eli Church	15	10	Mansfield
Phineas Corwin	"	14	Norwich
Titus Canfield	"	Nov. 9	Durham
Nathan Coal	"	Dec. 18	"
Wᵐ Johnson Daley	1	5	Pomphret
Clement Fairchild	"	10	Newtown
Zalmon Fairweather	"	31	Stratford
Wᵐ Gardner	15	10	Colchester
George Hall	1	8	Stratford
Asa Harris	10	10	Lebanon
Samˡˡ Hyde	1	14	"
Eli Moffatt	"	5	Killingly
Augustus Post	"	10	Norwich
James Robinson	15	18	Durham
Clement Stoddard	1	10	Norwich
Asa Sawyer	"	8	Waterbury
Dudley Squire	15	5	Durham
Hezʰ Terrell	1	8	Stratford
Marchant Wooster	"	14	"
Thomas Wakeley	"	10	"
Ezra Woodworth	15	17	Lebanon
Ardamus Stevens	1	Oct. 26	Norwich
Ichabod Sparks	Aug. 1	Dec. 10	Killingly

Connecticut Huts Decmʳ 24ᵗʰ 1780   A Fitch Capᵗ

[*State Library, Revolution* 17, 40.]

COL. WEBB'S COMPANY.

Pay Roll of the Short Levy Men who have serv'd in Cap* Webbs Company in the 4th Coonn* Reg* for the Camp^n 1780

Names	Comm* of Service		what time Paid		Towns
Tho* Deane	July	11	Dec.	3	Windham
James Bell	"			"	Norwich
David Wheeler		1		4	Windham
Benjn Woodworth		24		6	Lebanon
Rodger Huntington		11		"	Norwich
Elisha Allin	June	5		"	
Richard Robinson	July	12		9	Windham
Solaman Lord	"			8	"
Darius Bottom	June	11		10	Norwich
John Pengo	July	6		"	"
Joseph Miller		12		"	Windham
Nath^n Kanady	"			"	"
Joseph Marsh	June	5		"	
Timothy Green		4		"	
Henry Waldow		2		"	
Prentice Pengo	July	11		"	Norwich
Charles Waterman	Aug.	28		"	Plainfield
Henry McNeal	July	4		14	Ashford
John Huff		28	Oct.	10	Norwich
Lenard Perkins		11	Dec.	14	Plainfield
Nathl Allin (?)	June	28		10	
And^w Ealy		27		14	

Charles Fanning

[*State Library, Revolution 17, 53.*]

FIFTH REGIMENT — COL. BRADLEY.

FIRST COMPANY — COL. BRADLEY.

Pay Roll of the Levies in Col° Bradleys Company 5th Conn¹ Regiment
Commanded by Philip B Bradley Col°

Names	Commencement of pay 1780	To what Time paid 1780	Towns
Jacob Craw	July 1	Dec. 8	N. Fairfield
John Jinnings	"	9	Summors
Enoch Blackman (?)	"	[ ]	(?) Ripton
Nehemiah Sharwood	"	9	Ridgefield
Samˡˡ Gilbert	"	"	Ripton
Reubin McCraw	"	"	Windsor
John Parker	"	8	Summors
Willᵐ Hamblin	"	13	"
Abraham Holcomb	"	"	Canaan
Nathaniel Root	"	"	"
Joseph Olmsted	"	8	Ridgefield
Elijah Kellogg	"	13	"
Isiah (?) Nash	"	"	"
Reubin Coley	"	9	Summors
Ammon Craw (?)	Aug. 1	8	N. Fairfield

[The remainder of this roll is missing.]

[*State Library, Revolution 17, 54a.*]

SECOND COMPANY — LIEUT.-COL. JOHNSON.

A Pay Roll of the Levies in Lᵗ Col° Johnson's Company in the 5th
Connecticut Regᵗ Commanded by Philip B Bradley Col°

Names	Commencement of Pay	To what Time Paid	Towns
Elijah Blackman	July 1	Dec. 12	Stratford
Mills De Forest	"	14	"
Abel De Forest	"	12	"
Shermⁿ Fairchild	"	9	N. Milford
Andrew Gleson	"	Sep. 9	Torrington
Mead Heard	"	Dec. 9	Stratford
Elijah Heard	"	Oct. 26	"
Amos Holiday	20	Dec. 9	Simsbury
Ezekiel Whitney	1	Oct. 26	Ridgebury
Benajah Hays	20	"	Simsbury
David Osmer	1	Dec. 18	Farmington
John Parker	"	9	Stonington
Petʳ Wilkinson	"	13	N. Milford
Wᵐ Thorn	20	2	Simsbury
Nathⁿ Henman	Aug. 5	18	Stratford
Ephraim Sherwood	"	"	"
Samˡ Ogden	Sep. 1	"	Fairfield
Nathan Fairchild	12	9	Stratford
Samˡ French	July 1	"	"

Samˡ Woodcock Sajᵗ   No offiser present

[Indorsed] 1780

[*State Library, Revolution 17, 49.*]

THIRD COMPANY—MAJ. CHAPMAN.

Pay Roll of the Short Levies in Major Chapmans Company 5ᵗʰ Connᵗ Regᵗ Commᵈ by Philip B. Bradly Col

Names	Commencement of Pay		To what time paid		
Jehiel Burr	July	1	Dec.	9	Toringford
Champhilet (?) Stanliff	"			8	"
Elijah Bissell	"			9	"
Phenious Elmor	"			13	Windsor
Remembrance Sheldin	"			9	"
Fredrick Biggelow	"			"	Toringford
Seelah Woodruff	"			14	
Daniel Clark	"			9	Windsor
John Whiten	"			13	"
Gilbert Hart	"		Oct.	27	
Benjᵐ Gaylor	"		Dec.	3	Goshan
Robert Fields	"			9	Symsbury
Samuel Lamson	"			16	"
Brigador Lowmas	"			31	Toringford
Shedrick Bostwick	Aug.	1		3	N Milford
Andrew Canfield	"			9	"
Joel Ingersole	July	1		19	"
Ephram Turrel	Sep.	1		3	Fairfield
Joseph Hazie (?)	"			13	"
Elijah Mills	"			"	Windsor
Jonathan Strong	"			9	Toringford
Jonethan Demmon	"			13	Fairfield
Ezra Brown	July	1		"	Windsor
Joel Cook	"			9	"
Elijah Kelcy	"			3	Torringford

D Beach Ensⁿ

[Indorsed] Pay Roll of Major Chapmans Company 5ᵗʰ Connecᵗ Regiment 1780

[*State Library, Revolution 17, 20.*]

CAPT. WRIGHTS' COMPANY.

Pay Roll of the Short Levies in Capᵗ J A Wrights Company 5ᵗʰ Conn Regiment Commanded by Phillip B. Bradley Colᵒ

Names	Commencement of Pay 1780		To what time paid 1780		Towns
Peleg Brown	July	1	Dec.	13	Groatton
Asa Chapen	"			"	Summers
John Corkins	"			9	"
Daniel Cheney	July	24		"	Pomfret
Jobe Davis	July	1		13	Summers
Thomas Green	"			"	Harington
Timothy Harrington	"			9	Stafford
Samˡˡ Hodgkis	"			13	Litchfield
Isriel Treman (?)	"			3	Summers
Benjⁿ Orcott	"			9	"
Derias Orton	"			13	Litchfield
Sollomon Parsons	"			9	Summers
Jeremiah Phillips	"			"	"

Names	Commencement of Pay 1780	To what time paid 1780	Towns
Ellee Pratt	July 1	Dec. 9	Summers
Reuben Perry	"	3	"
James Redfield	"	"	Middletown
Clement Tuttel	24	9	Toringford
Asa Wood	1	13	Summers
Isaac Buck	"	Oct. 27	"

J Willcox Lieu[t]

[*State Library, Revolution,* 17, 7.]

CAPT. HAIT'S COMPANY.

Pay Roll of the Leavies in Cap[t] Samuel Haits Company 5th Connec[t] Reg[t] Commanded by Col[o] Philip B. Bradley

Names	Commencement of Pay 1780	To what time paid	Towns
Elisha Andras	July 1	Dec. 2	Simsbury
William Andras	"	9	"
Richard Andras	"	2	"
Roswell Case	"	13	"
Abiel Cook	"	"	N Fairfield
David Goowin	"	14	Simsbury
William Graham	"	2	"
Dudley Miller	"	13	"
Phineas Palmer	"	9	Stonington
Thomas Palmer	"	"	Voluntown
Jonas Randall	"	2	"
Richard Edgerton	"	9	Simsbury
Joseph Hawley	"	"	Ridgefield
John Gilbert	"	31	"
Samuel Bradley	"	13	"
Prince Walley	"	9	Danbury
David Sturgis	"	13	"
Chanley Judd	"	31	Waterbury
Clemmans Handy	"	Oct. 28	Windsor
Jehial Winchel	"	Nov. 5	Simsbury Deserted

Thadd[s] Keeler Lieu[t]

[*State Library, Revolution* 17, 31.]

CAPT. ST. JOHN'S COMPANY.

A Pay Roll of the Levies in Capt[t] John S[t] Johns Company in the 5th Connecticut Reg[t] Commanded by Philip B. Bradley Col[o]

Names	Commencement of Pay 1780	To What Time Paid	Towns
Sam[l] Baldwin	July 1	Dec. 13	Cornwell
Bruen Beach	"	"	Goshen
Elihu Barnerd	"	"	Simsbury
Rich[d] Bangs	10	"	Stratford
Judah Case	"	4	Simsbury
Caleb Case	"	13	"
Rulif Coon	"	17	N Milford
Domini Douglas	1	27	"
Sam[l] Kellog	"	4	Goshen

Names	Commencement of Pay 1780		To What Time Paid		Towns
Hicol^d Hitchcock	July	19	Dec.	13	Stratford
Nehem^h Olmstead		1		9	Ridgefield
Math^w Olmstead		16		"	"
Willm Cummins		"		4	"
Willm Elton		1		"	Farmington
Abner Guilbert		"		9	Litchfield
Joseph Osborn		"		13	Ridgefield
Buel Sacket		"		9	Litchfield
Saml Stebins		19		2	Ridgefield
Timothy Ray		1		9	Torrinton
John Weeler		16		2	Stratford
Southmit Guernsey		1		9	Waterbury

H. Rogers Leiut

[*State Library, Revolution 17, 38.*]

CAPT. MORRIS' COMPANY.

Pay Roll of the Short Levys that Belonged to Capt James Morris's Company 5th Connec^t Reg^t Commanded by Col^o Philip B Bradley

Names	Commencement of Pay		To What time paid		Town
Moses Allin	July	1	Dec.	16	Windsor
Josiah Apley		"		25	Torrington
Daniel Bogue		"		9	Windsor
Ezekiel Buck		"		"	N Millford
Reuben Barber		"		13	Windsor
John Culver		"		16	
Oliver Coller		"		2	Hartford
Lory Drake		"		9	Windsor
Martin Dill		"	Oct.	25	Goshen
James Eno		"	Dec.	13	Windsor
Eliakim Gaylord		"		2	"
Belah Hills		19		16	Torrington
Luther Lawrance		"		9	Norfolk
John Hall		1		"	Suffield
Philander Moore		"	Oct.	25	Windsor
Asa Moore		"	Dec.	16	"
Peleg Sweet		19		"	Torrington
Willm Stanard		1		2	"
Jonathan Walling		"		16	Hartford
Isaac Wardwell		"		2	Windsor
Christopher Whitbrite (?)		"		13	Middletown

No Officer Present Grove Rockwell Serj^t

[Indorsed] Pay Roll of the Short Levys in Capt Morrisses Company 1780

[*State Library, Revolution 17, 42.*]

CAPT. WARD'S COMPANY.

A Pay Roll of the Levies in Capt Thaddeus Weeds Company 5th Connecticut Regiment Commanded by Col^o Philip B Bradley Decr 31st 1780

Names	Commencement of Service		Expiration of Service		Towns to which they Belong
John Austen	July	1	Nov.	22	Simsbury
Achilles Comstock		"	Dec.	2	New Milford
Abel Collins		"		"	Southington

Names	Commencement of Service	Expiration of Service		Towns to which they Belong
Andrew Calahan	July 1	Dec.	13	Simsbury
Ithimar Colton	"		2	"
Eliakim Colton	"		9	"
Daniel Hillyer	"		13	"
Samuel Ives	"		9	Farmington
Alexander Phelps	"		2	Simsbury
Beebe Pangburn	"		9	Cornwell
Joseph Rockwell	"		26	Colbrook
John Russell	"	Aug.	14	Windsor
Arial Strong	"	Dec.	9	Norfolk
Ashbel Tillison	"		13	Farmington
Elias Tillison	"		"	Simsbury
Voluntine Whitman	"	Aug.	19	Farmington
Jesse Wilcocks	"	Dec.	13	"
Daniel Johnson	"	Aug.	1	
Williston Hurd	Aug. 20	Dec.	2	Stratford
Seth Tolcott	July 1		"	Hartford
John Fyler	Aug. 25		13	Torrington
Edward Pellom	July 5		9	Coventry

Corn⁹ Russel Lieut

[*State Library, Revolution 17, 51.*]

CAPT. CHAPMAN'S COMPANY.

Pay Roll of the Leavies in Cap⁹ Chapmans Company 5ᵗʰ Conn⁹ Reg⁹ Commanded by Phillip B. Bradley Colᵒ

Names	Commencement of Pay 1780	To What time Paid 1780		Towns
Thomas Buck	July 1	Dec.	2	Summers
Thamer Bingham	"		4	Goshen
Isaas Benham	"		8	Torrington
Rice Beach	"		"	Goshan
Jonathan Bostwick	"		13	N. Milford
Ebenezar Chubbuck	"		"	Tolland
Orcemus Brunson	"	Oct.	1	N. Milford
Gideon Dunham	"		31	Canaan
Jonathan Emmonds	"	Dec.	16	
Luther Gleason	"		14	Torrington
Ury Hill	"		8	Goshan
Asa How	"		"	Torrington
Timothy Hummaston	"		16	Northbury
Daniel Johnson	"		1	N. Milford
Edward Knapp	24	Sep.	14	Simsbury
Brainard Linsley	1	Dec.	13	Woodbury
Charles Millard	"		"	Cornwall
Ezekel Moses	24		"	Simsbury
Theodore Manross	1		2	Farmington
Charles Pease	"		8	Summers
Daniel Palmer	"		"	Stonington
John Russell	Aug. 14		2	Windsor
Sanford Richardson	July 1		8	Summers
Abner Squires	"		2	Tolland
Elijah Towner	"		8	Goshan
Walliston Hurd	"	Aug.	20	Stanford

D Bradley Lieut

[*State Library, Revolution 17, 55.*]

SEVENTH REGIMENT—COL. SWIFT.

FIRST COMPANY—COL. SWIFT.

Pay Roll of the short levies that have served in Colᵒ Swifts Compʸ 7 Conn Regᵗ

Mens Names	Towns to which they belong	Commencement of Pay		Discharged	
Elephaz Jerrum Priv.	Farmington	July	10	Oct.	10
" Drmr	"	Oct.	18	Dec.	7
James Bonnum	New Hartford	July	1		18
Jason Cruttenden	Southernton	"			7
Giles Curtiss	Canaan	"			3
Samuel Dean	Cornwell	June	24		"
Horriss Day	Southernton	"			13
Otis Ensign	N Hartford	"			16
Elijah Gaylord	"	"			7
Caleb Hall	Wallingford	July	10		10
Noah Higby	Canaan	"			7
Ezra Jones	"	June	26		"
John Marsh	N Hartford		24		18
Roswell Marsh	"		"		25
Samuel Moss	Wallingford	July	10	Oct.	31
Jeremiah Osborn	N Haven		1	Dec.	8
David Plum	Stratford	June	28		7
Stephen Parker	Cheshire		24		18
Ebenezer Pardy	Canaan	July	1		3
Luke Roberts	Danbury	"			"
David Sanford	Canaan	"			"
Jonathan Thomson	Norwalk	"			"
Lemuel White	N Hartford	June	24		7
Daniel Wallen	"	"			8

A Hall Sergᵗ No officer Present

[*State Library, Revolution 17, 2.*]

SECOND COMPANY.

LIEUT.-COL. HOLDRIDGE.

Pay Roll of the Short Levies in Lᵗ Colᵒ Holdridges Comyʸ 7ᵗʰ Connecticut Regᵗ Commanded By Heman Swift Colᵒ in the Service of the United States For 1780

Mens Names	Commencement of Pay		Ditcharged	Town to which they Belong
Benjamin Fairchild Fifer	July	1	Dec. 5	Stratford
John Ayres	"		18	Reding
Asa Benjamin	"		5	Stratford
Silas Berto	"		15	Reding
Gershum Beers	"		3	"
John Bordslee	"		18	Stratford
Elnathan Beech	Aug.	18	9	Cornwall
Hezekiah Berdslee	July	1	18	Stratford

Mens Names	Commencement of Pay	Ditcharged	Town to which they Belong
Dennis Burnett	Aug. 1	Dec. 3	Groton
William Chedsey	"	9	"
Phineas Gorham	July 1	15	Reding
Nathaniel Geers	24	12	Kent
Henery Ingraham	"	5	"
Solomon Johnson	Aug. 18	9	Cornwall
Lemuel Malery	July 1	Nov. 19	Stratford
Daniel Kine	"	Dec. 3	"
Noah Smith	24	19	Kent
Noah Spencer	1	3	N Hartford
Hoyt Scofield	"	9	Stratford
Abraham Thompson	"	— 17	"
Obediah Taylor	"	3	N Hartford
Levi Watson	"	9	"
John Wells	"	Oct. 31	Stratford
Jesse Morgin	Aug. 1	Dec. 3	Groton
Thomas Bidwell	20	5	Glasten[ ]
John Barnes	"	3	Wethersfield
Ephraim Bidwell	"	"	Glastenbury
Innitt (?) Holister	25	15	"
Robert Holdredge	July 1	Oct. 31	Hebron
Norman Phelps	Aug. 22	Dec. 27	"
William Wetherill	25	9	Wethersfield

John Phinney Serj^t No Officer Present

[*State Library, Revolution 17, 11.*]

THIRD COMPANY—MAJ. WOODBRIDGE.

Pay Roll of the Short Levies in Major Woodbridge's Comp^y In the 7th Conn^t Regiment Commanded by Col^o Swift Decr 31st 80

Names	Commen^t of Service	Expra^n of Service	Towns to which They Belong
Levi Arnold	June 25	Dec. 13	Haddam
Benj^a Butlor	July 10	9	Canaan
Zacheus Cande	June 24	"	"
Saml Dennison	22	"	Saybrook
Nehemiah Dickerson	26	3	Haddam
Saml Fox	July 1	27	
Minor Hellard	June 22	Oct. 31	Saybrook
James Thetsey	"	Dec. 3	"
Saml King	26	17	Haddam
Frances Lewis	"	13	"
Oliver Mead	Aug. 4	3	N. Milford
Abner Porter	June 25	7	Haddam
Jno Pratt	"	27	Saybrook
Job Stannard	22	7	"
Joseph Schovel	26	"	Haddam
Philip Smith	"	13	Saybrook
Jonathan Smith	25	"	Haddam
James Sellick	July 1	3	Danbury
Jesse Spencer	June 26	4	N. Hartford
Randolph Shaddee	July 7	27	
David Tiley	June 26	9	Saybrook
Ruben Tylor	July 28	4	Wallingford

J Willcox Lieu^t

[*State Library, Revolution 17, 9.*]

CAPT. CHAMBERLAIN'S COMPANY.

Pay Roll of the Short Levies that have Served in Captain Chamberlains Company 7th Connt Regt the present year, Decr 31st 1780

Mens Names	Commencement of Pay	To What Time Paid	Towns to which They Belong
Zachariah Doud	June 26	Dec. 13	Guilford
	"	3	"
Ira Adkins		"	
Benajah Tracy	July 7	"	Preston
Daniel Collins	June 26	"	Guilford
	"	"	"
Nathll Cramton		"	
Bradoe Stedmon	July 7	"	Preston
Elijah Stanard	June 28	"	Guilford
James Welman	July 29	"	Killingsworth
Ezra Bishop	June 26	13	Guilford
	"	"	"
Leonard Bishop		"	
Abel Parker	July 7	"	Preston
	"	"	"
Elisha Tracy			
Henry Bevins	June 26	9	Guilford
	"	"	"
Stephen Stone	"	"	"
Poffe Niger		"	
Clear Lewis	July 7	"	Wallingford
Titus Frances	June 30	"	"
James Fitch	9	13	Kent
James Hart	26	17	Guilford
John Wheeler	"	27	

James Bennit Lieut

[*State Library, Revolution 17, 5.*]

CAPT. CONVERSE'S COMPANY.

Pay Roll of the Short levies in Capt Converses Compy 7th Connect Regt in the Service of the United States Commanded by Colo Swift 1780

Mens Names	Commencement of pay	To what time paid	Towns to which they belong
Benjn Allyn	Sep. 1	Dec. 13	Fairfield
George Buckingham	July 1	17	Seabrook
Daniel Baily	"	9	"
John B. Juddson	"	"	Stratford
Isaac Butler	"	3	Norfolk
Joseph Batterson	Sep. 2	13	Fairfield
Abijah Batterson	Aug. 22	9	"
Ichabud Chapin	June 26	13	Goshen
Oliver Cone	July 1	9	Seabrook
Samll Downs	Aug. 22	25	Fairfield
Jehiel Hull	July 1	13	Norfolk
Justice Hail	June 26	"	Goshen
Samll Hase	July 1	3	Danbury
William Leach	"	9	Norfolk
Elisha Mayo	June 26	"	Goshen
John Miner	July 1	3	Norfolk
John Norton	June 26	13	Goshen
Daniel Piquet	"	9	"
Thaddeus Potter	"	"	"
James Sturdivent	July 1	3	Norfolk
Elisha Stoddard	June 28	9	Groton
Silas Seward	July 1	13	Norfolk

14

Mens Names	Commencement of pay	To what time paid	Towns to which they belong
Sam^{ll} Taylor	July 1	Dec. 13	Norfolk
Bates Turner	"	"	"
Amos Wood	"	"	Seabrook
Moses Wilcocks	June 26	9	Goshen
Abraham Bardin	July 1	Oct. 31	Norfolk
	Thos Converse Capt		

[*State Library, Revolution 17, 6.*]

CAPT. BILLING'S COMPANY.

Pay Roll of the Short Levies in Captⁿ Billing Company 7th Connecticut Regiment Commanded by Col^o Swift Dec^r-31st 1780

Names	Commencement of Service	Dates of Discharges	Towns to which They Belong
Edward Austen	June 29	Dec. 13	Preston
Daniel Braymon	July 1	"	Norwich
Frances Danity (?)	June 29	9	Preston
James Tylor	"	13	"
Joseph Lane	"	9	"
Joseph Guile	"	13	"
Josiah Bourougs (?)	July 10	8	Stratford
Jared Baldwin	"	10	N Milford
John Morehouse	"	17	N Fairfield
John Gregory	Sep. 2	8	N Milford
Joel Hurlbert	Aug. 20	9	Woodbury
Nathan^l Prentice	July 15	18	Preston
Neel McNeel	1	14	Stratford
Noah Bartrum	10	9	Reding
Gilbert Tracy	June 29	17	Preston
Thos Grant	"	13	"
Aaron Taylor	July 8	9	N London
Samuel Couch	Aug. 1	"	N Milford
Isaac Goodsell	July 15	"	Washington
Truman Beeman	10	13	Kent
Prentice Gallop	June 28	16	Groton
William Ward	July 10	9	Stratford
Rubin Jones	June 29	17	Preston
Steph^h Tylor	"	13	"
James Hubbert	July 10	9	Stratford
	C McDonald Serj^t	No officer present	

[*State Library, Revolution 17, 14.*]

CAPT. HALL'S COMPANY.

Pay Roll of the Short Levies in Capt Halls Company 7th Connecticut Reg^t Commanded By Col^o Swift Decr 31th 1780

Mens.Names	Commencement of Service	To what time Paid	Towns to which they Belong
James Brooks	July 1	Dec. 9	Haddam
[ ]	[ ]	[ ]	[ ]
Luis (?) Burton	5	"	Stratford
Hezekiah Clark	"	25	Haddam
Lemuel Chatfield	9	3	Stratford
Elihu Crane	5	"	Durham
Jedediah Coe	4	13	Gilford

Mens Names	Commencement of Service		To what time Paid	Towns to which they Belong
Asa Cogswell	July	7	Dec. 8	Canaan
Rosel Grant	"		9	Norfolk
William Hawley		5	"	Stratford
Asa Hide		7	18	Canaan
Luther Killum		5	"	Presson
John Lane		1	"	Killingsworth
Chileab Palmer		10	"	N Milford
James Parmerly	"		"	Gilford
Joshua Root		7	"	Canaan
Nathan Rix		5	9	Presson
William Stevens		1	"	Killingsworth
Ebenezer Scovill		7	18	Winchester
Sutliff Seward		5	"	Durham
Abel Tharp	"		8	Wallingford
Caleb Turner		1	"	Killingsworth
George White		7	"	Canaan

Solomon Pinto Ens[n]

[*State Library, Revolution 17, 22.*]

CAPT. BALDWIN'S COMPANY.

Pay Roll of the Short Levies who have Serv'd in Cap[t] Baldwin's Comp[y] 7th Cone[t] Reg[t]

Mens Names 31st Dec[r] 1780	Commencement of Pay		To what time Paid		Town to which they belong
John Buel	June	27	Dec.	8	Killingsworth
Joseph Bishop	July	1		9	Canaan
Zopher Betts		18		8	Sharon
Gideon Buel		10		"	Killingsworth
Joseph Buel		"		14	"
Peter Blacke	June	26		13	Haddam
Oliver Clark		27		"	"
Cornelius Dunham		28		16	Canaan
Benj[n] Dibble		20		4	Cornwall
Richard Ellot		27		8	Killingsworth
Francis Griswould		26		"	"
Peter Wines	July	6		9	Kent
Robert Newel	June	28	Oct.	27	Killingsworth
Samuel Merrit (?)		27	Dec.	8	"
Levi Osborn	July	1		9	Danbury
Ezra Porter	June	27		27	Killingsworth
Benjamin Peck (?)	July	1		9	Danbury
Jared Rice		20		"	Moodus
Luke Stevens	June	27		27	Killingsworth
Peter Spencer		21		9	Haddam
Jonah Sutlief		27		8	"
Reuben Wright		29		"	Killingsworth
Joab Wright		26		18	"
Nathan Wright		27		9	"
Eleazer Warner		"		18	"
Zebulon Thomson		29		27	"
James Spencer		28		9	Haddam
Rufus Thrall	July	1		"	Norfolk
Giles Thrall		25		"	"

Eben[r] Daggett Ens[n]

[*State Library, Revolution 17, 24.*]

CAPT. STEEVENS' COMPANY.

Pay Roll of the Short Leves Who have served in Capt Steevens Company 7th Connecticut Reg^t Decr 31st 1780

Mens Names	Commencement of Pay	Discharged	Towns to Which They Belong
Anthony Florous drum^r	1 Aug.	9 Dec. 80	Stoningtown
David Chapman priv.	10 July	3	Coalchester
Samuel Cruttondon	27 June	"	Killingworth
Joel Willcóx	"	"	"
Moses Stoddard	1 Aug.	9	Groton
Joseph Lane	27 June	"	Killingworth
Joseph Furbs	"	"	Haddam
Ezra Crane	"	"	Killingworth
Elias Redfield	"	"	"
Elisha White	"	"	"
John Willcox	"	13	Haddam
Abner Graves	10 July	"	Killingworth
Willm Loveridge	"	"	Coalchester
Thomas French	27 June	"	Guilford
Nathan Pierson	10 July	17	Killingworth
Joel Evats	27 June	"	"
Silas Parmele	"	25	"
Jonathan Chatfield	10 July	31 Oct.	"
John Widger	"	20 Nov.	Saybrook

Nathaniel Crane Serj^t No officer Present

[*State Library, Revolution 17.*]

EIGHTH REGIMENT — LIEUT.-COL. COM. SHERMAN.

FIRST COMPANY — LIEUT.-COL. COM. SHERMAN.

Pay Roll for the short Levies Colonel Sherman's Company 8th Connecticut R[   ]

Names	Comment of Service	Expiration of Service	Towns they belong to
John Adams	July 24	Dec. 12	Canterbury
David Craft	"	Nov. 4	Woodstock
Phinias Cole	"	Dec. 12	Woodbury
Benjamin Durfee	"	3	Canterbury
Asahel Herrick	"	9	"
Jared Hotchkiss	"	81	
Zenas Goodrich	June 7	Oct. 11	Farmington
Amaziah Ingram	10	Dec. 5	Sharon
Jerod Mott	7	12	Woodstock
Phinias Palmer	28	"	Woodbury
Uriah Page	10	Oct. 25	Branford
Peter Stephens	13	Dec. 9	Canterbury
Charles Woodard	8	"	"
John Benjamens	Aug. 16	12	Saybrook
Israil Douglass	"	Nov. 13	"
Calvin Webb	26	Dec. 12	"
Felix Griswould	"	Oct. 25	Winchester
Roswell Catlin	"	Dec. 9	"
Peter Corbion	"	3	"
Daniel Wright	Sep. 7	9	
Joseph Frizbie	3	Oct. 29	Branford
Ceasor Negro	"	Dec. 13	"
John Wright	July 10	"	Chatham
Joel Clark	"	Sep. 7	Southington

I. Sherman Lt Col Comd

[Indorsed] Pay roll of the short Levies Col Shermans Company 8th Reg^t Decr 22^d 1780

[*State Library, Revolution 17, 54.*]

CAPT. HODGE'S COMPANY.

Pay Roll for the Short Levies in Capt Hodges Company 8th Connecti-cut Regiment

Names	Commencement of Service 1780		Expiration of Service 1780		Towns they belong to
Luther Baldwin	July	17	Dec.	8	Colchester
David Cable		6		12	Fairfield
Samuel Cole		1		8	Farmington
David Culver	"			10	Colchester
Parson Crosby		17	Oct.	26	
Asa Hyde	"		Dec.	8	Woodstock
Oliver Kellogg		16		"	Colchester
Joseph Lyon		6		14	Fairfield
Moses Parsons	June	27		16	Farmington
Aden Palmer	July	16		10	Stonington
Nathan Roberts	"			8	Colchester
Timothy Smith		1		"	Farmington
Ebenezer Seely	Sep.	6		12	Fairfield
Simeon Stoddard		14		11	Woodbury
Reuben Taylor	July	16		10	Colchester
Peter Tharp		6		8	Fairfield
Amos Wells		16		10	Colchester
Nathan Wheeler	Sep.	6		6	Woodbury
Nath^{ll} Pritchard	"			5	"

Camp Highlands Decr 25th 1780 I Sherman Lt Col Comd

[*State Library, Revolution 17, 21*]

CAPT. MONSON'S COMPANY.

Pay Roll for the Short Levies in Capt Monsons Company 8th Conecti-cut Reg^t

Names	Commencement of Service 1778		Expiration of Service 1780		Town they belong to
Fradrick Avery	July	4	Dec.	8	Groton
David Avery	"			12	"
Asa Boudish		6		8	Norwich
Zalmon Burrit		4		4	Newtown
John Bedient		6		9	Fairfield
Christopher Bailey		1		12	Haddam
Benjamin Chapman		6		8	Stratford
Jese Cook		7		12	Coventry
William Ellis	"			8	Milford
Williaam Huston		4		8	Vollontown
Nathanel Jeffer					Groton
Joseph Liman		6		8	Coventry
Solomon Lommis	"			12	Tollon
Joseph Mitchel		10		"	Fairfield
William Rose		7		9	Canaan
Enock Sherman	"			12	Stratford
George Woodburn		5		8	Stonington
Selah Stanley					

John Hobart Lieut

[*State Library, Revolution 17, 32.*]

CAPT. COMSTOCK'S COMPANY,

Pay Roll for the Short Levies in Capt Comstock's Company 8th Connecticut Regiment

Names	Commencement of Service 1780		Expiration of Service 1780		Towns they belong to
George Bissel	July	8	Dec.	12	
Eliphalet Carpenter	"			17	Coventry
Isaac Hail		22		12	
Jedediah Harger		26		5	
Moses Kelley		1		9	Norwalk
Stephen Hait		10		25	"
Henry Hewit		20		12	Stoningtown
Parley Herwington		15		10	
Samuel Warren		22		9	
David Sullid		15		10	
Samuel Mallery		25		12	
Joel Sanford		"		3	
George Griffin		22		12	
Eldad Barbermore	Aug.	1		3	
Ruben Hill		5		11	
Dudley Stone		1	Sep.	18	
Abraham Bayley		3	Dec.	11	
Edward Babbit	July	27		12	
William Hough	Aug.	1		13	
Ebenezer Tatchen	Sep.	1		"	

Sam^{ll} Chmstock Capt

[*State Library, Revolution 17, 33.*]

CAPT. BENTON'S COMPANY.

Pay Roll for the Short Levies in Capt Bentons Comp^y eighth Connec^t Reg^t Com'd^d by L^t C Comd^t Sherman

Names	Comment^t of service 1780		Expiration of service 1780		Towns they belong to
Sam^{ll} Atkins	Aug	1.	Dec.	5	Farmington
Thom^s Brown	July	20		12	Chatham
Isaac Bristol		13		9	Litchfield
Elijah Bill		"		12	"
Wm Bartholomew		19		10	Lyme
Elijah Bartholomew		"		12	Hebron
Zachar^h Coe		13		"	Litchfield
Cesar Cady		17		9	Killingly
Elaphaz Kilborn		19		10	Colchester
Humphrey Palmer		"		5	"
James Redfield		"		"	Seabrook
Miles Wright		"	Oct.	25	Colchester
Joseph Stannard		"	Dec.	5	Seabrook
Thos Smith		"		31	Groton
Athin (?) Waters		"		9	Lyme
Asa Canada		1		12	Farmington
Daniel Chittenden		"	Oct.	25	Guilford
Seth Strickland		"	Dec.	8	Middletown
Hez^h Post		6		"	Seabrook
Joshua Osborn		22		12	Waterbury
Shubal Painter	Sep.	1		9	Newhaven
Asahel Ives		11		12	Woodbury
David Martin		"		9	"

James Olmsted Lieu^t

[*State Library, Revolution 17, 35.*]

CAPT. BRIGHAM'S COMPANY.

Pay Roll of the Short Levies in Capt Brighams Comp^y 8th Cone^t Reg^t Com^d by I Sherman Lt Col^o Comd^t

Names	Commencement of Service 1780		Expiration of Service 1780	Place of Aboad.
Asahel Woodworth	July	18	Dec. 12	Lebanon
Saml Whitney		"	"	Killingworth
Edward Spergar (?)		24	5	Groaten
Elisha Thorington		18	9	E. Haddam
Willm Spencer		"	16	"
Abraham Buckley	Sep.	1	9	Seybrook
James Brown	July	24	"	Ashford
Joseph Buird (?)		28	8	Farmington
Joseph Collins	Aug.	11	12	Derbey
Gideon Jackson		"	"	"
Daniel Dorman	July	5	9	Coventry
Wm Lucas		4	8	Middletown
Roswell Mallison		8	5	Groton
Nicholas Morgan		8	11	"
James Parker		5	12	Coventry
Chester Rogers		24	9	Ashford
George Sealy		"	"	Groton
Asehel Hull		18	5	Glastenbury
Seth Lovel	Aug.	12	16	Mansfield
Gideon Tucker	Sep.	1	9	Seybrook
John Bartoo		12	8	Farmington
Chatham Freeman		"	12	N. Haven
Joseph Goff	June	10	81	Litchfield
Jesse Torry, Fifer	July	18	9	Lebanon

Nathl Thornton Serj^t

[*State Library, Revolution 17, 43.*]

CAPT. SANFORD'S COMPANY.

Pay Roll of the Short Levies of Capt Sanfords Comp^y 8th Cone^t Reg^t com^d by I Sherman Lt Col Comd^t

Names	Commencement Ser^e 1780		Expiration of Service 1780	Place of Aboad
Dan Beaumont	July	20	Dec. 8	Lebanon
Elijah Battis		26	10	N. Haven
Richard Booge		15	Nov. 1	E. Haddam
Saml Blaksley	Sep.	12	Dec. 5	Southington
Stephen Chapel	June	27	9	Coventry
Oliver Churchel	July	26	"	Woodbury
Daniel Grover	June	27	8	Coventry
Saml Green	July	27	"	Milford
Ebenez^r Humberfield		26	11	N. Haven
Ichabod Peeva (?)	June	24	16	Voluntown
Comfot Robinson	July	19	5	Killensly
Jason Robinson		"	10	"
James Salley		15	81	E. Haddam
Jonathan Stone		19	5	Killensley
Moses Scofield		17	12	Lebanon
David Sanford		27	5	Milford
John Wottson		15	9	E. Haddam
Jonathan Willey		"	16	"

Saml Hait Ens^n

[*State Library, Revolution 17, 46.*]

CAPT. RICE'S COMPANY.

Return of the Short Levies in Capt Rices Company in the 8th Connt Reg⁺ Dec⁺ 22ᵈ 1780

Names	Commencement of Service 1780		Expiration of Service 1780		Towns
Job Bester	July	8	Dec.	16	Cantibury
Jonah Bishop	Sep.	11		11	N. Haven
Isaac Coopper	July	7		12	"
Christopher Crandel	Sep.	15		"	Plainfield
James Freeman	July	2		5	Grotton
Nathael Gates		17		9	E. Haddam
Elijah Harger		10		"	Hartland
Asahel Harvey		17		12	E. Haddam
Crippen Hurd		"		8	"
Joseph Jackson		10		5	Windham
Samˡⁱ Leavens		16		9	Killingly
Timothy Leek		28		16	N. Haven
John Lord		17		12	E. Haddam
Calvin Mallery		28		"	N. Haven
Ira Manvill		"		8	Woodbury
Philep Nickels		15	Nov.	10	Ashford
Burdan Potter		8	Dec.	9	Vollingtown
Daniel Purkens		23		"	Mansfield
Ezra Sumner		18		8	Ashford
Isaac Town		16	Oct.	25	Killingsly
Wᵐ Tyler		14	Dec.	9	Thomson

David Dixson Serj⁺

RETURNS FROM MILITIA, 1780.

FIRST REGIMENT.

Col Storrs's Return of Recruits for ye Amarican Army July 20, 1780 To Brigadr Genll J. Douglas Esqr of ye 5th Brigade of Militia in the State of Connecticut. The following is a Return of Names of the Recruits for the Continental Service Inlisted or Detachd & from what Town & Compy & how Conveyd or Sent forward to the Army from the first Regt in Said Brigade.

Mens Names	Of what Town	with whome sent
David Carpenter	Mansfield	Sent forward
Daniel Preston Jun	"	Capt Shumway
Ebenr Cary	"	at Home unwell
Levy Dow	Coventry	Sent on
Timo Rose	"	not Joind
John Gove	"	Sent on
Asa Manly	"	not Joind
Elisha Rodgers	Ashford	Capt Shumway
Amos Dowset	"	"
Lawrance Dowset	"	"
Asa Mason	Mansfield	"
Joseph Limon	Coventry	Sent on pr Col Brown
Lemll Parke	"	"
Samll Porter	"	"
Noah Carpenter	"	"
Elisha Dunham	Mansfield	by Capt Shumway
Nathan Parker	"	"
Samll Millington	"	"
Moses Bicknal	"	Sent on
James Brown	Ashford	
David Allen		
Thomas Wing	Ashford	
Peter Aspenwall	Mansfield	Sent on
Israel Balch Jun	"	
Benjn Bugbe	"	Capt Webb
Jonathan Basset	"	Capt Shumway
Ely Church	"	
Richd Crosbey	"	Capt Shumway
Robart Hammon	"	"
Walter Cory	"	"
Elijah Porter	"	"
Daniel Preston	"	"
Rhodolfus Howkins	Coventry	Sent on pr Col Brown
Asa Boodish	"	"
Peter Dun	"	"
Edward Pelham	"	"
Fredk Woodward	"	"
Danll Dorman	"	"
Caleb Hende	Ashford	Capt Shumway
Wm Southworth	"	"
James Chandler	"	"
Simeon Snow	"	"
Elisha Royce	"	"

Mens Names	Of what Town	with whome sent
Samuel Utley	Ashford	Cap* Shumway
John Goold	"	"
Moses Fitts	"	"
Benj* Barna	"	"
Jedad** Ward	"	"
Chester Rogers		
Jesse Cook	Coventry	p* Col Brown
Joseph Waldo	"	"
Joel Fowler	"	"
Elihue Benton	"	"
George Bissel	"	"
James Parker	"	"
Dan** Grover	"	"
Jeduthan Dimok	Mansfield	Cap* Shumway
Varney Fellows	"	"
Jesse Waldo Jr	"	"
Jerem* Hedges	"	"
Amasa Royce	"	
John Bugbe	"	Sent on
Benj* Peirce	"	Cap* Shumway
Phillip Nichols	Ashford	"
Elisha Royce	"	
Steaph* Eaton	"	"
Joshua Rindel	"	"
Robart Snow Jr	"	"
Joseph Tarbox		
Dan** B. Perkins	Mansfield	Cap* Shumway
Eleaz* Barrows	"	"
Joel Davis	"	
Asa Bowdish	"	Joined
Jonathan Baker	"	Cap* Shumway
W* Eaton	"	"
Th* Atwood	"	"
Ethan Barrows	"	"
Nath** Conant	"	"
Nath** Fenton	"	"
Augustus Storrs	"	"
Amos Thomson	"	"
Jobe Robbens	Ashford	
Sam** Bass	"	
John Hill		Join*

To the Hon*** Brigad* Gen** Douglas Esq* The within & foregoing Return is made in Consequence of your Orders of the 20** July & Submitted by your honr* most Obed* humble Serv*

Exp Storrs Col*

[*Connecticut Historical Society.*]

NINTH REGIMENT.

A Bounty Roll for Recruits raised in the 9** Militia Reg* to serve in the Continental Army for three years

Archibald Mott	George States
John Robinson	Thomas Chapman
Jack Spry	John McNulty
Timothy Ford	

John Mead Col* & Muster Master of the Recruits & three Months Men from the 9** Reg* &c 1780

[*State Library, Revolution 17, 79.*]

TWELFTH REGIMENT.

A Return of Inlisted & Detached Men to Serve in Continental Service untill y[e] last day of Dec[r] Next Certifying whether Inlisted or Detach[d] y[e] Comp[y] to which they belong place of abode by whom receipted or how conveyed to y[e] Army &c. Belonging to y[e] 12th Reg[t] of foot in the Militia of the State of Connecticut.

Inlisted or Detach[d]	Mens Names	Place of Abode
Inlisted	Asahel Woodworth	Lebanon
	Joseph Squebb	
	Squire Gooff	Hebron
	Tho[s] Marvin	
	Abel Spicer	Lebanon
	John Porter	
	Jesse Lyman	
	Linus Pineo	
	Nath[ll] Little	
	Eben[r] Silden	
	James Lathrop	
	Etkanah Jones	Hebron
	Asa Blish	
	Lawrance Powers	
	Ezra Woodworth	Lebanon
	Bigelow Waters	Hebron
	Solomon Saveroy	Lebanon
	Isaac Owen	Hebron
	Sam[ll] Thomas	Lebanon
Detach[d]	George Lampshire	
Inlisted	Joshua Rennolds	
	Elnathan Garcy	
	Benj[n] Woodworth	
	Isaa Lyman	
	Jonah Thomas	
	Moses Scofield	
	Elihu Jones	
	Sam[ll] Woodbridge	
	W[m] Winslow	Hebron
	Jacob Cooper	
	Jon[th] Metcalf	Lebanon
	Zadock Lee	
Detach[d]	Charles Hyde	
	Benj[n] Payne Jun[r]	gone out y[e] State &c
	Nathan Starkweather	
	Derias Dewey	
	Tho[s] Fitch	
	David Deans	
	Sam[ll] Lyman	
	Ezekiel Horton	Hebron
	Epafroditus Loveland	
	Joseph Smith	
Inlisted	Elisha Lyman	Lebanon
	Nath[ll] Fitch	
	Simon Newcomb	
Inlisted	Tim[o] Clark	
	John Powers	Hebron
	Nero Tom	Lebanon

Inlisted or Detach^d	Mens Names	Place of Abode
	Joseph Bloss	Hebron
	Sol° Day	
	Sol° Hayward	
	Jonth Hutchinson	
	Sam^{ll} Jones	
	Uriah Phinney	Lebanon
	James Downer	
	Dan Beamount	
	Asehel Kingsley	
	Jonth Hutchinson Junr	Hebron
	Wm Eldrige	
	Eben^r Clark	Lebanon
	Robert Holdrige	Hebron
	Nero Coss	Lebanon
	Roger Woodworth	
	Jared Phelps	Hebron
	Joseph Wright	Lebanon
	Asa Harris	
	Ezekiel Avery	
	Dan Lyman	
	Aaron Overton	Norwich
Detach^d	Dan^{ll} Emons	Hebron
	Asa Willey	
	Bethuel Phelps	
	Asa Fullor	
	Saml Horton	
	Walter Hunt	Lebanon
	Jn° Patrige Bisset	
Inlisted	Jonth Bill	
Detach^d	Ambrose Woodward	
Inlisted	Beriah Skinner	Hebron
	John Carrior	
	Joel Mack	

Errors Excepted

Lebanon 10th Augt 1780

A True Return of Drafted & Inlisted men &c as by the Returns Rec^d &c.   Test P^r me,   Jeremiah Mason Col°

Sundry of the within Named Detached men have Since the Date of this Return March^d on to Camp &c & have not Rec^d no Returns Since of the Capt &c.   J. M. C°

[*Connecticut Historical Society.*]

SIXTEENTH REGIMENT.

State of Connecticut To Nehemiah Beardsley Paymaster to the Recruits raised within the 16th Regiment to join the Connecticut Line in the Continental Army in the year 1780.   D^r.
Bounties paid them in July 1780, and for Blankets as follows

Job Hodges
Abel Guthrie
John Mooney
Levi Barnum
Reuben Judd
Ezekiel Whitney
Josiah Nichols
Daniel Anderson

Samuel Price
Daniel Gregory
Joseph Munrow
Frederick Tubbs
James Roberts
Joseph C. Hawley
Nehemiah Olmstead
Clement Fairchild

Mills Deforrest
John Carmon
Elijah Hurd
Jonathan Sherwood
Samuel Bradley
William Benedict
Abraham Vanshoik
Jacob Crow
Amon Crow
Nathaniel Porter
Matthew Clark
Zach⁴ Brush
Saunders Perry
Joseph Olmstead
Zalmon Burrit
Luke Roberts
Benjamin Peck
Levi Osborn
John Barnum
Henry Knap
Jared Baldwin
Joseph Starr

Phillip Wheeler
Elijah Kellogg
Uriah Nash
William Commins
Ebenezer Hawley
Samuel Stebben
Stephen Northrop
Abram Jillit
Junus Sillick
Isaac Blackman
James Beardsley
John Finch
Stephen Barnum
Jeremiah Lockwood
John Gilbert
Abijah Osburn
Jared Dunning
Matthew Olmstead
Timothy Barnum
Clark Hide
Stephen Bennet
Austin Bishop

[*State Library, Revolution 17, 72.*]

TWENTY FIRST REGIMENT.

A Return of the Men Inlisted or Detached from the 21 : Reg^t To Join the Continental Army July 12th 1780.

What Company	Mens Names	Place of Abode	Inlisted Detached	Term Engaged
Capt Johnson	Archalus Ama Negro	Canterbury	Inlisted	till last of Dec^r
	Ebenezer Fitch	"	Detached	"
Capt Ransford	Adams Stevens hir^d by norwich	Canterbury	Inlisted	till last of Dec^r
	Peter Stevens d^o Colchester	"	"	"
Capt Butt	Job Barstow	"	"	"
	Charles Fred^c Woodard	"	"	"
	Asahel Herrick	"	"	"
	John Adams	"	"	"
	Ebenezer Shaw	"	"	"
	Jared Mott Hir^d by ye lite Horse	"	"	"
Capt Bacon	David Eanos	"	"	During ye War
	Charles Justin	"	"	three years
	Thomas Scranton	"	"	
Capt Hibberd	Benjamin Darfee	Canterbury	inlisted	till last of Dec^r
	Epaphrus Curtiss hir^d by lite horse	"	"	"
	Nicholus Falkner	"		"
	Paul Harriss	"	Detach^d	
Capt Woodard	Joseph Dunam Hir^d by Preston	"	inlisted	"
Capt Tyler	Sam^ll Cleaveland hir^d by Pomfred	"	"	"
Capt Branch	John Jack Negro	Plainfield	"	for 3 years
	Stephen Elsworth hir^d by lite horse	"	"	till last of Dec^r
	Seth Lovell	"	"	"

What Company	Mens Names	Place of Abode	Inlisted	Term Engaged
Capt Waterman	Jonathan Whippal	Plainfield	inlisted	till last of Dec^r
	Charles Waterman	"	"	"
	Thomas Simmons	"	"	"
	Jabez Bottom	"	"	"
	James Fuller	"	"	"
Capt Bottom	James Patrick hir^d by lite horse	"	"	"
	Job Phillips	"	"	"
	Samuel Tracy	"	"	"
	John Fagins	"	"	"
	Daniel Herrington	"	"	"
	Joshua Patrick hir^d by lite Horse	"	"	"
Capt Dunlap	Reuben Bryant	"	"	"
	Edward Sparger	"	"	"
	Jeduthun Herd	"	"	"
	John Lovejoy	"	"	"
	Isaac Herrick	"	"	"
	Abraham Culver	"	"	"
	Joseph Boyd hir^d by lite Horse	"	"	"
	David Welch	"	"	"
	Samuel Kingsbury	"	"	"
	Charles Waterman	"	"	"
Capt Baley	Alexander Miller Junr	Voluntown	inlisted	till last of Dec^r
	John Phillips	"	"	"
	William Alma	"	"	"
Capt Edmond	Henry Hewett	"	"	"
	Hugh Canady	"	"	"
	George Griffeth	"	"	"

Capt Campbell	Elijah Fayer	"	"	"
15	Elisha Card	"	"	"
	Jonathan Parker	"	"	"
	Eleazer Lewis	"	"	"
	David Franklin	"	"	"
	Robert Jackson hir^d by norwich	"	"	"
Capt Dixson	Jonathan Jenks	"	"	"
	Abel Franklin	"	"	"
	Burden Potter	"	"	"
	Ichabod Peavy	"	"	"
	Jo^s Griffin hir^d by ye lite horse	"	"	"
	Miles Jordon	"	"	"
	Daniel Dowd "	"	"	"
	David Franklin	"	"	"
Capt Robbins	Thomas Palmer	"	"	till last of Decr next
	Daniel Palmer	"	"	"
	Jonas Randal	"		
	Willm Heughston hir^d by Groton	"	"	"
Capt Cady	George Little	Killingley	"	"
	Paul Griffis	"	"	"
Capt Eaton				

Canterbury July 24th 1780

To Gen^{ll} Douglas

Obadiah Johnson Colo.

MISCELLANEOUS RETURNS, 1780.

A Return of the Recruits Rased by the Defrant Towns to Fill up the Conn[t] Line of the Army for Durin the War or 3 years.

Mens Names	Date of inlistment	Tarm of Servis	Towns to which they Belong
Darius Orcutt	Nov[m] 23rd 1780	3 years	Ashford
Charles Repley	Dec[r] 27th 1780	"	Windham
Jube Deyer	Jan[ry] 11th 1781	"	"
Daniel Woodward	Nov 24th 1780	"	"
John Dingley	Dec[r] 15th 1780	"	"
Joseph Barrows	Dec[r] 26th 1780	"	"
Jed[ah] Hebard	Dec[r] 4th 1780	- "	"
Roswell Simons	Dec[r] 27th 1780	"	"
John Gilburt	Do 26th 1780	War	"
Elijah Randall	Dec[r] 8th 1780	3 years	"
Zopher Roberson	Dec[r] 8th 1780	"	"
Abner Lilley	Dec[r] 8th 1780	"	"
Eliphalit Spafford	Dec[r] 28th 1780	"	"
John Abbe	Jan 1th 1781	"	"
Nathanel Abbe	Jany 15th 1781	"	"
Joseph Abbe	Jan[y] 17th 1781	"	"
Stephen Hall	Jan[y] 10th 1781	"	Fairfeld
Abner Hills	Feb[y] 8th 1781	"	Lebanon
Joshua Bill	Feb[y] 8th 1781	War	"

Lebanon Feb[y] 9th 1781

A Trew Return Test John Ball L[t] & Recruiting Officer

[*Connecticut Historical Society.*]

A List of the Names of Six Months Men for the Town of Hartford Decm[r] 1780

Asa Bunce
William Hinsdel
James Ensign
James Duggans
Alvin Bigelow
George Blackburn
William Wickham
Daniel Roberts
Thomas Wadsworth 3[d]
Seth Talcott
David Cannady
Daniel Brewer Jun[r]
George Abbe
George Burk
Isaac Bellows
Horatio Wales
William Boardman
Hezekiah Wadsworth
Tim[o] Sedgwick
John Wilson Jun[r]
Stephen Burnham

W[m] Robbarts
Tho[s] Keeney
Amos Loveland
Roderick Seymour
W[m] Sedgwick
Elnathan Keyes
W[m] Ellis
Elisha Seymour
Ardon Seymour
Daniel Wadsworth
Jacob Augustus
Asaph Burley
Benjamin Porter Jun[r]
Tim[o] Anderson
James Olcott
Tim[o] Fisher
Zenas Burnham
Allen Webster
Samuel Dalliber
John Thomson
Josiah Gates

[*Connecticut Historical Society.*]

A Return of the Names of the Noncommissioned Officers and Soldiers who have Inlisted from the Town of Salisbury into the Continental Service in the Connecticut Line and other Regiments during the War and are now in Service

In Meggs Regiment
    Serg^t John McLean
    " Wm Tupper
    " Henry Hull
    " Gamaliel Terry
    Corp^l James Bradly
    " Daniel Hull
    " Amasa Grenoll
    Fif^r Jacob McLean
    Isaac Cool
    Champion Ackly
    Artemus Blodget
    Nathl Emerson
    Henry FitzJeroll
    Joseph T. Fitch
    Salmon Bostwick
    Benjⁿ Graves
    George Griswould
    Saml Griswould
    Moses Hull
    Jonathan Hull
    Billy Munger
    Simmeon Meggs
    Eliphalet Owen
    Asa Owen
    Phineas Strong
    Martin Tubbs
    Wm White
    Solo^m Whitney
    Jobe Towsley
    Wm Gates
    Hyman Cool

In Swift's Reg^t
    John Holly
    Hildrick Barret
    Peter Surdam
    Benjⁿ Scovel
In Bradley's Reg^t
    Isaac Welden
In Saml B. Webbs Reg^t
    Daniel Bostwick
In Warner's Reg^t
    Saml Stoddard
    Thos Chipman
    Wm Eno
    John Coon   Prisoner
    James Coon
    Ozias Baker
    Reuben Strong
    George Whitman Prisoner
    John Field
    George McCarter Presoner
In Hazens Reg^t
    Serg^t Wm Baker
    Wm Roberts
    Benjⁿ Daverson
    Heber Griswould
    Jacob Parish
    Micael Welch
    Reuben Clemons
In Sheldon's Reg^t of Light Dragoons
    Benjⁿ Hows
    Benjⁿ Everest
    David Owen
In Col^o Baldwins Core of Artificers
    Aaron Swetland

Salisbury Novr ye 27th 1780

[*State Library, Hebard Papers, 51.*]

Return of Men who have Deserted from the 2^d Connecticut Brigade Since Jany 1st 1778. Springfield Apr^{ll} 25th 1778

Mens Names	Places of Abode
Q^r Mr Serg^t Stratton	Lyme
D^m Maj^r Buckingham	Saybrook
Willm Manning	Norwich
Noah Pease	"
Ebenez^r Pelton	Groton
Jabaz Metcalf	Norwich
Jonathⁿ Nicholas	Mansfield
Willm Hollowell	N. London
David Fenn	Colchester
George Manwaring	N London
D^m Abraham Petenger	Lyme
Sam^{ll} Stark	Colchester

Mens Names	Places of abode
2^d Reg^t	
Amas Fuller	Fishkills N.Y.
John Widger	Saybrook
Daniel Evens	Woodstock
5th Reg^t	
Isaac Grant	Litchfield
Jacob Poson	Transient Person
James Stanton	Burlington
John Gould	Litchfield
Ephraim Whelor	Redding
James Hews	Hartford
Barack Taylor	Fairfield
Cash Africa	Litchfield Since Joined
Jabaz Williams	Redding
7th Reg^t	
John More	Branford
Edward Booth	N Milford
John Lawrance	Canaan
Christopher Blake	Mass.

N.B.   There is a mistake in the above date, it ought to be Jany 1st 80.

[*State Library, Revolution 17, 89.*]

OFFICERS AND SOLDIERS MARRIED.

[This list is undated, but is placed following other lists of 1780 and preceding lists of 1781 in the volume of records as now bound.]

List of Officers & Soldiers Married

N. Haven

Akin James Sej[t]
Alley William
Alling Jon[th]
Bains Sol[n] Serj[t]
Baher Edward d[o]
Brown Henry Corp[l]
Brochett Hez[h]
Bishop Nathan[l]
Blacksly Zelous
Britton Samuel
Bradly Oliver
Clerk David Serj[t]
Clark Joel
Coshall Thomas
Clark Martin
Doyle Hugh
Davis James
Dayton Israel
Dickerman Joseph
Eagelston David
Foot Isaac Serj[t]
Ford Daniel
Gibson Samuel
Huse Bodwell
Hoel Nicholas
Hull Samuel
Harding Frad[k]
How Joshua
Hunt Richard
Johnson Abr[m] Corp[l]
Joslin John
King George
Levensworth Eli Maj[r]
Lord Jabez
Lynds John
Mansfield Jo[s] Cap[t]
Munson W[m] Cap[t]
Miles John Leu[t]
Mix Tim[o] Leu[t]
Moultrop Jo[s] Serj[t]
Mallery Amos Corp[l]
Moltrop Stephen
Melone Daniel
Martin Lewis
Matthews Robert
Mansfield Dan

Moss John
Moss Daniel
Ohara Timothy
Prentice Jonas Cap[t]
Parmele Jer[h] Cap[t]
Potter Israel Leiut
Potter Moses
Parker Edmond
Robinson Jared Leiut
Robinson Samuel
Robinson Thomas
Sherman W[m] Cap[t]
Sherman John Leiut
Sporry Channcey
Smith Ambrose
Stevens William
Sugden Ab[m]
Stockwell Abel
Squier Daniel
Sanford Thomas
Squier Stent Sam[l]
Simpson Robert
Shepherd John
Trowbridge John Leiut
Troop John Leiut
Thomas John
        Samuel
Tolles Elnathan
Townsend Solomon
Thomas James
Todd Yale
Thomas Ephraim
Vorguson John
Wooster Thomas Cap[t]
Wood Elisha
Wilson John
White Sam[l] Jun[r]
Walter W[m]
Wilds Jonathan
Zandor Gad

WINDHAM COUNTY*
Woodstock

Bartholomew John
Bruce Ely
Clark Asael Ens[n]
Green John Corp[l]

---

*The Woodstock names with their Windham County heading appear to have been inserted after the first writing of the document.

Hambden W^m
Holmes David D^r
Lyon Asa Q.M.
Manning Wm Capt
Powers Nathan
Smith Dan^{ll} Corp^l

Waterbury

Barns Daniel
Basset W^m
Camp Samuel
Calkins Israel
Clark Richard
Cole John
Cook Joel
Camp Sam^{ll} Junr
Curtis Stephen
Dunbar Amos
Dutton Titus Serj^t
Davis Jon^n
    Stephen
Dunbar Miles
Edwards Nath^{ll} Leiu^t
Fallandon John
Fulford John Serj^t
Graves Simeon
Gaylord Benjn
Hickok Wm Junr
Hubbel James
Hickok Elisha
Hall Nathaniel
Judd Stephen
    Bruster
Lewis Saml Serj^t
Parker Eliab
Pardey Jonathan
Prichard George Junr
Parker Isaac
Pendleton Daniel
Pressen Amasa
Rice Nehemiah
Robarts Abiel
    Joel
Smith John
Southmaid W^m
Sanford Ezekiel
Smith Lus (?)
Scovill Stephen
Smith Samuel
Smith David Maj^r
Seward Nathan
Thair Asa
Tuttle Ezekiel
    Timothy
    Jabesh
    Timothy Ens^n
    Hezekiah
Terril Joel

Upson Ezekiel Serj^t
Welton Stephen Junr
Williams Obed

Durham

Cook Thos
Hinman Husted Corp^l
Jonson W^m
Strong Eliakim Serj^t
Squire Saxton J^r
Seward Saml
Squire Abiather

Derby

Allin David
Baldwin Silas
Farmer Thos Ens^n
Foot Ezra
Freeman Frank
Humphry E. Capt
Hotchkiss Levi Lieu^t (?)
Hawken Zadock
Moses Jonas
Murry Abr^m
O'Kane Jon^h
Prichard James Serj^t
Prindle J. Enos
Rigs Labor
Rigs James
Tomlinson David Ens^n
Warner Eben^r (?) Serj^t
Woster Henry
Washburn Benjn
Watreus Rich^d
White Jo^s
Whitny Henry P.M.
Wakelee Jonth

Wallingford

Antony John
Bradley Daniel
Barns Moses
Bristol Benjn
Barns David
Chamberlain Ep^m Capt
Francis John
Hart Benjn
Hall Rufus
Hastings John
Holt Samuel
Hitchcock Lem^l Leiut
    Thomas
Johnson John
Jones Thomas
Lewis Ebenezar
Munson Levi Leiut
Mansfield John Leiut
Mix Thomas Junr

Parker Elisha
Page Timothy
Peck Charles Serj^t of Artill
Parker Benjamin
Shallor Joseph Leiut
Smith Daniel
Stone David
Webb Gideon
Yale Nash

Branford

Barker Saml Capt
Bunnil Abrah^m
Bagdon Cesar
Foot Eben^r
Garrit (?) John
Hubbard John Ens^n
Harrison Jairus Serj^t
Hoadley Saml Serj^t
Janes Joseph
Norton Benjn Ens^n
Otis Joseph
Potter Stephen Capt
Smith Jordan
Turner Jacob
White John Ens^n

Guilford

Ball John Leiut
Benton Edward Serj^t
Bishop Thalmeno
Doud Moses
Fowler Caleb Corp.
Hall Stephen Capt
Hall Philemon Leiut.
Handy Samuel Serj^t
Hotchkiss Ira
Johnson Isaac
Norton Rufus Corpor.
      Elon
Niger Phillip
Pelton Benjamin
Strong John Serj^t
Thomson David Serj^t
Teal Samuel
Whaler Thomas

Milford

Bristol Jonathan
Ben Thomas
Beebe Joel
Belding John
Burk John
Davidson Isaac
Frost Samuel alias Cornelius
      Cahales
Hodg David
Hooker John

Hine Titus
Seward Daniel
Steward John
Sharp Joseph
Seward William
Sanford Saml Capt
Smith Wm Leiu^t

COUNTY OF NEW LONDON
Norwich

Bill Bariah Capt
Bishop Nath^{ll} Leiut
Bennet Benjn
Bryant John
Brewster Hez^h
Bebee Ammon
Bond John
Chapman Jo^s Leiut
Cook Case
Comstock Gideon
Carr James Miller
Corwin Jonth
Corwin Selah
Clark Jacob
Durkee John Col^o
Downing Chris^r
Ellis John Chap^n
Fox Jacob Leiu^t
Fanning Charles Leiu^t
Gardner Sherman
Gardner D. Tubbs
Hide James Ens^n
Maning W^m,
Mitchel George
Olin William
Peck Darius Leiu^t
Perrigo William
Pollard W^m
Plumb Peter
Qui Libeus
Read Ruben
Sydleman John
Spicer Samuel
Stillman Robert
Starkweather Asa
Troop Benjn Maj^r
Tracy Hugh Leiu^t
Tracy Wm Ens^n
Tracy Moses
Waterman Ebe^r J^r
Webb Jonathan
Wedge Joshua
Walton Silas

Killingsworth

Baldwin Caleb Lieu^t
Crane John
Hall Saml Corp^l

Leet Allen
Rumbelo Thomas
Stephens Aaron Cap[t]
Stevens Peter

Preston

Aldrige William
Burnham Asa
Eavan Isaac
Guyant Luke
Hollay Joseph
Jackson Thomas
Miles Charles Leiut
M°Daniel James
Meach Joshua
Roup Simeon
Storry Silas
Sears Obediah
Tyler Nathan

Saybrook

Baldwin Henry
Butler Stephen
Chapman Daniel Serj[t]
Comstock Samuel
Dudley Zebulon
Graham Silas
Grimes Cyrus
Grant James
Hull Oliver
Harvey W[m]
Jones Aaron
Kirkland   Cap[t]
Lord William
        Jeremiah Serj[t]
Lay Asa Leiut
Negro Briston
Newel Robort
Pratt Ethan
Shirman (?) Sam[l] Serj[t]
Shipman John
Stevens Elijah
Tooley Andrew
Thompson Epaphras
Warden Isaac
Waterhouse Stephen
White Oliver
Widger John
Wright Ezekiel

Lyme

Anderson Tho[s] Leiu[t]
Burnam Joseph
Beckwit Phin[s]
Boge Ichabod
Corwin Sela
Dodge Daniel
De Wolf Stephen

D Wolf Edward
Hyde Rufus
Herron John
Hayns Jonathan
Hudson Eleazer
Harrison W[m]
Lee Elisha Cap[t]
Lee Ezra Leui[t]
Lay Richard
Marther Elias L[t]
Miller Nathan
M°Coy Alex[r]
Peck Silas
Peck Silas J[r]
Reed Enoch Cap[t]
Rogers Lemuel
Rogers Joseph
Roach John
Sill David Col°
Selden Ezra Cap[t]
Spencer Ichabad L[t]
Sanders John
Sawyer Asa
Sullard Jacob
Smith Enoch
Wade John
Wilson George
Wade Martin

Groton

Avery Thomas Lie[t]
Avery Simeon Ens[n]
Allen Robart Serj[t]
Annew Andrew
Andrews James
Billing Stephen Lie[t]
Brightman Henry
Davis Daniel
Dayton Richard
Davison Robart
Freeman Guy
Faning Elisha
Freeman Edward
Freeman Micael
Gray Elijah
Harrington Isaac
Hannabal Joseph
Holly Joseph
M°Lane Mathew
M°Donold John
Pomp Samuel
Pelton Ebenezer
Pomp Jacob
Pelton David
Stanton Amos Cap[t]
Swift Robart
Sunsemun Aaron
Speers John

States or Starks Joseph
Sharper Tuis
Sterry Silas
Solomon Amos
Shortman William
Showls Nathan
Williams Henry Li'
Williams Uriah Serj'
Whitman Lemual d°
Yerington Jesse

Stoningtown

Brown Charles
Brumly William
Brown Joshua
Billings James
Brown Oliver
Cottrel Nathan
Cadwell Simeon
Cade Darius
Cinnamon Tho'
Davol John
Fellows Joseph Ens"
Fellows Nath"
Griffen James
Herrick Libeus
Hazzard Jeffery
Hanaball Joseph
Hudson John
Hiscox Thomas
Hawks Hannah p Son
Jackwise Robart
Ingram Mary p Son
Leeds Thomas
Lewis Valentine
McKinzey James
Newgent John
Palmer W. Jonathan Sej'
Peters Peter
Russel Giles Col°
Shaw Richard
Smith Daniel
Simmons James
Sowas Richard
Shelly Lemuel
Searl Constant
Tuncheman
West John [　　]
Warden Walter
Wheeler David

FOR THE COUNTY OF FAIRFIELD

Fairfield

Allen Eben'
　d° Thomas
　d° Moses
Burr Daniel

Buckley Seth
Bradley Eliphalet
　　　Nathan
Beers Hezekiah
Coggin David
Cable William
Durfree Thomas
Disborough Justus
　　　Joshua Serg'
Dimon Moses
Fuller John
Fegoe Peter
Fowler Nehemiah
French Samuel
Green Josiah
Glover John
Goodsall Epphaphras
Hubbel Wm Leiut
　　　Isaac Leiut
Hutonot Francis
Hilton Atkinson
Hall Stephen Serj'
Jackson P. Nathan Leu'
Johnson Nathaniel
Leverick Gabriel
Lyon Samuel
Lockwood Stephen
Morehouse David
Mitchel John Serj'
Meeker Stephen
Mills Joseph
Meeker Daniel
Osburn Stratten
Patching Elisha Serj'
Raymond William
　　　David
Sturgis Moses Serj'
Tayler Barrack
Webb Hezekiah
Williams Richard

Stanford

Blanchard Jacob
Bates David
Benton David
Cleaveland John
Fountain Eneas
Hickok Sam' Serj'
Hoyt Joseph Col.
Halley Abraham
Johnson Nathaniel
Jones Isaiah
Knap Usel
　　　James
Lockwood Timothy
　　　Eliphlalet Srj'
Lunsbury Peter
McAnotter John

Parkinton Dine
Scofield Selah
Smith Isaac
St John James
Smith Isaac Junr
Wardwell Jacob
       William
Weed Benjamin
      Thad^s Leiut

Danbury

Bishop David
Chapman Collins
Dixon George
Eames Everit
Hall David
Ludeman John
Lord John
Matthews James
Orian alias Ryan Jeremiah
   See Redding
Picket Thomas
Rossell Jeremiah

Redding

Bigsby Elias
Cooley Nathan
Hopkins Henry
Meeker Stephen
Sherwood Nehemiah
Raymond Saml

New Fairfield

Beardsley Phineas Capt
Barns James Leiut
Brown Charles Corpl.
Hall Talmage Serj^t
Jolly William
Knap James
Kinning Thomas
Lacy J. Fairchild Serj^t
Nichols Samuel
Robarts Benjaman
Saunders Wm Serj^t
Trowbridge John Serj^t
Wilder Aaron

Greenwich

Adams Jonathan
Butler Walton
Davis Isaac
Fletcher Joseph
Hays Abraham
Hariot Israel
Holmes Nath^{ll}
Jessup Nath^{ll}
Johnstone W^m

Lockwood Moses
      Saml Capt
Nickerson Arana
Parsons Theodosius
Rundel John
Ritch Edward
Rogers James
Town John
Waters William
Wessels Herculus
Wilson David
Waren Henry Leiut
Whiting Saml Leiu^t

Stratford

Benjamins John Serjt
Burrows Josiah
Beebee James Capt
Collins Wm Lock
Gilbert Obediah
Grover Jacob
Gorham Samuel
Hallop Joseph
Jones Jasper
King Orry
Phillips Thomas
Parker Samuel
      John
Russel Wm Junr
Shelley Eben^r Serj^t
Sunderland John
Walker Robart Cap
Washbon Samuel

Newtown

Botsford Joel
Foot Elijah
Kimberly   Leiut.
Lacey Josiah Capt
Prindle Abijah
Sanford James

Ridgfield

Bradley Col. Phil.
Cummes William
Perry Elisha
Remington Stephen
Smith Lewis

LITCHFIELD COUNTY

Salsbury

Blodget Artimus
Chappel Curtis
Clankhorn Eleaz^r Leiu
Fitch Joseph Trumbu..
Forgerson Daniel
Fitsgeral Henery

Hull Giles Serj[t]
Larnebe Willord
Maclane Jacobe Fif[r]
Monger Billey
Owen Eliphalet
Tupper William Corp[l]
Yates W[m]
Strong Phin[e]

Kent

Barnum Leiut
    Steaphen Serj[t]
    Amos Corp[l]
Barlow John
Curtice George
Cheney Richard
Die Daniel
Hill Eben[r] Capt
Lambskins Benj[n]
Mane John Jun[r]
Murry Noah Serj[t]

Litchfield

Bottem John
Burnham Asa
Mason John
Munger Daniel
Palmer Benj[n]
Plant Tim[o]
Rossiter Sam[ll]
Shelly John
Seelye David
Smith Henry
Smith Jonathan
Stannard Sam[l]
Stone Josiah
Tuttle Levi
Wright James

Cornwell

Lake Phineas
Price Levi
Swift Heman Col.
Simmons Sam[l]
Tanner Toral Leiut
Wix Uriah

Woodbury

Camp Phineas
Church Ebenezer
Demmon John
Easton Eliphalet
Franklin Jehiel
Filets Francis
Humphrey Elijah Cap[t]
Hitchcock David
Hull Stephen

Judgson Joseph
Lee Abner
Olds Aaron
Pollard Isaac
Rood Simeon
Stoddard Nathan Cap[t]
    Eli
Taylor Simeon
Walker Elisha
    Zachariah
Welch Luke

Colebrook

Canfield Abiel
Phillips Samuel
Simmons Joseph
    Ely

Torrington

Barber Nathaniel
Gaylord Benjamin
Frisby Benjamin

Winchester

Fay Gershom
.d[o] Timothy
d[o] William
Filley Remembrance
Mott Adam
Scovil Stephen
Wilkinson Jesse

New Milford

Bostwick Eben[r]
Bunts Josiah
Buel David
Buck Josiah Ens[n]
Canfield Elijah
Dunwell William
Daley James
Drinkwater W[m]
Hawley C. Joseph
Peet Lemuel
Starr Josiah Col.
Stillwell Stephen
Trowbridge Eben[r]
Wilkinson Ichabod
Whitley William

Goshen

Converse Thomas Cap
Deming Waite
Goold John
Knap Timothy
Layre Jacob
Miles Isaac Serj[t]
Norton Joseph

Peck Zebulon
Seelye John
Wyard Thomas

New Hartford
[No names given]

Harrington
Elmore Calib
Hodg Asael L[t]
Gridley Seth
Sott Elijah
Willcox James
Foot Eben[r]
Griswold White
Marshel Elisha

Washington
Beman Friend
Bunce Isaiah
Davidson John
Fenn Daniel
Jordan John
Newton Ezekiel
Olds Oliver
Welch Micael

Sharon
Allen Amos
Cleveland Josiah
Elmore Daniel
Fisher Isaac
Foster Benj[n]
Goodrich David
Gilson Eleazer
Johnson Robart
Kelcy Noah
Pettitt Enos
Rust Jonathan
Strong David L[t]
Waneright Thomas
Yale Waite

Norfolk
Aspenwall Aaron
Adams Asael
Aspenwell Calib
Hamblin Joel
Horskins Daniel
Orvis Eleazer
Plumb Amariah
Sturdevant Nathan
Tubbs Nathan
Watson Titus Cap[t]

Canaan
Culver Aaron
Chambers W[m]

Freeman Elisha
Green Samuel
Higbee Elihu
Holombeck John L[t]
Lester Andrew

Hartland
Bushnul Daniel
Hays Titus
Phelps Charles
Reed Benj[n]

COUNTY OF WINDHAM
Windham
Burnap Benj[n]
Bingham John Serg[t]
  d[o]   Abisha
Durkee Benj[n] L[t]
Durkee Jere[h]
Farnum Reuben
Holt Philemon
  See Willington
Littlefield Eben[r]
Martin George
Parish Eliphaz
Perry Eben[r] Serj[t]
Robinson Elias Ens[n]
Randal Elijah
Rouse Jabez Serj[t]
Riplee Charles d[o]
Robison Sam[l]
Smith James
Webb Nath[ll] Cap[t]
Waldo Albigence
West Joseph

Mansfield
Abbe John
Allen Ashur
Bassett Joshua
Barrows Jacob
Bugbee John
Bennet Joshua
Conant Sam[ll]
Conant Calib
Dexter John
Fenton Jon[th]
Fenton Sol[n] Lie[t]
Harris John
Porter Nathan
Reed Nathan
Smith Jn[o] Ju[r]
Shumway Jn[o] Cap[t]

Ashford
Allen Daniel Cap[t]
Brandum Charles

Cheeney Eben^r Corp^l
Hardy Nath^{ll}
Hall William
Lyon Henry
Mercy Thomas
Pool Daniel
Smith Peter
Smith Abijah
Spalding Eph^m
Wales Eben^r L^t
Waters W^m

Lebanon

Buts James
Badcock Jno
Ball Humphry
Blackman Jonth
Butler John
Coleman Noah Doc^r
Clerk Jno
Chappel Amaz^h
Carter (?) James
Foster Zep^h
Gross Sam^{ll}
Hill Phillip
Jones Danl
Palmer Elijah
Polly Alpheus
Strong Benajah
Vaughn Daniel
Woodworth Jed^h
Ward W^m
Woodworth Benjn

Plainfield

Cleft Lem^l Capt
Johnson Benjn
McGreeger John Capt
Marsh Peter
Stoddard Joshua

Pomphret

Bacon Nehemiah
Goodale Jacob
Jones Thomas
Lyon Abiel
Reed Oliver
Shadden John
Sharp Benjn
Smith Henery
Stoel Elisha

Voluntown

Bacon Henry
Dennison Amos
Green Robart
Robins Joseph
Summitt Prince

Union

Houghten James
Lilley Eben^r
Moore Wm Junr
Sprague James Leiu^t
Taylor Thomas

Killingsley

Perry Silvanus
Grover Amasa
Mash Abner

Cantebery

Adams David J^r
Adams David Doc^r
Adams Samuel
Bacon Abner Capt
Cleveland John Serj^t
Cade Abijah
Carte^r Reuben
Cleveland Tim^o Lei^t
Cleveland Moses Lei^t
Coburn Sam^{ll}
Cushman Daniel
Duggins James
Downing Stephen
Fitch Rufus
Gates Nath^{ll} Serj^t
Stevens Peter J^r
Shaw William
Shaw Jonathan
Shaw Benjn
Tickings Tias

[   ]ventry

[   ]ham Paul Capt
Clap Nathan
[   ]day Joseph
Parker Eben^r
Robison Eph^m
Thompson Nath^{ll} Serj^t

COUNTY OF HARTFORD

Hartford

Adams William L^t
Abbe Eleazer
Abbe Jeduthan
Augustus Cesar
[   ]arnard John Capt
Brewer Danl Serj^t
Bevens Ebenezer
Buckland Stephen Capt
Bull Epaphras d^o
Combs Wm Serj^t
    See Weathersfield
Case Richard

Clark Abraham Serj^t
Corne Malachi
Cadwell Matt^w Serj^t
Curtis Daniel
Cole Samuel
Darrow Chris^r Maj^r.
Delibar James
Day Wastebrook
Demming David L^t
Evans Abiathar
Evans Samuel J^r
Evans Henry
Green William Capt
Heath Peleg L^t
Hadlock Reuben
Hooker W^m
Jarrel Thos Serj^t
Keene Benjamin
Lummis Israel
Lucus Samuel
Mattucks Saml Capt
Miller Charles L^t
Mahar James
Mize William
Olmstad James Ensⁿ
Pomroy Ralph L^t
Rislee Stephen
Smith George Ensⁿ
Sedgwick Sam^{ll}
Spencer Obediah
Thomas Patrick
Wyllys Saml Col^o
Wadsworth Roger L^t
Walker Roswell Serj^t
Way Hammon
Waters Thomas

Suffield

Austin Richard
Allen Samuel
Granger Samuel
Granger Phinehas
Harmon John Capt
Nelson Daniel
Pearman Joseph
Rising James
Spear Elijah

Summers

Brown Jacob
Coole Reuben
Elmore William
Gibbs Josiah
Jones Eleazer
Pratt Russell
Wood Thomas

Bolton

Downer Ezra
How Zadock L^t
Warren John

Glossenbury

Canada David Serj^t
Crary Richard
Conlee John
Dealing Samuel
Freeman Samson
Fox Asa
Freeman Syphax alias Mosely
Grover Phinehas L^t
Hill Daniel
Holden John
Lamb Joseph
Loveland Thomas
Loveland Elisha
Loveland Levi
McDowel Alex^r Ensⁿ
Miller John
Peas Peter Serj^t
Smithers William
Stevens Timothy
Sambo Prince
Treat John
Tryon Ezra
Webster Joshua Serj^t

Weathersfield

Andrus Asa Serj^t
Buckley Edward Capt
Blinn Abrah^m
Blinn Justus
Brown Edward
Clark James
Crane Curtis
Comes Wm Serj^t
  see Hartford
Davis Eben^r
Griffin Simon Serj^t
Goodrich Ephraim
Kilby Christopher
Lockwood Moses Serj^t
Miller Nathaniel
Mygatt Zebulon
Riley John Leiut
Russel Asher
Stoddard Enock
Weston Benjⁿ Ensⁿ
Williams Daniel Serj^t
Wells Joshua

Hebron

Baxter Aaron
Culver David

Holdridge Hezek. Col.
Mack Orlander Leiut
Marble Thomas
Morril Asher
McJuborrough Jedd^n
Pomroy Benjn Doct^r
Porter Eleazer
Pieffer Lazarus
Starks Stephen
Taylor Ephraim
Wright Simeon
    Isaiah

Willington
Dimick Joseph
Fenton John
Holt Philemon Serj^t
  see Windham
Hatch Hayman Corp.
Orcut Caleb Serj^t
Root Nathan Leiut
Rice David

Tolland
Brown Eben^r
Eaton Solomon
Hinkly Ichabod Capt
Johnson Elihu
Luce Jonathan
Miner Andrew
Newton Elias
Price Rufus Leiut
Preston Tyrus
Peterson Andrew
Sabins Nehemiah

Farmington
Albert Thomas G. Serj^t
Andrus Theodore
    Obediah
Adams John
Brown Jonathan Capt
Barns Daniel Leiut
Brunson Roger
    Asa
Bates John
Cole John Leiut
Culver Timothy
Clark Lyman
Curtis Amos
Camp Isaac
Dutton Oliver Serj^t
Dunnum Cornelius
Fox Elisha
Hosmer Timothy Doc^r
Hart Jonathan Adj^t
Hotchkiss Zad^k Corp.
Howard George

Hayden David
Judd William Capt
Johnson John Corp.
Mix John Ens^n
Momosuck Daniel
Merrils Cyprian
Oswold   Col.
Parceval Paul Q.M.
Powers James
Potter Lemuel Serj^t
Rows Amos
Steel Josiah
Squier S. Samuel
Smith Asaph
    David
Stevens Rosewell
Thompson Isaiah Leiut
Wainright Samuel
Wilcox James
Welton Benjamin
Warren Abraham

Middletown
Anger George
Blackman Elijah
Barns Thomas
Boardman Moses
    A Samuel
Blake Ebenzar
Brown William
Bacon William
Clark Othniel Leiut
Cone Ozias
    Joseph
    Daniel
Crittenden Gideon
Dewey James
Ells Edward Capt
Fisher Christopher
Francis James
Foster John
Graves William
Gilston Jacob
Henshaw Wm Leiut
Hubbard Hezekiah Leiut
Hull David
Harris John
Hubbard Roswell
Johnson Jon^n Col.
  d^o Davis
Kimball Abra^m T.
Lung Joseph
Meigs J. Return Col.
Marks Comfort
Matthews William
Peck Ariel
Powers Thomas
Robinson John

Sumner John Col.
Savage Abijah Capt
Starr David Leiut
Sizer Jonathan
Warner Robart Capt
Wyllys Eben^r
    Joseph

East Windsor

Anderson W^m
Andrus W^m
Brown Jude
Baxter Francis
Bissel John
Brown Josiah L^t
Beman Jonathan
Churchill Elijah
Downer Caleb
Grant Azariah
Lomis Moses
Newton Isaac
Porter Hez^h
Pearce Daniel
Wallace Ab^m
Wadsworth J. B. Doc^r

Chatham

Bowers Benajah Cor (?)
    Ephraim
    Benjamin
Butler Peter
Carter Aaron
Cole Marcus Lieu^t
Graham Joseph
Goodrich Levy
Goff Samuel
Geddens Richard
Hale Aaron Leiu^t
Higgens Heman
    Jesse
Hubbard Elihue
Jennings Elnathan
Johnston James
Miller Enoch
    Daniel
Markham Josep
McCorne W^m
Norten Jedadiah
Pelton George
Parks Daniel
Ranney Jabesh
    Steaphen
Smith Ezra Leiu^t
Schalena Abrah^m
Stocken Marshall
Thomas Steaphen
Verry Jonathan

Wood Jacobe
Wright John

Haddam

Arnold Jehiel
Bailey Gideon Leiu^t
    Jacobe
    Robert
Bates Eleazer
    Amos
    Daniel
Bonfoy Benunuel
Brainord Encrease
Boardman Jonathan
Clark Samuel
Chase Walter
    Aaron
Church Samuel
Cone Elisha
Gladding William
Higgins Cornelius L^t
Porter Amos
Smith John Leiu^t

Simsbury

Andrus James Leiut
Bodwell Benjamin
Hill John 2^d
Higley Josiah
Harrington Elisha
Phelps Thomas
Prince Zacheriah
Woodbridg Theophilus L^t
Woodward Oliver

Infield

Abbe Thomas Capt
Booth Henery
Chandler Joseph
Earl William
Griswold Joseph
Hall Israel
Hager Simeon
Parsons David Capt
Parsons Jonathan
Perkins Daniel Junr
Simons Isaac
Ware Daniel Serj^t
Wood Lemuel
Geer Elihu

Colchester

Bill Jonathan
Carter Edward
Fenn David
Farnsworth Nath^ll
Harris Champlen

Hun Isaiah
Freeman Jack
Fox John
Graves Peter
Judd Daniel Serj^t
Quash Cato
Rowley Jesse
Roberts Nathaniel
Stark Tim°
    Samuel
    Steaphen
Tarble William
Witney Dan^{ll} Sarj^t Maj^r
Williams John

Windsor

Bristor John
Chandler Isaac
Coy Samuel
Denslow Marten
Gibs Samuel Leiut
Gillit Abel Junr
Griswold Phineas
Hoskens Tim°
Holcomb Matthew
Lamberton Obed
Lawrance Amos
Loomis Steaphen
Mather Nathaniel
Marshal Samuel
Maclane Niel
Pinney Aaron
Porter Daniel
Phelps Isaac

Prior Abner
Seymour Joseph
Thrall David
Thrall Isaac
Woodward Oliver
Wing Joseph
    Samuel
Wakefield Potashel

E. Haddam

Andrews Thos
Ackley Thomas
Clark Samuel
Fox Joshua
Holmes Eliph^t Capt
Hary Itha^r Capt
Harvey Ezra
Mitchel Samuel
Murfe Thomas
Mino Elihue
Mott Samuel
Mobs Pierce
Spencer David Lei^t
Salley James
Watkens Ephraim
Willey Jonathan
Wheeler Joshua
Williams Thomas

Stafford

Manning Phineas
Millington Sam^{ll}
Walker Nath^{ll}
Wallbridg Ames Maj^r

[*State Library, Revolution 30, 5.*]

16

NINTH REGIMENT—COL. WEBB.*

[See Record of Connecticut Men in the Revolution, page 245.]

FIRST COMPANY—COL. WEBB.

Return of the Officers and Privates of the Colo' Comp' Col' Sam¹ B Webb's Regm' Engaged for Three Years or During the War, the time of their Service, Pay Due & from the 1st Jan' 1780 to the 1st Jan' 1781

Name and Rank	Terms engaged for	Married	Towns engaged for	Commenc' of Service	Expiration of Service
Samuel B. Webb Col¹	3 years		Lebanon	1st Jan' 1780	1st Jan' 1780†
Timothy Allyn C Lieut	"		New Hartford	"	"
Elisha Flowers Serjt Mr	"	Mard	Wethersfd	"	1st March 1780
John Burnham Serjt	"		Middletown	"	15th May 1780
Elisha Hubbard "	"		Windsor	"	7th March 1780
Leonard Munroe "	"		Wethersfd	"	15th March
Thomas Holmes "	"		Hartford	"	1st Jan' 1781
William Hooker Private	"	Md	"	"	16th May 1780
" Serjt	"		Hartford	16th May 1780	1st Jan' 1781
Lach⁵ Saymore Corp¹	"		Stafford	Jan' 15th 1780	19th May 1780
Alva West Private	·		Stratford	"	20th June "
John Beers Corp¹	D War		"		1st Oct "
"	"		Middletown		1st Jan' 1781
Timothy Cale Drum'	3 years		Groton	1st Oct 1780	9th April 1780
Aden Ames Fifer	"		Lebanon	1st Jan' 1780	1st Jan' 1781
Walter Harris "	"		Stonington	"	28th April 1780
Cyrus Fish "	"		Windsor	"	1st Jan' 1781
Abial Allin Private	"		Lebanon	"	10th March 1780
Amherst Bartlet "	"		Wethersfd	"	4th May "
Abr'm Belding	D War		Stratford	"	1st Jan' 1781
Sam¹ Blackman	8 years		Stratford	"	30th April 1780
David Blackman	"		Hartford	"	"
Joseph Brewer	D War		Hartford	"	
James Chadwick	"			"	10th Jan' 1781

Name	Term	Residence		Date
Willm Chadwick	D War	Hartford	1st Jany 1780	10th Jany 1781
Timo Chapin	3 years	Windsor	"	10th March 1780
Phinehas Chapin	"	New Hartford	"	16th April "
Levi Crowell	"	Middletown	"	26th May "
Robart Colefax	"	Middletown	"	26th Feby "
Diureha Elderkin	"	Groton	"	23d May "
Josiah Gayland	"	New Hartford	"	7th April "
Solomon Goodrich	"	Hebron	"	11th April "
Asa Hull	"	Enfield	"	8th Nov. "
Eliphalet Hill	"	East Hartford	"	21st April "
Ebenezer Hoadley	D War	Guilford	"	1st Jany 1781
Silas Hubbard	3 years	Middletown	"	22nd April 1780
Stephen Hurlbert	"	Winchester	"	1st Jany 1781
Fredk. Jackson	"	Middletown	"	26th May 1780
Epahrass Jones	"	Hartford	"	20th May "
Willm Jones	"	Windsor	"	25th May "
Joseph Johnson	D War	Wethersfd	26th May 1780	1st Jany 1781
Levi Lattimer	3 years	Wethersfd	1st Jany 1780	13th July 1780
Thos Marshall	"	Norwich	"	15th April "
Stephen Moulton	"	Stafford	"	24th June "
Gardon Munsill	"	Windsor	"	19th May "
Normond Newell	"	Farmington	"	1st Jany 1780 †
Timothy Olmstead	"	Hartford	"	1st May "
James Pratt	"	Hebron	"	11th March "
Saml Pulford	D War	Stratford	"	1st Jany 1781
Daniel Robbarts	3 years	Middletown	"	26th Feby 1780
Ozwill Rockwill	"	Wethersfd	"	13th March "
Thomas Raynure	"	Worcester	"	8th July "
Ezra Smith	"	Middletown	"	14th April "
Army Sperry	D War	New Haven	"	1st Jany 1781
John Steele	3 years	Hartford	"	3d June 1780

*The "Short Term Levies" in this regiment which appear in the volume of "Rolls and Lists of Connecticut Men in the Revolution" (Connecticut Historical Society Collections volume VIII), pages 80-82, served in 1780, not in 1779 as is there stated.

†An error for 1781 as is shown by the "Whole term of Service."

	Terms engaged for	Married	Towns engaged for	Comment of Service	Expiration of Service
Josiah Treadway	3 years		Middletown	1st Jany 1780	28th May 1780
Bates Turnor	"		Norfolk	"	7th April "
Mathew Thomsen	"		Stratford	"	16th Jany 1781
John Vibbard	"		Hartford	"	20th March 1780
Daniel Ward	D War		Wethersfield	"	1st Jany 1781
					Timo Allyn C Lt

[State Library, *Revolution* 39, 1.]

[Indorsed] Colo Compy Cap. Timothy Allen Jany 1780.

Muster Roll of the Colo Company in the 9th Connectt Regt of Forces in the service of the United States Commanded by Saml B Webb for October November & Decemr 1780

[The following names, abstracted from this roll, do not appear in the preceding roll or in the previously printed volumes.]

Inlisted	Privates	Term	Remarks
Decr 2d 1780	Abijah Smith	3 years	Reinlisted & on furlough
July 18th	Nehemiah Higgins	6 M Levie	Discharged 4th Decr 1780
Augt 26th	Ozias Landon	"	Discharged 16th Decr 1780
July 18th	John Watson		Discharged 4th Decr 1780

[State Library, *Revolution* 39, 10.]

SECOND COMPANY — LIEUT.-COL. HUNTINGTON.

Return of the Officers and Privates of the Lᵗ Colᵒ Company Colᵒ Samˡ B. Webbs Regᵗ Engaged for three Years or during the War, the time of their Service, pay due, &c., from the 1ˢᵗ Janʸ 1780 to the 1ˢᵗ Janʸ 1781

Names	Rank	Term engaged for	From what Town	Date of Marriage	Commencement of Service	Expiration of Service
Ebenezʳ Huntingdon	Lᵗ Colᵒ		Norwich		1ˢᵗ Janʸ 1780	1ˢᵗ Janʸ 1781
Nathan Beers	Lieut		New Haven		"	"
"	P. Mr					
"	Cloth					
Jared Bunce	Privᵗ	D. War	Wethersfield	before 1ˢᵗ Janʸ 80	16ᵗʰ May 1780	16ᵗʰ May 1780
	Serjᵗ	D. War	Hartford		1ˢᵗ Janʸ 1780	1ˢᵗ Janʸ 1781
Jonathan Arnold	Corpˡ				6ᵗʰ Septʳ 1780	6ᵗʰ Septʳ 1780
	Serjᵗ	D. War	Hartford	before 1ˢᵗ Janʸ 80	1ˢᵗ Janʸ 1780	1ˢᵗ Janʸ 1781
Stephen Risley	Corpˡ				"	"
Jacob Achor	Privᵗ	3 years	Sᵗ Pennsylvania		"	"
Jonathan Arnold		D. War	New Hartford		"	"
Daniel Bostwick			Hartford		"	"
Reuben Cadwell		3 years	Hartford		"	"
Allin Evens		"	Hartford		"	"
Moses Fay			New Hartford		"	"
Asa Fox		D War	Glastenbury	before 1ˢᵗ Janʸ 80	"	"
Naniah Fox		"	Hartford		"	"
William Martin		"	Hartford	before 1ˢᵗ Janʸ 80	"	"
Zebilon Mygatt		"	Wethersfield	before 14ᵗʰ March 80	"	"
David Robarts		"	Middletown		"	"
Stephen Robarts		"	Middletown			
Josep Rawlinson		"	Wethersfield	before 1ˢᵗ Janʸ 80	"	"
Joshua Welles		"	Wethersfield			

Garrison West Point Novʳ 7ᵗʰ 1780   Nathan Beers Lieut.

[Indorsed] Lᵗ Colᵒ January 1780 Exᵈ N. B. Janʸ 1ˢᵗ 1780 to Jan 1ˢᵗ 1781

THIRD COMPANY—MAJ. WYLLYS.

Return of the Officers & Privates of the Majors Compy Coll Saml B. Webbs Regt engaged for three Years or during the War, the time of their Service pay due &c from Jany 1st 1780 to Jany 1st 1781

Names	Term engaged for	From what town	Date of Marriage.	Commencement of Service	Expiration of Service
John P. Wyllys Major		Hartford		Jany 1st 1780	Jany 1 1781
John Meiggs Leint Adjt		Middletown		"	"
Stephen Dormant Sergt	3 years	East Windsor		"	"
Wyman Parker "	D War	Hebron		"	" {Procured Christopher Horton to serve in his stead D. Wood
Peter Phillips "	"	Hartford	before 1st Jany 1780	"	May 6 1780
Elijah Bill "	3 years			"	May 12 "
Benjamin Mack Corpl	"	Say Brook		"	Mar. 7 "
David Wood	"	Windsor		"	Apr 10 "
Benjamin Dix Private	D War	Wethersfield		"	May 15 "
Corpl	"	"		May 16th 1780	Jany 1 1781
John Forbs Private	"	"		Jany 1st 1780	Septr 6 1780
Corpl	"	Say Brook		Septr 6 1780	Jany 1 1781
James Foster Drumr	"	Windsor		Jany 1 1780	"
William Throll "	3 years	Lyme		"	May 10 1780
Joseph Dreed Fifer	"	Groton		"	July 3 1780
Daniel Stoddard "	"	Wethersfield		"	Jany 1 1780
Prichard Beckley		Hartford		"	"
Allen Corning	D War	Windham		"	"
Hezekiah Cary	D War	Wethersfd		"	"
James Goodrich	3 years				"
Christopher Horton	D War	East Windsor		May 6 1780	" {Hired by Serjt Phillips to serve During the War

Name	Term	Residence		Jany 1 1780	Jany 1 1780
Jonathan Hand	D War	Wethersfd			Jany 1 1780
Thomas Morgan	"	"		"	"
Aaron Merrill	3 years	New Hartford	before 1st Jany 1780	"	"
Jabesh Norton	D War	Hartford		"	"
Francis Olmstead	3 years	New "		"	"
John Phillips	"	Hartford	Do	"	"
Phillip Jabor	D War	"		"	"
Elihu Waters	"	Jericho			Jany 7 1780
Alexander Hoy	3 years	Litchfield			Jany 25 "
Ebenezer Forquoir (?)	"	Kent	Do		Mar. 1 "
Eusebius Austin	"	Nw Hartford			Mar. 20 "
David Vibbard	"	Wethersfd			Mar. 20 "
Joel Couch	"	Middletown			Apl. 11 "
Samuel Norton	"	Lebanon			Apl. 28 "
Fitch Lamphier	"				May 26 "
Hosea Burge	"	New London			June 3d "
William Lewis	"	Bolton			Sept 20 "
Jehiel Chapin	"	Wethersfd			Jany 1 1781
Richard Bacon	D War				

[Indorsed] Return of Major Wyllys' Compy 9th Connt Regt Decr 14th 1780.

Camp Highlands Decemr 14th 1780 Jno P Wyllys Major

[State Library, Revolution 39, 3.]

Muster Roll of the Major's Company in the 9th Connecticut Regt in the Service of the United States Commanded by Coll Samuel B Webb for the month of Octr 1780

[The following names, abstracted from this roll, do not appear in the preceding roll or in the previously printed volumes.]

Inlisted	Privates	Term	Remarks
Aug 26th 1780	Thomas Stone	6 months	Discharged 14th Decr 1780
" 1780	Nathan Elwood		Prisoner of War
1777	Richard Bacon		

[State Library, Revolution 39, 12.]

FOURTH COMPANY—CAPT. BULKLEY.

Return of the Officers & Privates of the 1st Capt Company Col S. B. Webbs Regt engaged for three Years or during the War, the time of their service, Pay due &c from January 1st 1780 to Jany 1st 1781.

Names		Time engaged for	Date of Marriage	Commenct of Service	Expiration of Service	Town engaged for
Edward Bulkley	Capt			1st Jany 1780	1 Jany 1781	Wethersfield
Saml Mears	Lieut			"	20 Novr 1780	Hartford
Jonathn White	"	D War			20 Mar 80	New Haven
Simon Giffin	Sergt Majr	"	before 1st Jany	20 March 1780		Wethersfield
David Pratt	Qr Mr Sergt	"		1st Jany 1780	1 Jany 1781	Glastonbury
Wm Patterson	Dr Majr	"		"	"	New Haven
Elijah Boardman	Fife Majr	"		"	"	Wethersfield
Ithurel Flowers	Sergt	3 years		"	"	N Hartford
Amaziah Chappel	"	"	Do	"	7 May 1780	Labanon
Rhoderick Hopkins	Corpl	"		"	28 Febry 80	N Hartford
Daniel Sizor	"	D War		20 March 80	20 Mar 80	Middletown
Moses Griswould	Private	"		1st Jany 1780	1st Jany 81	"
	Corpl	"		6 Sept 80	6 Sept 1780	Wethersfield
	Private corpl	"		1st Jany 1780	1 Jany 81	"
Moses Hatch	Drmr	3 years			"	"
Christopher Brown	Fifer	D War				Groton
Arunah Hackley	"	3 years				Norwich
Daniel Puffer		D War				Lebanon
Moses Boardman	Private	3 years			13 June 80	Middletown
Zebediah Briggs		D War			1 Jany 81	Chatham
Wm Beaeton		"			"	Stratford
Prince Freeman		"			"	Groton
Gideon Goff		"			"	Wethersfield
Bazeleel Hamlin		"			"	Sandwich Mass B.
Saml Harrington						
Thos Loveland					"	Glastonbury
Elisha Mygott					"	Hartford

		1 Jany 81		
Simeon Puffer	3 years	1 Jany 81	1ˢᵗ Oct 1780	Labanon
Marshal Stocking	D War	"	1ˢᵗ Jany 81	Chatham
Joseph Treat	"	"		Wethersfield
Hez⁵ Wheeler		"		Stafford
Christopher Avery	3 years	"	8 Mar 80	Groton
Asa Butler	"	"	11 " "	Stafford
Phenious Shepherd	"	"	20 " "	N. Hartford
Alexandˡ Dochester	"	"	20 " "	Farmington
George Hopkins	"	"	7 Apr "	New Hartford
Ignatious Waterman	"	"	28 " "	Labanon
Justus Blin	"	"	20 May 80	Wethersfield
Jonathᵃ Wood	"	"	22 " "	Hartford
Nathˡ Moungomury	"	"	13 June 80	Chatham
Zebulon Bourrows	"	"	1ˢᵗ July 80	East Windsor
Felix Curtis	"	"	3 Augᵗ 80	Waterbury
Elihu Stowe	"	"	15 " "	Middletown
Noah Roberts Corpˡ		"	20 May 80	Labanon

Garrison West Point Novᵇʳ 17ᵗʰ 1780   Samˡ Mears Lieut.

[State Library, Revolution 39, 4.]

[Indorsed] 1ˢᵗ Compʸ Cap: Edward Bulkley Exᵈ N. B. Jany 1780

Muster Roll of the 1ˢᵗ Captˢ Company in the 9ᵗʰ Connecticut Battalion in the service of the United States commanded by Colˡ Samˡ B. Webb for the months of Octʳ November and December 1780
[The following names, abstracted from this roll, do not appear in the preceding roll or in the previously printed volumes.]

Enlisted	Privates	Term	Remarks
July 23ᵈ 1780	Zenus Lines	31ˢᵗ Decʳ	discharged Decʳ 9ᵗʰ 1780
Aug. 16ᵗʰ "	David Willets	" "	" 16ᵗʰ "
	Elijah Mygott		Transferd to the Regᵗ Invaleads Octʳ 3ᵈ 1780

[State Library, Revolution 39, 15.]

FIFTH COMPANY—CAPT. WALKER.

Return of the Officers & Privates of Capt Joseph Walker's Compy Coll Saml B. Webbs Regt Engaged for three or During the War, the time of their Service, Pay Due &c from the 1st of Jany 1780 to the 1st of January 1781.

Names		Term Engaged for	For what town	Date of Marriage	Commencement of service	Expiration of Service
Joseph Walker	Capt		Stratford		Jany 1st 1780	Jany 1st 1781
Stephen Ingham	Serjt	3 years	Saybrook		"	Apl 14th 1780
Amos West	"	"	Lebanon		"	May 27th 1780
Francis Nicholson	"	D War	Glastonbury		"	Jany 1st 1781
Waitstill Dickinson	Corp	"	Weathersfield		"	"
Simeon Holmes	"	"	"		"	
Elijah Porter	Serjt	"	Hartford		Sept 6th 1780	Sept 6th 1780
John Kirkum	Drumr	"	Weathersfield		Jany 1st 1780	Jany 1st 1780
Theodore Andruss	Flfr	3 years	New Hartford		"	"
Lewis Anguine	Private	D War	Stratford		"	Apl 10th 1780
Joel Beers		"			"	Jany 1st 1781
Timothy Beevins		"	Farmington		"	"
Peter Butler		3 years	Chatham	before 1st Jany	"	June 16th 1780
David Chapin		"	New Hartford		"	Jany 1st 1781
William Fay		"	Winchester	before 1st Jany	"	"
John Fay			New Hartford		"	
Remembrance Filley		D War	Winchester	before 1st Jany	"	Apl 12th 1780
Theodore Gilbert		3 years	New Hartford		"	Jany 1st 1781
John Graves		D War	Hartford		"	April 7th 1780
Jacob Griswold		"	Weathersfield		"	May 22nd 1780
George Hills		3 years	Simsbury		"	Jany 1st 1781
Orry King		D War	Stratford	before 1st Jany	"	March 26th 1780
Garmaliel Olmsted		3 years	New Hartford		"	Jany 1st 1781
William Prier		"	Enfield		"	Novr 8th 1780
Zeri Page		"	Lebanon	before 1st Jany	"	April 28th 1780
Asher Russel		D War	Weathersfield		"	Jany 1st 1781
Samuel Smith		3 years	Straford		"	"
Thoms Stanley		D War	Weathersfield		"	"

			before 1st Jany	Jany 1st 1780	Jany 1st 1781
Aaron Stevens	D War	New Hartford		Jany 1st 1780	Jany 1st 1781
John Thomas	"	New Haven		"	"
Ezra Tryon	3 years	Glastenbury		"	May 29th 1780
Moses Ward	"	Middletown		"	Feby 5th 1780
Joel Welton	D War	Farmington			Jany 1st 1781
James Wayland	"	Stratford		Feby 8th 1780	"
Abel Burton		"			

Highlands Decr 20th 1780 Francis Nicholson Serjt

[Indorsed] 2d Company Jany 1780 Cap. Joseph Walker

SIXTH COMPANY – CAPT. WILLIAMS.

Return of the Officers & Privates of the 3rd Company in Col¹ Sam¹ B. Webbs Reg¹ Engaged for three years or during the War, the time of their service, Pay due &c from Jan¹ 1ˢᵗ 1780

Names		Term Engaged for	Date of Marriage	Cmt of Service	Expiration of Service	Remarks
Sam¹ Wm Williams	Captⁿ	D War		Jany 1ˢᵗ 1780	Jany 1ˢᵗ 1781	Wethersfield
Thomas Gerralls	Sergᵗ	3 years		"	March 3	Hartford
Wm Chapman	"		Married	"		Say Brook
Joseph Gilbert	"	D W	Married	"	Feby 20th	N. Hartford
Matthew Cadwell	Corpˡ		Married		Jany 1ˢᵗ 1781	Hartford
Phineas Cadwell	"	3 years			March 7	N. Hartford
Stephen Butler		D War			Jany 1ˢᵗ 1781	Saybrook, promoted to Capt. 20th March
Wm Kircum	Dmʳ			"	"	Guilford
Richᵈ Jones	fifer	3 years			June 20th 80	Hartford
John Andras	Privᵗ	"	Married		Feby 4th 80	Farmington
Ezra Andrus		"	Married		April 7th 80	N. Hartford
Abraham Blin		"	Married		April 9th 80	Wethersfield
Charles Bulkley		"			March 26th 80	
Jonathⁿ Butler		"			Jany 1ˢᵗ 81	Say Brook
Jesse Chalker		"			March 4th 80	
Charles Churchill		"			June 2d 80	Wethersfield
Wm Clark		"	Married		April 5th 80	New London
Sam¹ Cole		"	Married		March 26th 80	Hartford
Elisha Cole		D War			Jany 1ˢᵗ 81	"
Gidⁿ Crittenden		3 years	Married		March 14th 80	Middle Town
Avuara (?) Copeland		"			Jany 1ˢᵗ 81	Pomfrett
Josiah Bordman		"			June 20th 80	Bolton
Daniel Davis			Married		July 12th 80	Groton
Peter Holt		D War	Married		Jany 1ˢᵗ 81	New London
Nathˡ Holt		3 years				Groton
Ephm Holdridge			Married			
Joseph Hawley		"				"
Thomas Hillet		D War				Preston

Name		Term			Town
Silas Lamb	Married	3 years	Jany 1st 1780	Jany 1st 81	Groton
Cyprian Morrills		"	"	May 4th 80	N. Hartford
Roger Morrills	Married	"	"	April 7th 80	"
Sam¹ Parker		D W	"	Jany 1st 81	Stratford
Isaac Payne		3 years	"	April 24th	N. Hartford
John Packer		"	"	Jany 1st 81	Groton
Sam¹ Phillips		"	"	March 16th 80	Colebrooke
Grhᵐ Robertson	Married	D War	"	Jany 1st 81	Coventry
Frederick Stoddard		"	"	"	Groton
Sam¹ Schoolcraft			"		Stonington
Stephen Scovil	Married	3 years	"	April 11th 80	Winchester
James Spencer			"	March 20th 80	N Hartford
Lemuel Sperry		D War	"	Jany 1st 81	Norfolk
Jesse Obbard		3 years	"	August 22d 80	Hartford
Sam¹ Weaver		"	"	Feby 1st 80	Weathersfield
Jesse Williams		"	"	Jany 1st 81	Groton
Peter Freeman			"	"	C Windsor
Caesar Freeman			July 12th 80		Wethersfield

The above is a true Copy of the original abstract sent to the Committee for settling the Depreciations for the year 1780

Camp at West Point Novʳ 29ᵗʰ 1780   Sam¹ Wᵐ Williams Capt

[Indorsed] 3ʳᵈ Compʸ Cap. S. W. Williams   Depreciation Abstract for 1780

[State Library. Revolution 39, 9.]

Muster Roll of the 3ᵈ Company in the 9ᵗʰ Regiment of Connecticut Forces in the service of the United States Commanded by Col° Sam¹ B Webb; for the Months of October November & Decemʳ 1780

[The following names, extracted from this roll, do not appear in the preceding roll or in the previously printed volumes.]

Enlisted	Privates	Term		Remarks
Feby 11ᵗʰ 78	Amasa Copeland	3 years		Blicksmith
	Ephraim Robertson	D War		Discharged Decʳ 3ʳᵈ and Enlisted for 3 years
July 28ʳᵈ 80	Jedediah Woodworth	6 Months		

[State Library, Revolution 39, 18.]

SEVENTH COMPANY – CAPT. HOPKINS.

Return, of the Officers and Privates of the 4th Capt° Company, Col¹ Sam¹ B. Webb's Reg¹ engaged for three Years, or during the War, the time of their Service Pay due &c from the 1ˢᵗ January 1780 to the 1ˢᵗ January 1781

Names	Rank	Term Engaged for	From what Town	Date of Marriage	Commencᵗ of Service	Expiration of Service
Elisha Hopkins	Capt		Hartford		1ˢᵗ Janʸ 1780	1ˢᵗ Janʸ 1781
Ebenʳ Frothingham	Lieutᵗ		Middletown		"	"
"	Qʳ Mʳ				29ᵗʰ Marᵇ 1780	"
Jeremiah Lord	Serjᵗ	D War	Saybrook		1ˢᵗ Janʸ 1780	
Nathan Savage	"	"	Middletown	before 1ˢᵗ Janʸ 80	"	
Samuel Helmes	"	3 years	Lebanon		"	12ᵗʰ June 1780
Prentice Stores	"	"	Wethersfield		"	28ᵗʰ Apˡ 1780
Benjamin Mix	Corpˡ	"	N Hartford		"	7ᵗʰ March 1780
Aaron Jones	Private	D War	Saybrook	Do	"	19ᵗʰ March 1781*
Joseph Bacon	Corpˡ	3 years	Middletown		20ᵗʰ Marᵇ 80	1ˢᵗ Janʸ 1781
Aaron Abercrombie	Drumʳ	D War	Raisley (?)		1ˢᵗ Janʸ 1780	15ᵗʰ April 1780
John Barnham	Private	"	Danbury		"	1ˢᵗ Janʸ 1781
Curtis Crane		"	Wethersfield	Do	"	
Joshua Howe		"	New Haven	Do	"	
Stephen Kellogg		"	Wethersfield		"	
Seth Montague		"	"		"	
Adam Mott		3 years	Manchester	Do	"	
Jesse Wilkerson		D War	Nine Partners	Do	"	
William Winans		"	Wethersfield		"	
Richard Belding		"	Farmington		"	
Chauncey Lewis						
Isaac Lewis						
Jerijah Thayer		3 years	Bolton		"	
Samuel Vallitt		D War	Bishopsgate		"	
Levitt Millard		3 years	Bolton		"	19ᵗʰ Septʳ 1780
James Anderson		"	Groton	Do	"	15ᵗʰ Apˡ 1780
Thomas Barnes		"	Middletown	Do	"	22ᵈ May 80

Name	Term	Residence		Date
John Benham	3 years	N. Hartford	1st Jany 1780	7th Apl 80
David Covil	"	"	"	5th May 80
Ebenezer Davis	"	Wethersfield	Do	12th May 80
Gurdon Geer	"	Groton	"	20th Marh 80
Seth Kellogg	"	Hartford	"	22d Apl 80
Christopher Kilby	"	Wethersfield	"	3d Marh 80
Amos Porter	"	"	"	10th May 80
Boswill Richardson	"	Lebanon	Do	26th May 80
Eli Simons	"	Colebrook	"	24th April 80
Jehosaphat Starr Ensign Q.M.	"	Middletown	Do	29th March 80

Eben' Frothingham Lieu'

[State Library, Revolution 39, 6.]

Garrison West Point Nov' 25th 1780

[Indorsed] 4th Compy Exd N. B. Elisha Hopkins Cap

Muster Roll of the 4th Capts Company in the 9th Connecticut Battalion in the Service of the United States Commanded by Coll Saml B. Webb for Octr Novr and Decr 1780.

[The following names, extracted from this roll, do not appear in the preceding roll or in the previously printed volumes.]

Inlisted	Privates	Term	Remarks
July 28d 1780	Ira Mott		
	John Porter	31st Decr	Discharged Decr 14th

[State Library, Revolution 39, 14.]

* An Error for 1780 as the "Whole Term of Service" shows.
† "Joined (?) from Coll Sherburnes Regt"

EIGHTH COMPANY – CAPT. HEART

Return of the Officers and Privates of the 5th Compy Col Saml B. Webbs Regt engaged for 3 years or during the War, the time of their Service, Pay pr Month &c from 1st of Jany 1780 to 1st of Jany 1781.

Names	Term engaged for	From what town	Date of Marriage	Commencement of Service	Expiration of Service
John Heart Capn		Say Brook		1 Jany 80	9 Apl 80
Joseph Bentley Ensgn		Groton		"	"
Jabez H. Tomlinson "		Stratford			1st Jany 81
Richard Price Sergt	3 years	Wethersfield		5 Aprl 80	22d Apl 80
Jesse Starr "	D War	Groton		1 Jany 80	23d Apl 80
Daniel Williams "	"	Wethersfield	before 1 Jany		1 Jany 81
Joshua Cone Corpl	"	Middletown			22d Apl 80
" Sergt	"	Middletown		22 Apl	1 Jany 81
Prosper Hosmer Private	"	N Haven		1 Jany 80	16 May 80
Samuel Beamount Sergt	"	Say Brook		16 May	1 Jany 81
David Parks Corpl	"	Groton		1 Jany	23 Dec 80
Willm Zepsor Drumr	"	Middletown			15 Apl
David Lindsay "	"	Wethersfield			1 Jany 81
Moses Clarck Fifer	"	Labanon		19 July 80	31st May 80
Reuben Brown "	"	Groton		1 Jany 80	1 Jany 81
Jabin Bennet Private	"	N. Hartford			20 June 80
Allen Bradley "	"	N Haven			1st Jany 81
Edward Brown		Wethersfield	before 1 Jany		‥
Daniel Bushnell		Hartland	Do		‥
Nehemiah Baron	3 years	Groton			‥
James Barnard	"	"			
Joshua Basset	"	Mansfield			31st July 80
Hezekiah Brewster	"	Norwich			26 May
Caleb Curtis	"	Northbury	before 1 Jany		‥
Brewster Chappell	"	Labanon			‥
Joshua Carpenter	"	"			
Amos Chappman	"	Groton		"	1st Jany 81

Name	Term	Place			
Martin Dibble	3 years	Say Brook		1 Jany 80	4 June 80
West Brook Day	"	Hartford	D°		24 Augt 80
Jack Freeman	D War	Lyme		23 Sep^t 80	1 Jany 81
Peter Freeman	3 years	Groton	D°	1 Jany 80	1 Jany 81
Elisha Faning	"	Wethersfield		"	"
Hezekiah Nott	D War	Labanon		"	18 June 80
Isaac Killogg	3 years	Hartford		"	20 March
Israel Loomis	"	Wethersfield		"	1 Jany 81
Josiah Robbins	D War	Hartford		"	"
Sam¹ Roberts	"	N Hartford		"	13th Ap^l
Elisha Roberts	"	Wellington		"	14 June
Willm Stiles	"	Groton		"	7 July
Ralph Williams	"	Wethersfield		"	19 March
Gideon Welles	"	Say Brook	D°	"	1 Jany 81
Isaac Wardin	"	Wethersfield		"	23 Ap^l 80
George Price					

[State Library, *Revolution* 39, 5.]

[Indorsed] 5th Comp^y Ex^d N. B. Capt John Heart Jany 1780

Muster Roll of the 5th Company in the 9th Connecticut Battalion in the Service of the United States Commanded by Col° Sam¹ B Webb for the Months of October Nov^r & December 1780.

[The following names, extracted from this roll, do not appear in the preceding roll nor in the previously printed volumes.]

John Riley Captain Lately Exchanged not Joind
Nehemiah Barns 3 years

Mch 21st 1778

[State Library, *Revolution* 39, 15.]

LIGHT INFANTRY COMPANY—CAPT. WELLS.

Return of the Officers & Privates of Capⁿ Roger Wells's compʸ of Light Infantry in the 9ᵗʰ Connecticut Regᵗ Commanded by Colˡ Samuel B. Webb engaged for three years or during the War the time of their service pay due &ᶜ from January 1, 1780 to January 1, 1781.

Name	Rank	Term engaged for	from what Town	Date of Marriage	Comm't of service	Expiration of service
Roger Wells	Lieutᵗ		Weatherford		Janʸ 1 1780	April 9ᵗʰ 1780
"	Captⁿ		"		April 9ᵗʰ 1780	Janʸ 1ˢᵗ 1781
Daniel Brewer	Serjᵗ	3 years	Hartford		Janʸ 1 80	"
Bela Scovell	Corp	D War	Guilford			
"	Serjᵗ					
Joseph Day	Corpˡ		Hartford		May 15 80	May 15ᵗʰ 1780
"	Serjᵗ		"		Janʸ 1 80	Janʸ 1ˢᵗ 1781
Samˡ Easton	Corpˡ				May 15 80	May 15ᵗʰ 1780
Walter Booth	Private		New Haven		Janʸ 1 80	Janʸ 1ˢᵗ 1781
"	Corpˡ		"			
David Lounsbury	Private		"		March 20ᵗʰ 80	March 20 80
"	Corpˡ				Janʸ 1 1780	Janʸ 1ˢᵗ 1781
Ezekiel Winchel	Drumʳ		Weatherfield		Augᵗ 28 80	Augᵗ 28 1780
Hough White	Fifer	3 years	Middletown		Janʸ 1 1780	Janʸ 1ˢᵗ 1781
Jnᵒ Allen	Private	D W	N Haven		"	"
Noah Barnham	"		Danbury		"	"
Timothy Fay		3 years	N. Hartford	Mᵈ	"	"
Ichabod Goodrich		D W	Wetherford		"	"
Joseph Hand			"		"	"
Joel Hoyt			Stamford	Mᵈ	"	"
Samˡ Hull			N. Haven		"	"
Benjamin Kircum			Guilford		"	"
Asa Leonard		3 years	Balton		"	"
Jonathan Miller		D War	Wetherfield		"	"
Brian Montique			Stratford		"	"
Thomas Norton		3 years	Middletown		"	"

			Janʸ 1 1780	Janʸ 1ˢᵗ 1781
Moses Porter	D W	Hartford	Janʸ 1 1780	Janʸ 1ˢᵗ 1781
Josiah Savage	3 years	Middletown	"	"
Joseph Simons	"	N. Hartford	"	"
Seth Stannard	D War	Winchester		

[Indorsed] L. Infantry Cap Roger Wells Exᵈ N. B. Janʸ 1780

CONNECTICUT LINE, 1781 - 1783.

[*See Record of Connecticut Men in the Revolution, pages 301-355.*]

SUPPLIES, 1781.

An Alphabetical List of the Names of the Officers and Soldiers in the Conn^t Line who have rec^d Family Supplies from the several Towns for 1781.

	Names	Rank	Towns to which they belong
5	Anderson Thomas	Lieut.	Lyme
	Atkins Josiah	Priv.	Waterbury
5	Avery Simeon	Lieut.	Groton
2	Allay William	Priv.	New Haven A^y
4(?)	Alling Jonathan	"	"
D	Adams Samuel	"	Canterbury
[ ]	Archer Grippin	"	Hebron
Inv^d	Auger George	"	Middletown Invalid
[ ]	Acley Thomas	"	East Haddam
†	Andreus Thomas	"	"
D	Adams Rhodrick	"	Symsbury
1	Andrus Asa	"	Weathersfield
5	Abbe Jeduthan	"	Hartford
1	Abbe Eleazer ·	"	"
	Alverd Thomas G.	Serg.	Farmington A^y
Inv^d	Andrus Theodore	"	" Invalids
1	Andrus Obediah	Priv.	"
S	Alling Abel	"	" Sapper
1	Arnold Seth	"	"
5	Aldredge W^m	"	Preston Disert Aug. 1 '81
1	Austin Phinehas	"	Suffield
D	Barber Amaziah	"	Symsbury
4	Bacon William	"	Middletown
In^d	Boardman Moses	"	" Invalid
3	Brown Benjamin	"	Canterbury
4	Baker Edward	"	New Haven
	Bishop Simeon	"	"
A	Barns Solomon	"	"
4	Blakeley Enos	"	"
A	Bishop Nath^{ll}	"	"
4	Blakslee Jared	"	"
1	Brown Henry	"	"
4	Blakslee Zealous	"	"
4	Beeck Asa	"	"
4	Brocket Hezekiah	"	"
2	Billins Stephen Ju^r	Capt.	Groton
5	Brightman Henry	Priv.	"
	Brice Robert	"	"
5	Bristor Stephen	"	Waterbury
1	Beckwith Phinehas	Ens.	Lyme
	Burnham Joseph	Conr^y	"
5	Butler William	Priv.	"
4	Booth Henry	"	Coventry
1	Brown Ebenezer	"	Killingly
5	Bayden Elhanan	"	"
D	Bugbee Pelatiah	"	Mansfield
3	Bordin Samuel	"	Norfolk

	Names	Rank	Towns to which they belong
2	Baldwin Caleb	Capt.	Killingsworth
	Brewster Hezeki[h]	Priv.	Norwich
1	Briant John	"	"
4	Bennet Benjamin	"	
[ ]	Beebee James	Capt.	Stratford Sapper
3	Booth Nathaniel	Ens.	"
4	Bayley Henry	Priv.	"
2	Brown Charles	"	New Fairfield
	Beardsley S. Wheeler	"	"
1	Barnum Timothy	"	"
2	Bishop David	"	Danbury
†	Benidict Ezra	"	"
1	Blanch Robin	"	Colchester
5	Beamon Cæsar	"	"
1	Booth Henry	Serg.	Enfield
3	Burges Ephraim	Priv.	"
1	Bunnel Amos	"	Southington
2	Brister John	"	Winsor
5	Brown Elias	"	"
Inv[d]	Barnes Moses	"	Wallingford Invalid
4	Bradley Daniel	"	"
3	Basset William	Serg.	Watertown
4	Barnes David	Priv.	Cheshire
4	Bristol Benjamin	"	"
4	Beldin John	"	Milford
H	Burk John	"	"
4	Bebee Joel	"	"
In[d]	Bristol Jonathan	"	" Invalid
3	Bates Daniel	"	Haddam
4	Baily Robert	"	"
	Bates Eleazer	"	"
1	Bowers Ephraim	"	Chatham
In[d]	Brown Edward	"	Weathersfield Invalid
4	Ball John	Lieut.	Guilford
2	Bishop Thalmeno	Priv.	"
4	Benton Edward	"	"
4	Buckley Job	"	Seabrook
2	Bushnel Constant	"	"
D	Bugbee John	"	Mansfield
	Bull Epaphras	Maj.	Hartford
1	Belden Simeon	Lieut.	"
3	Brewer Daniel	Serg.	"
	Bitons Timothy	Priv.	Farmington
	Brownson Roger	"	"
1	Belden Ezra	"	"
4	Bagdon Cezar	"	Branford
4	Blodget Artemas	"	Salisbury
D	Barns Steaphen	"	New Hartford
2	Bennet Isaac	"	Ridgfield
2	Beach David	Ens.	New Milford
2	Bostwick Eben[r]	Serj.	"
D	Bewel David	Priv.	"
D	Bennet John	"	" Deserted
A	Barlow John	"	Kent
2	Barnum Amos	Serj.	"
2	Barnum Stephen	"	"
3	Bushnell Daniel	Priv.	Hartland

	Names	Rank	Towns to which they belong
3	Brown Jonathan	Priv.	Norwalk
5	Baſ]ton John	"	"
5	Betts Elijah	"	"
2	Barnes Ambrose	"	"
1	Bacon Nehemiᵸ	"	Pomfrett
5	Billins Peleg	"	Preston
5	Ball Humphry	"	Lebanon
5	Buck Frank	"	"
	Bates David	"	Stamford
2	Batterson George	"	Fairfield
2	Chamberlain Ephrᵐ	Capt.	Wallingford
	Coedry Joseph	Priv.	Milford
2	Cohale Cornᵃ		
	alias Frost Samˡˡ	"	"
4	Clark Nathaniel	"	Durham
D	Churchill Elijah	"	Enfield
Invᵈ	Culver Timothy	"	Southington
1	Carter Edward	"	Colchester
†	Chapman Rufus	"	Stratford
†	Clark Ithurel	"	Danbury
	Corts Richard	"	Winchester
3	Comstock Sirajah	"	Norfolk
1	Cleft Lemuel	Capt.	Plainfield
4	Clark Martin	Priv.	New Haven
†	Clarrage Francis	"	"
5	Chapman Edward	"	Hebron
4	Cleaveland John	Ens.	Canterbury
D	Cushman Daniel	Priv.	"
5	Carter Reuben	"	"
3	Cleaveland Curtis	"	"
2	Clark Othniel	Lieut.	Middletown
2	Cone Ozias	Priv.	"
	Carrell John	"	Symsbury Deserted
1	Case Jeremiah	"	"
	Crocker Grace	"	"
D	Cone Elijah	"	East Haddam
	Chapman Joseph	Lieut.	Norwich
5	Chatfield John	Priv.	Killingsworth
5	Caesar Bristol	"	New Town
†	Cone Samuel	"	Haddam
†	Carey George	"	Chatham
1	Carter Aaron	"	"
1	Coombs William	"	Weathersfield
3	Crane Curtis	"	"
3	Clark William	"	"
4	Comstock Samuel	"	Seabrook
1	Curtis Daniel	"	Hartford
3	Cadwell Mathew	Serj.	"
5	Clark Abraham	Priv.	"
5	Case Richard	"	"
	Corning Malachi	"	"
A	Curtis Daniel	"	Farmington
4	Cooper James	"	Branford
	Chipman John	Capt.	Salisbury Prisoner
4	Chappel Curtis	Priv.	"
D	Cook Nathan	"	"
2	Convers Thomas	Capt.	Goshen

Names		Rank	Towns to which they belong
2	Caswell Ezra	Priv.	"
2	Carter Nathan	"	"
5	Comstock Samuel	Capt.	Norwalk
5	Chapel Russell	Priv.	Reading
2	Coley Nathan	Serj.	"
3	Duggan James	Priv.	Canterbury
[ ]	Doyl Hugh	"	New Haven
	Denison John Jr	"	" Deserted
Inᵈ	Davis James	"	" Invalid
	Davis Daniel	"	Groton Deserted
1	Dickenson George	"	Southington
4	Dudley Zebulon	"	"
5	Dodge Benjamin	"	Colchester
5	Dodge Elihu	"	"
2	Denslaw Martin	Ens.	Windsor
5	Davis Jonathan	Priv.	Watertown
†	Daniels Samuel	"	Milford
4	Davison Isaac	Serj.	Washington
4	Davison John	Priv.	"
A	Dickson George	"	Danbury
3	Dawns John	"	Stratford
Inᵈ	Demmon John	"	Woodbury Invalids
1	Durkee John	Col.	Norwich
	Doud Moses	Priv.	Guilford Deserted
	Doud Zechariah	"	" 6 months man
2	Dota Benjamin	"	Seabrook
D	Dimmick Joseph	"	Mansfield
1	Dunham Cornelius	"	Farmington
D	Dorman Garsham	"	Sharon
S	Dayley James	"	New Milford Sapper
2	Demming Wait	"	Goshen
2	D' Forest Samuel	Lieut.	Norwalk
3	Davis Joseph	Priv.	Preston
	Durfe Thomas	"	Fairfield
4	Elwood Joseph	"	"
5	Ellis Carpenter	"	Volunton
4	Egleston David	"	New Haven
1	Ells Edward	Capt.	Middletown
X	Ellis John	Revᵈ	Norwich
5	Eldridge Samuel	Priv.	Willington
	Emmit John	"	N. Haven
	Ely John	Col.	Seabrook
3	Evens Abiather	Serj.	Hartford
1	Evens Henry	Priv.	"
5	Elmore Calib	"	Harwington
1	Elles Nathan	"	Preston
1	Fox John	"	Colchester
2	Fenn Daniel	"	Washington
4	Foot Ezra	"	Derby
3	Filley Remembranee	"	Winchester
Inᵈ	Fulford, John	Serj.	Watertown Invalid
4	Field Edmund	Priv.	Wallingford
A	Fryar Charles	"	New Haven
A	Foot Isaac	"	"
2	Franklin Samˡˡ	"	Killingsworth
1	Fanning Charles	Lieut.	Norwich
5	Farnsworth Nathˡˡ	Priv.	"

	Names	Rank	Towns to which they belong
1	Foster John	Priv.	Middletown
D	Fuller Jacob	"	Symsbury alias Tullar
3	Fuller Ely	"	" alias Tullar
	Farnham Abiel	"	Canterbury
3	Freeman Edward	"	Groton
4	Farmer Thomas	Lieut.	Derby
	Fayer Elijah	Priv.	Voluntown Deserted
	Ford Daniel	"	New Haven
5	Ford Martin	"	"
5	Farnsworth Nath[ll]	"	Colchester
3	Fox Asa	"	Glastenbury
1	Fuller John	"	. Chatham
5	Freeman Sam[ll]	"	"
	Flag Jonathan	"	Hartford
	Fisher Isaac	"	Sharon Deserted
	Farnam Benj[n]	"	Ashford
4	Foot Eben[r]	"	Branford
4	Fits Gerrald Hen[y]	"	Salisbury
4	Fitch Joseph	"	"
3	Fox Simeon	"	New Hartford
3	Fuller James	"	Suffield
2	Fowler Nehemiah	"	Fairfield
	Feego Peter	"	"
8	Glass Silas	Priv.	Canterbury
3	Gates Nath[ll]	"	
4	Gitston Jacob	"	Middletown
S	Graves William	"	" Sapper
3	Gillet Jacob	"	Symsbury
In[d]	Gardner Sherman	"	Norwich Invalid
	Gillet Benj[n]	"	New Haven
3	Grant Azariah	"	East Windsor
In[d]	Gibbs Samuel	Lieut.	Windsor Invalid
	Gibbs William	Priv.	Colchester Deserted
3	Gay Jason	"	New Fairfield
5	Gaylord Jonathan	"	Watertown
4	Goldsmith William	"	Milford
5	Gillet John	"	"
1	Grover Amaza	"	Killingly
1	Graves John	"	"
5	Griffeth George	"	Voluntown
5	Gladen William	"	Haddam
In[d]	Graham Joseph	"	Chatham Invalid
4	Goodrich Levi	Ens.	"
3	Giffin Simon	Serj.	Weathersfield
4	Grant James	Priv.	Seabrook
4	Graham Cyrus	"	"
2	Gilson Eleazer	"	Sharon
[ ]	Goodrich David	"	"
4	Garrie John	"	Branford
[ ]	Griggory Mathew	Ens.	Norwalk
[ ]	Grant Luke	Priv.	Preston
[ ]	Granger Sam[ll]	"	Suffield
8	Gavet Steaphen		Stonington
4	Hoskins Timothy	"	Windsor
5	Harris Champlin	"	Colchester
5	Hallimage John	"	Enfield
5 (?)	Hall Hiram	"	"

	Names	Rank	Places to which they belong
3	Halley Nathan	Priv.	Stratford
3	Harrop Joseph	"	"
A	Harris Henry	"	"
†	Hewet Elisha	"	Danbury
1	Hawkins William	"	"
	Hall (?) Samuel	"	Wallingford
4	Hooker John	"	Milford
4	Hine Titus	"	"
5	Hull Eliakim	"	Durham
3	Hamlin Joel	"	Norfolk
	Howard Richard	"	Windham
4	Howel Nicholass	"	New Haven
5	Huse Bodwell	"	"
3	Hull Samuel	"	"
[ ]	Hide James ye 3d	Ens.	Norwich
1	Harrinton Elisha	Priv.	Symsbury
D	Humphry Timothy	"	"
D	Hunt John	"	"
1	Hill John	"	" Deserted
	Harvey Ezra	"	East Haddam
1	Hubbard Hezekiah	Lieut.	Middletown
2	Henshaw William	"	"
1	Hull David	Priv.	"
1	Higgins William	Lieut.	Lyme
4	Hodge David	"	Milford
5	Hanes Jonathan	"	Lyme
Id	Holden John	"	Glastenbury Invalid
3	Holmes Simeon	"	Weathersfield
3	Howe Joshua	"	New Haven
2	Hall Philemon	Lieut.	Guilford
2	Handy Samuel	Priv.	"
	Hall Eben	"	
4	Hough Simon	"	Seabrook
	Hadlack Reubin	"	Hartford
1	Hill Daniel	"	"
1	Jonathan Heart	Capt.	Farmington
4	Hobart John	Lieut.	Branford
4	Hoadley Samll	St	"
4	Harrison Jarius	"	New Milford
2	Hawley C. Joseph	"	Harwington
5	Hodg Asael	Capt.	Kent Invalid
Ind	Hills Ebenezer	"	Norwalk
5	Hubbell Seth	Priv.	Suffield
D	Hatherway Seth	"	"
D	Hatherway Willbre	"	Lebanon
3	Hills Phillip	"	Stonington
	Harvey Ephraim	"	Stamford
5	Hawley Abraham	"	Fairfield
A	Hubbel Isaac	Capt.	"
4	Hall Steaphen	Serj.	
H	Jones Thomas	Priv.	Wallingford
4	Johnson Abraham	"	New Haven
	Joslin John	"	Colchester
1	Johnson Bristol	"	Middletown
2	Johnson Jonathan	Lt. Col.	Durham
4	Johnson William	Priv.	Stratford
4	Jones Jasper	"	

	Names	Rank	Places to which they belong
[ ]	Johnson Isaac	Priv.	Guilford
3	Jones Aaron	"	Seabrook
3	Jarrels Thomas	Serj.	Hartford
H	Jones Joseph	Priv.	Branford
5	Johnson John	"	Norwalk
2	Jackson Jonathan	"	"
5	Jones Dan¹	"	Lebanon
	James Phillup	"	Fairfield
3	Kimball Jedede^h	"	Norwich
5	Kimberley Ephraim	Lieut.	New Town
†	Knowles James	Priv.	Haddam
D(?)	Kneeland Jesse	"	.Chatham
	Kellcey Preson	"	Guilford 6 month man
†	Kenney Benjamin	"	Hartford
2	Kelsey Noah	"	Sharon
D	King Joseph	"	Suffield
4	Lillie Abner	"	Windham
4	Lord Jabez	"	New Haven
5	Lines John	"	Colchester
5	Lane (?) Joel	"	Waterbury
1	Lung Joseph	"	Middletown
	Lawrence Amos	Serj.	Windsor Discharged
In^d	Lamberton Obed	Priv.	" " Invalid
In^d	Ludiman John	"	Danbury Invalid
1	Laverrick Gabriel	"	Milford
4	Loveman Jonathan	"	Durham
5	Lee Ezra	Lieut.	Lyme
5	Lay Richard	Priv.	"
4	Lay John	"	"
3	Lewis Peter	"	Stratford
In	Loveland Thomas	"	Glastenbury Invalid
D	Lattemore Levi	"	Weathersfield
†	Lord Jeremiah	"	Seabrook Invalids
4	Lay Asa	Capt.	"
4	Lord William	Priv.	"
1	Lyon Henery	"	Ashford
3	Luce Jonathan	"	Tolland
H	Lee Noah	Capt.	Salisbury
D	Leach Hezekiah	Priv.	Harwington
1	Levorick Gabriel		Fairfield vide above
4	Mansfield T.	Lieut.	Wallingford
1	Mix Thomas Junr	Priv.	"
1	Mix Enos	"	"
D	Meriman Josiah	"	"
H	Munson William	Capt.	New Haven
A	Miles John	"	"
A	Mix Timothy	Lieut.	"
4	Mothrop Joseph	Priv.	"
In^d	Mansfield Dan	"	" Invalid
S	Mathews Robert	"	" Sapper
4	Mallery Amos	"	"
5	Mallery Jonah	"	Waterbury
3	Meiggs John	Lieut.	Middletown
4	McCartee John	Priv.	Canterbury
1	Mack Abner	"	Hebron
1	Marble Thomas	"	"
1	Mason Rufus	"	Symsbury

	Names	Rank	Places to which they belong
4	Mallery Amos	Priv.	Milford
2	Marshal Byard	"	"
	Murry Abraham	"	Derby Deserted
†	Marchant John	"	Washington
D	Minor Elisha	"	Woodbury
†	Mathews Eliada	"	Cheshire
5	Mitchell Sam^ll	"	East Haddam
1	Mosely Syphax	"	Glastenbury
3	Maculpin Alexander	"	"
1	Miller Daniel	"	Chatham
D	Morrison William	"	Weathersfield
3	Maggot Zebulon	"	"
	Marks Abisha	"	"
4	McCullum Duncan	"	Seabrook
1	Millar Charles	Lieut	Hartford
1	Mize William	Priv.	"
1	Mahar James	"	"
3	Mix John	Lieut.	Farmington
1	Mossack Daniel	Priv.	"
4	McLane Jacobe	Serj.	Salisbury
	McCartee George	"	"
4	Munger Billa	"	"
4	Meigs Simeon	"	"
3	Meeker Steaphen	"	Ridgefield
	McCoy John	Priv.	New Milford
2	Mix Elisha	"	Goshun
4	Moss Daniel	"	Norwalk
1	McDaniel James	"	Preston
3	Meeker Stephen	"	Reading
3	Moor William	"	Union
3	McNulter John	"	Stamford
2	Morehouse David	"	Fairfield
4	Northrup Isaac	"	Milford
3	Nicholson Francis	Serj.	Glastonbury
A	Norton Jedediah	Priv.	Chatham
2	Norton Rufus	"	Guilford
2	Norton Elon	"	"
	Nigar Phillip	"	" 6 months man
4	Newel Robert	"	Seabrook
†	Norton Sam^ll	"	Hartford
A	Newell James	"	Farmington
4	Norton Benjn	Ens.	Branford
5	Nichols Samuel	Priv.	Norwalk
3	Nedson Robbin		Stoningtown
2	Owen Alvan	Priv.	Windsor
4	Olds Oliver	"	Washington
5	Olds Aaron	"	Woodbury
S	Osborn Nath^ll	Serj.	Stratford Sapper
3	Orcutt Caleb	"	Willington
4	Oates Joseph	Priv.	Branford
4	Owen Eliphalet	"	Salisbury
3	Olmsted Jesse	"	Norwalk
4	Ovit William	"	Stanford
5	Parker Nathan	Serj.	Coventry
4	Peirce John	Priv.	Wallingford
3	Pirkins Daniel	"	Enfield
4	Potter Moses	"	New Haven

	Names	Rank	Places to which they belong
A	Parker Edward	Priv.	New Haven
1	Pawers Thomas	"	"
	Paul Peter alias Peter Kellogg	"	Colchester
4	Pawers James	"	Southington
1	Perrigo William Jr.	"	Norwich
5	Patterson James	"	"
Inv^d	Penhellow Richard	"	"
4	Prior Abner	Maj.	Windsor
2	Porter Daniel	Priv.	"
1	Parsons Thomas	Serj.	"
D	Phillips William	Priv.	Symsbury
H	Parmalee Jerem^h	"	Milford
A	Prindle I Enos	"	Derby
5	Pumham Joseph	"	Lyme
5	Pollard Isaac	"	Woodbury
3	Preston Joseph	"	Winchester
†	Pendleton Daniel	Capt.	Watertown
4	Parker Isaac	Priv.	
4	Phillips Thomas	"	Stratford
5	Prindle Abijah	"	New Town
Inv^d	Palmer Isaac	"	Weathersfield
2	Pettet Enos	"	Sharon
4	Potter Steaphen	Capt.	Branford
†	Painter Gamaliel	"	Salisbury
2	Perry Elisha	Priv.	Ridgfield
3	Phinney Joseph	"	Lebanon
D	Patchen Elijah	"	Fairfield
2	Parrit David	"	"
1	Qui Libbeus	"	Norwich
4	Robinson Elias	Lieut.	Windham
†	Rexford Benjn	Priv.	Wallingford
H	Robinson Sam^ll	Lieut.	New Haven
5	Rogers Josiah	Priv.	Colchester
5	Roberts Nathan	"	"
2	Ransdale Ezra	"	"
3	Roberts David	"	Middletown
†	Runnels John	"	Norwich { supposed to be Joshua
4	Rowlee John	"	Winsor
A	Rumbeglow Thos	"	Killingsworth
4	Rozell Jeremiah	"	Danbury
	Rude Samuel	"	Hebron
5	Rice John	"	"
4	Reed Enoch	Capt.	Lyme
5	Ransom David	Priv.	"
4	Robinson Cato	"	Groton
5	Reaves James	"	East Haddam
5	Rice Nehemiah	Capt.	Watertown
5	Russell William	Priv.	Stratford
2	Ray Daniel	"	Haddam
1	Ranney Stephen	Serj.	Chatham
3	Russell Asher	Priv	Weathersfield
3	Riley John	Capt.	"
3	Rowlanson Joseph	Priv.	"
4	Roulenson Reubin	"	Guilford
2	Reeves Puryer	"	Seabrook

	Names	Rank	Places to which they belong
1	Runnels John	Priv.	Hartford
3	Risley Stephen	"	"
D	Rich Amos	"	Farmington
1	Ruggs Solomon	"	"
2	Russ Jonathan	"	Sharon
	Riley Phillip	"	Colebrook vid Original
2	Rust Epaphras	"	Cornwell
8	Raymond Sam¹¹	"	Reading Sapper deserted
5	Sweets John	"	Killingly
5	Sherman Reubin	"	Coventry
4	Shaylor T	Lieut.	Wallingford
5	Smith Daniel	Priv.	"
4	Sherman John	Lieut.	New Haven
4	Smith Ambrose	Priv.	"
4	Sugden Abraham	"	"
4	Stockwell Abel	"	"
A	Sherman Edmund	"	"
5	Shote James	"	Colchester
5	Shon Simeon	"	"
A	Squire Samuel	"	Southington
4	Starr David	Capt.	Middletown
†	Sizer William	"	"
†	Savage Stephen	Priv.	"
3	Simons Jonathan	"	Canterbury
1	Shaw Benjⁿ	"	"
2	Sanders William	"	New Fairfield
H	Stringham Peter	"	Danbury
4	Stewart John	"	Milford
5	Sandford Samuel	Capt.	"
4	Selden Ezra	"	Lyme
5	Spencer Ichabod	Lieut.	"
4	Swift Robert	Priv.	Groton
3	Sealy George	"	"
5	Stoddard Ely	"	Woodbury
5	Stewart Joseph	"	East Haddam
5	Smith David	Maj.	Watertown
†	Smith John	Priv.	"
5	Shilley Ebenezer	Serj.	Stratford
A	Simons Robert	Priv.	"
A	Sunderland John	"	"
1	Stevens Timothy	"	Glastenbury
Inᵈ	Simbo Prince	"	" Invalid
1	Smith John	"	Haddam
†	Smith Joshua	"	"
3	Stocken Marshal	"	Chatham
	Smith Ezra	Lieut.	"
3	Sizar Daniel	Priv.	Weathersfield
3	Shelley Edmund	"	Guilford
4 (?)	Shortman William	"	Hartford
[ ]	Spencer (?) John	Lieut.	"
D	Seward Jedediah	Priv.	Farmington
D	Smith Asaph	"	"
1	Stedman Thomas	"	"
1	Steel William	"	"
2	Strong David	Capt.	Sharon
D	Strong Phin⁸ Juʳ		East Windsor
	Smith Abijah	Priv.	Ashford Deserted
4	Smith Jordan	"	Branford

	Names	Rank	Places to whch they belong
D	Sheldon Elisha	Col.	Salisbury
†	Swetland Aaron	Serg.	"
4	Strong Phineas	Corp.	"
2	Smith Heman	Col.	Cornwell
D	Sereen James	Priv.	Suffield
3	Thompson David	"	Guilford
5	Taylor Elijah	Ens.	Norwalk
5	Tracy Perez	Priv.	Preston
3	Thompson James	"	Reading
H	Tisdale Eliph⁴	"	Lebanon
5	Tharp M Cornelius	"	Fairfield
2	Tredwell Cato	"	"
1	Talbut Benjamin	"	Killingly
5	Thompson Nath¹¹	Serj.	Coventry
A	Throop John	Lieut.	New Haven
4	Trobridge John	"	"
A	Todd Yale	Priv.	"
A	Thomas John	"	"
4	Tolles Elnathan	"	"
1	Townsend Solomon	"	"
4	Thomas Samuel	"	"
4	Thomas Ephraim	"	"
	Tarble William	"	Colchester
5	Talmage Icabad	"	Southington
5	Thair Asa	"	Waterbury
5	Throop Benjamin	Maj.	Norwich
	Tracy William	Ens.	"
1	Tracy Moses	Priv.	"
3	Tykan Tyas	"	Canterbury
	Turner Isaac	"	Killingsworth
1	Taylor Ephraim	"	Hebron
D	Tiffeny Humphry	"	Symsbury
4	Tolls Elnathan	"	Milford
D	Tucker Jarvis	"	"
5	Taylor Simeon	"	Woodbury
5	Taylor Josiah	"	"
3	Tubbs Nathan	"	Norfolk
†	Tryon Isaac	"	Glastenbury
2	Thomas Stephen	"	Chatham
D	Thomson Epaphras	"	Seabrook
A	Thomson Isaiah	Lieut.	Farmington
[	]ylor Jonathan	Priv.	Middletown
4	Towner Jacobe	"	Branford
4	Terry Gamalial	Serj.	Salisbury
4	Tupper William	"	"
D	Vanduser Thomas	Priv.	Windsor
4	Vangason John	"	Milford
	Verry Jonathan	"	Chatham
	Wright Jacob	"	Killingly
D	Wilson Barzillai	"	Woodstock for 1780 & 1781
†	Wilcox Jarius	Capt.	Wallingford
3	Wolcutt Joseph	Priv.	"
4	Wilson John	"	New Haven
4	Wood Elisha	"	"
D	Wild Jonathan	"	"
4	White Samuel	"	"
	Wallis Abraham	"	East Windsor
1	Warner Robert	Capt.	Middletown

Names	Rank	Places to which they belong
4 Willis Joseph	Priv.	Middletown
In^d Waterman Ebenezer Jr	"	Norwich Invalid
In^d Waterman Jo'	"	" Invalid
1 Wardwell Isaac	"	Windsor
In^d Wilder Aaron	"	New Fairfield Invalid
1 Woodbridge Timothy	"	Symsbury
1 White John	"	"
Wood Justus	"	Milford
4 White Joseph	"	Derby
5 Wilson George	"	Lyme
5 Wade John	"	"
1 Whitman Lemanuel	"	Groton
A Webb Gideon	"	Cheshire
3 Walter Charles	"	Norfolk
3 Wheeler John	"	"
2 Warren John	"	Bolton
2 Watkins Ephraim	"	East Haddam
5 Williams Thomas	"	"
1 Warren John	Serj.	Glastenbury
1 Wright John	Priv.	Chatham
3 Williams Daniel	Serj.	Weathersfield
3 Wells Joshua	Priv.	"
D Walton Silas	"	"
4 Wheeler Thomas	"	Guilford
4 White Oliver	"	Seabrook
Whittlesey Nathan	"	" { in R Island { Reg^t
1 Waters Thomas	"	Hartford
5 Willcox Giles	"	"
1 Wilton Solomon	"	Farmington
2 Williox James	"	"
1 Wilton Benjamin	"	"
1 Welton Joel	"	"
D Wainwright Samuel	"	"
3 Whitney Peter	"	Ashford
In^d Weterous W^m	"	" Invalid
4 White John	Lieut·	Branford
2 Wier Thomas	Priv.	Goshen
In^d Williams John	"	Norwalk Invalid
Woodworth Jedediah	"	Lebanon Desert^d
1 Welch Ebenezer	"	Washington
A Wilson David	"	Stamford
3 Wardwell Jacob	"	"
5 Waterbury W^m	"	"
A Williams Richard	"	Fairfield
4 Yale Nash	"	Wallingford
2 Young Ebenezer	"	Hebron
4 Yates William	"	Salisbury
3 York Richard	"	Preston

N: B: 1, 2, 3, 4, 5 denotes the Reg^t
D   Dragoons
In^d   Invalids
†   Artificers
H   Hazens
A   Artillery
Family Supplies 1781

BOUNTIES, 1781.

The United States D[r] To the State of Connecticut, for Bounties granted
to the Towns in said State for expence of recruiting the Continental Army
in 1781.

[Each man received £30 bounty.]

Date	Name of each Recruit	By what Town procured
1781		
March 15	Joshua Reynolds	Norwich
"	Solomon Andrews	"
"	Jabez Kirtland	"
"	Levi Munsell	"
"	James Bell	"
"	David Mattison	"
"	Comfort Chapman	"
"	Frederick Whipple	"
"	Jonas Ellis	"
"	Phineas Knight	"
"	Roger Edgerton	"
"	Benjamin Greenslit	"
"	John Munsell	"
"	Asa Squier	"
"	William Armstrong	"
"	Oliver Everett	"
"	Comfort Ames	"
"	Thomas Rathburn	"
"	Jacob Pettingall	"
"	John Patten	"
"	Benjamin Downs	"
"	Nathan Frink	"
"	Cato Derrick	"
"	Daniel Verguson	"
"	Benjamin Stoddard Jun[r]	"
"	Ozias Backus	"
"	James Miner	"
"	Jonathan Jer[h] Beebee	"
"	Daniel Hendricks	"
"	Isaac White	"
"	Ezra Hartshorn	"
"	Moses Tracy	"
"	Asaph Pettingell	"
"	Joel Hyde	"
"	Daniel Armstrong Jun[r]	"
"	Ephraim Story Jun[r]	"
"	Asa Patten	"
"	Jacob Wright	Killingly
"	Joseph Robbins	"
"	Clement Corbin	"
"	Stephen Blackmer	"
"	John Blackmer	"
"	Samuel Cheese	"
"	Abiel Chafee	"
"	Josiah D. Childs	"
"	Benjamin Adams	"
"	Joshua Fuller	"

Date	Name of each Recruit	By what Town procured
March 15	Chester Upham	Killingly
"	Justin Cady	"
"	John Graves	"
"	Amasa Grover	"
"	Ichabod Brooks	"
"	Abel Fling	"
"	Preserved Redway	"
"	John Peters	"
"	Jacob Wright Jun'	"
"	Gideon Martin Jun'	"
"	Ebenezer Corbin	"
"	David Peck	Ashford
"	William Chuble	"
"	Aaron Parks	"
. "	Ezra Davidson	"
"	Jonathan Buttock	"
"	Peter Whitney	"
"	William Johnson	"
"	Elijah Smith	"
"	James Hittrel	"
"	Darius Orcutt	"
"	David Tucker	Derby
"	Joseph Derrimo	"
"	Reuben Chalman	"
"	Primas Freeman	"
"	Dan Chatfield	"
"	Richard Pitts	"
"	George Clark	"
"	Marchant Wooster	"
"	Amasa Scott	"
"	Thomas Lee	"
"	Eliphalet Tomlinson	"
"	James Fields	"
"	Jonathan Loveland	Durham
"	Nath' Clark	"
"	Ebenezer Carr	"
"	Clement Carr	"
"	Silas Stanbourgh	"
"	Lemuel Stanbourgh	"
"	Samuel Bardin	Norfolk
"	Eliakim Seward	"
"	Nathan Tubbs	"
"	Serajah Comstock	"
"	Hendrick Biel	"
"	Joel Hamlin	"
"	Charles Walter	"
"	Philemon Kirkum	"
16th	John Wright	Killingworth
"	Cornelius Chittenden	"
"	Paul Pierson	"
"	Nathan Pierson	"
"	Joel Griffing	"
"	Eleazer Baldwin	"
"	Joseph Buell	"
"	Nathan Teal	"
"	James Elderkin	"
"	Caleb Elu	"
"	Jonah Carter	"

18

Date	Name of each Recruit	By what Town procured
March 16th	John Griswold	Killingworth
"	Joel Ixbel	"
"	Solomon Chittenden	"
"	Henry Stevens	"
"	Phineas Jones	"
"	Benjamin Gillet	"
"	Cornelius Thorp	Fairfield
"	Philip Hubbard	"
"	James Hubbard	"
"	Toney Gold	"
"	Nehemiah Fowler	"
"	Seth Burr	"
"	George Batterson	"
"	William Batterson	"
"	Caleb Disbrow	"
"	Tony Hill	"
"	Cato Treadwell	"
"	Dan Tooley	"
"	Solomon Culver	"
"	Jonathan Poor	"
"	Fortune Sanford	"
"	Benjamin Treadwell	"
"	Nehemiah Smith Odell	"
"	Thomas Solley	"
"	Thomas Banks	"
"	Josiah Patchin	"
"	Stephen Hall	"
"	John Polley	"
"	James Whipple	"
"	Joseph Elwood	"
"	Aaron Fox	"
"	Peter Montgomery	'
"	Elijah Patchen	"
"	Gideon Morehouse	"
"	Jedidiah Sherwood	"
"	Daniel Westcott	"
"	David Parrot	"
"	Samuel Taylor	"
15		Woodstock
"		"
"		"
"		"
"		"
"		"
"		"
16th	Michael Clark	Haddam
"	Daniel Ray	"
"	Joseph Forbes	"
"	Andrew Southworth	"
"	Peter Black	"
"	Solomon Wadhams	Goshen
"	Aaron Merrills	"
"	Cyprian Collins	"
"	David Francis	"
"	Elisha Peck	"
"	Jesse Royce	"
"	Jonathan Deane	"
"	Job Willcox Junr	"

Date	Name of each Recruit	By what Town procured
March 16th	Thomas Wyar	Goshen
"	Julius Beach	"
"	Caleb Munson	"
"	Seth Munson	"
"	Nathan Carter	"
"	James Crane	"
20th	Asahel Holcomb 3d	Symsbury
"	David Enos Junr	"
"	Agar Bonton	"
"	Ezekiel Davis	"
"	William Philips	"
"	Levi Wadsworth	"
"	Ezekiel Messenger	"
"	James Aldridge	"
"	Johnson Tiff	"
"	Morris F. Gerald	"
"	David Parkhurst	"
"	Eli Fuller	"
"	William Shepard Junr	"
"	Ezra Roberts	"
"	Jacob Fuller	"
"	Amaziah Barker	"
"	Jacob Holiday	"
"	John G. Holcomb	"
"	John Slater	"
"	Jeremiah Case	"
"	David Taylor	"
"	Ebenezer Edgerton	"
"	Zebulon Wallace	"
"	Rufus Mason	"
"	David Eggleston	"
"	Thomas Phelps	"
"	Jacob Gillet	"
"	Timothy Woodbridge	"
"	John Hunt	"
"	John White	"
"	Timothy Humphry	"
"	Philip Gregory	"
"	Jared Touser	"
"	Francis Stanley	Somers
"	Samuel Burges	"
"	Isaac Colton	"
"	Joel Pelton	"
"	William Hamlin	"
23d	William Merritt	Hebron
"	Jesse Thomson	Cheshire
"	Joel Barns	"
"	Dick Bristol	"
"	Cezar Doolittle	"
26th	John Abbee	Mansfield
"	Elihu Reed	"
"	Benajah Brown	"
"	David Brown	"
"	Stephen Reed	"
"	Jesse Badcock	"
"	Anthony Needham	"
"	William Mooney	"
"	Oliver Smith Junr	"

Date	Name of each Recruit	By what Town procured
March 26th	Hezekiah Wailey	Fairfield
"	Ebenezer Patchin	"
"	John Andrews	"
"	Abijah Hubbel	"
"	Levi Mallery	"
27th	Ichabod West	Tolland
"	James Covil	"
"	Moses Coy	"
"	Silvanus Gage	"
"	Reuben Robinson	"
"	Joel Barnard	"
"	Abel Stimson	"
28th	Daniel Cone 3^d	East Haddam
"	James Reeves	"
"	Thomas Williams	"
"	Samuel Mobbs	"
"	Pierce Mobbs	"
"	Nathan Luther	"
"	Nathl Warner Junr	"
"	Ansell Patterson	"
"	Ephriam Watkins	"
"	Ebenezer Post	"
"	Isaac Williams	"
"	David Hattuck	"
"	Abel Bingham	"
"	Robert Hull	"
"	Eli Hull	"
"	Cuff Negro	"
"	Richard Mack	"
"	Samuel Buckett	"
"	Stephen Sparrow 2^d	"
"	Judah Warner	"
"	Joel Spencer Junr	"
"	Charles Goodwin	"
"	Asael Hervey	"
"	Robert Watkins	"
"	Isaac Wardwell	Windsor
"	Jabez Colt	"
"	Peter Roberts	"
"	James Eggleston	"
"	Allen Prior	"
"	Timothy Horskins	"
"	Remembrance Sheldon	"
"	Reuben Hill	"
"	Calvin Willson	"
"	Elihu Mather	"
29th	Jack Negro	Hebron
"	Samuel Tyler	"
"	Seth Smith	New Hartford
"	Simeon Fox	"
"	Bassett Fox	"
"	Ichabod Talmadge	Southington
"	Jonathan Case	"
"	Luke Hart	"
"	George Dickinson	"
"	Amos Bunnel	"
"	Robert Cook	"
"	Archibald Cook	"
"	William Jones	"

Date	Name of each Recruit	By what Town procured
March 29th	Zebulon Dudley	Southington
"	Adonijah Rose	"
"	Abraham Tuttle	"
"	David Andrews	"
"	Bordle Hoose	"
30th	Benjamin Brown	Canterbury
"	David Spencer	"
"	Jedidiah Adams	"
"	John Maccarty	"
"	Curtis Cleaveland	"
"	Silas Glass	"
"	Nath¹ Gates	"
"	Benjamin Durfee	"
"	Jonathan Simons	"
"	Mason Green	"
"	James Duggens	"
"	J. Smith	"
"	John Cremer	"
"	Abiel Farnam	"
"	Javan Negro	"
"	Jedidiah Green	"
"	Rowland Cotton	Pomfret
"	Alfred Dresser	"
"	Nath¹ Stowell	"
"	Joseph Ross	"
"	Paul Davison	"
"	Ichabod Downing	"
"	Abijah Downing	"
"	Enoch Hurlbutt	"
"	John Ballard	"
"	Jonathan Stevens	"
April 2^d	Moses George	Cornwall
"	Jacob Young	"
"	John Carter Junr	"
"	Samuel Scovill Junr	"
"	Jack Freedom	"
"	Abner Lazel	"
"	Deliverance Stow	"
"	Rolin Jeffery	"
"	Elijah Holcomb	Windsor
"	Solomon Ruggs	Farmington
"	Aaron Hart	"
"	Solomon Ruggs Junr	"
"	Seth Arnold	"
"	William Steele	"
"	Ashble Merrills	"
"	Thomas Stedman	"
"	Gad North	"
"	Ezra Belding Junr	"
"	Prince Negro	"
"	Abel Allen	"
"	Sage Churchill	"
"	Solomon Welton	"
"	Timothy Fox	"
"	Moses Parsons	"
"	Thomas F. Bishop	"
"	Matthew Lee	"
"	Joel Welton	"

Date	Name of each Recruit	By what Town procured
April 3ᵈ	Roswell Cook	Farmington
"	Uri Hungerford	"
"	Isaac Tillotson	"
"	Amos Couch	"
"	Seth Root	"
"	Lemuel Lane	"
"	Robert Carr	"
"	Solomon Woodruff	"
"	Asael Tollotson	"
"	Gedar Woodruff	"
"	Obed. Gridley	"
"	James Gridley Junʳ	"
"	Jesse Shepard	"
"	Peter Rose	"
"	Reuben Hamlin	"
"	Obadiah Andrus	"
"	Isaac Nelson	"
"	Timothy Seward	"
"	Abner Tuttle	"
"	Isaac Bartholemew	"
"	Amos Rich	"
"	Abraham Bartholemew	"
4ᵗʰ	Daniel Roley	East Haddam
"	Thomas Green	Harwinton
"	Hezekiah Catlin	"
"	Shubael Crow	New Hartford
"	John Norwash	Glassenbury
"	Cuff Acklin	"
"	Thomas Brewer	"
"	William Peck	Somers
"	Reuben Perry	"
"	Jacob Granger	Suffield
5ᵗʰ	Alexander McCulpin	Glassenbury
"	Jacob Strong	East Windsor
6ᵗʰ	Joseph Willson	Willington
"	Reuben Dodge	"
"	Samuel Eldridge	"
"	Joseph Jacobs	"
"	Heman Hatch	"
"	Abel Stowell	"
"	Samuel Stowell	"
"	Alexander Ewing	"
"	Ebenezer Nye	"
"	Ezra Sibley	"
"	George Hatch	"
"	Cyrus Fenton	"
"	John George	Lebanon
"	Joseph Shantop	"
"	Reuben Tatson	"
"	Ezekiel Mazzeen	"
"	Elimath Elderkin	"
"	Ives Huntington	"
"	Philip Hill	"
"	Jedidiah Woodworth	"
"	Chester Waterman	"
"	Samuel Rice	"
"	Benjamin Cuthbert	"
"	Joshua Bill	"

Date	Name of each Recruit	By what Town procured
April 6th	Joseph Tinney	Lebanon
"	Daniel Beamont	"
"	Joel Clark	"
"	Uriah Palmer	"
"	John Clark 3d	"
"	Abner Hill	"
"	David Davison	"
"	William Fish	"
"	Marlack Tang	
"	Lemuel Stancliff	Torrington
"	John Barns	Canaan
"	Annanias Porridge	"
"	Samuel Porridge	"
"	David Beebe	"
"	John Onkshun	"
"	Gideon Jonathan	"
"	Thomas Studson	"
"	Jeremiah Wheedon	"
"	Joseph Johnson	"
"	Asa Hyde	"
"	David Jones	"
7th	John Crocker	Symsbury
"	Roderick Adams	"
"	Gad Alderman	"
10th	Benjamin Herrington	Enfield
"	Daniel Perkins 2d	"
"	John Mooney	"
"	Briant Brown	"
"	Thomas Ward	"
"	Oliver Field	"
"	Ephraim Burges	"
"	Ephraim Burges Junr	"
	Joseph Sheeker	
11th	Joel Doane	Saybrook
"	Reuben Bushnell	"
"	Cornelius Teigh	"
"	Job Bulkley	"
"	Benjamin Wilcox	"
"	Jesse Gorham	"
"	Gideon Buckingham	"
"	Richard Doane	"
"	Constant Chapman	"
"	Jude Pratt	"
"	Solomon Goff	"
"	David Haines	"
"	George Harris	"
"	George Buckingham	"
"	Amos Stephens	"
"	Samuel Lynde Junr	"
"	Puryer Reeves	"
"	Constant Bushnell	"
"	Zebulon Bushnell	"
"	Benjamin Doty	"
"	Jack Tobey	"
"	Joseph Whiteley	"
"	James Grant	"
"	Robert Newell	"
"	John George Wisetman	"

Date	Name of each Recruit	By what Town procured
April 11th	George Clark	Saybrook
"	George Wright Jun'	"
"	Duncan McCullum	"
"	Samuel Comstock	"
12th	Seth Baldwin	Hebron
"	Daniel Polly	"
"	Samuel Rude	"
"	Reuben Rolingson	Guilford
"	Joel Johnson	"
"	Ira Atkins	"
"	Edmund Shelly	"
"	Reuben Evarts	"
"	Gilbert Graves	"
"	Jehiel Willcox	"
"	Eber Hall	"
"	Timothy Shelly	"
13th	Brigadier Loomis	Torrington
17th	Jeremiah Cunnel	Ashford
"	Pelatiah Bugbee	Mansfield
19th	James Walker	Union
"	Perly Coy	"
"	William Moore	"
"	George Dillaby	"
"	David Thomson	"
"	Nehemiah Parker	"
"	Joseph Lawson	"
"	Peter Marsh	Plainfield
"	Stephen Bennet	"
"	Reuben Briant	"
"	Jeremiah Bennet	"
"	John Fagins	"
"	Daniel Dunham	"
"	Frederick Waldon	"
"	Amos Simons	"
"	Nath¹ Price	"
23d	Frank Buck	Lebanon
26th	Ebenezer Walker	Bolton
"	Richard Lawrence	Hebron
"	James Thomson	Union
"	David Butler	Harwinton
"	Timothy Rossetter	"
'	Caleb Elmour	"
"	Andrew Peters	Coventry
"	Simeon Commins	"
"	Jonathan Ball	"
"	Job Leason	"
"	Caleb Turner	Killingworth
28th	Samuel Fargo	Willington
"	Seth Dodge	"
"	Zephon Flower	New Hartford
30th	Elijah Cone 2d	East Haddam
"	Shubael Welton	Watertown
"	Jonathan Gaylord	"
"	Isaac Levingston	"
"	Lemuel Cook	"
"	Zarah Cook	"
"	Jn° Whitney	"
"	James Fulford	"

Date	Name of each Recruit	By what Town procured
April 30th	Josiah Preston	Winchester
"	Richard Coit	"
"	Richard Wares	Guilford
"	Bartlet Rowlinson	"
May 2^d	John Love	Somers
"	Thomas Watson	Stonington
"	Thomas Worden	"
"	Ephraim Harry	"
"	Anthony Defloris	"
"	Kudjoe Helmes	"
"	Jacob Sawas	"
"	Robbin Nedson	"
"	Benidict Eggleston	"
"	Ichabod Worden	"
"	Cato Jessup	"
"	Edward Nedson	"
"	Stephen Gavitt	"
"	Thomas Lambert	"
"	William Skesuck	"
"	Cato Cuff	"
"	Lodewick Paul	"
"	Benjamin George	"
"	Nath¹ Cottril	"
"	Christopher Avery	"
"	Jabez Morton	"
"	Daniel Hary	"
"	Thomas Paucheage	"
"	Jacob Robin	"
"	William Hudson	"
"	Samuel Peters	"
"	William Foster	"
"	Peter Apes	"
"	Isaac Herd	"
"	John Robertson	"
5th	John Bloss	Hebron
9th	Eleazer Hatch	Tolland
12th	John Rowley	Windsor
"	Samson Cuff	"
"	Eli Kelsey	Killingworth
"	Lyman Isbell	"
"	Josiah Chatfield 2^d	"
"	Jonathan Ward	"
"	Elias Stevens	"
"	Joseph Hull	"
"	Abraham Hurd Junr	"
"	James Wellman	"
"	Joseph Teal	"
"	John Carter Junr	"
"	Gideon Buell	"
"	William Jones	"
"	Nath¹ Chittenden	"
"	Joel Willcox	"
14th	Hubbard Burrows	Groton
"	Nath¹ Chapman	"
"	Jesse Holt	"
"	Jacob Lamb	"
"	Edward Freeman	"
"	John Mills	"

Date	Name of each Recruit	By what Town procured
May 15th	Jabez Cook	New Hartford
"	Nathan Mallery	Kent
"	Nathan Wheeler	"
"	Philetus Swift	"
"	Roger Luke	"
"	Samuel Ingraham	"
"	John Lay	Lyme
"	Nathl Smith	"
"	Saml Bartholemew	"
"	John Lay 2^d	"
"	Joseph Ransom	"
"	John Trube	"
"	William I. White	"
"	Amaziah Corwin	"
"	Joseph Pumham	"
"	William Butler	"
"	George W. Shepman	"
"	Isaac Scipis	"
"	Edward DeWolf	"
"	Ezekiel Beckwith	"
"	Benidict Minor	"
16th	Stephen Barnes	New Hartford
"	Solomon W. Beardsley	New Fairfield
"	Benjamin Knapp	"
"	Abel Guthrie	"
"	Calvin Bulkley	"
"	James Tilly	"
"	John Randall	"
"	Stephen Fox	"
"	Jason Gay	"
"	Moses Dutton	"
"	Heman Carter	"
"	Humphrey Gilbert	Mansfield
"	Marshal Keyes	"
"	John Bugbee	"
"	Titus Beadle	"
"	Joseph Dimick	"
17th	Skeen Douglass	New Milford
"	Daniel Utter	"
"	John Summers	"
"	John McCoy	"
"	David Blacknee	"
"	Joseph C. Hawley	"
"	William Whiteley	"
"	Samuel Hull	"
"	Daniel Johnson	"
"	Joel Sturdivant	"
"	Bostwick Ruggles	"
"	Ebenezer Steloon	"
"	Daniel Ower	"
"	Joseph Douglass	"
"	Isaac Lockwood	"
"	William Spear	"
"	David Buell	"
"	John Barnet	"
"	Frederick Slain	"
"	John Bartoo	"
"	Esquier Davenport	"

Date	Name of each Recruit	By what Town procured
May 17th	William Luke	New Milford
18th	Jonathan Newman	Ridgfield
"	Patrick Ambrose	"
"	John Dennison	"
"	Joseph Hawley	"
"	Isaac Bennet	"
"	Doge Williams	"
"	Solomon Benn	"
"	Nehemiah Olmstead	"
"	Hezekiah Boutin	"
"	Robert Willson	"
"	Talcott Hawley	"
21st	Sherry Reed	Coventry
"	Samuel Goodell	"
"	Ebenezer Youngs	Hebron
"	John Wright	"
"	Thomas McGuire	"
"	Peter Allen	"
22d	Henry Pollester	Voluntown
"	David Coy	"
"	Christopher Wier	"
"	John Desiton	"
"	John Kelly	"
"	Bryan Gordon	"
"	Jonathan Rogers	"
"	Daniel Dowd	"
"	John Frederick Jone	"
"	Andrew Hensley	"
"	Henry Pond	Colchester
"	James Shoat	"
"	Peter Kellogg	"
"	Josiah Rogers	"
"	Abner Hills Junr	"
"	John Lines	"
"	Richard Beebe	"
"	David Waters	"
"	Cezar Beman	"
"	Nathan Roberts	"
"	Gideon Quass	"
"	William Gibbs	"
"	Elihu Dodge	"
"	Peter Meguire	"
"	Comfort Beebe	"
"	Tony Edor	"
"	Israel Ransom	"
"	Simeon Shon	"
"	John Godfrey	"
"	Henry Hawton	"
"	Champlin Harris	"
"	James Freeman	"
"	Daniel Wright	"
"	Martin Stiles	"
"	Jasper P. Sears	"
"	Russell Williams	"
"	John Roberts	"
"	Derby Goff	"
"	Alpheus Wright	"
"	James French	"

Date	Name of each Recruit	By what Town procured
May 22ᵈ	Jeremiah Booth	Colchester
24ᵗʰ	Jeremiah Parmerlee	Milford
"	Joseph Cowdry	"
"	Samuel Wier	"
"	Levi Lattimer	Wethersfield
"	Wilber Hathaway	Suffield
"	Seth Hathaway	"
"	Levi French	"
"	Ready Lareey	"
"	Josiah Rising	"
"	Joseph King	"
"	James Screen	"
25ᵗʰ	Samuel Mott	Danbury
"	Henry Goslee	Chatham
"	Levi Benidict	Torrington
28ᵗʰ	Zechariah Waldo	Pomfret
"	Edward Crandell	"
"	Luther Grover	"
"	Samuel Lyon	"
"	Gardiner Cleaveland	"
"	John Robertson	"
"	David Dick	"
"	Ebenezer Grow	"
"	James McFarland	"
"	Cato	"
"	William Obriant	"
"	John Pearle	"
"	Richard Weax	"
"	Asa Gear	"
"	John Kimball	"
"	Benjamin Cady	"
"	Jared Kimball	"
"	Joseph Cheeney	"
"	Reuben Sharp	"
"	Joseph Craft	"
"	Archelaus Arney	"
"	Daniel Spencer	"
"	Ward Cotton	"
"	Stephen Barns	New Fairfield
"	John Katon	Windsor
30ᵗʰ	Jesse Kneeland	Chatham
"	William Gladding	Haddam
"	Daniel Bates	"
"	Aaron Stevens	Woodbury
"	Timothy Closby	"
"	John Tyler	"
"	John White	"
"	John Glazier	"
"	Zuar Bradley	"
"	Elnathan Miner	"
"	Electus M. Backus	"
"	Ezekiel Root	"
"	Gideon W. Mider	"
"	James Stoddard	"
"	Amos Davis	"
"	Gideon Curtiss	"
"	Samuel Cowell	"
31ˢᵗ	Benjamin Farnum	Ashford

Date	Name of each Recruit	By what Town procured
May 31ˢᵗ	Thomas Simons	Stafford
"	Silas Blodget	"
"	David Gardiner	Groton
"	George Sealy	"
"	Elihu Babcock	"
"	Abraham Neils	"
"	Anthony Goodsell	"
"	Robert Brice	"
"	Cary Latham	"
June 1ˢᵗ	Jacob Patching	Redding
2ᵈ	Inis Harper	Groton
"	Joseph Barrows	"
"	James Anderson	"
"	Jabez Edgcomb	"
"	Henry Brightman	"
4ᵗʰ	Stephen DeWolf	Hebron
"	James Leason	Ridgfield
"	Cato Freedom	Woodstock
5ᵗʰ	Josiah Hendrick	Redding
"	Daniel Couch Junʳ	"
"	John Springer	"
"	Whala Springer	"
"	John Lines	"
"	James Dixon	"
"	Henry Hopkins	"
"	James Thomson	"
"	William Eldridge	Tolland
"	Timothy Halsted	Harwinton
"	Ebenezer Talker	Kent
"	Swift Chamberlain	"
"	Thomas Prows	Lebanon
"	Jona. Danquegen	"
6ᵗʰ	Thomas Van Dunsen	Windsor
"	David H. Potter	Winchester
"	Humphrey Tiffany	Symsbury
"	Edward Crow	Ridgfield
"	William Kenn	New Milford
7ᵗʰ	Elias Carpenter	Woodstock
"	Eliphalet Carpenter	"
"	Isaiah Pratt	"
"	Ebenezer Bacon	"
"	Nathˡ Johnson	"
"	David Hammond	"
"	Stephen Child	"
"	William Westcott	"
8ᵗʰ	Thomas Manning	Stafford
"	Amasa Dimmick	"
"	Daniel Davis	Groton
"	David Chester	"
"	Jesse Williams	"
"	Daniel Morley	Glassenbury
9ᵗʰ	Reuben Sherman	Coventry
11ᵗʰ	Stephen Ben Davis	Newtown
"	Thomas Taylor	Norwalk
"	Thomas Wasson	"
"	Jesse Olmstead	"
"	Jonathan Brown	"
"	Daniel Sᵗ John	"

Date	Name of each Recruit	By what Town procured
June 11th	Elijah Betts	Norwalk
"	Isaiah Grant	Colchester
"	Nath¹ Roberts	Chatham
13th	John Wheeler	Norfolk
"	Bristo Johnson	Colchester
"	Benjamin Dodge	"
15th	John Trumbull	Preston
"	William Ely	"
"	Simeon Guile	"
"	James Brand	"
"	John Whitman	"
"	Joseph Davis	"
"	John Gates	"
"	Elias Meson	"
"	Silas Jacobs	"
"	James Nedson	"
"	Richard York	"
"	Joseph Quochetts	"
"	Joseph Hanniball	"
"	James Simons	"
"	Abraham Guile	"
"	Peleg Billings	"
"	Joseph S. Champlin	East Haddam
"	Joseph Stewart	"
16th	Jeremiah Hutchen	Torrington
19th	Adoniram Benton	East Windsor
"	Phineas Strong Junʳ	"
"	Elijah Benton	"
"	Henry Booth	Coventry
"	Samuel Burdon	"
20th	Solomon Bixly Junʳ	Stafford
21st	Eton Jones Junʳ	Litchfield
"	Asa Gillet	"
"	Reuben Smith Junʳ	"
"	Ebenezer Seeley	"
"	Roswell Kilborn	"
"	John Welch 2d	"
"	Midian Griswold	"
"	Orange Barnes	"
"	Solomon Lindsley Junʳ	"
"	George Negro	"
"	Samuel Jones	"
"	James Jones	Harwinton
26th	George Griffith	Voluntown
"	Ephraim Tucker	"
"	Elijah Fayer	"
"	Daniel Palmer	"
"	Reuben Bryant	"
"	Miles Jordan	"
"	Eliab Egleston	"
"	John Gray	"
"	Zadock Hurd	"
"	Alexander Knox	"
"	Reuben Adams	"
"	Samuel Palmer	"
"	Pharis Barnard	Coventry
July 5th	Ephraim White	Stafford
6th	Joseph Pease	East Windsor

Date	Name of each Recruit	By what Town procured
July 6th	Hazard Negro	East Windsor
"	William Jackson	Newtown
11th	John Royce	Hebron
12th	Joseph Wheeler	Stafford
17th	Benjamin Elsworth	East Windsor
19th	David Brown	Mansfield
31st	Daniel Miller	"
Augt 1st	John Lee	Ashford
8th	Charles Barnes	New Fairfield
16th	Edward Chapman	Hebron
20th	Solomon Eaton	Tolland
28	Nathan Chadwick	Lyme
"	Benjamin DeWolf	"
Septn 6th	Christopher Youngs	Redding
14th	Obadiah Taylor	New Hartford
"	Amos Tylor	"
25th	Cato Negro	East Windsor
27th	John Danielson	Newtown
"	Edward Jessup	"
"	Ezekiel Bennet	
Octr 3d	William Lement	Washington
"	Justus Taylor	"
"	Ephraim Doane	"
"	Simon Rose	
15th	David Plummer	Redding
"	Isaac Stedman	Groton
"	John Downer	"
16th	Thomas Hutchinson	Ridgfield
20th	Frederick Storrs	Mansfield
Novr 8	William Short	Killingly
"	John Sweet	"
"	Ebenezer Brown	"
"	Benjamin Talbutt	"
"	William Burrus	"
"	Jeremiah Robinson	
9th	Seth Baldwin	Hebron
17th	Ezra Ramsdell	Colchester
"	Moses Loomis	Coventry
20th	Thomas Fitz Simmons	Hebron
28th	Jedediah Kimball	Norwich
"	Thomas Brooks	
"	Josiah Doane	Saybrook
29th	Jethro Freeman	Derby
"	Marshall Bayard	Washington
30th	Noah Merrill	New Hartford
"	James Benham	"
Decr 11th	Jeff Liberty	Washington
19th	Lemuel Stancliff	Torrington
"	Andrew Fester	"
"	Nicholas Bosher	"
1782		
Jany 21st	Samuel Shelly	Stratford
24th	Isaac Olmstead	Redding
28th	Daniel Smith	Norwich
29th	Enoch Crovel	Willington
30th	John Jenks	Coventry
Febry 7th	Elijah Atwood Junr	Woodbury
13th	Ebenezer Shaw	Canterbury

Date	Name of each Recruit	By what Town procured
Feb 13th	Archelaus Ame	Canterbury
14th	Daniel G. Raymond	Norwalk
"	Jacob Hayden	"
March 1st	Isaac Higgins	Fairfield
6th	Selah Hart	Farmington
"	Josiah Barns Junr	"
"	David Hayden	"
"	David Hayden Junr	"
"	Zephaniah Hull	"
"	Jedidiah Seward	"
7th	Francis Barnard	Lyme
"	John Lay 4th	"
8th	Daniel Rider Junr	Stafford
12th	William Peck	Symsbury
"	John Allen	"
April 1st	Cazar Landing	Guilford
May 15th	John Pensyl	Stonington
30th	Isaac Avery	Groton
Augt 12th	Robert Johnson	Coventry
Sept 20th	Jos. Paro, alias Liberty	Haddam
Octr 23rd	Joshua Northrup Junr	Newtown
25th	Abijah Smith	Coventry
Decr 31st	William Osborn	Haddam
1783		
Janry 15th	John Warson	Torrington
21st	Ruel Africa	Coventry
May 24th	John Smith	Woodstock
June 3d	Eliphalet Spafford	Windham
"	Aaron Kingsley	"
"	Stephen Bennet	"
"	Lathrop Frink	"
"	Eleazer Robertson	"
"	Jedidiah Hebard	"
"	Daniel Woodward	"
"	John Dingley	"
"	Roswell Simons	"
"	Joseph Barrows	"
"	Charles Ripley	"
"	Juba Dyer	"
"	Jesse Gilbert	"
"	Elisha Back	"
"	James L. Dean	"
"	Ethiel London	"
"	Seth Laraba	"
"	Joseph Abbe	"
"	Nathl Abbe	"
"	John Abbe	"
"	Zophar Robinson	"
"	Abner Lilley	"
"	Elijah Randall	"
1784		
March 15th	Samuel Ames	Waterbury
"	David Davis	"
"	Moses Wooster	"
"	Asael Parker	"
"	Bethel Camp	"
"	Truman Hotchkiss	"
"	Stephen Bristol	"

Date	Name of each Recruit	By what Town procured
March 15th	Humphry Potter	Waterbury
"	James Prout	"
"	Jacob Morgan	"
"	Richard Lawrence	"
"	Levi Bronson	"
"	Joel Lane	"
"	Josiah Atkins	"
"	Osi Hitchcocks	"
"	Benjamin Burnham	"
"	Rozel Hotchkiss	"
"	John Flair	"
Septr 30th	Samuel Taylor Junr	Fairfield

[*Comptroller's Office, Haskill's Receipts, 35.*]

RETURNS FROM TOWNS, 1781.

NEW LONDON RETURN.

A Return of Inlisted Soldiers into the Continental Army by the Town of New London For the year 1781, viz;

Adi Chapman
Bliss Wilabey
Samuel Rogers
William Matterson

Jese Ward
William Clark
Joshua Kendal

A Return of Inlisted Soldiers in the Continental Army before the year 1781, viz,

James Gray
Sylvester Miner
Benj[n] Brooks
James Douglass Jun[r]
Benjamin Darrow
John Minard
William Prentice
Ichabod Beckwith
David Goodfaith
Joseph Copp Jun[r]
Roland Swift
Peter Holt
Daniel Plumb
Joseph Morgan
Simon Georgay
James Robertson
John Rogers 4th
Thomas Harris
Solomon Douglass
Samuel Weever

Robert Frasher
William Chappell
Nathan Douglass Jun[r]
Boanerges Beebe
James Giddis hired a man in his Room [Peter Holt]
John Daniels
John Butler
Daniel Henry
Alpheus Chappell
George Manwaring
Noah Chappell
Tim[o] Beckwith Jun[r]
Benj[n] Chappell Jun[r]

Cap[t] George Hurlbut
Cap[t] Rich[d] Douglass
Cap[t] W[m] Colfax
Cap[t] W[m] Richards
Lieu[t] Peter Robenson

The above is Copy delivered into the Com[ttee] New London Mar 20 1782

[Besides the above, another list contains the following additional names.]

W[m] Fargo Jun[r]
Dan[l] Comin

John Stewart.

[*Connecticut Historical Society.*]

LEBANON RETURN.

List of Soldiers of Lebanon now in y[e] Con[l] army as allowed by the Assembly May 1781

Elip[t] Tisdale
Rich[d] Woodworth
Nath[l] Porter
Humphrey Ball
Tho[s] Earl
Cash Palatine
Elip[t] Dower
Uriah Polley

W[m] Bentley
Dan. Jones
Nero Cross
Elijah Bill
Recomp[e] Woodworth
Dav[d] Lewis
Nath[l] Fitch Artif[r]
Allen Prat a [   ]

Wᵐ Williams
Beriah Badcock
Dennis Torney
Jez Palmer
Jnᵒ Whiteley Artifʳ
Jnᵒ Allen

Towns Quota
in Service

Deficient

81
45
—
36

Recruits, raisᵈ 1781

Jos. Shantop
Reuben Tatson
Ezˡ Mazzeen
Elemoth Elderkin
Jos. Huntington
Phillip Hill
Jed. Woodworth
Chester Waterman
Samˡ Bill
Benj Cuthburt
Joshua Bill

Jos. Finney
Dan Beumont
Joel Clark
Uriah Palmer
Jnᵒ Clark 3ᵈ
Davᵈ Davison
Wᵐ Fish
Marleck Jany
Frank Buck
Jnᵒ Danquenen
Thoˢ Brown
[*Connecticut Historical Society.*]

Names of Men belonging to the Town of Lebanon, engaged in the Continental Army during the War, as returnd lately by Genˡ Washington

Uriah Polley
Thoˢ Earl
Humphy Ball
Beriah Badcock
Nathˡˡ Porter
Wᵐ Williams
Cash Palatine

Dennis Torney
Wᵐ Jones
Richᵈ Woodworth
Cuff Wells
Jacob Rannee
Elipˢ Downer

Beside the above We have in yᵉ Conˡˡ [   ]
Persons Viz

Jabez Palmer for yᵉ War
John Whiteley Artifʳ
John Allen, an old Country Man
Wᵐ Bentley, for yᵉ W. (Norwich)
Danˡˡ Jones for yᵉ W. (Colchester)
Allen Pratt
Alpheus Polley

Thoˢ Baker, hird by Jonˢ Bill
Ezra Brown (Bolton)
Nero Cross, inlisted last Spring for 3
years
Elijah Bill, at home on Furlough
Recompence Woodworth

Lebanon Mar 5 1781

Upon the most carefull & mature Enquiry & Consideration, We Judge That We have full & sufficient Reason to claim, also, the next foregoing Persons belonging to this Town, as actually & bona fide engaged & serving in yᵉ Continental Army. (We have also missd & loose two or three, who were in our first Return which is lost & we cannot find their Names)

Test in behalf of yᵉ Town of Lebanon

Wᵐ Williams
Wᵐ Huntington } Select Men
Silas Phelps

add David Lewis inlisted p Capˡ Fitch & received Cloathˢ & Refreshments from Lebanon
also Jnᵒ Polley who listed at Fairfield
[*Connecticut Historical Society.*]

[Another list dated Feb. 28, 1781, gives the following additional names.]

John Bray Deserted now Lives at or Near Winsor
Hezekiah Buel Artʳ
Nathaniel Fitch artificer

[*Connecticut Historical Society.*]

REDDING RETURN.

£30 Bounties for Sundry Soldiers bel[g] to Reading

Date	Names of Soldiers	Date	Names of Soldiers
1781		June 5	James Dixon
June 1	Jacob Vatching	"	Henry Hopkins
5	Josiah Hendrick	"	James Thomson
"	Daniel Couch Jr.	Sep. 6	Christopher Youngs
"	Jno Springer	Oct. 15	David Plummer
"	Whala Springer	1782	
"	Jno Lines	Jan. 24	Isaac Olmsted

[*State Library, Revolution 28.*]

KILLINGLY RETURN.

These certify that the following Persons was Raised by the Town of Killingly for their Quota of Recruits to fill up the Continental Army Are as follows Viz

Clement Corbin	Abil Flingg
Chester Upham	Justin Cady
Joshua Fuller	John Peters
Benjamin Adams	Ichabod Brooks
Josiah D. Child	William Barrows
Ebenezer Corbin	Amasa Grover
Abial Chaffee	Benja Taulburt
Samuel Cheese	Preserved Redaway
Jacob Wight Jr	Steven Blackmore
Gideon Martin	John Sweat
Jacob Wight	Ebenezer Brown
Joseph Robins	Asa Copeland for 1 year
John Blackmore	Elhanon Boydon "
William Short	Ithamer Olney "
Jeremiah Robinson	Pline Greensar 6 months
John Graves	

Killingly July the 6th 1781

these Certify that the above 31 Recruits Were Raised by the Town of Killingly and certificates have Ben Received from the Recriuting officers for the Same they all being duly Musterd and Marchd in order to Join the Army

Willm Danielson ⎫
Pain Converse   ⎬ Selectmen
Eleaz^r Moffitt   ⎭ of Killingley

[*State Library, Revolution 25.*]

WALLINGFORD RETURN.

Acct of Supplies for the Officers & Soldiers Families Belonging to Wallingford from Apl 1 1781 until Jan 1 1782

Capt Eph Chamberlain	£13	10
Capt Jarius Wilcox	4	10
Lt Jno Mansfield	13	10
" Jos Shailor	13	10
Nath Yale	9	
Benj Rexford	3	
Moses Barns	9	
Thos Jones	9	

Edmond Field 9
Dan¹ Smith 9
  " Bradley 9
Thos Mix 9
Jos. Wollcott 9
Saml Holt 12
Enos Mix 7 14
Josiah Merriman 9
John Pierce 9

[*George M. Curtis, Meriden.*]

RETURNS FROM MILITIA, 1781.

FIFTH BRIGADE.

The following is a Return of those who have Engaged in the Continental service in the 5ᵗʰ Brigᵈ of militia after the sesions of assembly in may last their Names the Time they Engaged in service the Term they Inlisted for and the Town they count for and whether marcht or not
[All except the six noted below are described as having Marcht or Joined.]

Names 5ᵗʰ Regiᵗ	Time when Inlisted or Detached	Time for which Engaged	For the Quota of what Town
Enos Stebbins	June 26 1781	one year	Mansfield
Asa Cleaveland	29	to yᵉ last Dec	"
Robert Hale	28	year	"
John Fanton	July 2	last Dec	"
Solomon Fenton	3	year	"
Augustus Storrs	2	"	"
James Dunham	2	last Dec	"
Fredrick Storrs	June 12	3 years	"
Consider Hanks	28	last Dec	"
Joseph Whitemore	30	year	"
Chester (?) Southworth	July 2	"	"
James Church	5	"	"
Joseph Cushman	3	"	"
Joseph Tufts	June 23	"	"
Daniel Miller	July 5	3 years	"
Jonᵃ Dowset	7	year	"
Jonᵃ Ammedown	June 27	"	"
David Drown	30	3 years	"
Elisha Fenton	30	Last Dec	"
Calvin Chafee	10 July	year	"
Robart Eldrig	10	"	"
Phillip Perkins	20 July	"	"
Daniel Heff	July 3	Last Dec	Windham
James Hovey	3	"	"
Uriah Luce	3	"	"
John Neff	July 27	"	"
Jesse Peck	June 30	"	"
Chester Lillie	30	"	"
Elisha Back	March [ ]	3 years	"
James Luddington	20	"	"
John Quigley		"	"
Moses Ryce	July 10	year	Coventry
Charles Warnor	1	Last Dec	"
Elijah Hunt	1	"	"
Samˡˡ Carpenter	1	"	"
Stepᵃ Long	1	"	"
Wᵐ Porter	1	"	"
Joseph Bacon	2 July	"	"
Oliver Kingsbury	1	"	"
Jonᵃ Fitch	28 June	"	"

Names 5ᵗʰ Regᵗ	Time when Inlisted or Detached	Time for which Engaged	For the Quota of what Town
Mosess Loomis	25	3 years	Coventry
John Jinks	20 Aug	During war	"

11 Regᵗ
John Smith		3 years	Woodstock
Amos Morse		6 months	"
Harbe Childs		"	"
Abner Richmand		"	"
John Badger		"	"
Thoˢ Spencer		1 year	"
John Comba		6 months	"
Sylvenos Smith		"	"
Asa Copland		1 year	Killingly
Pleney Greene		6 months	"
Ishecor Onley		1 year	"
Ebnʳ Brown		3 years	"
James Boyd		1 year	"
Stephen Utley		6 months	Pomfret

12ᵗʰ Regᵗ
Benjᵃ Russell		1 year	Lebanon
Jonah Sweatland			"
Benjᵃ Bennet			"
Jabez Woodworth			"
Stephⁿ Buckingham			"
Jesse Wright			"
John Williams Jr			"
Benjᵃ Bissell			"
Benjᵃ Wood Jr			"
Elezʳ Woodward			"
Wᵐ Woodworth			"
Comfort Babe			"
Enos Gray			"
John Marin			"
John Clark			"
Ezekiel Lyman Jr			"
Samˡˡ Hills Jr			"
Benjᵃ Bissell			"
Prince Williams			"
Joseph Allin			"
Daniel Puffor			"
Nathⁿ Hovey			"
David Nucomb			"
Gurden Molton			"
Thoˢ Newcomb			"
Heman Woodworth			"
Zebadial Hide			"
Elisha Blackman			"
Nathⁿ Hovey			

The above named men are Continentals

Joshua Goff			Lebanon
John Colman Jr			"
Nathan Law			"
Daniel Perkins			"
Charls Hunt			

Names 12th Regt	Time when Inlisted or Detached	Time for which Engaged	For the Quota of what Town
Joseph Bartlet			Lebanon
Ichd Miner			"
Samll Lamfeer			"
Jabez Strong			"
John Jinkins			"
Philip Harris			"

For the 2 state Battallions from Leabanon

Names	Time when	Time for which	For the Quota
Daniel Vaughan	first March		Leabanon
Paul Hutsheson	"		"
Behuel Newcomb	"		"
Eleazer Richardson	"		"
Dan Bliss	"		"
Samll Bliss	"		"
Jason Youpon (? Jonson)	"		"
Samll Hayward	"		"
Dan Lyman	"		"
Philip Harris Jr	"		"
Caleb Gaspe	"		"
Dan Wattles	"		"
Wm Baxter	"		"
Beriah Bliss	"		"
Samll Bliss	"		"
John Rice	Continental		Hebron
Wm Merit	"		"
John Carver	"		"
Abner Hatch	"		"
Elisha Man	"		"
Appleton Holliston	"		"
Thos Brown Jr	"		"
Elijah Norton	"		"
Abel Wright	"		"
Sawyer Ellis	"		"
John Hutchison	"		"
Joas Dunham Jr	"		"
John Ellis 3d	"		"
Stephn Cumings	"	6 months	"
Moses Loomis	"	3 years	"
Benja Wood	"		"
Eazar Woodward	"		"
John Hutcheson	"		"
Larance Dowswet	"		"
Oliver Parish	"		"
Samll Goff	"		"
Daniel Folley	"		"
John Rice	"		"
Benja Steward		first March State Service	"
John Hibbard		"	"
Jabez Wotters		"	"
Squire Goff		"	"
Elijah Foller		"	"
Thos Mack		"	"
Thos Brown		"	"
John Powers		"	"

Names 12th Regtt	Time when Inlisted or Detached	Time for which Engaged first March	For the Quota of what Town
Jared Philips		State Service	Hebron
Norman Philips		"	"
21 Regit			
Joseph Whipple	Detd	Last Dec	Plainfield
Amasa Brown	"	"	"
Isaac Wight	"	"	"
Wm Watterman	"	"	"
George Dunworth	"	"	"
Benja Gallup	"	"	"
Andrew Clark			

[The six next above are not noted as having Marcht]

Joseph Pratt	Inlisted	"	"
John Green	"	"	"
Saml Bruster	"	"	"
Thos Beckus	"	"	"
Darbe Dunners (?)	"	"	"
Cuggo Negro	"	3 yers	Voluntown
Alexr Knox	"	"	"
Samll Palmer	"	"	"
Daniel Palmer	"	"	"
Ephm Tucker	"	"	"
Elijah Foster	"	"	Canterbury
Joseph Smith	"	"	"
Elezr Shaw	"	"	"
Benja Rathbon	"	"	"
Archalus Ama	"	"	"
Prince Negro	"	"	"
Thos Cranton	"	"	"
John Ormsbury	"	"	"
David Eanous	"		"
Daniel Herrick	"	first March	"
Berrey Boing	"	"	"
Elisha Balding	"	"	"
Jerh Parrish	"	"	"
Joseph Herrick	"	"	"
Samll Cleavland Jr	"	"	"
Joseph Munrow	"	"	"
John Adams	"	"	"
Charles Woodward	"	"	"
Samll Adams	"	"	"
Bethuel Bond	"	"	"
Joseph Hibbard			12th Sepr 1781

The following is A return of the men inlisted into the Massachusets Line in the Continental army from the Town of ashford for three years which by act of Congress said ashford hath a just Right to Count Viz

Wm Danscey
Benja Davison
John Davison
Roger Crane
Phileman Eatton
Oliver Ellis

James Brown
Origin Eatton
Nathn Ward
Ambros Brown
Elisha Roy[ ]
Chester Rogers

Moon Dimmuck   Th^{os} Morey
Jno Wintchester   Saml Perey

The above men are muster^d in the Countes of Suffolk Worster & middlesix certified July 1781

Pr Edward Green   ⎫ Muster
John Gleason   ⎬ masters
Barth^w Woodbury   ⎭

We whose Names are hereunto subscribed certifie that the above named men are Legal inhabitants of the state of Connecticut & Belong to the Town of Ashford & the bigest Part of them was born in s^d Town & have resided in the same Ever since Till inlisting

Elijah Whiton   ⎫ Justices
Benj^a Sumner   ⎬

Dated at Ashford   Benjn Clark   ⎫
11th Sepr 1781   Joseph Woodward   ⎬ Selectmen
Squier Hills   ⎭

[*State Library, Hebard Papers, 53*].

MISCELLANEOUS RETURNS, 1781.

A Return of the recruits rec⁴ and forwarded to Join The Connecticut Line in the Continental Army Hartford March 1ˢᵗ 1781 [Each man engaged for three years]

Soldiers Names	From what Regiment	For what Town
John Norwash	Col. Woodbridge	Glasenbury
Cuff Acklin	"	"
Ruel Affrican	Col. Storrs	Mansfield
Philip Gregory	Col. Phelps	Simsbury
John Slater	"	"
Ready Larey	Col. Newbury	Suffield
Remembrance Sheldon	"	Windsor
Jabish Colt	"	"
James Eggleston	"	"
Petor Roberts		
David Eggleston	Col. Phelps	Simsbury
Abel Allyn	Col. Hooker	Farmington
Sage Churchell	"	"
Solomon Welton	"	"
Timothy Fox	"	"
Moses Persons	"	"
Thomas F. Bishop	"	"
Mathew Lee	"	"
Joel Welton	"	"
Roswell Cook	"	"
Uri Hungerford	"	"
Isaac Tillitson	"	"
Amos Couch	"	"
Lemuel Lane	"	"
Ruben Carr	"	"
Obed Gridley	"	"
Asel Tillitson	"	"
Gider Woodruff	"	"
Solomon Woodruff	"	"
James Gridley	"	"
Jessy Shepard	"	"
Seth Root	"	"
Peter Rose	"	"
Ruben Hamtin		
David Taylor	Col. Phelps	Simsbury
John Griffin Holcom	"	"
Ebenezer Edgerton	"	"
Jeremy Cass	"	"
John White	"	"
Ruben Mason	"	"
Jacob Halladay	"	"
Zebulon Walles		
Robert Cook	Col. Hooker	Southington
Archibel Cook	"	"
Bodwell H[ ]	"	"
Luke Hart	"	"

Soldiers Names	From what Regiment	For what Town
George Dickerson	Col. Hooker	Southington
Clement Andrus	"	"
David Andrus	"	"
William Jones	"	"

Simeon Belding Lieu[t]
[State Library, Hebard Papers, 52.]

A Return of the Recruits to fill the Conn[t] Line of the Army

Mens Names	Towns to which they Belong
Henery Booth	Coverntry
Joseph Teal	Killingworth
Richard Weers	Guilford
William Poust	Killingworth
Eli Keley	"
Nathaniel Chittindan	"
Samuel Lynde Jur	Say Brook
Puryer Reeves	"
Zebelon Thompson	"
Benj[n] Doty	"
Park Toby	"
Jonathan Ward	Killingworth
Joel Isbell	"
Joseph Whitley	Say Brook
Cornelus Chapman	Say Brook
James Grant	"
Chester Bushnel	"
Amos Stevens	"
Richard Done	"
George Buckingham	"
George Harris	"
Solomon Goff	"
David Hains	"
Jude Pratt	"
Gideon Buckingham	"
Ruben Bushnal	"
Jese Graham	"
Benj[n] Wilcocks	"
John Bucley	"
Cornelius Tiegh	"
Joel Done	"
John Griswold	Killingworth
Joner Chester	"
Lymon Isbell	"
John Wright	"
Henery Stevens	"
Solomon Chittindan	"
Paul Pirson	"
Phinehus Jones	"
Caleb Elie	"
Joel Griffen	"
Nathan Person	"
Joseph Beull	"
Josiah Chatfield	"
Isaac Turner	"
Constant Bushnel	Say Brook

Mens Names	Towns to which they Belong
Jonathan Bullock	Ashford
William Cubb	"
William Jonson	"
James Hatrel (?)	"
Peter Whitney	"
Ezra Daverson	"
Abijah Smith	"
Aaron Parks	
Jonathan Ball	Coventry
Amesey Scott	Darby
David Davison	Lebanon

Middletown March 7th 1781

John Ball Lieut, & Recruiting Officer
of the 4th Conn't Reg't

[*Connecticut Historical Society.*]

Return of Recruits for the Continental Army Received or forward'd to
Camp since last Return   March 29th 1781

Names of the Men Rec'd since last Return	Term Engaged for	By what Town procured
Jedediah Kimball	3 Ys	Norwich
Thomas Brooks	"	"
Men forward'd since last Return		
Thomas McGuire	3 Ys	Hebron
Reuben Talsen	"	Lebanon
Phillup Hills	"	"
Joseph Phinney	"	"
Gideon Martin	"	Killingly
Cato Negroe	D. W.	Pomfret
David Coy	3 Ys	Voluntown
John Fred'k Tone	"	"
Andrew Hensey	"	"
Gideon Quas (? Tuas)	"	Colchester
Dan'l Armstrong	"	Norwich
Wm Armstrong	D. W.	"
James Bell	3 Ys	"
Jabez Kirttend	"	"
Phinehas Knight	"	"
Moses Tracy	"	"
Jon'th Jer'h Beebe	"	"
John Patten	"	"
Asa Patten	"	"
Asa Squier	"	"
Thomas Brooks	"	"
Oliver Everit	D. W.	"

A Size Roll of the following Men (Including The Deserters) Specifying
the Towns Engag'd for &c Left with L't Pride, Accounting for the Whole
I have Rec'd

Joseph Ross
Isaac White
Comfort Eams

Henry Pollister ⎫
John Kelley   ⎬ were Return^d Deserted
Richard Weir ⎭
Saml Rude
Crippin Archer
Eliab Eaglesten
John Bloss
John Wright
Danl Dowd
Ephraim Story
Reuben Bryant
Stephen Bennet
Jeremiah Bennet
John Fagens
Thos Fitz Simmons
Amas Simons
Jed^h Kimball

Joel Clark who Engag^d for Lebanon has Been to Camp & Return^d by Order of Col^o Grosvenor
Solomon Andrus of Norwich Muster^d out by Col^o Swift

James Hyde Ensⁿ
late R. Officer 1st Conn. Regm^t

His Excellency
Govr Trumbull,—

[*Connecticut Historical Society.*]

A Return of Deserters from the present 1st Connecticut Reg^t since the Return for Settlem^t of their Pay for Service of 1781.

Names	Time When	Towns they belong to
William Jones Fifer	1 Jan. '82	Branford
Gerard Leverick	"	Fairfield
John Grant	15 Jan. 82	Lyme
Samuel Goff	1 Jan. 82	Chatham
Samuel Thompson	21 Feb. 82	Canterbury
Hezekiah Phelps	30 Mar. 82	Symsbury
Jehiel Gibbs	"	Somers
John Gray	"	Voluntown
John Casey D^m	"	Providence
William Racke	1 Apr. 82	Bolton
James Brown	"	Westmoreland
William Flowers	10 Apr. 82	Hartford
Henry Walton	11 Apr. 82	Danbury
Gilbert Whitney	"	Symsbury
Andrew Gray	"	Stonington
Joseph Evans	"	Hartford
John Hamilton	20 Apr. 82	New Fairfield
Gideon Church	9 May 82	Westmoreland
Enos Mix	21 June 82	Wallingford
Austin Brown	25 July 82	Hebron

The above is a true Extract from the Regimental Book
Thos Grosvenor Lieut Col Com 1st Conn. Regt.

[*State Library, Revolution 25, 41*]

THIRD REGIMENT — COL. WEBB, 1782.

[See Record of Connecticut Men in the Revolution, page 580.]

FIELD AND STAFF.

[The muster rolls of the field and staff for February, March, May, June, July, September and October 1782 are preserved. Only the earliest of these is here copied, with such changes noted as appear on any of the later rolls.]

Muster Roll of the Field, Staff and Commissioned Officers in the 3ᵈ Connecticut Regiment in the service of the United States Commanded by Col Sam¹ B. Webb for Feb⁷ 1782.

Appointed	Names	Rank	Remarks
Jan. 1, 1777	Sam¹ B. Webb	Col.	
Oct. 10, 1778	Eben² Huntington	Lt. Col.	
Oct. 10, 1778	John P. Wyllys	Maj.	
Mar. 23, 1778	Nathan Beers	Lt. P. Master	
June 1, 1778	John Meigs	Lt. Adj.	
May 27, 1779	Eben² Frothingham	Lt. Q. Master	
Mar. 30, 1778	Jeremiah West	Surgeon	in arrest Feb. 23, 1782. Vacant March 1782
Aug. 1, 1778	John Rose	Mate	Promoted to Surgeon March 3, 1782
	Jonathan White	Serj. Maj.	On muster rolls for May 1782 and later
	Simon Griffin or Giffin	Qr. Mr. Serj.	"
	David Pratt	Drum Maj.	"
	John Kircum	Fife Maj.	"
	Light Infantry		
Apr. 9, 1780	Roger Welles	Capt.	
Apr. 9, 1780	Wᵐ Linn	Lieut.	
July 26, 1780	Jacob Kingsbury	Ens.	
	1ˢᵗ Company		
Jan. 1, 1777	Edward Bulkley	Capt.	
July 20, 1780	Daniel Bradley	Lieut.	Recruiting Officer March 1782, but not noted later in that capacity.

Appointed	Names	Rank	Remarks
	6th Company		
Oct. 10, 1778	Elisha Hopkins	Capt.	
Sep. 1, 1779	Eli Barnum	Lieut.	
Dec. 28, 1781	Nathan Gregory	Lieut.	
	4th Company		
Aug. 28, 1777	Joseph Walker	Capt.	Aid de Camp to Genl Parsons
Dec. 17, 1781	Martin Denslow	Lieut.	In arrest Feb. 23, 1782
	8th Company		
Feb. 10, 1781	Timothy Allyn	Capt.	
Dec. 6, 1781	William Lord	Lieut.	
Apr. 3, 1780	Jaques Harman	Ens.	
	3d Company		
Jan. 1, 1779	Stephen Betts	Capt.	
Aug. 1, 1779	Isaac Keeler	Lieut.	doing the duty of Adj.
	7th Company		
July 10, 1779	John Biley [Riley]	Capt.	
June 16, 1778	John Mix	Lieut.	Q. Master Genl Department
	5th Company		
Mar. 22, 1778	Saml Wm Williams	Capt.	
Feb. 10, 1781	Nathan H. Whiting	Lieut.	
	2d Company		
Nov. 15, 1781	Hezekiah Bogers [Rogers]	Capt.	Aid de Camp to Gen. Huntington.
May 4, 1781	Benjamin Dimmick	Lieut.	

LIGHT INFANTRY COMPANY—CAPT. WELLES.

[The muster rolls of this company for February, May, June, July, September and October 1782 are preserved. Only the earliest of these is here copied, with such changes noted as appear on any of the later rolls.]

Muster Roll of Capt Roger Welles's Company of Light Infantry in the 3d Connecticut Regiment in the Service of the United States Commanded by Col Saml B. Webb, For the Month of Feby 1782.

Inlisted	Rank	Name	Term	Remarks
Apr. 9, 1780	Capt.	Roger Wells		Transfered 1st Co. June 1, 1782
Apr. 9 "	Lieut.	Wm Linn or Lim		Not on muster roll for May 1782 or later
July 25	Ens.	Jacob Kingsbury		" "
	Serj.	Lewis Hurd	D. W.	
	"	Silas or Elias Phelps	"	
	"	Reubin Beach		Promoted from Corp. Feb. 9, 1782
	"	John Downs		
	Corp.	Stephen Butler		
		David Bullin		Reduced June 1, 1782
	"	Benjn Dire or Dix		Not on muster roll for May 1782 or later
	"	David Lounsbury		
		Joseph Clinton		
	Drum.	John Dixon		
	Fifer	Daniel Winchel		
		Jacob Achor	"	
		John Allyn	"	Not on muster roll for May 1782 or later
Dec. 20, 1780		Hendrick Bail	3 years	
		John Barnum	D. W.	Deserted Oct. 24, 1782
		Noah Barnum	"	Transferred 6th Co. July 1, 1782
		Nathl Beach		" 2d Co. "
July 1, 1780		Edward Burges	3 years	
		Reubin Cadwell	D. W.	Not on muster roll for May 1782 or later
		Jeret Chamberlain		
		Allyn Corning		
Dec. 22 "		Jeret Cunnell	3 years	" "
		Allyn Evins	D. W.	" "
		Rememberence Filley	"	

20

Inlisted	Term	Name	Rank	Remarks
	D. W.	Vaniah or Variah Fox		Not on muster roll for May 1782 or later
	"	Ichabod Goodrich		"
	"	Saml Gookins		"
	"	Saml Hemmin or Hennan		
		David Ward		Not on muster roll for May 1782 or later
		James Hyde		"
Mar. 18, 1781	3 years	Joseph Johnson		
	D. W.	Jedediah Kimball		
	"	Benjn Kircum		
	"	Jonathn Miller		
		Joel Mosher		Not on muster roll for May 1782 or later
	"	Stephen Meeker		
	"	Brion Montigue		
		Shelden Potter		
		David Roberts		Not on muster roll for May 1782 or later
		Isaiah Smith		
		Justin St. John		Not on muster roll for May 1782 or later
	"	Ezra Tryon		"
	"	Saml Vallett		"
	"	Benjn Waklee		
		Joshua Wheeler		
		Saml Whittney		Transfered 1st Co. June 1, 1782
July 11, 1780	3 years	Seth Grigory	Serj.	Not on muster roll for May 1782 or later
	D. W.	Thomas Wood		Dead Feb. 21, 1782
	"	Elihu Spear		Received from 4th Co. June 1, 1782
	1y. 8m. 16d.	Selah Scoviel or Scofield	Corp	" 2d Co. "
	1y. 9m. 19d.	Arehelus Amis or Ames		" 3d Co. "
	1y. 6m. 25d.	Ebenezer or Eben Bacon		" 7th Co. "
	1y. 7m. 20d.	Elias Carpinter		" 8th Co. "
	D. W.	Calvin Chaffe		" 7th Co. "
	"	James Chadwick		" 3d Co. " Transfered 3d
	"	Asa Copeland		" Co. July 1, 1782 from 6th Co. "
	1y. 7m.	Ward Cotton		" 1st Co. "

Time	Name	Company / Entry	Remarks
1y. 6m. 3d.	Roger Edgerton	" 5th Co., " 1782	" Transferred
D. W.	Thomas Evans	5th Co. July 1, 1782 / from 1st Co.	"
D. W. "	Mason Green	" 3d Co.	" Deserted
1y. 6m. 21d.	Andrew Hansey or Haney	June 13, 1782 / from 8th Co.	"
1y. 6m. 3d.	Philemon Kirkum	" 4th Co.	"
1y. 7m. 4d.	Joseph Lauson	" 2d Co.	"
1y. 6m. 16d.	Theophilus Luther	" 2d Co.	" Deserted
1y. 7m. 14d.	John Munsell	July 16, 1782 / from 6th Co.	"
1y. 27d.	Abijah Olmsted	" 2d Co.	" Deserted
D. W.	Lemuel Raymont or Raymond	July 16, 1782 / from 8th Co.	"
"	Elias Shaw	" 7th Co.	"
1y. 7m. 4d.	David Spencer	" 5th Co.	"
D. W.	Lemuel Sperry	" 4th Co.	"
1y. 6m. 14d.	Samuel Stowell	" 1st Co.	"
1y. 5m. 14d.	Charles Walter	" 4th Co.	"
D. W.	Elihu Waters	" 5th Co.	" Transferred
"	Seth Stannard	5th Co. July 1, 1782 / Joined from desertion May 23, 1782. Transferred 4th Co. July 1, 1782	"
1y. 8m. 27d.	Nath¹ or Nathan Stowell	Received from 1st Co. June 1, 1782	"
1y. 7m. 6d.	Selah Harke or Hearts or Hartee or Harte	" 4th Co. July 1, 1782	"
D. W.	Chancey Lewis	" 5th Co.	"
"	Ira Mott	" 5th Co.	"
1y. 6m. 7d.	Levi Munsell	" 6th Co.	"
1y. 7m. 1d.	Reuben Sharpe	" 7th Co.	"
1y. 4m. 14d.	Chester or Christopher Upham	" 3d Co.	"
1y. 2m. 16d.	Hazard Prior	on muster roll for Sept. 1782	"
D. W.	Nathª or Nathan¹ Smith	"	"

[State Library, Revolution 39; 50, 67, 77, 86, 95, 104.]

FIRST COMPANY—CAPT. BULKLEY.

[The muster rolls of this company for February, May, June, July, September, and October, 1782, are preserved. Only the earliest of these is here copied, with such changes noted as appear on any of the later rolls.] Muster Roll of Captain Edward Bulkley's Company 3rd Connecticut Regiment in the Service of the United States commanded by Col. Samuel B. Webb for the Month of February 1782.

Time Appointed	Term of Inlistment		Rank	
Mar. 20, 1780	D. W.	Edward Bulkley	Capt.	
May 17, 1778	"	Daniel Bradley	Lieut.	
Aug. 22 "	"	Jonathan White	Serj. Maj.	not on muster roll of May 1782 or later
		Simeon Giffin	Qr. Mr. Serj.	"
		David Pratt	Drum Maj.	"
		John Kircum	Fife Maj.	"
		Elijah Bordman	Serj.	
Nov. 3, 1780	3 years	Darius Orcutt or Oniott	"	
	D. W.	Moses Griswold	Serj.	
	"	Daniel Sizer	"	
	"	Samuel Easton	"	Discharged Feb. 13, 1782.
	"	Lewis Hurd	"	Received from the Light Co. June 1, 1782. Discharged Sept. 1, 1782.
	"	Hezekiah Nott	Corp	
	"	Thomas Stanley	"	
	"	Gideon Goff	"	
	"	Moses Hatch	Drum	
	"	David Lindsey	"	
	"	Asa Squire	Fifer	not on muster roll of May 1782 or later
	"	William Armstrong	"	"
	"	Daniel Bushnell	"	—
		Abraham Belding		
		Jonathan Bullock		
Jan 1, 1782	3 years	Simeon Barns		Time expires Apr. 18, 1782
Jan. 2 "	"	Jeremiah Bennet		
Apr. 3, 1781	"	John Ballard		
Jan. 17 "	"	Ward Cotton		Transfered to the Light Co. July 1, 1782

Date	Term	Name	Remarks
Feb. 18	"	Moses Coy	
Jan. "	"	Robert Chandler	
Jan. 11	"	Daniel Dunham	
Feb. 5	"	Joseph Douglas	
Jan. 17	D. W.	Alphred Dresser	
		Jack Freeman	not on muster roll of May 1782 or later
		Prince Freeman	
Dec. 14, 1780	3 years	Stephen Fox	
June 1, 1781	"	Cato Freeman	
	D. W.	Samuel Herington	
		Arunah Hackley	
Jan. 17, 1781	3 years	Samuel Lyon	
	D. W.	Daniel Morley or Muley	
Dec. 1, 1780	3 years	David Peck	
March 10, 1781	"	Nathaniel Price	
Feb. 10	"	Joseph Preston	
June 29		Joseph Pease	
	D. W.	Samuel Roberts	
	8 years	Reuben Roberson or Robinson	
Mar. 5	"	Abel Stowell	Transfered to the Light Co. June 1, 1782
Jan. 1	"	Samuel Stowel	not on muster roll of June 1782 or later
Jan. 1	"	Nathaniel Stowel	Joined from desertion May 24, 1782. Not on muster roll for Sept, 1782 or later
Mar. 13	D. W.	John Smith	not on muster roll for Sept. 1792 or later
June 1		Joseph Treat	
	"	Hezekiah Wheeler	
Jan. 8	3 years	Peter Whitney	
Dec. 20, 1780	"	Joseph Wilson	not on muster roll of May 1782 or later
Jan. 1, 1781		Ebenezer Nye	Died Feb. 22, 1782
Apr. 30, 1782	6m. 15d.	Nehemiah Seely	Joined May 16, 1782
Apr. 15	6m. 0d.	Joseph Clark	Fool transferred June 26, 1782
Apr. 27	6m. 12d.	George Foot	
Apr. 10	5m. 25d.	Joseph Bunnel	Joined May 16, 1782
Apr. 10	"	Thomas Evins	Transferred to the Light Co. June 1, 1782

Time Appointed		Term of Inlistment	
May 8, 1782	William Wetherll	6m. 28d.	with his Excellencys Barge June 5, 1782 and later.
	Joshua Whealer	D. W.	Received from the Light Co. June 1, 1782. Not on muster roll for Sept. 1782 or later
Apr. 1, 1782	Eleazer Cutler or Cutter	8m. 10d.	Joined June 10, 1782
May 1 "	Amos Gustin or Griffin	5m. 10d.	Joined June 10, 1782. Discharged Dec. 10, 1782
Apr. 1 "	Daniel Knight	"	Discharged Dec. 26, 1882
May 1 "	Christopher Kilby	8m. 10d.	Joined June 20, 1782
	Benoni Robins	5m. 10d.	Joined June 20, 1782. Discharged Dec. 27, 1782.

[State Library, Revolution 39; 45, 65, 72, 83, 91, 100.]

SECOND COMPANY – CAPT. ROGERS.

[The muster rolls of this company for February, March, May, June, July, September, and October, 1782, are preserved. Only the earliest of these is here copied, with such changes noted as appear on any of the later rolls.]

Muster Roll of Captain Rogers' Company in the 3rd Connecticut Regiment of Foot in the Service of the United States commanded by Colonel Samuel B. Webb for the Month of February 1782

Inlisted	Term			
		Hezekiah Rogers	Capt	Aid to Gen. Huntington
		Benjamin Dimmick	Lieut.	Transfered to 6th Co. Sep. 23, 1782
		Nathan H. Whiting	Lieut.	Joined from 4th Co. Aug 1, 1782
		Richard Lord	Serj.	
		William Bassett	"	
		Abiathar Evans	"	
		Peter Stalker	"	
		Ebenezer Stoddart	"	Discharged for Simeon C. Stoddart in his room Feb. 26, 1782
Dec. 20, 1780	3 years	Jesse St John	Corp.	
		James Crane	"	
		John Avery	Drum.	
		Frederick Whipple	Fifer	
Mar. 1, 1781	"	Antielus or Archelus Ames		Transfered to L. Co. June 1, 1782

Date			Name	Remarks
Dec.	21, 1780		Reuben Adams	
Feb.	1, 1781		Ephraim Burges	
Jan.	"	"	William Burrus or Burns	
Jan.	9	"	Elias Carpenter	
Jan.	2	"	Eliphelet Carpenter	
Feb.	1	"	Comfort Chapman	
Jan.	1	"	James Duggan	
			Moses Elsworth	Transfered to L. Co. June 1, 1782
Feb.	1	"	Joseph Finney or Phinney or Skinney	
			John Gimson	Deserted Aug. 1, 1782
			Asa Haze or Hays	Deserted April 10, 1782; but appears on later rolls.
Feb.	14	"	Joel Hait or Hart	not on muster roll for May 1782 or later name crossed from Sept 1782 roll and does not appear later
			Samuel Hull	
Dec.	18, 1780		Jacob Halladay	not on muster roll for May 1782 but appears on June 1782 and later
Mar.	13, 1781	D. W.	Abraham Murry	
Jan.	5	" 3 years	David Hammond	
Mar.	1	"	Andrew Hensey	Returned from desertion Feb. 27, 1782
			Phillip Hills	not on muster roll for May 1782 or later
Feb.	1	"	Samuel Jinkins	
July	5	"	David Mattison or Matheson	
			Cato Negro	
			Aaron Parks or Parker	
Mar.	6	"	William Short	
Feb.	1	"	Reuben Smith	not on muster roll for May 1782 or later
			Benjamin Stoddard	Died Dec. 27, 1782
Jan.	11	"	Johnson Tiff	
Jan.	11	"	Darius Truesdell or Tinsdell	
Jan.	21	"	Eli Tuller or Fuller	
Jan.	15	"	John F. Tone	
			William Woolcut	Died Feb. 5, 1782
			Simeon Curtis Stoddart	In room of Ebenezer Stoddard　not on muster roll for Sept. 1782 or later

Inlisted	Term	Name		
Apr. 10, 1782	D. W.	Reubin Beach	Serj.	appears on muster roll for May 1782 and later
	1y. 7m. 17d.	Ephraim Bates		" " " "
	D. W.	Joel Mosher		" " " "
	2y. 10m. 17d.	Tho⁴ Palmer		Joined April 27, 1782
	1y. 9m. 3d.	Jedediah Kimball		appears on muster roll for May 1782 and later
	10m. 17d.	Ebenezer Platt		Joined May 15, 1782.
	6m. 17d.	Miles Bennet		not on muster roll for June 1782, but appears on July and later
	10m. 5d.	Aaron Eaton		" " "
	6m. 17d.	Daniel Jackson		" " "
	D. W.	Justin St. John		appears on muster roll for May 1782 and later
	1y. 6m. 22d.	Andrew Treusey		" " " Transfered to L. Co. June 1, 1782
	6m. 28d.	David Shelton		Joined May 15 and deserted June 1, 1782
	7m. 24d.	Esaias Butts		Joined June 6, 1782
	D. W.	Jonathan Edwards		Joined June 14, 1782
	5m. 9d.	Nathan¹ Fenton		Joined June 20, 1782
	7m. 24d.	James Raymond or Braymon		Joined June 6, 1782
	5m. 9d.	Sasal or Saral Squires		Joined June 6, 1782
	" "	Nath¹ Connant		Joined June 20, 1782
	4m. 20d.	Jonathan Bamon or Beaumont		Joined July 17, 1782
	D. W.	David Clark		appears on muster roll for Sept. 1782 and later

[State Library, Revolution 39; 48, 57, 65, 75, 84, 95, 102.]

THIRD COMPANY – CAPT. BETTS.

[The muster rolls of this company for February, March, May, June, July, September, and October, 1782, are preserved. Only the earliest of these is here copied, with such changes noted as appear on any of the later rolls.]

Muster Roll of Captain Betts Company 3rd Connecticut Regiment in the service of the United States, Commanded by Colonel Samuel B. Webb for the Month of February 1782

Name		Term	Enlisted	
Stephen Betts	Capt.		Jan. 1, 1777	Transferred 3d Co. July 31, 1782
Isaac Keeler	Lieut.		Aug. 1, 1779	Transferred July 31, 1782 from 7th Co. Called
Jacques Harmon	Ens.			Lieut. Sept. 1782.
Aaron Raymond	Serj.	D. W.		
Joseph Hait	"	"		
Uzel Knap	"	"		not on muster roll for June 1782 or later
Elihu Spear	Corp.	"		not on muster roll for June 1782 or later
Selah Scofield	"	"		
James Downs	"	"		
George Hubbard or Hubert				
Anthony Floris or De Flovis	Drum.	3 years	Inlisted Jan. 18, 1781	
Reuben or Martin Reynolds or Rannals	Fifer	D. W.		
Thomas Blake		"		
David Betts		"		
Jacob Bosworth	Brigade baker	"		
Jonathan Brown		3 years	Jan. 1, 1781	not on muster roll for March 1782 or later
Parley Coy		"	Jan. 19, "	not on muster roll for March 1782, but reappears as
Joseph Davies			Dec. 4, 1780	Joseph Davis on muster roll May 1782. An entry against his name has been cut from the roll for Oct. 1782
Jonathan Dowsit		1 year	July 7, 1781	Discharged July 7, 1782
Lawrence Dowsit		"	July 5, "	Discharged July 5, 1782
David Dicks or Dickers		3 "	Dec. 28, 1780	
Edward or Ned Freeman		"	Mar. 17, 1781	

Name	Term	Date	Remarks
Benjamin Greenslit	3 years	Feb. 8, 1781	
John Gates	"	Dec. 10, 1780	
Abel Guthire	"	Nov. 19, "	
Jason Gay	"	Feb. 1, 1781	
Robert Holdridge	"	Dec. 26, 1780	
William Huse or Hughes	1 year	July 19, 1781	confined Provost Guard muster roll for June 1782, but not so noted on July 1782 roll
David Jackson	D. W.	Apr. 1	joined from desert[a] May 31, 1782 not on muster roll for June 1782 or later
Theophilus Luther	3 years	"	transferred to L. I. Comp. June 1, 1782
Joseph Lawson	"	Jan. 19 "	
John Mills	1 year	July 19 "	Discharged Dec. 19, 1782
Abraham Mills	"	July 17 "	Discharged Dec. 19, 1782
Gabriel Mills	"	July 19 "	Discharged Dec. 19, 1782
John McNulty	3 years	July 1, 1780	
Abijah Olmsted	"	July 11 "	transferred to L. I. Comp. June 1, 1782
Justus Olmsted	"	July 11 "	not on muster roll of Sept. 1, 1782.
Jesse Olmsted	"	Jan. 1, 1781	Deserted Sept. 1, 1782.
Jacob Pettingell or Pettersgill	"	Feb. 6 "	
Asaph Pettingell or Pettersgill	"	Feb. 6 "	
Samuel Peters	"	Dec. 10, 1780	
Jack Spry	D. W.	Jan. 29, 1781	Dead Feb. 8, 1782.
Abel Stimson	3 years	Apr. 2 "	Field Officers servant. Invalided June 21, 1782 not on muster roll of May 1782 or later
Feevish or Tuis Sharper	"	Jan. 1 "	
Daniel St. John	"	Jan. 19 "	
David Thompson	"	Jan. 19 "	
James Thompson	"		discharged July 25, 1782
Jacob Wardwell	D. W.	Dec. 16, 1780	
Chester Waterman	3 years	Jan. 19, 1781	
Thomas Worden	"	Mar. 10 "	
Jesse Williams	"		
Elexander Dernant or Deurant or Duvant	18m. 15d.	Mar. 12, 1782	Joined May 12, 1783
Jacob Haskel	6m. 17d.	May 1 "	" 31 " "
Samuel Bliss	6m. 17d.	May 6 "	" " "

Name	Inlisted	Term	Remarks
Samuel Parks	April 30 "	6m. 17d.	"
John Bliss	May 6 "	6m. 17d.	"
Moses Barnard	April 17 "	6m. 17d.	"
Beriah Bliss	April 27 "	6m. 17d.	"
Dan Lyman	April 27 "	6m. 17d.	"
John Berry		D. W.	"
Edward Burghes			Rec'd from L. Co. July 1, 1782
John Haskal	June 5, 1782		Joined July 17, 1782
Ichabod Case	March 12 "		"
Andrew Hazen	May 6 "		"

[State Library, Revolution 39; 44, 54, 63, 71, 81, 90, 99.]

FOURTH COMPANY – CAPT. WALKER.

[The muster rolls of this company, for February, March, May, June, July, September and October 1782 are preserved. Only the earliest of these is here copied, with such changes noted as appear on any of the later rolls.]

Muster roll of Captain Joseph Walker's Company 3d Connecticut Regiment of foot in the Service of the United States, Commanded by Col° Sam'l B. Webb for the month of Feb'y 1782.

Inlisted	Term	Name	Rank	Remarks
Aug. 22, 1777		Joseph Walker	Capt.	Aid de Camp to Maj. Gen. Parsons. B. Major on Oct. roll
Dec. 6, 1781		Martin Denslow	Lieut.	In arrest on Feb. roll only. Retired upon a resolution of Congress July 11, 1782.
		Isaac Keeler	Lieut.	Joined from 2d Co. July 31, 1782.
	D. W.	Francis Nicholson	Serj.	
	"	Jonathan Arnold	"	Name given as Jonathan Steuben on muster roll for June 1782 and later
	"	Simeon Holmes	"	
	"	Waitsoll or Waitstill Dickenson	"	
	"	Stephen Risley or Prisley	Corp.	
	"	Moses Porter	"	
	"	Army Sperry	"	
	"	Elijah Porter	Drum.	Discharged Mar. 28, 1782.

Name	Term	Inlisted	Remarks
Timothy Bevens	D. W.	Mar. 21, 1781	Servant to Gen. Parsons or to Capt. Walker Dec. 4, 1780
Hubbard Burrows	3 years	Dec. 28, 1780	
Samuel Bardon	D. W.		Invalided June 27, 1782
James Chadwick	3 years	Dec. 13, "	Transfered to Light Co. June 1, 1782, but entered on muster roll for July and later.
John Clark		Nov. 29, "	
Benjamin Durfee or Duffee	"		
Reuben Dodge	"		
Seth Dodge			
John Fagins	"	Jan. 22, 1781	
Joshua Fuller or Tusler	D. W.	Feb. "	
Isaac Ford	"		
Azariah Grant	"		
Mason Green			Transfered to Light Co. June 1, 1782
Ebenezer Hadley or Hoadley or Hodley			
Joel Hamlin	3 years	Dec. 20, 1780	Deserted Apr. 10, 1782
Herman or Hemen Hatch	"	Dec. 26, "	
David Hayden	"	May 11, 1781	
Jabez Mortars		Jan. 11, "	
Michael Minthern	D. W.		Deserted Nov. 1, 1782
Henry Ponds	3 years		
Asher Russell	D. W.		
Lemiel Manclift or Lemuel Stanclift			Waggoner
Jonathan Simonds	"	Mar. 1, "	
William Skeericks	"	Feb. 4, "	
John Thomas	D. W.		called Serj. on muster roll for Sept. 1782 and later.
Chester Upham	3 years	Dec. 16, 1780	Transfered to L. Inf. July 1, 1782 not on muster roll for Sept. 1782 or later.
James Wayland	D. W.		
Jacob Weight 1st	3 years	Dec. 16 "	
Jacob Weight 2d	D. W.		
Calvin Chaffee	1 year	July 10, 1781	Discharged Mar. 12, 1782
Oliver Kingsbury	6m.	July 1, "	Died Dec. 11, 1781

D. W.	David Lindsey	Drum.	on muster roll for March and later. Received from 1st Co.
1y. 11m.	Asa Squire	Fifer	on muster roll for March and later. Received from 1st Co.
D. W.	Jeremiah Chamberlin		on muster roll for May 1782 only
"	John Goodrich		" " " and later
"	David Hurd		" " " "
1y. 10m.	Alexander McColpin		" " " Invalided June 27, 1782 and later
2y. 11m.	Elijah Molley or Morley		" " " " and later
7m.	Nathan Potter		" " " " } Not on muster roll for Oct. 1782
D. W.	David Robarts		" " " "
11m.	Judah Robarts		" " " "
D. W.	Ezra Tryon		" " " "
"	Samuel Whitney		" " " " Not on muster roll Sept 1782 and later
"	Daniel Evit		Joined from desertion June 7, 1782
3 years	Royal Marter or Mantor		on muster roll for June 1782 and later Deserted Nov. 7, 1782
6m.	Joshua Olmsted		on muster roll for June 1782 and later Discharged Dec. 30, 1782
3 years	Jeremiah West		on muster roll for June 1782 Deserted July 27, 1782
"	Benjamin Yerred		" " " " "
4m. 20d.	David Hubbell		Joined July 20, 1782.
2m. 20d.	Noah Norton or Noah U. Norton		Joined July 20, 1782.
	Isaac Beers		on roll for Sept. 1782 and later.

[State Library, Revolution 59 ; 49, 53, 66, 76, 85, 94, 103.]

FIFTH COMPANY—CAPT. WILLIAMS.

[The muster rolls of this company for February, March, May, June, July, September and October 1782 are preserved. Only the earliest of these is here copied, with such changes noted as appear on any of the later rolls.]

Muster roll of Captain Samuel William Williams Company in the 3rd Connecticut Regiment in the service of the United States commanded by Colonel Samuel B. Webb for the month of February 1782.

Inlisted	Term	Name	Rank	Remarks
		Samuel William Williams	Capt.	Transfered to 3d Co. Aug. 1, 1782.
		Nathan H. Whiting	Lieut.	
	D. W.	Joshua Cone	Serj.	
	"	Jared Bunce	"	
	"	John Forbes	"	
	"	Thomas Wood	"	not on muster roll for June 1782 or later
	"	Walter Booth	"	Discharged Dec. 16, 1782 by hiring a man
	"	Daniel Ward	Corp.	
	"	Zebulon Mygatt	"	
	"	Frederick Stoddard	"	
	"	William Kirkum	Drum.	
	"	Joel Clark	Fifer	
Nov. 22, 1780	3 years	Jeddediah Addams		
Feb. 2, 1781	"	Christopher Avary		
Apr. 14, "	"	Elihu Babcock		
Jan. 6, 1778	"	Zebedee Brown		
Feb. 3, 1781	"	Joseph Borrows or Burrows		Waggoner
Jan. 29, "	"	Hezekiah Catlin		
Apr. 18 "	"	Stephen Childs		Discharged July 24, 1782
Dec. 20, 1780	"	Serajah Comstock		Deserted Apr. 16, 1782. On May roll and later sick in hospital never mustered
July 2, 1781	1 year	James Church		
June 30 "	"	Abner Coe		
Jan. 1 "	3 years	Samuel Fargo		Deserted July 27, 1782, but continued on later rolls
	D. W.	Asa Fox		Discharged July 2, 1782
July 12, 1780	3 years	Caesar Freman		Discharged June 29, 1782
Nov. 22 "	"	Nathaniel Gates		

Date	Term	Name	Rank	Remarks
Nov. 22, 1780	3 years	Silas Glass or Silas G. Cass		Transfered to L. I. Co. July 1, 1782
Mar. 5, 1781	D. W.	Selah Hart		Servant to Col. Huntington on muster roll for June 1782
		Thomas Hallet		
Apr. 17	3 years	Nathaniel Holt		Discharged June 29, 1782
Mar. 2	"	Jesse Holt		Transfered to L. I. Co. June 1, 1782
July 19	1 year	Stephen Hurlbut		
Dec. 26, 1780	3 years	Philliman Kirkum		Promoted to Corp. Sept. 21, 1782
	D. W.	William Martin		
	"	Stephen Roberts		
	"	Ephraim Robertson		
	"	Joseph Rowlandson		Transfered to L. I. Co. June 1, 1782
		Samuel Schoolcraft		
		Lemuel Sperry		
Apr. 28, 1781	3 years	Jonathan Stevens		Discharged July 2, 1782
July 2	1 year	Chester Southwoth		Transfered to L. I Co June 1, 1782
Dec. 1, 1780	3 years	Charles Walter		
Dec. 3 "	D. W.	Joshua Welles		
Jan. 1, 1781	"	Zedediah or Jedediah Woodworth		Dead Feb. 6, 1782
Mar. 22, 1782	1y. 6m. 8d.	Elimkin Seward		on muster roll for May 1782 and later
Apr. 1	1y. 8m. 17d.	Jeremiah Cunnell		"
May 1	9m. 8d.	Elijah Fayer		Joined June 10
Apr. 15	9m. 16d.	Oliver Coe		" " "
May 23	6m. 16d.	Daniel Heddy		" " "
Mar. 15	5m. 14d.	Janna Wilcox		Deserted Oct. 2.
May 4	5m. 14d.	Adrin or Adino Chapman		Joined June 6.
	8m.	Elisha Catlin		" not on muster roll for Oct. 1782.
	5m. 14d.	Josiah Butt		Joined June 10
	D. W.	Levi Hall		
		Seth Stannard		Transfered from L. I. Co. July 1, 1782
June 1, 1778		John Meiggs	Lieut. & Adj.	Transfered from Staff Aug. 1, 1782.
Apr. 29, 1782	4m. 20d.	Ebenezer Durfee		Joined July 7
May 13 "	4m. 20d.	Elijah Durfee		
June	4m. 20d.	William Cook		Joined July 24, Deserted Oct. 2.
	D. W.	Joseph Freat or Treat		on muster roll for Sept. 1782 and later.

[State Library, Revolution 39 ; 51, 59, 68, 78, 87, 96, 105.]

SIXTH COMPANY—CAPT. HOPKINS.

[The muster rolls of this company for February, March, May, June, July, September and October, 1782, are preserved. Only the earliest of these is here copied, with such changes noted as appear on any of the later rolls.]

Muster roll of Captain Elisha Hopkins's Company 3 Connect Regiment of Foot in service of the United States, commanded by Colonel B. Webb for February 1780*

Inlisted	Term		Rank	
		Elisha Hopkins	Capt.	
		Eli Barnham	Lieut.	
		Matthew Gregory	Lieut.	
	D W	Stephen Dormant	Serj.	
	"	Nathan Savage	"	
	"	Joseph Day	"	
	"	John Beers	"	
Jan. 4, 1782	"	Thomas Stone	"	
	"	Aaron Jones	Corp.	Deserted July 21
	"	Wᵐ Winans	"	
	"	Richᵈ Belding	"	
	"	William Thrall	Drum.	
	"	Isaac Finch	Fifer	
May 1, 1781	3 years	James Anderson		
Nov. 21, 1780	D. W.	Aaron Abercrumbie		
	3 years	Benjamin Brown		
Apr. 20, 1781	D. W.	Richard Baker or Bacon		Servant to Col. Webb
Feb. 27 "	3 years	Daniel Bails or Baits or Bates or Betts		
May 15 "	"	Thomas Brewer or Brown		not on muster roll for Oct. 1782
July 1	1 year	Josiah Barns		
Nov. 22, 1780	3 years	Daniel Betts or Bates		Discharged July 21
Jan. 1, 1781	"	Curtice Cleavland		
May 1 "	"	Gardiner Cleavland		
Dec. 20, 1780	"	Ichabod Downing		
		Roger Edgerton		On Lord Sterlings Guard Fish-hill, Transfered to L. Inf. June 1, and returned July 1, 1782
Jan. 16, 1781	"	Stephen Gavit		

Date	Term	Name	Remarks
Dec. 7, 1780	D. W. 3 years.	Joshua Howe	not on muster roll for June 1782. Appears on July 1782 muster roll and later
	D. "	Ephraim Harry	
21	D. W.	Stephen Kellogg	Deserted Feb. 27, 1782. Appears on muster roll for May and June Transfered to Light Inf. July 1.
		Chancey Lewis	
July 4, 1781	"	Sith Montague	Transfered to Light Inf. July 1
	"	Ira Mott	
	"	Jabez or Tabor Norton	comm'd cont with Col. Webb Dec. 13th 1781 not on muster roll for Sept 1782 or later
	3 years	Hazard Prior	
	D. W.	Will'm Rainvolt or Rain Volt or Reinvault	not on muster roll for Sept 1782 or later
Dec. 1, 1780	3 years	David Spencer	Transfered to L. Inf. June 1, 1782
Feb. 1, 1781	"	Jacob Strong	not on muster roll for May 1782 but appears on June 1782 and later
Feb. 18	"	Edmond Shelley or Thelly	
Nov. 26, 1780	"	Joseph Smith	not on muster roll for May 1782 or later
	D. W.	John Swaddle	
July 1, 1781	1 year	Thos Spencer	Discharged July 1
	D. W.	Hezekiah Cary	
	"	Elihu Waters or Warten	Joined from desertion Feb. 2, 1782. Transfered to L. Inf. June 1, and returned July 1, 1782
Apr. 9, 1782	D. W.	Jonathan Crutie	Deserted June 12, 1782
	"	Allen Corning	on muster roll for May 1782 and later
	"	Joseph Johnston	"
		Hendrick Bail	"
Apr. 1	1y. 6m. 5d.	Ruben Clark	Joined May 18, with Geographer July 12, 1782. Not on muster roll for Sept. 1782 or later
	9m. 15d.		
Apr. 19	6m. 15d.	Noah Kelsey	Joined May 18
Mar. 23	9m. 7d.	Samuel Stantliff	" "
Apr. 27	9m. 6d.	Nathan Edgerton	" " 20

* Signed and indorsed 1782, and later rolls of this company are dated 1782.

Inlisted	Term		
May 24 1782	5m. 9d.	Ebenezer Chapman	Joined June 5 Deserted Oct. 2,1782
Apr. 13 "	"	Daniel or David Gardner	" " 10 " "
Apr. 29 "	"	Jacob Fenton	" " 20
May 15 "	"	James Bliss	" " 20
Apr. 15 "	8m. 24d.	Jabez or Tabor Cole	" " 20
Apr. 30 "	2y. 8m. 20d.	Wilson Commins	" July 8
		Frank Negro	Joined Apr. 7, 1782 Servant. not on muster roll for Oct. 1782
	D. W.	Daniel Bostwick	Joined from desertion Sep. 24, 1782
	"	William Daskim	" " " " "
	"	Simion C. Stoddard	appears on muster roll for Sep. 1782

[State Library, Revolution 39 ; 46, 55, 64, 73, 83, 92, 101.]

SEVENTH COMPANY—CAPT. RILEY.

[The muster rolls of this company for February, March and June 1782 are preserved. Only the earliest of these is here copied, with such changes noted as appear on any of the later rolls.]

Muster Roll of Captain John Rileys Company of the 3rd Connecticut Regiment in the service of the United States commanded by Colonel Samuel B. Webb For the month of February 1782

Inlisted	Term			
	D. W.	John Riley	Capt.	
	"	John Mix	Lieut.	
	"	William or Thomas Holmes	Serj.	
	"	William Taylor	"	
	"	David Webb	"	
	"	William Patterson		
	"	Dan¹ Potter	Corp.	
	"	Christopher Horton		
	"	Ezekiel Winchal		
	"	Joseph Wolcutt	Drum	
		Samuel Bush	Fifer	
Sep. 1, 1779	3 years	Job Boomer		With the Quarter Master General since July 19, 1781.

Month	Day, Year	Term	Name	Remarks
Feb.	6, 1781	"	Ozias Bachus	
Apr.	22 "	"	Joseph Cheem or Cheney	
Jan.	8 "	1 year	David Chester	Transfered to L. Inf. June 1, 1782
June	30 "	3 years	Asa Copeland	
Dec.	1, 1780	"	Benjamin Cady	
Feb.	1, 1781		Silvenus Gage	
Feb.	5 "		Joel Hyde	
			Amos Harris	
Feb.	1	"	Eleazar Hatch	
			Peter Johnson	
Feb.	1	"	John or Richard Kimball	
Feb.	1	"	Jared Kimball	
Dec.	10, 1780	"	Marshall Kyes	
Jan.	27, 1781	"	Jabez Kirtland Brigade Waggoner	
Feb.	3	"	Phinehas Knight	
			Jonathan Luce	
Feb.	6	"	Levi Munsill	
Feb.	1	"	John Munsill	Transfered to L. Inf. June 1, 1782
			Benoni Moss	
Feb.	23	"	James Miner	
Jan.	15	"	Noah Merrills	
May	16	"	Gallaway Peters	
		D. W.	David Potter	Transfered to L. Inf. June 1, 1782
Feb.	3	3 years	Lemuel Raymond	
			Joshua Reynolds	
			Peter Shopp	
			Thadeus Scofield	
			Toney Turney	
Dec.	20, 1780	"	Nathan Tubbs	Deserted Apr. 10, 1782. Joined from desertion May 18, 1782
Mar.	5, 1781	"	John Wheeler	
Feb.	1	"	Ichabod West	
Jan.	1 "		Ichabod Warden	
			Thomas Wilson	Servant to Gen. Parsons Aide

Inlisted	Term		
Nov. 1, 1782	3 years	Richard York	not on muster roll for March 1782 or later
"	1y. 9m.	George Seeley	appears on muster roll for March 1782 and later
"	D. W.	Joseph Clinton Corp.	appears on muster roll for June 1782
May 6	34m. 21d.	David Heyden	Joined May 9
April 22	6m. 8d.	Nathaniel Silliman	" " 19
Mar. 25	8m. 22d.	Oliver Scott	" " 21
Feb. 3	3m. 22d.	Simon Stimson	" " 21
Apr. 12	5m. 28d.	Robert Welsh	" " 19

[State Library, Revolution 39; 47, 56, 74.]

EIGHTH COMPANY—CAPT. ALLYN.

[The muster rolls of this company for February, March, May, June, July, September, and October, 1782, are preserved. Only the earliest of these is here copied, with such changes noted as appear on any of the later rolls.]

Muster Roll of Captain Allyns Company in the 3ʳᵈ Connecticut Regiment in the service of the United States Commanded by Col¹ Samuel B. Webbs for the Month of February 1782.

Appointed	Term	Name		
		Timothy Allyn	Capt.	not on muster roll Oct. 1782
		William Lord	Lieut.	" " "
	D. W.	Jacquess Harmon	Ens.	Transfered to 2d Co. July 31
		Wyman Parker	Serj.	
	"	Abraham Hawley	"	
	"	Enoch Merriman	"	not on muster roll May 1782 or later
		John Downe	"	on muster roll for May and later
July 11, 1780	3 years	Hezekiah Betts	Corp.	Deserted April 10
	D. W.	Nathan Hawley	Corp.	
	"	Curtis Crane	Drum.	
	"	Thomas Brown	Fifer	reduced from fifer April 1
	1m. 10d.	David Coy	Fifer	Hired by Isaiah Pratt to serve in his stead March 21, 1782
		Matthew Jackson		
	D. W.	John Ammit		

Date	Term	Name	Note
Apr. 4, 1781	3 years	Ebenezer Bacon	Transferred to Capt. Wells L. I. Co. June 1, 1782
Jan. 29 "	"	Comfort Beebee	
		Richard Beebee	
Feb. 26	D. W.	Abial Chaffee	
July 18	3 years	John Churchell	Discharged July 18, 1782
	D. W.	William Clark	Transferred to Invalid Corps June 21, 1782
	3 years	Cesar Edwards	
Mar. 1	"	Jabez Edgecomb	
Jan. 1	"	Benedick Eggleston	
July 15	"	Benjamin Ellsworth	
Jan. 3	"	Bassat Fox	
		Simeon Fox	
Jan. 29	"	James Eggleston	Servant to Col. Verrick Nov. 18, 1781
March	"	David Garner	
Jan. 17	"	Jacob Gillet	
Jan. 29	"	Henry Horton	
Jan.	"	Cudjo Helms	
Dec. 18, 1780	"	John G. Holcomb	Transferred to Invalid Corps June 21, 1782
Jan. 16, 1781	"	Aaron Kingsley	
	D. W.	Peter Lewis	not on muster roll Sept. 1782 or later
	"	Eliel London	
	"	Stephen Ludlow	
	"	Nathaniel or Nathan Mallery	
	"	Elias Measom or Meason	
Nov. 25, 1780	3 years	John Mills	
Nov. 25	"	James Nedson	Not on muster roll March 1782 or later
Jan. 8, 1781	"	Robert Nedson	
Dec. 27, 1780	"	Isaac Nellson	
Dec. 27, 1781	"	Daniel Perkins	
Mar. 5 "	"	Isaiah Pratt	
Jan. 1 "	"	Adonijah Rose	
Mar. 1 "	D. W.	John Robertson	Transferred to Capt. Wells L. I. Co. June 1, 1782
	"	Comma Simonds	
		Elias Shaw	

Appointed	Term	Name	
Feb. 1, 1781	3 years	Ebenezer Shaw	Transferred to Light Infantry Co. July 1, 1782.
Mar. 1 "	"	Reuben Sharp	
Dec. 14, 1780		David Taylor	
		Calvin Chaffee	hired by Abial Chaffee to serve in his stead March 1782. Transferred to Capt. Wells L. I. Co. June 1, 1782.
Apr. 24, 1782	6m. 16d.	Isaac Beers	Joined June 8 Deserted July 18, 1782
Apr. 24 "	" "	Hezekiah Terrill or Turnill	" 8
June 29 "	5m. 9d.	Nehemiah Barns	" July 17
May 11 "	" "	Edward Dunkin	" June 17
May 11 "	" "	Daniel Hawley	" " 17
May 11 "	" "	Charles Lewis	" " 17
June 3 "	" "	Aaron Waley	" " 17

[*State Library, Revolution 39; 43, 53, 61, 70, 80, 89, 98.*]

CONNECTICUT LINE, 1783.

THIRD REGIMENT — COL. WEBB.

[*See Record of Connecticut Men in the Revolution, page 367.*]

FIELD AND STAFF.

[The muster rolls of the Field and Staff for Dec. 1782 – Jan. 1783 and Feb. 1783 are preserved. Only the earlier of these is here printed, with such changes noted as appear on the later.]

Muster Roll of the Field and Staff Officers, of the 3rd Connecticut Reg^t with such Noncommissioned Officers as are not attached to any Company

Ranks	Names	
Colonel	Samuel B. Webb	
Lieut. Col.	Ebenezer Gray	
Maj.	Joseph A. Wright	
Adjnt	John Meigs	
Quarter Master	Ebenezer Frothingham	
Pay Master	Nathan Beers	
Recruit Officer		
Surgeon	John Rose	
Mate	Jedediah Ensworth	Resigned Jan. 15,1783
	Aeneas Monson	Joined Jan. 15, 1783
Serj. Majors	Edward Miller	
	Jonathan White	Deserted Jan. 4, 1783
Qr. Mr. Serjeants	Simon Griffin or Giffin	
	William Tupper	
Drum Major	David Pratt	
Fife Majors	John Kircum	
	George Cook	

I certify the Present Muster Roll to be true in all its contents
Inspection of December 1782 & January 1783

W Barber Major & Ass^t Inspector of the North^n Army

[*State Library, Revolution 39 ; 106, 116.*]

LIGHT INFANTRY COMPANY—CAPT. WELLES.

[The muster rolls of this company for Dec. 1782–Jan. 1783 and Feb. 1783 are preserved. Only the earlier of these is here printed, with such changes noted as appear on the later roll.]

Roll and Muster of the Light Infantry Company in the 3rd Regiment of Connecticut Troops Commanded by Coll Saml B. Webb

Ranks	Names	Term of Enlistment	
Capt	Roger Welles		
Lieut	John Trowbridge		Transfd 1st Co Feb 1st 1783
"	William Linn		Transferd to 8th Compy 1st Jany 1783
Ensn	Jacob Kingsbury		Transfd 6th Co Feb 1st 1783
Sergts	Stephen Butler	D W	
	Elihu Spear	"	
	Silas Phelps		
	Moses Griswould	"	Recd from 3d Compy 1st Jany 1783
	Thomas Wood	"	Deserted Jany 10th 1783
Corporals	Selah Scofield		
	David Lounsbury	"	
	Benjamin Dix	"	
Drummer	John Dixon	"	
fifer	Daniel Winchel	"	
Privates	Jacob Achor	"	
	John Allyn	"	
	Archelus Ames	1 1 15	
	John Barnum	D W	
	David Bullen	"	
	Ebenezer Bacon	1 2 8	
	Reuben Cadwell	D W	
	Elias Carpenter	0 11 13	
	Calvin Chaffee	0 11 9	
	Asa Copeland	D W	
	Ward Cotton	0 11 18	
	Benjamin Dix	D W	promoted to Corpl 1 Jany 1783
	Allyn Evins	"	
	Thomas Evins	"	
	Remembrance Filley	"	
	Vaniah Fox	"	
	Ichabod Goodrich	"	
	Samuel Gookins	"	
	Andrew Hansey	0 11 10	
	Selah Harte	1 1 8	
	Samuel Hinman	D W	
	James Hyde	"	
	Benjamin Kircum	"	
	Philemon Kircum	0 11 22	
	Joseph Lawson	0 11 23	
	Chansey Lewis	D W	
	Stephen Meeker	"	
	Jonathan Miller	"	
	Ira Mott	"	
	Brion Montigue	"	
	John Munsill	1 0 4	

Ranks	Names	Term of Enlistment	
Privates	Levi Munsell	1 0 10	
	Sheldon Potter	D W	
	Lemuel Raymond	"	
	Reuben Sharpe	1 1 3	
	Elias Shaw	D W	
	Isaiah Smith	"	
	Nathan Smith	"	
	David Spencer	1 0 4	
	Lemuel Sperry	D W	
	Samuel Stowel	0 11 3	
	Nathaniel Stowel	1 1 15	
	Samuel Vallit	D W	Deserted Jany 31, 83
	Chester Upham	0 10 19	
	Benjamin Waklee	D W	
	Charles Walter	0 10 3	
	Hazard Pryor	1 5 8	transf^d 1st Comp^y 1st Jany 1783

I certify the above Roll to be the true State of said Comp^y this 26th day of Jany 1783

J. Kingsbury Ens^n

[*State Library, Revolution 39 ; 115, 125.*]

FIRST COMPANY—CAPT. BETTS.

[The muster rolls of this company for Dec. 1782–Jan. 1783 and Feb. 1783 are preserved. Only the earliest of these is here printed, with such changes noted as appear on the later roll.]

Roll and muster of the 1st Company 3rd Regiment of Connecticut Troops Commanded by Colonel Saml B. Webb for Dec^r & Jany 1782 & 3

Ranks	Names	Term of Enlistment	Casualties & Alterations
Captain	Stephen Betts		on Furlough
Lieu^t	John Mix		Comm^d Q. M. G. Rec^d from the 8 Company transferred to the 8th Comp^y Feb. 1, 83
Lieut	John Trowbridge		Rec^d from the Light Compy Feby 1 82–3
Ens^n	Jaques Harmon		
Lieu^t	Ebenezer Frothingham		Transfered to the Reg^{al} Staff
Serjeants	Jesse Smith	D War	
"	Joseph Clark	"	
"	Aaron Raymond	"	
"	Torey Scranton	"	
"	Joseph Hait	"	
"	Uzal Knapp	"	
"	Luther Reeves	"	
Corporals	James Downs	"	
"	Abel Hitchcock	"	
"	George Hubbard	"	
"	Enoch Thomas	"	
"	Samuel Jackson	"	
Drum	Anthony DeFloris	11m. 6d.	
"	Lemuel Sanborough or Samuel Stanborugh	12 7	

Ranks	Names	Term of Enlistment		Casualties &¹Alterations
Fife	Reuben Rennolds	War		
"	John Dauset	"		
Privates	Roger Avory	"		
	Thomas Blake	"		
	David Betts	"		
	Jacob Bosworth	"		
	John Bary	"		
	James Coburn	"		
	Joseph Davis	9	29	
	Juline Eston	War		
	Primas Freeman	"		
	Sirus Graham	"		
	Joseph Goldsmith	"		
	Silas Glasco or Glasses	"		
	William Hanson	"		
	Ebenezer Hill	"		
	James Freeman	"		
	David Jackson	"		
	Alexander Judd	"		
	Abner Lee	"		
	Job Leason	"		
	Robert Marsh	"		
	Anthony McDaniel	"		
	Reuben Parks	"		
	Nathaniel Pardy	"		
	Jeremiah Rozell	"		
	Ambrose Smith	"		
	Aaron Tuttle	"		
	Samuel Thomas	"		
	Jacob Wardwell	"		
	Benjamin Welton	"		
	Edward Burges	8m.	9d.	
	Jonathan Brown	10	25	
	Alexander Durand	10	23	
	Benjamin Dodge	10	25	
	David Dicks	10	23	
	Edward Freeman	10	12	
	John Gates	11	5	
	Benjamin Greenslit	11	28	
	Jaison Gay	11	26	
	Able (?) Guthrey	9	14	
	Gilbert Graves			
	Robert Holdridge	10	21	
	William Hughes	11	25	
	Clement Handy	28	7	
	William Lament	17	7	
	John McNulty	4	25	
	Aseph Pettengall	11	26	
	Jesse Olmstead	11	3	
	Jacob Pettengall	12	1	
	Hazard Prior	17	8	Recᵈ from the Lᵗ Infʸ Comʸ Janʸ 1 1783 Servt to Colᵗ Webb in Connᵗ
	Adonijah Rose	9	16	Recᵈ from the 6 Compʸ
	Tuis Sharper	13	27	
	Ephraim Story	15	7	
	Shubel Snow	28	7	

Ranks	Names	Terms of Enlistment		Casualties & Alterations
Privates	Daniel St John	10	25	
	James Thompson	11	25	
	Thomas Worden	13	2	
	Jesse Williams	12	25	
	Chester Waterman	11	11	
	Josiah Rogers			transf^d to the 6 Company Jan 1st 83
	John Bliss			Dich^d Decr 29th 82 Time expired
	Beriah Bliss	"	" 29	"
	Samuel Bliss	"	" 29	"
	Moses Barnard	"	" 29	"
	Abijah Bloggett	"	" 29	"
	Ichabod Case	1	3	
	John Haskal			Disch^d Decr 29th 82 Time expired
	Jacob Haskal	"	" "	"
	Andrew Hazen	"	" "	"
	Dan Lyman	"	" "	"
	Charles Miner	"	" "	"
	Reubin Cree	"	" "	"
	Saml Parks	"	" "	"
	John Porter	"	" "	"
	Oziah (?) Prentice			
	John Meeker			Discharged by his Excellencys order Jany 4th 83 for Inability

I certify the above Roll to be the true State of said Company this day of Jany 1783

J. Harmon Ens^n

[*State Library, Revolution 39; 107, 117.*]

SECOND COMPANY—CAPT. WALKER.

[The muster rolls of this company for Dec. 1782–Jan. 1783, and Feb. 1783 are preserved. Only the earlier of these is here printed, with such changes noted as appear on the later roll.]

Roll and Muster of 2nd Company 3rd Connecticut Regiment of Foot by Col^l S. B. Webb for Decr 82 & Jany 1783

Ranks	Names	Term of Inlistment	
Capt.	Joseph Walker		Brigade Major
Lieu^t	Aron Benjamin		
Ensign	Joseph Clark		
Serjeants	Jonathan Steuben	D W	
"	Francis Nickelson	"	
"	Simeon Holmes	"	
"	Waitstill Dickinson	"	
"	Ezbon Hubbell	"	
"	Elijah Demming	"	
"	Elihu Mather	"	
Corporals	Stephen Risley	"	
"	Moses Porter	"	
"	Armey Sperry	"	
"	John Thomas	"	
"	Benjamin Wheeler	"	
Drumer	David Linsly	"	
"	John Jinks	"	

Ranks	Names	Term of Inlistment		
Drumer	John Vaughn	D. W.		Joined from late 5th Reg^t Discharged 1st Jany 83
Fifer	Asa Squires	"		Died 24th Jany 1788
Privates	Henry Bivens	"		
	Abel Batchlor	"		
	James Chadwick	"		
	Benjamin Craft	"		
	Jehiel Doude	"		
	Daniel Evett	"		
	Reuben Everts	14m		
	Isaac Ford	D War		
	Jonathan Finch	"		
	Plymouth Freeman	"		
	Azariah Grant	"		
	John Goodrich	"		
	Prince George	"		
	Ebenezer Hodley	"		
	David Hurd	"		
	Titus Hine	"		
	Jonathan Haynes	"		
	Reuben Lake	"		
	Silvester Miner	"		
	Uriah Polly	"		
	Ashur Russell	"		
	David Roberts	"		
	Samuel Stone	"		
	Ezra Tryon	"		
	Jacob Wright 2nd	"		
	Silas Wood	"		
	James Grant	"		
	Hubbard Burras or Burrows	13m	9d	
	Isaac or James Beers	28	8	
	William Butler	12	0	deserted 8 Feby 83
	Elisha Back	14	0	
	Thomas Burrell	2	0	with the Geographer
	John Clark	10	10	
	Benjamin Durffee	9	16	
	Reuben Dodge	9	18	
	Seth Dodge	9	18	
	Joshua Fullar	11	8	
	John Faggins	11	9	
	David Hayden	15	27	
	Heman Hatch	10	14	
	Rufus Holdridge	13	0	
	Bodwell Hughes	25	0	
	Joel Johnson	12	0	
	Prince Johnson	10	0	
	Jabez Morters	11	28	
	Elijah Morley	26	28	
	Henry Pond	18	25	
	Jacob Patchen	13	0	
	Richard Pitts or Potts	11	0	
	Judah Roberts	1	18	
	Lemuel Stancliff	12	15	
	Jonathan Simons	12	18	

Ranks	Names	Terms of Inlistment		
	William Sheericks	11	25	
	Joshua Turner	25	0	
	Jacob Wight	12	23	
	Joseph Wakely	12	15	
	David Hubbell		Disch[d] Dec[r] 9th 1782	
	Noah U. Norton		" " "
	Joshua Olmsted		" " 30 82
	Amos Clark		" " 9 "
	David Hubbard		" " 30 "
	David Joice		" " 20 "
	Solomon Ranney		" " 30 "
	Nathan Wheeler		" " 30 "
	Walter Smith		" " 9 "
	Benjamin Webster		" " 6 "
	Ashbel Webster		" " 6 83
	John Clark 2[d]		" " 31 83

I certify the above Roll to be the true state of said Company this 26th day of January 1783

Joseph Clark Ens[n]

[*State Library, Revolution 39; 114, 124.*]

THIRD COMPANY—CAPT. SELDEN.

[The muster rolls of this company for Dec. 1782–Jan. 1783 and Feb. 1783 are preserved. Only the earlier of these is here printed, with such changes noted as appear on the later roll.]

Roll and Muster of the third Company of the 3rd Connecticut Regiment Commanded by Col[l] Sam[l] B. Webb for Dec[r] 1782 & Jan[y] 1783.

Ranks	Names	Term of Inlistment	
Capt	Ezra Selden		
Lieu[t]	John Meigs		Transf[d] to y[e] Reg[l] Staff Jan[y] 1st 1783
"	John Mix		Rec[d] from the 1st Co 1st Feby
Ens[n]	Abner Cole		
Lieu[t]	John Hobart		Rec[d] from y[e] 4th Reg[t] Jan[y] 1st 1783 transf[d] to 8th Co 1st Feby
Serj[t]	Daniel Sizer	D War	
"	Elijah Boardman	"	
"	Darius Orcutt or Oniott	8m 20d.	
"	Moses Griswold	D War	Transfd to the L I Comp[y] 1st Jan[y]
"	Allen Prior	"	
"	Ebenezer Shelley	"	
"	Phineas Squires	"	
Corporals	Hezekiah Nott	"	
"	Thomas Stanley	"	Reduced 8 March 83
"	Gideon Goff	"	
"	Reuben Moss	"	
"	Abraham Parker	"	
Drum	Moses Hatch	"	
"	Miles Cook	"	
Fife	William Armstrong	"	

Ranks	Names	Terms of Inlistment		
Fife	Silas Stanbrough	13m		
Privates	Daniel Morley	D War		
	Hezekiah Wheeler	"		
	Prince Freeman	"		
	Jack Freeman	"		
	Samuel Roberts	"		
	Abraham Belding	"		
	Benajah Bracket	"		
	David Barnes	"		
	Peter Lyon	"		
	Jabez Lord	"		
	David Hull	"		
	John Lerow or Scrow	"		
	John Bishop	"		
	Linus Morse	"		
	Eliacom Hull	"		
	Enoch Kellogg	"		
	Abdiel Flowers	"		
	Samuel Lee	"		
	Othniel Branard	"		
	Seth Hubbell	"		
	John Packard	"		
	Solomon Williams	"		
	Ezra Harvey	"		
	Samuel Cheese	"		
	Cezar Negro	18m.		deserted 26 Feb. 83
	Joseph Pease	16	14d.	
	Cato Freeman	16	1	
	John Ballard	13	20	
	Moses Coy	12	3	
	Nathan Frinck	12		
	Nathaniel Price	13		
	Reuben Robinson	12	20	
	Samuel Lyon	12	3	
	Robert Chandler	12		
	Joseph Douglass	11	22	
	Alfred Dressor	11	5	
	Joseph Preston	11	27	
	Peter Whitney	10	25	
	Daniel Dunham	10	28	
	Abel Stoel	10	17	
	Jeremiah Bennet	10	17	
	Jonathan Bullock	10	17	
	Stephen Fox	10	1	
	Benjamin Brown	10		
	David Peck	9	17	
	Joseph Abby	11	21	
	Gideon Dunham	2		
	Joseph Bunnel	1	28	
	Eleazer Cutler	1	19	
	Christopher Kelby	1	19	
	Nathaniel Hardy	1		Disch[d] 8th Febr 1783
	William Witherel			Discharged Jan[y] 18th 1783
	Neal McNeal			" Dec[r] 6th 1782
	Gideon Russell			" " 27th
	Jesse Thomas			" " 9th
	George Foot			" " 20th

Ranks	Names	Term of Inlistment	
Privates	Amos Gustin		Discharged Dec[r] 10th 1782
	Benoni Robins		" " 22[d]
	Ephraim Webster		" " 9th
	John Downing		" Jan[y] 2[d] 1783
	John Tucker		" Dec[r] 10th 1782
	Daniel W Knight		" " 26th
	Daniel Stevens		Transferred to y[e] 2nd Reg[t] Jan[y] 1st 1783
	Nehemiah Seley		Discharged Dec[r] 9th 1782
	Daniel Bushnell		" Jan[y] 6th 1783
	William Saivers	D War	Joined from the late 4th Feb 19,83
	Samuel Herrington	"	Found only on Feb. roll

I certify the above Roll to be the true State of said Company this 26th day of January 1783

Ezra Selden Capt

[*State Library, Revolution 39 ; 111, 122.*]

FOURTH COMPANY—CAPT. TEN EYCK.

[The muster rolls of this company for Dec. 1782–Jan. 1783 and Feb. 1783 are preserved. Only the earlier of these is here printed, with such changes noted as appear on the later roll.]

Roll and Muster of the 4th Company 3rd Conn[t] Regiment Commanded by Col[l] Sam[l] B. Webb

Ranks	Names	Term of Inlistment	
Capt	Henry Ten Eyck		
Lieu[t]	Isaac Keeler		
Serj[t]	Jared Bunce	D War	
	John Forbes	"	Adj[t] Gen[l] Guard July 12th 82
	Joshua Cone	"	Disch[d] Dec[r] 6th by hiring a man
	Walter Booth	,	
	Ahimaaz Punderson	"	
	Constant Chapman	11m 16d	
	Phinehas Squires	D War	Transfer[d] to the 3[d] Comp[y] Jan[y] 1st 83
	David Dixon	"	
Corp[ls]	Zebulon Mygott	"	Reduc[d] to a private 1 Mch 83
	Daniel Ward	"	
	Frederick Stoddard	"	
	Stephen Roberts	"	
	Jiles Wilcox	"	
Drummers	William Kerkum	"	
	Elijah Peeksley	"	
Fifer	Joel Clark	"	
	Samuel Shelley	"	
Privates	Jedediah Adams	9m 17d	
	Christopher Avery	17 7	
	Elihu Babcock	14 9	
	Joseph Borrows	18 7	
	Joseph Branch	D War	
	David Brown	10 5	
	Solomon Bigsby	15 27	
	John Boughton	D War	
	Jeremiah Cunnell	10 27	

Ranks	Names	Term of Inlistment	
Privates	Serajah Comstock	10 23	
	Joseph Chamberlin	10 16	
	Curtis Chapel	D War	
	Stephen Childs	14 22	
	Hezekiah Catlin	12 2	
	Joel Dolittle	D War	
	William Davis	"	
	James Dinah	"	
	Jonas Elis	"	
	Asa Fox	"	
	Elijah Fayer	13 5	
	Sam¹ Fargo	11 1	
	Caesor Freeman	5 17	
	Cuffee Freeman	D War	
	Silas Glass	9 27	
	Nath¹ Gates	9 27	
	Sam¹ Green	D War	Recᵈ from 7ᵗʰ Compʸ Janʸ 10ᵗʰ 83
	Nath¹ Holt	14 21	
	Jesse Holt	12 27	
	Pratt Jones	D War	
	Eli King	"	
	Willᵐ Martin	"	
	Thomas Meach	"	Transfᵈ to the 7ᵗʰ Compʸ Janʸ 1ˢᵗ 83
	Clemont Miner	"	Inlisted Decʳ 6ᵗʰ 1782 hired by Serjᵗ Booth
	Robert Newel		
	William Ovitt	"	
	Joseph Otis	"	
	Daniel Purkins	10 25	
	Isaac Roberts	D War	
	Joseph Rowlandson	"	
	Isaac Raymond	"	
	Ephᵐ Robertson	"	
	Seth Stannard	"	
	Philliman Stedmon	"	
	Isaac Stedmon	16 16	
	Sam¹ Schoolcraft	D War	
	Abel Stockwell	"	Deserted Decʳ 17ᵗʰ 82
	Andrew Simons	"	
	Jonathan Stevens	14 27	
	Joseph Treat	D War	
	Job Uffoot	"	
	Jedediah Woodworth	9 7	
	Joshua Welles	D War	
	Congo Zado	"	
	Josiah Butt	1 21	
	Daniel Heddy or Healdy	2 20	
	Oliver Coe	1 20	
	Elijah Durfy		Dischᵈ Decʳ 9ᵗʰ 82
	Sam¹ Convirs		" Janʸ 3ᵈ 83
	Elijah Andros		" Decʳ 6ᵗʰ 82
	James French		" " "
	Amos Green		" " "
	Edmond J Dunning		" " 17ᵗʰ 82
	Levi Hall		" Janʸ 11ᵗʰ 83

Ranks	Names	Term of Inlistment			
Privates	Roswell Lamphere	Disch^d	Dec^r	9th	82
	Stephen Squires	"	Dec^r	7th	82
	James Wilcox	"	Dec^r	28th	82
	Elisha Catlin	"	Dec^r	28th	82

I certify the above Roll to be the true State of said Company This 26th day of January 1783

Hen^y Ten Eyck Capt^a

[Indorsed] Roll & Muster of 4th Company 3rd Reg^t of Connecticut For Decem^r 82 & Jany 1783

[*State Library, Revolution 39; 113, 123.*]

FIFTH COMPANY — CAPT. HOPKINS.

[The muster rolls of this company for Dec. 1782–Jan. 1783, and Feb. 1783 are preserved. Only the earlier of these is here printed, with such changes noted as appear on the later roll.]

Roll and Muster of the 5th Company in the 3^d Connecticut Regiment Commanded by Col^l Saml B. Webb for Decemb^r 82 & Jany 83

Ranks	Names	Term of Inlistment			
Capt	Elisha Hopkins				
Lieu^t	Daniel Bradley				
Serjeants	Stephen Dormant	D	War		
	Nathan Savage	"			
	Joseph Day	"			
	John Beers	"			
	Thomas Stone	"			
	Daniel Bradley	"			
	Isaac Parker	"			
Corporal	William Wimans	"		Reduced, the 6th March 1782	
	Richard Belding	"			
	Jonathan Hull	"			
	Warren Murry	"			
	Asher Heacox	"			
Drummer	William Thrall	"			
Fifers	Isaac Finch	"			
	James Satterly	"			
	James Anderson	1	2	23	
	Aaron Abbercrumbie	D	War		
	Benjamin Brown	0	9	13	
	Richard Bacon	D	War		
	Daniel Baits	1	2	13	
	Josiah Barnes	1	2	18	
	Hendrick Bail	0	10	13	
	Curtice Cleaveland	0	9	15	
	Guardner Cleaveland	0	10	23	
	Allen Corning	D	War		
	Wilson Commins	2	2	23	
	Ichabod Downing	1	2	23	
	William Daskin	D	War		
	Roger Edgerton	0	10	12	
	Stephen Gavit	0	11	8	
	Joshua How	D	War		
	Ephraim Harry	0	10	9	

Ranks	Names	Term of Inlistment			
Privates	Seth Montague	D	War		
	Jabez Norton	"			
	John Swaddle	"			
	Jacob Strong	0	9	23	
	Edmond Sholly or Shelly	1	0	6	
	Simeon C Stoddard	D	War		
	Elihue Warters	"			
	Joseph Johnston	"			
	Samuel Stanklift or Stancliff	0	1	15	
	Nathan Edgerton	0	2	19	
	Jabez Cole	0	2	7	
	William Beardsley	D	War		
	Bristol Caesar	"			
	Moses Evens	"			
	Robert Freeman	"			
	Samuel D. Goff	1	0	9	
	Boswell or Roswell Hotchkiss	0	11	11	
	Joseph Kent	1	5	9	
	Elijah Lord	D	War		
	Elnathan Minor	"			
	Mills or Milo Palmer	2	3	9	
	Eliphilet Parrish	2	2	18	
	Cash Pallintine	D	War		
	William Russel	"			
	Alexander Williams	"			
	Nathaniel Warner	0	11	6	
	Jack Arabus	D	War		
	Lewis Martin	"			
	John Nayls	"			
	Shany or Sparry Reed	0	11	8	
	Ebenezer Carr	0	11	8	
	David Jones	D	War		
	Israel Dodge	"			
	Abraham Johnston	"			
	John Lay	0	11	4	
	Eleazer Robertson	D	War		
	Jared Palmer	"			
	Daniel Bostwick	"	Deserted Jany 22^d 83			
	Hezekiah Cary	"	" " "			
	Stephen Kellogg	"	Discharged Jany 5th 83			
	Noah Kelsug	"	" Decr 24th 82			
	Jacob Fenton	"	" " 9th			
	James Bliss	"	" " 5th			
	John Taylor	"	" " 9th			
	Samuel Minor	"	" " 5th			
	Freeman Gates	"	6th Jany 83			
	Benoni Pendal	"	29th Decem 82			
	James Dunning	"	10th			
	Thomas Anderson	"	5th			
	Sedgwick Orter	"	9th			

I certify the above Roll to be the true State of said Comp^y this 26th day of January 1783

Dan. Bradley Lieu^t

SIXTH COMPANY—CAPT. DORRANCE.

[The muster rolls of this company for Dec. 1782–Jan. 1783 and Feb. 1783 are preserved. Only the earlier of these is here printed, with such changes noted as appear on the later roll.]

Roll and Muster of the 6th Company 3d Connecticut Regiment Commanded by Col. Samuel B. Webb for Decr 82 & Jany 1783.

Ranks	Names	Term of Inlistment		
Capt	David Dorrance			
Lieu^t	Joshua Whitney			
Ensign	Jacob Kingsbury			Joined from the Light Company Febr 1783
Serj^ts	Elihu Sanford	D War		
	Hyman Parker	"		
	Abraham Hawley	"		
	John Kindle	"		
	Augustus Clark	"		
	John Downs	"		Deserted 11 March 1783
	Jehiel Bradley	"		
	Hezekiah Betts	4m	15d	
[Corporals]	John Daboll	D War		
	Nathan Hawley	"		
	Curtee Craen	"		
	Abijah Hubell	1y	1m	
	Alexander Mills	D War		
Drum Fif^r	Thomas Brown	"		
	Robert Bartlet	"		
	Mathew Jackson	1	0	25
	Samuel Wardell	D War		
Privates	John Ammit	"		
	Comfort Becks or Beebe	11	16	
	Richard Beebe	11	16	
	John Curchel	D War		
	Eli Denslow	"		
	Jones or Jeames Egleston	1	0	11
	Benedick Egleston	10	18	
	Jabez Edgcomb	1	0	18
	Benjamin Elsworth	1	4	18
	Basel or Basset Fox	11	5	
	Jacob Gillet	11	5	
	David Gardner	1	0	18	Servt to Genl McDougal
	Henery Horton	11	3	
	John Holcomb	9	2	
	Cudjo Helmes	10	18	
	Aaron Kingsley	11	4	
	Ebel or Eliel London	D War		
	Nathan Maleny or Mallery	"		
	Elias Meason	9	14	
	James Nodson	9	12	
	Isaac Nelson	10	14	
	Robert Neason	1	0	46
	John Robertson	1	0	18
	Ebenezer Shaw	"	"	"

Names	Term of Inlistment		
Comma Simons	D War		
David Taylor	10	2	
Simeon Fox	9	21	
John Mills	11	18	
Josiah Rogers	11	6	
Asa Rathburn	D War		
Aron Olds	"		
Ezekiel Butler	"		
Uriah Hungerford	"		
Georg Wilson	"		Deserted 9 March 1783
David Goodfaith	"		
Samuel Chapman	"		
Philo Gibbs	2	25	
Charles Repley or Risley	2	25	
Samuel Elwell		23	Deserted Feby 7 1783
Thomas Simons	1 1	0	
Barnabas Mitshel	D War		
Oliver Rouse	"		
Elijah Bryan	"		
Joseph Hawkins	"		
Amos Tharp or Sharp	"		
Timothy Johnston	"		
James Ceabury	"		
Martin Ford	"		
Daniel Moss	"		
Josiah Taylor	"		
Jonathan Ford	"		
Adonijah Ross			Transfer[d] to the 1 Com[y] 1 Jan 83
Nathan Lane			Discharged 1 Jan[y] 83
Edward Dunker (?)			" "
Nehemiah Barns			" "
David Hawly			Deserted 1st Dec[r] 1782
Charles Lewis			Discharged 1 Jany 1783
Hezekiah Turnill			" "
Aron Wayley			" "
Amos Westland			" "
Reuben Martin			" "
David Coy	D War		" "
Elijah Kiplee			Deserted 4th Jany 83
Jason Hitchcock			Discharg[d] 1 Jan[y] 83
James Patchen			
William Reed			
George Mitchel			
Rufus Hyde (?)			

I Certify the above Roll to be the true State of said Company this Twenty sixth Day of January 1783

David Dorrance Capt[a]

SEVENTH COMPANY—CAPT. DOUGLASS.

[The muster rolls of this company for Dec. 1782–Jan. 1783 and Feb. 1783 are preserved. Only the earlier of these is here printed, with such changes noted as appear on the later roll.]

Roll and Muster of the 7th Company 3d Connecticut Regt Commanded by Col Saml B. Webb for Decr 1782 and Jany 1783

Ranks	Names	Term of Inlistment	
Capt	Richd Douglass		
Lieut	Saml Hait		
Serjt	Tho⁸ Holmes	D War	
"	Willm Taylor	"	
"	Abraham Clark	"	
"	David Webb	"	
"	Benjn Brooks	"	
"	Willm Patterson	"	Deserted Jany 3d 1783
Corporal	Danl Potter	"	
"	Joseph Clinton	"	
"	Isaac Northrop	"	
"	Christr Horton	"	
"	James Hooker	"	
Drumer	Ezekiel Winchel	"	
"	Anthony Needham	"	
Fifer	David Phelps	"	
"	Joseph Woolcot	"	
Pt	Benjn Avery	"	
	Saml Bush	"	
	Nathl Beach	"	
	Benjn Bennet	"	
	David Bradley	"	
	Hezekiah Bracket	"	
	Azias Bowen or Ozias Backers	1y	Waiter to Col Webb in Connt
	Willm Carr	D War	
	David Chester	11m	
	Benjn Cady	10m	
	Costor Freeman	D War	Waiter to Capt Sill Aid de Camp
	Saml Rich	"	
	Tho⁸ Meach	"	Recd from the 4th Compy Jany 1st
	Sylvanus Gage	1y	
	Amos Harris	D War	
	David Hyden or Hayden	2y 4m	
	Joel Hyde	1y	
	Eliezer Hatch	1y	
	Peter Johnson	D War	
	Willm Johnson	"	
	Richd Kimball	1y	
	Jared Kimball	1y	
	Marshal Keyes or Hayes	10m	
	Phineas Knight	1y	
	Jabez Kirtland	1y	
	Jonathan Luce	D War	Deserted Decr 11th 1782
	James Miner	1y 1m	
	Noah Merils	11m	
	Benoni Moss	D War	

Ranks	Names	Term of Inlistment	
	Simeon Meigs	D War	
	David Potter	1y 3m	
	Moses Potter	D War	
	Levi Risley	"	
	Levi Robertson or Ralinson	"	
	Joshua Rynolds	1y	
	George Seely	"	
	Peter Shopp	D War	
	Ichabod Schofield	"	
	Tony Turney	"	
	Nathan Tubbs	11m	
	Philip White	D War	
	Benjⁿ Watrous	"	
	Thoˢ Wilson	"	
	Ichabod West	11m	
	Ichabod Worden	"	
	Oliver Scott	1m	
	Elijah Woolcot	D War	
	Cato Robertson or Robinson	"	
	Samˡ Green		Transfᵈ to the 4ᵗʰ Compʸ 1ˢᵗ Janʸ
	Richᵈ Case		Dischargᵈ 31ˢᵗ Decʳ 1782
	Samˡ Mitchel		" " "
	Elijah Pike		" " "
	John Wheeler		" " "
	Eliphalet Burnham		" 6ᵗʰ Janʸ 83
	Danˡ Barns		" 10ᵗʰ Decʳ 82
	Jeremiah Chapman		" 6ᵗʰ " "
	Benjⁿ Gaylord		" 13ᵗʰ " "
	Stacy Evans		" 15ᵗʰ " "
	Josʰ Kenny		" 6ᵗʰ " "
	Richᵈ Kenny		" 10ᵗʰ " "
	Danˡ Root		" 6ᵗʰ " "
	Samˡ Peck		" 6ᵗʰ " "
	Cornelius Phelps		" 29ᵗʰ " "
	Nathˡ Sylliman		" 6ᵗʰ Jany 83
	Zaccheus Gillet		" 10ᵗʰ Decʳ 82
	Benoni Gillet		" 10ᵗʰ " "
	Ebenezʳ Elwell		Deserted 13ᵗʰ Janʸ 1783

I Certify the above Roll to be the true State of said Company this day of Janʸ 1783

Richᵈ Douglass Captⁿ

[*State Library, Revolution 39 ; 109, 119.*]

EIGHTH COMPANY—CAPT. ROGERS.

[The muster rolls of this company for Dec. 1782–Jan. 1783 and Feb. 1783 are preserved. Only the earlier of these is here printed, with such changes noted as appear on the later roll.]

Roll and Muster of the 8th Company in the 3rd Connecticut Regiment Commanded by Col¹ Samuel B. Webb ; for Decr 1782 & Jany 1783

Ranks	Names	Term of Inlistment	
Captain	Hezekiah Rogers		Rec^d from 3^d Compy Feby 1, 83
Lieut.	John Hobart		Received from 3^d Company
"	William Lynn		Transf^d to 1st Lt. Co.
Ensn	Aron Keeler		
Serjeants	Richard Lord	D W	
"	William Bassett	"	
"	Abiather Evans	"	
"	Peter Stalker	"	
"	Reuben Beach	"	
"	Henery Hull	"	
"	Thomas Wells	"	
Corporals	Jesse St John	"	
"	James Crane	10m 12d	
"	Amasy Grenold	D W	
"	Nicholas Howell	"	
"	Reuben Carter	"	
Drummer	John Avery	"	
"	William Kane or		
	Thane	12 6	
Fifer	Frederick Whipple	D W	
	Isaac Higgans or		
"	Wiggins	17 6	
Private	Uriah Keeler	D W	
	Johnson Tiff	11 4	
	Thomas Palmer	26 23	
	Anor Adee	D W	
	Cato Negro	16 28	
	Jonathan Edwards	D W	
	Joel Shirt	"	Not on Feb. roll.
	Stephen Meigs	"	
	Aron Eaton	2 11	
	Nathan Walker	D W	
	Amos Holden	28 0	
	Moses Elsworth	D W	
	Weight Lewis	"	
	Enos Tuttle	"	
	John Durgley or		
	Dingly	"	
	Joel Mosher	"	
	Philip Hill	12 23	
	Justin St John	D W	
	James Liberty	"	
	Peter Mix	"	
	James Duggan	10 23	
	Uthiel or Ethiel Scott	D W	
	Aron Parks	"	
	David Hodge	"	
	Abner Lord	"	
	Cato Wilborow	"	

Private	Samuel Jenkins	D W	
	John F Tone	11 8	
	David Hammond	13 6	
	Esaias Butts	1 7	
	Eli Tuller or Fuller	11 13	
	Ebenezer Platt	2 13	
	Chandler or Charles		
	Judd	2 0	Burning Lime
	Ephraim Burgess	11 23	
	Jedediah Kimball	13 9	
	Reuben Adams	10 11	
	Amos Temple	D W	
	David Clark	"	Not on Feb. Roll
	William Short	13 6	
	Samuel Hull	11 23	
	William Waterbury	D W	
	Thomas Frink	"	
	Jacob Haladay	10 9	
	Ephraim Bates	11 23	
	Stephen Thompson	D W	
	Eliphalet Carpenter	10 26	
	Joseph Plinney or		
	Pheney	11 23	
	William Burras	10 23	
	James Raymond	1 7	
	Samuel Eells	D W	
	Darius Trussedell	11 4	
	Abram Murrey	D W	
	David Matterson	11 23	
	Jethro Toney	D W	Rec^d Novr 13th 1782 from the late 5th C Reg^t left out of the Muster Rolls for Novr thro' Mistake
	Amasy Stephenson		Discharged Dec 10th 1782
	Jonathan Beaumont		" " "
	Nathaniel Conant		" " "
	Joseph C Stubbs		" " "
	Thomas Leads		" " "
	William McFall		" " "
	Jesse Torrey		" " "
	Daniel Jackson		" " "
	Thomas Marble		" " "
	George Dameson (?)		" " "
	Nathan Fenton		" " "
	Miles Bennet		" " "
	Samuel Gorden		" " "
	Comfort Chapman		" Jan 1st 83
	Sariel Squires		" " "
	Ephraim Coy		" " 19th
	Bristor Negro		Private Servt Gen. Huntington
	Frank Buck	D W	Not on Jan. roll
	Joel Hait	"	" " "

I certify the above Roll to be the true state of said Company this 26th day of January 1783

Aaron Keeler Ensign

[*State Library, Revolution* 39 ; 112, 121.]

CONNECTICUT LINE.

MISCELLANEOUS.

HARTFORD COUNTY RETURNS.

A List of the Names of Men taken from the Returns from the Continental Army & those Claim^d by & allow^d to the Several Towns by the Committee for Hartford County

Hartford

Cesar Augustus
Daniel Curtis
Ockelow Porter
Nathaniel Merrils
Thomas Kittle
Josiah Stulee
Seth Kellogg
Samuel Simons
Daniel Hill
Jesse Taylor
William Flowers
William Shortman
Jupeter Stephens
James Maharr
William Mize
Henry Evans   Dead
Josiah Evans
Benjamin Webster
Joseph Whipple
Jeremiah Barrett
Sam^{ll} Easton   Discharg^d
Sam^{ll} Robarts
Joseph Day
Jabez Norton
Abiather Evans
David Williams
Reuben Cadwell
Elisha Cowls
Jonathan Arnold
Stephen Risley
Moses Porter

Elijah Porter
James Chadwick
John Hosmer
Thos Spencer
Elijah Demming
Abraham Clark
Thos Wells
John Kendall
David Crosly
Philemon Stedman
Jeduthan Abbey
Levi Risley
Moses Evans
Richard Case
Ephraim Prescott
Hezekiah Goodwin
Asa Saymour
Seth Kneeland
Simeon Goodrich
John Raynolds
Samuel Dorr
Charles Raynolds
Ashbel Easton
Elnathan Smith
Eliphelet Abbey
Richard Risley
John Knowles
Asa Risley
Theodore Treet
William Tryon
Amos Shepherd

the following not Return^d from the army but Claim^d and allow^d to Hartford

Paul McKinstry
Allen Evans
Allen Corning
Reuben Toney

Thos Waters
Eleazar Abbey }
Francis Psalter } Disch^d
Thos Wilson   Dead

Matthew Cadwell
Vaniah Fox
Joseph Brewer   Dead
Tho⁵ Jarrall
William Martin
William Matthews
Sam^{jl} Norton
Jonathan Flagg   Disch^d
James Gray
Peter Surkee
Benjamin Keney
Tho⁵ Obrian
David Taylor
William Lewis
Phillip Tabor

Giles Easton
Theodore Chamberlain
Ashbel Fox
Daniel Millar
William Combs
Henry Walton
Reuben Hadlock
Pattrick Marr
Ebenezar Haman
Samuel Holmes
William Anderson
Elisha Mygatt
John Foster
Nāthaniel Fenton

Middletown

Sam^{ll} Simons
Jacob Wood
Charles Loveland
Lamberton Clark
Francis Wright
Aaron Ward
Ebenezar Hubbard
Joseph Copp
David Butler
Jonathan Goff   Dead
John Foster
David Hull
Joseph Lung
Daniel Morgan
Christopher Middletown
Sawney Baston
Exter Freeman
Peter Middletown
Grove Rockwell
Naboth Lewis
Christopher Welch
Ozias Cone
Peter Torminer
Richard Cornwell
David Freeman
Elijah Phelps
Stephen Robarts
David Robarts
Edward Millor
Oliver Monn   Dead
George Doolittle
Jabez Adkin

William Bacon
Samuel Frothingham   Disch^d
Jonathan Taylor
Joseph Willis
Aaron Rowley
Lem^{ll} Wilcocks
Jonathan Hubbard
Josiah Smith
Nathaniel W Benton
Jacob Gilson
Isaac Robarts
Peter Freeman
Cuff Liberty
Phillemon Freeman
Cuff Freeman
Zachariah Stow
James Fosdick
David Gallipin
Jehiel Hurlbutt
Henry Hart
Joseph Bates
James Johnson
Abijah Hubbard
Daniel Robbison
Richard Down^d
David Adkins
Elijah Clark
James M°David
Allen Gilbart
Tho⁵ Petland
Jacob Rash
Stephen Salvage.

The following not Return^d from the army

William Hall
John Trat
Sam^{ll} Johnson
Abraham T. Kimball
Aaron Clark
Sam^{ll} Cook

Moses Boardman
Sumner Banks
William Salvage
John Swift
William Millar
James White

Moses Collins
James Hurlbutt
John Barson
Kay Cambridge
Allen Pratt
Robert·Stephens
William Cook

William Graves
Cuff Negro
Enoch Cornwell
Elisha Driggs
Jonathan Hurlbutt
George Anger
Seth Knowles

Farmington

Aaron Hart
Solomon Rugg   Disch^d
Solomon Rugg Ju^r
Thos Stedman
William Steel
Seth Arnold
Ezra Belding
Ashbel Merrill
Gad North
Matthew Lee
Seth Root
Solomon Welton
Sage Churchel
Thos F. Bishop
Isaac Tillotson
Ashbel Tillotson
Gedur Woodruff
Amos Couch
Salmon Root
James Gridley
Daniel Mosock   Dead
George Walton
Obed Gridley
Aaron Morce
John Robbison
Gideon Andrus
Free Love Robart
Prince Dennison
Hosea Gridley
Reubin Hamlin
Obadiah Andras
Jonathan Barns
Joseph Teal
Solomon Woodruff
Jesse Shepard
Joel Welton
Thos Stanley
Nathan Savage
Josiah Barns

Isaac Nelson
Selah Hart
Tim^o Bevens
Daniel Winchell
David Haydon
Simeon Barns
Ira Hungerford
Roswell Cook
Ichabod Bailey
Josiah Cowl
Jesse Matthews
Lem^{ll} Lane
Timothy Fox
Simeon Parsons
Asher Hecock
William Woodruff
Levi Parson
Barnabas Mitchel
Thos G Olvard
Thos G Olvard Ju^r
Nath^{ll} Lownsbury
Thos Warner
John Smith
Giles Abanathy
John Welch
Joseph Hunt
James Newel
Benjamin Cole
Jedediah Seward
Ebenezer Tuttle
Chancey Curtiss
Clark Curtiss
Asaph Smith
Sam^{ll} Wain Wright
Isaac Bartholimew
Tim^o Seward
Abraham Bartholimew
Aaron Rich

The following not Return^d from the army but allow^d to Farmington

Zachariah Hull
Abel Allen
Robart Carr
James Wilcocks
William D. Mott
James Evans
Roger Brunson
Cambridge Negro

Stephen Chapman Ju^r
Constant Robarts
Joseph Andras
Peter Negro
Sam^{ll} Stebbens
John Platner
Andrew Dowley
Cornelius Gordin

Amos Barns
Tho' Collet
James Taylor
Cornelius Dunham ⎫ Disch⁴
Liverpool Wadsworth ⎭

Abel Scipio   Dead
James H Hurlbutt "
Hartwell Barns Disch⁴
Prince Negro

Windsor

Ebenezar Welch
Barzilli Henry
Richard Cook
Alvin Hurlbutt
Tho' Parsons
William Cook
Isaac Wardwell
Clark Robarts
Ebenezar Wolworth
John Bristor
Alvin Owen
Daniel Porter
Sherman Rowland
Robart Westland
Peter Robarts
Remembrance Sheldon
David Daniels
Zebulon Hoskins

Eppaphras Lotwell
James Egleston
Allen Pryar
Timothy Hoskins
Calvin Wilson
Elihu Mather
John Rowley
Samson Cuff
John Dewset
Elias Brown
Joseph Holcomb
Burden Davis
John Keton
Reuben Hill
Elijah Holcomb
Zephaniah Webster
Jonathan Pinny
Tho' Vanduzar

These not Returned from the army

Jabez Colt
Plymouth Negro
Amos Lawrence Disch⁴
Tho' Bunc
Joseph Egleston

Joseph Westland
Ebenezar Drake
William Taylor
Obed Lamberton

Wethersfield

Ashbel Riley
Abner Andras
Moses Belding
Jonathan Millar
Dick Loomis
Tho' Wilson
Simeon Holms
Waitstill Dickerson
John Kirkum
Arthur Russell
Ezekiel Winchel
Stephen Dormont
Richard Belding
Stephen Kellogg
Seth Montague
Jared Bunce
Daniel Ward
Joshua Wells
Joseph Rowlison
Cesar Freeman
Simeon Griffin
Elijah Boardman
Hezekiah Knot
Tho' Holmes
Gideon Goff

Moses Hatch
David Linsey
Abraham Belding
Joseph Treet
Benjamin Dix
Ichobad Goodrich
Joseph Johnson
John Forbs
Richard Bacon
Curtiss Crane
Moses Griswold
Solomon Williams
Samuel Wells
Samuel Kirkum
Levi Lattimore
Edmond Weatherhead
William Clark
Jonathan Dallibier
Joseph Waters
Jabez Sizer
Charles Treet
Caleb Miller
William Morrison
Daniel Sizer

The following not Return^d from the army but allow^d to Weathersfield

Peter Mohawk
Simeon Griffin
Tho' Morgan
Zebulon Mygatt
Edward Brown
John Dowl
Joshua Cone

Josiah Robins
William Ware
Asa Andras
Isaac Palmer
Jared Goodrich
Ebenezar Stoddard
Samuel Weaver

Simsbury

Phillip Grigory
Jacob Davis
Benjamin Hayse
Stephen Langatha
Timothy Woodbridge
James Slaughter
Consider Holcomb
Rufus Mayson
John White
Jeremiah Case
Elisha Harrington
Elijah Clark
Zebulon Wallace
Joseph Wallace
Asa Hayze
Jacob Hollidy
Eli Fuller
William Taylor
Johnson Tiff
John G. Holcomb
Jacob Gillet
David Taylor
John Herlihy
James Aldridge

David Egleston
John Crocker
Gad Alderman
John Hunt
David Enos.
Levi Woolworth
Roderick Addams
Azer Bowton
Ebenezar Edgerton
Timothy Humphry
Jacob Fuller
William Phillips
Jared Towser
Solomon Parkharst
Levi Addams
Abel Case
Enum Moses
Furbuss More
Humphry Tiffeny
David Parkharst
Asahel Holcomb 3rd
Hezekiah Phelps
Gilbert Whitney

The following not in the army Return

Owin Rewick
John Huxley
George Sweet
William Andras   Disch^d
David Jones
John Hill 2nd   Disch^d
John Carrell
Charles Spencer
Josiah Linsley
Robart Linsley
Erastus Hatch
John Pooler
Ezekiel Davis
Jonathan Andras

Phillip Negro
Morris Jarrold
William Shepard
Amaziah Barber
John Slaughter
Jeremiah Parmerly
William Peck
John Allen
Ithamer Granger
Edward Knap
Israel Humphry
Joseph Segar 3rd   Disch^d
Joseph Sharp
Cuff Negro

East Windsor

Jude C. Brown
Jacob Strong
Mark Philly
Cato Negro
Hazard Prior
Azariah Grant
Joseph Pease

Stephen Ellis
Israel Osborn
Reuben Raynolds
Elijah Benton
Phinehas Strong
Adoniram Benton

Those below not in the army Return

Elijah Churchil
Stephen Dormond
Theodore Smith
Moses Elsworth
Ezra Elsworth
Oliver Hills
Benoni Hills

Christopher Horton
David Clark
Josiah Grovener
Sam[ll] Hadlock
Jeptha Hills
Benjamin Elsworth

Tolland

George Hubberd
Abel Stimson
Reuben Robinson
Moses Coy
Job Booman
Amos Harriss
Ichabod West
Ebenezar Hatch

Jonathan Luce
Joel Barnard
James Covel
Solomon Eaton
William Eldridge
Isaac Squires
Benjamin Butler

Those below not Return[d] from the army

John George
John William Hendrick
Phinehas Heth

Silvanus Gage
William Kinsey

Southington

Robart Cook
Archibald Cook
George Dickerson
Amos Bunnal
William Jones
David Andras
James Powers

Zebulon Dudley
Ichabod Talmage
Chancey Lewis
Isaac Lewis
Adonijah Roze
Samuel Root

Those below not in the army Return

Timothy Culver
Jason Hitchcock
Daniel Munson
Elijah Rice
Samuel Grannis
John Ukhart
Daniel Hitchcock

Moses Barker
Isaac Fisk
Barnabas Clark
Luke Hart
Bordle Hoose
Abraham Tuttle
Clemont Andras

Enfield

Benjamin Harrington
Henry Booth
John Hallamagee
John Jimpson
Ephraim Burges
Daniel Pirkins

David Bullin
Hiram Hall
Elijah Mecham
Levi French
Simeon Hager   Disch[d]
Jonathan Parsons D[o]

Those below not return[d] from the Army

Justin Davis
Lemuel Wood
Jonathan Terry
Alexander Banter

John Herman
Johannes Mecham
Oliver Field
John Moony

Colchester

Joshua Isham
Samuel Loomis
Lewis Ackley
Robart Bland   Disch^d
John Fox
William Isham
Joseph McHood
Ezekiel Danields
Bristol Johnston
Frederick Bowman
Israel Ransom
Esau Carter
Edward Carter
Israel Johnson
Ezra Ramsel
John Godfrey   Dead
James Shoot   D^o
John Lines
Cesar Bement

Josiah Rogers
Champlin Harris
Benjamin Dodge
Elihu Dodge
Tony Edor
David Waters   Dead
Simeon Shon
Peter Beguine (?)
Sam^ll D. Goff
James Freeman
Peter Kellogg
Nathan Robarts
Daniel Wright
Josiah Grant
Martin Stiles
Roswell Chapell
John Robarts
Nicholas Ackley

Those below not Return^d from the army

Nathan Scovil   Dead
Joseph Thompson
Dolphin Dart
Daniel Whitney   Disch^d
William Jones
Martin Canary

Comfort Bebee
Henry Horton
Richard Bebee
Jeremiah Booth   Dead
Henry Loud (? Lord)
James French

Glastenbury

Peter Forriss
Daniel Loveland
Nathan Hill
Peter Foster
Daniel Wright
Joseph Wright
Cuff Acklin
John Johnson   Disch^d
Samuel Fox
Cyphax Mosley
Newport Hale
Timothy Stephens
Aaron Ward
David Pratt

Daniel Morley
Thos Brewer
Alexander McCulpin
Frances Nicholson
Asa Fox
William Peters
John House
George House
Ezra Tryon Junr
James Stephens
Isaac Tryon
Abisha Marks
Elias Wares

Those below not Return^d from the Army

Thos^s Loveland
John Holding
James Dougharty
Ezra Tryon
Prince Simber

Josiah Hollister
Joseph Hills
Levius Eddy
Elisha Stephens

Suffield

Phinehas Austin
Lewis Leach
Narcissus Graham
Apollus Answitz
Samuel Thistle

Peletiah Pumroy
Dan^ll Wheeler
Silas Pease
Leucius Hurlbutt
Jeremiah Newbury

Phebus Pomroy
Michael Towsley
John Laphland
Joshua Spear
Sam¹¹ Gookins
James Fuller
Jeremiah Chamberlain
Samuel Granger
David Addams
John Russell

Edy Coy
Josiah Rising
Jacob Granger
James Serene
Joseph King
Darius Dunlay
Seth Hathaway
Wilber Hathaway
Titus Kent

The following not Return⁴ from the Army ·

James Dada
Filo Stoddard
Richard Austin
Eliphelet Phillips
Cesar Negro
Tho⁸ Watson

Phinehas Granger
John Spencer
Thada Larry
Jahiel Spencer
Matthew Goldwin

East Haddam

Sam¹¹ Chapman
Levi Fox
Richard Mack
Abel Bingham
David Shattock
Daniel Rols
Isaac Williams
Sam¹¹ Mobbs
Ephraim Wadkins
Asahel Hervy
Crppin Hurd
Robert Hull
Eli Hull
Samuel Rusket
Joel Spencer
Robart Wadkins
Cuff Smith
Judah Warner   Dead

Asahel Patterson
Israel Cone
Ebenezar Hinkley
Elihu Church
Nathan W. Minor
John Marsh
Stephen Sparrow
Daniel Thornton
Tho⁸ Williams
Phillip White
Tho⁸ Ackley
Sam¹¹ Mitchel
Zacheus Rols
Israel Rowley
Elijah Cone
William Lee
Daniel Cone

Those below not Return⁴ from the army

Ezra Harvey
John Ashley
Tho⁸ Andras
Charles Clark
Noah Huntly

Sam¹¹ Reves
Nathaniel Warner
Joseph Stewart
Joseph Chamberlain

Haddam

Loudon Bailey
Daniel Ray
Joseph Forbs
Peter Black
Michael Clark

Andrew Southard
James Wilcox   Time out July
    Next
William Bailey
Daniel Bates

Those below not Return[d] from the army

Jarius Congdon
William Osburn
Joseph Paro
Joshua Smith
Jonathan Smith Dead

John Smith
Cesar Chapman
London Sawyer
William Gladding

Willington

Ezra Sibble
Sam[ll] Eldridge Dead
Alexander Evans
Abel Stoel
Samuel Stoel

Cyrus Fenton Dead
Reuben Dodge
Seth Dodge
Heman Hatch
Samuel Firgo

Those below not Return[d] from the army

Joseph Wilson
Ebenezar Nye
Richard Lord

Caleb Olcott
Gideon Noble

Chatham

John Parks
Ephraim Bowers
Stephen Ranney
James Shield
Bathuel Goodrich
Joab Bowers
Samuel Goff
Charles O. Martin
John Wright Disch[d]
Jabez Wetmore
Sam[ll] Wood
Jacob Woods
Timothy Chapman
John Fuller
Jonathan Stocking
William Cook
Joel Doolittle

Othniel Brainard
Samuel Rich
Lend Rich
Sam[ll] Freeman
Lemuel Goodrich
Jedediah Norton
Elij. Whiting
George Carry
Jonathan Very
Samuel Cowdy
Henry Goseley
Jessie Kneeland
Josiah Davis
Eber Stocking
Stephen Thomas
Daniel Bliss

Those below not Return[d] from the army

Abner Cowl
Joseph Graham
Marshal Stocking
Stephen Tubbs
Aaron Carter

Oliver Graham
Thomas Snow
Nathaniel Robarts
Daniel Pelton

Bolton

William Rock
Ebenezar Walker

John Warren

Those below not Return[d] from the army

Samuel Addams Dead
Ezra Downer
John Smith

Benajah Abrow
William Beach

23

Hebron

Robart Cox
Stephen D: wolf
Jack Demming
Abner Mack
Seth Baldwin
Abijah Gardner
Joseph Belcher
Matthew Ford
Ebenezer Youngs

Robart Holdridge
Wyman Parker
John Royce
Cyprian Archer
Daniel Polly
Walker Tiffiny
Cesar Scipio
Thomas Marble   Disch⁴

Those below not in the army Return

Austin Brown
John Winship
William Merrit
Israel Jillit
Barzilla Mack
John George
Thomas McQuire
Richard Lawrence
Peter Pease

Rodowick Morrison
Edward Chapman
*Lawrence Dowsch time out 5ᵗʰ
   July next
*Nathan Reed time out 5ᵗʰ July
   next
*Roger Loomis time out Aug-
   ust 1ˢᵗ

Sommers

Jehiel Gibbs
Joel Pelton

Reuben Perez
William Hamlin

Those below not in the Army Return

John Love
William Beke
Isaac Colton

William Quirk
Edward Burges

Stafford

Solomon Bebee
Hezekiah Wheeler
Joshua Wheeler
Joseph Harrop
Daniel Rider Juʳ
Thoˢ Simons

Amasa Dimmuk
Thoˢ Manning
Silas Blotchet
Josiah Wheeler
Ephraim White

Jonathan Wells   } Committee
Howel Woodbridge }

[State Library, Hebard Papers, 81.]

FAMILY SUPPLIES.

An Alphabetical List of the Officers and Soldiers who have received Family Supplies whose names are not found in the Returns from the Army.

Names	Towns
Arnold Jehiel	Haddam
Austin Richard	Suffield
Bull Epaphˢ Major	Hartford
Buckland Stephen Capt	"
Brownson Roger	Farmington

* These names have been crossed out.

Names.	Towns.	
Barnes Moses	Wallingford	
Bradley Eliphalet	Fairfield	
Beebe James Capt	Stratford	
Blakesley Jerem^h	Danbury	
Burnap Benj^a	Windham	
Comstock Gideon	Norwich	
Samuel	Saybrook	
Cheney Richard	Kent	
Cone Joseph	Middletown	In Service of Elijah Hubbard E^d States Comissary or of Genl Parsons
Ozias	"	
Carrill John	Simsbury	
Carter Aaron	Chatham	
Clark Lyman	Farmington	
Joel	New Haven	
Dunbar Miles	Watertown	
Downing John	Fairfield	
Desborough Joshua	"	
Dickerman Joseph	New Haven	deserted Whip^d shot thro discharged on procuring one Ebenez^r Warner Substitute accepted & now in Service
Durkee Jeremiah	Windham	
Dickinson George	Danbury	
Davidson Robert	Groton	
Edwards Nathaniel Lieut	Watertown	
Fitch Nehem^h	Lebanon	
Ford Matthew	New Haven	
Flagg Jonathan	Hartford	
Gillet Adna	New Hartford	
Zechariah Serjt	Southington	
Gibson Samuel	New Haven	
Goold John	Goshen	
Gladding William	Haddam	In the army not Returned
Hull Giles	Salisbury	Supplies due at his Death
Hargar Simeon	Enfield	
Hovey Ezra	East Haddam	
Higgins Corn^s Lieut	Haddam	Supplies due before Discharged
Hotchkiss Zadock	Farmington	
Huse Boardwell	New Haven	
Johnson Robert	Sharon	
Lion Ezra	Ashford	
Lines John	New Haven	
Morgan Joshua	Salisbury	Balance due when Discharged
Munger Daniel	Litchfield	Discharged from Invalids 26 Feby 1780
McDonald John	Groton	
Meeker Daniel	Hartford	
Nash Eben^r	Norwalk	
Osborn Nathl	Stratford	
Olmsted Isaac	Norwalk	
Parker Benj^a	Wallingford	
Pickett Thomas	Danbury	
Patchin Elijah	Fairfield	Hired David Patchen in his room & Supplyd untill about Octr last
Persival Paul Q M	Farmington	

Names.	Towns.	
Palmer Benj[a]	Litchfield	Died 9 April 1780 at Litchfield
Powers James	Southington	
Polley Alpheus	Lebanon	Returned by Gen Washington
Pool Daniel	Ashford	
Porter Daniel	Windsor	
Raymong Sam[l]	Reading	
Rose Samuel	Coventry	Never Returned from the Town nor in Con[tl] Service nor Counted in the quota of s[d] Town
Remington Stephen	Ridgfield	
Sullard Jacob	Lime	
Smith Enoch	"	
John	Watertown	
Stillwell Stephen	New Milford	
Smith Job	Ridgfield	
Stanard Elijah	Guilford	
Stark Samuel	Colchester	
Timothy	"	
Tarble William	"	
Wording Isaac	Saybrook	
Yarington Jesse	Groton	

[*State Library, Revolution 20, 362.*]

RETURNS FROM MILITIA.

Names 5 Regt	Time for which Engaged	The Quota of Wha Town
John Woodward	first march	Windham
Shubeel Snow	"	"
Jed. Peck	"	"
Eph[m] Robinson	"	"
Abel Robinson	"	"
Frances West	"	"
Richard Robinson	"	"
Jn[o] Pettingal	"	"
Tube Negro	"	"
W[m] Yerington	"	"
Nath[n] Clark	"	Mansfield
Amos Conant	"	"
Nath[n] Marten	"	"
Isaac Arnold	"	"
Elias Burchard	"	"
Tho[s] Barrows Jr.	"	"
Oliver Smith	"	"
Elijah Davis	"	"
Joel Davis	"	"
Nath[ll] Eatton Jr	"	"
James Parker Jr	"	"
Bezeleel Balch	"	"
Eben[r] Fenton Jr	"	"
Gemaliel Fenton	"	"
John Redington	"	Coventry
Amos Dog	"	"
Nath[n] Bassett	"	"
Nath[ll] Conent	"	"
Jonath[n] Fenton	"	"
Steap[n] Chappee	"	"

Names 5 Regt	Time for which Engaged	The Quota of What Town	
Don Carlos Brigham	first march	Coventry	
Tim[y] White	"	"	
Sam[ll] Dreston	"	Ashford	Deserted
Sam[ll] Robbins	"	"	
Clark Robbins	"	"	
Benj[a] Perey	"	"	
Sam[ll] Crocker	"	"	
W[m] Snell	for West Point	"	
Archable Knox	"	"	
Step[n] Russell	"	"	
Eben[r] Eastman	"	"	
John Frink	"	"	
Sam[ll] Walker	"	"	
Sam[ll] Whipple	"	"	
John Abbett	"	"	
Amosiah Snow	"	"	
Abraham Ford	"	Windham	
James Flint	"	"	
David Jinins	"	"	
Daniel Robbins	"	"	
Tho[s] Gray	3 months	"	
Alfeas Bingham	"	"	
Perez Hibard	"	"	
Nath[n] Kennedy	"	"	
W[m] Wales	"	"	
W[m] Burnam	"	"	
Jesse Burnam	"	"	
Tim[y] Warner	"	"	
Eben[r] Devotion	"	"	
James Bicknal	"	Mansfield	
Joshua Barrows	"	"	
Asa Hanks	"	"	
Joseph Grover	"	"	
Peter Cambell	"	"	Des[t]
James Hylys (? Wylys) Jr.	"	"	
Bej[a] Collins	"	"	
Eben[r] Badcock	"	"	
Lyman Back	"	"	
Josiah Squire	"	"	
Eben[r] Carey	"		
Robert Badcock	"	Coventry	
Tim[y] Brown	"	"	
W[m] Dean	"	"	
Elea[r] Root	"	"	
Asa Lyman	"	"	

[Each man except the deserters is noted as having "marcht."]

[*State Library, Hebard Papers*, 77.]

NEW LONDON RETURNS.

Memorandoms Concerning Continental Soldiers from the Town of New London that are disputed.

James Gray
Moses Tracy
Benony Condle
Benja Brooks
Wm Fargo Jun
Backus Fox
Andrew Harris
Simon Hubbard
Christo^r Leech
Ezekiel Beckwith Jun
Aaron Jones
John Paul of Preston
John Swaddle
Daniel Davis
James Barnerd
Ichab^d Beckwith   Claim^d by Norwich
Thos Hallet   Claim'd by Preston
Rufas Chappel
John Truby   Claim'd by Lyme
Benj^a Darrow   Claim'd by Hartford
Thos Harris   Claim'd by Canterbury
Robert Frazier   Claim'd by Norwich
Robt Price   Claim'd by Preston

[*Connecticut Historical Society.*]

List **of Men** in the Continental Army belonging to the Town of New London

Lost   Ethel Plant
          James Grey
          Benjamin Brooks his Mother Grandmother & himself lived in
               this Town
Lost   Simeon Hubbard an Ind living with Pardon Tabor Enlisted
               with Collins 1777
          James Douglass Junr
          Benjamin Darrow
          John Maynard
          William Prentice
          Ichabod Beckwith was born and always lived in New London
          Timothy Beckwith Junr
          David Goodfaith
          Joseph Copp Junr
          Rowland Swift
          Peter Holt
          James Robertson
          Danie^l Plumb called David in the return from the Army
          Joseph Morgan
Lost   William Fargoe Junr
Lost   Backus Fox
          Simon Gorgay

The above are return'd from the Army

alow^d   Alpheus Chappel

George Monworring

Daniel Cornin a Transient Person, hired by this Town, in Durkees Reg^t

John Stewart a Transient Person hired by this Town, in Durkees Reg^t

Benjamin Chappel of this Town in Livingstons Reg^t in New York Line

alow^d   Daniel Hendry of this Town, now attending the Hospital at Danbury

William Whiting a Transient Person hired by this Town in Webb's Reg^t Discharg^d

Disputed   Thomas Hallet of Preston hired by this Town in Sherburns Reg^t

William Chappel of this Town unknown what Reg^t

Stephen Oliver of this Town unknown what Reg^t

Lost   Christopher Leech, born in this Town and an Apprentice here when he Enlisted in Lamb's Reg^t Artillery   adjudged to Lime

Isaac Beckwith J^r of this Town unknown what Reg^t

Josiah Smith of this Town hired by this Town who has since hir'd Andrew Harris of Norwich

Lost   John Tooby of this Town hir'd by Lyme

to be refer^d   Ezekiel Beckwith Junr of this Town hired by Lyme he

to the Govenour   Lives in New London bounds but in a Lyme Com-

& Council   pany.

Stonington William Hudson

Levi Lee

Wm Lane

James Derrick, was a Servand to Isaiah Bolles of this Town in New Hampshire Line

alow^d   John Rogers 4th was born and liv'd in this Town when he en-listed in Sheldons Reg^t Light Horse

Asa Crandal of this Town in Rhode Island Line

Dennis Dewis (an Indian) in Col. Durkees Reg^t

adjudg^d to   Moses Tracy, formerly of Norwich he Married his Wife & Settled

Norwich   in this Town sometime before he Enlisted where his Wife & Child now lives.

Thomas Harriss of this Town where he has a Wife & Interest in the 1st Reg^t

Amariah Lyon of this Town unknown what Reg^t

Curtis Chappel of this Town unknown what Reg^t

Henry Jones of this Town in Glovers Brigade

ad^d to   Aaron Jones of this Town where he has a wife & Family

Seabrook   unknown what Reg^t

ad^d lost   James Barnard of Groton hir'd by this Town unknown what Reg^t

John Nicolls, Transient Person hir'd by this Town in Chandler's Reg^t

John Wheaton Transient Person hir'd by this Town in Col Durkee's Reg^t

Samuel Brooks a Transient Person hired by this Town in S. B. Webbs Reg^t

alow^d   Solomon Douglas of this Town, hired last Summer during the Warr

alow^d   Samuel Weaver of this Town, hired last Summer for three Years

John Grant transient Person Hired by this town

allow^d   Robert Frassier of this Town where he had Married and lived
                 Some Years before and at the time of his Enlisting hired
                 last Summer During the Warr

alow^d   William Chapel 3^d at home on furlough being unwell of this
                 Town

alow^d   Nathan Douglass Junr of this Town an Invalid

alow^d   Boanerges Beebee of this Town where he has a wife and family
                 in New York Line

                 David Wilson a Transient Person in Durkees Reg^t

                 Benjamin Beebee of this Town in the Light Horse

alow^d   James Gidias of this Town in the 1st Reg^t

                 Robert Brice a Transient Person hir'd by this Town in Storrs
                 Reg^t

                 John Paul Indian hired by this Town in Durkees Reg^t

                 Russel Handy a Transient Person hired by this Town Starrs Reg^t

                 Thomas Handy d° d° & d°

alow^d   John Daniels of this Town in Durkees Reg^t

allow^d   John Butler of this Town in Starrs Reg^t

                 Thomas Mitchell a Transient Person hired by this Town in
                 Durkees Reg^t

ad^d to Nor^h Benoni Congdol his Mother & he living in this Town — he In-

Lost   listed at the age of 15 Years while he was at Norwich for
                 the Term of three Weeks on Trial as an apprentice

[Connecticut Historical Society.]

MILITIA REGIMENTS

SEVENTH REGIMENT, 1777.

CAPT. PLATT'S COMPANY.

A Pay Roll of Capt Danl Platts C^o of the 7th Reg^t in the State of Conn^t commanded by Wm Worthington Esq Col^l who march^d as far as New Haven on Ap^l 27 1777

[Each man was five days in service.]

Danl Platt	Cap	Ebenezer Williams
Elijah Scovel	Lieut	Noah Scovel J^r
Saml Doty	Ens^n	Jered Buckingham
Israel Done (?)	Serg^t	Taber Pratt
Asa Pratt	"	George Shaw
Ruben Pratt	"	Bemond Clark
Jesse Pratt	"	Ja^s Utter
Ja^s Comstock	Corp^l	Wm Bulkley
Danl Pratt	"	Nath^n Southard
Saml Burnel	"	Dav^d Beebe Pratt
Saml Parker	"	Ja^s Hamblen
Benj Williams J^r		Martin Debble
Ja^s (or Francis) Bushnell		Josiah Payt
Jesse Pratt 2		Isaac Webb
Ashbel Clark		Wm Southard
Zeph^h Pratt		Gid^o Pratt
Phinas Pratt		John Williams 2
Abr^m Pratt J^r		Ja^s Shaw
Steph^n Starkey		Ezra Pratt
Jo^s Glading		Abr^m Bulkley

[*Comptroller's Office, Copy 2, 17.*]

SEVENTEENTH REGIMENT, 1777.

ENS. CORBIN'S COMPANY.

A pay Abstract of Ens. Peter Corbins Co. it being the 7th Co. of the Alarm list in the 17th Regt. of the State of Conn. Fish-kill Oct 27 day. A.D. 1777. Marched Oct. 6th day. Discharged Oct 27. including 4 days for returning Home

Mens Name and Rank		time when marched	Discharged.
Peter Corbin,	Ens.	Oct. 6	Oct. 31
Jonathan Coe,	Sergt.	"	"
Eliphaz Alvord,	Sergt.	"	"
Robert McCune,	Sergt.	"	"
Philip Priest,	Corp.	"	29
Joel Roberts		"	31

Mens Name and Rank	time when marched	Discharged
Darius Gibbs	Oct. 6	Oct. 31
Samuel Clark	"	"
Samuel McCune	"	"
Nathan Blackman	"	22
Daniel Andrews	"	31
Nathaniel Balcan	"	"
Samuel Preston	"	14
Ichabod Loomis	"	"

Test Peter Corbin Ens

Eliphaz Alvord S. Clerk

[*Green Woods Chapter D. A. R., Winsted.*]

COL. JOHNSON'S REGIMENT, 1778.

CAPT. BRANCH'S COMPANY.

[*See Record of Connecticut Men in the Revolution, page 527.*]

A Pay Roll of Capt Moses Branch's Company in Col^o Johnson's Regiment of Militia from the State of Connecticut now in Service in the State of Rhode-Island from the First of February 1778 untill the 15th of March 1778 both Days Inclusive.

Mens Names		february first 1778	Finished Service
Moses Branch	Capt	Feby 1st	March 15th
Joseph Burges	Lieut	"	"
Ebenezer Lathrop	"	"	"
Jacob Tuckerman	Ensign	"	"
Nathaniel Phillips	Serj^t	"	"
Nicholas Randall	"	"	"
Elijah Simons	"	"	"
Comfort Titus	"	"	Feby 4th
John Burnap	"	"	March 15th
Archabel Jackson	"	4	"
Benjamin Palmer	Corp^l	1	"
Archabel Jackson	"	"	Feby 4th
Samuel Adams	"	"	March 15th
Jonathan Chilson	"	"	"
Elijah Kimball	"	4	"
Luther Bingham	fifer	"	"
Jesse Ensworth		"	"
Joshua Finney		"	"
John Munrow		"	"
Henry Head		"	"
Benjamin Chace		"	"
Caleb Hall		"	"
George Mordock		"	"
Samuel Brown		"	"
Willard Pierce		"	"
Noah How		"	"
James Briggs		"	"
Jedediah Johnson		"	"
Samuel Brown Jur		"	"
John Burt		"	"
Samuel Marshall		"	"

Mens Names	february first 1778	Finished Service
Squre Cleaveland	Feb' 1	Feb' 28th
Jonathan Fish	"	March 15th
Israel Fitts	"	"
Philip Utley	"	"
Adam Treadwell	"	"
Abraham Herrinton	"	"
David Kenedy	"	"
Zacheriah Maynord	"	"
Chester Lilley	"	"
Jared Webb	"	"
Sebuary Manning	"	"
Joseph Holland	"	"
Asaph Adams	"	"
Jonathan Sprague	"	"
Daniel Fairman	"	"
Charles Burges	.	"
Jedediah Adams	"	"
Josiah Butts	"	"
Fuller Smith	"	"
Elkany Smith	"	"
Daniel Downing	"	"
Ebenezer Parks	"	"
Samuel Palmer	.	"
Asahel Herrick	"	"
Dyer Williams	"	"
James Alexander	"	"
James Campbel	"	"
Archabel Campbel	"	"
James Tuller	"	"
Shubel Huchens	"	"
Zebediah Holt	"	"
Alexander Miller	"	"
John Whitney	"	"
Elijah Kimbal	"	Febu' 4th
Mark Eames	"	March 15th
Simeon Stevens	"	"
Joseph Eaglestone	"	"
Ichabod Randal	"	"
Cyrus Maynord	"	"
Elisha Pirkins	"	"
Benjamin Williams	"	"
Silas Glass	"	"
Asa Stevens	"	"
Joseph Raymond	"	"
Stephen Durkee	"	"
Thomas Jewett	"	"
Benj'n Colegrove	"	"
Philemon Adams	"	"
Thomas Bradford	"	"
Samuel Adams Jr	"	"
Josiah Collins	"	8th
Josiah Bradford	3rd	15th
David Enos	14th	13
Joshua Pattrick	1	Febu' 5th
Thomas Foster	4th	March 15th

Moses Branch Cap'

[*State Library, Drake Papers, 32.*]

THIRTEENTH REGIMENT, 1779.

CAPT. FULLER'S COMPANY.

A Pay Abstract of the Company commanded by Capᵗⁿ Abraham Fuller in the thirteenth Regiment of Militia Commanded by Coˡˡ Increase Mosley belonging to the State of Connecticut Who marched into the continental Service at Fredericksborough in the State of New york June yᵉ 4ᵗʰ 1779

Names of Officers and Privates	Time of marching	Days in Service	
Capⁿ Abraham Fuller	June 4	9	
Sarᵗ Joseph Bates	"	"	
Corpˡˡ Abraham Wilcox	"	"	
Corpˡˡ Joseph Eaton	"	"	
Fif Bartlet Chamberlin	"	"	
Nathaniel Gear	"	"	
Asa Parish	"	"	
Timothy Stevens	"	"	
Timothy Hatch	"	"	
Aaron Sacket	"	"	
Stephen Eaton	"	"	
Abel Lamphere	"	"	
Ebenezer Lion	"	"	
Jirah Chamberlin	"	"	
Daniel Beebe	"	"	
Aaron Case	"	"	
Isaac Coller	"	"	
Norise Coller	"	"	
Newcomb Raymond	5	8	
Robert Brownell	"	"	
Manasah Martins (?)	4	13	Who was

Draughted from my Company to go to Hartford with Prisoners

NAVAL RECORD.

FRIGATE TRUMBULL.

[See Record of Connecticut Men in the Revolution, page 598.]

Ship Trumbull's Muster Book 1777

[The roll in Record of Connecticut Men in the Revolution was evidently printed from this document. Data are here given that were not included in the former printing.]

Name	Place Ship'd at	Place born at	Age	Height	Complex[a]
Dudley Saltonstall		New London			
Jonathan Maltbie		Fairfield			
David Phipps					
Jacob White					
James Morris		Stratford			
John Crocker					
Joseph Cheilds		England			
Alexr P. Adams		New London			
Jonath Gaylord		Middletown			
Elisha Bennet					
Samuel Roberts	New London	Scotland	28	5 9	Fair
Robert Halladay	Conn.	England	26	5 6	Dark
Robert Saunders	New London	New London			
Aurther Roberson	"	Ireland			
Thomas Fitz Gerald		Fairfield			
Peter Whitney	Fairfield	New Haven			
Jonath Sabin	New Haven	Middletown			
Samuel Stow	Middletown		14	5 5	Brown
Edward Prentis	Cambridge, Mass.	Middletown	21	6 6	Fair
James Knapp	Middletown	Guilford	39	5 8	Brown
Jedediah Norton	"				

Name	Place Ship'd at	Place born at	Age	Height	Complex
James Ward	New Haven	New London	24	5 7	Fair
Jabin Sperry	"	New Haven	28	5 5	"
Philo Sperry	"	"	22	5 9	"
James Jeffery	"	Scotland	19	5 5	"
Moses Cook	"	New Haven	23	5 6	"
Will. Baird Nicholson	"	Rhoad Island	20	5 9	"
William West	"	Ireland	28	5 5	Dark
Trueman Loveland	"	Darby	16	5 8¾	Fair
Bowars French	"		19	5 9	"
John Stubbs	"	England	18	5 11	"
William Turner	"		18	5 5	"
John Huggins	Lyme	Branford	18	5 4	"
Edmund Taylor	Wethersfield	England	17	5 7	"
James Richardson	"	Devonshire	20	5 2	"
Richard Wear	"	Dublin	48	5 5	"
John Emmitt	"	Lancashire	26	5 3	"
Thomas Clark	"	Liverpool	21	5 6	"
John Burnham	"	Wethersfield	18	5 8¼	Dark
Samuel Caverle	N Haven	New Haven	19	5 2	Dark
Freeman Badger	"	Wallingford	20	5 3	Fair
John Thomson	"	Bristol	48	5 6	Brown
Thomas Jones	Lyme	England	24	5 8	Fair
Henry Peck	New Haven	New Haven	22	5 6	"
Elisha White	"	"	16	5 5	"
Samuel Wise	"		17	5 4	"
Samuel Tory	Middletown	Middletown	17	5 6	Brown
Jonathan Setchell	New Haven	Ipswich Mass.	19	5 4	
Robert Aitkins		Scotland	19	5 11	
Michael Creamer	Middletown	Middletown	17	5 4	Fair
Thomas Johnson	"		21	5 0	Blemish in one eye
Thomas Bazzill			23	5 8	Brown
Thomas Scott	Glastenbury	Glastenbury	23	5 10	"
George Stow	Middletown	Middletown	39	5 6	"
Joseph Miller	Glastenbury	Glastenbury	18	5 7	Fair

Name	Residence	Birthplace	Age	Ht. ft	Ht. in	Complexion
Noah Brooks	Middletown	Middletown	21	5	8	Brown
Willm Putnam	New London	Boston	24	5	5	"
John Brown	Fairfield	England	25	5	4	Fair
John Brice	East Haddam	Scotland	22	5	6	Brown
Thomas Wendover Jr.	"	New York	19	5	9	"
Levy Hodge	Glastenbury	Glastenbury	20	5	11	"
Joseph Scott	"	"	21	5	6	Fair
Joseph Peck	Wethersfield	Wallingford	16	5	5	Brown
Aron White	Middletown	Middletown	22	5	10	Fair
Samuel Collins	"	"	21	5	3	Brown
Ebenezer Miller	"	Chatham	30	5	9	Light
Ebenezer Sage	East Haddam	Middletown	17	5	6	Brown
Samuel Johnson	"	New York	53	5	10	Fair
Bouton Knapp	"	Stanford	26	5	4	"
Joseph Merris	Middletown	Killingsworth	15	5	9	"
David Miller	"	Middletown	12	5	2	Brown
Isaac Knapp	"	Newbury	23	5	5	Dark
Abijah Collins	Wethersfield	Wethersfield	28	5	6	Fair
Levy Holmes	Middletown	Middletown	24	5	4†	Fair
Bennett Eaglestone	"		50			"
Stephen Eaglestone	"		15			Brown
Justus Starr	Glastenbury	Glastenbury	21	6	6	Fair
William Goodrich	East Haddam	Colchester	25	5	2	"
Samuel Dunham	New Haven	New Haven	26	5	7	Brown
Nehemiah Storer	Fairfield	Fairfield	20	5	7	Fair
Nathan Gould	"	"	17	5	6	"
Edmund Burr	"	New York	17	5	9	"
Samuel Adams	New Haven	New Haven	15	5	9	Brown
John House	"	"	22	4	7	
Nathaniel Warren	"		25	5	9	
Eber Sperry		Pachaug	19	5	10	
Jonathan Smith		West of England	22	5	7	
John Jeffery	E Haddam	New Haven	22	5	8	Brown
Robert Upham	N Haven		22	5	4	Indian
Elisha Forbes			21	5	9	Brown

Name	Place Ship'd at	Place born at	Age	Height	Complex
Christian Hanson	N Haven	Denmark	31	5 2	Fair
William Presher	"	Cortlands Manor	21	5 5	"
Richard Goff	E Haddam	N London	13	4 10	Brown
Roger Robins	Wethersfield	Wethersfield	16	5 2	"
Samuel Davis	"	Worcester Eng.	41	5 9	"
John Giles	"	Somersish "	22	5 6	"
Mitchel Kingman		Norwich	32	5 6	
Stephen Oliver	New Haven	New London			
Thomas Oliver	"	Scotland			
Will. Taylor					
Silas Sanford	Lyme	Long Island			Fair
William Webb	Wethersfield	England	30	5 4	"
Asael Bush	"	Mass.		6 1	Sandy
John Daggett	New Haven	New Haven			Brown
Brittain	New London	New London			Negro
Daniel Porter					
Daniel Peterson	New Haven				Negro
Josiah Wood	Lyme	England	21	5 9¼	Fair

MISCELLANEOUS.

HARTLAND RETURN.

Asa Andrews
Jonathan Bill Junr
Samuel Benjamin Ju^r
Daniel Benjamin
John Damels
Festus Giddings
Benjamin Giddings
Phinehas Kingbury Ju^r
Zebulon Mack
Eliphas Pirkins
Jason Pirkins
Gideon Pirkins
Reuben Daniels
Ebenezer Dimock
Thomas Jones
Moses Cowdrey
Asa Cowdrey
Noah Chappel
Jessa Gates
Abner Waters
Titus Allen Ju^r

Oliver Bates
Hendale Bates
Timothy Crosby
Daniel Driggs
Ephraim Fox
Nathan Fox
Haris Fox
Daniel Beman
Joseph Gilbert
James Hungerford
Josiah Meeker
Aaron Meeker
John Porter
George Treet
Childes Taylor
Gamaliel Wilder
Erastus Hil s
Dan Monrow
Isaac Meacham
Thomas Wilder

Hartland Jenuary ye 26th AD 1778

This is to Certify that the above Named was in actual Service in the Year AD 1776

[Although this Return is stated to be for service in 1776 it seems probable that that date is an error of the writer for 1775.]

[*State Library, Revolution 6, 9.*]

In the Record of Connecticut Men in the Revolution, page 523, Capt. Jehiel Bryant's company, Sergeant John Downs is noted as having marched Oct. 5 and deserted Oct. 15, 1777. John Downes of Milford who served in the Revolution kept a diary, now in the possession of William H. Downes of Boston, which contains the following among other entries for Oct. 1777.

5 Alarm made. I march off.
8 I march towards Fishkill
15 Marched to North River
18 I Joined Lieut Col Fenn's Regt at Peekskill.

24

In printing the volume of Rolls and Lists of Connecticut Men in the Revolution (Collections, vol. 8) several rolls were, unfortunately, printed from a volume of copied rolls in the Comptroller's office instead of from the original rolls in the State Library. The following changes should be made in the printed volume to conform to the original rolls.

Capt. Miller's Company, page 160.

For Solⁿ Phelps	read Solomon Phelps Jr.
" Wm Burt	" William Buel.
" Saml Finley	" Samuel Finley Jr.
" David Blush	" David Blush Jr.
" Libbius Hills	" Lebbeus Hills Jr.
" Ja^s Mackarel	" James Mackaul.

Capt. Hutchinson's Company, page 161.

For Adam Bingham	read Aaron Bingham.
" Asariah Bell	" Azariah Bill.
" Ja^s House	" Joseph House.
" Isahel Jones	" Asahel Jones.
" Jon^a Savary	" Jno Savary.
" Jon^a Townsen	" Jno Townsen.

Capt. Dewey's Company, page 161.

For Annis Fitch	read Ammi Fitch.
" Ja^s Tickour	" James Tickner.
" Rodolph^s Wacker	" Rodolphus Thacher

Capt. Phelps' Company, page 162.

For Saml Tyler	read Samuel Fyler.
" Beniah Phelps	" Beriah Phelps.

Capt. Carpenter's Company, page 162.

For Ja^s Gay	read Joseph Gay.

[*State Library, Revolution 6 ; 137, 148, 149, 151, 155.*]

The following corrections should be made in the volume of Rolls and Lists of Connecticut Men in the Revolution (Collections, vol. 8).

Page 80. For Short Term Levies, 1779, read Short Term Levies, 1780.
Page 160. For Joseph Bartlet Jr., read Josiah Bartlet Jr.
Page 1·3. For Sam^{ll} Boston, read Sam^{ll} Bastow.
Page 209. Kezin Gridley should be Rezin Gridley.

ERRATA.

Page 48. Add at bottom of page — East Windsor Apr^{ll} 6th 1779.
Page 136. The document ending here should be credited to *Connecticut Historical Society.*
Pages 233, 235. The headline should read — Connecticut Line, 1777–1781.

INDEX.

Aames, Ebenezer, 49.
Abanathy, Giles, 347.
Abbe, Eleazer, 22, 163, 237, 260.
Abbe, George, 226.
Abbe, Jeduthan, 22, 163, 237, 260.
Abbe, John, 22, 54, 55, 73, 129, 163, 226, 236, 288.
Abbe, Joseph, 226, 288.
Abbe, Mason, 85, 127.
Abbe, Nathaniel, 226, 288.
Abbe, Thomas, 22, 66, 240.
Abbee, John, 182, 275.
Abbercrumbie, Aaron, 337.
Abberhart, John Lodewick, 2.
Abbett, John, 357.
Abbey, Eleazar, 345.
Abbey, Eliphelet, 345.
Abbey, Jeduthan, 345.
Abbot, 143.
Abbot, John, 12.
Abbot, John, Jr., 130.
Abbot, Stephen, 134.
Abby, Eleazer, 70.
Abby, Elezr, 143.
Abby, George, 180.
Abby, Joseph, 334.
Abby, Richard, 189.
Abel, Abel, 65.
Abell, Rufus, 74.
Abenathy, James, 61.
Abercrombie, Aaron, 254.
Abercrumbie, Aaron, 320.
Abernerthy, James, 102.
Abey, 80.
Abrow, Benajah, 59, 353.
Acaly, Samuel, 5.
Achor, Jacob, 245, 305, 328.
Ackley, Aeral, 118.
Ackley, Barzileel, 3.
Ackley, Champeou, 78.
Ackley, Lewis, 87, 351.
Ackley, Nicholas, 87, 351.
Ackley, Silas, 3.

Ackley, Thomas, 241, 352.
Ackley, Warren, 3.
Acklin, Cuff, 278, 279, 351.
Ackly, Champion, 227.
Ackly, Thomas, 21, 163.
Acley, Ariel, 80.
Acley, Azerial, 57.
Acley, Thomas, 260.
Acley, Uriah, 153.
Adams, 138.
Adams, Abel, 10.
Adams, Alexander P., 365.
Adams, Asael, 21, 177, 236.
Adams, Asaph, 363.
Adams, Benjamin, 11, 106, 272, 292.
Adams, Charles, 75.
Adams, David 21, 64, 146, 157, 163, 237.
Adams, David, Jr., 21, 237.
Adams, Elisha, 132.
Adams, James, 89.
Adams, Jedd, 146.
Adams, Jedediah, 64, 157, 277, 335, 363.
Adams, John, 21, 52, 70, 213, 223, 239, 297.
Adams, Jonathan, 21, 234.
Adams, Jonathan, Jr., 116, 144.
Adams, Oliver, 10.
Adams, Parker, 71, 136.
Adams, Permenio, 10.
Adams, Philemon, 363.
Adams, Reuben, 286, 311, 344.
Adams, Rhodrick, 10, 260, 279.
Adams, Samuel, 21, 49, 64, 157, 163, 237, 260, 297, 362, 367.
Adams, Samuel, Jr., 363.
Adams, Simion, 50.
Adams, William, 21, 70, 72, 82, 136, 160, 163, 237.
Adams, William, Jr., 148.
Addams, Abner, 19.

Addams, Asael, 74.
Addams, David, 19, 352.
Addams, Jeddediah, 318.
Addams, Joshua, 8.
Addams, Levi, 349.
Addams, Roderick, 349.
Addams, Samuel, 353.
Addis, Thomas, 198.
Adee, Aner, 61.
Adee, Anor, 343.
Adhins, David, 51.
Adkin, Jabez, 346.
Adkins, David, 346.
Adkins, Ira, 209.
Adkins, Josiah, 51.
Adkins, Luther, 50.
Adrus, Theodore, 163.
Adye, Aner, 99.
Aery, Ephriam, 46.
Affrica, Ruel, 60.
Affrican, Ruel, 299.
Africa, Cash, 53, 228.
Africa, Ruel, 288.
Aitkins, Robert, 366.
Akely, Samuel, 163.
Aken, James, 22.
Akerly, Samuel, 51.
Akin, James, 163, 229.
Albert, Thomas G., 22, 239.
Alcock, Giles, 53.
Alderman, Eppaph, 144.
Alderman, Gad, 279, 349.
Alderman, John, 10.
Alderman, Timothy, 188.
Aldin, 188.
Aldredge, William, 260.
Aldrich, Timothy, 184.
Aldrich, William, 163.
Aldridge, James, 275, 349.
Aldridge, Thomas, 10.
Aldridge, Jonathan, 137.
Aldridge, William, 232.
Aldrish, William, 77.
Alexander, James, 363.
Alger, Aaron, 137.
Allas, Phinehas, 148.
Allay, William, 260.
Allen, Abel, 277, 347.
Allen, Amasa, 49, 66.
Allen, Amos, 21, 236.
Allen, Asher, 72, 129, 163.
Allen, Ashur, 21, 54, 55, 236.
Allen, Benjamin, 67, 98, 113.
Allen, Daniel, 21, 199, 236.
Allen, David, 21, 218.
Allen, Diarca, 54, 72, 129.
Allen, Ebenezer, 21, 67, 163, 233.

Allen, Ebenezer, Jr., 96.
Allen, Eliphalet, 67.
Allen, Eseck, 10.
Allen, Gabrel, 4.
Allen, Ichabod, 182.
Allen, John, 47, 75, 139, 258, 288, 291, 349.
Allen, Jonathan, 21.
Allen, Lemuel, 46, 86, 130.
Allen, Minor, 119, 153, 154.
Allen, Moses, 21, 67, 163, 233.
Allen, Othniel, 49, 66.
Allen, Peter, 283.
Allen, Phineas, 54, 72, 129.
Allen, Robart, 232.
Allen, Samuel, 21, 46, 131, 132, 163, 238.
Allen, Thomas, 21, 67, 97, 233.
Allen, Timothy, 244.
Allen, Titus, Jr., 369.
Allen, William, 8.
Alley, William, 22, 163, 229.
Allin, Abel, 48, 242.
Allin, Amasa, 12.
Allin, Amos, 57, 79.
Allin, Arch, 14.
Allin, David, 230.
Allin, Ebenezer, 8.
Allin, Elisha, 201.
Allin, John, 198.
Allin, Joseph, 295.
Allin, Lemuel, 133.
Allin, Moses, 205.
Allin, Nathaniel, 201.
Allin, Sluman, 198.
Alling, Abel, 260.
Alling, John, 150.
Alling, Jonathan, 163, 229, 260.
Alling, Nathaniel, 6.
Alling, Titus, 6.
Alling, William, 8.
Allis, Nathaniel, Jr., 4.
Allyn, Abel, 299.
Allyn, Benjamin, 209.
Allyn, Daniel, 49.
Allyn, Ellihu, 189.
Allyn, Job, 14.
Allyn, John, 305, 328.
Allyn, Jonathan, 189.
Allyn, Joseph, 185.
Allyn, Miner, 51, 69.
Allyn, Robert, 50, 68.
Allyn, Theophilus, 189.
Allyn, Thomas, Jr., 14.
Allyn, Timothy, 242, 304, 324.
Alma, William, 224.
Aloord, Hewet, 65.

Alton, Joseph, 135.
Alverd, Thomas G., 260.
Alvord, Eliphaz, 361, 362.
Alvord, Thomas G., 163, 194.
Alvord, see Aloord.
Ama, Archalus, 223, 297.
Ambrose, Patrick, 283.
Ame, Archelaus, 288.
Amedown, Jonathan, 186.
Ames, Aden, 75, 242.
Ames, Alven, 128.
Ames, Antielus, 310.
Ames, Archelus, 310, 328.
Ames, Arehelus, 306.
Ames, Asa, 128.
Ames, Comfort, 272.
Ames, Cyrus, 9.
Ames, David, 192.
Ames, Ebenezer, 66, 194.
Ames, Ezra, 77.
Ames, John, 64, 156.
Ames, Matthias, 9.
Ames, Nathaniel, 182.
Ames, Samuel, 288.
Ames, Zebulon, 78.
Amis, Arehclus, 306.
Ammedown, Jonathan, 294.
Ammit, John, 324, 339.
Amos, 58.
Ancraman, John Frederick, 75.
Andeson, Thomas, 21.
Andeson, William, 21.
Anderson, Daniel, 221.
Anderson, J., 116.
Anderson, James, 254, 285, 320, 337.
Anderson, John, 136.
Anderson, Robert, Jr., 124.
Anderson, Thomas, 163, 180, 232, 260, 338.
Anderson, Timothy, 188, 226.
Anderson, William, 48, 163, 186, 240, 346.
Anderwood, Elius, 131.
Andras, Abner, 348.
Andras, Asa, 349.
Andras, Clemont, 350.
Andras, David, 350.
Andras, Elisha, 204.
Andras, John, 252.
Andras, Jonathan, 349.
Andras, Joseph, 347.
Andras, Obadiah, 347.
Andras, Richard, 204.
Andras, Thomas, 352.
Andras, William, 204, 349.
Andreus, Thomas, 260.

Andrews, Amos, 60, 83, 187.
Andrews, Andrew, 59, 82.
Andrews, Asa, 6, 369.
Andrews, Daniel, 362.
Andrews, David, 277.
Andrews, James, 232.
Andrews, John, 8, 276.
Andrews, Joshua, 65.
Andrews, Nathaniel, 186.
Andrews, Philn, 179.
Andrews, Richard, 186.
Andrews, Solomon, 272.
Andrews, Thomas, 241.
Andrews, Timothy, 84.
Andros, Elijah, 336.
Andrss, 48.
Andrus, Asa, 21, 163, 238, 260.
Andrus, Clement, 300.
Andrus, Daniel, 189.
Andrus, David, 300.
Andrus, Ezra, 21, 163, 252.
Andrus, Gideon, 347.
Andrus, Hezekiah, 11.
Andrus, James, 11, 21, 68, 80, 163, 240.
Andrus, John, 50.
Andrus, Jonathan, 145.
Andrus, Obediah, 21, 239, 260, 278.
Andrus, Richard, 10.
Andrus, Solomon, 302.
Andrus, Theodore, 21, 239, 260.
Andrus, Thomas, 21, 163.
Andrus, Timothy, 163.
Andrus, William, 10, 21, 163, 240.
Andruss, Ezra, 55.
Andruss, Theodore, 250.
Andruss, Timothy, 52, 70.
Andruss, William, 10.
Anew, Andrew, 163.
Angar, George, 163.
Anger, George, 239, 347.
Anguine, Lewis, 250.
Angur, George, 22.
Anibell, David, 3.
Anjevine, Lewis, 58, 92.
Annew, Andrew, 22, 68, 232.
Answitz, Apollus, 351.
Answorth, Alven, 198.
Anthony, John, 13, 60, 83.
Antoney, John, 22.
Antony, John, 230.
Apes, Peter, 281.
Apley, Josiah, 205.
Aply, Rozel, 147.
Arabus, Jack, 338.

Archer, Benjamin, Jr., 142.
Archer, Crippin, 302.
Archer, Cyprian, 354.
Archer, Grippin, 260.
Armstrong, Daniel, 301.
Armstrong, Daniel, Jr., 272.
Armstrong, Ebenezer, 76, 112.
Armstrong, Joseph, 95.
Armstrong, Josiah, 67, 97.
Armstrong, William, 272, 301, 308, 333.
Arnall, Jonathan, 51.
Arney, Archelaus, 284.
Arnold, 5.
Arnold, Abijah, 108.
Arnold, Gideon, 129.
Arnold, Isaac, 356.
Arnold, Jehiel, 22, 69, 163, 240, 354.
Arnold, John, 5, 132.
Arnold, Jonathan, 52, 70, 245, 315, 345.
Arnold, Josiah, 5.
Arnold, Levi, 208.
Arnold, Oliver, Jr., 74.
Arnold, Seth, 6, 260, 277, 347.
Arven, William, 71.
Arvin, William, 77, 135.
Ashford, 21, 22, 25, 27, 30, 33, 34, 36, 39, 42, 43, 46, 88, 130, 133, 138, 166, 169, 170, 173, 175, 177, 179, 181, 182, 183, 184, 185, 196, 199, 201, 216, 217, 218, 219, 226, 236, 264, 266, 269, 271, 273, 280, 284, 287, 297, 298, 301, 355, 356, 357.
Ashley, Abner, 129.
Ashley, John, 114, 352.
Ashly, John, 103.
Aspenwall, Aaron, 22, 177, 236.
Aspenwall, Caleb, 22, 177.
Aspenwall, Peter, 218.
Aspinwell, Aaron, 74.
Aspinwell, Caleb, 74, 236.
Asten, Banjmin, 15.
Astin, Thomas, 146.
Athington, Thomas, 67.
Atkins, Chancy, 189.
Atkins, Ira, 280.
Atkens, Joseph, 132.
Atkins, Josiah, 7, 260, 289.
Atkins, Josiah, Jr., 163.
Atkins, Samuel, 215.
Attwood, John, 3.
Attwood, Thomas, 182.
Atwater, Titus, 60.
Atwood, Ebenezer, 192.

Atwood, Elijah, Jr., 287.
Atwood, Isaac, 135.
Atwood, Thomas, 219.
Auger, George, 260.
Augustus, Bristo, 75.
Augustus, Caesar, 22, 70, 237, 345.
Augustus, Jacob, 194, 226.
Augustus, Zezar, 163.
Auldredg, William, 22.
Austen, Edward, 210.
Austen, John, 77, 205.
Austen, Richard, 22.
Austin, Amos, 13.
Austin, Benjamin, 13.
Austin, David, 115.
Austin, Ezra, 190.
Austin, Eusebius, 247.
Austin, Joshua, 144.
Austin, Phinehas, 260, 351.
Austin, Richard, 163, 238, 352, 354.
Austin, Thomas, 64, 156.
Austin, Uriah, 18.
Avered, Ambrose, 14.
Averet, Thadeous, 13.
Averies, Daniel, 90.
Averill, Jacob, 10.
Averill, Jonathan, 10.
Averill, Thomas, 9.
Avery, Amos, 66.
Avery, Benjamin, 61, 99, 341.
Avery, Charles, 3d, 74.
Avery, Christopher, 77, 249, 281, 318, 335.
Avery, Constant, 51, 69, 78.
Avery, Daniel, 80.
Avery, David, 214.
Avery, Elisha, 50, 68.
Avery, Ephraim, 131.
Avery, Ezekiel, 221.
Avery, Frederick, 75, 214.
Avery, George, Jr., 50, 68.
Avery, Isaac, 288.
Avery, John, 310, 343.
Avery, Miles, 74.
Avery, Prentis, 9.
Avery, Roger, 76, 148.
Avery, Simeon, 68, 163, 183, 232, 260.
Avery, Stephen, 199.
Avery, Thomas, 232.
Avory, Amos, Jr., 132.
Avory, Roger, 330.
Avory, Simeon, 22.
Avory, Thomas, 22.
Ayer, John, 78.

Baldwin, Abraham, 123.
Baldwin, Asa, 12.
Baldwin, Caleb, 72, 231, 261.
Baldwin, Eleazer, 273.
Baldwin, Elisha, 77.
Baldwin, Henry, 232.
Baldwin, Isaac, 123, 154.
Baldwin, Jared, 210, 222.
Baldwin, Levi, 1.
Baldwin, Luther, 214.
Baldwin, Samuel, 204.
Baldwin, Seth, 280, 287, 354.
Baldwin, Silas, 230.
Baldwin, William, 1.
Baldwin, Calib, 22, 164.
Baldwine, Elijah, 54, 72, 129.
Baldwine, Henery, 22.
Baldwine, Silas, 22.
Baley, 224.
Baley, Asa, 50.
Ball, Caleb, 8.
Ball, Humphry, 23, 237, 262, 290, 291.
Ball, James, 200.
Ball, John, 5, 164, 226, 231, 261, 301.
Ball, Jonathan, 280, 301.
Ball, Umphry, 163.
Ball, Vmphrey, 140.
Ballard, John, 277, 308, 334.
Ballen, Benjamin, 133.
Bamon, Jonathan, 312.
Bangs, Richard, 204.
Banjmin, Jese, 15.
Banks, Gershom, 4.
Banks, Samuel, 118.
Banks, Sumner, 346.
Banks, Thomas, 274.
Bannister, George, 61.
Banter, Alexander, 350.
Barber, Amaziah, 10, 260, 349.
Barber, Daniel, 10, 11, 143.
Barber, David, Jr., 85.
Barber, Elijah, 10.
Barber, Job, 11.
Barber, John, Jr., 144.
Barber, Jonathan, 186.
Barber, Nathaniel, 22, 235.
Barber, Reuben, 205.
Barber, Shubel, 14.
Barber, Stephen, 119, 142.
Barber, W., 327.
Barbermore, Eldad, 215.
Barbor, Simon, 6.
Barbur, Benjamin, 6.
Barbur, Simian, 6.
Barbur, Timothy, 6.

Bardin, Abraham, 210.
Bardin, Samuel, 273.
Bardon, Samuel, 316.
Bardsley, Abijah, 151.
Bardsley, Garsham, 47.
Bardsley, Gawham, 47.
Bardsly, Phineas, 7.
Barham, 95.
Barker, Amaziah, 275.
Barker, Ethen, 179.
Barker, James, Jr., 2.
Barker, John, 56, 77.
Barker, Joshua, 117.
Barker, Moses, 350.
Barker, Samuel, 22, 231.
Barker, Timothy, 1.
Barkhamsted, 145, 189.
Barlow, Daniel, 58, 67, 93.
Barlow, David, 68, 92.
Barlow, David, Jr., 58.
Barlow, John, 23, 107, 165, 235, 261.
Barlow, Micah, 134.
Barlow, Silas, 123.
Barna, Benjamin, 219.
Barnabee, James, 65.
Barnam, Levi, 191.
Barnard, 143, 194.
Barnard, Edward, Jr., 14.
Barnard, Francis, 288.
Barnard, James, 52, 70, 256, 359.
Barnard, Joel, 276, 350.
Barnard, John, 23, 70, 164, 237.
Barnard, Joseph, 86.
Barnard, Moses, 315, 331.
Barnard, Pharis, 286.
Barnard, Samuel, 10.
Barnard, Willial, 187.
Barnee, Frederick, 61.
Barnerd, Elihu, 204.
Barnerd, James, 358.
Barnes, Ambrose, 262.
Barnes, Charles, 287.
Barnes, David, 261, 334.
Barnes, James, 162.
Barnes, John, 140, 208.
Barnes, Josiah, 337.
Barnes, Moses, 261, 355.
Barnes, Orange, 286.
Barnes, Stephen, 282.
Barnes, Thomas, 254.
Barnet, John, 282.
Barnet, William, 123, 154.
Barnett, William, 8.
Barney, Luther, 3.
Barnham, Eli, 320.
Barnham, John, 254.

Basset, William, 24, 163, 230, 261.
Bassett, Joshua, 236.
Bassett, Joshua, Jr., 73.
Bassett, Nathan, 365.
Bassett, William, 310, 343.
Bassey, Peleg, 8.
Bassey, Silas, 8.
Bassit, Jonathan, 179.
Bassit, William, 84.
Bassitt, John, 58.
Baston, Sawney, 346.
Bastow, Samuel, 370.
Batchlor, Abel, 332.
Bate, Eleazer, 5.
Bates, Amos, 23, 70, 164, 240.
Bates, Daniel, 23, 70, 164, 240, 261, 284, 320, 352.
Bates, David, 23, 165, 233, 262.
Bates, Eleazer, 23, 70, 164, 240, 261.
Bates, Ephraim, 53, 312, 344.
Bates, Ezra, 108.
Bates, Hendale, 369.
Bates, John, 23, 239.
Bates, Joseph, 346, 364.
Bates, Oliver, 369.
Bates, Reuben, 6.
Bates, Samuel, 103.
Bath, John, 70.
Batterson, Abijah, 209.
Batterson, George, 262, 274.
Batterson, George, Jr., 4.
Batterson, James, Jr., 67, 96.
Batterson, John, 4.
Batterson, Joseph, 4, 67, 96, 209.
Batterson, Stephen, 67, 96.
Batterson, William, 4, 274.
Battis, Elijah, 216.
Baxter, Aaron, 23, 75, 141, 238.
Baxter, Alexander, 80.
Baxter, Benjamin, 49, 66.
Baxter, Francis, 23, 48, 164, 240.
Baxter, William, 296.
Bayard, Marshall, 287.
Bayden, Elhanan, 260.
Bayley, Abraham, 215.
Bayley, Henry, 93, 261.
Bayley, William, 51.
Bazzill, Thomas, 366.
Beach, Asa, 60, 83.
Beach, Benjamin, 58.
Beach, Bruen, 204.
Beach, D., 203.
Beach, David, 55, 261.
Beach, Ezekel, 6.
Beach, James, 144.

Beach, John, 58.
Beach, Julius, 275.
Beach, Lazarus, 89.
Beach, Nathaniel, 58, 90, 305, 341.
Beach, Obil, 69.
Beach, Reuben, 90, 305, 312, 343.
Beach, Rice, 206.
Beach, Roswel, 59, 83.
Beach, William, 353.
Beadle, Titus, 282.
Beadle, William, 51.
Beaeton, William, 248.
Beaher, John, 67.
Beaman, 48.
Beamon, Caesar, 261.
Beamont, Daniel, 279.
Beamont, Samuel, 256.
Beamont, Samuel, Jr., 79.
Beamont, William, 61.
Beamount, Dan, 221.
Beard, Abijah, 2.
Beard, Timothy, 73.
Beardsee, Gersham, 151.
Beardsle, Philo, 8.
Beardslee, Abijah, 58.
Beardslee, John, 4.
Beardslee, John, Jr., 58.
Beardslee, N., 162.
Beardsley, 98, 100, 126.
Beardsley, Abijah, 93.
Beardsley, Elijah, 122, 154.
Beardsley, James, 222.
Beardsley, John, 93.
Beardsley, Nehemiah, 221.
Beardsley, Phineas, 234.
Beardsley, Solomon W., 282.
Beardsley, Wheeler S., 261.
Beardsley, William, 338.
Beardsly, 118, 119, 120, 124.
Beardsly, Nehemiah, 162.
Beardsly, S., 91.
Bears, Hezekiah, 4.
Bearsley, Georshom. 2.
Bearzal, William, 161.
Beaumont, Dan, 216.
Beaumont, Jonathan, 312, 344.
Beazel, William, 82.
Bebe, Ammon, 165.
Bebe, James, 165.
Bebe, Joe, 164.
Bebee, Amon, 7, 231.
Bebee, Comfort, 351.
Bebee, Joel, 73, 261.
Bebee, Nathan, 181.
Bebee, Richard, 351.
Bebee, Solomon, 354.
Beckley, Prichard, 246.

Becks, Comfort, 339.
Beckus, Thomas, 297.
Beckwit, Phineas, 232.
Beckwith, Ezekiel, 282.
Beckwith, Ezekiel, Jr., 358, 359.
Beckwith, Ezra, 3, 86.
Beckwith, Guy, 198.
Beckwith, Ichabod, 23, 290, 358.
Beckwith, Isaac, Jr., 359.
Beckwith, Phineas, 23, 164, 260.
Beckwith, Timothy, Jr., 290, 358.
Beckwith, William, 3.
Beetley, Ephraim, 89.
Beden, William, 58.
Bedient, John, 214.
Bedient, Mordecai, 25, 109, 165.
Bedson, Daniel, 99.
Beebe, 88.
Beebe, Ammon, 24.
Beebe, Boanerges, 24, 290.
Beebe, Comfort, 283, 339.
Beebe, Daniel, 364.
Beebe, David, 279.
Beebe, James, 24, 355.
Beebe, Joel, 24, 231.
Beebe, Jonathan Jeremiah, 301.
Beebe, Naomi, 87.
Beebe, Nathan, 3.
Beebe, Nathaniel, 3.
Beebe, Richard, 283.
Beebee, Ammon, 76.
Beebee, Benjamin, 360.
Beebee, Boanerges, 360.
Beebee, Comfort, 325.
Beebee, James, 234, 261.
Beebee, Jonathan Jeremiah, 272.
Beebee, Nathaniel, 93.
Beebee, Richard, 325, 339.
Beech, Asa, 198.
Beech, Ashbell, 6.
Beech, David, Jr., 105.
Beech, Ebenezer, 97.
Beech, Elnathan, 207.
Beeck, Asa, 260.
Beeman, Elisha, 106.
Beeman, Ezekiel, 189.
Beeman, Friend, 24, 103.
Beeman, Jonathan, 24.
Beeman, Lemuel, 106.
Beeman, Matthias, 106.
Beeman, Samuel, 107.
Beeman, Truman, 210.
Beeny, John, 106.
Beers, Ephraim, 68, 96.
Beers, Gershum, 207.
Beers, Hezekiah, 22, 233.
Beers, Isaac, 317, 326, 332.

Beers, James, 92, 105, 382.
Beers, Jesse, 25, 109.
Beers, Joel, 58, 93, 250.
Beers, John, 92, 242, 320, 337.
Beers, John, Jr., 58.
Beers, Nathan, 245, 303, 327.
Beers, Thiah, 98.
Beers, Zachariah, 100.
Beevins, Ebenezer, 70, 164.
Beevins, Timothy, 250.
Begilow, Aloan, 193.
Beguine, Peter, 351.
Beke, William, 354.
Belcher, Elish, 10.
Belcher, Gill, 142.
Belcher, Joseph, 141, 354.
Belcher, Nathan, 10.
Belden, Ezra, 261.
Belden, John, 24, 73.
Belden, Simeon, 261.
Beldin, John, 261.
Belding, Abraham, 242, 308, 334, 348.
Belding, David, 197.
Belding, Ezra, 347.
Belding, Ezra, Jr., 277.
Belding, John, 164, 231.
Belding, Moses, 164, 348.
Belding, Richard, 254, 320, 337, 348.
Belding, Simeon, 300.
Beley, Asa, 68.
Bell, Asariah, 370.
Bell, Francis, 113.
Bell, J., 113.
Bell, James, 201, 272, 301.
Bellamy, Asa, 60, 83.
Bellows, Isaac, 185, 226.
Bellows, Nathaniel, 51, 69.
Bellows, Thomas, 15.
Bellus, Daniel, 10.
Bellus, Thomas, 10.
Belshaserhes, John, 118.
Beman, Cesar, 283.
Beman, Daniel, 369.
Beman, Friend, 236.
Beman, Jonathan, 240.
Beman, Uriah, 10.
Bement, Cesar, 351.
Bement, Jonathan, 189.
Bemont, Olliver, 140.
Bemus, Ephraim, 141.
Ben, Solomon, 121.
Ben, Thomas, 231.
Bend, John, 24.
Benedic, Derias, 162.
Benedict, Amos, 8.

Benedict, Asahel, 124.
Benedict, Comfort, 119.
Benedict, Daniel, 56.
Benedict, Darius, 78, 120.
Benedict, Ebenezer, 108.
Benedict, John, Jr., 8.
Benedict, Thomas, Jr., 8.
Benedict, William, 222.
Beneduk, Daniel, 59.
Benham, Isaas, 206.
Benham, James, 287.
Benham, Jared, 13.
Benham, John, 255.
Benham, Samuel, 13.
Benidict, Ezra, 261.
Benidict, Jeames, 74.
Benidict, Levi, 284.
Benjaman, Phinihas, 57.
Benjamen, J., 91.
Benjamen, John, Jr., 92.
Benjamens, John, 213.
Benjamens, Phin., 80.
Benjamin, Abial, Jr., 15.
Benjamin, Aron, 331.
Benjamin, Asa, 207.
Benjamin, Benjamin, 58, 65.
Benjamin, Daniel, 369.
Benjamin, David, 15.
Benjamin, Ezra, 15.
Benjamin, James, 8.
Benjamin, Jesse, 150.
Benjamin, John, 10, 165.
Benjamin, Rozel, 10.
Benjamin, Samuel, Jr., 369.
Benjamin, Stephen, 154.
Benjamins, Asa, 199.
Benjamins, Jesse, 77, 165.
Benjamins, John, 24, 234.
Benjamon, Daniel, 6.
Benn, Solomon, 283.
Bennedick, 88.
Bennedict, Eleazer, 124.
Bennedict, William, 102.
Bennet, Amos, 56, 76, 147, 159.
Bennet, Benjamin, 24, 75, 165, 231, 261, 295, 341.
Bennet, Benjamin, Jr., 7.
Bennet, David, 183.
Bennet, Elisha, 365.
Bennet, Ezekiel, 287.
Bennet, Isaac, 261, 283.
Bennet, Jaben, 81, 256.
Bennet, James, 19.
Bennet, Jeremiah, 280, 302, 308, 334.
Bennet, Job, 12.
Bennet, John, 12, 261.

Bennet, Joshua, 24, 54, 55, 130, 236.
Bennet, Miles, 312, 344.
Bennet, Nathaniel, 128.
Bennet, Stephen, 76, 148, 158, 222, 280, 288, 302.
Bennet, William, 12.
Bennett, Benjamin, 78, 120.
Bennett, Daniel, 75.
Bennett, John, 92.
Bennit, Abel, 10.
Bennit, Benjamin, 57, 68, 162.
Bennit, Daniel, 67.
Bennit, James, 55, 209.
Bennit, Nathaniel, 85.
Bennitt, 97.
Bennitt, Andrew, 4.
Bennitt, Benjamin, 3ᵈ, 93.
Bennitt, Daniel, 4, 95.
Bennitt, Hezekiah, 4.
Bennitt, James, 8, 101.
Bennitt, John, 58.
Bennitt, Tobe, 154.
Bennitt, Wolcutt, 4.
Bens, Thomas, 24.
Benson, William, 147.
Bentley, Aseal, 193.
Bentley, Jasper, 193.
Bentley, Joseph, 68, 256.
Bentley, William, 140, 290, 291.
Bently, Joseph, 50.
Benton, 215.
Benton, Adoniram, 185, 286, 349.
Benton, Azariah, 12.
Benton, David, 233.
Benton, Ebenezer, 17.
Benton, Edward, 24, 164, 231, 261.
Benton, Elihew, 193.
Benton, Elihue, 219.
Benton, Elijah, 82, 128, 286, 349.
Benton, Jonathan, 12, 187.
Benton, Josiah, 12.
Benton, Nathaniel W., 346.
Benton, Samuel, 12.
Benton, Zadock, 186.
Benton, Zebulon, 5, 51.
Berber, Shubel, 86.
Berdslee, Hezekiah, 207.
Berdsley, Phineas, 24.
Berry, John, 315.
Berto, Silas, 207.
Bester, Abel, 186.
Bester, Job, 217.
Bettis, James, Jr., 140.
Betts, 187.
Betts, Daniel, 320.
Betts, David, 313, 330.

Betts, Elijah, 262, 286.
Betts, Hezekiah, 324, 339.
Betts, Isaiah, 111.
Betts, James, 8, 23.
Betts, Peter, 116.
Betts, Rheuben, 8.
Betts, Stephen, 304, 313, 329.
Betts, Thomas, 8.
Betts, Thomas, Jr., 8.
Betts, Zopher, 211.
Beull, Joseph, 300.
Beumont, Dan, 291.
Bevens, Ebenezer, 23, 237.
Bevens, Timothy, 316, 347.
Bevin, Thomas, 4.
Bevins, Henry, 209.
Bewel, Daniel, 80.
Bewel, David, 24, 261.
Bewel, Matthew, 11.
Bewil, David, 163.
Bibbins, Timothy, 49.
Bicknal, James, 357.
Bicknal, Josiah, 131.
Bicknal, Moses, 218.
Bicknall, Josiah, 46.
Bidd, Bruster, 113.
Bidwell, Ephraim, 188, 208.
Bidwell, Jonathan, 14.
Bidwell, Jonathan, Jr., 86.
Bidwell, Joseph, 17.
Bidwell, Thomas, 208.
Biel, Hendrick, 273.
Bigelow, Alvin, 226.
Biggelow, Eli, 22.
Biggelow, Fredrick, 203.
Bigsbe, Elias, 24.
Bigsby, Elias, 89, 234.
Bigsby, Solomon, 335.
Biley, John, 304.
Bill, Azariah, 370.
Bill, Berinh, 22, 74, 231.
Bill, Daniel, 6.
Bill, Elijah, 139, 215, 246, 290, 291.
Bill, John, 66, 132.
Bill, Jonathan, 22, 139, 221, 240, 291.
Bill, Jonathan, Jr., 369.
Bill, Jont, 64.
Bill, Joshua, 142, 226, 278, 291.
Bill, Judah, 165.
Bill, Jude, 57, 80.
Bill, Samuel, 291.
Billens, James, 23.
Billens, Steaphen, 23.
Billing, 210.
Billing, Christopher, 149.

Billing, Ezekiel, 50, 68.
Billing, Joseph, 77.
Billing, Roger, 15.
Billing, Stephen, 68, 232.
Billings, Ebenezer, 47.
Billings, James, 233.
Billings, Joseph, 10.
Billings, Peleg, 10, 286.
Billings, Samuel, 189.
Billings, Steaphen, 165.
Billins, Peleg, 262.
Billins, Stephen, Jr., 260.
Bingham, Aaron, 141, 370.
Bingham, Abel, 276, 352.
Bingham, Abishai, 24, 85, 165, 236.
Bingham, Adam, 370.
Bingham, Alfeas, 357.
Bingham, Bartlet, 64, 146, 157.
Bingham, Elias, 85.
Bingham, John, 24, 85, 127, 165, 236.
Bingham, Levy, 127.
Bingham, Luther, 362.
Bingham, Maltier, 128.
Bingham, Samuel, 128.
Bingham, Thamer, 206.
Binns, Thomas, 73.
Birdsly, J., 91, 92.
Bishop, Almeno, 164.
Bishop, Austin, 222.
Bishop, Daniel, 2.
Bishop, David, 22, 120, 123, 154, 165, 234, 261.
Bishop, Elisha, 60, 83.
Bishop, Ezra, 209.
Bishop, James, 4, 197.
Bishop, Joel, 51.
Bishop, John, 66, 113, 334.
Bishop, John, Jr., 75.
Bishop, Johnson, 5.
Bishop, Jonah, 217.
Bishop, Joseph, 211.
Bishop, Leonard, 209.
Bishop, Nathaniel, 8, 22, 74, 164, 229, 231, 260.
Bishop, Neriah, 5.
Bishop, Richard, 46, 63.
Bishop, Simeon, 260.
Bishop, Thalmeno, 5, 231, 261.
Bishop, Thalmenus, 22.
Bishop, Thomas F., 277, 299, 347.
Bishop, William, 198.
Bishopp, Austin, 186.
Bishopsgate, 254.
Bissel, 48, 88.
Bissel, Benjamin, 163.

Boardman, William, 226.
Boardmun, John, 77.
Bobinson, Benjamin, 71.
Bocor, Hemon, 12.
Bodwel, Benjamin, 10.
Bodwell, Benjamin, 240.
Bodwill, Benjamin, 81.
Boeny, Ceaser, 192.
Boge, Ichabod, 232.
Boge, Oliver, 187.
Bogers, Hezekiah, 304.
Bogue, Daniel, 205.
Bogue, Ickabud, 23.
Boing, Berrey, 297.
Boise, Thadias, 193.
Bolch, Israel, 199.
Boles, Jeremiah, 142.
Bolles, Isaiah, 359.
Bolles, James, 24.
Bolles, Samuel, 76.
Bolls, Richard, 134.
Bolls, Samuel, 131.
Bolt, Benjamin, 103.
Bolton, 1, 27, 30, 43, 63, 66, 169, 192, 195, 198, 200, 238, 252, 254, 258, 271, 280, 291, 302, 353.
Bond, Bethuel, 297.
Bond, John, 74, 136, 231.
Bond, Joseph, 64, 147.
Bond, Stephen Moulton, 81.
Bonds, Joseph, 150.
Bondy, William, 61.
Boney, Javis, 69.
Bonfoey, Benanual, 164.
Bonfoy, Benanuel, 69.
Bonfoy, Benunuel, 23, 240.
Bonfoy, Henry, 7.
Bonfoy, Jerathmel, 52, 69.
Bonney, Peres, 47.
Bonnum, James, 207.
Bonton, Agar, 275.
Boodish, Asa, 218.
Booge, Richard, 216.
Booman, Job, 350.
Boomer, Job, 322.
Booth, 336.
Booth, Abell, 123.
Booth, David, 186.
Booth, Edward, 228.
Booth, Erastus, 48.
Booth, Henry, 22, 66, 164, 240, 260, 261, 286, 300, 350.
Booth, J., 92.
Booth, Jeremiah, 284, 351.
Booth, John, 14, 102, 186.
Booth, Joseph, 8.
Booth, Nathaniel, 58, 90, 261.

Booth, Prosper, 153.
Booth, Salvanus, 185.
Booth, Walter, 150, 258, 318, 335.
Bordin, Samuel, 260.
Bordman, David, 15.
bordman, Elijah, 308.
Bordman, Jonathan, 5, 70.
Bordman, Joseph, 15.
Bordman, Josiah, 63, 252.
Bordslee, John, 207.
Borrows, Joseph, 318, 335.
Bosher, Nicholas, 287.
Bostick, Richard, 197.
Boston, Samuel, 370.
Boston, Toby, 122, 154.
Boston, 14, 367, 369.
Bostwic, Levi, 8.
Bostwick, B., 100.
Bostwick, Daniel, 79, 227, 245, 322, 338.
Bostwick, David, 55, 105.
Bostwick, Ebenezer, 24, 55, 73, 105, 163, 235, 261.
Bostwick, Jonathan, 206.
Bostwick, Jos., 106.
Bostwick, Oliver, 55, 101.
Bostwick, Salmon, 227.
Bostwick, Shedrick, 203.
Bostwick, Solomon, 105.
Bostwick, William, 122.
Bosworth, Aaron, 131.
Bosworth, Daniel, 54, 73, 130.
Bosworth, Jacob, 130, 313, 330.
Botchford, Joel, 7.
Botsford, Abel, 154.
Botsford, Clement, 8.
Botsford, Elijah, 154.
Botsford, Jabez, 8.
Botsford, Jack, 154.
Botsford, Joel, 24, 123, 154, 162, 234.
Botsford, John, 8, 154.
Botsfords, Elijah, 162.
Botsfords, Jabez, 162.
Bottom, 159, 224.
Bottom, Darius, 201.
Bottom, Jabez, 199, 224.
Bottom, John, 24, 53, 235.
Bottom, Joshua, 147.
Boudish, Asa, 214.
Boughton, John, 335.
Bourn, Rawswold, 140.
Bourns, William, 66.
Bourougs, Josiah, 210.
Bourrows, Zebulon, 249.
Bouten, David, 24, 108.
Bouten, John, 109.

Bouten, Joseph, Jr., 111.
Bouten, Simeon, 108.
Boutin, Hezekiah, 283.
Bouton, Eleazor, 8.
Bouton, John, 24, 165.
Bowdish, Asa, 78, 219.
Bowdish, Joseph, 12.
Bowdril, Barzil, 74.
Bowe, Thadias, 193.
Bowen, 133.
Bowen, Azias, 341.
Bowen, Daniel, 86.
Bowen, John, 134.
Bowen, Michael, 98.
Bowers, Benajah, 22, 65, 164, 240.
Bowers, Benjamin, 22, 64, 164, 240.
Bowers, Ephraim, 22, 65, 164, 240, 261, 353.
Bowers, Joab, 353.
Bowers, Zepheniah, 79.
Bowing, Michael, 68.
Bowman, Frederic, 47, 351.
Bowman, Robert, 118.
Bowton, Azer, 349.
Boyd, James, 295.
Boyd, Joseph, 198, 224.
Boydon, Elhanon, 292.
Boyinton, Joseph, 114.
Brace, David, 18.
Bracket, Benajah, 334.
Bracket, Hezekiah, 164, 341.
Brackitt, Hezekiah, 73.
Bradford, 88.
Bradford, Josiah, 363.
Bradford, Thomas, 363.
Bradley, 55, 78, 80, 151, 227.
Bradley, Allen, 256.
Bradley, Ashbel, 69.
Bradley, Asa, 4.
Bradley, D., 206.
Bradley, Dan, 338.
Bradley, Daniel, 22, 67, 164, 230, 261, 293, 303, 308, 337.
Bradley, David, 4, 341.
Bradley, Elijah, 12.
Bradley, Eliphalet, 22, 67, 98, 165, 233, 355.
Bradley, Elisha, 4.
Bradley, James, 78.
Bradley, Jehiel, 61, 100, 339.
Bradley, Joseph, 4.
Bradley, Justice, 4.
Bradley, Nathan, 22, 67, 98, 165, 233.
Bradley, Oliver, 22.
Bradley, Onesimas, 4.

Bradley, Phil., 234.
Bradley, Philip B., 22, 165, 202, 203, 204, 205, 206.
Bradley, Samuel, 4, 204, 222.
Bradley, Zuar, 61, 99, 284.
Bradly, 151.
Bradly, Ashbil, 52.
Bradly, Charls, 151.
Bradly, Daniel, 83.
Bradly, James, 227.
Bradly, Josiah, 18.
Bradly, Oliver, 229.
Bradly, Reuben, 18, 186.
Bradshaw, William, 103.
Bragg, Ebenezer, 5.
Brainard, 88.
Brainard, Gideon, 3.
Brainard, Jonah, 3.
Brainard, Othniel, 65, 353.
Brainerd, Aaron, 5.
Brainerd, David, 6.
Brainerd, Reuben, 6.
Brainerd, Thomas, 6.
Brainerd, Timothy, 51, 70.
Brainord, Encrease, 23, 240.
Braizier, William, 95.
Branard, Othniel, 334.
Branch, 147, 158, 223.
Branch, Joseph, 75, 335.
Branch, Moses, 362, 363.
Branch, William, 74.
Brand, James, 286.
Brandon, Charles, 22, 131.
Brandum, Charles, 236.
Branford, 1, 22, 28, 29, 30, 32, 36, 39, 42, 43, 150, 164, 167, 168, 170, 172, 173, 175, 177, 179, 213, 228, 231, 261, 262, 264, 265, 266, 267, 268, 269, 270, 271, 302, 366.
Brath, Jonas, 7.
Braughton, John, 12.
Bray, John, 139, 291.
Braymon, Daniel, 190, 210.
Braymon, James, 312.
Brayzer, Benjamin, 58.
Breck, John, 54.
Breed, Jabez, 183.
Brewer, Benjamin, 81.
Brewer, Daniel, 23, 70, 164, 186, 237, 258, 261.
Brewer, Daniel, Jr., 226.
Brewer, Joseph, 242, 346.
Brewer, Thomas, 278, 320, 351.
Brewster, 88.
Brewster, Amos, 64, 75.
Brewster, Hez., 165.
Brewster, Hezekiah, 24, 75, 231, 256, 261.

25

Buffington, Benjamin, 137.
Bufinton, Benjamin, 56.
Bugbe, Benjamin, 54, 72, 218.
Bugbe, John, 24, 54, 55, 72, 130, 163, 219.
Bugbee, Abijah, 133.
Bugbee, Benjamin, 49, 66.
Bugbee, John, 183, 236, 261, 282.
Bugbee, Pelatiah, 260, 280.
Bugbee, Peter, 189.
Bugbee, Samuel, 56, 77, 138.
Buird, Joseph, 216.
Bulford, John, 61, 100.
Bulkley, Abraham, 361.
Bulkley, Calvin, 282.
Bulkley, Charles, 252.
Bulkley, Edward, 164, 248, 249, 303, 308.
Bulkley, Job, 279.
Bulkley, Nathan, Jr., 68.
Bulkley, Seth, 68, 95, 165.
Bulkley, William, 361.
Bull, Epaphras, 237, 261, 354.
Bull, Eppiphras, 23, 163.
Bull, John, 23.
Bullen, David, 328.
Bullen, David, Jr., 49, 66.
Buller, Asa, 57.
Buller, Benjamin, 57, 59.
Buller, Solomon, 6.
Buller, Zebulon, 190.
Bullin, Benjamin, 82.
Bullin, David, 305, 350.
Bullock, Jonathan, 46, 56, 77, 131, 138, 301, 308, 334.
Bunc, Thomas, 348.
Bunce, Asa, 52, 70, 194, 226.
Bunce, Isaiah, 55, 74, 106, 163, 236.
Bunce, Jared, 245, 318, 335, 348.
Bunday, Joshua, 78.
Bunday, William, 102.
Bunde, Simeon, 128.
Bundy, Nathaniel, 135.
Bundy, Thomas, 78.
Bunn, Paul, 6.
Bunnal, Amos, 86, 350.
Bunnel, Abraham, 2, 22.
Bunnel, Amos, 261, 276.
Bunnel, John, 2.
Bunnel, Joseph, 309, 334.
Bunnel, Levi, 60.
Bunnell, Abraham, 164.
Bunnil, Abraham, 231.
Bunnil, Samuel, 14.
Buns, Isaiah, Sr., 24.
Buns, Isaiah, Jr., 24.

Buntin, William, 60.
Bunts, Josiah, 235.
Burchard, Daniel, 11.
Burchard, Elias, 356.
Burchard, Roger, 196.
Burden, Benjamin, 13.
Burden, Samuel, 65, 132.
Burdges, Lott, 191.
Burdon, Samuel, 286.
Burdsey, Thedeous, 199.
Burdseye, Thads, 199.
Burge, Hosea, 140, 247.
Burges, Asa, 19.
Burges, Charles, 363.
Burges, Edward, 186, 305, 330, 354.
Burges, Ephraim, 261, 279, 311, 350.
Burges, Ephraim, Jr., 279.
Burges, Joseph, 362.
Burges, Samuel, 275.
Burgess, Ephraim, 344.
Burgh, Jared, 196.
Burghes, Edward, 315.
Burk, Elackander, 73.
Burk, George, 226.
Burk, John, 24, 164, 231, 261.
Burley, Aseph, 192, 226.
Burley, John, 116.
Burlington, 228.
Burn, Benjamin, 73.
Burn, Thomas, 81.
Burnal, Amos, 134.
Burnam, Asa, 10.
Burnam, David, 186.
Burnam, Elijah, 146.
Burnam, Jesse, 357.
Burnam, John, 68, 84.
Burnam, Joseph, 232.
Burnam, Nathan, 84.
Burnam, William, 357.
Burnan, Zeanas, 185.
Burnap, Benjamin, 24, 84, 165, 236, 355.
Burnap, Calvin, 85.
Burnap, James, 84.
Burnap, John, 362.
Burnel, Samuel, 361.
Burnet, James, 128.
Burnett, Dennis, 208.
Burnham, 88.
Burnham, Asa, 71, 77, 232, 235.
Burnham, Benjamin, 289.
Burnham, Eliphalet, 342.
Burnham, John, 50, 242, 366.
Burnham, Joseph, 260.
Burnham, Josiah, 64, 85, 128, 157.

Burnham, Stephen, 226.
Burnham, William, 87.
Burnham, Zenas, 226.
Burningham, Anthony, 199.
Burns, James, 121.
Burns, John, 87, 100.
Burns, Jules, 66.
Burns, Julius, 132.
Burns, William, 132, 311.
Burnside, Henry, 78.
Burnum, Asa, 23.
Burnum, Joseph, 23.
Burr, Andrew, 1.
Burr, Daniel, 22, 67, 95, 233.
Burr, David, 3ᵈ, 3.
Burr, Edmund, 367.
Burr, G., 95.
Burr, Jehiel, 203.
Burr, Seth, 274.
Burr, Stephen, 52, 69.
Burr, Zebinah, 11.
Burras, Hubbard, 332.
Burras, William, 344.
Burrell, Thomas, 332.
Burret, Abijah, 89.
Burret, Israel, 154.
Burrill, Joseph, 11.
Burrit, Charles, 66.
Burrit, Israel, 119.
Burrit, Zalmon, 214, 222.
Burritt, Charles, 58, 94.
Burritt, Isael, 8.
Burroos, Zebulon, 48.
Burros, Jonathan, 12.
Burroughs, 92.
Burroughs, Samuel, 164.
Burrows, Hubbard, 281, 316, 332.
Burrows, J. Procter, 81.
Burrows, Joseph, 318.
Burrows, Josiah, 234.
Burrus, John Proct, 59.
Burrus, Josiah, 24.
Burrus, William, 287, 311.
Burt, John, 362.
Durt, Josiah, 54, 73, 129.
Burt, William, 370.
Burton, Abel, 251.
Burton, Daniel, 193.
Burton, Henry, 15.
Burton, Isaac, 15.
Burton, Jacob, 10, 77.
Burton, Luis, 210.
Burton, Nathan, 15.
Burton, Robert, 104.
Bush, Asael, 368.
Bush, John, 136.
Bush, Samuel, 114, 322, 341.

Bushnal, Daniel, 23.
Bushnal, Ruben, 300.
Bushnel, Chester, 300.
Bushnel, Constant, 261, 300.
Bushnel, Daniel, 6.
Bushnell, Constant, 279.
Bushnell, Daniel, 71, 256, 261, 308, 335.
Bushnell, Francis, 361.
Bushnell, James, 361.
Bushnell, Reuben, 279.
Bushnell, Zebulon, 279.
Bushnul, Daniel, 236.
Butlar, John, 13.
Butler, Asa, 81, 249.
Butler, Benjamin, 1, 49, 66, 81, 139, 350.
Butler, David, 280, 346.
Butler, Ely, 7.
Butler, Ezekiel, 340.
Butler, Isaac, 209.
Butler, Isaiah, Jr., 6.
Butler, Israel, 57, 81.
Butler, John, 22, 121, 140, 162, 237, 290, 360.
Butler, Jonathan, 71, 79, 252.
Butler, Matthew, 2.
Butler, Peter, 22, 65, 164, 240, 250.
Butler, Solomon, 6.
Butler, Stephen, 22, 67, 79, 182, 232, 252, 305, 328.
Butler, Walter, 1, 22.
Butler, Walton, 234.
Butler, William, 6, 9, 260, 282, 332.
Butler, Zebulon, 185, 186, 187, 188, 189, 190.
Butlor, Benjamin, 208.
Buts, James, 237.
Butt, 156, 223.
Butt, Josiah, 319, 336.
Buttan, Danil, 197.
Buttock, Jonathan, 273.
Buttolph, Daniel, 11.
Buttolph, Joel, 145.
Button, Joshua, 186.
Button, Josiah, 186.
Butts, Esaias, 312, 344.
Butts, Josiah, 363.
Butts, Sherebiah, 146.
Byington, Benjamin, 112.
Byington, Isaac, 49.
Byintun, Ebenezer, 2.
Byintun, Jonathan, 2.
Byne, Jeremiah, 89.
Byshup, David, 154.

Carlton, Darius, 12.
Carlton, John, 12.
Carlton, Richard, 12, 66, 82, 132.
Carmon, John, 222.
Carpenter, 370.
Carpenter, Allen, 84.
Carpenter, Comfort, 12.
Carpenter, David, 179, 218.
Carpenter, Elias, 285, 311, 328.
Carpenter, Elijah, 133.
Carpenter, Eliphalet, 215, 285, 311, 344.
Carpenter, Henry, 136, 149, 160.
Carpenter, John, 18.
Carpenter, Joshua, 139, 256.
Carpenter, Nathan, 84.
Carpenter, Noah, 133, 218.
Carpenter, Samuel, 294.
Carpentor, Comfort, 183.
Carpentor, Henry, 82.
Carpinter, Elias, 306.
Carr, Clement, 273.
Carr, Ebenezer, 273, 338.
Carr, James, 75.
Carr, James Miller, 231.
Carr, Robert, 278, 347.
Carr, Ruben, 299.
Carr, William, 341.
Carr, William, Jr., 66.
Carrel, Joseph, 136.
Carrell, John, 262, 349.
Carril, John, 166.
Carril, Nathaniel, 137.
Carrill, John, 355.
Carrior, John, 221.
Carry, George, 353.
Cart, William, 56, 77.
Carter, Aaron, 25, 65, 166, 240, 262, 353, 355.
Carter, Asher, 47.
Carter, Daniel, 53.
Carter, Edward, 25, 166, 240, 262, 351.
Carter, Enoch, 63.
Carter, Esau, 351.
Carter, Heman, 282.
Carter, J., 106.
Carter, James, 25, 237.
Carter, John, Jr., 277, 281.
Carter, Jonah, 273.
Carter, Nathan, 263, 275.
Carter, Reuben, 25, 64, 146, 157, 166, 237, 262, 343.
Carter, Thadeous, 13.
Carter, William, 3.
Cartwright, Cyrus, 56.
Carver, John, 296.

Carver, Joseph, 1.
Carver, Nathaniel, 19.
Carwin, Sclah, 166.
Cary, Benjamin, 199.
Cary, Benjamin, Jr., 85, 128.
Cary, Ebenezer, 218.
Cary, Ezra, 149.
Cary, George, 166.
Cary, Hezekiah, 85, 246, 321, 338.
Cary, Jabez, 180.
Cary, Levi, 85.
Cary, Nathaniel, Jr., 54, 73, 129.
Cary, Oliver, 85.
Case, Aaron, 364.
Case, Abel, 349.
Case, Abraham, Jr., 11.
Case, Amasa, Jr., 143.
Case, Amos, 145.
Case, Asa, 144.
Case, Caleb, 204.
Case, Elisha, 81.
Case, Ezekiel, 14.
Case, Ezekil, Jr., 86.
Case, Ichabod, 315, 331.
Case, Jeremiah, 262, 275, 349.
Case, Jonah, 139.
Case, Jonathan, 276.
Case, Joseph Wain, 142.
Case, Judah, 204.
Case, Lemuel, 139.
Case, Lumey, 73, 130.
Case, Lummin, 54.
Case, Martin, 10.
Case, Micah, 11.
Case, Nehemiah, 59.
Case, Oliver, 10.
Case, Pliney, 11.
Case, Reuben, 143.
Case, Richard, 26, 70, 165, 237, 262, 342, 345.
Case, Ros, 144.
Case, Roswell, 204.
Case, Rufus, 143.
Case, William, 11.
Casey, John, 302.
Cash, 139.
Cass, Jeremy, 299.
Cass, Silas G., 319.
Caswell, Ezra, 263.
Caswell, Ezrael, 140.
Catlin, Abraham, 6.
Catlin, Eli, 6, 55.
Catlin, Elisha, 319, 337.
Catlin, Hezekiah, 278, 318, 336.
Catlin, Putnam, 53.
Catlin, Roswell, 71, 213.
Catling, Aling, 187.

Cato, 284.
Caverle, Samuel, 366.
Cay, David, 154.
Ceabury, James, 340.
Ceaser, 58.
Ceaser, Negro, 12.
Cebra, James, 73.
Center, John, 183.
Cesar, 56, 141.
Chace, Benjamin, 362.
Chace, Joseph, 65.
Chadwick, James, 52, 70, 242, 306, 316, 332, 345.
Chadwick, John, 26.
Chadwick, Nathan, 287.
Chadwick, William, 243.
Chafe, Cyrus, 130.
Chafe, Serel, 18.
Chafee, Abiel, 272.
Chafee, Calvin, 294.
Chafee, James, Jr., 134.
Chafee, William, 195.
Chaffe, Abiel, 194.
Chaffe, Calvin, 306.
Chaffe, Charles, 194.
Chaffee, Abial, 292, 325, 326.
Chaffee, Calvin, 316, 326, 328.
Chaffee, Samuel, 183.
Chamberlane, Ephriam, 165.
Chaimberlane, Luther, 54.
Chaimberlen, Luther, 130.
Chaimberlen, Seth, 130.
Chaise, Walter, 85.
Chalker, Isaac, 5.
Chalker, Jesse, 79, 252.
Chalman, Reuben, 273.
Chamberlain, 209.
Chamberlain, Eph, 292.
Chamberlain, Ephraim, 82, 230, 262.
Chamberlain, Jeremiah, 352.
Chamberlain, Jeret, 305.
Chamberlain, Joseph, 352.
Chamberlain, Samuel, 104.
Chamberlain, Swift, 285.
Chamberlain, Theodore, 52, 70, 346.
Chamberlin, Aaron, 87, 197.
Chamberlin, Bartlet, 364.
Chamberlin, Ephraim, 13, 26.
Chamberlin, Esre, 133.
Chamberlin, Jeremiah, 317.
Chamberlin, Jirah, 364.
Chamberlin, Joseph, 336.
Chambers, John, 78.
Chambers, William, 25, 63, 236.
Champen, Samuel, 150.

Champhilet, Stanliff, 203.
Champion, 145.
Champlin, Joseph S., 286.
Chandler, 46, 135, 359.
Chandler, Isaac, 86, 241.
Chandler, James, 181, 218.
Chandler, Joseph, 25, 66, 166, 240.
Chandler, Robert, 86, 134, 309, 334.
Chanler, 150.
Chapel, Curtis, 336.
Chapel, Guy, 181.
Chapel, Russell, 76, 263.
Chapel, Stephen, 216.
Chapel, William, 3d, 360.
Chapell, Roswel, 351.
Chapen, Asa, 203.
Chapen, Ezra, 63.
Chapen, Hiel, 63.
Chapens, Daniel, 18.
Chapin, David, 250.
Chapin, Ichabud, 209.
Chapin, Jehiel, 247.
Chapin, Oliver, 18.
Chapin, Phinehas, 243.
Chapin, Timothy, 243.
Chapin, Tomo, 48.
Chapman, 80, 203, 206.
Chapman, Abner, 56, 77, 87, 138.
Chapman, Adi, 290.
Chapman, Adino, 319.
Chapman, Adrin, 319.
Chapman, Albert, 67, 165.
Chapman, Amos, 159.
Chapman, Benjamin, 214.
Chapman, Cesar, 51, 70, 353.
Chapman, Collaris, 153.
Chapman, Collins, 25, 47, 124, 165, 234.
Chapman, Comfort, 272, 311, 344.
Chapman, Constant, 79, 279, 335.
Chapman, Cornelus, 300.
Chapman, Dan, 79, 150.
Chapman, Dan[ ], 25.
Chapman, Daniel, 232.
Chapman, David, 47, 69, 151, 212.
Chapman, Ebenezer, 322.
Chapman, Edward, 262, 287, 354.
Chapman, Elijah, 81, 103.
Chapman, Elisha, 153.
Chapman, Elius, 131.
Chapman, Gideon, 47.
Chapman, James, 67, 165.
Chapman, Jediah, Jr., 79.
Chapman, Jeremiah, 1, 342.
Chapman, John, 25.
Chapman, Jonathan, 158.

Chapman, Joseph, 25, 74, 142, 165, 197, 231, 262.
Chapman, N., 102.
Chapman, Nathaniel, 281.
Chapman, Oliver, 183.
Chapman, Reuben, 4.
Chapman, Rufus, 262.
Chapman, Samuel, 3, 97, 340, 352.
Chapman, Stephen, 49.
Chapman, Stephen, Jr., 347.
Chapman, Thomas, 219, 227.
Chapman, Timothy, 58, 353.
Chapman, William, 79, 252.
Chapman, Zachh, 179.
Chapmon, Elijah, 12.
Chappee, Steaphen, 356.
Chappel, Alpheus, 359.
Chappel, Amaziah, 26, 139, 237, 248.
Chappel, Benjamin, 359.
Chappel, Bruister, 140.
Chappel, Comfort, 26.
Chappel, Curtice, 26, 78.
Chappel, Curtis, 234, 262, 359.
Chappel, Joshua, 26.
Chappel, Noah, 369.
Chappel, Roswel, 87.
Chappel, Rufas, 358.
Chappel, Solomon, 63.
Chappel, William, 359.
Chappel. William 3d, 26.
Chappell, Alpheus, 290.
Chappell, Benjamin, Jr., 290.
Chappell, Brewster, 256.
Chappell, Noah, 65, 290.
Chappell, William, 290.
Chapple, Noah, 132.
Chappman, Amos, 256.
Chaps, John, 92.
Chard, Joseph, 8.
Chard, Samuel, 8.
Charter, Levi, 48, 86.
Chase, Aaron, 240.
Chase, Jared, 8.
Chase, Lot, 76, 147, 159.
Chase, Samuel, 188.
Chase, Walter, 26, 70, 127, 240.
Chatfield, Caleb, 2, 58, 91.
Chatfield, Dan, 273.
Chatfield, John, 53, 72, 166, 262.
Chatfield, Jonathan, 212.
Chatfield, Josiah, 300.
Chatfield, Josiah, 2d, 281.
Chatfield, Lemuel, 210.
Chatfield, Levi, 48.
Chatfield, Oliver, 2.
Chatham, 22, 25, 29, 30, 32, 34, 36,
38, 39, 41, 42, 43, 64, 88, 164, 166, 167, 168, 171, 172, 173, 175, 176, 193, 213, 215, 240, 248, 249, 250, 261, 262, 264, 266, 267, 268, 269, 270, 271, 284, 286, 302, 353, 355, 367.
Chatman, Timothy, 91.
Cheapeak, Simon, 68.
Chedsey, William, 208.
Cheem, Joseph, 323.
Cheeney, Ebenezer, 237.
Cheeney, Joseph, 284.
Cheese, Samuel, 272, 292, 334.
Cheets, Isaac, 130.
Cheilds, Joseph, 365.
Cheney, Aseal, 193.
Cheney, Daniel, 203.
Cheney, Ebenezer, 25, 77, 131, 138, 166.
Cheney, Elijah, 56, 77, 137.
Cheney, John, 56, 77, 137.
Cheney, Joseph, 323.
Cheney, Richard, 25, 165, 235, 355.
Cheshire, Joseph, 114.
Cheshire, 164, 170, 172, 176, 196, 197, 207, 261, 267, 271, 275.
Chester, Christopher, 50, 69.
Chester, David, 285, 323, 341.
Chester, Jones, 300.
Chester, Lemuel, 51, 69.
Chester, 171.
Chidsey, Ephraim, 1.
Chidsey, Roswell, 1.
Child, Josiah, 136.
Child, Josiah D., 292.
Child, Pennel, 71.
Child, Penuel, 135.
Child, Stephen, 285.
Childs, Harbe, 295.
Childs, Josiah D., 272.
Childs, Stephen, 318, 336.
Chilson, Jonathan, 13, 362.
Chipman, John, 165, 262.
Chipman, Thomas, 78.
Chipman, Timothy, 65.
Chipman, Jonathan, 147.
Chittenden, Benjamin, 13.
Chittenden, Cornelius, 273.
Chittenden, Daniel, 215.
Chittenden, Daniel Jr., 5.
Chittenden, Eber, 53.
Chittenden, Gideon, 2.
Chittenden, James, 52, 72.
Chittenden, Jared, 5, 51.
Chittenden, John, 53, 72.
Chittenden, Nathaniel, 281, 300.
Chittenden, Reuben, 52, 72.

Crampton, Benjamin, 51.
Crampton, Calvin, 51.
Cramton, Nathaniel, 209.
Cran, Amon, 162.
Cran, Ruben, 162.
Crandal, Abel, 81.
Crandal, Asa, 359.
Crandal, John, 81.
Crandel, Abel, 59.
Crandel, Christopher, 217.
Crandell, Edward, 284.
Crandol, John, 139.
Crane, Amarah, 72.
Crane, Amariah, 54, 129.
Crane, Curtice, 26.
Crane, Curtis, 165, 238, 254, 262, 324, 348.
Crane, Daniel, 52, 70.
Crane, Elihu, 210.
Crane, Elijah, 7.
Crane, Enos, 66.
Crane, Ezra, 212.
Crane, James, 275, 310, 343.
Crane, Joel, 53, 72.
Crane, John, 52, 72, 231.
Crane, Jonathan, 46, 131.
Crane, Nathaniel, 52, 72, 212.
Crane, Roger, 297.
Cranton, Thomas, 297.
Crary, Richard, 26, 166, 238.
Crary, William, 148.
Craw, Ammon, 202.
Craw, Haman, 121.
Craw, Jacob, 202.
Craw, Reuben, 53, 121.
Crawferd, Jason, 86.
Crawfoot, John, 90.
Crawford, Jason, 134.
Crawford, John, 58.
Crawford, Newton, 113.
Crawford, William, 123, 154.
Creamer, Michael, 366.
Cree, Reubin, 331.
Cremer, John, 277.
Crissey, Truman, 100.
Crittenden, Gideon, 26, 239, 252.
Crittendon, Gideon, 166.
Crocker, Grace, 262.
Crocker, John, 279, 349, 365.
Crocker, Rozwel, 76.
Crocker, Samuel, 357.
Crofford, Jason, 46.
Cromwell. Prince, 123.
Crosbey, Richard, 218.
Crosby, Levi, 3.
Crosby, Michel, 136.
Crosby, Obed, 6, 71.

Crosby, Parson, 214.
Crosby, Richard, 182.
Crosby, Simon, 53.
Crosby, Timothy, 369.
Crosby, David, 345.
Cross, Jonathan, 18.
Cross, Joseph, 57, 81.
Cross, Nero, 290, 291.
Crossman, John, 96.
Croswell, Mark, 12, 82, 148, 160.
Crovel, Enoch, 287.
Crow, Amon, 222.
Crow, Edward, 285.
Crow, Elias, 86.
Crow, Jacob, 222.
Crow, Shubael, 278.
Crowel, Enoch, 190.
Crowel, Manoah, 185.
Crowell, Edward, 7.
Crowell, Levi, 243.
Crowell, Solomon, 7.
Crowfoot, Samuel, 124.
Crudock, William, 117.
Crutie, Jonathan, 321.
Cruttenden, Gilbert, 4.
Cruttenden, Jason, 207.
Cruttenden, Jedidiah, 4.
Cruttenden, Salmon, 4.
Cruttenden, Zebulon, 5.
Cruttondon, Samuel, 212.
Cubb, William, 301.
Cuff, Abel, 58.
Cuff, Cato, 281.
Cuff, Samson, 281, 348.
Cuffe, Cato, 180.
Cuggo, 148.
Culbert, Robert, 52, 70.
Culver, Aaron, 25, 63, 64, 236.
Culver, Abel, 53.
Culver, Abraham, 224.
Culver, Daniel, 25.
Culver, David, 25, 214, 238.
Culver, John, 205.
Culver, Moses, 82, 149, 160.
Culver, Samuel, Jr., 14.
Culver, Solomon, 274.
Culver, Timothy, 25, 166, 239, 262, 350.
Cumber, Lemon, 60, 83.
Cumings, Stephen, 296.
Cummes, William, 26, 234.
Cummins, William, 162, 165, 205.
Cummus, Williams, 78.
Cumstalk, Aaron, 110.
Cunnel, Jeremiah, 280.
Cunnell, Jeremiah, 319, 335.
Cunnell, Jeret, 305.

Daset, John, 86.
Daskam, William, 58.
Daskim, William, 322.
Daskin, William, 337.
Daton, Ezekiel, 116.
Daton, Israel, 13, 27.
Daton, Richard, 27, 68.
Dauset, John, 330.
Davel, John, 27.
Davenport, Bernard, 106.
Davenport, Esquier, 282.
Davenport, John, 61, 95, 99.
Davenport, Richard, 66.
Davenport, Stephen, 109, 114.
Davenport, Thomas, 106.
Daverson, Benjamin, 227.
Daverson, Ezra, 301.
Davice, Martin, 81.
Davice, William, 14, 49.
David, Sill, 232.
Davidson, Ezra, 273.
Davidson, Isaac, 73, 166, 231.
Davidson, John, 153, 236.
Davidson, Robert, 355.
Davies, Joseph, 313.
Davies, Josiah, 65.
Davinson, Isaac, 27.
Davinson, John, 27.
Davinson, Peter, 129.
Davinson, Robert, 27.
Davinson, William, 27.
Davis, Amos, 2, 13, 66, 198, 284.
Davis, Burden, 348.
Davis, Daniel, 27, 68, 167, 232, 252, 263, 285, 358.
Davis, David, 288.
Davis, Ebenezer, 27, 167, 238, 255.
Davis, Elijah, 356.
Davis, Ezekiel, 275, 349.
Davis, Isaac, 27, 115, 234.
Davis, Jacob, 80, 349.
Davis, Jacob, Jr., 10.
Davis, Jacob, 3d, 145.
Davis, James, 27, 124, 154, 167, 229, 263.
Davis, Jobe, 203.
Davis, Joel, 183, 219, 356.
Davis, John, 81.
Davis, Jonathan, 27, 84, 129, 166, 263.
Davis, Jonn, 230.
Davis, Joseph, 263, 286, 313, 330.
Davis, Joshua, 54, 129.
Davis, Josiah, 353.
Davis, Justin, 350.
Davis, Lathrop, 76, 140.
Davis, Lemuel, 18.

Davis, Martin, 59.
Davis, Robert, 68.
Davis, Samuel, 18, 182, 368.
Davis, Stephen, 27, 84, 230.
Davis, Stephen Ben, 285.
Davis, Thomas, 60.
Davis, Thomas Justus, 49, 66.
Davis, William, 50, 68, 76, 336.
Davison, Asa, 46, 131.
Davison, Benjamin, 297.
Davison, David, 279, 291, 301.
Davison, Isaac, 263.
Davison, John, 263, 297.
Davison, Paul, 46, 277.
Davison, Robert, 167, 232.
Davison, William, 131, 166.
Davisson, Daniel, 198.
Davol, John, 233.
Dawner, Caleb, 27.
Dawner, Ezra, 27.
Dawns, Benjamin, 121.
Dawns, John, 263.
Day, David, 95, 148, 160.
Day, Horriss, 207.
Day, Isaac, 59.
Day, Joseph, 52, 70, 258, 320, 337, 345.
Day, Nathan, 195.
Day, Solomon, 221.
Day, Wastebrook, 238.
Day, Westbrook, 27, 257.
Dayley, James, 263.
Dayton, Israel, 167, 229.
Dayton, Richard, 232.
Deains, Levi, 76.
Dealing, Samuel, 27, 195, 238.
Dean, 98.
Dean, Benjamin, 92.
Dean, Bradley, 98.
Dean, James L., 288.
Dean, Jeremiah, 120, 162.
Dean, Levy, 128, 196.
Dean, Samuel, 207.
Dean, Solomon, Jr., 132.
Dean, William, 357.
Deane, Jonathan, 274.
Deane, Thomas, 201.
Deans, David, 220.
Deans, Levi, 85.
Deaolph, Amasa, 138.
Deates, Samuel, 76.
Deathic, Ephraim, Jr., 47.
Deavenport, Richard, Jr., 132.
Debble, Martin, 361.
Defloris, Anthony, 281.
De Floris, Anthony, 329.
De Floris, see Floris.

26

Dickinson, Jesse, 58.
Dickinson, Waitstill, 250, 331.
Dickison, Jesse, 187.
Dicks, David, 313, 330.
Dickson, George, 263.
Dickson, John, 113.
Dickson, Joseph, 4.
Dickson, Miles, 94.
Die, Daniel, 27, 235.
Diggins, Benjamin, 183.
Dike, 135.
Dikeman, Daniel, 119.
Dikeman, Frederick, 118.
Dikeman, Jonathan, 119.
Dileno, Jonathan, 132.
Dill, Martin, 205.
Dillaba, George, 59.
Dillabur, George, 82.
Dillaby, George, 280.
Dilyno, Aaron, 190.
Dimick, Joseph, 84, 239, 282.
Dimmick, Amasa, 285.
Dimmick, Benjamin, 304, 310.
Dimmick, Jeduthan, 183.
Dimmick, John, 18.
Dimmick, Joseph, 263.
Dimmick, Phillip, 183.
Dimmick, Shoball, 81.
Dimmick, Solomon, 183.
Dimmick, Timothy, 180.
Dimmock, Benjamin, 131.
Dimmock, Elias, 131.
Dimmok, Joseph, 27.
Dimmuck, Benjamin, 46.
Dimmuck, Elias, 46.
Dimmock, Moon, 298.
Dimmuck, Simeon, 18.
Dimmuk, Amasa, 354.
Dimock, Ebenezer, 369.
Dimock, Edward, 12.
Dimock, Shubal, 59.
Dimok, Jeduthan, 219.
Dimon, Gold, 98.
Dimon, John, 27.
Dimon, Moses, 4, 27, 96, 233.
Dinah, James, 336.
Dingley, John, 226, 288.
Dingly, John, 343.
Dire, Benjamin, 305.
Disberow, Simon, 67.
Disborough, Henry, 67,
Disborough, Joshua, 27, 233.
Disborough, Justus, 27, 233.
Disborow, Joshua, 67, 167.
Disborow, Justice, 67.
Disborow, Justin, 167.
Disbrow, Caleb, 274.

Disbrow, Henry, 96.
Disbrow, Isaac, 96.
Disbrow, Joshua, 96.
Disbrow, Justin, 96.
Disbrow, Russell, 4.
Disbrow, Simon, 4, 96.
Diteman, Fradrick, 153.
Diteman, Jon[n], 154.
Dix, Benjamin, 246, 305, 328, 348.
Dixon, David, 61, 103, 335.
Dixon, George, 27, 54, 234.
Dixon, James, 64, 148, 285, 292.
Dixon, Jared, 61, 103.
Dixon, John, 305, 328.
Dixon, Joseph, 104.
Dixon, Miles, 58.
Dixson, 225.
Dixson, David, 217.
Dixson, James, 147.
Dixson, John, 148.
Dixson, R., 160.
Dixson, Robert, 149.
Doan, Prince, 79.
Doane, Ephraim, 287.
Doane, Joel, 279.
Doane, Josiah, 287.
Doane, Richard, 279.
Dochester, Alexander, 249.
Dodg, Daniel, 27.
Dodg, James, 133.
Dodg, Nathan, 27.
Dodg, William, 54, 73, 129.
Dodge, 162.
Dodge, Benjamin, 263, 286, 330, 351.
Dodge, Daniel, 232.
Dodge, Elihu, 263, 283, 351.
Dodge, Israel, 59, 64, 75, 83, 158, 338.
Dodge, James, 47.
Dodge, Jeriel, 64.
Dodge, Peregreen, 87.
Dodge, Perigree, 83.
Dodge, Reuben, 278, 316, 332, 353.
Dodge, Seth, 280, 316, 332, 353.
Dody, Jeriel, 147, 158.
Doel, Shem, 61.
Dog, Amos, 356.
Doghardy, Andrew, 113.
Dolittle, Joel, 336.
Donatis, Francis, 167.
Done, Israel, 361.
Done, Joel, 300.
Done, Richard, 300.
Donity, Francis, 75.
Donnety, 63.
Donvon, Daniel, 147.

Egelston, Timothy, 86.
Egelstone, David, 81.
Eggleston, Benedick, 325.
Eggleston, Benidict, 281.
Eggleston, David, 275, 299.
Eggleston, James, 276, 299, 325.
Egleston, Benedick, 339.
Egleston, David, 263, 349.
Egleston, Eliab, 286.
Egleston, James, 339, 348.
Egleston, Jones, 339.
Egleston, Joseph, 348.
Elderkin, 19.
Elderkin, Diariah, 50.
Elderkin, Diarka, 68.
Elderkin, Diureha, 243.
Elderkin, Elemoth, 291.
Elderkin, Elimath, 278.
Elderkin, James, 273.
Elderken, Vine, 28.
Eldredg, John, 54, 72.
Eldredg, Jonothan, 130.
Eldridge, Samuel, 263, 278, 353.
Eldridge, William, 190, 285, 350.
Eldrig, Robart, 294.
Eldrige, Daniel, 46.
Eldrige, William, 221.
Eley, Daniel, 14.
Elie, Caleb, 300.
Elies, Nathan, 78.
Eliot, Thomas, 135.
Elis, Jonas, 336.
Elles, J. Bard, 8.
Elles, Nathan, 263.
Ellington, 48.
Ellis, Carpenter, 78, 263.
Ellis, John, 28, 74, 167, 231, 263.
Ellis, John, 3d, 296.
Ellis, Jonas, 272.
Ellis, Oliver, 297.
Ellis, Peter, 9.
Ellis, Phenis, 82.
Ellis, Phineas, 160.
Ellis, Samuel, 190.
Ellis, Sawyer, 296.
Ellis, Stephen, 181, 349.
Ellis, William, 214, 226.
Ellot, Richard, 211.
Ells, Edward, 28, 239, 263.
Ellsworth, Benjamin, 325.
Elmer, Calib, 28.
Elmer, Daniel, 28, 79, 119, 154.
Elmer, Daniel, Jr., 57, 80.
Elmer, William, 11, 28, 80.
Elmon, Calib, 167.
Elmor, Phenious, 203.
Elmore, Caleb, 71, 236, 263.

Elmore, Daniel, 167, 336.
Elmore, Joseph, 188.
Elmore, William, 238.
Elmour, Caleb, 280.
Elsworth, Hez, 48.
Elsworth, Benjamin, 190, 287, 339, 350.
Elsworth, Ezra, 350.
Elsworth, John, 180.
Elsworth, Moses, 48, 311, 343, 350.
Elsworth, Stephen, 223.
Elton, William, 205.
Elu, Caleb, 273.
Elwell, Ebenezer, 342.
Elwell, Samuel, 340.
Elwood, Isaac, 67, 96.
Elwood, Joseph, 4, 263, 274.
Elwood, Nathan, 67, 247.
Elwood, Thomas, 3.
Ely, Elisha, 167.
Ely, Gabriel, 3.
Ely, John, 263.
Ely, William, 286.
Emerson, Joseph, 180.
Emerson, Nathaniel, 227.
Emmeson, Nathanael, 78.
Emmit, John, 263.
Emmitt, John, 366.
Emmonds, Jonathan, 206.
Emmons, Noadiah, 3.
Emons, Daniel, 221.
Enfield, 22, 25, 28, 29, 30, 31, 37, 40, 43, 49, 66, 164, 166, 168, 169, 173, 177, 180, 185, 186, 189, 190, 240, 243, 250, 261, 262, 264, 267, 279, 350, 355, 365.
England, 366, 367, 368.
Engle, Joseph, 131.
Eno, David, Jr., 81.
Eno, Elisha, 144.
Eno, Isaac, 144.
Eno, James, 10, 205.
Eno, Joel, 143.
Eno, Levi, 187.
Eno, Samuel, 145.
Eno, William, 227.
Enoe, Joab, 131.
Enos, David, 49, 192, 349, 363.
Enos, David, Jr., 275.
Ensign, James, 194, 226.
Ensign, Otis, 207.
Ensworth, Jedediah, 15, 327.
Ensworth, Jesse, 362.
Ensworth, Joseph, 197.
Ephraim, Joshua, 59, 82.
Erl, James, 49.

Erl, Jams, 66.
Erl, William, 67.
Ervin, William, 56.
Eston, Juline, 330.
Eumun, Stedly, 112.
Eustace, Francis, 101.
Evan, Isaac, 28.
Evans, Abiather, 28, 70, 167, 238,
  310, 343, 345.
Evans, Alexander, 353.
Evans, Allen, 345.
Evans, Benonia, 71.
Evans, Daniel, 86, 134.
Evans, Henry, 28, 167, 238, 345.
Evans, James, 347.
Evans, Joseph, 302.
Evans, Josiah, 345.
Evans, Moses, 345.
Evans, Samuel, Jr., 28, 70, 238.
Evans, Stacy, 342.
Evans, Thomas, 307.
Evarts, Daniel, 78.
Evarts, Jensourah, 53.
Evarts, Reuben, 280.
Evats, Joel, 212.
Evens, 66.
Evens, Abiather, 263.
Evens, Allin, 245.
Evens, Daniel, 228.
Evens, Elijah, 11.
Evens, Henry, 263.
Evens, Isaac, 77, 146, 157.
Evens, Moses, 338.
Evens, Samuel, 132.
Evens, Stephen, 68.
Everest, Benjamin, 227.
Everet, Richard, 108.
Everett, Oliver, 272.
Everit, Eliphalit, 80.
Everit, Oliver, 301.
Everts, Reuben, 332.
Eves, David, 58.
Evett, Daniel, 332.
Evins, Allyn, 305, 328.
Evins, Thomas, 309, 328.
Evis, Daniel, 167.
Evit, Daniel, 317.
Ewen, Edward, Jr., 76.
Ewing, Alexander, 278.
Exton, William, 65.

Fabrique, Abraham, 93.
Fagens, John, 302.
Faggins, John, 332.
Fagins, John, 224, 280, 316.
Fagins, William, 181.
Failor, Stephen, 12.

Faiman, Richard, 29.
Fairbanks, Barachiah, 6.
Fairbanks, Benjamin, 136.
Fairchield, Alexander, 58, 91.
Fairchild, Benjamin, 207.
Fairchild, Clement, 200, 221.
Fairchild, Edmund, 7.
Fairchild, Gershom, 90.
Fairchild, James, Jr., 8.
Fairchild, Jesse, 8.
Fairchild, Joseph, 47.
Fairchild, Nathan, 202.
Fairchild, Peter, 154.
Fairchild, Samuel, 104.
Fairchild, Sherman, 202.
Fairfield, 3, 21, 22, 25, 27, 28, 29,
  30, 31, 32, 33, 34, 35, 36, 37, 38,
  40, 41, 43, 67, 92, 94, 95, 96, 97,
  98, 125, 126, 151, 163, 165, 167,
  168, 169, 171, 172, 174, 176, 188,
  189, 191, 197, 202, 203, 209, 214,
  226, 228, 233, 262, 263, 264,
  265, 266, 267, 268, 270, 271, 274,
  276, 288, 289, 291, 302, 355, 365,
  367.
Fairfield Co., 233.
Fairman, Daniel, 363.
Fairman, Elezar, 136.
Fairman, Henry, 8.
Fairman, John, 12.
Fairman, Richard, 67.
Fairweather, Samuel, 123.
Fairweather, Zalmon, 200.
Falkner, Aaron, 146.
Falkner, Nicholus, 223.
Fallandon, John, 230.
Fallows, Isaac, 12.
Fancher, Rufus, 53.
Faning, Elisha, 232, 257.
Fanning, 88.
Fanning, Charles, 28, 74, 168, 231,
  263.
Fanning, David, 51, 69.
Fanning, Elisha, 28, 69, 168.
Fanning, Frederick, 51, 69, 76.
Fanning, John, 74.
Fanning, Nathan, 51, 69.
Fanning, Thomas, 51, 69.
Fanning, Walter, 9.
Fanton, Hezekiah, 97.
Fanton, John, 294.
Fareweather, Samuel, 154.
Fargo, Aaron, 48.
Fargo, Samuel, 280, 318, 336.
Fargo, William, 76.
Fargo, William, Jr., 290, 358.
Fargoe, William, 28.

Ford, Daniel, 29, 152, 167, 229, 264.
Ford, Isaac, 150, 316, 332.
Ford, John, 187.
Ford, Jonatnan, 60, 83, 340.
Ford, Martin, 167, 264, 340.
Ford, Matthew, 354, 355.
Ford, Timothy, 219.
Foreseth, Andrew, 68.
Forgarson, Daniel, 29.
Forgerson, Daniel, 78, 234.
Forgo, Peter, 168.
Forquoir, Ebenezer, 247.
Forriss, Peter, 351.
Forsdich, 88.
Forseth, Andrew, 50.
Forsyth, Jesse, 76.
Fortin, Amon, 196.
Fosbury, John, 14.
Fosbury, Stephen, 14.
Fosdick, James, 346.
Foster, Ben, 80.
Foster, Benjamin, 29, 168, 236.
Foster, Chancy, 48.
Foster, Christopher, 5.
Foster, Comfort, 85, 128.
Foster, Elijah, 297.
Foster, Francis, 162.
Foster, James, 49, 79, 153, 246.
Foster, John, 29, 70, 167, 239, 264, 346.
Foster, Jonah, 162.
Foster, Joseph, 192.
Foster, Nathaniel, 57, 81.
Foster, Peter, 351.
Foster, Thomas, 363.
Foster, Warham, 48.
Foster, William, 281.
Foster, Zephaniah, 29, 139, 237.
Fountain, Eneas, 233.
Fountain, Enos, 114.
Fountaine, Enos, 28.
Fowler, 5.
Fowler, Abiathar, 2.
Fowler, Amos, 2.
Fowler, Caleb, 28, 167, 231.
Fowler, Elisha Adams, 3.
Fowler, Joel, 219.
Fowler, Jonath, 48.
Fowler, Josiah, 5.
Fowler, Josiah, Jr., 2, 5.
Fowler, Matthew, 122, 162.
Fowler, Nehemiah, 3, 28, 67, 233, 264, 274.
Fowler, William, 5.
Fox, Aaron, 53, 274.
Fox, Amos, 47, 48.

Fox, Asa, 28, 168, 238, 245, 264, 318, 336, 351.
Fox, Ashbel, 346.
Fox, Backus, 75, 358.
Fox, Basel, 339.
Fox, Bassat, 325.
Fox, Basset, 276, 339.
Fox, David, Jr., 3.
Fox, Ebenezer, 168.
Fox, Elisha, 28, 167, 239.
Fox, Ephraim, 6, 369.
Fox, Gideon, 47.
Fox, Harris, 71, 369.
Fox, Jacob, 28, 74, 231.
Fox, Joel, 87, 141.
Fox, John, 28, 241, 263, 351.
Fox, Jonathan, 8.
Fox, Joseph, 76.
Fox, Joshua, 3, 28, 241.
Fox, Lemuel, 193.
Fox, Levi, 352.
Fox, Naniah, 245.
Fox, Nathan, 189, 369.
Fox, Robert, 130.
Fox, Rosel, 194.
Fox, Samuel, 208, 351.
Fox, Sariah, 143.
Fox, Simeon, 264, 276, 325, 340.
Fox, Stephen, 52, 70, 282, 309, 334.
Fox, Thomas, 195.
Fox, Timothy, 277, 299, 347.
Fox, Vaniah, 306, 328, 346.
Fox, Variah, 306.
Frame, John, 85.
Frances, Amos, 14.
Frances, James, 13, 29.
Frances, John, 14, 29.
Frances, Titus, 209.
Francis, Christopher, 12.
Francis, David, 274.
Francis, James, 167, 239.
Francis, John, 82, 168, 230.
Franck, Joshua, 139.
Frank, Joshua, 47.
Frank, Mical, 162.
Franklen, Jehial, 29.
Franklin, Abel, 76, 148, 158, 159, 198, 225.
Franklin, David, 198, 225.
Franklin, Jehiel, 107, 168, 235.
Franklin, Samuel, 28, 72, 167, 263.
Fransway, Anthony, 73.
Fraser, Samuel, 152.
Frasher, Robert, 290.
Frassier, Robert, 360.
Frazier, Robert, 358.
Freat, Joseph, 319.

Frederick, John, 87.
Fredericksborough, N. Y., 364.
Free, Arkelaus, 87.
Free Body, London, 143.
Freedom, Cato, 285.
Freedom, Chatham, 60.
Freedom, Dick, 60, 83.
Freedom, Jack, 277.
Freeman, Amos, 97.
Freeman, Benjamin, 9.
Freeman, Caesar, 253, 336, 348.
Freeman, Cato, 309, 334.
Freeman, Chatham, 83, 216.
Freeman, Costor, 341.
Freeman, Cuff, 346.
Freeman, Cuffee, 336.
Freeman, Cult, 103.
Freeman, Daniel, 9.
Freeman, David, 346.
Freeman, Edward, 28, 168, 232, 264, 281, 313, 330.
Freeman, Elisha, 28, 236.
Freeman, Exter, 346.
Freeman, Frank, 28, 230.
Freeman, Gager, 9.
Freeman, Gift, 153.
Freeman, Guy, 28, 232.
Freeman, Jack, 28, 91, 241, 257, 309, 334.
Freeman, James, 217, 283, 330, 351.
Freeman, Jethro, 287.
Freeman, Joseph, 76.
Freeman, Micael, 28, 168, 232.
Freeman, Mosely, 28.
Freeman, Nathan, 9.
Freeman, Ned, 313.
Freeman, Peter, 253, 257, 346.
Freeman, Phillemon, 346.
Freeman, Phineas, 9.
Freeman, Plymouth, 332.
Freeman, Primas, 273, 330.
Freeman, Prince, 248, 309, 334.
Freeman, Providence, 28.
Freeman, Robert, 58, 338.
Freeman, Roger, 54, 73, 130.
Freeman, Sampson, 28, 168.
Freeman, Samson, 238.
Freeman, Samuel, 65, 264, 353.
Freeman, Shubael, 91.
Freeman, Sifax, 28.
Freeman, Syphax, 238.
Freeman, Toney, 93.
Freman, Caesar, 318.
Freman, Elish, 64.
Freman, Elisha, 63.
Freman, Robert, 91.

Freman, Roman, 196.
French, Abner, 56, 77, 85, 128, 138.
French, Abner, Jr., 75.
French, Bowars, 366.
French, Isaac, 49, 67.
French, James, 283, 336, 351.
French, Jehiel, 58.
French, John, 147.
French, Josiah, 58, 94.
French, Levi, 189, 284, 350.
French, Samuel, 28, 97, 202, 233.
French, Thomas, 212.
French, Truman, 93.
Frenchman, Philip, 67, 95.
Frinck, Nathan, 334.
Frink, Elisha, 77.
Frink, Jabez, 182.
Frink, James, Jr., 78.
Frink, John, 357.
Frink, Lathrop, 288.
Frink, Nathan, 272.
Frink, Seth, 77.
Frink, Silas, 85, 127.
Frink, Theophilas, 77.
Frink, Thomas, 77, 344.
Frisbey, Benjamin, 28.
Frisbey, Jabez, 6.
Frisbie, Caleb, 1.
Frisbie, Hooker, 2.
Frisbie, Titus, 1.
Frisby, Benjamin, 235.
Frisby, Levi, 11, 49.
Frissel, Amasa, 86.
Frissell, 133.
Friswell, John, 195.
Frizbie, Joseph, 213.
Frost, Ephraim, 181.
Frost, Joseph, 4.
Frost, Samuel, 26, 29, 73, 231, 262.
Frost, Stephen, 111.
Frothingham, Ebenezer, 254, 255, 303, 327, 329.
Frothingham, John, 101, 105.
Frothingham, Samuel, 346.
Fryar, Charles, 167, 263.
Fulford, James, 280.
Fulford, John, 29, 84, 167, 230, 263.
Fullar, Joshua, 332.
Fuller, 158.
Fuller, A., 104.
Fuller, Abraham, 364.
Fuller, Amas, 228.
Fuller, Barnabas, 17.
Fuller, Bethuel, 3.

Fuller, David, 187.
Fuller, Edward, 74, 105.
Fuller, Eli, 275, 311, 344, 349.
Fuller, Ely, 264.
Fuller, Jacob, 264, 275, 349.
Fuller, James, 199, 224, 264, 352.
Fuller, John, 3, 28, 67, 85, 95, 97, 138, 167, 233, 264, 353.
Fuller, Joshua, 272, 292, 316.
Fuller, Nat^n, 18.
Fuller, Timothy, 3.
Fuller, Timothy, 2^d, 3.
Fuller, William, 187.
Fullers, Aaron, 147.
Fullor, Asa, 221.
Funning, Charles, 201.
Furbs, Joseph, 212.
Fyler, Ambros, 59.
Fyler, John, 206.
Fyler, Norman, 86.
Fyler, Samuel, 370.

Gage, Salvenas, 191.
Gage, Silvanus, 276, 350.
Gage, Silvenus, 323.
Gage, Sylvanus, 341.
Gage, Tom, 61.
Gainer, James, 150.
Gains, Daniel, 144.
Gains, Jonathan, 17.
Gallet, James, 81, 141.
Gallipin, David, 346.
Gallop, Prentice, 210.
Gallup, Benjamin, 149, 297.
Gallup, Prentice, 51, 69.
Gallup, Thomas, 51.
Gallup, Wheler, 148.
Galord, Joel, 69.
Galpen, Peet, 7.
Garcy, Elnathan, 220.
Gardiner, David, 29, 168, 285.
Gardiner, De Tubs, 29.
Gardiner, Sherman, 29, 168.
Gardiner, Thomas, 8.
Gardner, 183.
Gardner, Abijah, 142, 354.
Gardner, D. Tubbs, 231.
Gardner, Daniel, 322.
Gardner, David, 74, 322, 339.
Gardner, Dennis, 87.
Gardner, George, 69.
Gardner, Nathaniel, 74.
Gardner, Peregrine, 76.
Gardner, Septimer, 138.
Gardner, Sherman, 75, 231, 264.
Gardner, Thomas, 75.
Gardner, Thomas, 75.

Gardner, William, 47, 200.
Garner, David, 325.
Garner, William, 111.
Garret, John, 29.
Garret, Samuel, 181.
Garrie, John, 264.
Garrison, Lewis, 95.
Garrit, John, 56, 168, 231.
Gaspe, Caleb, 296.
Gates, Daniel, 3^d, 3.
Gates, Ebenezer, 193.
Gates, Freeman, 338.
Gates, Jessa, 369.
Gates, John, 10, 286, 314, 330.
Gates, Jonah, 3.
Gates, Jonas, 153.
Gates, Jonathan, 148.
Gates, Josiah, 226.
Gates, Luther, 77, 198.
Gates, Nathaniel, 29, 64, 237, 264, 277, 318, 336.
Gates, Nathael, 217.
Gates, Samuel, 8, 110.
Gates, Silas, 19, 64, 146, 156.
Gates, Steven, 10.
Gates, Uriah, 189.
Gates, William, 227.
Gates, Zechariah, 3.
Gaunecy, Timothy, 94.
Gauney, Timothy, 58.
Gavit, Stephen, 264, 320, 337.
Gavitt, Stephen, 281.
Gay, Jaison, 330.
Gay, James, 370.
Gay, Jason, 264, 282, 314.
Gay, Joseph, 370.
Gay, Richard, Jr., 11.
Gayland, Josiah, 243.
Gaylor, Benjamin, 203.
Gaylor, John, 190.
Gaylor, William, 52, 72.
Gaylord, Benjamin, 30, 230, 235, 342.
Gaylord, Eleazer, 14.
Gaylord, Eliakim, 205.
Gaylord, Elijah, 207.
Gaylord, John, 48, 75.
Gaylord, Jonathan, 264, 280, 365.
Geanings, Elnathan, 64.
Gear, Asa, 284.
Gear, Nathaniel, 364.
Gearham, Nehemiah, 94.
Geddens, Richard, 240.
Geer, Allen, 10.
Geer, Benajah, 54, 73, 128, 130.
Geer, Elihu, 29, 240.
Geer, Gideon, 140.

Gilston, Jacobe, 30, 239.
Gimson, John, 311.
Ginning, Joseph, Jr., 85.
Ginnings, Daniel, 199.
Ginnings, Stephen, 199.
Gitston, Jacob, 264.
Gladding, Jediah, 79.
Gladding, William, 168, 240, 284, 353, 355.
Gladen, William, 69, 264.
Gladin, Jedidiah, 153.
Glading, Joseph, 361.
Glading, William, 29, 183.
Glasco, Silas, 330.
Glasgow, Silas, 92.
Glass, Samuel, 56, 64, 77, 146, 157.
Glass, Silas, 264, 277, 319, 336, 363.
Glasses, Silas, 330.
Glassgow, Silus, 58.
Glastonbury, 17, 26, 27, 28, 30, 31, 33, 34, 35, 37, 39, 40, 42, 43, 88, 143, 166, 168, 169, 170, 171, 175, 176, 177, 193, 194, 195, 208, 216, 238, 245, 248, 250, 251, 264, 265, 266, 267, 269, 270, 271, 278, 285, 299, 351, 366, 367.
Glasten[   ], 208.
Glazier, John, 284.
Gleason, James, 187.
Gleason, John, 298.
Gleason, Jonn, 76.
Gleason, Luther, 206.
Glenney, William, 199.
Gleson, Andrew, 202.
Glover, 359.
Glover, Christopher, 119.
Glover, John, 30, 168, 233.
Goar, Elijah, 136.
Goarham, Isaac, 124.
Godard, Edward, 153.
Goddard, Skiler, 66.
Godfrey, 98.
Godfrey, Cresterfey, 4.
Godfrey, John, 283, 351.
Godfrey, Nathaniel, Jr., 4.
Goff, Derby, 283.
Goff, Gideon, 5, 248, 308, 333, 348.
Goff, Hezekiah, Jr., 7.
Goff, Jonathan, 346.
Goff, Joseph, 216.
Goff, Joshua, 65, 87, 295.
Goff, Richard, 368.
Goff, Samuel, 29, 65, 168, 240, 296, 302, 353.

Goff, Samuel, Jr., 65.
Goff, Samuel D., 338, 351.
Goff, Solomon, 279, 300.
Goff, Squire, 296.
Gold, John, 102.
Gold, Toney, 274.
Gold, William, 67, 97.
Goldsmith, James, 73.
Goldsmith, Joseph, 73, 330.
Goldsmith, William, 73, 264.
Goldwin, Matthew, 352.
Gomer, Pharoah, 49.
Goodale, Alvin, 138.
Goodale, Elezr, 17.
Goodale, Ezra, 137.
Goodale, Jacobe, 30, 138, 237.
Goodale, John, Jr., 133.
Goodale, Silas, 74.
Goodell, Alvin, 77.
Goodell, Ezra, 56, 77.
Goodell, Fraderick, 197.
Goodell, Jacob, 76.
Goodell, Oliver, 56.
Goodell, Samuel, 283.
Goodfaith, David, 29, 290, 340, 358.
Good Luck, London, 58.
Goodrich, Abel, 187.
Goodrich, Bethuel, 65, 353.
Goodrich, David, 79, 168, 236, 264.
Goodrich, Ephraim, 238.
Goodrich, Ichabod, 258, 306, 328, 348.
Goodrich, James, 246.
Goodrich, Jared, 349.
Goodrich, John, 65, 80, 317, 332.
Goodrich, Lemuel, 65, 352.
Goodrich, Levi, 64, 168, 264.
Goodrich, Levy, 240.
Goodrich, Simeon, 345.
Goodrich, Solomon, 74, 243.
Goodrich, William, 367.
Goodrich, Zenas, 213.
Goodsall, Epphaphras, 233.
Goodsel, Eppaphras, 67.
Goodsel, James, 4.
Goodsel, Thomas, 4.
Goodseil, Anthony, 285.
Goodsell, Epaphras, 95.
Goodsell, Isaac, 210.
Goodsill, Anthony, 60, 83.
Goodsill, Eppiphras, 30.
Goodwell, Jonathan, 95.
Goodwin, Charles, 276.
Goodwin, Hezekiah, 52, 70, 345.
Goodyear, Edward, 107.

Green, 136.
Green, Amos, 75, 197, 336.
Green, Asahel, 108.
Green, B., 115.
Green, Benjamin, 183, 193.
Green, David, 10, 57.
Green, David, Jr., 81.
Green, Edward, 298.
Green, Ezra, 115.
Green, Francis, 75.
Green, Frederick, 86, 134.
Green, Jack, 71.
Green, Jacob, Jr., 57.
Green, James, 89.
Green, Jedᵈ, 146.
Green, Jedediah, 157, 277.
Green, Jeremiah, Jr., 39.
Green, Joel, 65.
Green, John, 29, 133, 147, 196, 229, 297.
Green, Joseph, 57, 168.
Green, Joseph, Jr., 4.
Green, Joshua, 81.
Green, Josiah, 29, 68, 98, 109, 233.
Green, Mason, 277, 307, 316.
Green, Robert, 29, 82, 149, 160, 237.
Green, Roger, 64, 146, 156.
Green, Samuel, 29, 63, 73, 98, 110, 216, 236, 336, 342.
Green, Solomon, 4.
Green, Thomas, 49, 71, 203, 278.
Green, Timothy, 201.
Green, Wardwill, 193.
Green, William. 18, 29, 70, 238.
Green, Zach, 57.
Greene, John, 86.
Greene, Pleney, 295.
Greenfield, Archibald, 179.
Grenold, Amasy, 343.
Greensar, Pline, 292.
Greenslit, Benjamin, 193, 272, 314, 330.
Greenwich, 21, 22, 27, 28, 31, 32, 33, 36, 37, 38, 42, 43, 44, 88, 115, 116, 118, 126, 234.
Greer, James, 74.
Gregory. Daniel, 191, 221.
Gregory, Elias, 9.
Gregory, Ezra, 9.
Gregory, Isaac, 9.
Gregory. J.. 111.
Gregory, Jack, 185.
Gregory, John, 210.
Gregory, Matthew, 110, 320.
Gregory, Matthew, Jr., 111.
Gregory, Nathan, 304.

Gregory, Philip, 275, 299.
Gregory, Stephen, 7.
Grenoll, Amasa, 227.
Grey, James, 358.
Grey, William, 65.
Gregory, Benjamin, 154.
Gridley, Hosea, 49, 347.
Gridley, James, 299, 347.
Gridley, James, Jr., 278.
Gridley, Kezin, 370.
Gridley, Obed, 299, 347.
Gridley, Obed., 278.
Gridley, Rezin, 370.
Gridley, Seth, 30, 71, 236.
Gridly, Seth, 168.
Griffen, Abner, 144.
Griffen, James, 30, 233.
Griffen, Joel, 300.
Griffen, John, 144.
Griffen, Nathaniel, 11.
Griffeth, George, 224, 264.
Griffeth, William, 47.
Griffin, Amos, 310.
Griffin, Cornelius, 76.
Griffin, Edward, 53, 72.
Griffin, George, 215.
Griffin, Joseph, 77, 137, 225.
Griffin, Joseph, Jr., 56.
Griffin, Matthew, 143.
Griffin, Simeon, 348, 349.
Griffin, Simon, 238, 303, 327.
Griffin, William, 118.
Griffing, Joel, 273.
Griffis, Paul, 225.
Griffith, George, 286.
Griffith, William, 8, 153.
Griggory, Mathew, 264.
Griggs, Paul, 19.
Grigory, Phillip, 349.
Grigory, Seth, 306.
Grimes, Abraham, 47.
Grimes, Cyrus, 29, 79, 232.
Grimes, Joseph, Jr., 10.
Grimes, Silus, 29.
Grinall, Amasa, 78.
Grisson, Lewis, 67.
Griswell, Giles, 13.
Griswold, 15.
Griswold, Andrew, 74.
Griswold, Benjamin, 1.
Griswold, Cesar, 183.
Griswold, Elijah, 14.
Griswold, Elisha, 143.
Griswold, Ezra, 5.
Griswold, George, 52, 72.
Griswold, Jacob, 250.
Griswold, John, 274, 300.

Hait, Nehemiah, 109.
Hait, S., 112.
Hait, Samuel, 113, 204, 216, 341.
Hait, Stephen, 108, 215.
Haladay, Jacob, 344.
Halchet, John, 151.
Hale, Aaron, 30, 64, 240.
Hale, Garsham, 199.
Hale, James, 46, 85, 131.
Hale, Joseph, 188.
Hale, Newport, 351.
Hale, Robert, 46, 131, 294.
Hale, Thomas, Jr., 49, 66.
Halkins, Samuel, 189.
Hall, 55, 88, 210.
Hall, A., 207.
Hall, Aaron, 60, 82.
Hall, Abram, 14.
Hall, Amos, 51, 142.
Hall, Andrew, 129.
Hall, Asa, 13, 67.
Hall, Benajah, 59, 83.
Hall, Benjamin, 4.
Hall, Caleb, 207, 362.
Hall, Charles, 13.
Hall, Christopher, 197.
Hall, Daniel, 13.
Hall, Daniel Johnson, 60, 83.
Hall, David, 30, 47, 83, 119, 154, 169, 224.
Hall, Eben, 265.
Hall, Ebenezer, 3, 71.
Hall, Eber, 5, 280.
Hall, Eleazer, 97.
Hall, Elisha, 60, 83.
Hall, Enos, 13.
Hall, Ezenas, 196.
Hall, Garsham, 2d, 199.
Hall, George, 93, 200.
Hall, Henrey, 82.
Hall, Hiland, 74.
Hall, Hiram, 49, 66, 264, 350.
Hall, Irael, 66.
Hall, Isaac, 49, 129.
Hall, Israel, 13, 30, 169, 240.
Hall, Jatham, 83.
Hall, Jedediah, 97.
Hall, Joel, 14.
Hall, John, 47, 53, 205.
Hall, Josiah, 188.
Hall, Jotham, 60.
Hall, Levi, 319, 336.
Hall, Moses, 83.
Hall, Moses, 2d, 13.
Hall, Moses, 3d, 13, 60.
Hall, Nathan, 3.
Hall, Nathaniel, 30, 84, 129, 230.

Hall, Philemon, 5, 30, 169, 231, 265.
Hall, Robert, 169.
Hall, Rufus, 13, 30, 83, 169, 230.
Hall, Samuel, 13, 30, 71, 136, 170, 231, 265.
Hall, Simeon, 50, 69.
Hall, Stephen, 30, 58, 67, 93, 117, 139, 169, 226, 231, 233, 265, 274.
Hall, Street, 14.
Hall, Talmage, 7, 30, 234.
Hall, Thomas, 51.
Hall, Titus, 13, 169.
Hall, Timothy, 19.
Hall, William, 30, 131, 237, 346.
Halladay, Jacob, 144, 299, 311.
Halladay, Robert, 365.
Hallamagee, John, 350.
Hallet, Thomas, 78, 319, 358, 359.
Hallett, John, 68.
Halley, Abraham, 233.
Halley, Edmond, 184.
Halley, Joseph, 160.
Halley, Manchester, 184.
Halley, Nathan, 265.
Halley, Robart, 10.
Hallimage, John, 264.
Hallop, Joseph, 32, 234.
Halloway, William, 32.
Hallowell, William, 75.
Hally, Abraham, 31.
Halsey, Jeremiah, 9.
Halsted, Joseph, 71.
Halsted, Timothy, 285.
Haman, Ebenezar, 346.
Hambden, William, 32, 230.
Hamblen, James, 361.
Hamblen, Levi, 12.
Hambleton, John, 8, 122.
Hamblin, Joel, 169, 236.
Hamblin, John, 80.
Hamblin, Levi, 80.
Hamblin, William, 202.
Hamhidon, James, 94.
Hamilton, George, 53.
Hamilton, James, 112.
Hamilton, John, 155, 302.
Hamlin, Bazeleel, 248.
Hamlin, Cornelius, 57, 80.
Hamlin, Joel, 32, 74, 265, 273, 316.
Hamlin, John, 18.
Hamlin, Levi, 18, 50.
Hamlin, Reuben, 194, 278, 347.
Hamlin, Richard, 6.
Hamlin, William, 275, 354.
Hammon, Robart, 218.

Hammond, David, 285, 311, 344.
Hammond, Robert, 184.
Hamtin, Reuben, 299.
Hanaball, Joseph, 233.
Hancy, Samuel, 70.
Hand, Jonathan, 247.
Hand, Joseph, 79, 153, 258.
Handcox, John, 66.
Handee, Caleb, 183.
Handey, Samuel, 169.
Handy, 5.
Handy, Clement, 330.
Handy, Clemmans, 204.
Handy, Jairus, 5.
Handy, Jonathan, 5.
Handy, Richard, 58, 94.
Handy, Russel, 360.
Handy, Samuel, 31, 231, 265.
Handy, Thomas, 360.
Hanes, Jonathan, 170, 265.
Hanes, Silas, 4.
Haney, Andrew, 307.
Hanford, Eleazor, 9.
Hanford, Ozias, 109.
Hanford, Stephen, 9.
Hanford, Theophilus, Jr., 9.
Hanford, Theophilus, 3d, 9.
Hanford, Timothy Hathorly, 108.
Hanks, Asa, 357.
Hanks, Consider, 294.
Hannabal, Joseph, 31, 232, 286.
Hansen, Samuel, 79.
Hansey, Andrew, 307, 328.
Hanson, Christian, 368.
Hanson, Samuel, 153.
Hanson, William, 330.
Haradan, Paul, 86.
Hard, David, 91.
Harde, John, 130.
Harde, Nathaniel, 130, 169.
Harden, Frederick, 32, 169.
Hardey, Nathaniel, 72.
Harding, Fradk, 229.
Harding, Frederick, 8.
Hardy, Nathaniel, 30, 237, 334.
Hargar, Simeon, 355.
Harger, Elijah, 217.
Harger, Jedediah, 215.
Harington, Elisha, 10.
Harington, Stephen, 10.
Hariot, Israel, 234.
Harke, Selah, 307.
Harlop, Joseph, 169.
Harman, Jaques, 304.
Harmon, J., 331.
Harmon, Jacques, 313, 324, 329.
Harmon, John, 32, 238.

Harper, Inis, 285.
Harret, Israel, 117.
Harrington, Andrew, 75.
Harrington, Benjamin, 350.
Harrington, Elisha, 80, 240, 349.
Harrington, Isaac, 232.
Harrington, Samuel, 248.
Harrington, Timothy, 203.
Harrinton, Elisha, 31, 170, 265.
Harrinton, Isaac, 31.
Harriot, Israel, 31.
Harris, Amos, 59, 82, 323, 341.
Harris, Andrew, 358, 359.
Harris, Asa, 200, 221.
Harris, Bruster, 190.
Harris, Champlin, 32, 168, 240, 264, 283, 351.
Harris, George, 197, 279, 300.
Harris, Henry, 169, 265.
Harris, Jason, 71.
Harris, John, 5, 32, 54, 55, 129, 169, 236, 239.
Harris, Joseph, 7.
Harris, Nathaniel, 66, 132, 140.
Harris, Paul, 181.
Harris, Philip, 296.
Harris, Philip, Jr., 296.
Harris, Thomas, 64, 290, 358, 359.
Harris, Walter, 139, 242.
Harrison, Asahel, 2.
Harrison, Champlin, 168.
Harrison, Jairus, 2, 30, 231, 265.
Harrison, Jarus, 170.
Harrison, John, 71, 111.
Harrison, Reuben, 194.
Harrison, William, 30, 76, 232.
Harrison, Wooster, 2.
Harriss, Amos, 350.
Harriss, Andrew, 76.
Harriss, Jason, 136.
Harriss, Paul, 223.
Harriss, William, 76.
Harrop, Joseph, 169, 265, 354.
Harry, Ephraim, 281, 321, 337.
Harscall, David, 135.
Hart, Aaron, 277, 347.
Hart, Benjamin, 31, 83, 169, 230.
Hart, Gilbert, 203.
Hart, Henry, 346.
Hart, James, 209.
Hart, Joel, 311.
Hart, John, 79.
Hart, Jonathan, 31, 169, 239.
Hart, Luke, 276, 299, 350.
Hart, Selah, 288, 319, 347.
Hart, Timothy, 13, 60, 83.
Hart, Titus, 14, 60, 82.

Hawley, Israel, 91.
Hawley, James, 102, 104.
Hawley, John, 78.
Hawley, Joseph, 120, 204, 252, 283.
Hawley, Joseph C., 6, 31, 55, 71, 74, 221, 235, 265, 282.
Hawley, Liverius, 55.
Hawley, Liverus, 120.
Hawley, Nathan, 90, 169, 324, 339.
Hawley, Nathan, Jr., 58.
Hawley, Ozias, 188.
Hawley, Peter, 54.
Hawley, Richard, 58, 94.
Hawley, Stephen, Jr., 8.
Hawley, Talcott, 283.
Hawley, Talmage, 122.
Hawley, Wallaston, 92.
Hawley, William, 4, 211.
Hawton, Henry, 283.
Hayden, David, 31, 239, 288, 316, 332, 341.
Hayden, David, Jr., 288.
Hayden, Jacob, 288.
Hayden, Thomas, 31.
Haydon, Alyn, 6.
Haydon, David, 347.
Haydon, Thomas, 14.
Hayes, John, 121.
Hayes, Marshal, 341.
Hayley, John, 128.
Haynes, Jonathan, 332.
Hayns, Jonathan, 31, 232.
Hays, Abraham, 31, 234.
Hays, Asa, 80, 311.
Hays, Asahel, 11.
Hays, Benajah, 202.
Hays, Benjamin, 80, 144, 349.
Hays, Jacob, 11, 144.
Hays, John, 162.
Hays, Luke, 11.
Hays, Micah, 144.
Hays, Oliver, 11.
Hays, Seth, 11.
Hays, Titus, 31, 71, 236.
Hays, William, 3d, 11.
Hays, Zenos, 144.
Hayse, Abraham, 117.
Hayward, Samuel, 296.
Hayward, Solomon, 221.
Hayze, Asa, 349.
Hazard, Jeffry, 32.
Haze, Asa, 311.
Haze, Enoch, 188.
Hazelton, Arnold, 5.
Hazelton, Charles, Jr., 5.

Hazen, 178, 227, 271.
Hazen, Andrew, 315, 331.
Hazie, Joseph, 203.
Hazzard, Jeffery, 233.
Heacock, David, 32.
Heacock, Elisha, 32.
Heacock, Samuel, 32.
Heacock, William, Jr., 32.
Heacox, Asher, 49, 337.
Head, Henry, 362.
Healdy, Daniel, 336.
Heard, Elijah, 202.
Heard, Isaac, 147.
Heard, Jacob, 56, 147.
Heard, Jeduthen, 82, 148.
Heard, Mead, 202.
Heard, Robert, 148.
Heart, 88.
Heart, Bliss, 49.
Heart, Elijah, 50.
Heart, Elisha, 49.
Heart, John, 256, 257.
Heart, Jonathan, 265.
Heart, Reuben, 50.
Heart, Timothy, 49, 192.
Hearts, Selah, 307.
Heath, John, 73.
Heath, Peleg, 31, 70, 238.
Heath, Peleg L., 169.
Heath, Thomas, 192.
Hebard, Jedediah, 226, 288.
Hebbard, Aaron, 86, 134.
Hebbard, Andrew, 64, 147.
Hebbard, Asa, 134.
Hebbard, Elihu, 86, 134.
Hebbard, Timothy, 86, 134.
Hebbard, William, 146.
Hebbern, Francis, 67.
Hebron, 23, 25, 31, 34, 35, 37, 40, 42, 141, 142, 169, 171, 176, 185, 197, 208, 215, 220, 221, 238, 243, 246, 260, 262, 266, 268, 270, 271, 275, 276, 280, 281, 283, 285, 287, 296, 297, 301, 302, 354.
Hecock, Asher, 347.
Hecock, Daniel, 173.
Hecock, David, 61.
Hecox, E., 168.
Heddy, Daniel, 319, 336.
Hedges, Jeremiah, 183, 219.
Heerd, Isaac, 159.
Heerd, Jacob, 159.
Heff, Daniel, 294.
Heldrig, William, 113.
Hellard, Minor, 208.
Hellermegy, John, 180.
Helmes, Cudjo, 339.

Helmes, Kudjoe, 281.
Helmes, Samuel, 140, 254.
Helms, Cudjo, 325.
Hende, Caleb, 131, 218.
Hendee, Caleb, Jr., 46.
Hendreck, David, 9.
Hendric, Benjamin, 60.
Hendrick, Eleazer, 55, 106.
Hendrick, John, 7.
Hendrick, John William, 350.
Hendrick, Josiah, 285, 292.
Hendrick, Nathan, 9.
Hendrick, Nathaniel, 110.
Hendricks, Daniel, 272.
Hendry, Daniel, 32, 359.
Henington, Benjamin, 49.
Henman, Nathan, 202.
Henman, Samuel, 58.
Henmin, Hust., 66.
Henmin, Samuel, 306.
Hennan, Samuel, 306.
Henries, Zadock, 107.
Henry, Barzil, 86.
Henry, Barzilli, 348.
Henry, Daniel, 290.
Henry, William, 52, 70.
Hensey, Andrew, 301, 311.
Henshaw, Benjamin, 2.
Henshaw, William, 31, 169, 239, 265.
Hensley, Andrew, 283.
Hepburn, Joseph, 119.
Hepburn, Peter, 73.
Herd, Isaac, 281.
Herd, Jeduthan, 224.
Herick, Amos, 53.
Herington, Clark, 146.
Herington, Ezekiel, 146.
Herington, Samuel, 309.
Herington, Timothy, 57.
Herlihy, John, 349.
Herman, John, 350.
Hernden, Paul, 133.
Herreck, Isaac, 9.
Herren, Perley, 71.
Herrick, Asahel, 213, 223, 363.
Herrick, Daniel, 297.
Herrick, Ebenezer, 15.
Herrick Isaac, 191, 224.
Herrick, Israel, 15.
Herrick, John, 61, 99.
Herrick, Joseph, 181, 297.
Herrick, Lemuel, 77.
Herrick, Libens, 32, 233.
Herrick, Robert, 64, 146, 156.
Herrin, Perley, 136.
Herrington, Abraham, 148.

Herrington, Benjamin, 66, 279.
Herrington, Clark, 64, 156.
Herrington, Daniel, 224.
Herrington, Ezekiel, 64, 156.
Herrington, Samuel, 73, 335.
Herrington, Timothy, 81.
Herrinton, Abraham, 363.
Herrinton, Samuel, 129.
Herris, Thomas, 146.
Herron, John, 232.
Hervey, Asael, 276.
Hervy, Asahel, 352.
Herwington, Parley, 215.
Hesket, James, 68.
Heth, Phinehas, 350.
Heughston, William, 225.
Hewet, Elisha, 265.
Hewett, Henry, 224.
Hewit, Henry, 215.
Hewit, Nathaniel, 184.
Hewit, Robert, 184.
Hewlett, John, 133.
Hews, James, 228.
Heyden, David, 169, 324.
Heyden, David, Jr., 49.
Heydon, Charles, 60, 83.
Hibard, Perez, 357.
Hibbard, 157, 158.
Hibbard, Andrew, 156, 200.
Hibbard, Asa, 85, 86, 127.
Hibbard, Dyar, 85.
Hibbard, Eben, 85.
Hibbard, Elish, 7.
Hibbard, John, 296.
Hibbard, Joseph, 297.
Hibbard, Levi, 85.
Hibbard, Timothy, 85.
Hibbard, Uriah, 85.
Hibberd, 223.
Hibberd, Dier, 127.
Hibberd, Ebenezer, 127.
Hibberd, Hez, 128.
Hibberd, Timothy, 127.
Hibberd, Vriah, 128.
Hibbert, Francis, 67.
Hiccock, Samuel, 170.
Hickcox, Elisha, 84.
Hickcox, William, Jr., 84.
Hickock, Bethel, 108.
Hickok, Elisha, 230.
Hickok, Samuel, 233.
Hickok, William, Jr., 230.
Hickox, Joseph, 66.
Hickox, Samuel, 114.
Hicks, John, 152.
Hicock, David, 100.
Hicock, Thad=, Jr., 105.

Hide, Asa, 211.
Hide, Clark, 222.
Hide, James, 58, 91, 94, 169, 231.
Hide, James, 3d, 265.
Hide, Nathaniel, 18.
Hide, Theophilus, 11, 14.
Hide, William R., 169.
Hide, Zebadial, 295.
Higbee, Elihu, 236.
Higby, Elihu, 30.
Higby, Isaac, 63.
Higby, Lemuel, 190.
Higby, Noah, 207.
Higgans, Isaac, 343.
Higgens, Heman, 240.
Higgens, Jesse, 240.
Higgins, Cornelius, 30, 69, 240, 355.
Higgins, Cornelius, Jr., 5.
Higgins, Cornetuis, 169.
Higgins, Heman, 30, 65.
Higgins, Isaac, 288.
Higgins, Jesse, 30, 65.
Higgins, Jesse, Jr., 65.
Higgins, Nehemiah, 244.
Higgins, William, 169, 265.
Highlands, 182, 198, 247, 251.
Highlands, see Camp Highlands.
Higley, Benjamin, 68.
Higley, Eben, 188.
Higley, Josiah, 81, 143, 240.
Higley, Ozias, 144.
Hill, 98.
Hill, Abner, 279.
Hill, Daniel, 31, 89, 238, 265, 345.
Hill, David, 11, 89.
Hill, Ebenezer, 31, 106, 169, 235, 330.
Hill, Eli, 9.
Hill, Elijah, 188.
Hill, Eliphulet, 243.
Hill, Henry, 79.
Hill, John, 5, 170, 187, 219, 265.
Hill, John, 2d, 11, 31, 80, 240, 349.
Hill, Jonah, 13.
Hill, Jonathan, 56, 77, 137.
Hill, Moses, 5, 51.
Hill, Nathan, 351.
Hill, Nathaniel, 75.
Hill, Philip, 31, 237, 278, 291, 343.
Hill, Reuben, 187, 215, 276, 348.
Hill, Squier, 131.
Hill, Thomas, 56, 77, 137.
Hill, Tony, 274.
Hill, Ury, 206.
Hill, William, 112.

Hillard, Azariah, 179.
Hillard, Jonathan, 149.
Hillet, Thomas, 252.
Hills, Abner, 226.
Hills, Abner, Jr., 283.
Hills, Belah, 205.
Hills, Benoni, 48, 350.
Hills, Daniel, 169.
Hills, Ebenezer, 49, 265.
Hills, Eliphalet, 52, 70.
Hills, Erastus, 188, 369.
Hills, George, 81, 250.
Hills, Jacob, 180.
Hills, Jeptha, 350.
Hills, Joseph, 351.
Hills, Lebbeus, Jr., 370.
Hills, Libbius, 370.
Hills, Oliver, 350.
Hills, Phillip, 139, 265, 310, 311.
Hills, Samuel, Jr., 17, 295.
Hills, Squier, 298.
Hills, William, 141.
Hillton, Atkisson, 67.
Hillyer, Daniel, 206.
Hilton, Atkinson, 31, 98, 169, 233.
Hilton, Benjamin, 58.
Hinckley, David, 84.
Hinckley, Iccabud, 169.
Hinckley, Ichd, 81.
Hinckley, J., 185, 186, 187, 188, 189, 190, 191.
Hinckley, Jared, Jr., 139.
Hinckley, John, 84.
Hinde, Caleb, 131.
Hine, Ambrose, 60, 83.
Hine, Isaac, 162.
Hine, N., 99, 100, 105, 106.
Hine, Titus, 32, 73, 170, 231, 265, 332.
Hinkley, Ebenezar, 352.
Hinkly, Ichabod, 32, 239.
Hinkston, Joseph, 11.
Hinman, Benjamin, 3d, 61.
Hinman, D., 100.
Hinman, E., 107, 108.
Hinman, Enos, 100.
Hinman, Houghton, 168.
Hinman, Husted, 3, 31, 230.
Hinman, Joel, 100.
Hinman, Jonas, 100.
Hinman, Samuel, 90, 328.
Hinman, Timothy, 61, 107.
Hinsdale, William, 52, 70, 194.
Hinsdel, Elisha, 71.
Hinsdel, Samuel, 71.
Hinsdel, William, 226.
Hinson, William, Jr., 76.

How, Israel, 18.
How, J., 117, 118.
How, Jaazaniah, 56, 77, 137.
How, John, 17.
How, Joshua, 229, 337.
How, Noah, 362.
How, Zadock, 1, 63, 169, 238.
Howard, Benjamin, 17.
Howard, Elijah, 63.
Howard, George, 32, 169, 239.
Howard, Jonathan, 131.
Howard, Richard, 85, 127, 169, 265.
Howard, William, 129.
Howd, Joel, 2.
Howe, George, 103.
Howe, Joshua, 30, 169, 254, 265, 321.
Howe, Silas, 117.
Howe, Zadock, 30.
Howel, Nicholas, 32, 265.
Howell, John, 74.
Howell, Nicholas, 169, 343.
Howkins, Rhodolfus, 218.
Hows, Benjamin, 227.
Hows, George, 61.
Hoy, Alexander, 247.
Hoyt, Comfort, 153.
Hoyt, Joel, 258.
Hoyt, Joseph, 233.
Hoyt, Joseph, Jr., 9.
Hoyt, Justice, 9.
Hoyt, Nathan, Jr., 9.
Hoyt, Peter, 32.
Hoyt, Philemon, 32.
Hoyt, Samuel, 32.
Hoyt, Thomas, 9.
Hrreck, Sanford, 9.
Hubbard, Aaron, 17.
Hubbard, Abijah, 346.
Hubbard, Benjamin, 48.
Hubbard, David, 17, 333.
Hubbard, Dean, 7.
Hubbard, Ebenezar, 346.
Hubbard, Elihu, 30, 65, 240.
Hubbard, Elijah, 17, 355.
Hubbard, Elisha, 242.
Hubbard, Elizr, 17.
Hubbard, George, 59, 82, 313, 329, 350.
Hubbard, Hezekiah, 30, 169, 239, 265.
Hubbard, Hezekiah, Jr., 7.
Hubbard, James, 274.
Hubbard, Joel, 6.
Hubbard, John, 7, 30, 68, 231.
Hubbard, Jonas, 74.

Hubbard, Jonathan, 346.
Hubbard, Joseph, 90.
Hubbard, Manoah, 193.
Hubbard, Philip, 274.
Hubbard, Roswell, 30, 169, 239.
Hubbard, Selah, 7.
Hubbard, Silas, 243.
Hubbard, Simeon, 358.
Hubbard, Simon, 358.
Hubbard, Solomon, 7.
Hubbard, Timothy, 7.
Hubbart, John, 61.
Hubbel, Abijah, 276.
Hubbel, Amos, 7.
Hubbel, Enoch, 8.
Hubbel, Ezra, 7.
Hubbel, Isaac, 31, 67, 68, 169, 233, 265.
Hubbel, James, 230.
Hubbel, Seth, 169.
Hubbel, William, 31, 169, 233.
Hubbell, Aaron, 3.
Hubbell, David, 317, 333.
Hubbell, Ezbon, 331.
Hubbell, Gershom, 4.
Hubbell, Isaac, 4, 92, 94.
Hubbell, Isband, 97.
Hubbell, Isbon, 67.
Hubbell, Jos., Jr., 4.
Hubbell, Lemuel, 154, 162.
Hubbell, Nathan, 123, 154.
Hubbell, Primus, 103.
Hubbell, Samuel, 104.
Hubbell, Seth, 109, 265, 334.
Hubbell, William, 4, 67.
Hubbell, William G., 162.
Hubbert, Elisha, 61.
Hubbert, James, 210.
Hubbert, Joseph, 59.
Hubble, Thadeus, 9.
Hubell, Abijah, 339.
Hubert, George, 313.
Huchens, Shubel, 363.
Hucker, James, 61.
Hudson, Daniel, 192.
Hudson, David, 61.
Hudson, Eleazer, 31, 232.
Hudson, George, 84.
Hudson, John, 31, 233.
Hudson, Joshua, 18.
Hudson, William, 281, 359.
Huff, John, 201.
Huggins, John, 366.
Hughes, Bodwell, 332.
Hughes, William, 314, 330.
Huit, Leuis, 10.
Hubbard, John, 7.

Hurlbert, John, 83.
Hurlbert, Stephen, 243.
Hurlburt, Cuff, 181.
Hurlburt, Gideon, 96.
Hurlburt, Gideon, Jr., 102.
Hurlburt, Noah, 104.
Hurlburt, Reuben, 144.
Hurlburt, Robert, 102.
Hurlburt, S., 104.
Hurlburt, Steave, 84.
Hurlburt, Steaven, 60.
Hurlburt, Stephen, 98.
Hurlbut, 61.
Hurlbut, Abner, 76.
Hurlbut, Alvin, 86.
Hurlbut, Aseph, 61.
Hurlbut, David, 69.
Hurlbut, George, 290.
Hurlbut, Stephen, 319.
Hurlbut, Thomas, 128.
Hurlbutt, Alfred, 85.
Hurlbutt, Alvin, 348.
Hurlbutt, Aseph, 102.
Hurlbutt, Enoch, 277.
Hurlbutt, James, 347.
Hurlbutt, James H., 348.
Hurlbutt, Jehiel, 346.
Hurlbutt, Jonathan, 347.
Hurlbutt, Leucius, 351.
Huse, 8.
Huse, Boardwell, 169, 355.
Huse, Bodwell, 32, 229, 265.
Huse, Freeman, 8.
Huse, William, 314.
Huston, William, 214.
Hutchen, Jeremiah, 286.
Hutchenson, Thomas, 78.
Hutcherson, Thomas, 57.
Hutcheson, John, 296.
Hutchinson, 370.
Hutchinson, Amos, 15.
Hutchinson, Asa, 142.
Hutchinson, Ebenezer, 142.
Hutchinson, Elijah, 141.
Hutchinson, Jonathan, 221.
Hutchinson, Jonathan, Jr., 221.
Hutchinson, Moses, 198.
Hutchinson, Thomas, 121, 162, 287.
Hutchison, John, 296.
Hutchson, Amos, 15.
Hutenot, Francis, 169.
Hutinock, Frances, 4.
Hutonet, Francis, 31.
Hutonot, Francis, 67, 233.
Hutsheson, Paul, 296.
Hutternock, Francis, 98.

Huxley, John, 349.
Hyat, Abraham, 9.
Hyat, Alvin, 9.
Hyatt, Samuel, 111.
Hyde, Asa, 214, 279.
Hyde, Charles, 220.
Hyde, James, 31, 302, 306, 328.
Hyde, James, 3d, 74.
Hyde, Jedidiah, Jr., 74.
Hyde, Joel, 272, 323, 341.
Hyde, Ollever, 140.
Hyde, Rufus, 31, 232, 340.
Hyde, Samuel, 200.
Hyde, William, 196.
Hyden, David, 341.
Hylys, James, Jr., 357.

Indian, 4.
Indian, James, 138.
Indian, John, 48.
Indian, Joseph, 141.
Indian, Samson, 156.
Indian, Tom, 104.
Ingals, 138.
Ingersole, Joel, 203.
Ingham, Samuel, 49.
Ingham, Stephen, 79, 250.
Ingly, Joseph, 46, 113.
Ingraham, Daniel, Jr., 140.
Ingraham, Eleazer, 104.
Ingraham, Henry, 208.
Ingraham, Samuel, 282.
Ingraham, William, 104.
Ingram, 33, 233.
Ingram, Amaziah, 213.
Ingram, Jared, 10.
Ingram, Mary, 33, 233.
Ipswich, Mass., 366.
Ireland, 365, 366.
Isbell, Joel, 300.
Isbell, Lyman, 281, 300.
Isbell, Peruda, 104.
Isham, Ebenezer, 87.
Isham, Jona, 87.
Isham, Joshua, 47, 351.
Isham, William, 87, 351.
Ivers, Thomas, 58.
Ives, Aaron, 13.
Ives, Abij., 83.
Ives, Asahel, 215.
Ives, Elnathan, 19.
Ives, Lazarus, 19.
Ives, Levi, 13.
Ives, Samuel, 206.
Ixbel, Joel, 274.

Jaaroms, David, 49.

Johnson, Artemas, 1.
Johnson, Benjamin, 32, 60, 76, 83, 148, 158, 237.
Johnson, Bristo, 286.
Johnson, Bristol, 265.
Johnson, Caleb, 181.
Johnson, Caleb, Jr., 7.
Johnson, Dan, 13.
Johnson, Daniel, 10, 116, 206, 282.
Johnson, Davice, 70.
Johnson, David, 32, 84.
Johnson, Davis, 52, 239.
Johnson, Eliakim, 60, 83.
Johnson, Elihu, 32, 81, 170, 239.
Johnson, Elijah, 10, 12.
Johnson, Grant, 59.
Johnson, Isael, 83.
Johnson, Isaac, 32, 231, 266.
Johnson, Israel, 47, 60, 192, 351.
Johnson, James, 7, 32, 64, 84, 146, 346.
Johnson, James, Jr., 65.
Johnson, James, 2ᵈ, 7.
Johnson, Jedediah, 362.
Johnson, Jeremiah, 4.
Johnson, Joel, 280, 332.
Johnson, John, 4, 9, 32, 53, 67, 77, 83, 96, 110, 146, 150, 170, 230, 239, 266, 351.
Johnson, John, Jr., 5.
Johnson, Jonathan, 32, 170, 239, 265.
Johnson, Joseph, 85, 128, 243, 279, 306, 348.
Johnson, Luther, 60.
Johnson, Nathaniel, 4, 11, 32, 67, 98, 114, 233, 285.
Johnson, Obadiah, 158, 159, 161, 225.
Johnson, Peter, 61, 323, 341.
Johnson, Phinehas, 73.
Johnson, Prince, 332.
Johnson, Reuben, 1.
Johnson, Robert, 32, 170, 236, 288, 355.
Johnson, Rufus, 199.
Johnson, Samuel, 6, 13, 117, 346, 367.
Johnson, Samuel, 2ᵈ. 13.
Johnson, Solomon, 72, 135, 208.
Johnson, Thomas, 366.
Johnson, Timothy, 73.
Johnson, William, 3, 32, 59, 66, 67, 81, 96, 117, 170, 190, 265, 273, 341.
Johnston, Abraham, 338.

Johnston, Bristol, 351.
Johnston, James, 240.
Johnston, Jonathan, 132.
Johnston, Joseph, 321, 338.
Johnston, Timothy, 340.
Johnstone, William, 234.
Johson, Isaac, 170.
Joice, David, 333.
Jole, William, 162.
Jolly, William, 33, 122, 155, 234.
Jona, 162.
Jonas, Jonah, 154.
Jonathan, Gideon, 279.
Jone, John Frederick, 283.
Jones, Aaron, 32, 79, 170, 232, 254, 266, 320, 358, 359.
Jones, Asa, 76, 147, 159.
Jones, Asahel, 370.
Jones, Charles, 170.
Jones, Dan, 290.
Jones, Daniel, 32, 58, 90, 140, 170, 237, 266, 291.
Jones, David, 279, 338, 349.
Jones, Eleazer, 32, 80, 238.
Jones, Elezer, 18.
Jones, Elias, 56, 77, 137.
Jones, Elihu, 220.
Jones, Epahrass, 243.
Jones, Etkanah, 220.
Jones, Eton, Jr., 286.
Jones, Ezra, 207.
Jones, George, 6.
Jones, Henry, 32, 359.
Jones, Isaac, 63.
Jones, Isahel, 370.
Jones, Isaiah, 32, 114, 170, 233.
Jones, Issacher, 18.
Jones, James, 56, 77, 137, 286.
Jones, Jasber, 170.
Jones, Jasper, 32, 93, 234, 265.
Jones, Jesse, 52.
Jones, John, 2, 90, 95, 97, 136.
Jones, Jonah, 122.
Jones, Joseph 2, 32, 170, 266.
Jones, Manual, 147.
Jones, Morris, 74, 79.
Jones, Nathan, 80.
Jones, Phineas, 274.
Jones, Phinehus, 300.
Jones, Pratt, 336.
Jones, Richard, 252.
Jones, Rubin, 210.
Jones, Samuel, 59, 60, 83, 221, 286.
Jones, Stephen, 12, 18.
Jones, Thomas, 9, 32, 76, 77, 137, 170, 230, 237, 265, 292, 366, 369.

Kellogg, Seth, 52, 70, 255, 345.
Kellogg, Stephen, 254, 321, 338, 348.
Kelly, John, 40, 53, 283.
Kelsey, Eli, 281.
Kelsey, Noah, 33, 80, 170, 266, 321.
Kelsey, Oliver, 72.
Kelsug, Noah, 338.
Kelue, Peter, 162.
Kendal, Daniel, 19.
Kendal, Joshua, 290.
Kendall, John, 345.
Kendall, Joshua, 198.
Kendol, Noadiah, 144.
Kendrich, Benjamin, 87.
Kenedy, David, 363.
Keney, Benjamin, 170, 346.
Keney, Thomas, 180.
Kenn, William, 285.
Kennedy, Joseph, 12.
Kennedy, Nathan, 357.
Kenney, Benjamin, 266.
Kenning, Thomas, 122.
Kenny, Jonas, 184.
Kenny, Joshua, 342.
Kenny, Richard, 342.
Kent, Abel, 18.
Kent, Benajah, 18.
Kent, Joseph, 180, 338.
Kent, Nathan, 57.
Kent, Oliver, 179.
Kent, Titus, 352.
Kent, 23, 25, 26, 27, 31, 34, 35, 103, 104, 106, 107, 126, 165, 169, 170, 189, 208, 209, 210, 211, 235, 261, 265, 282, 285, 355.
Keny, 143.
Keny, James, 143.
Kerkum, William, 335.
Kerns, Luke, 60.
Ketcham, Ezra, 47.
Ketchem, Daniel, 4.
Ketchum, Ezra, 119, 154.
Ketchum, Samuel, 109.
Keton, John, 348.
Keyes, Aaron, 46.
Keyes, Elnathan, 226.
Keyes, Marshal, 282, 341.
Keys, Elnathan, 181.
Kibbe, Bildad, 11.
Kibbe, Daniel, 11.
Kibbe, James, 2d, 11.
Kibbe, Philip, 57, 81.
Kidder, James, 130.
Kilbey, Christopher, 170.
Kilborn, Abraham, 53.

Kilborn, David, 53.
Kilborn, Elaphaz, 215.
Kilborn, Roswell, 286.
Kilborn, Samuel, 53.
Kilby, Anthony, 188.
Kilby, Christopher, 33, 238, 255, 310.
Killam, Cyrus, 51.
Killingly, 30, 35, 37, 71, 134, 135, 136, 137, 138, 161, 173, 183, 190, 192, 193, 194, 195, 197, 199, 200, 215, 216, 217, 225, 237, 260, 264, 269, 270, 272, 273, 287, 292, 295, 301.
Killingworth, 22, 28, 30, 34, 38, 39, 52, 72, 150, 151, 164, 166, 167, 170, 173, 174, 188, 209, 211, 212, 216, 231, 261, 262, 263, 268, 270, 273, 274, 280, 281, 300, 367.
Killogg, Isaac, 257.
Killum, Luther, 211.
Kiltam, Cyrus, 69.
Kimbal, Abraham, 33.
Kimbal, Elijah, 363.
Kimball, Abraham T., 170, 239, 346.
Kimball, Elijah, 362.
Kimball, Jared, 284, 323, 341.
Kimball, Jededeh, 266.
Kimball, Jedediah, 287, 301, 302, 306, 312, 344.
Kimball, John, 284, 323.
Kimball, Richard, 323, 341.
Kimball, Samuel, 199.
Kimberlee, John, 154.
Kimberley, Ephraim, 266.
Kimberly, 33, 234.
Kimberly, Charles, 60.
Kimberly, E., 170.
Kimberly, John, 123.
Kimboe, Charles, 131.
Kinball, Charles, 185.
Kindle, John, 339.
Kine, Daniel, 208.
King, Eli, 336.
King, George, 33, 75, 170, 229.
King, Hez, 170.
King, John, 152.
King, Joseph, 266, 284, 352.
King, Orry, 33, 93, 170, 234, 250.
King, Samuel, 4, 208.
King, Theodore, 187.
Kingbury, Phinehas, Jr., 369.
Kingley, Asael, 181.
Kingman, Mitchel, 368.
Kingsberry, Jabez, 75.
Kingsberry, Joseph, 48.

Kingsbury, Andrew, 132.
Kingsbury, J., 329.
Kingsbury, Jabez, 71, 136, 161.
Kingsbury, Jacob, 303, 305, 323, 339.
Kingsbury, Joseph, 193.
Kingsbury, Michael, 113.
Kingsbury, Oliver, 136, 294, 316.
Kingsbury, Samuel, 224.
Kingsley, Aaron, 288, 325, 339.
Kingsley, Asehel, 221.
Kingsley, Elipaz, 85.
Kingsley, Hezekiah, 159.
Kingsley, James, 75.
Kingsley, Ebenezer, 19.
Kinne, Asa, 10.
Kinne, Benoni, 12, 148.
Kinne, Ezra, 15.
Kinne, Jacob, 10.
Kinne, James, 149.
Kinne, Spencer, 15.
Kinney, Joseph, 182.
Kinning, Thomas, 33, 234.
Kinsey, William, 350.
Kiplee, Elijah, 340.
Kircum, Benjamin, 258, 306, 323.
Kircum, John, 303, 308, 327.
Kircum, Philemon, 328.
Kircum, William, 252.
Kirkham, Benjamin, 51.
Kirkham, William, 51.
Kirkland, 232.
Kirkum, John, 250, 348.
Kirkum, Philemon, 273, 307, 319.
Kirkum, Samuel, 348.
Kirkum, William, 318.
Kirtland, 33.
Kirtland, Jabez, 272, 323, 341.
Kirtland, James, 81.
Kirttend, Jabez, 301.
Kittle, Thomas, 345.
Knap, Aaron, 119, 154.
Knap, Abraham, 74.
Knap, Benjamin, 121.
Knap, Borden, 114.
Knap, Charles, 116.
Knap, David, 121.
Knap, Ebenezer, 3.
Knap, Edward, 349.
Knap, Elijah, 74.
Knap, Henry, 222.
Knap, James, 33, 57, 80, 115, 233, 234.
Knap, John, 3, 55, 105.
Knap, John, Jr., 121.
Knap, Jonas, 57.
Knap, Jones, 80.

28

Knap, Lemuel, 137.
Knap, Moses, 7, 89.
Knap, S., 114.
Knap, Samuel, 116.
Knap, Timothy, 33, 69, 170, 235.
Knap, Usel, 33, 233.
Knap, Uzel, 313.
Knapp, Benjamin, 282.
Knapp, Bouton, 367.
Knapp, Edward, 206.
Knapp, Isaac, 367.
Knapp, James, 365.
Knapp, Jared, 53.
Knapp, Nathan, 115.
Knapp, Ushal, 114.
Knapp, Uzal, 329.
Kneel, Robart, 66.
Kneeland, Jesse, 266, 284, 353.
Kneeland, Jonathan, 3.
Kneeland, Samuel, 87.
Kneeland, Seth, 345.
Knight, Daniel, 310.
Knight, Daniel W., 335.
Knight, Elijah, 75.
Knight, Phineas, 272, 301, 323, 341.
Knight, Squier, 136.
Knight, Squir, 71, 148.
Knight, Squire, 160.
Knight, William, 82, 147, 159.
Knolton, Joseph, 3.
Knot, Hezekiah, 348.
Knowles, Charles, 7.
Knowles, Giles, 65.
Knowles, James, 266.
Knowles, John, 345.
Knowles, Seth, 65, 347.
Knowlton, 88.
Knowlton, Joshua, 46.
Knox, Alexander, 286, 297.
Knox, Archable, 357.
Koberling, Cornelus, 14.
Kyes, Aaron, 130.
Kyes, Marshall, 323.

Lacey, Fairchild F., 34.
Lacey, John F., 154.
Lacey, Josiah, 34, 67, 234.
Lacey, Richard, 4.
Lacy, J. Fairchild, 234.
Lacy, John, 7.
Lacy, John Fairchild, 122.
Lacy, Josiah, 171.
Lacy, Seth, 8.
Lad, Eliab, 12.
Ladd, John, 132.
Ladd, Oliver, 132.

Ladd, Samuel, Jr., 75.
Laflen, James, 82.
Laflen, John, Jr., 82.
Laflin, Abraham, 82.
Laflin, James, 59.
Laflin, John, 59, 61.
Lair, Jacob, 69.
Lake, Phineas, 171, 235.
Lake, Reuben, 332.
Lamb, 150, 152, 359.
Lamb, Asa, 51, 69, 198.
Lamb, Benjamin, 128.
Lamb, Jacob, 281.
Lamb, Joseph, 33, 183, 238.
Lamb, Silas, 253.
Lambart, Samuel, 6.
Lambert, Thomas, 281.
Lamberton, Obed, 34, 170, 241, 266, 348.
Lamberton, Obed, Jr., 85.
Lambkins, Benjamin, 170.
Lambskins, Benjamin, 34, 235.
Lament, William, 330.
Lamfear, Samuel, 61.
Lamfeer, Samuel, 296.
Lamphere, Abel, 364.
Lamphere, Roswell, 337.
Lamphere, Samuel, 108.
Lamphier, Fitch, 247.
Lamphier, Roswell, 182.
Lampshire, George, 220.
Lamson, Ebenezer, 11.
Lamson, Samuel, 203.
Lancashire, 366.
Landing, Cazar, 288.
Landon, Ozias, 244.
Lane, Amos, 80.
Lane, Joel, 266, 289.
Lane, John, 46, 131, 211.
Lane, Joseph, 210, 212.
Lane, Lemuel, 278, 299, 347.
Lane, Nathan, 340.
Lane, Robert, 65, 132.
Lane, William, 33, 359.
Lanfere, Oliver, Jr., 2.
Langatha, Stephen, 10, 349.
Langathe, Stephen, 80.
Langdon, Philip, 18, 80.
Langly, David, 69.
Lankton, Jonathan, 50.
Lanord, Asa, 63.
Lanphear, Fitch, 140.
Laphland, John, 352.
Laraba, Seth, 288.
Larabe, Nathaniel, 9.
Larabee, John, 154.
Laraby, Asa, 54.

Laraby, Willet, 54.
Lareey, Ready, 284.
Larey, Ready, 299.
Larnebe, Willord, 235.
Larned, 135.
Larnord, Joseph, 141, 142.
Larow, John, 53.
Larrebee, Willard, 78.
Larrebee, Willet, 34.
Larribe, Seth, 85.
Larrobe, Seth, 127.
Larroby, Thomas, 180.
Larry, Thada, 352.
Lashbrooks, William, 56, 77, 137.
Latham, Amos, 50, 68.
Latham, Cary, 285.
Lathrop, Ebenezer, 362.
Lathrop, James, 179, 220.
Lathrop, Joseph, 75.
Lathrop, Samuel, 76.
Lattemore, Levi, 266.
Lattimer, Levi, 243, 284.
Lattimore, Levi, 348.
Laughlin, James, 80.
Laurance, Edward, 11.
Lauson, Joseph, 307.
Lauton, Joshua, 134.
Laverrick, Gabriel, 266.
Law, Nathan, 295.
Lawin, Joseph, 93.
Lawrance, Amos, 86, 170, 241.
Lawrance, Bille, 46, 63, 64.
Lawrance, John, 135, 228.
Lawrance, Luther, 205.
Lawrence, Amos, 34, 266, 348.
Lawrence, David, 86, 134.
Lawrence, Luthar, 10.
Lawrence, Richard, 280, 289, 354.
Laws, Joseph, 139.
Lawson, David, 179.
Lawson, Joseph, 280, 314, 328.
Lay, Asa, 34, 79, 171, 232, 266.
Lay, Elias, 3.
Lay, John, 179, 266, 282, 338.
Lay, John, 2d, 282.
Lay, John, 4th, 288.
Lay, Richard, 34, 170, 232, 266.
Layre, Jacob, 34, 235.
Lazel, Abner, 277.
Leach, 151.
Leach, Ebenezer, 59.
Leach, Hezekiah, 6, 266.
Leach, Jabez, 71, 137.
Leach, Lewis, 351.
Leach, William, 60, 84, 209.
Leads, Thomas, 344.
Leaming, George, 93.

Lyman, Richard, 2ᵈ, 139.
Lyman, Richard, 3ᵈ, 139.
Lyman, Samuel, 220.
Lyme, 21, 23, 26, 27, 31, 33, 34, 35, 37, 38, 39, 40, 43, 44, 163, 164, 166, 167, 169, 170, 171, 173, 174, 177, 179, 180, 181, 182, 183, 184, 190, 215, 227, 232, 246, 257, 260, 265, 266, 268, 269, 271, 282, 287, 288, 302, 356, 358, 359, 366, 368.
Lynde, Gideon, 78.
Lynds, John, 229.
Lynde, Samuel, Jr., 279, 300.
Lynn, William, 343.
Lyon, 97, 98, 134.
Lyon, Aaron, 3, 14.
Lyon, Abiel, 33, 76, 138, 237.
Lyon, Amariah, 359.
Lyon, Asa, 33, 86, 134, 230.
Lyon, Ezra, 170.
Lyon, Henry, 33, 131, 237, 266.
Lyon, Isaac, 104.
Lyon, John, 97, 134.
Lyon, Joseph, 214.
Lyon, Joseph, Jr., 68.
Lyon, Nathan, 89.
Lyon, Pelatiah, 110.
Lyon, Peter, 334.
Lyon, Samuel, 33, 97, 233, 284, 309, 334.
Lyon, Stephen, 97, 134.
Lyon, Thomas, 33.
Lyon, Tony, 96.

McAnotter, John, 35, 233.
McCannack, John, 151.
McCartee, George, 267.
McCartee, John, 266.
McCarter, George, 227.
Maccarty, John, 277.
McCensey, George, 35.
McCensey, James, 35.
McClain, James, 78.
McCluer, James, 18.
McColpin, Alexander, 317.
McCorn, William, 34.
McCorne, William, 65, 240.
McCowen, Neal, 118.
McCoy, Alexander, 35, 74, 232.
McCoy, John, 267, 282.
McCraw, Reuben, 202.
McCullum, Duncan, 267, 280.
McCulpin, Alexander, 278, 351.
McCune, Robert, 361.
McCune, Samuel, 362.
McDaniel, Anthony, 54, 330.
McDaniel, Daniel, 71.

McDaniel, James, 232, 267.
McDaniel, John, 171.
McDanield, James, 35.
McDanields, James, 77.
McDaniels, Jams, 171.
McDaniels, Samuel, 9.
McDavid, James, 346.
McDonald, C., 210.
McDonald, Charles, 55, 120, 154.
McDonald, John, 35, 113, 355.
McDonel, John, 68.
McDonold, John, 232.
McDougal, 339.
McDowel, Alexander, 35, 238.
MacFall, William, 34, 344.
McFarland, James, 284.
McFee, Anguis, 73.
McGlaflin, John, 153.
McGreeger, John, 237.
McGregor, John, 35, 171.
McGregory, Aaron, 8.
McGregory, Samuel, 189.
McGriegier, 198.
McGriegier, John, 76.
Mcgriggay, Joel, 66.
Mcgriggry, Joel, 49.
McGuire, Thomas, 283, 301.
McHood, Joseph, 351.
McIntire, Abel, 48.
McIntosh, Timothy, 181.
McJuborrough, Jeddⁿ, 239.
Mack, Abner, 141, 171, 266, 354.
Mack, Barzilla, 354.
Mack, Benjamin, 79, 246.
Mack, Daniel, 186.
Mack, Hezekiah, 3.
Mack, Joel, 141, 221.
Mack, Orlander, 239.
Mack, Richard, 276, 352.
Mack, Samuel, 142.
Mack, Thomas, 296.
Mack, Zebulon, 369.
Mackarel, James, 370.
Mckartey, James, 139.
Mackaul, James, 370.
Mackaul, Walter, 141.
McKay, James, 3.
McKeine, Barnabas, 5.
McKensey, John, 58.
McKenzie, John, 94.
McKey, Wyllin, 190.
Mackinborough, Benjamin, 142.
Mackinborough, Jedadiah, 142.
McKinstry, Paul, 345.
Mackintire, Henery, 57, 80.
McKinzey, James, 233.
Mackrady, John, 117.

Macks, Jeremiah, 171.
McLane, Jacobe, 35, 235, 267.
McLane, Matthew, 35, 232.
McLane, Moredock, 63.
Maclane, Niel, 241.
McLarlene, John, 158.
McLean, David, 52, 70.
McLean, Jacob, 78, 227.
McLean, John, 78, 227.
McLean, Neil, Jr., 86.
McLean, William, 47, 118, 153.
McLorey, Andrew, 77.
McMullin, John, 67.
McNale, Archabel, 14.
McNeal, Henry, 201.
McNeal, Neal, 334.
McNeel, Neel, 210.
McNeil, Neil, 63.
McNulter, John, 267.
McNulty, John, 219, 330.
McNulty, John, 314.
McNunlly, John, 113.
McNutters, John, 171.
MacOrlander, 35.
McQueen, William, 2.
McQuire, Thomas, 354.
McRenneck, John, 73.
McRow, William, 198.
Maculpin, Alexander, 267.
Maggot, Zebulon, 171, 267.
Mahar, James, 35, 70, 171, 238, 267.
Maharr, James, 345.
Maksfield, Caleb, 154.
Main, John, 104.
Malcom, Thomas, 75.
Maleny, Nathan, 339.
Malery, Lemuel, 208.
Malison, Thomas, 50, 68.
Mallary, A., 99.
Mallary, David, 102.
Mallerson, Benjamin, 34.
Mallery, Amos, 35, 73, 172, 229, 266, 267.
Mallery, Calvin, 217.
Mallery, David, 73.
Mallery, Giles, 9.
Mallery, John, 1.
Mallery, Jonah, 84, 171, 266.
Mallery, Levi, 276.
Mallery, Levey, 3.
Mallery, Nathan, 282, 325, 339.
Mallery, Nathaniel, 325.
Mallery, Samuel, 215.
Mallery, Simeon, 66.
Mallet, Abell, 93.
Mallison, Roswell, 216.

Maltbie, Jonathan, 365.
Maltbie, Zaccheus, 1.
Maltby, David, 115.
Malthrop, Joseph, 172.
Malthrop, Steaphen, 172.
Man, Elisha, 296.
Man, Zadock, 142.
Manchester, 254.
Manclift, Lemiel, 316.
Mane, John, Jr., 235.
Maning, Samuel, 58.
Maning, William, 80, 231.
Manjent, Nicholas, 54.
Manley, William, 14.
Manly, Asa, 218.
Manly, John, 147.
Manning, Bille, 134.
Manning, Dyar, 74.
Manning, Phin., 81.
Manning, Phineas, 35, 241.
Manning, Roger, 74.
Manning, Samuel, 91.
Manning, Seabury, 199.
Manning, Sebuary, 363.
Manning, Thomas, 285, 354.
Manning, William, 35, 133, 171, 227, 230.
Manning, William, Jr., 75.
Manross, Theodore, 206.
Mansfield, Charles, 152.
Mansfield, Dan, 35, 172, 229, 266.
Mansfield, John, 13, 35, 82, 171, 230, 292.
Mansfield, Josh, 35.
Mansfield, Joseph, 172, 229.
Mansfield, Mathew, 189.
Mansfield, Richard, 152.
Mansfield, T., 266.
Mansfield, 21, 22, 24, 26, 27, 29, 32, 37, 38, 39, 41, 54, 55, 72, 73, 88, 129, 133, 138, 163, 167, 173, 174, 179, 180, 181, 182, 183, 184, 199, 200, 216, 217, 218, 219, 227, 236, 256, 260, 261, 263, 275, 280, 282, 287, 294, 299, 356, 357.
Mantor, Royal, 317.
Manvill, Ira, 217.
Manwaring, George, 34, 227, 290.
Marble, Thomas, 35, 141, 171, 239, 266, 344, 354.
Marchant, John, 267.
Marchant, Stephen, 73.
Marcy, Thomas, 34.
Margaro, John, 112.
Marin, John. 295.
Markham, **Isaac**, 49, 66.
Markham, Joseph, 34, 171, 240.

Markham, Joshua, 65.
Markham, Samuel, 7.
Marks, Abisha, 267, 351.
Marks, Comfort, 7, 35, 239.
Marks, Hezekiah, 142.
Marr, Pattrick, 346.
Marsh, Abner, 35, 71, 135.
Marsh, John, 207, 352.
Marsh, Joseph, 201.
Marsh, Peter, 35, 76, 159, 172, 237, 280.
Marsh, Robert, 330.
Marsh, Roswell, 207.
Marsh, Samuel, 6.
Marshal, Byard, 267.
Marshal, Elisha, 35.
Marshal, Samuel, 241.
Marshall, Elijah, 14.
Marshall, Joseph, 118.
Marshall, Mead, 115.
Marshall, Samuel, 86, 362.
Marshall, Samuel Bryan, 73.
Marshall, Thomas, 243.
Marshall, William, 117.
Marshel, Alexander, 143.
Marshel, Elisha, 236.
Marshel, John, 200.
Marshell, Amos, 68.
Martain, Gidion, 72.
Martain, Hewlett, 133.
Marten, George, 35.
Marten, John, 54.
Marten, John, Jr., 72.
Marten, Lewis, 35.
Marten, Nathan, 356.
Marter, Royal, 317.
Marther, Elias, 232.
Martin, Charles, 65.
Martin, Charles O., 353.
Martin, David, 215.
Martin, George, 85, 171, 236.
Martin, Gideon, 135, 292, 301.
Martin, Gideon, Jr., 273.
Martin, John, 75.
Martin, John, Jr., 129.
Martin, Joseph, 140.
Martin, Lewis, 229, 338.
Martin, Nathaniel, 85.
Martin, Philip, 196.
Martin, Reuben, 340.
Martin, Samuel, 194.
Martin, William, 134, 245, 319, 336, 346.
Martins, Manasah, 364.
Marus, Moses, 87.
Marvin, Barnabas, 111.
Marvin, Matthew, 108, 154.

Marvin, O., 109.
Marvin, Ozias, 9.
Marvin, Thomas, 220.
Masa, Joseph, 127.
Mash, Abner, 237.
Mason, Asa, 179, 218.
Mason, Ashbel, 53.
Mason, Jeremiah, 142, 221.
Mason, John, 35, 53, 150, 171, 235.
Mason, Reuben, 299.
Mason, Rufus, 11, 266, 275.
Massachusetts, 99, 126, 228, 297, 368.
Masters, Nicholas, 100.
Maten, Abner, 194.
Mather, Elias, 35, 171.
Mather, Elihu, 86, 276, 331, 348.
Mather, Increase, 14.
Mather, John, 114.
Mather, Nath, 86.
Mather, Nathaniel, 241.
Matheson, David, 311.
Mathews, Eliada, 267.
Mathews, Hubbard, 49.
Mathews, James, 153.
Mathews, Jese, 49.
Mathews, Robert, 266.
Mathews, William, 50.
Matson, John, 11.
Matterson, David, 344.
Matterson, William, 290.
Mattherson, William, 78.
Matthews, Eliada, 171.
Matthews, James, 34, 118, 234.
Matthews, Jesse, 347.
Matthews, John, 171.
Matthews, Robert, 34, 172, 229.
Matthews, William, 34, 239, 346.
Mattison, David, 272, 311.
Mattocks, Samuel, 35, 70.
Mattoon, Joel, 13.
Mattoon, Samuel, 13.
Mattucks, Samuel, 238.
Mauenborough, Jedadiah, 35.
Maxfield, Caleb, 118.
May, John, 14.
Maynard, John, 358.
Maynord, Cyrus, 363.
Maynord, Zacheriah, 363.
Mayo, Elisha, 135, 209.
Mayson, Rufus, 349.
Mazuzen, Mark, 2.
Mazzeen, Ezekiel, 278, 291.
Meach, Joshua, 35, 232.
Meach, Thomas, 76, 336, 341.
Meach, William, 76, 147, 158.

442   REVOLUTION LISTS AND RETURNS.

Mertin, Joseph Plum, 73.
Merwin, David, 55, 105.
Merwin, Jesse, 104.
Mesenger, Aron, 11.
Mesenger, David, 11.
Mesenger, Israel, 11.
Mesenger, Ruben, 11.
Meson, Elias, 286.
Meson, Joseph, 50.
Messenger, Ezekiel, 80, 275.
Mesum, Joseph, 75.
Metcalf, Dan, 139.
Metcalf, Jabez, 139, 227.
Metcalf, Jonathan, 181, 220.
Micael, 28.
Micha, 75.
Middlesex Co., 298.
Middleton, William, 179.
Middletown, Christopher, 346.
Middletown, Peter, 346.
Middletown, 6, 22, 23, 25, 26, 27,
    28, 29, 30, 31, 32, 33, 34, 35, 37,
    38, 41, 43, 44, 88, 163, 164, 166,
    167, 168, 169, 170, 171, 172, 173,
    174, 176, 188, 193, 204, 205, 215,
    216, 239, 242, 243, 244, 245, 246,
    248, 249, 251, 252, 254, 255, 256,
    258, 259, 260, 262, 263, 264, 265,
    266, 268, 269, 270, 271, 301, 346,
    355, 365, 366, 367.
Mider, Gideon W., 284.
Miel, Charles, 77.
Mielkin, John, 184.
Miels, Charles, 171.
Migat, Zebulon, 36.
Miggs, Phinehas, 66.
Mildrum, Mark, 49.
Miles, Caleb, 69.
Miles, Charles, 9, 35, 232.
Miles, Isaac, 35, 69, 235.
Miles, James, 60, 83.
Miles, John, 8, 35, 172, 229, 266.
Miles, Samuel, 13.
Miles, Thomas, 166.
Milord, 24, 26, 27. 29, 31, 32, 39,
    40, 41, 73, 88, 150, 151, 164, 166,
    167, 168, 170, 172, 174, 175, 176,
    214, 216, 231, 261, 262, 263, 264,
    265, 266, 267, 268, 269, 270, 271,
    284, 369.
Millar, Charles, 267.
Millar, Daniel, 65, 346.
Millar, Jonathan, 348.
Millar, Samuel, 11.
Millar, William, 346.
Millard, Charles, 206.
Millard, Levit, 63, 254.

Miller, 370.
Miller, Abner, 46, 63, 64.
Miller, Alexander, 198, 363.
Miller, Alexander, Jr., 224.
Miller, Caleb, 348.
Miller, Charles, 34, 70, 171, 238.
Miller, Daniel, 34, 52, 70, 171, 240,
    267, 287, 294.
Miller, David, 142, 367.
Miller, Dudley, 204.
Miller, Ebenezer, 367.
Miller, Edward, 327.
Miller, Enoch, 240.
Miller, James, 26, 75.
Miller, John, 34, 238.
Miller, Jonathan, 258, 306, 328.
Miller, Joseph, 201, 366.
Miller, Nathan, 34, 232.
Miller, Noah, 186.
Miller, Nathaniel, 7, 34, 171, 238.
Millet, Jonathan, 12.
Millington, Samuel, 36, 56, 137,
    218, 241.
Millington, Samuel, 3d, 81.
Millinton, Samuel, 77.
Millor, Edward, 346.
Mills, 103, 104.
Mills, Abraham, 314.
Mills, Alexander, 61, 103, 116,
    339.
Mills, Elihu, 86.
Mills, Elijah, 203.
Mills, Ephraim, 11.
Mills, Gabriel, 314.
Mills, George, 114.
Mills, Gideon, 11.
Mills, John, 4, 281, 314, 325, 340.
Mills, Joseph, 35, 67, 96, 233.
Mills, Roger, 14.
Mills, Samuel, 35, 171.
Mills, Samuel Riggs, 94.
Mils, Nathaniel, Jr., 135.
Minard, John, 290.
Miner, Andrew, 34, 239.
Miner, Charles, 180, 331.
Miner, Christopher, 184.
Miner, Clement, 81, 336.
Miner, Elihu, 34.
Miner, Elnathan, 284.
Miner, Ichabod, 296.
Miner, James, 34, 272, 323, 341.
Miner, John, 209.
Miner, Sylvester, 34, 290, 332.
Miner, Rausel, 81.
Miner, Timothy, 180.
Mingo, 50.
Mino, Elihue, 241.

Mordock, George, 362.
Mordock, Samuel, 140.
More, Furbuss, 349.
More, John, 228.
More, John, Jr., 35.
More, Nathaniel, 185.
More, William, Jr., 35.
Moredock, Ariel, 140.
Moredock, Jonathan, 140.
Moredock, Prince, 196.
Moree, Aaron, 50.
Morehouse, 111, 112.
Morehouse, David, 4, 34, 67, 94, 171, 233, 267.
Morehouse, Euriah, 4.
Morehouse, Ezra, 4.
Morehouse, G., 89, 90.
Morehouse, Gideon, 274.
Morehouse, John, 210.
Morehouse, Michael, 9.
Morehouse, Peter, 3.
Morehouse, Thomas, 9.
Morey, Thomas, 130, 298.
Morgan, Daniel, 346.
Morgan, Ebenezer, 50, 68.
Morgan, Ephrain, 78.
Morgan, Jacob, 289.
Morgan, James, Jr., 47.
Morgan, Jonathon, 11.
Morgan, Joseph, 290, 358.
Morgan, Joshua, 65, 355.
Morgan, Nathan, 85.
Morgan, Nathl, 89.
Morgan, Nicholas, 216.
Morgan, Thomas, 247, 349.
Morgen, Nathan, 128.
Morgin, Jesse, 208.
Morley, Daniel, 285, 309, 334, 351.
Morley, Elijah, 317, 332.
Morley, John, 17.
Morley, Thomas, 17.
Morras, Peter, 82, 149.
Morril, Asher, 239.
Morrills, Cyprian, 253.
Morrills, Roger, 253.
Morris, 134.
Morris, Andrew, 2.
Morris, Asa, 134.
Morris, James, 205, 365.
Morris, John, 73.
Morris, Peter, 160.
Morris, Robert, 69.
Morrison, Andrew, 56, 193.
Morrison, Rodowick, 354.
Morrison, William, 171, 267, 348.
Morrisson, Andrew, 77.

Morrisson, John, 137.
Morrow, Thomas, 184.
Morse, Amos, 295.
Morse, Chester, 57.
Morse, David, 5.
Morse, James, 64, 75, 146.
Morse, John, 133.
Morse, Linus, 334.
Mortars, Jabez, 316.
Morters, Jabez, 332.
Morton, Jabez, 281.
Moseley, 126.
Moseley, Increase, 364.
Mosely, 28, 99, 100, 102, 104, 106, 108.
Mosely, Ebenezer, 128.
Mosely, Samuel, 131.
Mosely, Sifax, 171.
Mosely, Syphax, 238, 267.
Moser, George, 4.
Moses, Abel, 6.
Moses, Enum, 349.
Moses, Ezekel, 206.
Moses, John, 144.
Moses, Jonas, 35, 230.
Moses, Shubal, 10.
Mosher, Joel, 306, 312, 343.
Mosher, Stephen, 181.
Mosier, Daniel, 93.
Mosier, Joel, 90.
Mosier, Joseph, 67, 98.
Mosley, Cyphax, 351.
Mosock, Daniel, 347.
Moss, Barnibas, 13.
Moss, Benoni, 60, 83, 323, 341.
Moss, Daniel, 35, 229, 267, 340.
Moss, Isaiah, 60, 83.
Moss, John, 35, 229.
Moss, Linas, 69.
Moss, Pompy, 58.
Moss, Reuben, 60, 83, 333.
Moss, Samuel, 207.
Mossack, Daniel, 267.
Mothrop, Joseph, 266.
Mott, Adam, 34, 84, 235, 254.
Mott, Archibald, 219.
Mott, Benjamin, 75.
Mott, Edward, 9.
Mott, Elihu, 65.
Mott, Ira, 255, 307, 321, 328.
Mott, Jacob, 146.
Mott, Jared, 223.
Mott, Jarib, 151.
Mott, Jerod, 213.
Mott, Jarub, 156.
Mott, Jerub, 64.
Mott, Jerule, 64.

Norton, Jabesh, 247.
Norton, Jabez, 321, 338, 345.
Norton, Jedediah, 172, 267, 353, 365.
Norton, John, 209.
Norton, Joseph, 69, 172, 235.
Norton, Levi, 74.
Norton, Noah, 317.
Norton, Noah U., 317, 333.
Norton, Rufus, 172, 231, 267.
Norton, Samuel, 172, 247, 267, 346.
Norton, Shadrach, 18.
Norton, Tabor, 321.
Norton, Thomas, 258.
Norwalk, 8, 24, 25, 27, 28, 34, 36, 41, 42, 44, 88, 95, 108, 109, 110, 111, 112, 126, 151, 165, 167, 169, 171, 172, 175, 177, 207, 215, 262, 263, 264, 265, 266, 267, 270, 271, 285, 286, 288, 355.
Norwash, John, 278, 299.
Norwich, 22, 24, 25, 26, 27, 28, 29, 31, 33, 34, 35, 36, 37, 38, 41, 42, 43, 44, 74, 88, 137, 148, 159, 165, 167, 168, 169, 171, 172, 173, 176, 179, 180, 181, 182, 183, 184, 185, 186, 191, 193, 196, 197, 198, 199, 200, 201, 210, 214, 221, 223, 225, 227, 231, 243, 245, 248, 256, 261, 262, 263, 264, 265, 266, 268, 270, 271, 272, 287, 291, 301, 302, 355, 358, 359, 360, 368.
Nott, Epaphras, 13.
Nott, Hezekiah, 257, 308, 333.
Nottingham, George, 59, 118.
Noys, Nathaniel, 50.
Noyse, Nathaniel, 69.
Nucomb, David, 295.
Nugent, John, 36.
Numes, Benjamin, 153.
Nutton, Ezekiel, 172.
Nye, Ebenezer, 278, 309, 353.

Oates, Joseph, 267.
Oatis, Joseph, 172.
Obbard, James, 253.
Obrian, Thomas, 346.
OBriant, John, 152.
Obriant, William, 284.
OCain, Jeremiah, 151.
Odell, Isaac, 4, 67, 94.
Odell, Nehemiah Smith, 274.
Ogden, Edman, 4.
Ogden, Edmon, 4.
Ogden, Joseph, 98.
Ogden, Samuel, 202.
Ohara, Timothy, 229.

Oharra, Timothy, 36.
O'Kane, Jonh, 230.
Okeain, Jeremiah, 36.
Olcott, Caleb, 353.
Olcott, James, 226.
Olcut, James, 6.
Olcut, James, Jr., 6.
Olds, Aaron, 36, 103, 235, 267, 340.
Olds, Oliver, 36, 104, 236, 267.
Olford, Eber, 188.
Olin, William, 36, 231.
Oliver, Stephen, 359, 368.
Oliver, Thomas, 368.
Olmstad, James, 238.
Olmstead, Abijah, 111.
Olmstead, Francis, 247.
Olmstead, Isaac, 110, 172, 287.
Olmstead, James, 36, 172.
Olmstead, Jeremiah, 120.
Olmstead, Jesse, 285, 330.
Olmstead, Joseph, 222.
Olmstead, Matthew, 205, 222.
Olmstead, Nehemiah, 120, 205, 221, 283.
Olmstead, Timothy, 243.
Olmsted, Abijah, 307, 314.
Olmsted, Ashbel, 81.
Olmsted, Francies, 81,
Olmsted, Garmaliel, 250.
Olmsted, Isaac, 292, 355.
Olmsted, James, 70, 215.
Olmsted, Jeremiah, 162.
Olmsted, Jesse, 267, 314.
Olmsted, Joseph, 202.
Olmsted, Joshua, 317, 333.
Olmsted, Justus, 314.
Olmsted, Nehemiah, 56, 78.
Olmsted, Silas, Jr., 9.
Olmsted, Gemalial, 59.
Olmstid, David, 162.
Olmstid, Nehh, 162.
Olney, Ithamer, 292.
Olvard, Thomas G., 347.
Olvard, Thomas G., Jr., 347.
Oney, Ithamar, 192.
Oniott, Darius, 308, 333.
Onkshun, John, 279.
Onley, Ishecor, 295.
Orcott, Benjamin, 203.
Orcott, John, 80.
Orcut, 88.
Orcut, Caleb, 36, 239.
Orcutt, Ben Jon, 57.
Orcutt, Benjamin, 81.
Orcutt, Caleb, 84, 172, 267.
Orcutt, Darius, 226, 273, 308, 333.
Orcutt, Jacob, 12.

Parish, Asa, 364.
Parish, Eliphaz, 236.
Parish, Jacob, 227.
Parish, Oliver, 296.
Parish, Roswell, 50, 69.
Parit, 88.
Park, Elijah, 9.
Park, Fradrick, 51, 69.
Park, Isaac, 73, 129.
Park, James, 51, 69.
Park, Moses, 9.
Park, Reuben, 78.
Parke, David, 78.
Parke, Jonathan, 18.
Parke, Lemuel, 218.
Parkenton, Denny, 108.
Parker, Aaron, 311.
Parker, Abel, 209.
Parker, Abraham, 333.
Parker, Abram, 60, 83.
Parker, Amos, 60, 83.
Parker, Asael, 288.
Parker, Benjamin, 13, 37, 83, 172, 231, 355.
Parker, Ebenezer, 237.
Parker, Edmund, 13, 37, 172, 229.
Parker, Edward, 268.
Parker, Eliab, 37, 84, 230.
Parker, Elijah, 87.
Parker, Elisha, 37, 83, 172, 231.
Parker, Elisha, Jr., 60.
Parker, Gamaliel, 104.
Parker, Hyman, 339.
Parker, Isaac, 37, 54, 84, 173, 230, 268, 337.
Parker, James, 216, 219.
Parker, James, Jr., 356.
Parker, John, 37, 60, 66, 83, 202, 234.
Parker, John, Jr., 132.
Parker, Jonathan, 51, 225.
Parker, Nathan, 66, 132, 218, 267.
Parker, Nehemiah, 280.
Parker, Samuel, 37, 91, 93, 173, 234, 253, 361.
Parker, Stephen, 207.
Parker, Timothy, 60, 83.
Parker, William, 60, 83.
Parker, Wyman, 142, 246, 324, 354.
Parkharst, David, 349.
Parkharst, Solomon, 349.
Parkhurst, David, 275.
Parkins, Jason, 6.
Parkins, Phinehas, 6.
Parkinson, Dene, 37.
Parkinton, Dine, 234.

Parks, Aaron, 273, 301, 311, 343.
Parks, Daniel, 36, 65, 173, 240.
Parks, David, 256.
Parks, Ebenezer, 363.
Parks, James, 52, 61, 70, 108.
Parks, John, 65, 353.
Parks, Joshua, 12.
Parks, Reuben, 330.
Parks, Samuel, 187, 315, 331.
Parmalee, Jeremiah, 268.
Parmele, 5.
Parmele, Charles, 2.
Parmele, Constant, 53, 72.
Parmele, Hezekiah, 2.
Parmele, James, 52, 72.
Parmele, Jeremiah, 37, 229.
Parmele, Joseph, Jr., 5.
Parmele, Phineas, 2.
Parmele, Silas, 212.
Parmele, William, 5.
Parmerlee, Jeremiah, 284.
Parmerly, James, 211.
Parmerly, Jeremiah, 349.
Paro, Joseph, 288, 353.
Parret, John, Jr., 3.
Parrish, Eliphaz, 38, 85, 128.
Parrish, Eliphilet, 338.
Parrish, Jeremiah, 297.
Parrish, Nehemiah, 19.
Parrit, David, 268.
Parrot, David, 274.
Parry, Ebenezer, 85.
Parseval, Paul, 172.
Parson, Levi, 347.
Parsons, 189, 304, 315, 316, 323, 355.
Parsons, Bartholomew, 109.
Parsons, David, 37, 66, 110, 173, 240.
Parsons, Jabez, 49, 66.
Parsons, Jesse, 117.
Parsons, John, 5.
Parsons, Jonathan, 37, 66, 173, 240, 350.
Parsons, Moses, 214, 277.
Parsons, Osborn, 110.
Parsons, Richard, 19.
Parsons, Samuel, 60.
Parsons, Simeon, 347.
Parsons, Sollomon, 203.
Parsons, Theodosius, 37, 117, 234.
Parsons, Thomas, 86, 268, 348.
Parsons, William, 11, 14.
Patch, William, 119.
Patchen, Aser, Jr., 110.
Patchen, Azor, 111.
Patchen, David, 355.

Peese, Erastus, 18.
Peese, Joel, 18.
Peese, Peter, 18.
Peese, Samuel, 18.
Peese, Sylvanus, 18.
Peess, Abial, 18.
Peet, Abell, 90.
Peet, John, 58, 93.
Peet, Lemuel, 37, 55, 73, 101, 173, 235.
Peeva, Ichabod, 216.
Peevy, Ichabod, 148.
Peirce, Benjamin, 219.
Peirce, Daniel, 172.
Peirce, John, 267.
Peirce, Justus, 107.
Peirce, Samuel, 59, 63, 82.
Pelham, Edward, 218.
Pellet, Enos, 37.
Pellom, Edward, 206.
Pelton, Benjamin, 36, 52, 72, 231.
Pelton, Daniel, 65, 353.
Pelton, David, 36, 68, 74, 232.
Pelton, Ebenezer, 36, 68, 227, 232.
Pelton, George, 36, 65, 240.
Pelton, James, 51, 69.
Pelton, Joel, 275, 354.
Pelton, Moses, 11.
Pemberton, John, 50, 68.
Pendal, Benoni, 338.
Pendall, Toby, 75.
Pendleton, Daniel, 38, 84, 173, 230, 268.
Pene, James, 73.
Penfield, Isaac, 145.
Penfield, Peter, 154.
Penfield, Seth, 190.
Pengo, John, 201.
Pengo, Prentice, 201.
Penhallow, Richard, 75.
Penhellow, Richard, 268.
Pennsylvania, 245.
Pensyl, John, 288.
Perce, John, 13.
Percefield, 88.
Perey, Benjamin, 357.
Perey, Samuel, 298.
Perez, Reuben, 354.
Perigo, William, 37.
Perkens, 128.
Perkens, Daniel, Jr., 37.
Perkens, Daniel B., 54, 73, 129.
Perkens, Ebenezer, 132.
Perkens, Frances, 128.
Perker, Elisha, 13.
Perker, Joseph, 154.
Perkhust, John, 8.

Perkins, Charles, 47.
Perkins, Daniel, 295, 325.
Perkins, Daniel, Jr., 67, 240.
Perkins, Daniel, 2d, 279.
Perkins, Daniel B., 219.
Perkins, Ebenezer, 67, 74, 122.
Perkins, Francis, 64, 157.
Perkins, Gideon, 145.
Perkins, Joel, 185.
Perkins, John, 60.
Perkins, Lenard, 201.
Perkins, Oliver, 19.
Perkins, Phillip, 294.
Perkins, Samuel, 8, 60, 83.
Perkins, Wescut, 146.
Perkins, Westly, 146.
Perrey, Abijah, 58.
Perrey, John, 3.
Perrey, Salvenus, 137.
Perrey, Silverus, 72.
Perrigo, Ebenezer, 75.
Perrigo, William, 172, 231.
Perrigo, William, Jr., 75, 268.
Perrin, Jethnel, 134.
Perring, Stephen, 143.
Perry, 101.
Perry, Abijah, 93.
Perry, Daniel, 133.
Perry, Ebenezer, 37, 129, 236.
Perry, Elipha, 78.
Perry, Elisha, 37, 61, 120, 162, 173, 234, 268.
Perry, Reuben, 204, 278.
Perry, Sandrus, 190.
Perry, Saunders, 222.
Perry, Silvanus, 37, 173, 193, 237.
Perry, Thomas, 197.
Persival, Paul, 355.
Person, Nathan, 300.
Persons, Aaron, 13.
Persons, Isaac, 80.
Persons, Jacob, 154.
Persons, John, 3.
Persons, Moses, 299.
Persons, Semion, 49.
Pervett, John, 63.
Petenger, Abraham, 227.
Peter, 141.
Peter, Galloway, 61.
Peters, Andrew, 280.
Peters, Gallaway, 323.
Peters, John, 73, 273, 292.
Peters, Joseph, 82, 148.
Peters, Nathan, 9.
Peters, Peter, 37, 233.
Peters, Samuel, 281, 314.
Peters, William, 141, 351.

Piney, Levi, 10.
Piney, Nathaniel, 11.
Piney, Peter, 11.
Pinney, Aaron, 38, 86, 241.
Pinney, Ebenezer, 190.
Pinney, Isaac, Jr., 14.
Pinney, Noah, 193.
Pinney, Philister, 81.
Pinney, Isaac, 57, 81.
Pinny, Jonathan, 348.
Pinto, Solomon, 211.
Piquet, Daniel, 209.
Pirce, Benjamin, 183.
Pirkins, Daniel, 267, 350.
Pirkins, Eliphas, 369.
Pirkins, Elisha, 363.
Pirkins, Francis, 85.
Pirkins, Gideon, 369.
Pirkins, Jason, 369.
Pirson, Paul, 300.
Pitcher, Abner, 74.
Pitt, Calib, 8.
Pitts, Richard, 273, 332.
Pitts, Samuel, 179.
Pixlie, Elijah, 61.
Placey, William, 85, 127.
Plainfield, 26, 32, 35, 41, 56, 76,
    88, 136, 146, 147, 158, 159, 163,
    171, 198, 199, 201, 217, 223, 224,
    237, 262, 280, 297.
Plank, John, 194.
Plant, Ethel, 358.
Plant, Timothy, 37, 54, 235.
Platner, John, 347.
Platt, Daniel, 361.
Platt, Ebenezer, 312, 344.
Platt, William, 162.
Platts, Dan, 152.
Plinney, Joseph, 344.
Plum, Charles, 7.
Plum, David, 207.
Plum, Joseph, 154.
Plumb, Amariah, 37, 74, 236.
Plumb, Daniel, 290, 358.
Plumb, Peter, 37, 75, 173, 231.
Plumer, Ebenezer, 137.
Plummer, David, 287, 292.
Poalk, Ammi, 12.
Pole, Frederick, 117. .
Polegreen, Cooper, 76.
Pollard, Ebenezer, 69.
Pollard, Isaac, 37, 99, 235, 268.
Pollard, William, 37, 75, 231.
Pollerd, Ebenezer, 51.
Pollester, Henry, 283.
Polley, Alpheus, 76, 291, 356.
Polley, John, 274, 291.
Polley, Uriah, 74, 290, 291.

Pollister, Henry, 302.
Polly, Alpheus, 37, 139, 173, 237.
Polly, Daniel, 142, 280, 354.
Polly, Uriah, 140, 332.
Pomeroy, Benjamin, 37.
Pomeroy, Ralf, 37.
Pomeroy, Ralph, 70, 172.
Pomfret, 22, 30, 32, 33, 38, 39, 40,
    41, 56, 76, 137, 138, 148, 158,
    165, 192, 193, 196, 197, 198, 199,
    200, 203, 223, 237, 252, 262, 277,
    284, 295, 301.
Pomp, David, 37.
Pomp, Elisha, 87.
Pomp, Jacob, 37, 232.
Pomp, John, 50.
Pomp, Samuel, 37, 68, 232.
Pompey, Samuel, 173.
Pomroy, Benjamin, 239.
Pomroy, Medad, 166.
Pomroy, Nathaniel, 18.
Pomroy, Phebus, 352.
Pomroy, Ralph, 238.
Pomroy, John, 18.
Pond, Charles, 73.
Pond, Eleazer, 74.
Pond, Henry, 283, 332.
Pond, John, 75.
Ponds, Henry, 316.
Pool, Daniel, 36, 173, 237, 356.
Poole, Daniel, 131.
Pooler, John, 11, 349.
Poolman, John, 10.
Poor, Jonathan, 67, 96, 274.
Pope, David, 112.
Pope, Seth, 197.
Porridge, Annanias, 279.
Porridge, Samuel, 279.
Porter, 159.
Porter, Aaron, 52.
Porter, Abner, 52, 208.
Porter, Amos, 36, 70, 172, 240,
    255.
Porter, Andrew, 58, 95.
Porter, Benjamin, Jr., 226.
Porter, Daniel, 37, 86, 173, 241,
    268, 348, 356, 368.
Porter, Eldad, 60, 83.
Porter, Eleazer, 37, 141, 239.
Porter, Alexander, 141.
Porter, Elijah, 49, 52, 71, 184, 218,
    250, 315, 345.
Porter, Ephraim, 94.
Porter, Ezra, 211.
Porter, Hez, 48.
Porter, Hezekiah, 36, 185, 240.
Porter, John, 220, 255, 331, 369.
Porter, Jonathan, 137.

Preston, David, 46, 63.
Preston, Fyrus, 12.
Preston, Jonathan, 61, 84.
Preston, Joseph, 268, 309, 334.
Preston, Josiah, 281.
Preston, Samuel, 362.
Preston, Tiras, 37.
Preston, Tirus, 81, 173, 239.
Preston, 9, 15, 22, 23, 28, 30, 31, 33,
     35, 38, 40, 41, 42, 77, 88, 150,
     159, 163, 165, 167, 168, 169, 170,
     171, 175, 179, 182, 183, 184, 199,
     209, 210, 211, 223, 232, 252, 260,
     262, 263, 264, 267, 270, 271, 286,
     358, 359.
Price, Elijah, 12.
Price, George, 257.
Price, Levi, 235.
Price, Levy, 36.
Price, Nathaniel, 280, 309, 334.
Price, Paul, 54.
Price, Richard, 256.
Price, Robert, 358.
Price, Rufus, 12, 36, 81, 239.
Price, Samuel, 12, 221.
Prichard, George, 172.
Prichard, George, Jr., 36, 84, 230.
Prichard, James, 36, 151, 230.
Pride, Reuben, 74, 192.
Prier, William, 67, 250.
Priest, Asa, 143.
Priest, Philip, 361.
Primas, Jesse, 58.
Primus, Jesse, 92.
Prince, 74.
Prince, Phillip, 184.
Prince, William, 77.
Prince, Zackery, 81.
Prince, Zacheriah, 240.
Prindel, Joseph, 68.
Prindle, Abijah, 8, 36, 124, 154,
     173, 234, 268.
Prindle, Enos, 104.
Prindle, Enos J., 36, 230, 268.
Prindle, Enos Jones, 2, 97.
Prindle, Enos Y., 172.
Prindle, Ezra, 122, 162.
Prindle, Peter, 8.
Prindle, Zalmon, 124, 154.
Prior, Abner, 38, 86, 173, 241, 268.
Prior, Allen, 276, 333.
Prior, Hazard, 307, 321, 330, 349.
Prisley, Stephen, 315.
Pritchard, Benjamin, 73.
Pritchard, Jabez, 2.
Pritchard, Nathaniel, 214.
Pritcket, Jerod, 200.

Prout, James, 83, 289.
Prout, William, 60, 83.
Prouty, Edward, 144.
Providence, 302.
Provost, Dan, 108.
Prows, Thomas, 285.
Prudden, Toney, 73.
Pryar, Allen, 348.
Pryor, Allyn, 86.
Pryor, Hazard, 329.
Psalter, Francis, 345.
Puffer, Daniel, 140, 248.
Puffer, Lazrus, 141.
Puffer, Simeon, 140, 249.
Puffor, Daniel, 295.
Pulford, Elisha, 58, 94.
Pulford, Samuel, 58, 92, 243.
Pumham, Joseph, 268, 282.
Pumroy, Peletiah, 351.
Punderson, Ahimaaz, 335.
Purcivael, Paul, 37.
Purdey, Jesse, 173.
Purdy, Jesse, 118.
Purkens, Daniel, 217.
Purkins, Cudgo, 196.
Purkins, Daniel, 336.
Putman, Reuben, 57, 81.
Putnam, 56, 77.
Putnam, Aaran, 197.
Putnam, Charles, 138.
Putnam, William, 367.

Quacheets, Joseph, 68.
Quameny, Charles, 139.
Quas, Gideon, 301.
Quash, Cato, 38, 173, 241.
Quass, Gideon, 283.
Queekets, Joseph, 50.
Qui, Libbeus, 173, 231, 268.
Quiba, Thomas, 79.
Quigley, John, 294.
Quindley, Thomas, 38.
Quirk, William, 80, 354.
Quivey, Jonathan, 187.
Quochetts, Joseph, 286.
Quosh, Ephraim, 91.
Quy, Libeus, 38.
Quy, Negro, 38.

Racke, William, 302.
Raimond, Ebo, 75.
Rainvolt, William, 321.
Raisley, 254.
Ralinson, Levi, 342.
Ramong, Samuel, 173.
Ramsdall, Ezra, 287.
Ramsdil, Ezra, 194.

Reed, Oliver, 38, 76, 77, 237.
Reed, Ruben, 38.
Reed, Shany, 338.
Reed, Sherry, 283.
Reed, Sparry, 338.
Reed, Stephen, 275.
Reed, William, 340.
Reed, William, Jr., 111.
Reeves, James, 276.
Reeves, Luther, 329.
Reeves, Puryer, 268, 279, 300.
Reggs, Moses, 48.
Reinvault, William, 321.
Reives, James, 184.
Rementon, Stephen, 78.
Remington, Abijah, 18.
Remington, Steph, 162.
Remington, Stephen, 38, 120, 173, 234, 356.
Remong, William, 3.
Ren, Solomon, 56, 78, 162.
Rennals, Benjamin, 57.
Rennels, Simeon, 186.
Rennolds, Joshua, 220.
Rennolds, Reuben, 330.
Renson, William, 159.
Renton, Chandler, 51.
Repley, Charles, 226, 340.
Rerde, Isaac, 199.
Resegue, Abraham, 56.
Reves, Samuel, 352.
Rewick, Owin, 349.
Rexford, Benjamin, 174, 268, 292.
Rexford, Benjamin, Jr., 83, 174.
Reynalds, Benjamin, 81.
Reynold, William, 105.
Reynolds, Benjamin, 115.
Reynolds, David, 61, 103.
Reynolds, Israel, 116.
Reynolds, Jacob, 135.
Reynolds, James, 135.
Reynolds, John, 75, 173, 196.
Reynolds, Joshua, 76, 179, 272, 323.
Reynolds, Justus, 61, 103.
Reynolds, Martin, 312.
Reynolds, Matthew, 188.
Reynolds, Reuben, 313.
Reynolds, Simeon, 76.
Reynolds, Solomon, 107.
Reynolds, Solomon, Jr., 61.
Rhoades, Benjamin, 12.
Rhode Island, 359, 362, 366.
Rial, Stephen, 154.
Rian, Jerem, 36.
Rian, Jerry, 173.
Rian, Patrick, 154.
Rice, 217.

Rice, Daniel, 80.
Rice, David, 39, 84, 239.
Rice, Elijah, 350.
Rice, Isaac, 187.
Rice, Jared, 211.
Rice, John, 268, 296.
Rice, Jonah, 143.
Rice, Jonathan, 188.
Rice, Jotham, 60, 83.
Rice, Nehemiah, 39, 173, 230, 268.
Rice, Samuel, 278.
Rice, Simeon, 190.
Rich, Aaron, 347.
Rich, Amos, 269, 278.
Rich, Joseph, 65.
Rich, Lemuel, 65.
Rich, Lend, 353.
Rich, Nathaniel, 65.
Rich, Samuel, 65, 341, 353.
Rich, Thomas, 65.
Richard, Nathaniel, 57.
Richards, Js, 111.
Richards, James, 8.
Richards, Jedidiah, 74.
Richards, John, 9.
Richards, Nathaniel, 80.
Richards, Sam, 192.
Richards, Samuel, 107, 194.
Richards, Silas, 135.
Richards, Steaphen, 38.
Richards, William, 38, 182, 290.
Richardson, Asa, 140.
Richardson, Boswill, 255.
Richardson, Eleazer, 296.
Richardson, Hezekiah, 132.
Richardson, James, 118, 366.
Richardson, Jesse, 18.
Richardson, Jonathan, 139.
Richardson, Rawswold, 139.
Richardson, Sanford, 18, 206.
Richardson, Stephen, 145.
Richardson, William, 1.
Richmand, Abner, 295.
Richmond, Samuel, 59, 91.
Rickard, Silas, 71, 72.
Rider, Daniel, Jr., 288, 354.
Ridgebury, 202.
Ridgefield, 22, 26, 37, 38, 39, 56, 78, 98, 118, 119, 120, 126, 162, 165, 172, 173, 174, 185, 202, 204, 205, 234, 261, 267, 268, 283, 285, 287, 356.
Riggs, Abner, 48.
Riggs, Daniel, 121.
Riggs, John, 91.
Right, John, 133.
Right, Samuel, 11, 142.
Rigs, Daniel, 162.

Roberts, Ezra, 275.
Roberts, Isaac, 336.
Roberts, James, 221.
Roberts, Joel, 38, 361.
Roberts, John, 14, 47, 121, 283.
Roberts, John, Jr., 7.
Roberts, Judah, 332.
Roberts, Luke, 207, 222.
Roberts, Nathan, 38, 214, 268, 283.
Roberts, Nathaniel, 241, 286.
Roberts, Noah, 249.
Roberts, Peter, 276, 299.
Roberts, Samuel, 257, 309, 334, 365.
Roberts, Samuel, Jr., 71.
Roberts, Simeon, 7.
Roberts, Stephen, 319, 335.
Roberts, Thomas, 54.
Roberts, William, 227.
Roberts, Zibee, 71.
Robertson, Aurther, 365.
Robertson, Cato, 342.
Robertson, Eleazer, 288, 338.
Robertson, Elias, 38, 56.
Robertson, Ephraim, 38, 65, 253, 319, 336.
Robertson, George, 195.
Robertson, Grh^m, 253.
Robertson, James, 38, 290, 358.
Robertson, Jared, 38.
Robertson, John, 38, 281, 284, 325, 339.
Robertson, Levi, 342.
Robertson, Nathaniel, 119.
Robertson, Samuel, 38.
Robertson, Simeon, Jr., 38.
Robertson, Thomas, 38.
Robin, Jacob, 281.
Robin, Michael, 61.
Robins, Benoni, 310, 335.
Robins, Elijah, 18.
Robins, Enos, 199.
Robins, Joseph, 71, 135, 237, 292.
Robins, Josiah, 349.
Robins, Nathaniel, 86.
Robins, Roger, 368.
Robinson, Abel, 85, 356.
Robinson, Cato, 268, 342.
Robinson, Clark, 131.
Robinson, Comfort, 216.
Robinson, David, 61, 103.
Robinson, Eleazer, 85, 127.
Robinson, Elias, 46, 85, 138, 174, 236, 268.
Robinson, Ephraim, 356.
Robinson, James, 200.
Robinson, Jared, 229.

Robinson, Jason, 216.
Robinson, Jeremiah, 287, 292.
Robinson, John, 198, 219, 239.
Robinson, Levi, 60, 83.
Robinson, Nathaniel, 47, 154.
Robinson, Reuben, 276, 309, 334, 350.
Robinson, Richard, 201, 356.
Robinson, Samuel, 85, 152, 174, 229, 268.
Robinson, Simeon, 199.
Robinson, Simson, Jr., 174.
Robinson, Thomas, 229.
Robinson, Zopher, 85, 288.
Robison, Benjamin, 135.
Robison, Cato, 50.
Robison, Elias, 77.
Robison, Ephraim, 237.
Robison, Samuel, 236.
Rock, Thomas, 183.
Rock, William, 353.
Rockwell, Amasa, 188.
Rockwell, Daniel, 132.
Rockwell, Grove, 205, 346.
Rockwell, John, Jr., 110.
Rockwell, Joseph 9, 206.
Rockwell, Merit, 77.
Rockwell, William, 189.
Rockwill, Ozwill, 243.
Rodgers, Bigsbey, 72.
Rodgers, Bixbie, 129.
Rodgers, Chester, 130.
Rodgers, Elisha, 218.
Roe, Abijah, 143.
Roger, Isaac, 68.
Rogers, Asael, 38.
Rogers, Bigsbe, 54.
Rogers, Chester, 46, 216, 219, 297.
Rogers, Daniel, 55, 105.
Rogers, Elisha, 181.
Rogers, Ephraim, 1.
Rogers, Ethen, 179.
Rogers, Gideon, 184.
Rogers, Gurdon, 180.
Rogers, H:, 205.
Rogers, Hezekiah, 109, 304, 310, 343.
Rogers, Isaac, 50.
Rogers, Jacob, 1.
Rogers, James, 38, 118, 234.
Rogers, Jeffery, 73.
Rogers, John, 4th, 290, 359.
Rogers, Jonathan, 283.
Rogers, Joseph, 38, 199, 232.
Rogers, Josiah, 76, 148, 158, 268, 283, 331, 340, 351.
Rogers, Jsaiah, 85.

Ruggs, Solomon, Jr., 277.
Rumbeglow, Thomas, 268.
Rumbelo, Thomas, 38, 232.
Rumbelow, Thomas, 72.
Rumsey, David, 102.
Rumsey, John, 89.
Rumsey, Nathan, 89.
Runald, Jacob, 71.
Runalds, David, 71.
Runalds, James, 71.
Runalds, Samuel, 72.
Rundal, John, 117.
Rundel, John, 234.
Rundell, Jeremiah, 116.
Rundle, John, 38.
Runnels, David, 137.
Runnels, John, 268, 269.
Runnels, Joshua, 268.
Runnels, Ravid, 136.
Runnels, Samuel, 135.
Rusel, 46, 63.
Rusell, William, 73.
Rush, George, 105.
Rusket, Samuel, 352.
Russ, Jonathan, 79, 269.
Russego, Abraham, 78.
Russel, 152.
Russel, Asher, 39, 173, 238, 250.
Russel, Corns, 206.
Russel, Eleazer, 131.
Russel, Elijah, 136.
Russel, Elmer, 60. 83.
Russel, Giles, 39, 233.
Russel, James, 49, 67.
Russel, Jeremiah, 154.
Russel, Jesse, 10.
Russel, John, 5, 11, 72, 135.
Russel, Simeon, 136.
Russel, William, 338.
Russel, William, Jr., 39, 234.
Russele, Elijah, 57.
Russell, Arthur, 348.
Russell, Asher, 268, 316, 332.
Russell, Benjamin, 295.
Russell, Corll, 86.
Russell, Cornelius, 14.
Russell, E., 151.
Russell, Edward, 151.
Russell, Eleaser, 46.
Russell, Gideon, 334.
Russell, John, 206. 352.
Russell, Joseph, 2.
Russell, Stephen, 357.
Russell, William, 173, 268.
Russigu, Abraham, 162.
Russigue, Abraham, 120.
Rust, Amaza, 132.

Rust, Epaphras, 173, 269.
Rust, Jonathan, 39, 174, 236.
Ryan, Jeremiah, 58, 234.
Ryan, John, 122.
Ryce, Moses, 294.
Ryley, John, 173.
Ryne, William, 154.
Ryon, Jeremiah, 39.
Rynolds, Joshua, 342.

Saben, Nehemiah, 81.
Sabens, Nathaniel, 147.
Sabens, Nehemiah, 41.
Sabin, 137.
Sabin, Billinds, 77.
Sabin, Billings, 56.
Sabin, Jonathan, 365.
Sabins, 159.
Sabins, Nathaniel, 56, 76.
Sabins, Nehemiah, 12, 175, 239.
Sacket, Aaron, 364.
Sacket, Buel, 205.
Sackett, J., 106.
Saffard, David, 200.
Sagar, Thomas, 120.
Sage, Abraham, 7.
Sage, Ebenezer, 367.
Sage, Stephen, 7.
St George, George, 50.
St John, 56, 78.
St. John, Aaron, 111.
St John, Daniel, 285, 314, 331.
St. John, Dover, 109.
St John, Gideon, 189.
St John, James, 41, 115, 234.
St. John, Jesse, 111, 310, 343.
St John, John, 175, 204.
St. John, Justin, 110, 306, 312, 343.
St. John, Nehemiah, 9.
St. John, Nehemiah, Jr., 9.
St Squir, Samuel, 150.
Saivers, William, 335.
Sales, William, 54.
Salisbury, 24, 26, 28, 29, 31, 34, 35, 36, 40, 42, 44, 57, 78, 163, 165, 168, 171, 172, 173, 175, 176, 177, 227, 234, 261, 262, 264, 266, 267, 268, 270, 271, 355.
Salks, Othniel, 154.
Salley, James, 40, 216, 241.
Saltonstall, Dudley, 365.
Salvage, Stephen, 346.
Salvage, William, 346.
Sambo, Prince, 238.
Sampson, David, 196.
Sampson, Jonson, 196.
Samson, 64.

Scovel, Peter, 128.
Scovel, Steaphen, 41.
Scovell, Bela, 258.
Scovell, Daniel, 5.
Scovell, John, Jr., 5.
Scoviel, Selah, 306.
Scovil, 108.
Scovil, Ebenezer, 59.
Scovil, Jonathan, 108.
Scovil, Nathan, 351.
Scovil, Seely, 114.
Scovil, Silas, 114.
Scovil, Silvanus, 108.
Scovil, Stephen, 175, 235, 253.
Scovill, 5.
Scovill, Ebenezer, 211.
Scovill, Peter, 85.
Scovill, Samuel, Jr., 277.
Scovill, Stephen, 84, 230.
Scovill, Westall, 5.
Scovils, Steaven, 61, 84.
Scrantom, Abraham, 5.
Scrantom, Jared, 5.
Scrantom, Noah, 5.
Scrantom, Timothy, 51.
Scrantom, Torrey, 51.
Scranton, Thomas, 223.
Scranton, Timothy, 5.
Scranton, Torey, 329.
Screen, James, 284.
Scribner, Abraham, 9.
Scribner, Asa, 41, 110, 175.
Scribner, Elias, 9.
Scribner, Moses, 109.
Scribner, Stephen, 109.
Scribner, Zacheus, 9, 110.
Scriptor, John, 84.
Scrow, John, 334.
Seagor, Thomas, 162.
Sealey, Sylvarnus, 57.
Sealey, Zadock, 52.
Sealy, George, 216, 269, 285.
Sealy, John, 69.
Sealy, Sylvanus, 78.
Sealy, Zadock, 70.
Seaman, William, 117.
Sear, John, 112.
Searl, Constant, 41, 233.
Searls, Ruben, 1.
Sears, Jasper P., 283.
Sears, John, 104.
Sears, Joseph, 121, 162.
Sears, Knoles, 162.
Sears, Obediah, 175, 184, 232.
Seaser, 148.
Seaton, George, 7.
Seaward, Samuel, 2, 66, 175.
Sedgwick, Samuel, 70, 238.

Sedgwick, Timothy, 194, 226.
Sedgwick, William, 192, 226.
Seeley, 54.
Seeley, Ebenezer, 286.
Seeley, Ephraim, 58.
Seeley, George, 324.
Seeley, Gideon, 58.
Sceley, Lemuel, 94.
Seely, Amos, 123.
Seely, Ebenezer, 214.
Seely, Ephraim, 90, 92.
Scely, George, 342.
Seely, Gideon, 90.
Seely, Justus, 93.
Seely, N., 97.
Seely, Nehemiah, 309.
Seelye, Selvinis, 162.
Seelye, Amos, 154.
Seelye, David, 54, 235.
Seelye, John, 54, 236.
Seelye, Selvinis, 162.
Seers, Obediah, 41, 77.
Seers, Remington, 15.
Segar, Joseph, 3ᵈ, 349.
Segwick, Samuel, 40.
Selden, 181.
Selden, E., 182.
Selden, Ezra, 40, 174, 232, 269, 333, 335.
Seley, Ephraim, 61.
Seley, Gideon, 58.
Seley, Lemuel, 58.
Seley, Nehemiah, 335.
Selleck, Charles, 114.
Selleck, Daniel, 118.
Selleck, David, 93.
Selleck, Henry, 111.
Selleck, Jacob, 9, 111.
Selleck, James, 9.
Sellick, Benjamin Seymor, 153.
Sellick, James, 208.
Serdam, Peter, 63, 79.
Sereen, James, 270.
Serene, James, 352.
Sergeant, Samuel, 129.
Sesar, Jonathan, 109.
Setchell, Jonathan, 366.
Seward, Daniel, 40, 231.
Seward, Eliakim, 273.
Seward, Elimkim, 319.
Seward, Elnathan, 51, 74.
Seward, Jedediah, 269, 288, 347.
Seward, Nathan, 40, 174, 230.
Seward, Samuel, 40, 230.
Seward, Silas, 209.
Seward, Sutliff, 211.
Seward, Timothy, 278, 347.
Seward, William, 40, 231.

Smith, Jordan, 39, 175, 231, 269.
Smith, Joseph, 2, 5, 8, 47, 121, 151, 154, 162, 220, 297, 321.
Smith, Joshua, 49, 147, 269, 353.
Smith, Josiah, 114, 346, 359.
Smith, Levy, 39.
Smith, Lewis, 234.
Smith, Lue, 84, 174.
Smith, Lus, 230.
Smith, Matthew 3ᵈ, 3.
Smith, Moses, 10.
Smith, Nathan, 50, 68, 156, 307, 329.
Smith, Nathaniel, 51, 282, 307.
Smith, Noah, 208.
Smith, Oliver, 356.
Smith, Oliver, Jr., 275.
Smith, Peter, 39, 114, 131, 237.
Smith, Philip, 208.
Smith, Ralph, 55, 105.
Smith, Reuben, 5, 54, 311.
Smith, Reuben, Jr., 286.
Smith, Richard, 17, 154.
Smith, Robert, 61, 101.
Smith, Roger, 85.
Smith, Samson, 60.
Smith, Samuel, 3, 8, 39, 84, 107, 183, 230, 250.
Smith, Seth, 13, 60, 83, 276.
Smith, Simeon, 131.
Smith, Sylvˢ, 65.
Smith, Sylvenos, 295.
Smith, Taber, 79, 152.
Smith, Theodore, 350.
Smith, Thomas, 215.
Smith, Timothy, 51, 70, 214.
Smith, Tone, 46.
Smith, Walter, 333.
Smith, Wells, 52, 69.
Smith, William, 5, 12, 39, 48, 73, 151, 174, 231.
Smithers, William, 40, 238.
Snell, Ebenezer, 81, 189.
Snell, Joseph, 46, 59, 82.
Snell, William, 357.
Snow, Amosiah, 357.
Snow, Ebenezer, 73.
Snow, Ebenezer, Jr., 54, 74, 129.
Snow, Jonathan, 54, 72, 76, 129.
Snow, Joseph, 2.
Snow, Robart, Jr., 219.
Snow, Robert, 199.
Snow, Shubel, 330, 356.
Snow, Simeon, 182, 218.
Snow, Thomas, 353.
Sole, William, 59.
Soles, Richard, 82.

Solley, Thomas, 274.
Solomon, Amos, 40, 68, 233.
Solomon, Nathaniel, 51.
Somers, 11, 23, 26, 28, 30, 32, 37, 43, 80, 164, 166, 168, 173, 177, 187, 188, 189, 202, 203, 204, 206, 238, 275, 278, 281, 302, 354.
Somersetshire, Eng., 368.
Sorow, Thomas, 65.
Sott, Elijah, 236.
Southard, Andrew, 352.
Southard, Nathan, 361.
Southard, William, 361.
Southington, 164, 166, 168, 173, 175, 177, 187, 190, 205, 207, 213, 216, 261, 262, 263, 268, 269, 270, 276, 277, 299, 300, 350, 355, 356.
Southmaid, 41.
Southmaid, William, 230.
Southmayd, William, 84.
Southward, William, 183.
Southwell, Asael, 181.
Southwell, Paschall, 68.
Southworth, Andrew, 274.
Southworth, Chester, 294, 319.
Southworth, James, 131.
Southworth, Joseph, 46.
Southworth, William, 46, 131, 218.
Soward, Daniel, 73.
Soward, William, 73.
Sowas, Richard, 41, 233.
Sowers, William, 175.
Sowl, William, 81.
Spafford, Elijah, 85, 127.
Spafford, Eliphalet, 226, 288.
Spalden, Ephraim, 131.
Spaldin, Ephraim, 39.
Spalding, Ephraim, 237.
Sparger, Edward, 224.
Sparks, Ebenezer, 197.
Sparks, Ichabod, 200.
Sparks, Isaiah, 12.
Sparks, Joseph, 59, 82.
Sparrow, Stephen, 352.
Sparrow, Stephen, 2ᵈ, 276.
Spalding, Andrew, 158.
Spalding, Andrew, 148.
Spaulding, Stephen, 147.
Spear, Elihu, 306, 313, 328.
Spear, Elijah, 174, 238.
Spear, Joshua, 352.
Spear, William, 282.
Spears, John, 68.
Spears, Jonathan, 3, 67.
Spears, Nathaniel, 3.
Speers, Elijah, 41.
Speers, John, 40, 232.

Steele, William, 277.
Steevens, 212.
Steevens, Aaron, 55, 72.
Steevens, Abraham, 53.
Steevens, Eliakim, 53, 72.
Steevens, Hubbel, 52, 72.
Steevens, Peter, 72.
Steevens, Samuel, 53.
Steevens, Simon, 53, 72.
Steloon, Ebenezer, 282.
Stemson, Aaron, 132.
Step, James, 72.
Stephen, Isaac, 4.
Stephens, Aaron, 232.
Stephens, Amos, 279.
Stephens, Dan, 102.
Stephens, Daniel, 61.
Stephens, Elisha, 351.
Stephens, Henery, 57, 80.
Stephens, James, 351.
Stephens, Jupeter, 345.
Stephens, Peter, 213.
Stephens, Preeda, 6.
Stephens, Robert, 347.
Stephens, Thomas, 67.
Stephens, Timothy, 51, 351.
Stephens, William, 79.
Stephenson, Allen, 12.
Stephenson, Amasy, 344.
Sterling, 94, 320.
Sterling, Nathaniel, 109.
Sterry, Silas, 40, 175, 233.
Stery, Silas, 68.
Steuben, Jonathan, 315, 331.
Stevens, Aaron, 251, 284.
Stevens, Adams, 223.
Stevens, Amos, 300.
Stevens, Ardamus, 200.
Stevens, Asa, 363.
Stevens, Benjamin, 17.
Stevens, Daniel, 335.
Stevens, Ebenezer, 79.
Stevens, Elias, 281.
Stevens, Elijah, 79, 232.
Stevens, Elnathan, 198.
Stevens, Henry, 274, 300.
Stevens, James, 119.
Stevens, Jonathan, 277, 319, 336.
Stevens, Josiah, 17.
Stevens, Luke, 211.
Stevens, Nathan, 64, 156, 157.
Stevens, Peter, 17, 64, 223, 232.
Stevens, Peter, Jr., 156, 237.
Stevens, Reuben, 122, 154.
Stevens, Rosewell, 239.
Stevens, Simeon, 12, 363.
Stevens, Stephen, 46, 63, 64.

Stevens, Thomas, 46, 63, 64.
Stevens, Timothy, 17, 238, 269, 364.
Stevens, William, 185, 211, 229.
Stevenson, Adam, 54.
Stevins, Reuben, 74.
Steward, Benjamin, 296.
Steward, John, 41, 174, 231.
Stewart, Alexander, 15.
Stewart, Ceaser, 75.
Stewart, Charles, 108.
Stewart, John, 73, 269, 290, 359.
Stewart, Joseph, 180, 269, 286, 352.
Stewart, Robert, 2.
Stewart, William, 12, 57, 80.
Stibbins, Elisha, 12.
Stigley, Benjamin, 68.
Stiles, Ashbel, 14.
Stiles, Beriah, 65.
Stiles, Daniel, 145.
Stiles, Joseph, 61, 107.
Stiles, Martin, 65, 283, 351.
Stiles, Robert, 65.
Stiles, Robert, Jr., 52.
Stiles, Stephen, Jr., 142.
Stiles, William, 84, 257.
Stillman, Robert, 75, 231.
Stillman, Stephen, 121.
Stilman, Robert, 41.
Stillwell, Stephen, 100, 235, 356.
Stilwell, Stephen, 41, 74, 155, 175.
Stilwill, 195.
Stilwill, Elias, 195.
Stimson, Aaron, 66.
Stimson, Abel, 276, 314, 350.
Stimson, Joel, 12.
Stimson, Simon, 12, 59, 81, 324.
Stirges, David, Jr., 3.
Stirges, Hill, 3.
Stirges, Moses, 4.
Stocken, Marshal, 39, 240, 269.
Stocker, Beter, 4.
Stocker, Peter, 67.
Stockin, Marshall, 175.
Stocking, Eber, 65, 353.
Stocking, John, 2.
Stocking, Jonathan, 65, 353.
Stocking, Marshal, 65, 249, 353.
Stocking, William, 65.
Stockwell, Abel, 41, 174, 229, 269, 336.
Stockwell, William, 137.
Stodard, Curtes, 197.
Stodard, Daniel, 69.
Stodard, Eli, 175.
Stodard, Elisha, 69.

Stodard, Enoch, 174.
Stodard, Fradrick, 69.
Stodard, Moses, 68.
Stoddard, Anthony, 61, 99.
Stoddard, Benjamin, 311.
Stoddard, Benjamin, Jr., 272.
Stoddard, Clement, 200.
Stoddard, Daniel, 51, 246.
Stoddard, Ebenezer, 311, 349.
Stoddard, Eli, 99, 235.
Stoddard, Elisha, 51, 209.
Stoddard, Ely, 41, 269.
Stoddard, Enoch, 41, 238.
Stoddard, Filo, 352.
Stoddard, Frederick, 51, 253, 318, 335.
Stoddard, James, 284.
Stoddard, Joshua, 41, 76, 159, 237.
Stoddard, Moses, 50, 212.
Stoddard, Nathan, 41, 51, 235.
Stoddard, Samuel, 64, 156, 227.
Stoddard, Simeon, 214.
Stoddard, Simeon C., 322, 338.
Stoddart, Ebenezer, 310.
Stoddart, Simeon C., 310.
Stoddart, Simeon Curtis, 311.
Stoderd, Joshua, 147.
Stoderd, Samuel, 146.
Stoel, Abel, 334, 353.
Stoel, Asa, 84.
Stoel, Elisha, 41, 237.
Stoel, Nathaniel, 138.
Stoel, Samuel, 353.
Stone, 5, 134, 136.
Stone, B., 101.
Stone, Daniel, Jr., 5.
Stone, David, 40, 60, 231.
Stone, Dudley, 215.
Stone, Henry, 137.
Stone, Jonathan, 216.
Stone, Joseph, 40.
Stone, Joshua, 108.
Stone, Josiah, 40, 54, 235.
Stone, Samuel, 332.
Stone, Seth, 5.
Stone, Simeon, 135.
Stone, Stephen, 209.
Stone, Thomas, 175, 247, 320, 337.
Stone, William, 51.
Stone, William, 119.
Stonington, 23, 24, 25, 26, 27, 29, 30, 31, 32, 33, 34, 35, 36, 37, 39, 40, 41, 43, 44, 177, 179, 180, 181, 182, 183, 184, 199, 202, 204, 206, 212, 214, 215, 233, 242, 253, 264, 265, 267, 281, 288, 302, 359.
Storer, Nehemiah, 367.

Stores, Augustus, 184.
Stores, Prentice, 254.
Storrs, 88, 218, 299, 360.
Storrs, Augustus, 219, 294.
Storrs, Exp., 133, 219.
Storrs, Frederick, 287, 294.
Storrs, William, 54.
Storrs, William Fitch, 129.
Storry, Silas, 77, 232.
Story, Asa, 10.
Story, Ephraim, 302, 330.
Story, Ephraim, Jr., 272.
Story, Oliver, 76.
Story, Solomon, 9.
Stoves, Benjamin, 112.
Stow, Deliverance, 277.
Stow, George, 366.
Stow, Isaac, 5.
Stow, Samuel, 73, 365.
Stow, Zachariah, 346.
Stowe, Elihu, 249.
Stowel, Elisha, 138.
Stowel, Nathaniel, 309, 329.
Stowel, Samuel, 309, 329.
Stowell, Abel, 278, 309.
Stowell, Elisha, 76, 77.
Stowell, Nathan, 307.
Stowell, Nathaniel, 56, 77, 277, 307.
Stowell, Samuel, 278, 307.
Straight, William, 136.
Straten, Stephen, 4.
Stratford, 24, 26, 29, 30, 32, 33, 37, 39, 40, 41, 43, 44, 58, 88, 90, 91, 92, 93, 94, 97, 124, 126, 151, 165, 167, 168, 169, 170, 171, 172, 173, 174, 177, 185, 187, 198, 199, 200, 202, 204, 205, 206, 207, 208, 209, 210, 211, 214, 234, 242, 243, 244, 248, 250, 251, 253, 256, 258, 261, 262, 263, 265, 266, 267, 268, 269, 287, 355, 365.
Stratton, 227.
Stratton, Samuel, 122.
Street, John, 120, 162.
Strickland, Asahel, 10.
Strickland, David, 54.
Strickland, Ichabod, 144.
Strickland, Moses, 61.
Strickland, Seth, 215.
Strickling, Moses, 100.
Stringer, John, 78.
Stringham, Peter, 269.
Strong, Arial, 206.
Strong, Barnabas, 40, 140.
Strong, Benajah, 237.
Strong, Charles, 100.

Talman, Ebenezer, 99.
Talor, William, 81.
Talsen, Reuben, 301.
Tamage, Nathaniel, 187.
Tang, Marlack, 279.
Tankard, George, 69.
Tanner, 88.
Tanner, Toral, 235.
Tanner, Tryal, 42.
Taphan, Ezekel, 152.
Tarble, William, 42, 175, 241, 270, 356.
Tarbox, Benjamin, 114.
Tarbox, David, 142.
Tarbox, Joseph, 219.
Tarnham, William, 138.
Tatchen, Ebenezer, 215.
Tatson, Reuben, 278, 291.
Tattendon, John, 84, 176.
Taulburt, Benjamin, 292.
Tayler, Barrack, 233.
Tayler, James, 49.
Taylor, 88.
Taylor, Aaron, 210.
Taylor, Barack, 41, 68, 92, 176, 228.
Taylor, Benjamin, 54.
Taylor, Childes, 6, 369.
Taylor, David, 275, 299, 326, 340, 346, 349.
Taylor, Edmund, 366.
Taylor, Elijah, 9, 42, 47, 110, 175, 270.
Taylor, Ephraim, 42, 141, 176, 239, 270.
Taylor, Isaac, 3.
Taylor, James, 80, 107, 348.
Taylor, Jesse, 345.
Taylor, John, 41, 56, 118, 175, 338.
Taylor, John, Jr., 48.
Taylor, Jonathan, 346.
Taylor, Joshua, 47, 124, 153.
Taylor, Joshua, Jr., 116.
Taylor, Josiah, 109, 270, 340.
Taylor, Justus, 287.
Taylor, Levi, 9.
Taylor, Nath, 63.
Taylor, Nathan, 67, 109.
Taylor, Nathaniel, 3.
Taylor, Noah, 47, 109.
Taylor, Obediah, 208, 287.
Taylor, Reuben, 214.
Taylor, Samuel, 48, 210, 274.
Taylor, Samuel, Jr., 289.
Taylor, Simeon, 42, 175, 235, 270.
Taylor, Thomas, 42, 82, 176, 237, 285.

Taylor, Thomas, Jr., 136.
Taylor, Timothy, 7.
Taylor, William, 76, 118, 322, 341, 348, 349, 368.
Teal, Jacob, 50.
Teal, Joseph, 50, 53, 72, 281, 300, 347.
Teal, Nathan, 273.
Teal, Oliver, 53, 72, 75.
Teal, Samuel, 42, 51, 175, 231.
Teal, Tites, 53.
Teal, Titus, 74.
Teen, John, 98, 109.
Tefford, John, 146.
Teigh, Cornelius, 279.
Temp, Amos, 92.
Temple, Amos, 344.
Temple, Frederick, 106.
Ten Eyck, 188.
Ten Eyck, Henry, 335, 337.
Terrel, Job, 187.
Terrell, Hezekiah, 200.
Terrey, Joseph, 51.
Terril, Joel, 42, 230.
Terril, Thomas, 142.
Terrill, Hezekiah, 326.
Terry, Ephraim, 85, 127.
Terry, Ephraim 3d, 140.
Terry, Gamalial, 79, 227, 270.
Terry, Jonathan, 350.
Terry, Jonathan, Jr., 67.
Terry, Levi, 49, 67.
Terry, Stephen, 10.
Thacher, Rodolphus, 370.
Thade, Daniel, 87.
Thair, Asa, 84, 230, 270.
Thane, William, 343.
Thares, Elisha, 73.
Tharp, Abel, 60, 82, 211.
Tharp, Amasa, 59, 83.
Tharp, Amos, 59, 83, 340.
Tharp, Cornelius M., 270.
Tharp, Peter, 214.
Thayer, Asa, 176.
Thayer, Jerijah, 63, 254.
Thayer, Zepheniah, 63.
Thayr, Asa, 42.
Thelly, Edmond, 321.
Thetsey, James, 208.
Thistle, Samuel, 351.
Thomas, Aaron, 5.
Thomas, Absalom, 41, 75.
Thomas, Daniel, 75, 77.
Thomas, David, 51, 70.
Thomas, Elijah, 75.
Thomas, Enoch, 61, 103, 329.
Thomas, Ephraim, 41, 150, 176, 229, 270.

Toby, Park, 300.
Todd, Samuel, 54.
Todd, Thaddeus, 60, 83.
Todd, Yale, 8, 42, 176, 229, 270.
Tolbert, Ebenezer, 195.
Tolcott, Seth, 206.
Tole, Amos, 5.
Tolland, 12, 23, 28, 32, 34, 36, 37,
    38, 41, 59, 66, 73, 80, 81, 130,
    132, 140, 164, 167, 169, 170, 173,
    175, 185, 186, 187, 188, 190, 191,
    206, 214, 239, 266, 276, 281, 285,
    287, 350.
Tolles, Elnathan, 176, 229, 270.
Tollotson, Asael, 278.
Tolls, Elnathan, 42, 73, 270.
Tom, Nero, 220.
Tomlinson, 93, 94.
Tomlinson, Benjamin, 2.
Tomlinson, David, 2, 42, 230.
Tomlinson, Eliphalet, 273.
Tomlinson, Gideon, 2.
Tomlinson, Isaac, 2.
Tomlinson, Jabez H., 256.
Tomlinson, Joseph, 48.
Tomlinson, Timothy, 100.
Tomlinson, William, 2.
Tomson, Alexander, 48.
Tona, Jethro, 61.
Tonance, Joseph, 102.
Tone, John F., 311, 344.
Tone, John Frederick, 301.
Tone, Negro, 131.
Toney, 58.
Toney, Jethro, 344.
Toney, Reuben, 345.
Tooby, John, 359.
Tooley, Andrew, 42, 232.
Tooley, Benjamin, 72.
Tooley, Dan, 274.
Tooly, Andrew, 79, 176.
Tooly, Benjamin, 52.
Tooly, John, 53.
Tooly, William, 53.
Toringford, 203, 204.
Torminer, Peter, 346.
Torney, Dennis, 291.
Torrey, Jesse, 344.
Torrington, 22, 28, 30, 59, 88, 180,
    202, 205, 206, 235, 279, 280, 284,
    286, 287, 288.
Torry, Amos, 18.
Torry, Jesse, 140, 216.
Tortolott, Barnew, 137.
Tory, Samuel, 366.
Totton, Thomas, 11.
Touser, Jared, 275.

Town, Isaac, 217.
Towner, Elijah, 206.
Towner, Jacobe, 270.
Townsen, John, 370.
Townsen, Jonathan, 370.
Townsend, Hendrick, 47.
Townsend, Solomon, 42.
Towee, John, 59.
Tower, Gideon, 13.
Town, Archabel, 135.
Town, Archelaus, 71.
Town, John, 117, 234.
Town, William, 115.
Townd, John, 42.
Towner, Dan, 155.
Towner, Enoch, 4.
Towner, Jacobe, 42, 175.
Towner, Timothy, 5.
Towner, William, 7.
Townsend, Elias, 8.
Townsend, Solomon, 229, 270.
Towser, Jared, 349.
Towsley, Job, 79, 227.
Towsley, Michael, 352.
Tozer, Jared, 184.
Tracey, Hezekiah, 42.
Tracey, Moses, 42, 176.
Tracey, Solomon, 127.
Tracey, William, 42, 176.
Tracy, Benajah, 209.
Tracy, Daniel, 76.
Tracy, Elisha, 209.
Tracy, Ezekiel, 9.
Tracy, Gilbert, 210.
Tracy, Giles, 9.
Tracy, Hezekiah, 74.
Tracy, Hugh, 231.
Tracy, Levi, 9.
Tracy, Moses, 75, 231, 270, 272,
    301, 358, 359.
Tracy, Peres, 10.
Tracy, Perez, 270.
Tracy, Salom^n, 85.
Tracy, Samuel, 198, 224.
Tracy, William, 74, 231, 270.
Trall, Reufus, 74.
Trantom, John Thomas, 148.
Trapp, Thomas, 3^d, 76.
Trat, John, 346.
Traverse, Joseph, 117.
Treadway, Josiah, 244.
Treadwell, Adam, 363.
Treadwell, Benjamin, 274.
Treadwell, Cato, 274.
Treadwell, Nathaniel, 97.
Treadwell, Thomas, 97.
Treat, B., 107.

Treat, John, 42, 238.
Treat, Joseph, 249, 309, 319, 336.
Treat, Mingo, 55.
Tredwell, Cato, 270.
Treet, Charles, 348.
Treet, George, 369.
Treet, Joseph, 348.
Treet, Mingo, 105.
Treet, Theodore, 345.
Treman, Isriel, 203.
Treusey, Andrew, 312.
Trobridge, 88.
Trobridge, John, 270.
Trobrig, John, 74.
Troop, Benjamin, 42, 231.
Troop, John, 42, 229.
Troubridge, Benjamin, 65.
Trowbridg, Ebenezer, 176.
Trowbridg, John, 175, 176.
Trowbridg, Samuel, 42.
Trowbridge, Bille, 7.
Trowbridge, Daniel, 7.
Trowbridge, Ebenezer, 42, 55, 105, 235.
Trowbridge, Isaac, 54.
Trowbridge, John, 42, 155, 229, 234, 328, 329.
Trowbridge, Samuel, 110.
Trube, John, 282.
Truby, John, 358.
Truesdell, Darius, 311.
Truman, Joseph, 76.
Trumbull, John, 286.
Trumbull, Jonathan, 302.
Trumbull, 365.
Trussedell, Darius, 344.
Tryon, Ezra, 42, 238, 251, 306, 317, 332, 351.
Tryon, Ezra, Jr., 351.
Tryon, Isaac, 176, 270, 351.
Tryon, James, 49.
Tryon, William, 52, 70, 194, 345.
Tuas, Gideon, 301.
Tubbs, Elemuel, 17.
Tubbs, Frederick, 185, 221.
Tubbs, Martin, 79, 227.
Tubbs, Nathan, 74, 176, 236, 270, 273, 323, 342.
Tubbs, Simon, 46, 63.
Tubbs, Stephen, 353.
Tubs, Nathan, 42.
Tucker, Benjamin, 183.
Tucker, Daniel, 61, 103.
Tucker, David, 273.
Tucker, Ephraim, 286, 297.
Tucker, Gideon, 216.
Tucker, Jarvis, 176, 270.

Tucker, John, 152, 335.
Tucker, Joseph, 57, 80.
Tucker, William, 2.
Tucker, Zoath, 82, 148, 160.
Tuckerman, Jacob, 362.
Tuells, Elijah, 7.
Tuells, Samuels, 7.
Tufts, Joseph, 294.
Tullar, Ely, 264.
Tullar, Jacob, 264.
Tuller, Eli, 10, 311, 344.
Tuller, Elijah, 10.
Tuller, Israel, 188.
Tuller, Jacob, 10.
Tuller, James, 363.
Tuller, Joseph, 10, 186.
Tuller, Reuben, 144.
Tumey, Gersham, 58.
Tuncheman, 233.
Tupper, Solomon, 57, 180.
Tupper, William, 42, 78, 176, 227, 235, 270, 327.
Turell, Nathan, 58.
Turner, 136.
Turner, Bates, 74, 210.
Turner, Caleb, 52, 72, 211, 280.
Turner, Isaac, 270, 300.
Turner, Jacob, 231.
Turner, John, 52, 70.
Turner, Joshua, 333.
Turner, Moses, 74.
Turner, Nathaniel, 71.
Turner, Nehemiah, 96.
Turner, Orel, 53.
Turner, Philip, 74.
Turner, William, 74, 152, 195, 366.
Turney, Asa, 97.
Turney, Gersham, 58.
Turney, John, 58.
Turney, Samuel, Jr., 98.
Turney, Tony, 323, 342.
Turnill, Hezekiah, 326, 340.
Turnor, Bates, 244.
Turnor, Habackock, 132.
Turnor, John, 54, 130, 203.
Turrel, John, 61, 186.
Turrill, Josiah, 154, 162.
Turrill, Smith, 154.
Turrills, George, 154.
Tusler, Joshua, 316.
Tuttel, Clement, 204.
Tuttel, Peltiah, 193.
Tuttle, Aaron, 330.
Tuttle, Abner, 278.
Tuttle, Abraham, 277, 350.
Tuttle, Charles, 13.
Tuttle, Ebenezer, 347.

Walter, Silas, 44.
Walter, William, 44, 176, 229.
Walters, Thomas, 44.
Walton, George, 347.
Walton, Henry, 10, 302, 346.
Walton, Nathan, 10.
Walton, Silas, 231, 271.
Walton, Ward, 71, 136.
Walton, William, Jr., 136.
Wampe, John, 130.
Wampee, John, 56, 77.
Wamper, John, 137.
Wampey, Samuel, 81.
Wand, James, 51.
Waneright, Thomas, 236.
Wanerite, Thomas, 79.
Wanslow, William, 56.
Ward, Aaron, 346, 351.
Ward, Daniel, 244, 318, 335, 348.
Ward, David, 2, 306.
Ward, Jacob, Jr., 80.
Ward, James, 11, 18, 366.
Ward, Jedadiah, 219.
Ward, Jese, 290.
Ward, John, 18, 49, 66, 177, 192.
Ward, Jonathan, 281, 300.
Ward, Joseph, 13.
Ward, Macock, 107.
Ward, Moses, 251.
Ward, Nathan, 297.
Ward, Thomas, 279.
Ward, William, 44, 140, 210, 237.
Wardell, Samuel, 339.
Warden, Ichabod, 323.
Warden, Isaac, 44, 232.
Warden, Walter, 44, 233.
Wardin, Isaac, 153, 257.
Warding, Isaac, 79.
Wardwell, Eliacom, 11.
Wardwell, Isaac, 205, 271, 276, 348.
Wardwell, Jacob, 44, 114, 176, 234, 271, 314, 330.
Wardwell, William, 44, 114, 234.
Ware, Daniel, 43, 66, 177, 240.
Ware, William, 349.
Wareing, Ebenezer, 115.
Wareing, Eliakim, 112.
Wareing, Samuel, 115.
Waren, Henry, 234.
Wares, Elias, 351.
Wares, Richard, 281.
Waring, Moses, 108.
Warms, Samuel, 18.
Warner, 178, 227.
Warner, Aaron, 145.
Warner, Abner, 11.
Warner, Amasa, 57, 80.

Warner, Andrew, 85, 127.
Warner, Daniel, 11.
Warner, Ebenezer, 13, 43, 151, 230, 355.
Warner, Eleazer, 211.
Warner, Elizur, 55.
Warner, Israel, 11, 14.
Warner, John, 18.
Warner, Judah, 276, 352.
Warner, Moses, 13.
Warner, Nathaniel, 338, 352.
Warner, Nathaniel, Jr., 276.
Warner, R., 193.
Warner, Robert, 43, 240, 270.
Warner, Samuel, 18.
Warner, Thomas, 347.
Warner, Timothy, 357.
Warnor, Charles, 294.
Warnor, Matthew, 129.
Warren, Abraham, 43, 177, 239.
Warren, Asbel, 185.
Warrin, Edward, 48.
Warren, Ephriam, 136.
Warren, Jacob, 72.
Warren, John, 43, 106, 177, 238, 271, 353.
Warren, Nathaniel, 367.
Warren, Samuel, 215.
Warrin, 136.
Warrin, Henery, 43.
Warrin, Jacob, 136.
Warrups, Thomas, 103.
Warson, John, 288.
Warson, Thomas, 57, 121.
Warten, Elihu, 321.
Warters, Elihue, 338.
Warthington, Erastus, 197.
Warwehew, Peter, 103.
Washband, Edmund, 100.
Washbon, Benjamin, 57, 81.
Washbon, Luke, 12.
Washbon, Nathan, 57, 81.
Washbon, Nehemiah, 57.
Washbon, Samuel, 234.
Washborn, Lemuel, 139.
Washborn, Samuel, 94.
Washburn, Benjamin, 43, 230.
Washburn, Samuel, 43, 177.
Washington, George, 46, 89, 291.
Washington, 24, 27, 29, 33, 36, 44, 163, 172, 210, 236, 263, 267, 271, 287, 356.
Wason, Thomas, 78, 162.
Wasson, Thomas, 121, 285.
Wassonk, Abel, 68.
Wassonks, Abel, 50.
Wate, John, 186.
Wate, William, 152.

31

Webster, Ashbel, 17, 333.
Webster, Benjamin, 52, 70, 333, 345.
Webster, Charles, 192.
Webster, Ed, 139.
Webster, Elisha, 50.
Webster, Ephraim, 335.
Webster, Israel, 74, 141.
Webster, Joshua, 43, 238.
Webster, Moses, 130.
Webster, Nathan, 18.
Webster, Roswell, 50.
Webster, Simeon, 18, 57.
Webster, Simeon, 3ᵈ, 81.
Webster, Zephaniah, 348.
Wedg, Josoph, 44.
Wedge, Joshua, 44, 231.
Weed, Benjamin, 44, 113, 234.
Weed, Elijah, 56, 78, 120, 162.
Weed, Ezra, 108.
Weed, John, 113.
Weed, Jonas, 113, 145.
Weed, Joseph, 81.
Weed, Justus, 186.
Weed, Th[   ], 176.
Weed, Thaddeus, 44, 205, 234.
Weekes, Joseph, 42.
Weeks, Alexander, 68.
Weeks, James, 101.
Weeks, John, 104.
Weeks, Micajah, 57, 121, 162.
Weeks, Mousiah, 78.
Weeler, John, 205.
Weers, Richard, 300.
Weever, Samuel, 290.
Weight, Jacob, 1ˢᵗ, 316.
Weight, Jacob, 2ᵈ, 316.
Weir, Richard, 302.
Welch, Christopher, 346.
Welch, David, 224.
Welch, Ebenezer, 271, 348.
Welch, John, 347.
Welch, John, 2ᵈ, 286.
Welch, Lemuel, 14.
Welch, Luke, 44, 102, 177, 285.
Welch, Micael, 44, 227, 236.
Welch, Robert, 58, 94, 124, 153.
Welch, Roger, 66.
Welch, Samuel, 194.
Welchard, Samuel, 113.
Weld, 137.
Welden, Abraham, 79.
Welden, Isaac, 227.
Welkenson, Levi, 61.
Wellden, Isaac, 79.
Weller, Thomas, 102.
Welles, Gideon, 257.

Welles, Joshua, 245, 319, 336.
Welles, Roger, 303, 305, 328.
Welles, Samuel, 17.
Wellman, Barnabus, 52, 72.
Wellman, James, 281.
Wellman, John, 52, 72.
Wellman, Paul, 52, 72.
Wellman, William, 53, 72.
Wells, 88, 325, 326.
Wells, Amos, 214.
Wells, Benjamin, 198.
Wells, Cuff, 47, 291.
Wells, Cuffee, 75.
Wells, David, 58.
Wells, David, Jr., 94.
Wells, Elisha, 49.
Wells, Gideon, 148.
Wells, John, 208.
Wells, Jonathan, 2, 354.
Wells, Joshua, 44, 176, 238, 271, 348.
Wells, Roger, 258, 259, 305.
Wells, Samuel, 348.
Wells, Stephen, 57, 79.
Wells, Thomas, 52, 70, 343, 345.
Wells, Timothy, 49.
Welman, James, 209.
Welman, John, 185.
Welman, Paul, 49.
Welsh, Michael, 107.
Welsh, Reuben, 128.
Welsh, Robert, 324.
Welsh, Rodger, 132.
Welten, Benjamin, 43.
Welten, Steaphen, Jr., 43.
Welton, Benjamin, 177, 239, 330.
Welton, Joel, 50, 251, 271, 277, 299, 347.
Welton, Shubael, 280.
Welton, Solomon, 49, 177, 277, 299, 347.
Welton, Stephen, Jr., 84, 230.
Wendover, Thomas, Jr., 367.
Wentworth, Amos, 199.
Wentworth, Ezekiel, 132.
Wentworth, Levi, 76.
Weson, Samuel, 6.
Wessels, Herculus, 43, 234.
Weson, Samuel, Jr., 6.
West, Alva, 57, 242.
West, Amos, 140, 250.
West, David, Jr., 65.
West, Frances, 356.
West, Ichabod, 276, 323, 342, 350.
West, Ira, 12.
West, Jabez, 12.
West, Jeremiah, 81, 303, 317.

Wilcocks, Lemuel, 346.
Wilcocks, Moses, 210.
Wilcocks, Philemon, 54.
Wilcockson, Isaiah, 94.
Wilcox, Abraham, 364.
Wilcox, Benjamin, 279.
Wilcox, Ebenezer, 52.
Wilcox, Elias, 44, 112. 177.
Wilcox, Elisha, 182.
Wilcox, James, 71, 239, 337, 352.
Wilcox, Janna, 319.
Wilcox, Jarius, 176, 270, 292.
Wilcox, Jiles, 335.
Wilcox, Jonathan, 51.
Wilcox, Shumer, 51.
Wilcox, Stephen, 183.
Wilcox, Timothy, Jr., 5.
Wild, Jonathan, 270.
Wilder, Aaron, 44, 122, 155, 177, 234, 271.
Wilder, Gamaliel, 369.
Wilder, Jonathan, 6.
Wilder, Thomas, 369.
Wildman, Mathew, 55, 101.
Wilds, Jonathan, 44, 176, 229.
Wiley, Edward, 42.
Wilkenso, Jesse, 84.
Wilkenson, Ichabod, 74.
Wilkenson, Jesse, 60, 177.
Wilkenson, Levi, 84.
Wilkerson, Jesse, 254.
Wilkeson, Iccabud, 44.
Wilkeson, Jesse, 44.
Wilkey, Jeremiah, 72.
Wilkie, Jeremiah, 136.
Wilkinson, Ichabod, 55, 235.
Wilkinson, Jehabad, 105.
Wilkinson, Jesse, 235.
Wilkinson, Peter, 202.
Willasey, William, 5.
Willcocks, Amos, Jr., 144.
Willcocks, Daniel, 7.
Willcockson, David, 58.
Willcockson, John, 58.
Willcockson, John, Jr., 58.
Willcox, Azriah, 10.
Willcox, Daniel, 52, 72.
Willcox, Giles, 53, 72, 271.
Willcox, J., 204, 208.
Willcox, James, 43, 177, 236.
Willcox, Jehiel, 280.
Willcox, Job, Jr., 274.
Willcox, Joel, 212, 281.
Willcox, John, 212.
Willcox, Joseph, 11, 52, 72.
Willcox, Lemuel, 60, 83.
Willcox, Philemon, 176, 177.

Willcox, Roger, 10.
Willcox, Seth, 11.
Willcoxson, David, 58.
Willcoxson, Josiah, 58.
Willets, David, 249.
Willey, Asa, 221.
Willey, Jesse, 3.
Willey, Jonathan, 42, 176, 216, 241.
Willey, Joseph, 50, 69.
Willford, Joseph, 2.
William, Jacob, 69.
William, Joh, 53.
Williams, Abel, 147.
Williams, Abijah, 134.
Williams, Alexander, 13, 82, 148, 160, 338.
Williams, Ama, 130.
Williams, Amos, 4.
Williams, Asa, 180.
Williams, Benjamin, 124, 363.
Williams, Benjamin, Jr., 361.
Williams, Daniel, 43, 176, 238, 256, 271.
Williams, David, 345.
Williams, Doge, 283.
Williams, Dyer, 363.
Williams, Ebenezer, 90, 351.
Williams, Ezra, 96.
Williams, Henry, 43, 68, 107, 121, 148, 162, 177, 233.
Williams, Isaac, 276, 352.
Williams, J., 137.
Williams, Jabez, 90, 124, 228.
Williams, Jacob, 51.
Williams, Jesse, 148, 158, 253, 285, 314, 331.
Williams, John, 43, 44, 50, 68, 94, 108, 111, 123, 154, 177, 241, 271.
Williams, John, Jr., 3, 295.
Williams, John, 2, 361.
Williams, Jonath, 119.
Williams, Joseph, 51, 69.
Williams, Joshua, 75.
Williams, Nathan, 19, 50, 68.
Williams, Obed, 43, 84, 230.
Williams, Obediah, 177.
Williams, Paul, 50.
Williams, Prince, 295.
Williams, Ralph, 51, 69, 73, 130, 257.
Williams, Richard, 43, 67, 95, 97, 117, 176, 233, 271.
Williams, Roberson, 3.
Williams, Robert, 50, 68.
Williams, Russell, 283.
Williams, S., 138.
Williams, Sampson, 12.

Williams, Samuel Williams, 252, 253, 304, 318.
Williams, Sanford, 191.
Williams, Solomon, 50, 68, 334, 348.
Williams, Thomas, 43, 50, 68, 176, 241, 271, 276, 352.
Williams, Uriah, 43, 68, 177, 233.
Williams, Warren, 19.
Williams, William, 6, 291.
Williams, William, Jr., 139.
Williamson, John, 91.
Williamson, Zelophehead, 57, 80.
Williard, Samuel, 79.
Willington, 27, 29, 32, 36, 39, 84, 88, 172, 182, 183, 186, 187, 188, 190, 236, 239, 257, 263, 267, 278, 280, 287, 353.
Williox, James, 271.
Willis, Joseph, 271, 346.
Willis, Joseph, Jr., 7.
Willmot, Joel, 83.
Willmott, Joel, 60.
Willoughby, John, 50, 69.
Willson, Abnur, 6.
Willson, Calvin, 276.
Willson, David, 177.
Willson, George, 177.
Willson, John, 10, 176.
Willson, Joseph, 278.
Willson, Michael, 11.
Willson, Robert, 283.
Willys, 80, 152.
Wilmot, Walter, 8.
Wilson, Abiel, 14.
Wilson, Asa, 180.
Wilson, Barzillai, 270.
Wilson, Calvin, 348.
Wilson, David, 43, 116, 234, 271, 360.
Wilson, George, 43, 232, 271, 340.
Wilson, Gilbert, 117.
Wilson, James, 14, 101.
Wilson, John, 43, 134, 180, 229, 270.
Wilson, John, Jr., 180, 226.
Wilson, Joseph, 309, 353.
Wilson, Nehemiah, 117.
Wilson, Samuel, 61, 99.
Wilson, Thomas, 323, 342, 345, 348.
Wilson, William, 132.
Wilton, Benjamin, 271.
Wilton, Solomon, 271.
Wimans, William, 337.
Winans, William, 254, 320.
Winchal, Ezekiel, 322.
Winchel, Daniel, 305, 328.

Winchel, Ezekiel, 258, 341, 348.
Winchel, Ira, 50.
Winchel, Israel, 49.
Winchel, Jehial, 11, 204.
Winchel, John, 86.
Winchel, Seth, 113.
Winchel, Thomas, Jr., 11.
Winchell, Daniel, 347.
Winchell, Oliver, 14.
Winchester, 29, 34, 41, 44, 60, 84, 144, 168, 175, 177, 188, 189, 211, 213, 235, 243, 250, 253, 259, 262, 263, 268, 281, 285.
Wincop, Abraham, 4.
Windham, 24, 27, 28, 29, 34, 35, 37, 38, 39, 43, 44, 84, 127, 137, 138, 139, 140, 165, 167, 169, 171, 174, 176, 182, 196, 197, 198, 199, 200, 201, 217, 226, 236, 239, 246, 265, 266, 268, 288, 294, 355, 256, 357.
Windham Co., 229, 236.
Windsor, 14, 24, 26, 27, 30, 31, 34, 36, 37, 38, 42, 44, 85, 164, 166, 168, 170, 172, 173, 179, 185, 186, 187, 188, 189, 190, 193, 202, 203, 204, 205, 206, 241, 242, 243, 246, 261, 263, 264, 266, 267, 268, 270, 271, 276, 277, 281, 284, 285, 291, 299, 348, 356.
Wines, Peter, 211.
Wing, Joseph, 86, 241.
Wing, Samuel, 14, 44, 86, 241.
Wing, Thomas, 218.
Wingfield, Daniel, 96.
Winship, John, 141, 354.
Winslow, William, 77, 220.
Winchester, John, 298.
Winter, Asa, 134.
Winter, Isaac, 197.
Winter, Juvenal, 198.
Winter, Simeon, 11.
Winthrop, Frederick, 7.
Winton, Asa, 86, 93.
Winton, Nathan, 67, 98.
Winton, Peter, 4.
Wires, Elius, 142.
Wise, Samuel, 366.
Wisetman, John George, 279.
Witemore, Ebenezer Turill, 2.
Withamson, Zelophehead, 57.
Witherel, William, 334.
Withy, Ephram, 78.
Withy, Philip, 19.
Witney, Daniel, 241.
Witter, Ephraim, 198.
Witter, Josiah, 9.

Wix, Uriah, 43, 235.
Wolbridge, Porter, 81.
Wolcott, George, 14.
Wolcott, Joseph, 13.
Wolcott, Joseph, Jr., 60, 83.
Wolcutt, 190.
Wolcutt, Abiel, 186.
Wolcutt, Erastus, 48.
Wolcutt, Joseph, 270, 322.
Wolcutt, Peter, 190.
Wolf, Daniel D., 180.
Wolf, Levi, 162.
Wolfe, Levi, 154.
Wolf, see De Wolf.
Wollcott, Joseph, 293.
Wollworth, Reuben, 11.
Wolman, Miles, 162.
Wolworth, Ebenezar, 348.
Wolworth, Phinehas, 11.
Wompee, John, 75.
Wood, Abner, 18.
Wood, Amos, 210.
Wood, Asa, 204.
Wood, Benjamin, 296.
Wood, Benjamin, Jr., 295.
Wood, Charles, 54, 72, 130, 180.
Wood, D., 117, 246.
Wood, David, 52, 71, 115, 246.
Wood, Elisha, 43, 176, 229, 270.
Wood, Ezra, 4, 67, 96.
Wood, Jacob, 43, 65, 240, 346.
Wood, Jacob, Jr., 65.
Wood, Jonathan, 177, 249.
Wood, Josiah, 78, 117, 368.
Wood, Justus, 150, 271.
Wood, Lemuel, 43, 66, 240, 350.
Wood, Samuel, 353.
Wood, Silas, 332.
Wood, Simon, 111.
Wood, Stephen, 111, 112, 113.
Wood, Thomas, 43, 80, 112, 113, 136, 177, 238, 306, 318, 328.
Wood, Timothy, 17.
Woodard, 223.
Woodard, Abraham, 51.
Woodard, Charles, 213.
Woodard, Charles Frede, 223.
Woodard, Elias, 147.
Woodard, Joseph, 78.
Woodard, Lee, 146.
Woodart, Comfort, 137.
Woodbourn, Morris, 180.
Woodbridg, Theophilus, 44, 177, 240.
Woodbridg, Timothy, 10.
Woodbridge, 208, 299.
Woodbridge, George, 180.
Woodbridge, Howel, 354.

Woodbridge, Samuel, 220.
Woodbridge, Theophilus, 80.
Woodbridge, Thomas, 111.
Woodbridge, Timothy, 271, 275, 349.
Woodbrig, Theophilus, 10.
Woodbrige, Theodore, 71.
Woodburn, George, 214.
Woodbury, Bartholomew, 298.
Woodbury, 26, 27, 28, 29, 30, 31, 32, 33, 36, 37, 39, 41, 42, 44, 61, 99, 100, 102, 104, 107, 108, 126, 165, 167, 168, 170, 171, 175, 177, 186, 188, 206, 210, 213, 214, 215, 216, 217, 235, 263, 267, 268, 269, 270, 284, 287.
Woodcock, Samuel, 54, 202.
Woodertory, Thomas, 112.
Woodford, Levi, 187.
Woodford, Timothy, 63.
Woodin, Hezekiah, 2.
Woodin, Jeremiah, 48.
Woodin, William, 2.
Wooding, Philow, 48.
Woodruff, Charles, 50.
Woodruff, Gedor, 278, 299, 347.
Woodruff, Job, 73.
Woodruff, John, 104.
Woodruff, Seelah, 203.
Woodruff, Solomon, 278, 299, 347.
Woodruff, William, 49, 347.
Woodruff, Zebulon, 49.
Woods, Jacob, 353.
Woods, Justus, 73.
Woods, Samuel, 150.
Woodstock, 24, 25, 29, 31, 32, 33, 35, 37, 39, 86, 133, 134, 182, 183, 184, 192, 195, 197, 198, 213, 214, 228, 229, 270, 274, 285, 288, 295.
Woodsworth, Benjamin, 176.
Woodsworth, Jedadiah, 176.
Woodward, Ambrose, 221.
Woodward, Amos, 85, 127.
Woodward, Charles, 297.
Woodward, Daniel, 226, 288.
Woodward, Eazar, 296.
Woodward, Elezr, 295.
Woodward, Frederick, 218.
Woodward, John, 356.
Woodward, Joseph, 298.
Woodward, Joshua, 10.
Woodward, Lee, 64, 158.
Woodward, Oliver, 44, 86, 177, 240, 241.
Woodward, Roswell, 5.
Woodward, Thomas, 107.
Woodword, Oliver, 81.

www.ingramcontent.com/pod-product-compliance
Lightning Source LLC
Chambersburg PA
CBHW071824270326
41929CB00013B/1893